Psycho/History

PSYCHO/HISTORY

READINGS IN THE
METHOD OF
PSYCHOLOGY,
PSYCHOANALYSIS,
AND HISTORY

Edited by
Geoffrey Cocks and
Travis L. Crosby

YALE UNIVERSITY PRESS
NEW HAVEN AND LONDON

The editors gratefully acknowledge the support of the Albion College Faculty Development Committee.

Designed by Nancy Ovedovitz and set in ITC Garamond type by David E. Seham Associates, Inc. Printed in the United States of America by Vail-Ballou Press, Binghamton, N.Y.

Library of Congress Cataloging-in-Publication Data

Psycho/history : readings in the method of psychology,
    psychoanalysis, and history.
    Bibliography: p.
    Includes index.
    1. Psychohistory.   I. Cocks, Geoffrey, 1948–
II. Crosby, Travis L., 1936.
D16.16.P25 1987   901'.9   86-23411
ISBN 0-300-03681-7
ISBN 0-300-03682-5 (pbk.)

The paper in this book meets the guidelines for permanence and durability of the Committee on Production Guidelines for Book Longevity of the Council on Library Resources.

10   9   8   7   6   5   4   3   2   1

To our students, past, present, and future

Contents

Introduction

In our teaching of undergraduates, we have discovered that psychohistory is an ideal vehicle for introducing the timeless questions of human motivation in the past. Practical difficulties in making readily available those articles which best illustrate the most important issues in applying psychological concepts to history led us to the idea of this anthology.[1] Readings found here, combined with basic readings in Freud, Erikson, and Kohut, and supplemented by other works cited in our bibliography will, we believe, offer a thorough and balanced introduction to psychohistory. The readings will also provide a springboard for a discussion of general historiographical issues.

A useful approach to the promises and problems of psychohistory lies in the opposing paradigms of Carl Hempel and William Dray. Hempel believes that history is a scientific process of empirical inquiry, verification, and prediction. Historical inquiry is thus a search for general laws which will illuminate clear lines of cause and effect for all historical events.[2] Dray, on the other hand, believes that history is not a scientific endeavor; it is instead concerned with an empathic understanding of the motives and actions of historical figures. The historian, according to Dray, should strive to see things from the subject's point of view (and not merely ask "What would I have done?") so as to make that particular historical experience come alive as a sensible and meaningful narrative.[3]

Practicing historians nowadays do not generally see themselves as purveyors of a scientific point of view, even as they have increasingly drawn models and methods from the social sciences. Historians use the term "causation" in a more tentative, less conclusive way than Hempelians would like. For most historians, the concept of causation is not an expression of, nor a search for, general laws in history. Historians make use of what Dray would call "unifying" concepts, or they may speak of "conditions" or "circumstances." Even when historians use the term "cause," they almost always mean it in a way that suggests varying degrees of determinancy.

Early psychohistorical efforts especially were often marred by an ahistorical tendency to postulate psychological causes and their law-like effects upon historical characters by seeing childhood experiences as invariantly causative upon adult behavior. In their enthusiasm, they were clearly taking a cue from Freud, who always insisted that his work was a natural science. But in so doing, they ignored Freud's own view of causal complexity, or "overdetermination," as Freud put it.

One may wonder why historians should have been drawn to an essentially therapeutic and ostensibly scientific body of psychological theory such as Freud's. There are sound reasons. The historian H. Stuart Hughes, for one, has summarized the similar convictions, concerns, and aims shared by psychoanalysis and history: the conviction that the past has an influence on the present; a concern for plural explanations drawn from the welter of small and large clues to the mysteries of human behavior; and the aim of "liberat[ing] man from the burden of the past by helping him to understand that past."[4] It has also been argued that psychoanalysis, far from being merely another aspiring natural science, employs a holistic and not a mechanical approach to the individual case history, seeking to build a coherent and meaningful narrative of a life rather than just the confirmation of general laws.[5]

Embedded within the Hempelian certainties of psychoanalysis as a therapeutic discipline, psychohistorians have also seen a role for the subjective interpretations represented by the involvement, through transference and countertransference, of analysts with their patients. Thus, as "human sciences," both psychoanalysis and history can employ a combination of objective and subjective thinking.

In its present stage of development, psychohistory clearly bears the scars of its divided allegiance between a historical tradition which sees itself as beyond the reach of general laws and a therapeutically oriented (and "scientific") field such as psychoanalysis. This fragmented theoretical framework has too often produced one-dimensional, silly, or even cruel caricatures of politicians, peoples, and geniuses. Contributing to these faulty analyses are the inherent evidentiary problems of psychohistory: the difficulty of gathering data on childhood; the resultant danger of circular reasoning in hypothesizing antecedents from adult words and actions; the absence of personal contact enjoyed by the psychoanalyst; the misuse of subjectivity; the danger of reductionism; the question of whether psychoanalytic theory is valid for other times and places (and, indeed, whether the application of any contemporary model can illuminate the special "mentalities" of earlier periods).[6] Psychohistorians must take care to recognize the limits of their approach, as a number of the selections in this anthology suggest. Paradoxically, perhaps, they must be sophisticated and daring in their use of evidence. Psychohistorians can look for clues of the irrational, for example, not merely in the absence of rationality but in the context of a life or group: clues found in self-defeating behavior, such as that of Woodrow Wilson in his campaign for U.S. entry into the League of Nations; or in patterns of expression and action;[7] or in instances of "mass hysteria."[8]

Advances since the days of classical Freudian theory have helped smooth the way for psychohistorians. The evolution within the various schools of depth psychology in the 1920s and 1930s toward a greater emphasis on ego functions, character, and object-relations operating throughout an individual's life, rather than on id impulses buried deep within the psyche and childhood, has offered the psychologically attuned historian greater interpretive flexibility.[9] If viewed as heuristic devices rather than scientific laws, the diversity of theories can help refine our knowledge of behavioral complexity in the past. An example is the ongoing work in what has become the burgeoning historical subgenre of "Hitlerature."[10]

Historians have turned away from the early easy conviction that Hitler could be understood in crude psychopathological terms alone; they have become increasingly sophisticated about the fascinating mixture of the rational and irrational, the conscious and unconscious within Hitler. A responsible portrayal of any historical figure or phenomenon must include consideration of the internal world of its subject or subjects as revealed by patterns of behavior (actions, thoughts, motives) and their origins in the whole context of a life or lives. So Hitler's life must be viewed in its phenomenological and genetic totality (that is, what he did and why) and a coherent whole must be constructed out of the interaction of his private and public worlds. Every human being constitutes the intersection of various aspects of a given historical context: family, culture, society, politics, economics—all of these environments creating a dynamic pattern of feeling, perception, and knowledge within the individual which determines motives and actions over a lifetime. These influences reach the historian in various ways, from documents to dreams. Thus when the historian reads (and accepts the accuracy of the account) that Hitler dreamed late in the war that no A-4 rocket would ever reach England,[11] the interpretation of such a dream will not reflect some crude sexual analogy but will reveal a tangle of past and present motivational conditions about Hitler's conscious considerations of technical and strategic problems and alternatives, his calculated tendency toward the histrionic, and his personal feelings about power and aggression in general and about England in paticular.

Part I of this anthology is devoted to readings which raise basic questions about the possibility of using psychoanalytic theory in historical inquiry. We begin with one of the foremost critics of psychoanalysis. In his classic 1953 statement, the English psychologist Hans Eysenck charged that psychoanalysis is riddled with theoretical and methodological errors that undermine its claim to scientific status. For Eysenck, scientific explanation in psychology must rest upon experimental evidence that builds toward a comprehension of the laws governing human behavior. Psychoanalysis, Eysenck avers, can at best only offer some commonsense understanding of human actions and characteristics.

Where Eysenck sees weakness in the psychoanalytic enterprise, the philosopher of history Hans Meyerhoff sees strength. In an address to a psychoanalytic audience in 1961, Meyerhoff outlined what he saw as the similar aim and approach of psychoanalysis and history—a convergence of concern that is distinct from purely scientific method. The historian and the scientist are distinct from each other most crucially, according to Meyerhoff, in terms of their relationship to their respective subject matters.

The historian and psychoanalyst Peter Loewenberg emphasizes the same theme in his 1977 essay. Loewenberg stresses the importance of a relativistic approach to the study of history, arguing that even within science itself positivism has given way to the recognition that scientific paradigms should be judged not so much in terms of correspondence to truth but, more like history, in terms of persuasive coherence. Like Meyerhoff, Loewenberg also places a great emphasis on the empathic means of understanding shared by history and psychoanalysis. The subjective involvement of the historian with human beings in history is similar to the phenomenon of countertransference in psychoanalysis, that is, to the process whereby the analyst reacts to the patient's memories and emotions in terms of his or her own feelings. While some analysts claim that no such genuine process of countertransference can take place outside an encounter with a living subject, historians can and do react empathically to the experiences of those whom they study. The historian does not merely report facts: he or she interprets history by means not only of intellect, but by subjective understanding as well.[12]

Every historian uses this empathic ability to determine whether certain information or interpretations "fit" in terms of an understanding of the whole of the subject's life. The relevance, indeed the existence, of Hitler's dream about his rockets never reaching England, for instance, can be confirmed at least in part in terms of the historian's sense that such a happening "fits" into the patterns of Hitler's motives and subjectivity. The goal of history is to understand specific cases, as opposed to science's mission to explain phenomena in accord with general laws. Subjectivity, in short, seems endemic in historical studies. Historians must therefore be aware of the emotional environment of their own lives and times, as well as that of the past, some arguing that psychohistorians must undergo psychoanalysis.

There are of course inherent dangers in such interpretive flexibility. Charles Strozier offers a critique of subjectivity in the psychohistorical work of Erik Erikson. As Strozier notes, Erikson's methodology is based upon what Erikson himself calls "disciplined subjectivity." Strozier observes, among other things, that Erikson never precisely defines what he means by discipline. Part I concludes with two essays by psychohistorians whose work has recently raised anew debate over historical method. The first is by Lloyd deMause, founder of the Institute for Psychohistory in New York. DeMause has earnestly insisted that psychohistory constitutes a new science. Based on a theory of the history of childhood that envisions a future utopia of adult-child harmony, deMause's work and that of his followers has been dogged by failed predictions and the unreliability of so-called fantasy-analyses of groups past and present. Binion, for his part, insists on a peculiar degree of empathy in a variation of the kind of psychohistory propounded by deMause. Binion represents one extreme end of the kind of empathic understanding of the past advocated by Dray, while deMause attempts to use Dravian means to Hempelian ends.

Psychohistory, as we have noted, is largely based upon psychoanalysis—which is itself concerned with the exploration of individual human lives. Naturally enough, then, most psychohistory takes the form of psychobiography. Part II, therefore, presents a selection of essays on the subject of psychology and historical biography. Child psychiatrist Robert Coles begins the discussion with a cautionary tale about the pitfalls of psychobiography. Too easily can psychopathological labeling become a mere device for moral condemnation or clumsy debunking. Coles also raises the troubling question of the nature of genius and whether psychoanalysis can ever contribute to an understanding of it. Although the historian Joseph M. Woods thinks that Coles may be overly harsh in some of his criticisms, Woods agrees that outdated and overly simplistic psychoanalytic approaches to the past have harmed psychohistory's credibility. Woods suggests more fruitful models may be those based either upon the narcissistic personality or upon the actions of self-defeating behavior. In a practical demonstration of how psychobiography can suggest various alternative hypotheses in explaining the life of a man of genius, the psychologist William McKinley Runyan focuses on a single dramatic incident in the painter Vincent van Gogh's life—when he cut off the lower half of his left ear as a present for a prostitute. Runyan's ingenious exercise highlights some of the problems dogging the elucidation of the motives of historical figures.

Part II concludes with a series of articles presenting different psychological intepretations of Woodrow Wilson's career. Alexander George, a political scientist, offers a valuable methodological guide to writing and evaluating psychobiographies by focusing on Wilson as an example. Robert C. Tucker, also a political scientist, presents an alternative interpretation of Wilson's motives and behavior based upon the ego psychology of the neo-Freudian Karen Horney. A major challenge to the thesis that Wilson was psychologically lamed all his life as a result of his stern upbringing by a strict Calvinist father has been mounted by the psychiatrist and neurologist Edwin Weinstein. Weinstein sees Wilson's failures—the most notable of which was his inability to lead the United States into the League of Nations after World War I—in great measure as a function of a series of disabling strokes Wilson suffered beginning in 1896.[13] In the presentation of his argument, Weinstein is joined by the clinical psychologist James Anderson and the historian and Wilson biographer Arthur Link. In a rebuttal, Juliette and Alexander George dispute the evidence for Weinstein's hypothesis, reiterating their belief in the primacy of psychological factors behind Wilson's actions. The debate raises the important issue of the role played by physiological states and disorders in the lives of historical figures.[14] While certain aspects of an individual's life can certainly be explained by the presence of a discrete medical condition, in most cases the historian will want to integrate such a factor into the broader context of the subject's motivational and developmental life.

Part III addresses the especially difficult question of the psychological study of groups in history. Biography, after all, comprises only a small portion of the historian's task. More often, historians look to the larger weave of peoples and times in the fabric of the past. How are psychohistorians to take the long step from general psychological group theories to the dynamics of particular groups? What is the psychological link between individuals constituting group behavior? What, especially, is the link between leaders and followers? This is, of course, the stuff of social psychology. Most psychohistorians have remained firmly within the psychoanalytic tradition in attempting to explain group behavior in the past.

Bruce Mazlish, a historian, concludes that Freudian approaches are more successful. Gerald Platt, however, in discussing from a sociological point of view several psychoanalytic theories as they have been applied to past societies, finds them wanting. The historian John Demos, like many others in the psychoanalytic tradition, posits the importance of the family as the mediator of social values and pressures and, drawing from the developmental ego psychology of Erik Erikson and Heinz Kohut's study of narcissism, explores here the psychological dynamics of witchcraft in the culture of early New England.

As in psychobiography, so in group psychohistory, German history has proven to be a fertile ground. Many of these works have grown up around the phenomenon of National Socialism. Harvey Asher's review of non-psychoanalytic methods of inquiry into the Nazi movement provides a concise summary of various complementary alternatives to the Freudian model. Asher's article is a call to psychohistorians to remain open to the various possibilities of psychohistorical modeling.

We conclude our anthology with an essay by Peter and Carol Stearns on the historical study of emotions as part of a broadly conceived social history. Whether their eclectic approach will enhance or transcend psychohistory remains to be seen, but their ideas are a testament to the continuing vitality of the psycho-historical debate.

NOTES

1 Early anthologies of psychohistory for our purposes are too narrowly bound to psychoanalytic theory. These include Bruce Mazlish (ed.), *Psychoanalysis and History* (New York, 1963); and Benjamin B. Wolman (ed.), *The Psychoanalytic Interpretation of History* (New York, 1971). Robert Jay Lifton and Eric Olson (eds.), *Explorations in Psychohistory: The Wellfleet Papers* (New York, 1974) is not focused on the historiographical issues that we wish to emphasize. Other anthologies are idiosyncratic in their approach to psychohistory, such as Lloyd deMause (ed.), *The History of Childhood* (New York, 1974); Lloyd deMause (ed.), *The New Psychohistory* (New York, 1975); and Rudolph Binion, *Soundings: Psychohistorical and Psycholiterary* (New York, 1981). George Kren and Leon Rappoport (eds.), *Varieties of Psychohistory* (New York, 1976) defines psychohistory too loosely through the inclusion of essays only marginally relevant to an examination of a psychologically informed historical method.

Robert Brugger (ed.), *Our Selves—Our Past: Psychological Approaches to American History* (Baltimore, 1981); and Peter Loewenberg, *Decoding the Past: The Psychohistorical Approach* (New York, 1983), while excellent in their way, are primarily collections of case studies rather than of historiographically oriented essays.

2 Carl G. Hempel, "The Function of General Laws in History," in Patrick Gardiner (ed.), *Theories of History* (Glencoe, Ill., 1958), pp. 344–55.

3 William Dray, *Laws and Explanation in History* (London, 1957).

4 H. Stuart Hughes, "History and Psychoanalysis: The Explanation of Motive," in *History as Art and as Science: Twin Vistas on the Past* (New York, 1964), p. 47.

5 Michael Sherwood, *The Logic of Explanation in Psychoanalysis* (New York, 1969), pp. 190, 231.

6 Lawrence Walker, "*Mentalités:* The Hidden Agenda of Stannard's *Shrinking History*," *Psychohistory Review,* vol. 12, no. 4 (1984), pp. 43–48.

7 See, for example, Richard L. Bushman, "On the Uses of Psychology: Conflict and Conciliation in Benjamin Franklin," *History and Theory,* vol. 5 (1966), pp. 225–40.

8 As in John Putnam Demos, *Entertaining Satan: Witchcraft and the Culture of Early New England* (New York, 1982).

9 Peter Loewenberg, "Psychohistory: An Overview of the Field," in *Decoding the Past,* pp. 20–31.

10 Geoffrey Cocks, "The Hitler Controversy," *Political Psychology,* vol. 1 (1979), p. 67.

11 Walter Dornberger, *V-2,* trans. James Cleugh and Geoffrey Halliday (New York, 1954), pp. 91, 206.

12 Loewenberg, "Psychohistory," pp. 14–16.

13 Edwin A. Weinstein, *Woodrow Wilson: A Medical and Psychological Biography* (Princeton, 1981).

14 For another example, see Ida Macalpine and Richard Hunter, *George III and the Mad Business* (New York, 1969).

PART I

PSYCHOLOGY, PSYCHOANALYSIS, AND HISTORY

1

What Is Wrong with Psychoanalysis?

H. J. Eysenck

It is impossible to deny that Freudian theories have had a tremendous influence on psychiatry, on literature, and perhaps also on that whole complex of laws, folkways, and *mores* which we often refer to as "sexual morality." Moralists are inclined to doubt whether this influence has been essentially for the good, but after the initial outcry which was perhaps inevitable most people have settled down to an easy and even enthusiastic acceptance of psychoanalysis. This acceptance is not altogether in line with psychoanalytic teaching, which would lead one to anticipate resistance and hostility. Such resistance and hostility as there are can be found almost exclusively among psychologists and anthropologists, i.e. among those who have made a professional and detailed study of the theories and claims of psychoanalysts; among lay people the terms "psychology" and "psychoanalysis" have come to be almost synonymous, and in the literary world Freudian terms and concepts have been accepted so completely that modern novels are frequently indistinguishable from psychiatric case records.

This would appear to be an almost unique phenomenon in science. In no other science are we likely to find certain theories and hypotheses popularly accepted but rejected by many experts in that science. There are a few cases where this has been known to happen; the Lysenko affair has shown that in genetics also *vox populi* may be *vox dei,* to the extent of having genuine scientists excommunicated and threatened for not accepting views the evidence for which was practically non-existent, but which found favour with lay judges. Possibly another parallel may be found in the history of the heliocentric theory of the universe in which laymen supported those who believed the earth to be the centre of the world, against the consensus of opinion of those best qualified to judge.

Reprinted from *Uses and Abuses of Psychology* by H. J. Eysenck (Penguin Books, 1953) pp. 221–41, copyright © H. J. Eysenck, 1953.

3

In thus equating psychoanalysis with popular opinion we may seem to be moving in a topsy-turvy world. Is not Freud the great innovator, comparable with Galileo or Darwin? Is it not true that like these great scientific geniuses he also was at first stoned by the common multitude, only to be recognized and honoured after many years of persecution? Perhaps this apparent paradox is not quite as paradoxical as it may seem.

There are two kinds of psychology, just as there are two ways in which we may approach any other set of phenomena. Eddington has contracted these two approaches in his famous example of the two tables—the sensible table, which we can see and touch, which has weight and thickness, and is part of our everyday environment, and the scientific table, made up of electrons and protons, consisting essentially of nothingness interrupted by extremely fast-moving electric charges. We may accept the scientific table on the authority of the physicist's say-so, and because we have found in the past that predictions based on the physicist's view of the world tend to be correct; nevertheless, most of us find it impossible to look at the world consistently in this fashion, and prefer to deal rather with sensible entities which in some mysterious way we think we understand. It is obvious to us that the earth is flat, that the sun moves around the earth, and that you cannot make a silk purse out of a sow's ear. We may give up these views reluctantly and under protest when the factual support for the contrary views becomes too strong, but we usually do so with very bad grace, and a secret hankering after the good old ways.

The same opposition occurs with even greater force in psychology. German philosophers have brought out this point quite clearly in contrasting *verstehende* psychology with *erklärende* psychology, i.e. a common-sense psychology which tries to *understand* human beings, and a psychology which tries to *explain* their conduct on a scientific basis. It is often said that psychology has a long past, but a short history; it is the common-sense type of psychology which has been the stand-by of writers, philosophers, and all others who had to deal with human beings, and which accounts for the long past, but it is the explanatory, scientific type of psychology which arose towards the end of the last century which is referred to as having had the short history. These two kinds of psychology are so frequently mixed up that a few words may be useful in clarifying the issue.

In our dealings with people we can hardly be said to proceed on a haphazard basis of pure chance. Experience teaches us to expect certain reactions from certain types of people; close acquaintance may enable us to predict with considerable accuracy the reactions of our friends, or of members of our family. We may know quite well that Mary is a bit old-maidish, so that it is better not to tell *risqué* stories in front of her, while Joan is a bit of a fly-by-night who can always be relied upon to liven up a party. Dick is reliable and so honest that one would not be well advised to discuss in front of him ways and means of obtaining income tax relief which departed ever so little from the paths of rectitude, while Fred is forever cutting corners, and is quite likely one day to overdo it and find himself in jail. Dolores is "one for the boys" and "an easy lay"; Mac is a tightwad and High Church; Jim has no money sense at all and tends to take a scientific view of most things; Dolly is a "one-man woman" and house-proud. We all make these generalizations with respect to the people we know well, and we are quite prepared to act on them. We may even pride ourselves on our "understanding of human nature," and on the accuracy of our diagnosis. We often believe that such judgements can with accuracy be formed almost at first sight, and many people go as far as to think that external physical signs, such as a weak chin, or red hair, or a Jewish nose, are infallible signs of a person's character. We may not know consciously how we arrive at our judgements, but we will defend to the death our claim to their correctness.

Similar judgements are made every day on the physical plane also. We judge things to be heavy or light, we consider the air to be humid or dry, we expect material objects to fall when they are unsupported. We should be surprised to find that water did not wet us, or the sun did not heat us. We have a whole set of expectations built up through experience, and fortunately for us these expectations are frequently right.

Some physical concepts may appear similar to those of everyday life, e.g. those of time and space. It is, however, important to realize that they are far from identical. Newton has pointed out in the *Scholium* which precedes his *Principia,* that sensed time and sensed space, i.e. our everyday notions of these concepts, are not to be confused with "true or mathematical" time and space; anyone who confuses the two "is guilty of vulgar ignorance." Physical science does not attempt to *understand* everyday phenomena in common-sense terms, although ultimately it started out from this type of observation; physical science tries to *explain* natural phenomena in terms of laws of wide generality which subsume the individual phenomenon in question.

Exactly the same is true of psychology. The "understanding" psychologist is trying to gain an intuitive insight into the working of another person's mind on the basis of his common-sense knowledge of human nature. He may have derived his knowledge from self-observation and introspection, or from the observation of other people in a great variety of situations, or even from reading Shakespearian plays and modern novels; there is no denying that he is often amazingly astute and accurate in his intuitions. This type of insight, based on wide experience and probably natural aptitude and interest in human beings, is a very valuable quality in many walks of life, and almost indispensable in the psychiatrist, the personnel manager, the social leader, and the politician. However, valuable and useful as it may be, psychological insight and understanding by themselves have nothing whatsoever to do with psychology as a science, just as little as facility in dealing with physical "things" is an essential asset for the physical scientist. From observation I venture to assert that many of the greatest psychologists are if anything below average in this quality of "insight" into human motives and purposes, and similarly physicists of the highest standing are frequently incapable of adjusting the carburettor in their cars, or even of fixing a burned-out fuse. The expectation frequently voiced, namely, that psychologists should have learned a lot about "human nature," using the term in this sense, is quite unjustified. The psychologist knows no more about "human nature" than the next man, and if he is wise he will not let his claims outrun his discretion.

If the psychologist as a scientist is not trying to understand other people, then what precisely is he trying to do? He is trying to explain their conduct in terms of a system of general scientific laws. In doing so he may use terms which he has taken over from everyday speech, terms like intelligence, emotion, trait, type, ability, and so forth, just as the physicist took over terms like space, time, weight, mass, and many others from the language of his day. But it would be an error to equate the muddled, inexact, ill-defined terms of common usage with the exact, precisely defined, clear-cut concepts of the scientist. There are similarities, and a certain amount of overlap, but there certainly is nothing approaching complete correspondence.

This fact often leads to misunderstanding. The psychologist makes a statement regarding, say, the inheritance of intelligence, using that word in a relatively precise way to stand for a set of measurable phenomena. The layman understands the statement to refer to his own idea of intelligence, which may be and usually is rather different from that of the psychologist, and offers objections which are not at all relevant to the intent of the original statement. The psychologist finds it difficult to counter these criticisms because all the terms he uses have special connotations which would require explanation, frequently involving highly complex mathematics, and all of which can only be understood in terms of the whole system of thought of which they form a part. These bars to understanding are particularly mischievous because their presence is often quite unsuspected, and the argument may go on for hours and hours without reconciling the positions of the protagonists in the slightest. Scientific statements are highly complex statements deriving their meaning essentially from a whole set of facts, hypotheses, and theories; they cannot meaningfully be debated in the absence of full knowledge of all these facts, theories, and hypotheses.

How are these considerations relevant to psychoanalysis? Perhaps I can best make clear the connexion by stating quite briefly and dogmatically that psychoanalysis in my view is trying to *understand,* rather than to *explain;* that consequently it is essentially non-scientific and to be judged in terms of belief and faith, rather than in terms of proof and verification; and that lastly its great popularity among non-scientists derives precisely from its non-scientific nature, which makes it intelligible and immediately applicable to problems of "understanding" other people. This judgement I believe to be a statement of fact, rather than a value judgement. Religion and art are two other non-scientific disciplines which in spite of their lack of concern with scientific truth have contributed greatly to human happiness; to say that they are less valuable than science implies a scale of standards and values which itself is subjective and non-scientific. To judge

whether a given discipline is or is not scientific is possible without value implications; it necessitates nothing but a commonly agreed definition and standard
of scientific procedure. Such a definition and such standards exist, and may be
found in the writings of logicians and philosophers of scientific methodology;
those who are acquainted with these writings will agree that in spite of occasional
disagreements on minor issues there is an overwhelming amount of agreement
on the main points.

Many psychoanalysts would probably agree with this analysis, and maintain
that their work differed in many important respects from orthodox scientific
procedures. Jung is but one of a large number of analysts who consciously reject
scientific methodology in favour of subjectivity, intuition, and unconscious "understanding." There can be no argument here; those who look for religion, faith,
beauty, or other non-scientific values need fear no scientific criticism. Neither,
on the other hand, should they make any claims to having established scientific
truths; they cannot reject the methods of science and yet claim the results. This
desire to have the best of both worlds is very frequent among analysts, but it
would be difficult to proffer any logical argument in its defence. Non-scientific
analysts may, of course, quite frequently be right in their surmises, hunches, and
intuitive insights, just as many people who have never heard of psychology or
of psychoanalysis are often astonishingly astute in their understanding of human
motives. To be correct in particular instances is not necessarily a sign of the
scientific worth or correctness of one's views, theories, or hypotheses. (The obverse of this statement is more nearly true; to be wrong in particular instances
discredits a scientific theory to such an extent that it needs to be replaced completely by another, or at least heavily revised.)

While thus many analysts disclaim any intention of being scientific in their
work, no such thing could be said of the great majority who in their writings
claim that what they say is not merely useful, interesting, exciting, and ingenious,
but also true in the scientific sense of that term. Freud himself certainly held
such a view, and most of his followers would probably agree with his contention.
This makes it possible to apply our agreed criterion, and to see to what extent
psychoanalysis lives up to its pretensions.

It is here already that many analysts enter their first objection. They say that
traditional ideas as to what constitutes scientific method and scientific truth are
unduly narrow, and that the proof they are willing to offer is none the less scientific for lying outside the confines of orthodoxy. In other words, starting out
with the claim that "psychoanalytic conclusions are scientific truths," a claim
which is interesting only because we have come to appreciate that "scientific"
truths tend to be correct because they have been arrived at by a particular method, the analysts immediately proceed to alter the meaning of "scientific" in such
a way as to make it include the psychoanalytic findings in question. Such habits
of subtle redefinition are, of course, quite familiar in politics; prestige words
like "democracy" are frequently applied to dictatorships by a process of definition

which turns their customary meaning inside out. The high-priest of all who indulge in this pastime, of course, is Humpty Dumpty, whose discussion of the
meaning of "glory" has become a classic in the art of sowing semantic confusion.

> "I don't know what you mean by 'glory,' " Alice said. Humpty Dumpty smiled con-
> temptuously. "Of course you don't—till I tell you. I meant 'there's a nice knock-down
> argument for you!' " "But 'glory' doesn't mean 'a nice knock-down argument,' " Alice
> objected. "When *I* use a word," Humpty Dumpty said in rather a scornful tone, "it means
> just what I choose it to mean—neither more nor less." "The question is," said Alice,
> "whether you *can* make words mean so many different things." "The question is," said
> Humpty Dumpty, "which is to be Master—that's all."

A well-known exponent of this practice, Mrs. Baker Eddy, redefined "science"
in terms of religion, thus arriving at Christian Science. Communists redefine
"science" in terms of Marxian "dialectical materialism," thus arriving at the
"people's democracies" with their "dictatorship of the proletariat." The palmist
of Brighton pier redefines "science" in terms of her particular mercenary art,
thus arriving at "scientific fortune-telling." The claim that psychoanalysis is scientific has no ascertainable meaning whatever unless we define the term "science" in the way agreed on by the great majority of those who have considered
the history and practice of science. This is the important question; whether psychoanalysis is scientific in some other meaning of the term, created merely in
order to enable the answer "yes" to be given, is neither here nor there.

What, then, is the evidence on which psychoanalysis is based? Essentially it is
clinical rather than experimental. I have already discussed the differing attitudes
of the clinician and the experimentalist in the introduction, and shall not here
repeat what I have said there. Suffice it to remember that clinical work is often
very productive of theories and hypotheses, but weak on proof and verification;
that in fact the clinical method by itself cannot produce such proof because investigations are carried out for the avowed purpose of aiding the patient, not of
putting searching questions to nature. Even when a special experiment is carefully
planned to test the adequacy of a given hypothesis there often arise almost insuperable difficulties in ruling out irrelevant factors, and in isolating the desired
effect; in clinical work such isolation is all but impossible. The often-heard claim
that "psychoanalytic hypotheses are tested on the couch" (i.e. the couch on which
the patient lies during the analytic session) shows a clear misunderstanding of
what is meant in science by "testing" hypotheses. We can no more test Freudian
hypotheses "on the couch" than we can adjudicate between the rival hypotheses
of Newton and Einstein by going to sleep under an apple tree.

What type of evidence other than the clinical do Freud and his followers ad-
duce in support to their claims? There are two main varieties. The first relates
to the integrated nature of the whole body of hypotheses, theories, practices,
and treatments which makes up modern psychoanalysis. An integrated system of
constructs in science has unique advantages; it also has considerable dangers
inherent in it. The advantages lie in the mutual support which the various parts

of the system given to each other; the dangers lie in the tendency for interpretations to be biased in terms of the analyst's preconceived notions. This danger is particularly marked in psychoanalysis because interpretation of observations forms such a large portion of the whole structure.

It is increased by another feature of psychoanalysis which is unique in science, and is reminiscent rather of the practices of the ancient order of Loyola. Each psychoanalyst must pass through a training analysis in which all his actions, dreams, and fantasies are interpreted in Freudian terms, and in which he forms strong emotional bonds with his teacher, bonds which predispose him to accept such interpretations as correct, and which will make it impossible for him to make objective, unbiased judgements about the true relevance of analytic concepts. That this danger is not imaginary is attested by the admission of well-known psychoanalysts. Glover, for example, in arguing against the views of another Freudian which he regarded as pernicious and dangerous, accounted for the adherence of certain analysts to these views in terms of their "emotional certainty of the truth of the analyst's views" acquired in their training analyses under the heretic. But what is sauce for the goose is sauce for the gander, and if the views of the adherents of Melanie Klein are due to their "emotional bias" acquired during the training analysis, surely the same explanation can be given of the views held by Glover and his adherents? In fact, *ad hominem* arguments of this kind form the stock-in-trade of Freudian argumentation; it is because they are recognized not to have scientific validity that they have not usually been turned back on to psychoanalysts themselves.

It is not often realized to what extent this "emotional biasing" through training analysis forms a complete barrier between analyst and critic. Thus Freud states that "the teachings of psychoanalysis are based upon an incalculable number of observations and experiences, and no one who has not repeated those observations upon himself or upon others is in a position to arrive at an independent judgement of it." Thus Freud demands effectively that one must believe in his system before one can criticize it, a demand which is hardly in line with orthodox scientific procedures! Similar claims are made by the Jungians, where Jacobi states that "theoretic conceptions and explanations are adequate only up to a certain point for the comprehension of Jung's system of thought, for in order to understand it completely one must have experienced its vital working on one's self." When it is realized that there are some fifteen or more hostile "analytic" systems making similar claims, it will be clear that no one can be competent to judge between them because no one would have enough time and money to undergo fifteen separate and incompatible personal training analyses!

Claims made for Freudian hypotheses in terms of their forming part of a "system" must therefore be rejected as irrelevant. There are quite a number of such "systems," all disagreeing on fundamental issues, and all relying on proof of the clinical ("couch") variety. But if they are all based on evidence obtained "on the couch," how can we hope to judge between their divergent claims? If the clinical experience of the claimants is the only type of proof attempted, and if these clinical experiences are in flagrant contradiction, then we must either rely on faith, declare the whole matter incapable of a solution, or ask for more acceptable proof. When Freudians claim that their patients produce in their dreams symbols clearly similar to those described by Freud, while Jungians claim with equal fervour that their patients produce in their dreams symbols similar to those posited by Jung, we must look for more experimental evidence before deciding between these claims—unless, indeed, we try to account for both findings in terms of quite a different type of hypothesis, making suggestibility to the known expectations of the analyst responsible for the results of Freudians and Jungians alike!

Such more experimental, factual type of evidence is the second variety offered by analysts, and we must look at it with particular care. Let me quote a particular argument in illustration; an argument taken from Freud's writings and selected because I have found that to many audiences it makes a very strong appeal. Freud argues for the hypothesis that all dreams are in reality wish-fulfilments, and quotes in support reports about the common experiences of explorers and others that when they are starving in their camps they tend to dream about food. Thus the need for food generates the wish for food, and the dream, ever ready to fulfil these wishes, obliges with vistas of two-pound steaks and strawberry shortcake. Here, then, we have outside support for our hypothesis, and the scientific proprieties appear to be fulfilled.

Let me restate this argument in more formal terms. On the basis of detailed observation of the dreams of many patients, we arrive at the hypothesis that "dreams are wish-fulfilments." From this hypothesis we deduce that starving men should dream of food. . If this can be shown to be so, our hypothesis is supported; if this can be shown not to be so, our hypothesis is decisively disproved. Now Freud does not provide us with experimental evidence of any kind; he relies on anecdotal evidence of the most unreliable variety, second-hand, selective, and incomplete. Little value can be attributed to it. Fortunately we have more recent reports of adequately controlled, well-carried-out experiments into human starvation, experiments in which the participants lost almost a quarter of their body weight. Detailed records were made of their dreams, and comparisons with properly-fed individuals failed to show any tendency, however small, for the starving subjects to report more food-dreams than the control group. Thus experimental procedures show Freud's anecdotal evidence up as inconclusive and irrelevant; they also disprove his fundamental hypothesis regarding the nature and purpose of the dream.

Similar findings have again and again attended the detailed investigation along experimental lines of Freudian generalizations. Orlansky, Sears, and many others have summarized the experimental literature dealing with Freudian concepts, and the outcome, by and large, has been that for every hypothesis supported there are at least two where the evidence is doubtful, or clearly contrary to expectation. This is by no means a bad average as scientific hypotheses go, but it does seem to dispose of the Freudian system as such. Much may be salvaged, and taken over into newer systems of personality description; indeed, psychology will for many years to come be deeply indebted to the intrepid genius who infused new life into a rather philosophical and academic discipline. But however highly we may value these hypotheses and insights, psychoanalysis as a self-contained system claiming to afford a scientific view of human nature is dead, even though the embalmed corpse may still be exhibited to the faithful.

How does psychoanalysis counter the factual arguments brought against it? In the first place, by claiming that its therapeutic procedures work, thus lending important support to the theories and hypotheses on which it is based. I have examined the evidence regarding the effectiveness of psychotherapy in another chapter of this book, and we may notice only the conclusion, to the effect that the available evidence, which is technically faulty and of very doubtful value, being based almost entirely on the opinion of each psychotherapist regarding the success of his own therapy, gives no support whatever to the contention that psychotherapy alleviates the mental suffering of neurotics. Some two patients out of three do tend to improve during therapy, but similarly two patients out of three improve without being given any psychotherapy at all. Thus this argument can hardly be used in order to bolster up the contentions of the Freudians.

The second defence of the psychoanalysts relates to a feature of their system which will be familiar to those who have made a study of semi-religious systems, ranging from biblical prophecy to dialectical materialism. The original statements are couched in such vague, general and complex ways that deductions cannot be made with any degree of definiteness; interpretation thus becomes necessary, and a class of self-styled "experts" arises, claiming to expound the pure truth of the original, and relating it to current problems and current thought. As Ellis, himself an analyst, points out, "analytic theory has so far been formulated in such a loose and unverifiable manner as to encourage some analysts to verge dangerously close to mysticism, than which nothing is less scientific." He goes on to direct attention to the fact that analysis has tended to attract more than its due share of individuals who seem to be mystical-minded, a fact he attributes to four main causes: "*(a)* analysis has *not* held strictly to scientific principles, but has allowed considerable non-scientific leeway to its devotees; *(b)* it has attracted to its ranks many neurotics who have great need of mystical, non-logical defences, and who must continually fall back on religio-mystical philosophies to bolster their inabilities to face the grim realities of contemporary life; *(c)* it has tolerated vague, generalized formulations which are ever but a step removed from mysticism, and which may easily be mystically interpreted; *(d)* it has frequently been cultish and obscurantist: which is precisely what mystics inevitably tend to be, too." Be that as it may, the fact is indisputable that Freudian theories are not simple, straightforward statements of hypotheses from which testable deductions can be made; they are highly involved, loose *obiter dicta* which require interpretation before being intelligible, which are frequently contradictory, and which do not easily lend themselves to processes of scientific proof and disproof. This makes them almost completely resistant to disproof; if deductions from psychoanalytic hypotheses are not verified it can always be maintained that the deduction rests on an erroneous understanding of the hypothesis, and that an alternative "interpretation" of the hypothesis would indeed predict the ex-perimentally-found facts. Thus Freudian hypotheses are indeed quite invulnerable, being too indefinite for factual deductions to be made with any certainty; by the same token they are also unscientific and useless.

It is the third defence of the psychoanalysts, however, which constitutes a master-stroke of tactical brilliance. They make use of concepts such as "reaction formation," which allow a person who theoretically should show behaviour pat-tern A to react away from this pattern to such an extent that he shows instead the opposite pattern, Z. Thus the person who because of various hypothetical childhood events is supposed to be timorous may through reaction formation be outwardly aggressive and tough; thus the hypothesis is verified regardless of whether the patient is found to be either timorous or aggressive. Jung makes use of a similar mechanism by stating that persons who are outwardly introverted are unconsciously extraverted, while those who are outwardly extraverted are unconsciously introverted—thus making it possible to "explain" any type of conduct simply by referring it either to the conscious or to the unconscious por-tion of the patient's personality. It is this feature of analytic thought, more than any other, which serves the analyst as a defence mechanism, because all reactions whatever can thus be explained after a fashion, even if none can be predicted. However, it is not *ex post facto* explanation which constitutes science, but pre-diction which can be verified. Here the concept of reaction formation is of course quite useless, because it does not help us in deciding between a number of pos-sible alternatives. Concepts like reaction formation are essentially *ad hoc* hy-potheses which inevitably explain the individual case because they have been put forward especially in order to explain it, but which do not fit into any sys-tematic framework, and which are anathema to scientists because of the ease with which they can be advanced, and the difficulty of proving or disproving them. If we make up an *ad hoc* hypothesis for every new case—which essentially is the method of psychoanalysis—then we shall never go beyond the present position where we can explain everything and predict nothing.

So far we have criticized analytic procedures on general grounds; it may be useful to particularize and state a few of the objections which psychologists have brought forward against various features of contemporary psychoanalysis. In the first place, then, *psychoanalytic conclusions are based on unreliable data.* Its data are introspections (of the analyst) and verbalized statements (of the anal-ysand). Data of this kind are essentially subjective, and therefore present special difficulties to the scientist. These difficulties are not insuperable; verbatim re-cordings can be made of the analytic session, and Roger and other non-analytic workers have shown how useful and indeed invaluable such recordings can be in tracing the course of therapy, in validating hypotheses advanced by the therapist, and in checking the accuracy of the extremely fallible memory of the therapist. In relying on his memory alone, the therapist easily becomes selective, and what is recorded by him in the case history tends to be what fits in with his preconceived ideas. Thus what is reported by the analyst in articles and books is seldom the whole evidence; it is a highly selected part of the evidence, usually taken from a few highly selected cases. No general conclusions can be drawn from such data, particularly as the analyst seldom attempts the essential cross-check of going through his data to find evidence against his preconceived notions, and in favour of a hypothesis different to the one suggested by Freudian theory.

This would not be so dangerous if the data presented by the analyst were at least direct records, however selected, of what occurred in the analytic session. But usually *psychoanalytic data prejudge the issue* by mixing inextricably raw data and analytic interpretation. The reader who is familiar with Freud's own writings, or with those of any of his followers, will be able to check for himself the ratio of fact and interpretation in the cases there reported. As Wittels admits in his biography of Freud, "Freud's specific method of investigation . . . was not suitable for setting up boundaries and strict definitions. Through insight into himself, he came to understand a psychological phenomenon, and from the beginning his discoveries carried a strong inner conviction of certitude." As Ellis comments on this passage, "while an inner conviction of certitude is indubitably a fine trait for a prophet to possess, its liabilities for a scientist should be sufficiently obvious to warrant no further comment." It is this inner conviction of certitude which presumably makes the analytic writers eager to convince by argument, rather than to prove by fact, and which leads to this inextricable combination of verbal report and interpretation.

Psychoanalysts overgeneralize their conclusions. Freud based his imposing edifice on the verbal statements of a few hundred middle-class Viennese neurotics. Instead of confining his conclusions to the population of which this was a sample—as would have been the proper scientific procedure—he extended them to all human beings, at all times, everywhere. In other words, he thought to have divined universal truth from an extremely unrepresentative sample of human beings. What is true of his neurotic patients (assuming for the moment that his observations were accurate, and his hypotheses correct) is obviously not necessarily true of non-neurotic Trobriand Islanders; indeed, Malinowsky has shown with a wealth of detailed illustrations that Freudian theories are very strongly culture-bound, and have to undergo considerable modification if they are to be applied in any way to other groups. What is true of middle-class people is not necessarily true of working-class people; in another chapter I have discussed the facts supporting this statement at some length, and will therefore not deal with them again here. Nor does the fault lie with Freud alone. Most of his followers have emulated his example, and there are several cases where what has been alleged to have been found true in one case has been generalized to the whole of humanity! Overgeneralization of this kind puts psychoanalysis outside the pale of science; before findings are extended beyond the group on which they were originally established, there must be acceptable proof that such extension is warranted.

Psychoanalysts apply their putative principles to general social phenomena without proof of their applicability. Even if Freud's theories and hypotheses were strictly applicable to human beings as individuals, it would not follow that we could account for social phenomena such as war, industrial unrest, or artistic production by their means. Many analysts, however, have extended these theories to deal with almost all the social problems which beset us, always from a theoretical point of view, i.e. without any reference to fact, and usually without the humility of the scientist presenting a hypothesis. These dubious speculations are presented as facts, and society is urged to take action accordingly. . . . I have seen it suggested in a serious document intended for official consumption that part of the unrest in the coalfields was due to the unconscious conflicts aroused in the miner by having to use his pick-axe (a phallic male symbol) on "mother earth" (a mother symbol). To the layman, who finds difficulties in distinguishing between psychology, psychoanalysis, and psychiatry, such far-fetched ideas are likely to bring all three into disrepute, although there is probably no serious psychologist who would subscribe to views of this type. Freud himself has issued a warning against "indiscriminate psychoanalysing" of all and sundry; it is unfortunate that his followers have not always followed this sober advice.

Where Freudian hypotheses are used to guide research, this research is often illustrative of preconceptions, rather than a crucial test of the hypothesis. Thus the hypothesis that broken homes produce neurosis may lead to a demonstration that neurotics frequently come from broken homes. This fact, of course, is not crucial unless it can also be shown that people who do not suffer from neurosis tend to come from broken homes in a significantly smaller number of cases. But this second part of the experiment is hardly ever performed by Freudians. Figures published by the American Army showed that a large proportion of neurotics did indeed come from broken homes; they also show, however, that normal and especially well-adapted soldiers also came from broken homes in almost equally large proportion. These figures indicate that the broken home had only a vanishingly small part, if any, to play in the genesis of neurosis.

This neglect of control groups to provide the negative part of the inductive argument is a very characteristic part of Freudian experimentation. Again and again a causal sequence is asserted because certain events are found to occur frequently in the early years of the lives of neurotics; hardly ever is there any attempt to show that these events occur less frequently, or not at all, in the lives of non-neurotics. The analyst may retort that we are all neurotic, after all, unless psychoanalysed according to the dictates of Freud (of Jung, or Stekel, or Adler, or whoever may be the father-figure of the analyst who is talking), and that therefore these events would be expected to occur universally. But this argument clearly proves too much; we may all be neurotic, but some of us are more neurotic than others, and it is the causes of these individual differences which we wish to know about. If the causes adduced by Freudians are universal, then by that token they cannot help us in accounting for the fact that one person has a nervous breakdown, while another overcomes his difficulties in less neurotic ways.

Psychoanalytic arguments from facts beg the question. Let us turn to the preceding argument that broken homes cause neurosis, and let us assume that it had been established beyond doubt that broken homes were more frequent in the histories of neurotics than in the histories of non-neurotics. To argue from this that the broken homes were in any way responsible for the subsequent neurosis would be a clear example of an ancient logical fallacy, namely, that of the *post hoc, ergo propter hoc* argument. To the statisticians, this fallacy is known as "arguing from correlations to causes." All that could be regarded as established would be that broken homes and neurosis are correlated; this correlation tells us nothing whatsoever about the causal sequences involved. The Freudian interpretation is an environmentalistic one; it would be just as reasonable to invoke a hereditary one, somewhat along these lines. Predisposition to neurosis is inherited—neurotic parents, neurotic children. But neurotic parents are likely to have their marriages fail, so that their children will grow up with the background of a broken home. Consequently, we shall find that neurotics will tend to come with disturbing frequency from broken homes—not because the broken home causes the neurosis, but because the parents' neurosis causes both the broken home and (through heredity) the child's neurosis. I do not claim that this second hypothesis, along hereditarian lines, is more likely to be true than the Freudian (although there is considerable evidence for the view that neurotic predisposition and emotional instability are to a considerable extent inherited traits); I am concerned with the calm disregard by psychoanalysts of non-Freudian hypotheses which might explain the alleged facts equally well. Science advances by eliminating counter-hypotheses through carefully controlled experiments; it does not advance by begging the question. When it is realized that the alleged facts themselves are of very doubtful standing, and often merely the projections of the analyst's own wishes and desires, it will be realized why scientists are chary of accepting the analytic account of human nature as anything but brilliant speculation.

Protests against these methods of conducting research and of advancing arguments and proofs are not confined to psychologists; many orthodox psychiatrists are equally severe in their censure. Elliot Slater sums the matter up extremely well when he says: "There has ... been an increasing tendency among clinicians to minimize the effects attributable to genetical causes, and to teach a psychiatry in which they receive little or no mention. This tendency has been marked in Britain, but it has assumed formidable strength in the U.S.A. Instead of a harmonious development, in which the psychoses and neuroses, constitution and environment, psychogenesis and physiogenesis receive their due share of attention, interest among practical workers has been devoted more and more exclusively towards psychotherapy, psychoanalysis, social psychiatry, personnel selection, group therapy, and preoccupations with anthropology, sociology, and political theory. In its one-sidedness, this development is not healthy.

"It would not perhaps be putting it too high to say that we are witnessing the manifestation of an anti-scientific tendency which is winning an increasing number of supporters. The customary canons of scientific reasoning are ignored by these schools. Uncomfortable facts are left unconsidered. Hypotheses are multiplied regardless of the principle of economy. Explanations which may be valid for certain members of a class of phenomena are regarded as true for the class as a whole. Interpretations which conform with theory, and which might be true, are regarded as established. Possible alternatives are not considered, and no attempt is made to seek for evidence of critical value which shall decide between them. Criticisms from outside are ignored, and only the initiate may be heard. Utterance is dogmatic and lacks scientific humility and caution. These are the mental mechanisms which we associated with the growth of a religious orthodoxy, and not with the progress of science."

If this chapter has been critical, it has been so because I am concerned about the future of psychology. However much psychologists may show their desire not to be held responsible for the views advanced by psychoanalysts, society often fails to mark the distinction between scientific statement, based on fact and rigorous logical and statistical reasoning, and the kind of *obiter dicta* discussed in this chapter, based on assumptions and loose and wishful thinking. If the latter are in due course discredited, this discredit will almost certainly attach to the whole of psychology and psychiatry, instead of only to the group responsible.

I would not like to be understood as condemning psychoanalysis hook, line, and sinker. Like most psychologists, I appreciate the breath of fresh air which Freud introduced into the musty dry-as-dust atmosphere of nineteenth-century academic psychology. The brilliance of his mind has opened doors which no one now would wish to close again, and his keen insight has given us a storehouse of theories and hypotheses which will keep researchers busy for many years to come. All this one can appreciate without accepting the totality of his views as revelations from a higher authority, and without losing one's critical sense. There is much that is supremely important in Freud's contribution to psychology, but there is also much that is bad. To eliminate the latter, without losing the former, must be the task of a scientifically-orientated psychology. The answer to the question which forms the title of this chapter—What is wrong with psychoanalysis?—is simple: Psychoanalysis is unscientific. It is only by bringing to bear the traditional methods of scientific inference and experimentation that we can hope to reap all the benefit of its founder's genius.

2

On Psychoanalysis as History

Hans Meyerhoff

There are various ways of dealing with the relationship between psychoanalysis and history, for there is much common ground between the two disciplines. Psychoanalysis, as we know, has its own philosophy of history. It is to be found primarily in the works which Freud wrote during the last phase of his life, say from *Totem and Taboo* in 1913 to *Moses and Monotheism* in 1939. We now have a considerable body of literature on this subject, chiefly by "outsiders," i.e., sociologists and philosophers, and I will not add anything to this discussion.[1]

Another link between the two disciplines is the use of psychoanalysis in history. Thus a few years ago, a distinguished historian startled his professional colleagues in a presidential address delivered before the American Historical Association by pleading seriously that a "deepening of the historical understanding" was possible only through a more extensive use of psychoanalysis.[2] Freud himself was surprisingly reluctant about applying psychoanalysis to specific problems and personalities in history. In a very thoughtful letter to Arnold Zweig, he explicitly warned against doing this sort of thing in the case of Nietzsche.[3] And while he did play the game of analyzing historical figures in his letters, he did not do so in his official works—with one notable exception: the as yet unpublished study of Woodrow Wilson which Freud wrote in collaboration with William Bullitt.[4]

Again, I will not say anything else on this interesting and difficult subject. Thus I do not discuss great speculative ideas in philosophy nor specific practical problems in history. I deal with a different topic, more modest and less exciting. Psychoanalysis and history also have a great deal in common (1) because a historical method is an integral part of psychoanalytic theory and therapy, (2) because, though formulated as a strictly psychological theory, psychoanalysis cannot be divorced from a study of history and society. The primary purpose of this paper, then, is to consider these similarities in method between the two disci-

Reprinted from *Psychoanalysis and the Psychoanalytic Review*, vol. 49, no. 1 (Summer 1962) pp. 3–20.

plines or, more simply, to look at psychoanalysis from a different perspective: not as a branch of the general sciences, biological, medical, or psychological, but as a branch of history.

It is customary to say, especially among clinicians, that psychoanalysis is (or should be) a science, no more and no less. This is a perfectly legitimate view supported as it is by Freud's own authority and by the persistent endeavors since Freud to improve the scientific status of psychoanalysis. Psychoanalysis *is* like any other science in several respects. It has developed a theoretical system of its own consisting of abstract concepts, principles, and (possibly) general laws. And this system presumably is "open": it may be revised in the light of new evidence and as a result of rethinking old concepts. The theoretical system provides the basis and support for the specific work in therapy. Thus psychoanalytic explanations are guided and controlled by psychoanalytic theory. There is a theory of dreams; there is a theory of neuroses; and, above all, there is a general theory of the mind to explain the infinite variety of individual behavior.

There is no need to belabor this point. There are, of course, many difficult problems which arise in the context of psychoanalytic theory; but that's a different topic. I do not wish to question the scientific status of psychoanalysis. Let us agree that, in principle, it is like any other science regardless of how unfriendly critics may judge its actual performance. Yet, though it has its own theory in the scientific sense, psychoanalysis, if not a branch of history, has very close affiliations with history. Moreover, these affiliations are neither accidental nor negligible. They are an essential aspect of psychoanalysis as a "science." Psychoanalysis is an interesting logical specimen because it is and must be both science and history. Thus a historical perspective may help to clarify certain problems—both logical and ideological—which haunt psychoanalysis and which seem to be peculiarly impervious to treatment by strictly scientific methods. The remainder of this paper is an attempt to make the historical dimension inherent in psychoanalysis more explicit and more respectable.

II

"Psychoanalysis is the most radically historical psychology: this is its basic challenge to all other psychologies."[5] What, then, is historical about psychoanalysis?

To begin with, psychoanalytic theory itself is historical. In contrast to other types of psychology, psychoanalysis employs a historical method and characteristically historical concepts in the study of human behavior. The method is based on the simple proposition that we know the patient when we know his history. Thus "case histories" are an integral part of psychoanalytic theory. They are not, as we shall see, symptoms of an underdeveloped science. Again, psychoanalytic concepts are historical or evolutionary: they have a temporal sense and direction built into them. They may refer to fixed points in time; they may try to catch developmental (dynamic) processes such as reaction-formations, sublimations, integrative or regressive processes; or they may simply describe crucial stages on life's way—from the oral to the genital stage of development. In brief, they deal with the vicissitudes—i.e., the historical fate—of the libido. In a striking literary image Freud, as you know, compared the mind and life of man to the historical model of the ancient city of Rome.

The basic project of psychoanalysis is historical. It consists in discovering the past as it survives in the present life of the patient. This is possible because of memory. Our patients, as Freud said, suffer from memories. Man is a distinctly historical animal because he remembers. Memory introduces a historical dimension into human life beyond the biological processes of growth, maturation, and death. Because of memory human beings are conscious of having a history. And because of memory, the "past" makes all the difference in the present and future life of the individual.

In practice, this historical (or genetic) method "works" by making and remaking the history of the patient. Thus the concrete application of history to psychoanalysis occurs in the context of clinical work. The clinical situation is essentially a historical situation; or, in Erikson's words, the "thearapeutic encounter" is a historical process. It consists in remembering, recording, and reconstructing a significant slice of human history: the patient's history as unveiled in interaction with the therapist.

Erik Erikson has paid special attention to these affinities between psychoanalysis and history as they apply to clinical work and to the psychoanalytic treatment of a historical problem.[6] Moreover, he has presented some of his own ideas by referring to the work, *The Idea of History,* by the English philosopher and historian, R. G. Collingwood. There are two major features of Collingwood's conception of history which are particularly appropriate to the work in psychoanalysis: First, for Collingwood (as for Croce) history is always "contemporary" in the sense that it is a reconstruction of the past "as it survives in the present." Thus history involves a specific reference to the present—and possibly to the future; for the present presumably always includes a direction toward the future. Second, for Collingwood (as for Dilthey) history is always the re-enactment of some *thought* of the past in the mind of the contemporary historian. Thus the task of the historian is not simply to preserve the dry-as-dust facts of the past: the assassination of Lincoln, the fate of the Armada, the burning of Moscow, the massacre of St. Bartholomew's, and so forth; the essential task of the historian is to rethink the states of mind of the human agents involved in these happenings or to explain their feelings, ideas, motivations, and intentions. In short, the historian is engaged in a "psychological" project of a highly introspective nature; for it is his task to discover the inner and hidden "meaning" behind the overt sequence of events.

Collingwood, of course, is not the only philosopher in the field of history; but his ideas on the subject have been very influential in recent years and they are obviously pertinent to the historical project in psychoanalysis. This project also aims at disclosing the inner and hidden meaning of past events: the feelings, fantasies, and ideas associated with, or repressed in, memories; and the therapist's role consists primarily in rethinking the processes, both conscious and unconscious, unfolding in the patient's mind. Moreover, a psychoanalytic inquiry into the past is always oriented toward the present—and the future. Remembering in therapy is also an act of appropriating the past in order to forget. To cure the patient of his memories is to deliver him from the tyranny of the past. In this sense, psychoanalysis serves the cause of human freedom: its primary purpose is to expand and reinforce the areas of life, both present and future, in which the individual can choose freely and responsibly because he has become the master of his own history.

The practical demands imposed upon a therapist differ, of course, from the case of a historian imbued with what Professor Lovejoy has called a "purely archaeological motive"; i.e., a pure passion for discovering the truth about the past for its own sake. Yet, even if there be such simon-pure passion—which is doubtful—it is not incompatible with the belief that more and better knowledge about the past may also be a means for a deeper insight into and a more intelligent response to the present. Thus, according to Mr. Carr, history has a dual function which corresponds closely to the basic project in psychoanalysis: "to enable man to understand the society of the past and to increase his mastery over the society of the present."[7] And even Professor Lovejoy, concerned as he is with saving the theory of history from any involvement with present interests, concedes that "history is a branch of anthropology, in the largest sense of the term, and the historian is contributing in his own fashion to mankind's effort to fulfill the Delphian imperative."[8] What else but "Know thyself" is the categorical imperative inherent in psychoanalysis? Why? Because self-knowledge is believed to be the key to human freedom and to the discovery of one's own identity. Thus what ordinary history does for the collective life of mankind, psychoanalysis does for the life of the individual.

III

These historical features of psychoanalysis give rise to two significant problems: (1) the problem of objectivity, (2) the problem of explanation. With regard to both problems, psychoanalysis finds itself in the same camp with history.

The clinical situation is unique in that it involves another person—the therapist—in the very process he is studying. I don't mean to say that he gets involved in the outside life of his patient (though, I understand, this has happened). Nor do I mean that a trained therapist cannot look upon the "case" as if it were merely an "object" for scientific study. We know that he must be capable of detachment or of what some writers in history have called an "effort of self-transcendence" or an "act of self-emptying."[9] Yet it is an open question, in history as in therapy, whether the analyst can ever detach himself so completely from the evidence he is studying that he is nothing but a free-floating, neutral observer. According to Erikson, this is not possible in the therapeutic encounter; for the "objective" study of the patient's past is a process in which the therapist is "subjectively" involved in a logical sense: his own affective and emotional responses are part of the historical process unfolding on the couch; and this situation "highlights one methodological point truly unique in clinical work."[10] The emotional responses of the clinician are part of the *evidence* for the case he is analyzing. They serve as "an evidential source and as a guide in intervention."[11] I cannot here present Erikson's reasons for making this startling assertion. In the specific case discussed by him in detail, Erikson derives this conclusion from the interpretation of a dream. This interpretation, he shows, is based not only upon an expert knowledge of psychoanalytic theory, but also upon an emotional response, more precisely, upon responding to a sense of anger felt by the therapist at a crucial juncture in the analysis of the patient.

Thus the therapist in reconstructing the specific case before him may (and must) fall back upon private resources of his own not at the disposal of anyone else. He must also "feel" his way through the evidence; or, if you prefer, he must learn to trust his unconscious. Obviously, there is no one who can double in brass for one's unconscious. Nor can the therapeutic situation, strictly speaking, be reenacted at a later time; for "later" means that time has passed and that the people concerned with a review of the case are not the same. Thus the "objective" evidence presented later, on a tape or a film, cannot be analyzed as it would or might have been during the actual process of therapy. There is no escape from this element of historicity: time and place make all the difference in psychoanalysis as in history.

Emotional responses, however, whether anger, affection, or what not, are but one aspect of this strange encounter. Even as the case before him can be reconstructed and treated only by a "psychoanalysis of the total personality"—to cite the pioneer work of Franz Alexander—so the therapist himself is involved as a whole human being in this historical process. He is engaged as a total personality as well—at least theoretically; for he must mobilize all the resources of his personality, emotional and intellectual, imaginative and moral, logical and ideological, in order to solve the particular puzzle before him. He must respond to the clinical situation in terms of his whole life. In this sense, therapy is an "existential" encounter.

A similar situation prevails in history; for what is the evidence in history? Of course, dates and documents, facts and figures—the primary sources; and nobody doubts the truth of the simple factual statement that Lincoln was assassinated in Ford's Theater in Washington on the 14th of April 1865. Yet the truth of such factual statements is not what makes history: accuracy in these matters, getting the facts straight, "is a duty, not a virtue."[12] What makes history is to explain and interpret these happenings; that is, to write a significant narrative, not a compilation of facts. In other words, facts must be selected and interpreted so that we are shown what they "mean." Evidence in history as in psychoanalysis is always interpreted evidence. Facts are significant only in a context of interpretation.

In the case of an interpretive study of Lincoln's death the evidence appealed to consists of more than primary sources. "Potentially and in principle," as Collingwood pointed out, "the whole perceptible world is evidence for the historian."[13] What he had in mind was that the evidence is found not in the documents only—or in the associations on the couch; *part* of the evidence is supplied by the historian's own personal experience. Again, what are the principles which guide the historian in his interpretations? Of course, he is guided by the "facts"; of course, he observes the principles of ordinary logic and draws upon every possible kind of knowledge in the general (scientific) sense. A historian writing about the origins of World War II must also use general laws and theories about nature, man, and society. Only in the case of ordinary history (unlike psychoanalysis which has its own theory) this general body of knowledge is usually derived from nonhistorical sources—from common sense or from some other science such as physics, geography, economics, or psychology. Yet, after these various resources have been exhausted, "the interpreting of evidence," to cite Collingwood again, "is [also] a task to which a man must bring everything he knows; . . . and not knowledge only, but mental habits and possessions of every kind; and none of these is unchanging." Why not? Because they change in his own life as in history. Thus the historian is "always a part of the process he is studying"[14]—which corresponds to what Erikson singled out as the unique feature inherent in clinical work.

It follows that, however conscientious and self-critical he may be in his work, the historian cannot be completely neutral. He cannot step outside history—his own place in history. While studying history he is also—in part—a product of history, and the ideas he employs for interpreting history are themselves part of the historical process. This creates a much more intimate relationship between observer and observed than in a study of nature where it seems to be easier to enforce a strict dichotomy between subject and object. In this sense, the historian is more involved—logically involved—in the study of history than a scientist is in a study of nature. By "logically involved" I mean that he is "at the same time both the subject and the object of historical knowledge"[15]; he is caught up in the historical process in his thinking about history; and he is indebted to history for the ideas and concepts he employs for an understanding of history.

Perhaps he is more emotionally involved as well; for a historian cannot but care about the community of men as he need not care about a colony of mice. He cannot be as indifferent about the behavior of human beings as he may be about the behavior of molecules. And "caring," of course, is an emotional term, or "subjective." It's more than that; for it is a complex attitude including emotional, intellectual, moral, and ideological components. It is a response in terms of one's whole personality—the way one thinks and feels about human life and the world in general.

It may be possible to leave this personal view of the world at home when we are doing scientific work in the laboratory. History cannot be written without it; and it would be wishful thinking to close one's eyes to the presence of a personal equation in psychoanalysis. There are many ways in which personal factors of age, sex, class, culture, and ideology intrude upon the "scientific" work in these two disciplines. Thus there is at least a *prima facie* case for skepticism.

Both history and psychoanalysis have used similar methods to cope with this threat of skepticism. Both have developed objective controls to reduce the effect of the personal equation and, if possible, to expunge it altogether. In history, these controls are known as the "critical method." Developed in the nineteenth century along with what are known as the "auxiliary sciences" of history—archaeology, epigraphy, paleography, and so forth—this method has been constantly improved and expanded. It promised to raise history to the status of "a science, no less and no more."[16] Whether this is so or not, the scientific method of history is now a *sine qua non* for doing any serious and respectable work in the field. Similarly, psychoanalysis has developed objective controls to curb capricious guesswork and private intuitions. They include a didactic analysis, a supervised analysis, controlled observations, experimental work, and objective tests of various kinds. These controls operate in conjunction with psychoanalytic theory; and both theory and controls are designed to achieve a degree of objectivity which we associate with knowledge in other sciences. The ideal goal, in history as in psychoanalysis, is to eliminate the personal equation, to make the findings in both disciplines as "objective" as possible. Thus in both fields we can and do expose crackpots, charlatans, and propagandists; we can and do distinguish between science and fiction.

Yet, after we have done all we can and should along these lines, there remains a residue which seems to be impervious to any treatment by objective methods. Take the case of disagreements in history and in psychoanalysis: they are very much like disagreements in ordinary life—or in philosophy. In fact, as the history of the psychoanalytic movement shows, serious disagreements and deviations invariably reflect basic philosophical differences. They are not caused—nor resolved—simply by appealing to the facts and the logic of the case. They are not decided on the basis of strictly objective criteria. I know we make allowance for this defect by saying that psychoanalysis, along with other human sciences, is still in a relatively primitive state as compared with the physical sciences; but, while this is true, the long record of radical and intractable disagreements in history may make us wonder whether it is the whole truth. We do not find in history any agreement upon a universal conceptual framework of interpretation as we do in the development of the physical sciences. Thus I suspect the defect is more deep-seated than we like to admit—due to the fact, as I have suggested, that in history as in psychoanalysis (or in ordinary life) we are more deeply involved in the subject matter we are studying than we are in a study of nature. This involvement may be quite nonspecific. Thus it need not be expressed in obvious prejudices and interests, whether personal or social. It may be a more general bias, an unconscious slant, as it were, derived from one's whole experience of life or one's total response to the world. Nevertheless, this is a very "subjective" sort of thing. And it is a flaw which is an integral part of the logical structure in history and in psychoanalysis.

IV

I now turn to another area, the context of explanation, in which the intimate connection between psychoanalysis and history is particularly conspicuous. Why case histories? Because the general theory—though necessary—is not enough to explain the individual case. Now it is frequently said, and correctly, that this is so in every science. We would not hail the discovery of general laws if these laws could not be used to explain, and predict, the behavior of particular events; yet in applying these laws, say, the laws of ballistics, we must always modify our calculations deduced from the laws in terms of specific conditions—type of gun, weather, wind, terrain, and so forth—which prevail at a certain time and place.

In psychoanalysis, however, this familiar problem appears in a different light. The artillery unit need not know anything about the history of the gun or how it came to be mounted at Fort Sumter in order to understand how it works. Yet psychoanalysis "works" only insofar as we reconstruct the history of the individual case. To put the matter differently, in both history and psychoanalysis, it is not only more difficult to specify the initial and boundary conditions relevant to the particular case; but this specification involves a historical analysis. Thus we do not get out of the "historical" circle. A historical method is needed in order to determine the specific conditions modifying the application of the general law. This does not mean that we can do without a general theory. To repeat: psychoanalysis does have its own (scientific) theory; and the individual case, whether a dream or a neurotic symptom, may be explained by appealing to this general theory even as the case serves as evidence for the theory. Yet a case history also employs a characteristically historical type of explanation; for it shows not only how to explain a particular case in terms of a general theory; it also shows how the pieces of evidence—like the pieces of a jig-saw puzzle or like evidence in court—fit and hang together so that the story we tell provides its own explanation. In this sense, a case history is "self-justifying" and "autonomous" as Collingwood said of a narrative in ordinary history.[17] He did not wish to say that we ever have the final truth; what he meant was that, if history is rewritten, this will be done by telling a "better" story—more complete, more coherent, more intelligible, or what not.

These two methods of explanation deserve to be distinguished; for, in the one case, we explain by showing how the evidence fits into a general theory; in the other case, we explain as we do in history, in court, in a novel, or in ordinary life: by telling a story, a coherent, intelligible story which is "true" for the individual case only. Freud's complaint that, though trying to be a pure scientist, he always came up with results that read as if they were literature, reveals something of this "logical" ambivalence inherent in psychoanalysis. For these reasons, I believe, case histories are an integral part of psychoanalysis, not a symptom of a science still in its infancy. They call attention to the fact that, in a study of human behavior, there are two kinds of knowledge and two types of explanation corresponding to them: a concept of "knowledge" in the scientific sense and an "understanding" of the individual case in the historical sense.

I know this is a controversial thesis which I cannot argue here; but it does not matter whether we say "understanding" or prefer some other expression, "perception," "insight," or what not, to describe the same phenomenon: an understanding of the particular case, the historical *Gestalt,* as it were, or the unique "life-style" of the patient in Erikson's words. What matters is that we find the same kind of language used repeatedly in both history and psychoanalysis—they cannot do without some such concept however ambiguous it may be—and that, logical critics to the contrary notwithstanding, there is no provision in the standard model of scientific knowledge for this characteristically historical type of understanding. Both ways of knowing, the theoretical and the historical, intersect in the field of human life; both interact with each other. Thus without knowledge in the scientific sense we have no theory to check on intuitive nonsense. Yet without an understanding in the historical sense we deal with abstractions only; that is, with man as an abstraction. We do not understand the concrete case, at least not in actual life. In short, to paraphrase Kant: history without theory is blind; theory without history is empty.

In psychoanalysis we cannot fail to see this dialectical schema; but a similar situation, I believe, prevails not only in history, but in other sciences of man and society as well. Scientific studies, say, in sociology, economics, or academic psychology may achieve a spurious kind of objectivity as long as they construct nothing but abstract models and theories. The price they pay for playing these games is that they must abstract from the reality of the human situation; for in actual life we are always involved—as the therapist is in a special sense—with individuals who live in history and have a history. Thus the theoretician in pursuit of the ideal of pure objectivity must deal with human beings in a very artificial setting. He must remove them from the reality in which they actually live and he must lift himself, by his own bootstraps, out of the same historical process. Without this trick he would be just as vulnerable to the historical flaw as psychoanalysis is. Thus he is safe in his science only by escaping from reality—which is an odd conception of "empiricism"; for the reality of life is not caught in the abstract, theoretical models of science, but in the concrete structure of human history.

I suggest, therefore, that psychoanalysis is actually more empirical because it is more than an abstract theory and less than objective. It is both more and less than a science in the ordinary sense because it is also a branch of history. It pays for this entanglement with human life in history as we all do in our efforts to know ourselves and others; for it would be "bad faith" to claim that, in this search for self-knowledge at home or in history, we ever achieve anything like the kind of knowledge produced in a lab. It would not even be desirable; for the ideal of objective knowledge also means that we deal with human beings as if they were nothing but "objects" for a scientific theory. Thus the historical flaw inherent in psychoanalysis may be less objectionable than methodological purists would have us believe. It makes psychoanalysis more "human," as it were; or it shows that, in addition to being an abstract science, psychoanalysis also cares about understanding individuals as we encounter them in actual life, not as we set them up for a psychological experiment. It reminds us that, in the human world, truth is never abstract as in the world of science; it is always concrete; hence, relative to a specific human situation, to time, place, and the individuals involved in it. More correctly, the abstract and the concrete intersect in human life as do theory and history. This reminder renders a significant service in our time; for it is a defense of the rights of the individual to seek his own truth and to choose his own way of life against the dark powers of abstraction prevailing everywhere in the organized systems of science and society. If psychoanalysis is to serve this human cause—an "existential" project, if you like—it must not succumb to pharmacology, but it must be conscious of its own place and function in history.

V

There is something artificial about the therapeutic situation. It is also isolated from reality. Clinical work, of course, is dictated by special needs and objectives which justify this isolation. It is based on a kind of "formal contract" according to which conditions in the outside world are largely disregarded or held in abeyance.[18]

Yet the historical process in therapy is not a private affair; it is a public event as well. Both patient and therapist are also products of the culture in which they live; and both respond not only to each other, but also to the world outside. Hence, what happens in therapy is determined, in part, by the social and cultural situation in which it takes place. "We cannot" (not even as "clinicians") "lift a case history out of history."[19] In other words, we cannot understand the history of the patient without knowing something about the world which made him sick.

A psychoanalytic study of the individual, therefore, cannot be divorced from a study of society. The fate of the libido is always decided in a concrete historical situation. This does not mean that psychological processes do not have their own "inner logic"; what it does mean is that outside conditions, both social and ideological, are built into the psychological structure of man. "We cannot even begin to encompass the human life cycle without learning to account for the fact that a human being under observation has grown stage by stage into a social world. . . .

We cannot even begin to encompass a human being without indicating for each of the stages of his life cycle the framework of social influences and of traditional institutions which determine his perspective on his more infantile past and his more mature future. In this sense, we can learn from patients only to the extent to which we realize (and the patient realizes) that what is said and done in treatment is based on a formal contract between healer and patient and must be carefully transposed before being applied to the general human condition. This is the reason why the fragments of case histories or psychoanalytic interpretations which flutter around in increasing number in our newspapers and magazines seem lost like bats in the daytime."[20]

I have cited this long passage to make a simple point. These are not the sentiments of a Marxist critic; Erikson is not grinding an axe for professional sociologists; he is presumably working within the framework of traditional psychoanalytic theory. Yet he buries at least one controversy as artificial as it is misleading: the red herring of whether psychoanalysis is a part of biology or sociology. It is rooted in both and always has been since Freud. Biological drives always interact with historical necessities (for work and for moral restraints) imposed by society. In this sense, psychoanalysis is a branch of the social sciences.

It is also a part of the social process itself. We know something about the profound impact psychoanalysis has had upon the modern world in many fields other than clinical psychology. We have also come to acknowledge that, beyond the controlled and responsible methods of clinical work, psychoanalysis—especially in its many popular adaptations—has become an influential ideology in our culture. This ideology is a mixed blessing. "We must grudgingly admit that even as we are trying to devise . . . a therapy for the few, we were led to promote an ethical disease among the many."[21] Yet, surprisingly, there are few, if any, studies which deal with the role played by psychoanalysts in society and with the ideological commitments inherent in psychoanalysis. A psychoanalyst cannot afford to close his eyes to these commitments; for they are an integral part of clinical work. Thus in order to refine the objective controls in psychoanalysis and improve its scientific status, psychoanalysis must also become "historically self-conscious."[22] It must cultivate a social consciousness, if you like, an awareness of its own place and function in the world outside the office. Otherwise, alive as the therapist may be to the unconscious processes inside the patient and within himself, he may be quite blind to the social forces without. Thus he cannot confine his study of man to the artificial isolation of the clinical situation; or if he does, he cannot but fall victim to the powers in the world that impose this isolation.

Here again we find an interesting interaction between the two disciplines. Regardless of how effective a tool psychoanalysis may be in solving specific historical problems, it is safe to say that the historian cannot simply disregard it in an effort to understand himself. "We cannot leave history," to cite Erikson once more, "to nonclinical observers and professional historians who often all too nobly immerse themselves into the very disguises, rationalizations, and idealizations of the historical process from which it should be their business to separate themselves."[23] Or, as Mr. Carr observes on behalf of the historical profession, "since Marx and Freud wrote, the historian has no excuse to think of himself as a detached individual standing outside society and outside history. This is the age of self-consciousness: the historian can and should know what he is doing."[24] The injunction holds in reverse as well: in an age of historical self-consciousness, the psychoanalyst has no excuse to think of himself as nothing but a clinical practitioner. Thus even as a historian needs psychoanalysis to become conscious of his emotional blindspots, so the therapist needs a knowledge of history to become conscious of his ideological commitments and their social implications.

When Freud returned, as he said, "after a life-long detour through the natural sciences to the cultural problems" which had "fascinated" him in his youth, this move, I suspect, was more than an excuse for indulging in fancy philosophical speculations. Throughout his life Freud was deeply imbued with a sense of culture and history. More specifically, what did he come back to in the works of his last phase? On the one hand, he revised the metapsychological foundations of psychoanalysis; on the other hand, he analyzed the function of the "cultural superego," the ideological superstructure in society. Thus these works are not merely exercises in speculative philosophy; they are also essays in applied psychology. They deal with concrete social and historical problems; e.g., with the relationship between a leader and the masses in history (as in *Group Psychology*) or with the cultural function of religion (as in *The Future of an Illusion*) or with the pathology of morality (as in *Civilization and its Discontents*). Even *Moses and Monotheism,* it is sometimes forgotten, is more than a stubborn defense of a speculative hypothesis first put forth in *Totem and Taboo;* it was also written as a contribution toward an understanding of the historical function of anti-semitism in the Western world—then erupting in its most virulent and destructive form.

These studies are, on the whole, very critical. They expose and debunk prevailing ideologies. They are a "psychoanalytic critique of society."[25] Thus the issue is not whether psychoanalysis is biologically or culturally oriented. The issue is what kind of social critique is conducted in the name of psychoanalysis; more bluntly, whether psychoanalysis is still capable of serving as a critical voice in society—say, as the biological conscience of a moribund culture.

Psychoanalysis, therefore, needs a sense of history for two reasons: first, to make the therapist conscious of his own place in society; second, to preserve the critical potential inherent in psychoanalysis. A sense of history is essential to keep psychoanalysis from becoming nothing but a "safe" science. Perhaps it is not the most promising state of affairs if psychoanalysis is simply taken for granted as it is in our culture; for as Ernest Jones observed wisely, "one cannot help suspecting that much of the so-called acceptance [of Freud's ideas] is really a subtle form of rejection, a protection against assimilation of their profound impact."[26] There is something offensive about psychoanalysis: it offends common sense and the idols of the Establishment. This is part of its heritage as a science; yet to appropriate and exercise this heritage, the psychoanalyst must be conscious of history. Without a historical consciousness he cannot be true to himself as a scientist.

NOTES

1 For some of this literature, see Herbert Marcuse, *Eros and Civilization* (Boston 1955); Norman O. Brown, *Life Against Death* (Middletown 1959); Philip Rieff, *Freud: The Mind of the Moralist* (New York 1959) and the chapters on Freud in David Riesman, *Individualism Reconsidered* (Glencoe; Ill. 1954).

2 William L. Langer, "The Next Assignment," *American Historical Review*, LXIII, no. 2.

3 Ernest Jones, *The Life and Work of Sigmund Freud* (New York 1957) vol. III, p. 459.

4 *Moses and Monotheism* may be another exception; but Freud's essays on Leonardo and Dostoevsky are not historical studies.

5 Donald Meyer in a review of *Young Man Luther* by Erik Erikson in *Theory and History*, I, 3, p. 294.

6 The two major contributions by Erik Erikson on which I have drawn heavily are: "The Nature of Clinical Evidence," in *Evidence and Inference*, ed. by Daniel Lerner (Glencoe, Ill. 1959), hereafter cited as "Evidence," and *Young Man Luther* (New York 1958), hereafter cited as *Luther*. For his statement that the "therapeutic encounter" is historical, see "Evidence," p. 77.

7 Edward Hallett Carr, *What is History?* (New York 1962), p. 69.

8 Arthur O. Lovejoy, "Present Standpoints and Past History," in *The Philosophy of History in Our Time*, ed. by Hans Meyerhoff (Doubleday Anchor: New York 1959), p. 181.

9 *The Philosophy of History in Our Time*, op. cit., p. 174.

10 E. Erikson, "Evidence," p. 93.

11 Ibid.

12 A delightful aperçu by A. E. Housman quoted by Mr. Carr in *What is History?*, op. cit., p. 8.

13 R. G. Collingwood, *The Idea of History* (Oxford 1946), p. 247.

14 Ibid., p. 248.

15 Raymond Aron, "Relativism in History," in *The Philosophy of History in Our Time*, op. cit., p. 154.

16 J. B. Bury, "The Science of History," in *Varieties of History*, ed. by Fritz Stern (Meridian: New York 1956), p. 210.

17 R. G. Collingwood, op. cit., pp. 249, 236.

18 Cf. E. Erikson, *Luther*, p. 20. The terms of this contract, as is well known, may include the condition that the patient must not make any major changes or take major decisions in his life until he has completed therapy.

19 E. Erikson, *Luther*, pp. 15–16.

20 Ibid., p. 20.

21 Ibid., p. 19.

22 Ibid., p. 18.

23 Ibid., p. 20.

24 E. H. Carr, op. cit., p. 186.

25 E. Erikson, *Luther*, p. 21.

26 Ernest Jones, op. cit., vol. III, p. 433.

3

Why Psychoanalysis Needs the Social Scientist and the Historian

Peter Loewenberg

If—which may sound fantastic today—one had to found a college of psychoanalysis, . . . analytic instruction would include branches of knowledge which are remote from medicine and which the doctor does not come across in his practice: the history of civilization, mythology, the psychology of religion and the science of literature. Unless he is well at home in these subjects, an analyst can make nothing of a large amount of his material.

FREUD (1926)

Whether or not the psychoanalysts have found the means to rescue [those whose consciousness is corrupt] or to save those in whom this evil has advanced less far, their attempt to do so is an enterprise that has already won a great place in the history of man's warfare with the powers of darkness.

R. G. COLLINGWOOD (1938)

I

There are many areas of convergence and complementarity between the modes and assumptions of the historian and the psychoanalyst which have been neglected in the usual concentration on differences and oppositions. The aim of this essay is to discuss the congruences between the disciplines of history and psychoanalysis, not to elaborate on their obvious differences. Interdisciplinary work in psychoanalysis has stressed psychodynamic insight into the humanistic and social sciences. Nearly four decades ago the anthropologist Edward Sapir

Reprinted from the *International Review of Psycho-Analysis*, 4 (1977), pp. 305–15.

(1951) wrote his seminal essay, "Why Cultural Anthropology Needs the Psychiatrist." In this important statement, written in 1938, he said:

> Culture cannot be accepted as anything more than a convenient assemblage, or at best total theory, or possible modes of behaviour abstracted from the experienced realities of communication, whether in the form of overt behavior r or in the form of fantasy. . . . We cannot thoroughly understand the dynamics of culture, of society, of history, without sooner or later taking account of the actual interrelationships of human beings. . . . It will be the future task of the psychiatrist to read cause and effect in human history (pp. 575–6).

The manifold contributions which Sapir foresaw have indeed been delivered to history and assimilated, particularly in the areas of biography, mass movements and the interpretation of cultural artifacts. No fair-minded observer can deny that these gifts have been substantial and have benefited the sophistication and complexity both of the perceptual and interpretive phases of the historical enterprise.

I wish here to develop the as yet unrealized obverse of this contribution— what psychoanalytic theory and clinical practice may gain from a familiarity with historical theory and research methodology. There is a common empathic method between history and psychoanalysis that is usually only recognized as going from psychoanalysis to history. This paper will show the reverse to be equally important. In many vital points, especially where psychoanalysis is most vulnerable *vis-à-vis* the natural sciences, the disciplines share a common methodology of empathic insight and understanding. Historians do not deal with live patients who can respond to propositions and they do not try to cure or change their subjects. Yet, there is a great deal to be gained for psychoanalysis, which is besieged by demands for empirical evidence from the side of the "hard" sciences and clinical medicine, by exploring the rich developments of humanistic and social science methodology with which psychodynamics has much in common. The methodological rationales of the humanities can buttress and fortify the intuitive and empathic realms of affect and expression which are the stuff of psychoanalytic evidence and clinical practice.

The historical sciences in particular have over the last century elaborated the justifications and cognitive foundations for the processes of deriving inference from evidence in building a longitudinal picture of events, making causal linkages and hypothesizing reconstructions of the past. A conversance with this interface is of greatest importance for psychoanalysis at this critical juncture in its history. I submit that psychoanalysis, rather than being exclusively a subspecialty of psychiatry, stands at the intersection of the humanities, the social sciences and the natural sciences in particularly crucial ways. I shall draw upon the best of historians and social scientists for my case examples, not among the mediocre, nor even upon the norm, for only the best have utilized the methodology to its full potential.

II

The most obvious, yet most controversial, lesson imparted by history is the necessity to view behaviour in a temporal and cultural context.

> A graduate student writing a dissertation on Alexander the Great consulted me for a psychodynamic view of Alexander's apparent homosexuality and his instrumental use of women. According to this student's data, Alexander rarely cohabited with a woman and then only did so when it would further his political or diplomatic purposes. My response was to send the student back to fill in what were the behavioural modes of a royal house in Greek Macedonian culture in the fourth century B.C. with regard to homosexuality and the treatment of women.

The norms of 20th-century mental health cannot be trusted to tell us about average expectable or deviant behaviour in other times. Such apparent givens as the primal scene, the phases of childhood, the onset of puberty, menstruation and the vicissitudes of adolescence turn out not to be immutable at all when viewed in historical perspective. As recently as the 17th century it was normal for parents and children to live and sleep in the same room and bed. Privacy did not exist in the Early Modern European family (Shorter, 1975, pp. 39–44). Mothering was often a matter of indifference and infanticide and abandonment of children was a common practice until the late 18th century (Shorter, 1975, pp. 168–90). There is evidence that the average age of the onset of menses was 17.5 as late as the 1830s in Great Britain and has been moving progressively to earlier ages. It was 16.5 in the 1860s, 15.5 in the 1890s, 14.5 in the 1920s and 13.25 in the 1960s. Starting in 1900, the curve in the United States is roughly parallel, showing a downward tendency for the 20th century, falling among white girls to 12.5 in 1940–45 (Laslett, 1971, p. 222). J. M. Tanner finds that "menarche in Europe has been getting earlier during the last hundred years by between three and four months per decade" (Laslett, 1971, p. 222). The governing variable seems to be the quality of nutrition, particularly protein, and the quantity of calories in early infancy. The critical factor is definitely not hot climates, as was formerly believed. The median menarchical ages according to the latest figures are: 18 years in the Highlands of New Guinea, 17 years in Central Africa, 15.5 years among South African Bantu and Transkei, and 12.5 years among well-off Chinese in Hong Kong—i.e. more or less comparable with Americans and Europeans (Tanner, 1971, pp. 928–9). The consistent increase in average life expectancy, as well as the earlier onset and prolongation of adolescence, means a continuing change in the phase-specific tasks and adaptations in our patients. These temporal differences may also be seen spatially at the present time. The analogues to the historian's movement in time are the anthropologist's movement in space from one culture to another and the sociologist's movement within a culture across class and status groups.

For the psychoanalyst who works with the finest minutiae of his patient's life and communication, the nuances of the cultural variables with which he must deal are also finer. The uniqueness of each patient far transcends the gross categories of classification that social scientists use. Precisely because of this, the normative modes of behaviour against which the patient's unique acts are placed tend to be unconsciously assumed as the backdrop of behaviour.

The patient, a lady born and raised in a Calvinist culture in north-western Europe, repeatedly presented what she termed her "drinking problem" in the course of analysis, complaining that it was not getting adequate therapeutic attention. By "drinking problem" she meant the guilt feelings she had when drinking, her fantasies of derogatory things that people watching her, including her maid, were thinking. When asked why she could not enjoy a drink she made for herself, the patient talked of not being "nice" and "respectable." At this point I initiated a cultural exploration, inquiring into attitudes towards alcohol in the patient's childhood home and culture, when she had her first drink, what the laws of the land were, including when the taverns closed, the legal age of alcohol consumption, etc. The patient found great relief in this exploration. She related various sexual attitudes, feelings about menstruation, bleeding, nudity, defecation, and what she termed "anal" sexuality, to her childhood home and social culture. The patient frequently thereafter referred to what she termed her "Puritanical" self in her analysis, relating it to various forms of denial of pleasure or the "spoiling" of gratifications.

A patient was described in consultation as engaging in the apparently bizarre behaviour of secretly saving her earnings in order to buy a high-powered $20,000 foreign sports car for her husband. When a query elicited the information that she was from a south European country where *machismo* is a masculine ideal, her behaviour could be viewed as a grandiose and loving act in terms of her culture, rather than as aberrant as it first appeared to her analyst. Now various issues of her identification of her husband with her father could come into analytic focus.

A patient referred to his mother as "Mrs. Jones." When I asked why he chose such an oblique way of talking about his mother, he elaborated on his image of her as a character in Samuel Richardson's novel *Clarissa, or the History of a Young Lady:* this had determined his area of academic research, his marriages, etc. It is of the greatest importance for the analyst to learn the patient's particular idiomatic terms for significant others. Did he call his father "Pop" or "Dad" or "Papa"? Was his sister "Baby" or "Betty," "Liz" or "Elizabeth"? Was his mother "Mom," "Mommy" or "Mrs. Jones"? The specific form of the name may be the key that unlocks the emotional closet of the repressed feelings of the past.

In these vignettes we see the relevance of filling in the social and cultural context of each unique clinical situation as precisely as possible. The psychoanalytic models are strong heuristic devices for pointing to the psychodynamics of a neurosis, but they cannot be applied rigidly as formulae. Each case must be fleshed out in its personal and cultural particularity. This emphasis on the unique particularity of each case is a standard canon of historical method and as such provides one of the "deep" points of contact between the disciplines of psychoanalysis and history.

III

A fundamental source of difficulty in placing psychoanalysis as a scientific discipline is a persistent misperception of the nature of science: psychoanalysts too often remain under the sway of 19th-century physicalistic notions of science. Modern science uses metaphors of varying usefulness; truth or falsity is not an issue. As Einstein (1922, p. 1) said: "The object of all science, whether natural science or psychology, is to co-ordinate our experiences and to bring them into a logical system." Freud provided universally recognized scientific achievements that posed model problems and solutions to a community of practitioners. This, the historian of science Thomas Kuhn (1970, p. viii) terms a scientific "paradigm." "Normal science," he writes, "means research firmly based upon one or more past scientific achievements, achievements that some particular scientific community acknowledges for a time as supplying the foundation for its further practice" (p. 10). How different this is from the positivistic concept of the "Yes" or "No" litmus test and the capacity to quantify which too often in clinical psychiatry passes for definitions of science! The issue here is not, "show me the location of the superego (as I can see a tubercle bacillus)," but rather, "does the concept of superego serve a useful explanatory, clinical, and research function?"

Further consequences of recent work in the nature and history of science by Kuhn, Imre Lakatos and Michael Polanyi are that the choice between competing paradigms is not rational, but is based on "all or nothing" conversion experiences, analogous to intuitive religious experiences (Kuhn, 1970, p. 150). Einstein speaks of "the search for those highly universal ... laws from which a picture of the world can be obtained by pure deduction. There is no logical path leading to these ... laws. They can only be reached by intuition, based upon something like intellectual love ("Einfühlung") of the objects of experience" (Popper, 1959, p. 32). Kuhn calls this a "paradigm shift." These are made not on the basis of whether a theory can be verified but on its probability of being fruitful as a research strategy. The scientist is making a choice pointing to "one of the directions in which future discussions of verification should go" (Kuhn, 1970, p. 145).

A most important point developed in the history of science during the past two decades is that falsification cannot invalidate a paradigm. Any paradigm, such as the Ptolemaic view of geocentric planetary motion or the Newtonian worldview can be stretched to subsume new data. No theory can be falsified, nor disproved within itself. As Karl Popper (1959) puts it:

> In point of fact, no conclusive disproof of a theory can ever be produced; for it is always possible to say that the experimental results are not reliable, or that the discrepancies which are asserted to exist between experimental results and the theory are only apparent and that they will disappear with the advance of our understanding (p. 50).

Kuhn (1970) stresses that all theories have anomalies:

> No theory ever solves all the puzzles with which it is confronted at a given time; nor are the solutions already achieved often perfect. On the contrary, it is just the incom-

pleteness and imperfection of the existing data-theory fit that, at any time, define many of the puzzles that characterize normal science. If any and every failure to fit were ground for theory rejection, all theories ought to be rejected at all times (p. 146).

The issue becomes which paradigm shall in the future guide research on problems which neither competitor can yet claim to resolve. These are decisions that "can only be made on faith" and "personal and inarticulate aesthetic considerations" (Kuhn, 1970, p. 158). Note how Kuhn uses the idioms of religious conversion and subjective appeal. What does a physicist mean when he says an explanation is "elegant"? One of the meanings intended by the scientist is that the proposition has the aesthetic appeal of economy, harmony and inclusiveness.

The aesthetic appeal of a psychoanalytical reconstruction consists in its logical ability to be in agreement with a narrow range of potential facts. This is what gives an interpretation accepted by the patient "truth value" for a life lived, and justifies the painstaking efforts at thorough clinical exploration and testing of prediction-statements derived from psychoanalytic theory. Likewise, the aesthetic appeal of the historical narrative moves the historian to undertake the process of historical inference and reconstruction when he seeks to establish the character of the background and initial conditions for a longitudinal development. This common aesthetic interest which motivates efforts to secure logical completeness in explanatory historical and psychoanalytical models, the relevance of testing reconstructions, and the desire for factual accuracy in narrative and explanation, should draw those who share it into effective cooperation.

Kuhn (1970) points out that in the great paradigm shifts in the history of science "most of the articulable technical arguments pointed the other way. When first introduced, neither Copernicus' astronomical theory nor De Broglie's theory of matter had many other significant grounds of appeal" (p. 158). Michael Polanyi (1958) demonstrates on a wide front that no "objective framework" can account for a scientist's acceptance or rejection of theories (pp. 12–14). The development of the science of psychoanalysis is a matter of providing the appropriate atmosphere or ecology consisting of what Polanyi (1974) terms "a fund of intuitive approaches and emotional values which can be transmitted from one generation to the other only through the medium of personal collaboration. Scientific research, in short, is an art" (pp. 22–3).

What this means is that two or more competing paradigms imply different world-views with built-in gaps in communication. We begin to see why experimental psychologists and psychoanalysts talk across chasms of mutual incomprehension. The same applies to conceptual differences among psychoanalysts, such as between representatives of the Freudian, Kleinian and object-relational schools. These are gestalt switches for conceptualizing the same clinical data analogous to the perceptual transformations of a Rorschach subject who can see bats and facial profiles from the same ink blot. I concur with Lakatos in his modification of Kuhn when he pleads for numerous paradigms: "The history of science has been and should be a history of competing research programmes (or, if you wish, paradigms), but it has not been and must not become a succession of periods of normal science: the sooner competition starts, the better for prog-ress" (Lakatos, 1970, p. 155). Psychoanalysis can only be better for it if we abandon positivistic ideas of science and adopt a relativistic and pluralistic view of our enterprise. The difference between religion and science is the willingness to let the specific situation dictate the interpretation and the interpretive mode.

IV

Although often unaware of what they are doing, psychoanalysts actually utilize what social scientists conceptualize under the term "model-building." This social scientific tool was developed by the German historical sociologist Max Weber (1864–1920) during the same years that Freud was doing his great creative work. Weber termed these models "ideal types" or "constructed types." They are ab-stractions from reality, not descriptions of its particularity. Their purpose is to serve as heuristic devices to elucidate certain aspects of phenomena that will then lead to further investigation and analysis.

> The constructed scheme, of course, only serves the purpose of offering an ideal typical means of orientation. It does not teach a philosophy of its own. The theoretically con-structed types of conflicting "life orders" are merely intended to show that at certain points such and such internal conflicts are possible and "adequate".... As will readily be seen, the individual spheres of value are prepared with a rational consistency which is rarely found in reality. But they *can* appear thus in reality and in historically important ways, and they have. Such constructions make it possible to determine the typological focus of a historical phenomenon. They enable us to see if, in particular traits or in their total character, the phenomena approximate one of our constructions: to determine the degree of approximation of the historical phenomenon to the theoretically con-structed type. To this extent, the construction is merely a technical aid which facilitates a more lucid arrangement and terminology (Gerth & Mills, 1958, pp. 323–4).

Weber made conceptual constructs from social reality that were never en-countered in such purity in the complexity of life. His ideal type of capitalist economic behaviour, for example, is a typological simplification. It is a model uniting many characteristics which give capitalism its uniqueness as an economic practice, although any particular attribute may be absent in any given historical case. The ideal type also comprises its multiple tendencies and its long-range goals in history, even if such a pure case nowhere exists.

> An ideal type is formed by the one-sided *accentuation* of one or more points of view and by the synthesis of a great many diffuse, discrete, more or less present and oc-casionally absent *concrete individual* phenomena, which are arranged according to those one-sidedly emphasized viewpoints into a unified analytical *construct* (Shils & Finch, 1949, p. 90).

Thus when social scientists and historians talk of "economic man," "charisma," "capitalism" or "feudalism," they are "using logically controlled and unambiguous conceptions, which are thus more removed from historical reality," rather than "less precise concepts, which are more closely geared to the empirical world" (Gerth & Mills, 1958, p. 59). Of course, the historical models of "feudalism" and "capitalism" are constantly being revised as new meanings are discovered and conceptualized in the ongoing development of the social sciences, just as psychoanalytic categories and concepts are ever being refined, torn down and rebuilt. Intellectually this is a sign of a living discipline.

Model-building is also exactly what psychoanalysts and psychiatrists do when they use diagnostic-descriptive categories such as "borderline personality," "hysterical neurosis," "schizoid" or "passive-aggressive personality." When the clinician draws upon Fenichel's (1945, ch. 14) brilliant 42-page delineation of the obsessive-compulsive neurosis, he is placing the unique individuality of his patient against an ideal type which he uses as a heuristic device to illuminate his data and to guide him to see further relationships latent in the material. Fenichel's nosology is a synthesis of many diffuse concrete individual phenomena which cannot be found in any single patient. The psychoanalytic theorist supplies a limiting construct to which the individual clinical case is compared for the presence of significant components. Social scientists have had extensive experience and have developed a sophistication in model-building which could be of use to psychoanalysts who are often needlessly defensive in their use of ideal types when dealing with their medical colleagues who rely on the "hard" evidence of laboratory tests.

V

Cultural and historical relativism, the modern history and philosophy of science, and conceptual abstraction from reality can be used to build bridges between the social sciences, the humanities and psychoanalysis. But, most importantly, those who are divided by disciplines and vocabulary can come to the other side of the chasm with firm mutal foundations in the empathic mode of understanding. This is the ultimate ground on which the disciplines meet. Here we have the unquantifiable area of personal knowledge which, as Freud (1905) said in a pungent passage on symptomatic acts in the Dora case, constitutes the essence of communication to those who wish to and know how to observe:

> He that has eyes to see and ears to hear may convince himself that no mortal can keep a secret. If his lips are silent, he chatters with his finger-tips; betrayal oozes out of him at every pore. And thus the task of making conscious the most hidden recesses of the mind is one which it is quite possible to accomplish (pp. 77–8).

This area of cognition is invoked when we say of a person "he is an experienced clinician" or when we respect the seasoned judgement of an historian who tells us a document is implausible or that an account does not "sound right."

An example is when the author was asked to review a recent biography of Adolf Hitler which, based on a manuscript account by Hitler's sister-in-law, asserts that he visited England and lived in Liverpool for a period of five months in 1912 and 1913 (Payne, 1973, pp. 93–102). From knowing Hitler's boastfulness about his authority on a wide range of matters, and knowing that in none of his speeches or writings, including the *Table Talks,* does he anywhere refer to personally being conversant with the English people, I inferred (Loewenberg, 1974) that the asserted trip never took place and the account of a stay in England is bogus. Correspondence with the Home Office (personal communication, 30 May 1975) has confirmed that there is no record of a Hitler visit to the United Kingdom.

Wilhelm Dilthey (1833–1911), the German historian and philosopher of history, early formulated the idea that the historian is himself the primary instrument of research, that he uses himself as the perceptor and interpreter of data. Dilthey said, the historian relives the past in his own mind. What makes Dilthey so strikingly modern to us, is the stress he laid on historical knowledge as an inner experience of the historian. "This conception," said Collingwood (1956) "of the historian as living in his object, or rather making his object live in him, is a great advance on anything achieved by any of Dilthey's German contemporaries" (p. 172).

Dilthey stressed that the historian's understanding *(Verständnis)* is based on his inner relationship *(innere Verhältnis)* to his subject of research, and this relationship is possible through recreation *(Nacherzeugen)* and identification *(Nacherleben).* Historians face the practical task "of the inner reliving of the development of individuation [of our subject]" ("Innerlich ... diesen Aufgang zur Individuation zu durchleben"). He called on historians to place themselves mentally in the historical situation *(Sichhineinversetzen).* "On the basis of this placing of oneself in the situation, this transposition, the highest form in which the totality of mental life can be effective in understanding, arises—imitation or identification." ("Auf der Grundlage dieses Hineinversetzens, dieser Transposition entsteht nun aber die höchste Art, in welcher die Totalität des Seelenlebens im Verstehen wirksam ist—das Nachbilden oder Nacherleben." Dilthey, 1958, pp. 213–14). Dilthey was the earliest conceptualizer of the use of sympathy *(Mitfühlens)* and empathy *(Einfühlung)* as tools of cognition in historical research.

VI

R. G. Collingwood's (1889–1943) work and method is particularly congenial to the psychoanalytic mode of experience because it highlights the tools of emotional empathy and mental identification which lead to intellectual insight as to "how it really was." He saluted Freud as "the greatest psychologist of our age" (Collingwood, 1938, p. 64). With Collingwood we may see not only a philosopher of history conceptualize what happens when an historian works, but we may also observe a first-rate historian doing his research and making his discoveries. Collingwood is closest to the psychoanalytic theory of memory when he stresses

that a feeling, such as anger, when it is relived in the present, as in the transference, may be a pathway to the thoughts of the past.

> If I now think about a feeling which I had in the past, it may be true that thinking about
> it occasions, or else perhaps depends for its possibility on the independent occurrence
> of, an echo of that feeling in the present: that for example, I could not think of the
> anger I once felt except so far as I now experience at least a faint vibration of anger
> in my mind.... The actual past anger of which I am thinking is past and gone; that
> does not reappear, the stream of immediate experience has carried it away forever; at
> most there reappears something like it. The gap of time between my present thought
> and its past objective is bridged not by the survival or revival of the object, but only
> by the power of thought to overlap such a gap; and the thought which does this is
> memory (Collingwood, 1956, p. 293).

Collingwood was aware of, and illustrated, the psychodynamics of projection:
"We learn to bolster ... self-deceit by attributing the disowned experience to
other people. Coming down to breakfast out of temper, but refusing to allow
that ill humour so evident in the atmosphere is our own, we are distressed to
find the whole family suffering agonies of crossness" (Collingwood, 1938, p. 218).

To theorize elegantly about history is one thing. To apply a theory intelligently
so that it yields solid results is quite another. It is instructive to see how Collingwood "operationalized" his empathic theory of historical research. He tried
to reason as the Roman strategists did, then reconstruct the past in his own mind
and test his fantasy by empirical research. His research was concerned with the
purpose and function of Hadrian's Wall, a 73-mile-long structure built across the
narrowest part of England on a line from the Tyne on the North Sea to the Solway
on the Irish Sea and maintained by the Romans between 122 and 383 A.D. Collingwood reversed the previous scholarship by first creating a problem where
there was previously only accepted dictum—that this wall, as other walls at the
extremities of the Roman Empire, was a military fortification designed to keep
out barbarian invaders. Collingwood asserted that he could not imagine this. His
subjective fantasies and feelings led him to his problem:

> When disturbance ripened into war, when large forces from the north advanced upon
> the Wall and attempted (as no doubt they did, not always unsuccessfully) to penetrate
> it, *we cannot imagine* that the Roman cohorts actually lined up on the rampart-walk
> to repel them, still less that Hadrian's engineers *ever contemplated* such a proceeding
> [italics mine] (Collingwood, 1921, p. 9).

Collingwood tells us, he is employing his empathetic function of identification
in making a reconstruction. He explicitly says that his tool of cognition is his
power of imagination, his ability to get into the mind of Hadrian's engineers
and, if a given pattern of thought is "unthinkable" for them in his mind, this
fantasied implausibility is for him an important historical datum. Collingwood is
using his educated and disciplined fantasy as a primary dimension of historical
research.

Collingwood placed himself in the mental and intellectual position of the Roman generals and engineers who designed and built the wall. He immersed himself in their situation, seeking the "inward experience" of making the past object live in him. He maintained that the historian makes discoveries by rethinking the thoughts of his subjects in his own mind:

> The historian of politics or warfare, presented with an account of certain actions done by Julius Caesar, tries to understand these actions, that is, to discover what thoughts in Caesar's mind determined him to do them. This implies envisaging for himself the situation in which Caesar stood, and thinking for himself what Caesar thought about the situation and the possible ways of dealing with it. The history of thought, and therefore all history, is the re-enactment of past thought in the historian's own mind (Collingwood, 1956, p. 215).

Collingwood pointed out that those strategists who had appropriate business in the Roman province would cross the wall at one of the forts. In addition to its function as a boundary, the wall was intended as:

> an obstacle to smugglers, or robbers, or other undesirables. A man from beyond the frontier, found on the Roman side of the line, could not plead ignorance or innocent intentions if the line was clearly marked; and if, in addition, it was a slight obstacle, crossing it otherwise than at the authorized and controlled gateways was proof of a sinister purpose (Collingwood, 1921, pp. 7–8).

Now we see Collingwood, the empathic historian, at work, using his powers of identification based on an immersion in the life problems and problem-solving thought of Roman strategists in the time of Hadrian:

> [The Wall] lacks the essential characteristic of a fortification. It cannot be defended. In order to defend a wall you must be able to bring reinforcements to a threatened point; but the top of the Wall was reached only by stairways at forts and mile-castles, and by ladders (it would appear) at the turrets; and ladders 500 yards apart are a very poor means of bringing reinforcements to the top of a narrow wall. Nor was the Wall broad enough to march reinforcements along it, behind the "firing line," even if (as was not the case) the Roman soldier had been provided with *armes de jet* adequate for dealing with an attack on such a work. The walls of a fort of this period are rendered defensible by the earth bank behind them, giving access to every point, and by the frequent gates, which enable the garrison to sally out and take assailants in the rear; both these features are absent from the Wall (Collingwood, 1930, p. 78).

What then was the purpose of this large Roman work in the north of England? Making his brilliant original formulation, Collingwood tells us:

> The Wall, in spite of appearances, was not strictly a fortification. It was an elevated sentry-walk, where men patrolling the frontier were secure against sudden attack and could command a good view of the country which it was their business to watch. It was also a very effective obstacle against raiding, not because raiding parties could not get across it—for a few men with a ladder could easily overpower a sentry or two and get across before help could arrive—but because, once they were across and the alarm given, it

would be almost impossible for them to get back, especially if they were laden with plunder (Collingwood, 1959, p. 32).

The wall was a frontier work, not a military work. It was not a fortification, a work designed to resist attack by armed forces. It was a police work, designed to keep out Caledonian raiders who would be seriously impeded by such a wall.

In Collingwood's research and interpretation on the problem of the Wall, extending over two decades, we see the historian's procedure of reconstruction of the past by inferring the thoughts and feelings of particular men in the past from the historical evidence of the present. It is a process of immersion in their problems and identification with their solutions, a practice analogous to puzzle solving. And how do we know that Collingwood is right? Of course, we do not know for a certainty. Indeed we may be certain that in due course his view will be revised. But our conviction is based on the fact that for now the pieces fit. Puzzle solving, incidentally, is a methodological simile used by Freud (1923):

> If one succeeds in arranging the confused heap of fragments, each of which bears upon it an unintelligible piece of drawing, so that the picture acquires a meaning, so that there is no gap anywhere in the design and so that the whole fits into the frame—if all these conditions are fulfilled, then one knows that one has solved the puzzle and that there is no alternative solution (p. 116).

VII

The historian, like the psychoanalyst, engages in reconstruction through the method of retrogression, through retro-diction, beginning with the present, including his own emotional evidence from the present, and moving toward the past. Marc Bloch (1886–1944), one of the greatest of modern historians, made his contribution to historical method by insistence on the importance of the historian's understanding of the living as a key to the past. Bloch said:

> The lines of connection work both ways. Misunderstanding of the present is the inevitable consequence of ignorance of the past. But a man may wear himself out just as fruitlessly in seeking to understand the past, if he is totally ignorant of the present.... This faculty of understanding the living is, in very truth, the master quality of the historian (1953, p. 43).

He stressed that history as understood by the historian is directly related to his receptivity based on his own life awareness and openness to experience, and his ability to "resonate" emotionally with the impact of events as he lives them. He constantly emphasized the need for the historian to "know from within," just as the psychoanalyst must get in touch with his own feelings in order to resonate with what the patient is telling him. It is because the therapist has himself been a patient that he knows the nuances of what the patient is trying to communicate.

To have known and analysed the trauma of separation, the pain of humiliation, the fires of envy and the terrors of castration anxiety, is an indispensable condition for compassionately and fearlessly guiding a patient through honest inner exploration of his defences. There is more than a grain of truth in the stubborn assertion of patients from minority groups that a therapist of their own group can best understand them. An analyst who has had and "worked through" certain experiences, such as divorce, parent loss, emigration and resettlement, will have greater rapport with a patient who is dealing with those problems than a therapist who has only dealt with these life crises in theory or by way of the literature.

The analogue in historical training is the importance attached to fieldwork in the land or society one wishes to study, on the principle that, apart from the value of documents and archives, there is no substitute for direct, personal immersion in the culture and participation in the social life of the people whose history one wishes to interpret.

As an American historian who found himself in West Berlin in August 1961 at the time of the erection of the Berlin Wall, I noted the undue anxiety of the German population about the food supply in very personalized terms. While we were concerned with whether a war between the U.S. and Soviet forces would break out, many Germans were asking, "How will I feed my family?" "Where will we get meat?" "My butcher will not take care of me, he does not regard me as a favoured customer, what will I do?" The acute food anxiety I observed being aroused by this political crisis suggested questions to which the historical experiences of Germans in the civilian deprivations during and after the two World Wars supplied at least some of the answers. A recollection of the stories of hunger recounted by my parents, who were children during the First World War, suggested further generational questions for research and phase-specific answers (Loewenberg, 1971).

Bloch was an officer in the French Army in both World Wars. He described and analysed, in what is a masterpiece of its genre, the fall of France in 1940. Bloch also described the feelings of being helpless and trapped as the German armies cut off the Anglo-French forces in Belgium in May 1940:

Shall I ever, I wonder, forget that evening of 20 May? Just as it was getting dusk, with the flames of Arras lighting the distant horizon, my immediate superior came into the room. In a very low voice, and pointing on a school wall-map to the mouth of the Somme, he said: "The Boches are *there!*"—then, turning away, he murmured, "Don't talk about it more than you can help." I had been trying to get G.H.Q. on the telephone, and it was only after I had made the attempt several times and failed, that I realized to the full the sense of complete abandonment that comes to a soldier when he hears the word—"surrounded" (1968, pp. 12–13).

This existential experience was for Bloch a *sine qua non* of dealing with the past, for "we can truly understand the past only if we read it by the light of the present" (Bloch, 1968, p. 2). This principle is convincingly applied in Bloch's critique of the eminent medievalist, Fustel de Coulanges. Fustel had found in France "no trace" of the open field system common in the European Middle Ages. To this conclusion, Bloch (1966) commented:

Fustel de Coulanges was not a man on whom the external world made much impact. It is quite probable that he never took any special notice of the characteristic pattern of ploughlands visible all over northern and eastern France which so irresistibly call to mind the open-fields of England. And since Fustel had no particular interest in agriculture, the debates on grazing on the arable which were engaging both Chambers at the very moment ... also failed to attract his attention. Fustel based his answers on documents, very ancient documents. Now these were texts he knew very well; how was it then that they failed to reveal for him any trace of the phenomena they in fact quite plainly attest? ... Fustel concentrated solely on his documents, without considering them in the light of the more recent past (pp. xxvii–xxviii).

Bloch was calling, not only for the historian to get out and look at fields and talk to peasants, but also to listen carefully to the political issues and debates of his own time, for their benefit to him in illuminating the past. He taught (1966): "Since the facts of the distant past are also the most obscure, there is really no escape from the discipline of working back from the better to the less well-known. ... The historian ... is perpetually at the mercy of his documents; most of the time he must read history backwards if he hopes to break the secret cypher of the past" (p. xxviii). For the psychoanalyst working with a patient, this is what he does when he begins with the presenting complaint, with what hurts now, and works back to make past defences and adaptations distonic so that they may be analysed. As Bloch (1953) put it in 1941:

> For here, in the present, is immediately perceptible that vibrance of human life which only a great effort of the imagination can restore to the old texts. I have many times read, and I have often narrated, accounts of wars and battles. Did I truly know, in the full sense of that word, did I know from within, before I myself had suffered the terrible, sickening reality, of what it meant for an army to be encircled, what it meant for a people to meet defeat? Before I myself had breathed the joy of victory in the summer and autumn of 1918 (and, although, alas! its perfume will not again be quite the same, I yearn to fill my lungs with it a second time) did I truly know all that was inherent in that beautiful word? In the last analysis, whether consciously or not, it is always by borrowing from our daily experiences and by shading them, where necessary, with new tints that we derive the elements which help us to restore the past (p. 44).

Psychoanalysis is, significantly, the only modern treatment modality which requires the healer to have experienced the treatment prior to himself becoming a therapist. Bloch made it a tenet of method that the historian will understand history only to the extent that he experiences in the present and understands himself as an historical subject. This, finally, is a solid ground for mutual enlightenment, support and intellectual alliance between those who pursue the spirits of Clio and Psyche as their life's work. Each discipline can make better sense of its own problems if it understands the methods of the other.

ACKNOWLEDGEMENTS

The author wishes to express his gratitude to Professors Fawn M. Brodie, Alan Dundes, John Fitzpatrick III, John Heilbron, Albert D. Hutter, Franklin Mendels,

Eugen Weber, M. Norton Wise; Drs Naomi Malin, Norman Reider and Mr David Horowitz for reading and discussing a draft of this paper.

REFERENCES

Bloch, M. (1953). *The Historian's Craft.* New York: Knopf.
———. (1966). *French Rural History: An Essay on its Basic Characteristics.* Berkeley and Los Angeles: University of California Press.
———. (1968). *Strange Defeat: A Statement of Evidence Written in 1940.* New York: Norton.
Collingwood, R. G. (1921). The purposes of the Roman Wall, *Vasculum* 8, 4–9.
———. (1930). *The Archaeology of Roman Britain.* New York: Dial Press.
———. (1938). *The Principles of Art.* London: Oxford University Press.
———. (1956), *The Idea of History.* New York: Oxford University Press.
———. (1959). *Roman Britain.* London: Oxford University Press.
Dilthey, W. (1958). Das Verstehen anderer Personen und ihrer Lebensäusserungen. In *Gesammelte Schriften,* vol. 7, Stuttgart: Teubnen.
Einstein, A. (1922). *The Meaning of Relativity.* Princeton: Princeton University Press.
Fenichel, O. (1945). *The Psychoanalytic Theory of Neurosis.* New York: Norton.
Freud, S. (1905). Fragment of an analysis of a case of hysteria. *S.E.* 7.
———. (1923). Remarks on the theory and practice of dream-interpretation. *S.E.* 19.
———. (1926). The question of lay analysis. *S.E.* 20.
Gerth, H. H. & Mills, C. W. (eds.) (1958). *From Max Weber: Essays in Sociology.* New York: Oxford University Press.
Kuhn, T. S. (1970). *Structure of Scientific Revolutions.* Chicago: University of Chicago Press.
Lakatos, I. (1970). Falsification and the methodology of scientific research programmes. In I. Lakatos & A. Musgrave (eds.), *Criticism and the Growth of Knowledge.* London: Cambridge University Press.
Laslett, P. (1971). Age at menarche in Europe since the eighteenth century. *J. interdisciplin. Hist.* 2, 221–36.
Loewenberg, P. (1971). Psychohistorical origins of the Nazi youth cohort. *Am. hist. Rev.* 76, 1457–1502.
———. (1974). Review of Robert Payne, *The Life and Death of Adolf Hitler, Comite d'Hist. de la 2e Guerre Mondiale,* Bull. no. 212, 32–34.
Payne, R. (1973). *Life and Death of Adolf Hitler.* New York: Praeger.
Polanyi, M. (1958). *Personal Knowledge: Towards a Post-Critical Philosophy.* Chicago: University of Chicago Press.
———. (1974). *Scientific Thought and Social Reality.* New York: International Universities Press.
Popper, K. (1959). *The Logic of Scientific Discovery.* New York: Basic Books.
Sapir, E. (1951). Why cultural anthropology needs the psychiatrist. In D. G. Mandelbaum (ed.), *Selected Writings of Edward Sapir in Language, Culture and Personality.* Berkeley and Los Angeles: University of California Press.
Shils, E. A. & Finch, H. A. (eds.) (1949). *Max Weber on the Methodology of the Social Sciences.* Glencoe, Ill.: Free Press.

4

Disciplined Subjectivity and the Psychohistorian: A Critical Look at the Work of Erik H. Erikson

Charles B. Strozier

As Erikson notes in *Young Man Luther,* we have to risk a "bit of impurity" in any hyphenated approach, for such efforts are the "compost heap of today's interdisciplinary efforts which may help to fertilize new fields and to produce future flowers of new methodological clarity."[1] To dwell for a moment on this metaphor, we need to understand the shape, size, and perhaps the smell of that compost heap as well as how it accumulates; we need to consider both its content and the way it is constructed. Erikson's contribution to the interdisciplinary heap is rich indeed and centers, conceptually, on his ideas of the epigenesis of the life cycle and especially the place and meaning of identity in life history and history. The assessment of such concepts and their continuing relevance—or lack of it—is an important agenda for psychohistory. But to understand and assess Erikson's ideas we must also examine systematically how he uses them. A complete treatment of Erikson's methodology would require analysis of his use of evidence, the process by which he makes inferences, his utilizations of theoretical constructs in interpretating data, and related issues. This discussion is limited by necessity and focuses on one particular aspect of Erikson's methodology: disciplined subjectivity.

From a methodological point of view, disciplined subjectivity lies at the very center of Erikson's work. He defines and develops the concept—and himself—in both *Young Man Luther* and *Gandhi's Truth,* in more theoretical books like *Childhood and Society* and *Identity: Youth and Change,* and throughout papers and speeches delivered over the years. What he means by the term is a *"specific*

Reprinted from *Psychohistory Review* 5:3 (1976) 28–31.

self-awareness" that the psychohistorical observer himself must include in his own field of perception.[2] Good historians, Erikson notes, have always expressed "some awareness of their place in history," but for psychohistorians such awareness is necessarily sharpened by psychological insight.[3] For the clinician—as for the psychohistorian—"The evidence is not 'all in' if he does not succeed in using his own emotional responses during a clinical encounter as an evidential source and as a guide in intervention, instead of putting them aside with a spurious claim to unassailable objectivity."[4]

Erikson has outlined the limits of this subjectivity most clearly in his 1968 *Daedalus* essay, "On the Nature of Psycho-Historical Evidence: In Search of Gandhi." There Erikson charts the requirement that the reviewer of a piece of history must be "reasonably clear about" the stage and conditions of his own life when he selectively involves himself in history as well as the place (or sequence) of that moment in his total life history, and the state of his community in momentary and sequential terms. By communities, Erikson means "a whole series of collective processes from which the reviewer derives identity and sanction and within which his act of reviewing has a function: there, above all, he must know himself as living in the historical process."[5]

Perhaps the most obvious reason Erikson dwells on the self-awareness of the reviewer is to caution psychohistorians not to "immerse themselves into the very disguises, rationalizations, and idealizations of the historical process from which it should be their business to separate themselves."[6] From an ethical point of view, we owe the past the same rigorous and respectful honesty that it should be our business to impose on ourselves as students, teachers, or therapists. But beyond the ethical argument the irrational counter-transference implicit in any encounter with a piece of history must be recognized and turned to methodological advantage.[7] The likes and dislikes of psychohistorians are irrelevant; but uncritical and unanalyzed identifications or petty, irrational hatred hopelessly distort understanding.

From another point of view—one that stresses the creative potential of disciplined subjectivity rather than its role in modifying counter-transference—the self-awareness of the observer permits the utilization of one's emotional responses as a source. If the analyst listens with his "third ear," the psychohistorian likewise searches his own unconscious feelings toward individual lives and collective events in the past to understand the relationship between otherwise confusing or superficially irrelevant data. Subjectivity, in Erikson's use of the term, thus permits (but is not defined by) an empathic encounter with the historical record. The methodological problem, however, is the difference between empathy in a therapeutic encounter in which two people are very much alive and present, talking, gesturing, and feeling (at least one of them is); and the experience of historians in cold, dusty archives struggling inevitably with illegible handwriting. Perhaps there is a vitality missing in the work of historians, an absence of interpersonal exchange, that makes me at least question to what extent we can really talk about empathically relating to the sources.

Part of the argument for Erikson's continued effort to place disciplined subjectivity at the center—methodologically speaking—of psychohistory is the parallel he sees between historical and psychoanalytic methodologies. Erikson has noted twice in *Daedalus* discussions the affinity he feels with the historian who, "like the clinician, must serve the curious process by which selected portions of the past impose themselves on our renewed awareness and claim continued actuality in our contemporary commitments."[8] Neither psychoanalytic nor historical methodologies are scientific in a natural scientific sense and both strive for an understanding that is loose, complex, subjective, and right only insofar as the criteria for judging the evidence are generally accepted. As John Klauber has noted—and I think Erikson would agree—that while the idea of science is unitary explanation of multiple phenomena, history and psychoanalysis attempt to find multiple explanations for single events.[9] I would only add that explanation consists in ordering all the different causes of an event. And in history, psychoanalysis, and psychohistory the most important factor is not necessarily the oldest or most repressed.

But Erikson also recognizes the distinctions between history and psychoanalysis as he simultaneously seeks to resolve the differences. The most important distinction Erikson develops is that between a case history and a life history. In a case history we learn what went wrong and why, the diagnosis which reflects the orientation of the observer; and the therapeutic suggestions for improved health. "A life history, in contrast, describes how a person managed to keep together and to maintain a significant function in the lives of others."[10] Going beyond biography—which in fact Erikson does in most of his writings—he argues forcefully, from *Childhood and Society* on, for looking at any problem from three vantage points: the somatic, the individual or ego, and the societal. In *Luther,* for example, Erikson sees an interconnectedness between the religious and political crises of the great reformer, his followers, and Western Christendom itself. Such a complex perspective requires a kind of triple bookkeeping[11] and in the end focuses more on the uncertain process of human existence than on history seen historically or psychoanalytically. Our individual place in this process makes us both observers and participants. An avowed subjectivity is therefore a more honest position but also reflects a more sophisticated understanding of life itself, of which history is a part.

It is, however, neither self-evident nor really ever explained by Erikson what precisely disciplines subjectivity. To take the question of self-analysis, it is mandated that those who make a profession of psychoanalyzing others must first have learned to analyze themselves, and this for both theoretical and ethical reasons. Psychoanalytic candidates therefore experience patienthood as an integral part of training and subsequently, in practice, learn to empathize with their individual patients in clearly articulated ways. But in history the "patients" are dead, which at least mutes the force of the ethical argument (although I agree with Erikson that it does not entirely eliminate it). Even more importantly, however, true historical understanding involves a sense of individual life history in any period *and* larger developments which shape events as we know them. Erikson, of course, is not only aware of these differences, he has discussed them at length. My point is that it is precisely because of the differences between history and psychoanalysis, that is, for both theoretical and ethical reasons, that Erikson modifies the demand for self-analytic capacity in psychohistorians. In the *Daedalus* piece Erikson argues that, "the psycho-historian will have developed or acquired a certain self-analytical capacity which would give to his dealings with others, great or small, both the charity of identification and a reasonably good conscience."[12] The word I would underline in this quote is "certain." How much is "certain?" Does that amount differ for psychobiography and group analysis? To be fair, we have to keep in mind that there is always a degree of ambiguity when discussing such an elusive concept as self-understanding. The question remains, however, whether Erikson's all-embracing humanism muddles somewhat a clear understanding of subjectivity as the methodological basis of psychohistory. As usual with Erikson—at least in my experience—he seems right. But I am also acutely aware of the unanswered questions.

A more practical but still important issue psychohistorians face in implementing what Erikson means by disciplined subjectivity is determining the criteria for judging whether a given observer has or has not adequately understood himself and, further, whether this awareness has been creatively utilized in relating to the past? A task force of the American Psychiatric Association has addressed this question recently and concluded with the mechanical recommendation that the psychohistorian should, at least, indicate in a preface the source of his particular involvement in his subject and note whatever biases were relevant to the research. But such a position assumes self-awareness is present before the preface is written. And, as I have already asked about self-knowledge, how much revelation is enough? Is the demand for such self-revelation equally relevant for all forms of psychohistorical inquiry? And, finally, as Erikson himself has noted, how can we be sure effusive self-revelation is not serving as an ingenious cover-up and/or disarming propaganda?[13] For Erikson the issue seems relatively simple. He is a practicing analyst, self-aware and sophisticated, able to introduce himself into his writings carefully, selectively, judiciously. His personal asides are, to me, rich and enlightening. But for psychohistorians generally, it is more complex. Most are not analyzed (though I have no knowledge of the relevant statistics), but in any event to require a personal analysis of a psychohistorian would make the field merely an adjunct of psychoanalysis, a position Erikson does not support. We are left, it seems to me, urging self-awareness without defining it; hoping for creative utilization of the self in psychohistorical inquiry without establishing the criteria by which it will be judged; and failing to establish the relevance of disciplined subjectivity for areas such as group analysis.

I find, in conclusion, that I have raised more questions than I have answered. Such is the challenge of working in a new field. Disciplined subjectivity and its role in psychohistorical inquiry is an issue that interests me professionally and personally. I approached the subject after my own analysis and as I begin training as a research candidate at the Chicago Institute for Psychoanalysis. I rather hoped in re-reading Erikson's writings that I would find a greater consistency, a more coherent argument for the training course I am in fact following. That I found some ambiguity is the subject of this short paper. That the issues are so intelligently joined, that the contradictions are developed with such complexity, is a tribute to Erikson.

NOTES

1 Erik H. Erikson, *Young Man Luther: A Study in Psychoanalysis and History* (Austen Riggs Center, Monograph No. 4, New York: Norton, 1958), p. 16.
2 Erik H. Erikson, *Insight and Responsibility* (New York: Norton, 1964), p. 52.
3 Erik H. Erikson, *Dimensions of a New Identity: The 1973 Jefferson Lectures in the Humanities* (New York: Norton, 1974), p. 15.
4 Erikson, *Insight and Responsibility,* p. 73.
5 Erik H. Erikson, "On the Nature of Psycho-Historical Evidence: In Search of Gandhi," *Daedalus* 97, No. 3 (Summer 1968), p. 709.
6 Erikson, *Young Man Luther,* p. 20.
7 Erikson, *Daedalus,* p. 707.
8 Ibid., p. 695.
9 John Klauber, "On the Dual Use of Historical and Scientific Method in Psychoanalysis," *International Journal of Psycho-Analysis* 49:80–88, 1968.
10 Erikson, *Dimensions of a New Identity,* p. 13.
11 Erik H. Erikson, *Childhood and Society* (New York: Norton, 1950), p. 46.
12 Erikson, *Daedalus,* p. 709.
13 Erik H. Erikson, " 'Identity Crisis' in Autobiographic Perspective," *Life History and the Historical Moment* (New York: Norton, 1975), pp. 17–47.

5

The Independence of Psychohistory

Lloyd deMause

Ever since 1942 when the philosopher Carl Hempel published his essay "The Function of General Laws in History,"[1] it has been recognized by most philosophers of history that history cannot be a science in any strict sense of the term and that history can never regard it as part of its task to establish laws in the Hempelian sense. Written history may, in the course of its narrative, use some of the laws established by the various sciences, but its own task remains that of relating the essential sequence of historical action and, *qua* history, to tell what happened, not why.[2]

Psychohistory, it seems to me, is on the contrary specifically concerned with establishing laws and discovering causes in precisely the Hempelian manner. The relationship between history and psychohistory is parallel to the relationship between astrology and astronomy, or if that seems too pejorative, between geology and physics. Astrology and geology are disciplines seeking sequential orders in the sky and the earth, while astronomy and physics are not narrative at all, but are sciences attempting to establish laws in their own respective areas. Psychohistory, as the science of historical motivation, may concentrate on the same historical events that written history covers, but its purpose is never to tell what happened one day after another. When the first astronomers came along and found astrologers describing the positions of the stars day by day and trying to explain all the relationships between them, they created a revolution by saying, "Forget about the sequence of the skies. What interests us *qua* scientists is this one dot of light and whether it goes in a circle or an ellipse—and *why*. In order to find this out, we will have to drop the narrative task of astrology."

What is more, science never did pick up this task of narration—because it couldn't. Astronomy, even if it finally discovers all the laws of the universe, will still not narrate the sequences of skies, any more than psychohistory will ever

Reprinted from *The New Psychohistory* by Lloyd deMause, pp. 7–27, Psychohistory Press, New York: 1975.

narrate the events of this or that period. Psychohistory, as a science, will always be problem-centered, while history will always remain period-centered. They are simply two different tasks.

It does not, of course, follow that psychohistory simply uses the facts historians have narrated up to now in order to construct laws of historical motivation. Like astronomy and physics, psychohistory finds it necessary to conduct its own search for material peculiar to its own interests in both past and present society. Whole great chunks of written history are of little value to the psychohistorian, while other vast areas which have been much neglected by historians—childhood history, content analysis of historical imagery, and so on—suddenly expand from the periphery to the center of the psychohistorian's conceptual world, simply because his or her own new questions require material nowhere to be found in history books.

Now I am well aware that in claiming the field of historical motivation exclusively for the psychohistorian I immediately run up against the oft-repeated claim by historians that they work with motivations all the time, so there is nothing new in that. I had heard this claim so often in the two decades since I first studied the philosophy of history that I was finally moved to measure exactly how often historians actually do examine motivations in their works. I therefore kept a tallysheet as I read 100 history books of varying kinds and recorded exactly how many sentences were devoted to any kind of motivational analysis whatsoever—not just psychoanalytic, but any level of attention at all. In no case did this motivational content reach as much as 1% of the book—so the field seemed to be ours by default. What wasn't pure narrative of one event after another turned out to be mainly the recitation of as many economic facts as possible in the hopes that their mere conjunction with the historical narrative would be mistaken for explanation.

Now anyone who has read any portion of the over 1,300 books and articles contained in the "Bibliography of Psychohistory"[3] will soon realize that psychohistory has reversed this 1-to-99 ratio, so that the bulk of psychohistorical writing is devoted to an intense concentration on motivational analysis while the physical events of history are necessarily given quite sketchy background treatment. There is, for instance, only one page at the beginning of Runciman's three-volume *History of the Crusades*[4] describing how the participants decided to begin four hundred years of wars, and then several thousand pages devoted to the routes, battles and other events which make up the "history" of the Crusades. A psychohistorian would *assume* the history, and spend his decades of research and thousands of pages in the most fascinating question for psychohistory—why so many set off on such a strange task as relic-saving. That the historian, when reviewing such a psychohistory, would accuse it of "ignoring" the full history of the Crusades should bother the psychohistorian as little as the accusation by the astrologer that Galileo "ignored" all the other stars in describing the path of one mere planet. It wasn't his task, and narrative history isn't ours.

What seems not to have occurred to the critics of psychohistory is that we might choose to focus on the historical evolution of the psyche because only thereby can we reach the unsolved problems of precisely these same fields of politics, economics and sociology, fields which are shot through with unproven psychological assumptions and which have failed to become reliable sciences precisely because of the unsolved psychohistorical problems within them. Professionals in each of these fields recognize this quite well, and even admit it to each other in their journals—it is only historians, ignorant of the shaky psychological underpinnings of the fields from which they uncritically borrow, who imagine there can be "economic, political and social factors" which are somehow apart from "psychological" factors in history. As one instance, it is probably true that my own work on the evolution of childhood was at least partly a response to problems encountered in the theory of economic development, as set forth in such books as Everett E. Hagen's *On the Theory of Social Change: How Economic Growth Begins,* where the crucial link needed to produce a take-off in economic development is shown to be just the kind of personality which I was later able to trace in the history of childhood as the result of the "intrusive mode" of parenting. Just as surely is the study of class intimately tied up with evolving psychohistorical patterns of dominance and submission, and the study of power dependent upon an understanding of group-fantasy needs and defenses. The notion that psychohistory somehow "ignores" economics, sociology or political science is possibly the most ignorant charge that could be leveled against it.

When the *Times Literary Supplement* attacks the *Journal* for "seeing behind every action a hidden motive,"[5] all one can answer is "Of course! Action is simply behavior, and since only psyches can have motives, motivation, hidden or not, must be examined in and of its own right to give meaning to all action." Historians habitually skip this examination, as when A. J. P. Taylor describes why Hitler did not intend to go to war in 1939:

> Many however believe that Hitler was a modern Attila, loving destruction for its own sake and therefore bent on war without thought of policy. There is no arguing with such dogmas. Hitler was an extraordinary man; and they may well be true. But his policy is capable of rational explanation; and it is on these that history is built. . . . In considering German armament we escape from the mystic regions of Hitler's psychology and find an answer in the realm of fact. The answer is clear. The state of German armament in 1939 gives decisive proof that Hitler was not contemplating general war, and probably not intending war at all.[6]

The sleight-of-hand involved in this way of writing history is never to examine the actor's actual motives at all, but simply to conclude from looking at material reality, here armaments, what his motives were. That this eliminates the possibility that Hitler might have intended war regardless of the state of his armaments is simply overlooked. Historians are presumed to be unable to "do psychology," which is "mystical" anyway, so they are forced to accept the most "rational" explanations. . ."and it is on these that history is built."

These and many other reasons integral to the logic of psychohistory lead me to believe that it will sooner or later be necessary for psychohistory to split off from history and form its own department within the academy in much the same way that sociology broke off from economics and psychology from philosophy in the late 19th century. As a matter of fact, there is a real sense in which psychohistory never was the exclusive or even the major possession of history departments: the majority of the books and articles in the "Bibliography of Psychohistory" were written by scholars who were not professional historians at all, and this is also the case for the articles written for this *Journal,* the contributing editors of which include psychiatrists, political scientists, educators, psychologists, psychotherapists, humanists and anthropologists as well as historians. Only a minority of the subscribers to the *Journal* are in fact historians. Courses in psychohistory are being offered today in many different departments, and even when offered in the history department they are likely as not conducted jointly by a historian and a psychoanalyst. Therefore my suggestion that separate psychohistory departments should be established is less a schismatic device than it is a move to unite the fractured parts of psychohistorical inquiry, so that all those who are really in the same field can communicate with each other, rather than their being minorities in separate departments and thinking of themselves as "political psychologists," "psychoanalytic sociologists," "applied psychoanalysts," and so on. The choice of *problems*—not the material studied—defines the discipline, and all these scholars are working on the same kinds of problems.

   In uniting these many fields, psychohistory would, it seems to me, for the first time make some sense out of the crazy-quilt pattern of separate disciplines presently studying "the psychology of society." It would assume, of course, that "psychohistory" is not a narrower term than "psycho-social," and that in fact the term "psycho-social" is simply redundant, since the "social" is not "out there" but only "in here," in the head. The usual accusation that psychohistory "reduces everything to psychology" is philosophically meaningless—*of course* psychohistory is reductionist in this sense, since all it studies is historical motivations. Only when the "social" is admitted to being part of the "psychological" can the paradigm for psychohistorical study be recognized as follows:

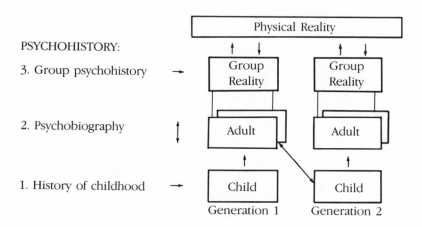

Besides defining the three divisions of psychohistory, this paradigm does two things that distinguish it from the other social sciences, particularly sociology. First, it reverses the relationship between physical and psychological reality, so that instead of material progress setting the pace of history and somehow dragging behind the psyches of its actors, human psychology is made primary—setting Marx on his head and Hegel back on his feet—and material reality is viewed as primarily the outcome of man's decisions, past or present, conscious or unconscious. Secondly, the major basis for historical change is the *interrelations of persons,* not forgetting the relations between generations, and man is viewed for the first time not as *homo faber* but as *homo relatens.*

There are other differences in psychohistory that are only now becoming apparent. First of all, as a science, psychohistory proceeds not by patient accumulation of piles of facts, but by first defining problems interesting to its own internal development, then formulating bold hypotheses from available evidence to solve these problems, and finally attempting to test and *disprove* (not prove—proofs are for high school chemistry students) the hypotheses from new evidence now painstakingly acquired. In fact, psychohistory has a double burden of proof, for it has to conform not only to all the usual standards of historical research, but it must also be psychologically sound—unlike the usual shoddy psychology now found in every historical journal which makes one want to shout at every page, "But people just don't *work* that way!" This double burden of proof will require its own special kind of training, of course, with thorough grounding in the full range of tools of historical research and developmental psychology, since both are essential to the job of cracking open the clam-shell of historical motivation.

It is of course quite true, as historians have pointed out, that psychohistory has no special method of proof that is unavailable to the historian or to any other discipline for that matter. Like all sciences, psychohistory stands or falls on the clarity and testability of its concepts, the breadth and parsimony of its theories, the extent of its empirical evidence, and so on. What psychohistory *does* have which is different is a certain *methodology of discovery,* a methodology which attempts to solve problems of historical motivation with a unique blend of historical documentation, clinical experience and the use of the researcher's own emotions as the crucial research tool for discovery. Let me give a personal example to illustrate this.

For the past decade, I have been intensely interested in the small but growing literature on the causes of war which has begun to be produced by social scientists of many disciplines. I had long ago discovered that historians, wrapped up in the specifics of one particular war or period, were little interested in generalizing on their narrative. In fact, it seemed as though historians used the words "desire for power" as terminations of thought as though the sight of millions of people organizing themselves for years in order to gobble up millions of their hostile neighbors at enormous sacrifice to themselves was the most transparent of human actions, requiring no explanation of motivation whatsoever. Those few historians who went beyond their narrative jumped immediately into economic "explanations," something not too difficult to do, since no war failed to have an economic dispute hanging around somewhere nearby. But they simply never got around to asking why war was the means by which this or that economic dispute was resolved. Neither did they seem to notice that the war was in fact never economically beneficial, and that when the leaders were deciding to go to war they simply never bothered to sit down and draw up a list of economic objectives, assign them a dollar value, subtract the costs of the war, and come up with a "war profit statement" (the very rationality of such an act makes it laughable). Yet the historians continued to pour out whole libraries describing economic conditions prior to wars, never bothering to examine the actual words and actions of the leaders who made the decision to go to war to see if all those economic factors actually had any causal effect on their motivations.

I was as little able to make any sense out of other kinds of historians' explanations for war, which were not only psychologically naive but often as not logically contradictory. Given "diplomatic" causes, opposite conditions were supposed to cause identical results, World War I having been caused by the "inflexibility" of the alliance system, so that when one little fight broke out all of Europe was dragged in, while World War II was caused by the "over-flexibility" of the alliance system term, allowing Hitler to pick off one country after another without fear of bringing in others. Similarly, "social" causes were cited with contradictory results: the cause of France's going to war with Austria in 1772 was the revolutionary turmoil within her borders, while her war with England in 1803 was caused by the *end* of revolutionary turmoil, thus allowing her energies to be turned outward

My own studies of the causes of war centered on the actual motivations of those who made the decisions, and of those around them who created the climate of expectation which allowed them to carry the decision into actuality. During the past year, I collected a large stack of photocopies and notes on the actual words of leaders and others during the times decisions to go to war were being made—a task which is not as simple as it may sound, since historians generally remove from their narrative much of the most important material a psycho-historian needs to determine motivation, such as personal imagery, metaphors, slips, side comments, jokes, scribbles on the edges of documents, and so on, and these were not too easily recovered from their original sources in a limited time span. Still, at the end of the year I had accumulated a wide range of material, and had even learned from it a few new things about war.

The first thing I learned was that these leaders seemed to me to be less father-figures in the Oedipal sense than garbage-disposal directors, being expected by those around them to handle huge amounts of projected emotions which the individuals were unable to keep bound by means of the usual intra-psychic defenses. Large groups seem to present a different level of problem to the psyche than interpersonal relations, so that intrapsychic defenses become less effective and the psyche is thrown back on modes of relating that prevailed in pre-verbal infancy, when problems were handled by projecting them into the mother's body and re-introjecting them back into one's own ego. The individual relates to a large group with similar massive projection devices, and delegates leaders and other role-players to assist him in this task. This process is continuous throughout the history of all large groups, and requires specific *group-fantasies* to carry it out and to defend against the primitive anxieties that result. One group-fantasy leaders are expected to carry out is to find places to dump these huge quantities of projected emotions, which I took to calling external and internal "toilet-objects." That the emotions thus dumped were of infantile origin goes without saying, but to my surprise I found that they seemed to come from all levels of the psychic organization, so that in 1914 German leaders could call the Serbs not only "regicidal" (Oedipal), which one could understand, but also "poisonous" (oral), "filthy" (anal) and "licentious" (phallic).[7] Once the leaders had designated which countries were to be the toilet-objects for these projected emotions, the emotional dumping could continue as a regular part of the political system, and it was then the task of diplomacy to see to it that these now-dangerous objects were fully controlled, in the same manner that little children, favorite toilet-objects for adults, are controlled by being now "chastised," now "brought to their knees," now "taught a lesson," and so on. As long as these external toilet-objects did not threaten to get out of control, war could be kept at a distance, and "diplomacy" seemed to work.

But something always seemed to happen to disturb the delicate process of emotion-dumping, and a group-process began which inexorably led the way to war, even when all those concerned seemed to want to avoid it. This "helpless drift" toward war was the predominant emotional tone for every war I was studying, so that it seemed as though some extremely powerful group-fantasy was being acted out which even the most powerful of leaders was quite helpless to change once it got rolling. To use a German example once again, Kaiser Wilhelm II, who had been encouraging Austria-Hungary to go to war with Serbia, was so startled when Serbia agreed to virtually all of Austria's excessive demands that, having announced that "every reason for war drops away," he gave orders for Vienna to be told to be conciliatory. But the pull of the group-fantasy was too great. His subordinates acted as though *they simply did not hear what he he said,* and the war began anyway. As Bethmann-Hollweg remarked at the time: "All governments ... and the great majority of their peoples are peacefully inclined, but the direction has been lost, and the stone has started rolling."[8] War seemed to be a group-psychotic episode, with patterns of thinking, levels of imagery, and degrees of splitting and projection that are usually only found in the limited psychotic episodes of individuals, but which are temporary and which sooner or later appear quite incomprehensible to those same people. The manic optimism and inevitable under-estimation of the length and severity of the war, the increase in paranoia as to the motivations of the enemy (an "index of paranoia" has even been constructed and graphed[9]), the total absence of awareness that in going to war real people would actually *die,* these and other seeming irrationalities are all indications that a powerful group-fantasy is being acted out. But just what this relentless group-fantasy was completely stumped me. Some controlling process held together all these images and insights that I had picked up from the material in front of me. But I had no idea what it was, and why it seemed so compelling to all the participants.

As in previous cases when I had been bewildered by the material before me, I was convinced that personal defensive reasons were behind my inability to find an answer, and I tried many ways to break my defenses down. I attempted to identify with those leaders on whom I had the most complete material, reading every biography from Napoleon to Hitler that I could get hold of, trying to listen to their "free associations" to the events around them. I immersed myself in the mass of material for weeks at a time and analyzed my dreams each morning for my *own* "associations" and defenses. Nothing seemed to work. I was completely stuck for several months.

In January of this year, I was reading *Business Week* and noticed the interview with Henry Kissinger in which he explained that he had learned that "it is easier to get into a war than to get out of it" and that the only case in which the U.S. would go to war again was "where there is some actual strangulation" occurring. This imagery struck me as familiar. It particularly reminded me of something Kaiser Wilhelm and those around him kept saying in 1914, that "the Monarchy has been seized by the throat and forced to choose between letting itself be strangled and making a last ditch effort to defend itself against attack," and that a "net has been suddenly thrown over our head, and . . . we squirm isolated in the net."[10] I remembered that when I initially read them I was struck by how inappropriate these feelings were, since Germany was in no way strangling and since England, who was accused of throwing the net over her head, was at that time quite friendly toward Germany. Since I was familiar with the many "encirclement" theories with which nations justified their going to war, I was once again tempted to pass off the imagery as rationalization when I stopped myself and said "No! Both Henry and Wilhelm seem quite sincere here. They are reporting to me that it *felt* as if they were being strangled and that consequently they had to go to war, and for once I ought to *trust* their feelings and see where they take me." I once again pulled out my pile of notes, and soon found that this had indeed been the controlling fantasy I had overlooked for so long—images of being "strangled" and "choked" leaped up from every page I had before me. What was more, the strangulation of war seemed to be caused by a fantasy of being in the birth canal, "unable to draw a breath of relief," "unable to see the light at the end of the tunnel," but nevertheless "against one's will" beginning "the inexorable slide towards war," starting with the inevitable "rupture of diplomatic relations," moving with "naked force" into "the descent into the abyss" and finally "breaking out" into the "war that is the price of one's freedom."

Needless to say, I was still extremely reluctant to accept the reality of such an unlikely, even bizarre group-fantasy as "war as birth." Yet even a provisional emotional acceptance of the basic birth thesis made all the difference in the world to how I proceeded with my research. For one thing, only now could I begin to use my knowledge of the psychoanalytic literature on common birth images in dreams, in which suffocation and claustrophobia always represent being trapped in the birth canal, facts which completely eluded me during the prior year while trying to make sense of the historical material. I had noticed, of course, that leaders said they felt "small and helpless" during the slide towards war, but had thoroughly blocked out the importance of the imagery. That there was a life-and-death struggle going on for "some breathing space" was apparent—as Bethmann-Hollweg told the Reichstag in announcing war on August 4, 1914: "He who is menaced as we are and is fighting for his highest possession can only consider how he is to hack his way through."[11] But there was also present all the imagery of birth-dreams familiar to psychoanalysts—choking, drowning, hanging, suffocating, being crushed in rooms or tunnels. In psychoanalysis, these images represent the patient's attempt to repeat and by repeating to master the fearful pressure of labor contractions and the gasping for air after birth. This reliving indicates that birth traumata are still very much alive in most adults, especially those whose regressive need to re-merge with the mother has been kept alive by inadequate parenting.[12] Not only have psychoanalysts traditionally found these images in dreams,[13] but more recently Arthur Janov has discovered that patients in Primal therapy regularly have "birth Primals" in which they re-experience their own births in great detail, and with enormous psychological and physical changes taking place after these re-livings.[14]

In somehow trying to make sense out of all these strands of thought, I noticed that it didn't seem as though *reality*—physical reality—was forcing leaders to feel like strangled babies. Henry Kissinger and the Kaiser were actually no more in danger of war when they began voicing feelings of choking in a birth canal than they had been a year earlier when they did not voice such feelings. What was actually "strangling" the American economy was more the effects of the 1.5 trillion dollars spent on war goods in the previous two decades than the current oil situation, and the notion that little Serbia was actually able to "strangle" central Europe was wholly fantastic. In fact, when I checked my material I found that nations who were *actually* surrounded, like Serbia herself, or Poland in 1939, did *not* voice such images, while countries which *do* say they feel encircled when going to war, like Germany in 1939, do *not* then say so when the war goes against them and they in fact become encircled (for instance there is not a single birth image in *Hitler's Secret Conversations,* running from July 1941 to November 1944). It is *group-reality,* a psychic reality, not material reality, which for reasons yet unknown causes nations to pour into their leaders feelings of being strangled in a birth canal, and which causes these leaders to then feel that only the extreme solution of going to war and hacking their way through offers the possibility of relief.

It was now not long before I became aware that wars proceed in the same sequence as birth. They develop out of a condition resembling pregnancy, the air heavy with feelings of great expectancy, what William Yancey, head of the Alabama delegation to the secessionist Democratic Convention in 1860, before a hushed convention, referred to as "a dormant volcano" which threatened to become "a great heaving volcano."[15] Soon it seems that "every day is pregnant with some new event."[16] The nation's leaders find themselves in what Kaiser Wilhelm termed "the nervous tension in the grip of which Europe has found itself during the last few years,"[17] or what Admiral Shimada in a pre-Pearl Harbor meeting described as a "tight, tense, and trapped feeling" in the air. The nation soon found that it had to "relieve herself of the inexorable pressure to which he has been subjected . . . to extricate herself from the desperate position in which she was entangled . . . to at least gain a breathing spell."[18] The nation seems to be gripped, as Congressman Brinton said in 1917, in what felt like an "invisible energy-field." "There is something in the air, gentlemen," he told his fellow Congressmen, "something stronger than you and I can realize or resist, that seems to be picking us up bodily and literally forcing us to vote for this declaration of war."[19] Shortly thereafter, diplomatic relations are "ruptured," "the past placed its hand on the shoulder of the present and thrust it into the dark future"[20] and the "descent into the abyss" begins as the nation starts its "final plunge over the brink."

When war is finally decided upon, the feeling is inevitably one of enormous relief. When Germany declared war on France in 1914, it came, said the Crown Prince, as a welcome end to the ever-increasing tension, an end to the nightmare of encirclement. "It is a joy to be alive," rejoiced a German paper the same day; Germany was "exulting with happiness."[21] And in America, half a century earlier, when Fort Sumter fell, both North and South experienced the same relief that "something unendurable had ended." Crowds went wild with laughter, waving banners, being swept up in the excitement. "The heather is on fire. I never before knew what a popular excitement can be," wrote a Boston merchant, watching the jubilant crowds, and the *London Times's* correspondent described the same thing in the South—"flushed faces, wild eyes, screaming mouths" outshouting the bands playing "Dixie."[22]

If the announcement of war was equivalent to the actual moment of birth, I wondered to myself how far this concreteness of detail could be carried. For instance, would it be too far-fetched to imagine that one might find in the historical material evidence of the actual explosive first gasp for breath of the newborn, usually accompanied by a slap on the back. I did not have to look far for confirmation of my hunch. Searching my notes once again for the actual feelings expressed by those present at the precise moment that war had been declared, I discovered several clear instances where an *actual birth explosion* had been hallucinated. For instance, when Lincoln issued his proclamation calling for troops to defend the Union, an action recognized by all as the beginning of the Civil War, he retired to his room alone, "and a feeling came over him as if he were utterly deserted and helpless ... he suddenly heard a sound like the boom of a cannon ... The White House attendants, whom he interrogated, had heard nothing .... He met a few persons on the way [outside], some of whom he asked whether they had not heard something like the boom of a cannon. Nobody had heard anything, and so he supposed it must have been a freak of his imagination."[23] Similarly, when Chamberlain stood before the British Cabinet in 1939 and announced: "Right, gentlemen, this means war," one of those present remembered: "Hardly had he said it, when there was the most enormous clap of thunder and the whole Cabinet Room was lit up by a blinding flash of lightning. It was the most deafening thunder-clap I've ever heard in my life. It really shook the building."[24] The birth-explosion seemed to take place only after the emotional recognition that the birth crisis was terminated—it did *not* take place, for instance, upon the first actual shooting, at the siege of Fort Sumter. In fact, the birth-explosion could be hallucinated even if the message that war had started was in error. When Hitler in 1938 was handed the message that Czech forces were mobilizing, and it looked as though the long-avoided European war would begin, Paul Schmidt, his interpreter, said it seemed as though a "big drum-bang" had sounded in the dead silence of those few minutes.[25] This birth-explosion was so necessary, in fact, that leaders, including both Woodrow Wilson and F.D.R., always carefully delayed bringing their countries into wars until they could feel the exaltation (and exhalation) of the war-cry of birth. As Wilson put it, when one of his Cabinet told him in early 1917 that America would follow him if he led them to war:

> Why that is not what I am waiting for; that is not enough. If they cannot go in with a whoop, there is no use of their going in at all.[26]

The more I examined the words of leaders the more I recognized that all of them seemed to *realize* that war was a group-fantasy of birth against which one struggled almost in vain. During the Cuban missile crisis, for example, it was only after Khrushchev wrote to Kennedy pleading that the two nations not "come to a clash, like blind moles" battling to death in a tunnel[27] that war between them could be averted. Even more explicit is the code-word used by Japanese ambassador Kurusu when he phoned Tokyo to signal that negotiations had broken down with Roosevelt and that it was all right to go ahead with the bombing of Pearl Harbor. Forced to invent a voice code on the spot which Tokyo would recognize as meaning that war should begin, Kurusu announced that the "birth of a child" was imminent and asked how things were in Japan. "Does it seem as if a child might be born?" "Yes," came the reply, "the birth of the child seems imminent." The only problem was that American intelligence, listening in, spontaneously recognized the meaning of the war-as-birth code.[28]

The imagery of war as birth seemed to reach back to earliest times. Numa erected a bronze temple to Janus, the Roman god of doorways and archways, and whenever Rome went to war the huge double doors were opened, a common dream-image of birth. Thereafter, whenever a war began, nations borrowed the Roman imagery and declared, as did the *Chicago Tribune* the day Lincoln called for troops: "The gates of Janus are open; the storm is on us." Certainly no American war has seemed to lack birth-imagery, beginning with the American Revolution, filled with images of birth and separation from the mother-country and what Samuel Adams termed the fight for "the child Independence ... now struggling for birth[29] right down to the Vietnam war, which began as "a swampy hole you got sucked into," soon turned into a "bottomless pit" and a "tar baby" you couldn't let go of,[30] and ended with a baby airlift.

While some of the symbolism of war is quite open and transparent—it hardly needs a psychoanalyst to interpret the message General Groves cabled to President Truman to report that the first A-bomb was successful ("The baby was born") or to see the imagery of the Hiroshima bomb being called "Little Boy" and the plane from whose belly it dropped being named after the pilot's mother—still some of the symbolism of war only becomes intelligible when one becomes familiar with psychoanalytic clinical research into dreams of birth. Although I was familiar with much of this literature, from Rank's essay on the birth-trauma to Janov's extensive work on the re-experiencing of birth during primal therapy, I discovered a whole new range of images once dreams. For instance, I discovered a little-known book written 25 years ago by the psychoanalyst Nandor Fodor entitled *The Search for the Beloved: A Clinical Investigation of the Trauma of Birth and Pre-Natal Conditioning,* a book which was ignored at the time it was published only because it was so far in advance of its time. It includes, for example, a complete description of the violence of "normal" birth methods that anticipates at every point that of Frederick Leboyer,[31] plus a proposal for psychotherapy to heal the birth trauma that spells out in advance much of the work of Arthur Janov.

One of the birth symbols that Fodor calls attention to is the image—or rather more often the nightmare—of fire. According to both Leboyer and Fodor, the neonate's skin is extremely sensitive, and feels as though it is burning up both during the long hours of labor and immediately after birth, especially when the room is colder than 98°F. or when the baby is wrapped in rough clothes.[32] Once this is realized, the historical image of war as a "ravaging fire" is more easily comprehended. Moreover, just as in dreams birth can be symbolized by being caught in a burning house, much of warfare involves simply setting fire to people and things, even when it costs more to do so than the benefit involved, as in the case of the "strategic bombing" of Europe in World War II. War and burning seem so intimately connected that troops are driven to set fire to villages even when the latter belong to those who are supposedly allies, as in Vietnam. The impulse to set people and places afire seemingly transcends any other objective in war.

Similarly, Fodor's book contains many references to another dream image for birth—falling or jumping out of towers. This is, of course, a repetition of the moment of birth itself, which involves falling upside down and activates the baby's instinctual fear of falling and reflexive hand-grasping. Only if one keeps one's "inner ear" tuned for this imagery does it become obvious that leaders at crucial moments use the "jumping out of towers" theme to convey war-as-birth messages. For instance, just as Japan was deciding to go to war with America, its leaders were presented with a voluminous report containing well-documented evidence that Japan was outnumbered by America in every area of war potential and actuality by at least 10 to 1 and therefore couldn't possibly win. Since they were in the group-process stage that made the "slide to war" inexorable, Tojo looked at this overwhelming proof that Japan couldn't win the war and announced: "There are times when we must have the courage to do extraordinary things— like jumping, with eyes closed, off the veranda of the Kiyomizu Temple!"[33] Similarly, the French Foreign Minister, at the time of the Munich Agreement, referred to war as "jumping from the Eiffel Tower."[34]

By the time I had finished re-examining my historical material, it had become obvious that all the "innocent babies" killed—and sometimes rescued—during wars were not merely side issues, accidents of war, but rather that *babies were the heart of war's central fantasy.* Consider how often wars open with rumors of the enemy "disemboweling pregnant women," whether by Turkish bayonet or Khmer Rouge wooden stake.[35] Consider how often wars end with "baby-saving" missions, whether by American baby-lift from Vietnam or Nazi Lebensborn projects in Europe, where babies from occupied countries were stolen, measured with obstetrical-type instruments for racial fitness, and either killed as unfit or sent back to Germany for raising as Aryan. Consider how often the killing of babies—as in the Calley trial—becomes the emotional turning-point of a war, and how once it was recognized that *Americans were actually killing babies* (which of course they had been doing all the time) the public removed its support from the war. It soon becomes apparent that, as Fodor found in his birth-dream research[36] and as Melanie Klein discovered clinically,[37] breaking out of the birth canal involves simultaneously breaking *into* the mother's body, and that the merging of these two fantasies is the essence of the war-as-birth fantasy in which neighboring countries must be invaded to escape from "encirclement" while at the same time the invader has the need to control and destroy the bad babies in the mother's body, the hated siblings, the damaged contents of the womb. That foreign countries contained infantilized bad-babies who had to be eliminated—or sometimes saved—was indicated by far more than my Kleinian proclivities. The historical material was full of such imagery. For instance, Hitler began World War II not only because he felt Germany needed *Lebensraum,* "room to live," but also because he had to save the good (German) babies in neighboring states and kill the bad (Jewish, Polish, etc.) ones. The blood-ties binding the mother to those babies who were to be saved was clear in the imagery of the opening words of *Mein Kampf:*

German-Austria must return to the great German motherland, and not because of economic considerations of any sort. ...*Common blood belongs to a common Reich.* As
long as the German nation is unable even to band together its own children in one
common State, it has no ... right to think of colonization.[38]

But aside from those few good babies who deserve to be saved, most babies are
hated occupiers of the mother's body, and must be eliminated. In fact, even the
use of poison gas for genocidal purposes began (in early 1939) with the gassing
of mentally ill and deformed *children,* and only two years later was extended
to include Jews and others,[39] all equally bad-babies, all made bad by the very
same emotional dumping described earlier in the section on external and internal
toilet-objects. For in the end the baby must die after all, and modern war has
been quite as effective in carrying out the filicidal impulses of humanity as child
sacrifice and infanticide used to be.[40]

Now the point of this side trip into the methodology of psychohistorical discovery is that far more is involved in contributing to a specific moment of discovery in psychohistory than the technical training of the psychohistorian.
Certainly both my historical and psychoanalytic knowledge helped—I had to
know how to get around in the literature of both fields—but in a more profound
sense every moment of my own emotional development led to the breakthrough
in recognizing the birth imagery in war. This goes beyond my own obvious interest in the causality of war over the past two decades, and has nothing at all
to do with any theoretical bent toward birth trauma imagery, since I was neither
a Rankian nor a Janovian. Far more crucial were, for example, the long hours
somewhere around the seventh or eighth year of my personal psychoanalysis
when I struggled to re-experience and find meaning in dreams of drowning and
sinking in a whirlpool or quicksand, or, when my son was two years old, those
hundreds of hours I spent with him pretending we were babies in mommy's
belly, crawling around in the dark under the bedclothes and pretending to fall
off the bed crying "Help! Save me!," because that was the endless game that
seemed to give him a strong sense of the pleasure of mastery. Psychohistory,
like psychoanalysis, is a science in which the researcher's *feelings* are as much
or even more a part of his research equipment than his eyes or his hands. Like
eyes, feelings are not infallible; they often introduce distortions, and so on, but
since psychohistory concerns human motivation and since the discovery and
weighing of complex motives can *only* be accomplished by identification with
human actors, the usual suppression of all feeling preached and followed by
most "science" simply cripples a psychohistorian as badly as it would cripple a
biologist to be forbidden the use of a microscope. The *emotional* development
of a psychohistorian is therefore as much a topic for discussion as his or her
intellectual development. That it includes personal psychoanalysis as a foremost
prerequisite goes without saying, as in the case of the psychoanalyst. But I think
it goes beyond this formal requirement.

I must candidly report that as a result of my own personal contacts over the past decade with perhaps a thousand historians from all over the world, both in connection with the history of childhood project and in starting this *Journal,* I no longer believe that most traditional historians are emotionally equipped, even with training, to use their feelings as psychohistorical research tools, although there is a whole new generation of psychohistorians just now beginning to write who *are* able to do so. To expect the average historian to do psychohistory is like trying to teach a blind man to be an astronomer, so averse are they to psychological insight into themselves or their historical material from *any* school of modern psychology. There are complex historical reasons for this fact, having to do with the differential process of self-selection within the universities in recent decades and with the process whereby departments of history have lost so many emotionally open students to psychology. In light of this fact, whenever I speak to a scholar of the emotional development necessary to make a good psychohistorian and get a blank look of total incomprehension, I try to find a way to leave the subject of psychohistory altogether. My listener usually is in another world of discourse where emotional reactions are not considered crucial to the results.

A final illustration will further demonstrate this point. For many years I wondered why I, a radical and anti-nationalist, was nevertheless moved almost to tears when I stood with my son watching a parade with marching bands. The temptation was to shrug off the feeling or to give it a label that would deflect the discomfort, but I was so concerned with this feeling of being swept up by military music that I took to leaving my table at the New York Public Library each time I heard music from a military band going down Fifth Avenue just to see if I could catch my feeling and locate its power over me. If I seemed a bit odd to associates who were with me at the time, so be it—I had to try to answer this question, which was psychohistorical to its core. It was only after the discovery of the war-as-birth thesis that my mind returned to the question of why the bands moved me so—I now had a hunch that I knew the answer. I took a stop-watch out to the next parade and timed the beats of the band. They occurred at about 110–130 beats per minute. Then I timed some popular music, of the usual soothing quality, on the radio—from 70 to 80 beats per minute. When I checked with my wife's obstetrician, I found that the normal heartbeat is about 75 beats per minute and that the elevated heart-beat of a woman during a contraction in labor is between 110–150 beats per minute. I obviously was a baby being born while watching the parade, being picked up and carried along by my mother's heart-beat whether I felt like it or not, and the tears in my eyes were for the impending separation from my mother! Perhaps not the most important discovery in the world, but one thoroughly psychohistorical—and though its *confirmation* might be open to anyone using usual scientific canons of truth, its *discovery* was only open to the psychohistorian with the quite peculiar personality patterns and even lifestyle necessary for using one's emotions as tools for the investigation of group reality.

All of which is not to indicate that I felt satisfied that I had found the ultimate "cause" of war with the war-as-birth paradigm. Oddly enough, science doesn't specifically aim at discovering causes—it tries to solve problems interesting to its own internal development, and causes are often the byproduct of this problem-solving. What I had done by my research was, I think, something even more crucial to psychohistory than finding a cause: *I had changed the question I was asking.* I had defined a new problem, embedded in a new theoretical structure which I felt could be both fruitful and empirically testable, and I was now able to ask a whole series of new questions such as: Why do nations project birth feelings into their leaders at some moments in their histories and not at others? What means are used to communicate these projections? Are these birth images defenses against other psychic conditions in the leadership group or in the nation? Were some wars exceptions to the war-as-birth paradigm, and if so what motivational imagery did they substitute for it? Are there differential evolutionary patterns of war imagery? Why do group-fantasies occur in such grotesquely exaggerated slow-motion, taking months and years to act out events that originally took hours, while exactly the same images in dreams are condensed into minutes?

The ability to generate new questions is precisely the hallmark of a science. Physical science expanded so rapidly in the seventeenth and eighteenth centuries not because scientists were somehow brighter than those around them. In some senses, these early scientists were quite limited in their education and in a wide knowledge of the world around them. The same principle holds for psychohistorians, who hope to succeed where historians have failed by giving scientific explanation to historical motivation. Psychohistorians can achieve this, not because they are smarter than historians but because they conceive of their task in a wholly different way and have access to research tools and scientific models unavailable to the historian. Just as there was no way for even the most learned astrologers to understand the motions of the planets as long as they (1) conceived of their task as essentially narrative- rather than problem-centered, and (2) refused to use a telescope, so even the most learned historian cannot understand the causality of history as long as he (1) conceives of his task as narrative- rather than problem-centered and (2) refuses to use his own emotional-identification capacity in a scientific way at every step in the research process.

Other psychohistorians have, I believe, found ways similar to mine to intensify this emotional-identification and defense-stripping process. Rudolph Binion, in researching his psychobiographies of Lou Andreas-Salomé and Hitler, spent several years accumulating mountains of primary source material on their motivational patterns and then locked himself up for months with his evidence and read and re-read every detail until "the pieces ... *all* fit together, with the facts *all* stacked up behind them: this alone carried final conviction."[41] Henry Ebel surrounds himself with his historical material and "Primals" for hours while free-associating to the material in front of him, in a concentrated effort to reach deeper levels of motivation than the usual reading reveals.[42] All these methods, like my own dream-interpretation to remove defenses against discovery, are attempts by psychohistorians to fashion research tools that, like microscopes and telescopes, give access to material hitherto denied them. For psychohistory is more a *re-discovery* than a discovery—*it is a process of finding out what we all already know and act upon.* Our discovery of exterior conditions is wholly dependent on how much we can strip away of our interior defenses against recognition of what we are doing all the time. Every person going to war speaks in birth imagery, responds to birth drumbeats, and communicates in birth symbols to others going to war, and every historian fills his books with writing that tells of "the pulse-beat of the coming violence growing louder and faster as the nation moves inexorably to the birth-pangs of war." We all know it—yet no one knows it. Only the psychohistorian who trains himself to use what is "in here" to discover what is going on "out there" can hope to succeed where so many have failed in understanding and bringing under control those group-fantasies we choose to call our history.

NOTES

1 Carl Hempel, "The Function of General Laws in History," in Herbert Feigel and Wilfred Sellars, ed., *Readings in Philosophical Analysis.* New York: Appleton-Century-Crofts, 1949.

2 Alan Donagan, "Explanations in History," in Patrick Gardiner, ed., *Theories of History.* New York: The Free Press, 1959.

3 Lloyd deMause, ed., *Psychohistory: A Bibliographic Guide.* New York: Garland Publishing, 1975.

4 Steven Runciman, *History of the Crusades.* 3 vols. Cambridge: Cambridge University Press, 1950.

5 Elie Kedourie, "New Histories for Old," *Times Literary Supplement,* March 7, 1975, p. 3.

6 A. J. P. Taylor, *The Origins of the Second World War.* New York: Atheneum, 1968, pp. 216, 217.

7 Max Montgelas and Walter Schücking, eds., *Outbreak of the World War: German Documents Collected by Karl Kautsky.* Oxford: Oxford University Press, 1924, pp. 63, 307, 266, 161.

8 Montgelas and Schücking, eds., *Outbreak of The World War,* pp. 250ff. The inexorability of the movement to war, as well as most of the other irrationalies of the war process, is best summarized and adequately referenced in Geoffrey Blainey, *The Causes of War.* New York: The Free Press, 1973.

9 Ole R. Holsti and Robert C. North, "The History of Human Conflict," in Elton B. McNeil, ed., *The Nature of Human Conflict.* Englewood Cliffs, N.J.: Prentice-Hall, 1965, p. 166.

10 Luigi Albertini, *The Origins of the World War of 1914.* Vol. II. Oxford: Oxford University Press, 1952, p. 132; Imanuel Geiss, ed., *July 1914: The Outbreak of the First World War: Selected Documents.* New York: Charles Scribner's Sons, 1967, p. 295.

11 Ralph H. Lutz, *Fall of the German Empire, 1914–1918: Documents of the German Revolution.* Vol. I. Stanford: Stanford University Press, 1932, p. 13.

12 For the various levels of parenting throughout history, see Lloyd deMause, ed., *The History of Childhood.* New York: The Psychohistory Press and Harper & Row, 1974 and 1975.

13 Nandor Fodor, *The Search for the Beloved: A Clinical Investigation of the Trauma of Birth and Pre-Natal Conditioning.* New Hyde Park: University Books, 1949, pp. 35–45.

14 Arthur Janov, *The Feeling Child: Preventing Neurosis in Children.* New York: Simon and Schuster, 1973, pp. 41–81.

15 Bruce Catton, *The Coming Fury.* Garden City, N.Y.: Doubleday & Co., 1961, p. 32.

16 William Eddis, *Letters from America.* Cambridge, Mass.: Harvard University Press, 1969, p. 151.

17 Montgelas and Schücking, ed., *Outbreak of the World War,* p. 56.

18 Herbert Feis, *The Road to Pearl Harbor.* Princeton: Princeton University Press, 1950, pp. 293, 265.

19 Richard W. Leopold and Arthur S. Link, eds. *Problems in American History.* New York: McKay, 1965, p. 762.

20 Feis, *Pearl Harbor,* p. 293.

21 Barbara Tuchman, *The Guns of August.* New York: The Macmillan Co., 1962, p. 121.

22 Catton, *Fury,* p. 325.

23 Carl Sandburg, *Abraham Lincoln: The War Years.* Vol. 1. New York: Harcourt, Brace & Co. 1939, pp. 236–37.

24 Sidney Aster, *1939: The Making of the Second World War.* New York: Simon and Schuster, 1973, p. 387.

25 Paul Schmidt, *Statist auf diplomatischer Bühne 1923–45.* Bonn, 1949, p. 413.

26 Joseph P. Tumulty, *Woodrow Wilson As I Knew Him.* New York: Doubleday, 1921, p. 235.

27 Robert F. Kennedy, *Thirteen Days: A Memoir of the Cuban Missile Crisis.* New York: W. W. Norton, 1969, p. 89.

28 John Toland, *Rising Sun: The Decline and Fall of the Japanese Empire.* New York: Random House, 1970, pp. 174–75.

29 Henry Steele Commager and Richard B. Morris, eds., *The Spirit of Seventy-Six* Vol. I. New York: Bobbs-Merrill Co., 1970, p. 294.

30 David Halberstam, *The Best and the Brightest.* New York: Random House 1969, pp. 249, 601, 617.

31 Frederick Leboyer, *Birth without Violence.* New York: Alfred Knopf, 1975.

32 Personal communication with Dr. Leboyer at the Tarrytown Conference on Birth without Violence, April 19, 1975; Fodor, *Search,* pp. 16, 93–103.

33 Toland, *The Rising Sun,* p. 112.

34 Laurence Thompson, *The Greatest Treason: The Untold Story of Munich.* New York: William Morrow & Co., 1968, p. 112.

35 Robert Sam Anson, "Withdrawal Pains," *New Times,* March 21, 1975, p. 25.

36 Fodor, *Search,* p. 253ff.

37 Melanie Klein, *Narrative of a Child Analysis.* New York: Basic Books, 1960.

38 Adolf Hitler, *Mein Kampf.* New York: Reynal & Hitchcock, 1939, p. 3.

39 Lucy S. Dawidowicz, *The War Against the Jews, 1933–1945.* New York: Holt, Rinehart and Winston, 1975, p. 132.

40 As I was writing up this article I found that I had encountered the essence of the baby imagery more than a year earlier in *The First Part of the Revelation of Moses the Son of Jehoshar* (Fort Lee, N.J.: Argonaut Books, 1973, pp. 58–59, 102, 106) in the brilliant aphorisms of Henry Ebel describing how "Dresden, Berlin, Hiroshima and Nagasaki were also made chokewomb hot-wombs" and how "men wonder at the calm bestiality with which the Nazi murdered babies and infants and children. But that was the whole point. The helpless adults they butchered were equally 'children' to them. If they baby-phagged as hard as they could, then perhaps they wouldn't be babyphagged themselves. If they pushed more babies into the chokewomb hotwomb, then perhaps Mama would spare THEM."

41 Rudolph Binion, "Hitler's Concept of *Lebensraum,*" *History of Childhood Quarterly: The Journal of Psychohistory* 1 (1973):196; "My Life with Frau Lou," in Perry Curtis, ed., *The Historian's Workshop.* New York: Knopf, 1970, pp. 293–306.

42 Henry Ebel, "Primal Therapy and Psychohistory," *History of Childhood Quarterly: The Journal of Psychohistory* 2 (1975):563–70; and *The First Part of the Revelation of Moses the Son of Jehoshar.*

6

Doing Psychohistory

Rudolph Binion

A universe permanently unconscious of itself in all its parts, existence everywhere and forever unexperienced, boundless being in a sensory void: this is inconceivable. Such incognizance is spoiled just by being imagined. To envision even bygone worlds of unsuspecting, unsuspected matter, or an oblivious cosmos to come, is for the mind's eye to supply the defect. Because existence cannot be unthought, philosophers tend to suppose that it is inherently known. For Anaxagoras already, psyche was the containing and ordering principle of the universe, so that awareness of things was one with their cause. Many a master of modern historical thinking has followed Anaxagoras in this. Thus for Hegel, human history had meaning; its meaning was expanding consciousness; its contents was what consciousness required to expand. Here is where Karl Marx claimed to set Hegel aright. Marx argued instead that what was developing in the long haul was the economy, with human relations, institutions, and finally consciousness tagging along. But modes of production developed logically and intelligibly for Marx just as consciousness did for Hegel. For Marx too history made sense, and for him too the point of it was to be understood. Relative understanding ("class consciousness") lent history its dynamics; absolute understanding would be its fulfillment. It was Darwin who dealt such age-old human presumption its hardest blow. In Darwin's scheme, consciousness had evolved from more rudimentary sensibility and, behind that, insensibility. Darwin's derivation of mind from brute matter by way of accidents adding up (through "natural selection from random variations") turned Anaxagoras inside out. Anaxagoras's containing and ordering principle reappeared accordingly—in the exact adaptation of consciousness to nature and the possibility of systematizing the messy facts of life.

Ours is Darwin's world. Our consciousness no longer fools us about its mindlessness. Our species' history merges with natural history. Our species' future is open: its natural lot is to change continually, with or without mutations, de-

Reprinted from *The Journal of Psychohistory,* vol. 5 (1978) 313–23.

pending on who survives to reproduce. Our animal instincts of survival and re-
production have us coming and going, even where they miscarry or where we
refine them beyond recognition. Our creatural consciousness is distinguished
in the main by being reflexive. We do not want something without knowing that
we want it—or refusing to know. Our faculty of refusing to know what we want
was Freud's province. Prying into its pathology, Freud uncovered a human reserve
of instinctual thinking unfit for consciousness beyond infancy, and that in a nether
realm of disclaimed memories and inexpressible stirrings out of the individual
and racial past. Here was a whole new germinal source of history. Freud well
realized this. But Freud approached history through his clinical findings imag-
inatively extended instead of using history to extend them. Psychoanalysis has
yet to repair his omission. Historians can look to psychoanalysts, Freud foremost,
for object lessons in interpreting human folly, but not for interpretations ready-
made.

Human history is what people did. To understand it is to understand why
people did what they did. This is possible because mind is enough of a kind
for its workings to be inwardly intelligible at any historic remove. Understanding
history through motives and motives through history: this is psychohistory. Psyche
causing history, making it intelligible: this updates Anaxagoras.

For such intelligibility the records must suffice. There is a no telling in advance
when they will. They could be bulky with the key pieces missing. My own odd
experience has been that the key pieces always survive, however little else does.
But I have stuck to richly documented history for safety's sake. This precaution
is hardly restrictive, as just about any topic is worth doing, or redoing, in the
present crude state of the art. A more restrictive consideration in the choice of
topics is that they must be lived with at emotionally close quarters for years. My
own intended next topic was the traumatic aftereffects of the Black Death as reflected in the outbursts of social violence, convulsive and contagious, that spread
in its wake a generation after. But then I balked at absorbing myself in that morbid
matter after five years with Hitler's Germany. In any case the project was infel-
icitously conceived. Proper psychohistorical procedure is to pursue causes rather
than effects. A researcher can probe a given event, say young Napoleon's flight
from Corsica, for unconscious input, but not for unconscious output. Should a
link be suspected with Napoleon's flight from Egypt six years later, this would
need to be probed in its own right.

As a rule, the aspirant psychohistorian is best advised to pick a biographic
subject. This rule is highly breakable. But the individual psyche remains the basis
of our conceptualizations until further notice. So it were as well for the trainee
to train by penetrating one or another historic life in full. Actually there is no
penetrating a historic life except in full, as nothing significant in a life is detached
from the rest subjectively. The life need not be written up in full when the time
comes. But its thrust or drift at any juncture must fall in with its thrust or drift
overall—with its controlling purposes, its dominant patterns, its recurrent motifs—when they are read as (as Nietzsche's phrase) "a sign language of the affects."

To grasp a life inwardly requires mastery of its full documentary remains. It also calls for conversance with the whole run of personalities, institutions, and events, and the whole congeries of ideas, usages, and values, involved. To top that off, it takes an intellectual and emotional stunt both strenuous and delicate. The researcher must emphatize and analyze at once. He must imagine himself Napoleon setting sail from Alexandria and ask himself: "What am I doing *unconsciously* in setting sail from Alexandria?" His empathy must be perfect to yield Napoleon's answer, yet only partial for him to catch the answer when it comes. That is, he must make believe in earnest and still know that he is making believe. This comes to an artificial, controlled ego-split.

As good a passage of an assumed life as any to probe first in this posture is one with a suspected precedent, such as Napoleon's flight from Egypt: the precedent will never simply fall into place associatively without leading beyond itself. Another good starter is quirks or foibles except that they can easily get magnified out of proportion. Better are lapses or aberrations from a smooth course of action or system of thought: they will be found to expose its underpinnings. Fictionalists offer an ideal point of departure in their fiction, the rule being that every element of it has at least one referent in their lives. Take Ibsen. Inquiry on him would almost have to begin with his impregnating a servant girl when he was eighteen. This misadventure looms even larger behind his later dramas than the two unsettling circumstances of his childhood: his rumored illegitimacy and his father's financial ruin. All three come into *The Wild Duck* practically undistorted in the backdrop to the sorry menage of a photographer and dreamer (read: naturalist and poet). Tragedy ensues when an idealistic illusion-destroyer (Ibsen again) drags the old misadventure upstage center. Ibsen took his own hint here and returned to disguising his experience of the unwanted child again and again until his last heroine went mad from reliving it again and again in disguise. Here, in *When We Dead Awaken,* the child is a statue for which she has posed in the nude. Traumatized by the sculptor's mere thanks for the chaste episode, she relives it in reverse as a nude artist who teases men to despair.

Not only characters and situations, but also themes and techniques, have their antecedents in a creative writer's life. Bertolt Brecht's shock at the surgical butchery he witnessed as a medical orderly in 1918 went into pacifist plays aggressively staged, then didactic plays justifying violence, before he mastered it in a theater balancing both modes and messages. Jean Genet's obsession with his own homosexuality shows behind the dominant devices of his theater: the play of false identities and the inversion of customary relations and values. Philosophers for their part work up private experience into ideas. Witness Malthus conceiving of "moral restraint" as a corrective to his fearful "power of population" while on a chaste research trip abroad with his future wife. Or witness Søren Kierkegaard, the last child of a seduced housemaid: his pious father's shattering disclosure of this transgression eventuated in S.K.'s concept of a "teleological suspension of the ethical" whereby Abraham suspended ethics to the roundabout end of getting his son Isaac (S.K.). This equivalence was full of dialectical twists: Abraham was tempted to be ethical; he surmounted his temptation; he got by renouncing. A writer's life too has its themes with their concealed allusions to his past. They go by the same rules of origination as those in his works: it is as simple as that. Take Kierkegaard renouncing his fiancée untouched by pretending to have been only trifling with her: this repeated in the negative his father's seduction of the wench he then dutifully married. Repudiated masters are imitated like repudiated parents. Auguste Comte wound up enunciating a new Christianity like Saint-Simon. John Stuart Mill followed Comte in finding a mismated muse to humanize his theories.

But such fragments of a life may not go to the heart of it. What counts is how it cohered, beginning with what it cohered around. An activist who was also a theorist invites a focus on the action his theorizing served. The simple sense of a lifelong course of action takes exceeding care to discern. What was a Lenin's basic endeavor? It was something like a use of coercion for the sake of final deliverance from coercion. Here are the two terms of a classic bout with the father ghost, the proper sequence—deliverance from, then succession to, the coercionist—being simply reversed. This reversal was offset in practice by the need to end the Czar's despotism before Lenin's could begin. And yet I would expect Leninism to have been actuated less by the father complex than by "a shattering experience"[1] of seventeen-year-old Vladimir Ilyich: his elder brother's execution for plotting to kill the Czar. Both brothers had become intellectual rebels upon their father's death a year earlier. The elder one alone had turned to politics. He espoused Marxism, but resorted to terrorism against "a system which permits no freedom." So he explained at his trial, adding: "Terror is our answer to the violence of the state. It is the only way to force a despotic regime to grant political freedom to the people."[2] His avenger, even while liquidating Czarism, perfected its repressive methods from inside the Kremlin on the theory that freedom would someday ensue. Here is a tempting paradox. Only the paradox may be mine rather than Lenin's—a function of my formulation rather than his intention. There is no telling from the biographic outside. To know what values or aims, attitudes or methods, were vital to Lenin, and discover what they meant to him deep down, I would need to become Lenin artificially, with the whole Lenin corpus down pat.

But even then, how would I know the right answer if I found it? Right answers come piecemeal, each piece a breakthrough with a compelling rush of unsuspected associations. Psychohistorical analysis proceeds about like dream analysis on a grand scale except that the associations thrown up involve new material facts that then check out. This is retrodiction. It dispels any and all self-doubt on the researcher's part. I worked through the known Hitler records by empathic introspection to missing experiences that I documented only afterwards, including Hitler's Pasewalk hallucination, his mother's poisoning, and her maternal trauma. Through Hitler's calls for Germany's eastward expansion I even heard the muted reference to Germany's lost eastern conquest of World War I before I could pin it down archivally. I say "even" because I heard it on the receiving end of his calls, by thinking and feeling myself into the public to which he appealed. But when is such an inquiry complete? Loosely put, when nothing puzzles us any longer about a Lenin or a Hitler—when we know what was bothering him inwardly, and how he handled it outwardly, with all his crucial utterances and decisions and moves as forced consequences. Perhaps more formal criteria can be defined. Informally it is again as in dream analysis: the mystery is exhausted—and the self-analyst with it.

Breakthrough, retrodiction, exhaustion: these are conclusive for the researcher. They prove nothing for anyone else. He can show that his solution fits to the nth degree of irrefragability. That will establish it as possible, no more. He can show further how to confirm or disconfirm it. But no subsequent empirical support will carry final conviction either. Here the psychohistorian is uniquely up against it. His special problem is not, as the clinical-minded insist, the risk of "countertransference" so long as the data keep running his way. Any other historian also risks reading his own *meshugas* into his materials. So for that matter does the natural scientist. Einstein may well have had a world womb at heart when he conceptualized his plenum universe finite and unbounded, self-contained and expanding, quasi-spherical and quasi-elliptical like a mollusk. The payoff is whether kinetic energy does equal $mc^2/\sqrt{1-v^2/c^2}$. With the psychohistorian too the proof is in the pudding. But the psychohistorian's pudding cannot be just measured and weighed. It must also be tasted to be tested. That is, others must step inside his subject after him and try out his reading of the evidence on themselves in turn. This costs emotional strains on top of critical pains, though none that begin to approach the researcher's own. With affective material, feeling is believing. In any case belief is "something *felt* by the mind," as David Hume remarked.[3] That is doubly so in psychohistory.

But the problem is not simply one of belief as against disbelief. An open-minded reader will ordinarily believe a right psychohistorical solution only to underweight it. Granted your derivation of a Lenin's politics, he will say, was there nothing *else* agitating the agitator? And what about hard objective forces shaping his will?

This second question embarrasses many a psychohistorian into an unmeaning methodological pluralism. The hedging preface would have it that the psychohistorical is one factor among many—that it adds one new dimension. An unfortunate influence this way would seem to be the *Annales* school with its aim of *histoire totale*. In practice *histoire totale* means that to describe past social reality anything goes, from climate to the id. The key word here is "describe": *histoire totale* is total description of past social reality slowly changing. To explain such change is another matter. The law of parsimony applies to all explaining. More, social change must be seen for what it is, people doing things differently, or it will forever resist explanation. Statistics are no way around this imperative.

The fall of a net fertility rate way back when means that some women were cop-
ulating less or breastfeeding longer or something. All that statistical analysis can
show is who and what. The psychohistorical "Why?" remains. To reply to it in
the negative, whatever people did not act *from* or *on* does not help explain their
acts. By *"from"* I mean the inner impetus inwardly regulated; by *"on"* I mean
a resistant or compliant medium. The rest is beside the explanatory point. Grav-
itation and respiration are vital to human enterprise, but not for understanding
it. The same goes for social context as distinct from social motives or purposes.
Inquiry is inclusive, explanation exclusive.

That principle of exclusion applies to motivational material itself. Unless we
can pick out the crucial pieces behind a historic performance we slip into item-
ization tending toward a *psychohistoire totale*. The psychohistorical catchall has
its advocates. Their catchword is "overdetermination." This was Freud's peculiar
term for mutlidetermination in mental life—peculiar because it implies that some
determinants are expendable and so are not determinants after all. But, terminology apart, Freud recognized that, say, a tightly condensed dream is not caused
by all the latent material stacked up behind it, let alone by all the modes of
concealed expression employed in it. In his scheme, a dream is caused by a
preconscious thought that combines with an unconscious wish or vice versa. The
rest just gets in on the act. Roughly these same rules apply to a psychic economy
waking as sleeping except that awake means oriented to outer reality at the level
of consciousness. Short of pathology, routine living is governed by the reality
principle in accordance with unconscious intent, while the twists and turns of
a life's course are governed by unconscious dictates in keeping with the reality
principle. This causality as per Freud holds in psychohistory if room is made in
his scheme for unconscious demands arising out of postinfantile experience. And
what counts in psychohistory are causes, not the whole range of "overdeter-
minants," though these too must be rehearsed in print now and again—behind
a mind set or a brain storm, a decision or an inspiration, analyzed or reconstructed in full for illustrative purposes.

To the same point, psychotherapy will rightly deal in infantile material that is
wrong for psychohistory. Consider Kierkegaard again. Why did his father's disclosure about his mother's seduction hit him so hard? The answer would have
mattered to him on the couch. It is immaterial to his "teleological suspension
of the ethical" if this is directly accountable by that disclosure affecting him unconsciously (and his broken engagement consciously). Or consider Ibsen again.
His theater appears to have been haunted most by the erotic and financial casualty
of his unwanted child, with his rumored illegitimacy and his father's business
failure brought in by association. Such a traumatic setback to a highminded, ambitious youth is irreducible to infantile material. In Lenin's case, the father complex is conspicuous in his marked ambivalence toward his elder brother as the
new head of their family after their father's death. That brother's execution was
no less a powerful experience in its own right that certainly shaped his striving

in more ways than he knew. And where was the generative center of Hitler's politics? "The Jew" was his mother's last doctor, "living space" was Ludendorff's lost conquest; the rest was peripheral.

Emotional shock-absorption comes into the clinical texts only in its failing form: the traumatic neurosis. But its normal form, unconscious reliving, is the ferment of endless historic storm and stress. Therein lies another warning against simply applying clinical theory to history. But no more warning should be needed against this misguided procedure than that the most to be gained by it is less than nil. Imagine a psychobiographic sleuth on the trail of a narcissistic personality disorder behind Stalin's seemingly paranoid rule. Instead of entering into his subject in all its vastness, he would be documenting Stalin's irritability, his whims and rages, his grandiosity, his intolerance of frustration and dissent. However strong a presumption he might finally establish that baby Djugashvili resented his severance into self and other, that primal upset leads nowhere in particular careerwise or otherwise. So he could not turn around and derive Stalinism from it. Besides, Stalin's terror arose with his victims' eerie compliance. To be seen into, it would need to be seen arising. It were probably best approached through his crude debut as terrorizer in Tsaritsyn in 1918. Causes show most distinctly through beginnings. When I could not trace Hitler's calls for eastward expansion to a personal source, their beginnings led me to their source in his audiences prompting them. To have tapped that source is my proudest research coup. That would be the lure of a Stalin, a Lenin, a Napoleon, as psychohistorical subject: their unconscious rapport with those they ruled.

Twice now I have cited Hitler's unconscious rapport with his public: *jamais deux sans trois!* The clue to it came from *Mein Kampf.* There Hitler related that in his agitational incunabula he had delivered two stock speeches in ever new versions by reading corrections off his listeners' faces. Reports by Party and press, by Army and police, of his early speech-making attested to his intense interaction with his audiences. His one stock speech denied German war guilt; the other vindicated the Treaty of Brest-Litovsk as a gracious partnership with the defeated Soviet Union. Both connected *a contrario* with his project, first published in *Mein Kampf* of 1924–1926, for a German conquest of the Soviet Union with Britain's concurrence. I had already found this project expounded in private utterances recorded over the year preceding the Putsch of November 1923. Could it have developed out of his two early oratorical repertory pieces following the indications from his listeners' faces? I thought and felt myself back into his audiences in the Munich area before the Putsch and across Germany in the late 1920s. After long months of straining my mind's ear I could all at once hear, and shrilly, where his call for eastward expansion resonated with a traumatic national experience. This was the 1918 defeat, for which Germans were the less prepared since Ludendorff's subjugation of Soviet Russia had seemed to render them invulnerable. That trauma did not, then, just pop up behind Hitler's expansionist project and introduce itself. It erupted convulsively, a pent-up panic so overpowering when released that I blocked it out again and again before I could admit it to consciousness sufficiently even to identify it. With it, disparate elements of Weimar Germany's troubled and confusing politics rushed to mind, connected up, fell into place. These included a missing link in my evidence that I then had to hunt down: the transition from Hitler's two early repertory pieces to his project for a new eastern conquest. This project was now intelligible as an invitation to a traumatic reliving—one designed ostensibly to undo the 1918 defeat, actually to outdo it. A year or more passed before I realized that I was taking that transition for granted. Then I scouted for documentation. I found it for May 31, 1921, when Hitler delivered those two repertory speeches combined, both for the last time. In vindicating Brest-Litovsk on that occasion he blurted out that the big German loss from the defeat in the west had been the land conquered from the Soviets. And he grounded the point in the very arguments that he later advanced to urge a reconquest.

   That documentary find confirmed for me my intuition of the German trauma. True, my final proof of it lay with Hitler registering it and reacting.[4] But the insight had been won through self-projection into his national public. This opened mass phenomena to direct psychohistorical inquiry. Such effects may be only sporadic and transitory in modern times—repercussions of group shock or fear for a few generations. Or all large-scale human developments may be collaborative at the unconscious level. Take a broad cultural movement such as Romanticism. Why did Romantic values spread across Europe in the decades around 1800? All at once youngsters sought out the common path and the rare destiny; exalted community and aloneness; affected enchantment and estrangement, exuberance and languishing, yearning and pining; swooned over their sister if they had one, and felt burnt out by twenty-some if they lived that long. Gerald N. Izenberg is studying several important Romantics against a background of changing familial circumstances. If that is where the stimulus to Romanticism came from, he can be trusted to find it. But I wonder. A proto-Romanticism burgeoned early along in the Age of Reason with its bursts of tears and brooding over ruins, as if the regnant formalism and rationalism were not wholly tolerable. The binding constraints and restraints had rigidified beyond easy endurance. The Romantics repudiated them in a surge of passion (and posturing), often enough without having experienced them at first hand. This emergence of Romanticism out of "the stirrings of unchanneled emotion . . . disrupting the old order"[5] makes culture look continuous on the level of nerves, with one century's moodiness developing into the mannered mood of the next. Jacques Barzun stretches that line of descent farther back. Referring to "romantic" exploration and creation in the sixteenth century, he adds that "when classicism had twinges, they were like pre-natal recollections of romanticism."[6] This image is psychohistorically overdrawn, to be sure. Yet it is meaningful within a time-honored, universal frame of reference: that of collective historical experience, with collective memories to match. The psychological truth to this ever-current scheme of history requires to be explored. Its exploration would seem to offer at least as promising an approach to broad movements in history as the search for patterns of change in private cirumstances.

I do not say more promising. The only thing wrong with psychoprosopography is the word. Collective experience involves individuals. How it involves them is part of what requires exploring. So the comparative study of individual Anabaptists or Abolitionists can only complement the exploration of those mass manifestations per se. The same holds for more generalized historical studies of formative influences on children, from nurturing and socializing practices[7] to great existential upheavals.[8] Such studies yield norms and aggregates—types and tendencies of personal development. These cannot be searched out for the motives that make history. Only specific individuals can for individual motives, specific collectivities for collective motives.

Such collectivities run large so far as can tentatively be told. Monster-ridden medieval Europe was one for Walter Abell in *The Collective Dream in Art.*[9] The convenient access to collective traumas or anxieties through common motifs in art has been neglected since this pioneering work. But Paul Monaco found in the popular cinema of the 1920s, with its relatively closed national markets, a comparable medium for penetrating national group process. By analyzing the French and German filmic fantasy wares of those years, he established that the Germans were then haunted by the war they had lost in 1918 and the French by their subsequent national insecurity.[10] And now Lloyd deMause has spotted a new locus of national fantasy in the imagery interspersed in public rhetoric. It, he holds, signals unconscious national imperatives to responsive political leaders.[11] No doubt it does. But do the signals come in perinatal crisis cycles as deMause contends? That is too schematic for the few glimpses we have had of group process. My own guess is that collective identities are vestigial—that they were the giants and many-headed monsters of yore. If so, they will draw researchers to prehistory. Only this much is already certain: that they await further insight before theoretical bearings can be taken.

For such insight, the more genius the better. But the first thing needful is expertise—in history generally, and in individual-based psychohistory—as distinct from small-minded professionalism. Historical professionalism, like any other, is defined by what has been and is being done. Psychohistory itself is infested with a would-be professionalism oriented toward clinical models. Such models of individual personality disserve it because of their tangential relevance. Not even tangential relevance can be found for the psychoanalytical theories of group process drawn from self-observing artificial groups.[12] With collective causality, psychohistory comes into its own. That puts it farther beyond the professional pale than ever before. Its big, and only, hope is that, with a whole uncharted realm of human reality open before it, it is also more exciting than ever before.

NOTES

1 Louis Fischer, *The Life of Lenin* (New York, 1964), p. 9. See also ibid., p. 17: "a lasting shock."
2 Quoted in David Shub, *Lenin* (Baltimore, 1966), pp. 15–16. See further Fischer, pp. 14–17,

and, on young Lenin and revolutionary terrorism, Richard Pipes, "The Origins of Bolshevism: The Intellectual Evolution of Young Lenin," in *Revolutionary Russia: A Symposium,* ed. Richard Pipes (New York, 1968), pp. 33–66.

3 David Hume, *A Treatise of Human Nature,* Book I, Part III, Section VII.

4 Rudolph Binion, *Hitler among the Germans* (New York, 1976), pp. 58–66.

5 Jacques Barzun, *Classic, Romantic and Modern* (New York, 1961), p. 53.

6 Ibid., p. 56.

7 As fine a monograph as any is John Demos, *A Little Commonwealth: Family Life in Plymouth Colony* (New York, 1970). The grand overview is Lloyd deMause, ed., *The History of Childhood* (New York, 1974).

8 The best differentiated cohort analysis of the aftereffects of a social calamity is Glen H. Elder, Jr., *Children of the Great Depression: Social Change in Life Experience* (Chicago, 1974).

9 Walter Abell, *The Collective Dream in Art: A Psycho-Historical Theory of Culture Based on Relations Between the Arts, Psychology, and the Social Sciences* (Cambridge, Mass., 1957; New York, 1966).

10 Paul Monaco, *Cinema and Society. France and Germany during the Twenties* (New York, 1976).

11 Lloyd deMause, "Jimmy Carter and American Fantasy," in Lloyd deMause and Henry Ebel, eds., *Jimmy Carter and American Fantasy* (New York, 1977).

12 Here the great source is W. R. Bion, *Experience in Groups* (New York, 1959). The single, signal application of small group theory to history is in the pre-Bion school deriving from Georg Simmel and based on "the development of the attitudes of the individuals concerned": see R. C. Raack, "When Plans Fail: Small Group Behavior and Decision-Making in the Conspiracy of 1808 in Germany," *Conflict Resolution,* Vol. 14, pp. 3–19.

Part I
Bibliography

The argument about the scientific validity of psychoanalysis has sparked a lively debate. The most convenient and comprehensive source book is *Psychoanalysis, Scientific Method, and Philosophy,* ed. Sidney Hook (New York, 1959). A more recent and detailed examination of the scientific status of psychoanalysis, which focuses on such specific aspects as dream theory, personality types, and Oedipal dynamics is Seymour Fisher and Robert P. Greenberg, *The Scientific Validity of Freud's Theories and Therapy* (New York, 1977). This may be complemented by Paul Kline's *Fact and Fancy in Freudian Theory* (London, 1972). Eysenck himself returns to the attack in "Psychoanalysis—Myth or Science?" *Inquiry,* vol. 4, no. 1 (Spring 1961), pp. 1–15. Paul Meehl supports Eysenck, emphasizing the importance of refutability or disconfirmation as the best criterion in demarcating science from other kinds of cognitive enterprises such as metaphysics. If an experiment cannot be replicated exactly, it cannot be disconfirmed: it is here that experimental psychology parts company with psychoanalysis. See Meehl's article, "Some Methodological Reflections on the Difficulties of Psychoanalytic Research," in *Minnesota Studies in the Philosophy of Science* (University of Minnesota Press, 1970), vol. 4, pp. 403–16. The historian Saul Friedlander, clearly sympathetic to psychoanalysis, has strong reservations about its role as a scientific means of explanation. His first chapter, "The Theoretical Framework," in *History and Psychoanalysis* (New York, 1978) sets forth his argument. Even some analysts doubt that the work of Freud and his followers can be considered scientific as that term is defined according to the canons of natural science. This is Fritz Schmidl's view in his "Psychoanalysis and History," *Psychoanalytic Quarterly,* vol. 31 (1962), pp. 532–48.

The consensus seems to be that psychoanalysis no longer has, if it ever had, the status of a scientific field of endeavor. This is an important issue as it relates to psychohistory. If psychohistorians believe that the dictates of psychoanalysis have the force of general laws in history, they will naturally assign it a significant causative role. This no doubt accounts for the previously mentioned tendency among some psychohistorians to accept uncritically the equation: if x (childhood experiences), then y (adult behaviors). To think of psychoanalytic theory in terms of an ineluctable model of human actions, rather than as a heuristic device for understanding human behavior, may distort the contributions that psychoanalytic theory could make to the study of history. Thus some critics, influenced by what they see as the scientific pretension of psychoanalysis, dismiss psychohistory out of hand. See, for example, Jacques Barzun, *Clio and the Doctors* (Chicago, 1974) and David Stannard, *Shrinking History* (New York, 1980). A thoughtful and moderate counter to Barzun and Stannard is Peter Gay's *Freud for Historians* (New York, 1985). In it, Gay pleads for a history that is "an elegant, fairly rigorous aesthetic science" (ix).

It is important to remember that not all explanation is scientific, a point made by (among others) John Passmore, "Explanation in Everyday Life, in Science, and in History," *History and Theory,* vol. 2, no. 2 (1962), pp. 105–23; and George Miller, "Is Scientific Thinking Different?" *Bulletin. The American Academy of Arts and Sciences,* vol. 36, no. 5 (Feb. 1983), pp. 26–37. The ideal of descriptive or narrative explanation in history as opposed to a scientific explanation has recently been given attention by Lawrence Stone, "The Revival of Narrative: Reflections on a New Old History," *Past and Present,* vol. 85 (Nov. 1979), pp. 3–24; and Hayden White, "The Question of Narrative in Contemporary Historical Theory," *History and Theory,* vol. 23, no. 1 (1984), pp. 1–33. The implications of a narrative explanation for psychohistory are clear: it may be a more workable approach to the past than a scientific explanation. As Michael Sherwood reminds us, Freud himself used different kinds of explanations, among them unified narratives based upon minute detail to lend coherence, through patterning, to a patient's life. Sherwood's argument in full may be found in *The Logic of Explanation in Psychoanalysis,* cited in our introduction. See also Thomas A. Kohut, "Psychohistory as History," *American Historical Review,* vol. 91 (1986), pp. 336–54.

PART II

THE PSYCHOLOGY OF THE INDIVIDUAL IN HISTORY

7

On Psychohistory

Robert Coles

In a letter dated October 9, 1898, Freud made mention of Leonardo da Vinci: he was "perhaps the most famous left-handed individual," and he "is not known to have had any love affairs." The letter was one of many addressed to Wilhelm Fliess. As Freud step by step began to formulate what we know today as psychoanalysis, he turned to his friend to present his thoughts openly and with some passion, as if he needed to ask whether all those ideas made any sense or were hopelessly out of kilter—useless notions prompted by the disturbed minds a psychiatrist sees, not to mention his own dreams and fantasies, which he had relied upon rather significantly in *The Interpretation of Dreams.*

That book, published in 1900, was unquestionably Freud's masterpiece; rich with years of clinical observations, written in a forceful style, it is by no means out of date now, nor will it ever be. A writer had sensed something important about human experience and found for himself an original language—a means by which his ideas might take hold of the reader's imagination. Soon after its publication Freud broke with Fliess. Why write letters about ideas when they are already set down in a book? Why discuss possible discoveries when they have been made, and are even attracting a limited but impressively brilliant cadre of admirers? Anyway, if Freud had once overestimated Fliess extravagantly, soon enough the latter's distinct limitations became apparent, and that was that—no awful scene, just a moment or two of recognition that became much more only as time passed.

Leonardo da Vinci was harder for Freud to put aside. Though by 1907 he was caught up in psychoanalytic work (by then the Vienna Psychoanalytical Society had been established), there is evidence that the achievements and the spirit of one genius were very much on the mind of another. Freud was reading a study of Leonardo that year, and called it one of his favorite books. On December 11,

1907, he spoke at some length about the general subject of psychoanalytic biography. Two years later he again referred to Leonardo, this time in a letter to Jung dated October 17, 1909: a patient under treatment had the same "constitution," the same psychological makeup, as the famous artist, but not his genius. He also told Jung that he was hoping to obtain a book, published in Italy, on Leonardo's youth.

In early December of 1909 Freud spoke to his Vienna colleagues at the Psychoanalytical Society about Leonardo, not the first time, incidentally, that such a presentation had been made. Isidor Sadger, one of the earlier members of the society (he joined in 1906, the same year Rank did), had studied the lives and writings of Heinrich von Kleist and C.F. Meyer. A short story of Meyer's, "Die Richterim," had also interested Freud; he once wrote to Fliess about that, too, remarking how Meyer's own life seemed to come across in the fiction he wrote.

By 1910 Freud was engaged in more than a casual inquiry; he went through every book on Leonardo he could lay his hands on, and he started writing one of those inviting, even charming essays of his that have a way of stirring up far more controversy than they seem meant to. In America the essay was translated by A.A. Brill and published as *Leonardo da Vinci: A Study in Psychosexuality.* More recently Alan Tyson has made another translation that is more faithful to the German at points, yet reads much better in English: *Leonardo da Vinci and a Memory of His Childhood.* In 1957, nine years before the surprise publication of *Thomas Woodrow Wilson,* supposedly a collaborative "study" by Freud and William Bullitt, the editors of the Standard Edition of the *Complete Psychological Works of Sigmund Freud* described the short book on Leonardo as "not only the first but the last of Freud's large-scale excursions into the field of biography."

It is an excursion well worth looking at today. What Freud tried to do over a half century ago still is being done, sometimes under the name of "psychohistory." Moreover, both his successes and his difficulties as an analyst of a long-dead historical figure's mental life are being experienced by others in our time. The Leonardo book stirred up an immediate reaction of disapproval—"more than the usual amount," we are told.[1] In 1910 everything Freud wrote was met with incredulity or anger by his colleagues. With the appearance of this new book many could find him guilty of an additional crime: not content with declaring the behavior of his patients to be the result of sexual tensions deviously expressed, he was now implicating one of the greatest artists of all time.

In fact Freud took pains to express his admiration for Leonardo. He was not writing an exposé. He had no intention of hurting the reputation of a great man. He was writing of "one who is among the greatest of the human race," and doing so because he firmly believed that "there is no one so great as to be disgraced by being subject to the laws which govern both normal and pathological activity with equal cogency."

Freud was intent on finding at all costs a way of looking at the human mind. He had started doing so with a few patients, then had the courage and honesty to include himself in their company, and around the time of the Leonardo study was ready to look elsewhere: at ordinary men and women who have no symptoms and never see psychiatrists; at patients with disorders other than those he would be likely to see in his office; and in this instance, at a historical figure whose life in certain respects seemed to lend itself to the kind of investigation Vienna's psychoanalysts were making with (as they saw it) astonishing success.

The point was to move from the given clinical case to the broader statement, from the specific to the universal—the "laws" Freud mentions. He wanted to move from the apparent, the readily observable, to "deeper layers"—to those unconscious forces he was convinced control just about every aspect of our lives. He wanted to leave the psychiatrist's office and find in the life of a man who was never a patient further evidence that it is correct for analysts to deny that "health and disease, normal and nervous, are sharply distinguished from each other, and that neurotic traits must be considered proofs of a general inferiority." And finally, he wanted to go back far in time, find in the remains, so to speak, of a man of great historical importance—his words, remarks attributed to him, his sketches and paintings—evidence that explains some of the contradictions and ambiguities of his life.

Freud acknowledges that not much is known about Leonardo's childhood. He refers to "the obscurity" of the artist's boyhood. Still, in his scientific notebook Leonardo did mention a childhood memory:

It seems that I was always destined to be so deeply concerned with vultures; for I recall as one of my very earliest memories that while I was in my cradle a vulture came down to me and opened my mouth with its tail, and struck me many times with its tail against my lips.

When mentioning the bird Leonardo used the word *nibio,* which in the modern Italian form *nibbio* refers to a kite, not a vulture. Freud keeps on using the German word *geier,* meaning vulture. He was misled by several German translations.

There is no doubt that this memory of Leonardo's stirred Freud's imagination. He argues his case not only forcefully but elegantly. He does indeed make the sexual interpretations that by now are unsurprising to those who have experienced psychoanalysis firsthand. The vulture is the mother, yet Leonardo, strangely, has "succeeded in endowing precisely this bird which is a mother with the distinguishing mark of masculinity." Such a paradox is explained, and soon (if we are disposed to go along) a man's memory is made the clue to his later psychological characteristics.

Nor does Freud stop there. Immensely learned, and especially so about the various ancient cultures, he makes what Alan Tyson calls "the Egyptian connection." Leonardo was not alone, and may well have known so, Freud suggests, because the hieroglyph for the Egyptian word for "mother" also happens to represent a vulture. Moreover, Freud's friend Oskar Pfister came up with another notion, and in 1919 Freud added it as a footnote to his book's argument: in Leonardo's *St. Anne with Two Others,* at the Louvre, Mary's "curiously arranged and rather confining drapery" turns out to have the "outline of a vulture." Pfister called it an "unconscious picture-puzzle," and by the time he was through with his analysis one part of the drapery is "a bird's outspread tail, whose right-hand end, exactly as in Leonardo's fateful childhood dream, leads to the mouth of the child, i.e., of Leonardo himself."

It is easy to scoff at all this. Freud was not altogether won over to Pfister's imaginative vision, as it could be called; but apart from Pfister's contribution Freud had constructed his own elaborate interpretation on what turned out to be, in retrospect, rather shaky ground. Still, the immediate response to his book had nothing to do with the details of the argument, but rather was moral: how dare these psychoanalysts, their minds always so grimly centered on pathology, most of it sexual, take on a much revered man, dead several hundred years, and saddle him with a host of psychiatric complexes and disorders? No matter how generous Freud was to Leonardo's genius, no matter how carefully and incisively he tried to connect the artist to every single one of us, the anger and mockery continued; nor were they without effect.

Irrational rejection breeds even in the best of men disappointment and sadness. Freud often reassured his colleagues that some day the world would take seriously their various formulations and conjectures—and one measure of his genius was just that self-assurance. On the other hand, under constant assault he and his coworkers became victims of their effort to defend themselves. Wrongly dismissed, they in turn dismissed others, however well intentioned such skepticism and misgivings were. Well-educated and cultivated men, they couldn't help becoming cliquish, even parochial, and highly self-protective. The next step, alas, was a kind of arrogance that demolishes all criticism as "irrational," or treats such criticism with a barrage of unnecessarily self-justifying counterargument— for example Kurt Eissler's effort to challenge the more cautious and justifiable criticism of Freud's Leonardo study.

Eissler's *Leonardo da Vinci* is a long book, in comparison to which Freud's own seems a mere monograph. Much of Eissler's argument is set forth, far less polemically and legalistically, by the four editors (James and Alix Strachey, Anna Freud, and Alan Tyson) in their introduction to Mr. Tyson's translations of Freud's book. They grant that certain "arguments and conclusions are invalidated by careful analysis of Freud's assumptions." (A kite is not a vulture.) Still, assuming a certain psychoanalytic sensibility in their readers, the editors quite justifiably refuse to give way completely. Leonardo's memory or fantasy or daydream (who can ever know exactly which?) seems justifiably of psychological interest, as does the "interesting problem" of how it came about that the Egyptians linked the ideas of "vulture" and "mother." Egyptologists attribute the connection to chance: a phonetic coincidence. Psychoanalysts have a right to speculate otherwise, though not at Leonardo's or anyone else's expense, unless with some evidence.

Most important, for all his ambitiousness and speculative ingenuity, Freud never lost the guardedness that clinical work demands. "The aim of our work," he said at the end of his study, "has been to explain the inhibitions in Leonardo's sexual

life and in his artistic activity." To a degree he succeeded. Leonardo's hopes and
his fears make a good deal of sense to the receptive reader by the time he has
read the various interpretations offered by a writer who had more than a touch
of the novelist in him: the text is clean and direct, its narrative power hard to
resist. Very important, there are discussions that amount to a separate contribution; Leonardo's life stimulated Freud to think about a number of psychoanalytic issues he had not before dealt with very seriously, and for the first time
he broached the subject of "narcissism." Later on that aspect of human development would prompt in him and other analysts no end of concern.

On the other hand, he ran into difficulties, some of them not unforeseen.
Leonardo had himself in his own language admitted to the "sexual inhibitions"
Freud calls to our attention repeatedly, so he was not in the position of making
a case that may well be false. Perhaps on that account the writing at times is so
relaxed and satisfactory: we are not being nervously grabbed by the collar and
told to ignore all existing documents and legends in favor of a premise that can
never be proved, only believed.

However, quite another tone appears when the second part of the author's
"aim" is being fulfilled. We are warned that some critics, and even more significantly some of Leonardo's contemporaries, simply didn't look upon his "artistic
activity" as "inhibited"—not that they were likely to use such a word. Instead,
they offered excuses for his failure to finish much of his work, or were frankly
puzzled by it, or felt prompted to remember that others (like Michelangelo) also
worked slowly, even enigmatically. They also have insisted that Leonardo was a
man of the very widest interests; when he was not painting he was occupying
himself with an astonishing range of scientific investigations and forecasts, often
wedded to his artistic capabilities through intricate sketches or drawings.

Such efforts to look at Leonardo as a thoroughly successful and productive
artist and scientist, entitled to make his own decisions about what to work on
and for how long at a time, are to Freud "excuses," admittedly "valid" but not
sufficient. Whereas he freely admits that little is known about Leonardo's childhood and youth, he is less willing to stress what is nevertheless true: that absolutely nothing is known about any thoughts or "associations" Leonardo may
have had about his decision to pursue careers as an artist and a scientist, and
to do so at his own speed. His problems as a child and later as a man who
feared sexual relations with women and sought out intense relationships with
men are treated sensitively by Freud, and in such a way as slowly to produce a
plausible picture: against considerable odds a particular man struggled hard to
find the best kind of life he could, given impediments he simply could not shake
off.

In contrast, when Freud considers Leonardo the man of Western scientific and
cultural history, a rather different approach becomes evident. Things are not so
much clarified and furnished a perspective as made the subject of all too fixed
and unqualified interpretations. Leonardo's interest in how birds fly, his proph-

ecies that man may one day do the same, move Freud to ask: "But why do so many people dream of being able to fly?" The answer: the wish to be able to fly is nothing else than a "longing to be capable of sexual performance." Leonardo's career as a sharp naturalistic observer is explained this way: "His rebellion against his father was the infantile determinant of what was perhaps an equally sublime achievement in the field of scientific research." True, the *Mona Lisa* is a portrait, the product of observation and imagination, but the artist found his model's smile so powerful and unforgettable "for the reason that it awoke something in him which had for long lain dormant in his mind—probably an old memory.

The memory, of course, had to do with his mother, and her influence on Leonardo's later life is put this way: "For his mother's tenderness was fateful for him; it determined his destiny and the privations that were in store for him." Elsewhere Freud is more restrained; Leonardo's mother is connected only to *part* of his destiny—as a celibate and lonely man. But at the end, after pointing out modestly that "psychoanalysis does not throw light on Leonardo's artistic powers," Freud feels he has to insist that both the "manifestations" and "limitations" of those "powers" are indeed made "intelligible" to us by psychoanalytic inquiry—and then he goes on to make this claim:

> It seems at any rate as if only a man who had had Leonardo's childhood experiences could have painted the Mona Lisa and the St. Anne ... have embarked on such an astonishing career as a natural scientist, as if the key to all his achievements and misfortunes lay hidden in the childhood phantasy of the vulture.

That last phrase is, of course, not at all substantiated, nor has the fate of any psychoanalyst ever since been to find such a "key" to anyone's career, however "astonishing." It can be argued that the same holds for anyone's life, even that of a terribly hurt and suffering mental patient who can barely stay quiet long enough to read a book or look at a painting with any concentration. Ironically and without prejudice one might observe that it is a key dream of the author's that is revealed in such a comment: somewhere a person's creativity—his or her "astonishing career," all the achievements that get recorded in history—can be located and then exposed.

Yet the study throughout works against such a conclusion. Again and again Freud connected Leonardo's presumed childhood experiences and his later psychological characteristics to those that millions of other people have. Health and illness, he emphasized, are not so "sharply distinguished from each other," nor are the so-called normal from those referred to as "neurotic." Insofar as each of us is a "civilized human being," he points out, we are susceptible to one or another neurotic tendency; the repressive function of the mind, so constantly in operation, guarantees such an outcome. Leonardo was indeed "obsessional," but so are millions of other people. The real question, of course, is what Leonardo did with his life; not just with his neurosis, but with his remarkable energy—

his emerging intelligence, his perceptiveness, his sensitivity, his imagination, his resourcefulness of spirit, his artistic sensibility, his capacity to take note of how all sorts of things (including the body's muscles and joints) work.

These are not words or phrases Freud uses. He more or less takes for granted Leonardo's genius. He mentions it but does not "analyze" it. That is not the kind of analysis he is up to. Mostly he is willing to admit that as a psychoanalyst he will never be able to make such an analytic attempt. He calls his study a "pathographical review" and defends it as such against those who would call it "a piece of useless impertinence." Such people, he insists with some truculence, really want utterly untarnished heroes. Such people go about idealizing certain gifted historical figures and for that reason "find all pathography unpalatable." Still, he puts in the mouths of such people an argument that he never answers, intent as he is on analyzing their "real" (worshipful) intent. The argument is that a psychoanalytic study of a great man "never results in an understanding of his importance and his achievements," so there is no point in making "a study of things in him that could just as easily be found in the first person one came across."

As one reads Freud carefully in this important psychoanalytic biography his dilemma becomes apparent. He wants to comprehend an elusive and gifted man. He has a limited amount of information to go on. He is not interested in undercutting his subject, turning him into some perverse eccentric whom everyone without his talents can pity. He is a man of discrimination and refinement. He wants to learn—from his own frailties, as they come across in dreams, slips of the tongue, fantasies, as well as from Leonardo's life, in so far as it can be discerned.

On the other hand he is in his own way as insatiably curious as Leonardo was; he wants answers—and not just to small questions. He once likened himself to a conquistador, but like all conquistadors, there was just so much territory he could conquer. He had at his disposal a nineteenth-century mechanistic view of nature, a cause-and-effect mentality that scientists of his day found helpful in the course of their work. This produces that. One thing brings about another. X lies at the root of Y. And if it doesn't *seem* that way, if there are many other forces at work and all of them make for a murky atmosphere, then the greater the challenge. With more knowledge comes increased specificity—and that is the direction a scientist travels. So, back and forth he goes, even from paragraph to paragraph. One moment he says he is trying to fathom Leonardo's "trivial peculiarities" and the "riddles of his nature" so as to discover "what determined his mental and intellectual development." The word "determined" stands out, especially when it is used in connection with Leonardo's *intellectual* development. No wonder, a page or two on, we encounter quite another line of thinking:

In Leonardo's case we have had to maintain the view that the accident of his illegitimate birth and the excessive tenderness of his mother had the most decisive influence on the formation of his character and on his later fortune, since the sexual repression which set in after this phase of childhood caused him to sublimate his libido into the urge we know, and established his sexual inactivity for the whole of his later life. But this repression after the first erotic satisfactions of childhood need not necessarily have taken place; in someone else it might perhaps not have taken place or might have assumed much less extensive proportions.

We must recognize here a degree of freedom which cannot be resolved any further by psychoanalytic means. Equally, one has no right to claim that the consequence of this wave of repression was the only possible one. It is probable that another person would not have succeeded in withdrawing the major portion of his libido from repression by sublimating it into a craving for knowledge; under the same influences he would have sustained a permanent injury to his intellectual activity or have acquired an insurmountable disposition to obsessional neurosis.

We are left, then, with these two characteristics of Leonardo which are inexplicable by the efforts of psychoanalysis; his quite special tendency towards instinctual repressions, and his extraordinary capacity for sublimating the primitive instincts.

One can try to pin a life down, but only so far. There is that "degree of freedom"—frustrating to a scientist who wants to have every possible "variable" tracked down and fitted right in its place. Even more vexing, that "quite special tendency" and that "extraordinary capacity" were by no means only Leonardo's, nor are they only the property of a few geniuses. Those tendencies or capacities are widespread. Many talented people respond to thousands of different childhood experiences through their own unique blend of repressions and sublimations. Anyway, as Freud goes on to say, there is a biological element in all this that defies our comprehension—even now, decades later. He writes of "the organic foundations of character on which the mental structure is only afterwards erected."

His language here is as vague as the state of knowledge warranted. What I suppose he might have said, were he less of a hopeful, ambitious scientist and of a more philosophical nature, would go something like this: we can understand some of this man's psychological troubles, but his gifts as an artist and a scientist are beyond anyone's ken; they are God-given or part of Nature's mysterious design, though maybe someday, centuries later, we'll know more—and meanwhile let's not try to do the impossible with the valuable but thoroughly limited tools available. If he sometimes approaches saying that, he also backs into quite another corner: *only* a man with Leonardo's kind of childhood could have painted the *Mona Lisa*.

The difficulties Freud faced and candidly admitted in his study of Leonardo have persisted, despite the efforts of psychoanalytically sophisticated biographers. Nor have all of Freud's successors been as fair and self-critical as he was when he wrote about Leonardo. In the name of "applied psychoanalysis" the lives of an assortment of political leaders, generals, artists, and writers, not to mention characters in novels, short stories, and plays, have been examined; and as one goes through those attempts, dozens and dozens of them, one keeps coming back to the Leonardo study—and to Freud's superior qualities as a thinker and a writer.

He may not have been able to transcend the limits of his own historical era. He may have made mistakes of fact, even at times of judgment. He may have tried unsuccessfully to harness language to a number of ambitions. As a scientist searching for tangible discoveries, but also as a man of artistic temperament, especially sensitive to the opportunities and hazards that words present, he was not unlike Leonardo, caught between opposing directions of his own making. But Freud did not in frustration, resentment, and envy turn on the man he was trying to learn more about. Words like "oral" or "anal" or "phallic" are not fastened upon Leonardo. His ideas about religion are discussed in the context of the fifteenth and sixteenth centuries in which he lived.

If Freud shows pride and more than a dash of the messianic explorer, determined at fifty-three to find an intellectual New Jerusalem, he is also able to be tentative, and frankly so. Almost inadvertently, and ironically just at the point when he becomes categorical, we are given a chance to see the confines of his own thinking. When we are told that psychoanalysis finds "inexplicable" Leonardo's particular bent for repression and his remarkable powers of sublimation we are confronted with the author's own impasse. Freud can describe Leonardo in new ways but in the end that impasse remains: a man's various gifts defy the imagery of pathography. If I am able to play tennis all day and score quite well at it, too, I do so not because tennis has a symbolic meaning to me, based on a "problem," or because I lack various diseases or handle certain physiological stresses in a way that differs from that of many others, who find that their symbolic sense of what tennis "means," based on their past or still present "problems" and their physiological makeup, however like mine, do not get translated into my kind of game.

To put it differently, infirmities, or the thoughts they prompt, or even the absence of infirmities don't explain the presence of assets. Here words and phrases come to mind that Freud for his own reasons learned to distrust: will, determination, ingenuity, spirit, ambitions—dreams of a broader kind than he tended to analyze. He had found it necessary to move away from those ways of speaking (and looking at the world) because many of his first patients had for years been slapped on the back or kicked somewhere and told to find willpower, shape up, and get better. The more he listened to his patients the less respect he had for the moralistic pieties of Victorian consciousness. He wanted to expose all that for the sham it was. Anyway, he was not a fuzzy or abstract philosopher, certainly not a theologian, but a neurophysiologist become psychiatrist become a new kind of scientist, a psychoanalyst, so he did not wish to talk about Leonardo's willful spirit, which at times had given way to indifference or apparent apathy.

In a sense, then, Freud's study was a dramatic standoff. There was Leonardo, across the centuries, a man whose obvious capacities and achievements could not be taken for granted or buried under an avalanche of terminology developed in response to the plight of seriously disturbed patients. And there was Freud, anxious to extend his observations to include people like Leonardo, but smart enough to hold back, or venture out only for so long on thin ice.

The best psychoanalytic theorists, first Freud himself, then his daughter Anna, and Heinz Hartmann, have tried to find concepts that would make it easier for them to consider not only Leonardo but those many people who may have their moments of tension, but who in general live useful and untroubled lives. The ego has been emphasized; its capacities have been described in detail. The id may exert its pressures, but we have those various "mechanisms of defense" to call upon. Moreover, the ego is not only in the position of reacting to demands or outright assaults made upon it. The ego has its own energy, some of it "conflict free." When we mobilize our intelligence, use the mind's power of logic and analysis, we are summoning "conflict-free" energy.

The expression "conflict free," used so often by Heinz Hartmann, is a revealing one; with respect to man's everyday work, his various successes as a competent and resourceful creature, it is as far as psychoanalysis can go conceptually, given its history, its concerns, and not least, the nature of its imagery. Hartmann, like Freud, was a man of vast knowledge, and sensitive to the respect and good manners, if not admiration, that novelists or artists, like other human beings, have the right to assume from those who study them. The same can be said for Ernest Kris, a colleague of Hartmann's who had a special interest in artists and the sources of their creativity; and for Anthony Storr, whose recent book[2] shows that such an interest continues to preoccupy certain analysts. Kris worked hard at distinguishing between the paintings or drawings of hospitalized psychotics and those done by artists, and Storr emphasizes the difference between what he calls "pornographic images" and "great art."

But one wonders whether there is any need for psychoanalysts to bother themselves with such distinctions, however well intended. Critics, maybe even ordinary viewers, are quite able to do so on their own. No doubt both of those analysts were angered by and ashamed of what some of their colleagues have done in the name of psychoanalytic "interpretation" of writers, artists, political leaders. Yet at a certain point, all these psychological efforts at biography, literary criticism, or the "analysis" of artistic production come upon the very stumbling blocks Freud had the good sense to discuss openly in his Leonardo book. Here, for example, is Dr. Storr, writing about "creativity" over half a century after that book was published:

> Man is a creature inescapably, and often unhappily divided; and the divisions within him recurrently impel the use of his imagination to make new syntheses. The creative consequences of his imaginative striving may never make him whole; but they constitute his deepest consolations and his greatest glories.

Always it is trouble, problems, conflicts, "divisions" that generate novels and paintings, or for that matter, the efforts of history's gifted leaders. A phrase like "impel the use of his imagination" may be an attractive way of putting it, but the cause-and-effect assertion is both utterly clear and utterly unsubstantiated— and the use of such a phrase only serves to show that those of us who are trained to dwell upon psychopathology, to think of people as variants of one or another "psychiatric model" (the anal or oral or phallic "character,") are also "impelled" to use our imaginations for certain reasons.

To his credit Kurt Eissler has furthered discussion of this issue substantially, as I mentioned in a previous essay:

> The question, however, has not been answered, what connection exists between the genius's psychopathology and his achievements. Psychopathology, in general, is looked upon as defect. . . . Observation of the genius, however, suggests the possibility that psychopathology is indispensible to the highest achievements of certain kinds.

He then takes the next logical step:

> Consequently if what we observed in the genius struck us as neurotic or psychotic or perverse or even criminal, we would then have to reconsider our classification under these accustomed headings. If, for example, an apparently obsessional symptom was indispensable to geniushood . . . there would be no sense in calling it a neurotic symptom. Whatever the essence of neurosis may be, the concept of neurosis makes sense only when it is correlated with a deficit.

Needless to say, what goes for the genius goes for the near-genius and on down. One has a right to ask the broader question: What connection is there between an ordinary human being's daily achievements and his psychopathology, or between a psychiatrist's, a lawyer's, a politician's accomplishments and the various emotional upsets he as a human being is bound to have? Open-minded on this issue as Eissler is, he can't give up the conviction that psychopathology is a *sine qua non* of life—as Freud among others (Job, Isaiah, Saint Paul, not to mention some of those geniuses Eissler mentions) has made quite clear. Why is its presence in anyone, gifted or not, an occasion for surprise, and more than that, aggrandizement—the insistence that other elements in a person's life are tied to, or are expressions of, or are causatively linked with "deficits" or neurotic developments in childhood or "mechanisms of defense," such as sublimation?

For some reason it has been psychoanalysts, among psychological theorists, who have been most anxious to study the lives of creative men and women, or of historical figures. Piaget, whose studies of intelligence as it develops over the years might be considered particularly well suited to such studies, has avoided them, perhaps because his speculations always follow from what he has watched and heard, even as Anna Freud has in recent years insisted that "direct observation" ought to precede theoretical formulation and elaboration. Perhaps a scientist like Piaget knows full well that the "variables" that make up a man's creative life—be it a writer's or a political leader's or a psychoanalyst's—defy the language and concepts of any particular psychological theory.

Anna Freud once referred to "the universally envied gift of creative energy."[3]

There is no point in turning that gift into an unapproachable mystery. Scientists have a right to move closer toward any "phenomenon" they happen to find interesting. Nor need such an approach be insulting, abusive, or destructive. The issue is one of evidence—is there enough of it?—but also of motives, as Miss Freud has mentioned; and envy is only one of them. Theorists, like the presidents and dictators they study, can be overcome by ambition and a kind of intellectual aggressiveness that has to be checked by the prudent skepticism of critics.

In this regard, some of Freud's most valuable discoveries—the nature of "resistance" and the workings of "transference" and "countertransference" in psychoanalytic therapy—have become ironic instruments in the most narrow kind of ideological self-justification. Doubts or misgivings are chalked up to a lack of psychoanalytic experience or sophistication, if not to outright "hostility" or "ambivalence" of one or another kind. This *ad hominem* tendency obviously undercuts the possibility of any rational argument, except of the kind sanctioned by those who do the thinly disguised name calling.

Even friends can get caught in such intellectual warfare, where sides are taken and one is considered either a friend or a foe. Referring to an interesting and suggestive biography, *Woodrow Wilson and Colonel House,* the editor of a collection of essays called *Psychoanalysis and History* makes an interpretation of sorts: "Brodie's review-essay of the Georges' book about Wilson points up the overtly psychoanalytic aspects of their work, which they felt constrained to conceal in a footnote."[4] The editor himself notes a few sentences later that the book's subtitle is "A Personality Study." Furthermore, in an author's note at the very beginning, even before the table of contents, Alexander and Juliette George acknowledge forthrightly the influence Harold Lasswell and Nathan Leites had on their study of Wilson's relationship to his longtime principal adviser. A special "Research Note" discusses that influence for six pages—before the section called "Notes and Bibliography" even begins.

What have they concealed—or rather, why are they described as concealing anything? True, they write as historians. That is to say, they want to examine the psychological quality of a particular president's involvement with one of his aides, but they also want to move from one point in time to another, and carry their readers with them. In other words, their interests are chronological and narrative as well as psychological. They have a broad view of American political life to present and, just as important, to document convincingly—in a way that will make the reader understand what he is reading and feel satisfied that a sincere effort has been made to start with facts, assemble them into a point of view, and present the latter as that and only that, not as the answer to a "problem."

No doubt about it, psychoanalytic terminology is avoided by the Georges. We are not told, as we are in *Thomas Woodrow Wilson: A Psychological Study* by William Bullitt and Sigmund Freud, that "the libido insulated in his [Wilson's] reaction-formation against his passivity to his father had been without outlet and had reached such a pitch of intensity that it had to break out against someone."

We are told much about Wilson and his father, considerably less but nevertheless much about Colonel House. The President and his aide found in each other a fateful dovetailing of psychological qualities. Certainly they worked out "neurotic needs" through one another, as we all do, and eventually (when things were going downhill on other accounts) at each other's expense. But the Georges can't seem to forget that the involvement of the two men has to be viewed from other directions: the nature of the presidency, the social and cultural characteristics of a given moment in American history, the particular stresses that wars, accidents, unexpected tragedies (the death of Wilson's first wife) can bring upon a man's character and personality, whatever the determinants of childhood that bear down on him, on all of us.

I doubt very much that even the most eager proponent of "applied psychoanalysis," or one of its contemporary equivalents or closely related "areas" of inquiry, "psychohistory," would want to change the perspective the Georges have given us. How might they have made their debt to psychoanalysis more explicit? As other historians and essayists have done over the centuries, they have drawn upon knowledge that is available, traditional modes of study or reflection and new modes, and made of it all an exercise in exposition, explanation, and comment.

If they conceal anything from the reader it is any temptation they may have felt to fix static labels on the men they were studying or to come up with sweeping, unqualified statements such as this: "In fact, psychoanalytic theory fully accounts for the observation that no known charismatic leader can be described as a genuine genital character."[5] Or, "The personality of the charismatic leader can be characterized briefly, since we already indicated that his behavior must conform to childish fantasies about how omnipotent adults behave."[6] Or, with regard to Robespierre: "Unfortunately, the implacable superego coupled with the released sadism and the projective paranoid mechanisms common to the Leader and the masses created the need for further human sacrifices, and thus the Revolution in a truly cannibalistic way devoured its own children."[7]

Nor is Robespierre unique: "The psychological truth expressed in this last speech of the doomed leader exceeds his singular case and applies to every revolutionary leader and to every dictator."[8] In this century the love they give us, the good and decent intentions they possess and offer to us as something to imitate and make our own, the cultural heritage they hand down—so many facts, so many assumptions, so much that has to do with proficiency and self-assurance and comprehension of the world—all of that somehow is either taken for granted or overlooked in favor of "complexes" of various kinds.

There is, further, a pejorative streak in the language of psychopathology that not only demeans the "object" of description but the writer doing it and his or her "discipline." There is also a stinginess of spirit in some of the descriptions psychiatrists and psychologists (and those who follow their lead in other disciplines) give to individuals of the most obvious attainments. Which contemporary historians or critics advocate unthinking, reflexive sentiment or glorification? These days the danger comes from quite another direction: will the application of psychological "insight" to history or the arts be done in such a way as to produce caricatures of human beings—and those only to be turned into proof of some larger generalization about the "laws" that govern the human mind?

Or will one kind of knowledge be called "superficial" simply because it possesses its own richness and complexity of vision—in contrast to another kind of knowledge that somebody else happens to find congenial or happens to be trained to call upon? Or will a book's manner of organization and language be pushed into intellectual arguments or vendettas that really have nothing to do with what an author has intended?

In the case of the Georges' book on Wilson, two historians have nicely drawn upon psychoanalytic principles without in any way doing an injustice to their own responsibilities. To imply that they are hiding something out of fear is to be less than fair not only to their profession but to their scholarship. No one would deny that some historians, like some doctors or lawyers or writers, have no use for *any* effort to look at historical figures from a psychoanalytic perspective—overtly or otherwise. Still, it is absurd at this time for analysts and those interested in "applying" psychoanalysis or developing a "field" called "psychohistory" to imagine themselves embattled, scorned outcasts, neglected on all fronts—rather as Freud and his first followers were.

Psychoanalysis and its various "applications" have been embraced all too ardently by the American public—and not only by its so-called "lay" segment. Sometimes that enthusiasm was for the bad: it is astonishing, for example, how many writers submitted willingly to the brutal, stupid lashings an analyst like Edmund Bergler gave them in his books supposedly meant to "explain" writers and their "personality structure." But sometimes much of value came of this enthusiasm: it is remarkable how openly and generously many important American medical schools welcomed analysts during the 1930s and 1940s, often to good effect so far as the education of young doctors goes. In any event, to this day a historian or political scientist, not to mention a psychoanalyst, who writes a biography or discusses some contemporary issue, or one connected with the remote past, from a psychological point of view stands at the very least an excellent chance of getting the public's attention.

Walter Langer's "secret wartime report," now become *The Mind of Adolf Hitler,* has hardly been ignored. In view of the substantial scholarship on the Nazis that has gone relatively unnoticed—the work of historians, economists, political scientists—one has to look not only at the book itself but at the reasons for its appeal. Nor has Bruce Mazlish's "psychohistorical inquiry" into Richard Nixon's life been ignored—any more than will the portentously named *The Kennedy Neurosis: A Psychological Portrait of an American Dynasty.* Each of them is yet another variant of the kind of inquiry Freud began long ago: harnessing psychology to an understanding of certain people who have taken a significant part in history.

To start with the worst, the book on the Kennedy family is, alas, an exercise in nastiness, and an instructive lesson in how psychological words and phrases, presented as a means of scientific exposition, can become in certain hands instruments of moral condemnation, and even malicious abuse. The author of *The Kennedy Neurosis,* Nancy Clinch, refers to her "study of the Kennedy's characterology" as a "form of psychohistory"; it is even "psychohumanism." People have what she calls "self-actualizing needs." There are "parental patterns" and a "specific cultural milieu," and they, of course, affect a "hierarchy of needs." When things go wrong a neurosis develops: "a self-defeating defense pattern of feeling and behaving." Something called a "pseudo-self" comes into being. There is "basic anxiety" and it keeps generating "unconscious hostility." After we learn about all that, we are told where we are going:

> It is my purpose to analyze what the historical record seems to reveal: that the Kennedy drive to power was largely neurotic in origin and thus largely neurotic in goal; and that when power was obtained, the Kennedys were severely limited in the use of their authority for positive aims because of emotional conflicts and ambivalences.

Note the word "because": assertive, unthreatened by any modifiers, anxious to make its connection. There is no point in looking at the structure of our government, let alone at our society. Those political scientists and journalists who try to figure out what presidents can and cannot do, those historians who try to apprehend the subtleties of America's development as a democracy, the regional tensions, the push and pull of economic and social forces—they have been seduced by complexity, ambiguity, even uncertainty. The author says we need "autonomy, self-direction, and freedom." Those observers and scholars of American history need the freedom to use the word "because" more boldly—though one can drop the word and get the same startling result:

> The Kennedys, like American scientists, achieved the "impossible" through teamwork in their election triumphs. But once elected, they seemed to "fall under a fairyland spell" that kept them from accomplishing any significant part of their professed aims.

The "spell" is next defined: "neurotic conflict." It seems that Mr. and Mrs. Joseph P. Kennedy (called "Joe and Rose") made "excessive demands for perfection and social success" on their sons and daughters. The result: a need on the part of those children for their own "frustration, punishment and even destruction":

> I do not see the Kennedy failures in performance as caused mainly by bad luck or by the vagaries of politics and human nature. Rather, the factual failures were largely the result of psychohistorical circumstances that existed for the Kennedy sons even before they were born and that strongly affected the shaping of their individual characters.

So much for "bad luck" or the "vagaries of politics and human nature"—the stuff of novelists or playwrights, the passing fancy of newspapermen, the preoccupation of old-fashioned, overly scrupulous scholars or essayists, who may be aware of "unconscious emotional conflicts," but who get side-tracked by their search for facts, their insistence on maintaing detachment as well as respect for those they study.

Perhaps this book has its place; some day social historians will want to study its by no means unique mixture of Nichols and May psychology, non sequiturs, simpleminded social commentary, and dizzying historical overstatement. For example, Mr. Joseph P. Kennedy is singled out from the rest of us parents for "unconsciously" projecting "his needs and longings onto his sons." Even though the author admits that some of the book's points "may seem strained, and even cruel," she persists, in the interest of truth. Thus, "Jack, Bobby, and Teddy" (as they are called by this expert on their lives who has never even met them) "would all take up cigar smoking, the Freudian symbol of potency and power."

Then there was President Kennedy. Here is what his White House staff was all about:

> Thus Kennedy was not only in close and constant touch with his family, but he also created a new family of staff retainers who seem to have served partly as substitute parent images daily filling the old dual role of nursemaids and slave drivers.

One of them was Kennedy's secretary, Mrs. Lincoln. He may have liked her, but his general attitude toward women, along with a few other things, is summarized in the following four sentences:

> Kennedy essentially disliked and distrusted women. Therefore his strong emotional need for support and approval led him to follow the counsel of male authority figures. Unfortunately, a large number of these authority figures—such as McNamara, Rusk, Acheson, Taylor, Bundy, and Rostow—were as confused and misguided as Kennedy about national values and priorities. The 1971 publication of the Pentagon Papers clearly revealed this about their Vietnam policy.

There it is: from sexism to Vietnam in less than a paragraph. Not that the author forgets other parts of the world. She says the President had "an emotional fixation" on Castro, who was "Kennedy's alter-ego: the bold leader Kennedy longed to be but could not bring himself to become." Why could he not? "Making laws may arouse unconscious resistance in the lawmaker who has suffered much in his own life from rigid legalisms."

As for the President's brother and trusted adviser, he was similarly "neurotic." Did he have compassion for the poor and vulnerable in this nation? Yes, but "this is understandable in view of his 'underdog' position in the family and the emotional insecurity he never lost." Did he like athletics and inspire young people to follow suit? True, but there was a reason:

> Here we can see a belief in the masculine mystique of physical toughness, and also a probable need for reassurance and affection through physical contact with other males that was more difficult to express directly. Football for the Kennedy sons—and especially Robert, who even kept a football in his Attorney General's office and often tossed it around with his staff—carried deep psychological undertones of emotional need and gratification.

Finally, the author, who can toss a few passes of her own, reserves the longest throws for the book's last paragraphs: "Yet the Kennedy mystique can also be seen as essentially the outcome of some four thousand years of the Graeco-Judeo-Christian ethos which has directed and energized Western civilization, and which has now spread over the world." There is cause for hope, though: "By studying the lives of national leaders, such as the Kennedys, we can find reflections of our own search for identity and confirmation, and help change both ourselves and our nation toward maturity and health rather than neurosis."

There are other reasons to study the lives of important men of history. As Walter C. Langer makes clear in his book on Hitler, the Office of Strategic Services was interested in winning the war; "maturity" and all the rest could come to Germany (and America) later. Colonel William J. ("Wild Bill") Donovan knew Dr. Langer, then a Boston psychoanalyst, and asked him to put together a psychological appraisal of Hitler, including an estimate of what he might do if things should go badly for him, as they already were going in 1943 when Langer began his hurried job. Yet, for all the rush, this book is decidedly better than the one on the Kennedys. Langer's portrait of Hitler is far more thoughtful and sensitive than Miss Clinch's caricatures of the Kennedy family.

Langer avoids psychiatric name calling.[9] He emphasizes Hitler's strengths, his abilities, his obvious capacity to mesmerize and lead a nation. There are mistakes of judgment or emphasis, but these are usually owing to false information which was supplied to the relatively uninformed analyst and his quickly assembled staff. The prose is clear, a clue to the author's essential modesty and common sense. Once in a while there is an utterly fatuous remark, but it is usually delivered in a way that makes one less angry than regretful:

> I may be naïve in diplomatic matters, but I like to believe that if such a study of Hitler had been made years earlier, under less tension, and with more opportunity to gather first-hand information, there might not have been a Munich; a similar study of Stalin might have produced a different Yalta; one of Castro might have prevented the Cuban situation; and one of President Diem might have avoided our deep involvement in Vietnam. Studies of this type cannot solve our international problems. That would be too much to expect.

At only one point does the author reveal the smugness and arrogance that are all too common in such efforts, and even then they derive from a remark of one of Langer's colleagues: "Now I know what his [Hitler's] perversion is." Not that anyone *knows*. We are never given any hard, concrete evidence—only guesses and secondhand speculations, some from highly unreliable sources, as the historian Robert G. Waite makes clear in his useful afterword. "It just came to me out of my clinical experience," the surprised Dr. Langer heard when he asked his colleague how she had come to that conclusion. Fortunately, it was Dr. Langer and not his colleague who tried to figure out the personality of a man whom he had never met and about whom he had only the most shadowy and suspect of information. Professor Waite says that such an attempt is justified: "Basically, he is convinced the perversion existed because he knows as an experienced analyst widely read in the literature of abnormal psychology that many patients with the same patterns of behavior as Hitler have exhibited a penchant for the same perversion."

Once again we are back to the same problem. Clearly those "patterns of behavior" Hitler had (shiftlessness for a while, anxiety, phobias, sexual inhibitions) have been and are shared by millions of people. *Some* of them may end up, as conjecture about Hitler would have it, lying on the floor and pleading with women to empty themselves (the nearer the better, and all over, if possible), but some may choose other ways to find pleasure, and by no means do all those with Hitler's "patterns of behavior," or anyone else's share his supposed "penchant." A million prior interviews with disturbed men and women would not enable anyone to know the facts of a particular person's private life. Nor does Dr. Langer's prediction that Hitler would probably commit suicide when and if he were cornered constitute "dramatic and convincing evidence of the validity of his approach to an understanding of Hitler's personality." But Dr. Langer mentions several other possibilities, and is unwilling to pin himself down—a refreshing trait, in view of the certainties that other writers are drawn to.

Hitler himself repeatedly mentioned his intention; he would go down to death on his own rather than surrender, bringing all of Germany with him, if he had the choice. Clearly Dr. Langer was right in suggesting suicide as "the most plausible outcome," though he lists insanity and death in battle as other possibilities. But then, my ninth-grade Latin teacher made a similar prediction—he was more unequivocal—in class around the same year, when we were reading Caesar's *Gallic Wars;* and so did the journalist Dorothy Thompson, who mentioned the very same likelihood several times in her syndicated columns during the early 1940s. I would imagine that thousands of people thought about Hitler as a probable suicide when they read their newspapers and saw how desperate his situation had suddenly become.

With Langer's study of Hitler we face once more the nagging questions other "psychohistorical" inquiries pose; and Dr. Langer can no more settle those questions for us than could Freud in the case of Leonardo. How did a wretched, deeply troubled, at times pathetic youth—the "neurotic psychopath" of this book—end up Führer of the Third Reich, a man not only possessed of authority and power but believed and heeded by millions? If not Hitler, might it have been someone else? If only Hitler, then surely it was not his "perversion" or his disordered mind (the province of the psychoanalyst) that accounts for his successes.

Hitler's life, like many other lives, presents several purely psychological mysteries, apart from the "psychohistorical" one of his particular rise to power. After the First World War, this nondescript, pitiable ne'er-do-well suddenly turned into a remarkably persistent and adept politician, then into a charismatic leader, finally the Füher of most of Europe. Langer refers to a "transformation of character," as well he might. But how to account for it? We are told that there is an explanation: the weak and panicky Hitler, "in order to quiet his fears," suddenly "imagined himself as a person who far surpassed his enemies in all the 'virile' qualities." We are given the name for such a psychological maneuver, "identification with the aggressor," and its importance is described in language not unlike that used by Freud in connection with Leonardo: "This is the key to an understanding of Hitler's actions since the beginning of his political activities to the present time."

Presumably Hitler was thereby freed to become what he eventually did become. If only that maneuver worked as well for thousands of other nobodies, who have tried desperately to convert their vulnerability and self-hate into something they can use on others. The Weimar Republic was full of such people; America has its share: people who "identify" with various "aggressors"—and, having done so, get nowhere. As for psychological recovery or "transformation," psychiatrists can spend long, intimate months, if not years, with patients and not know why at a particular moment a person is suddenly, it seems, "better." *In retrospect,* we come up with formulations, explanations: such and such was "interpreted." We are less likely to mention the many times we have offered similar "insights" to other patients, even to the same patient, all to no avail.

Langer was no doubt right about the turn of mind Hitler experienced. But he goes way beyond the bounds of logic—and his own profession's knowledge—when he makes that commonly indulged-in "mechanism" the "key" to an understanding of Hitler's "recovery," let alone all the subsequent "actions" of that satanic genius. Nor is the "messiah complex," also cited by him, very helpful—as any psychiatrist knows who works with the severely disturbed and utterly ineffectual "paranoid schizophrenics" who inhabit our state hospitals, insisting every day that they could save the world, if they were only heeded.

No one wants to circumscribe the continuing attempt of psychologists and psychiatrists to make sense of the irrational and bizarre, the seemingly normal but in fact pathological. It is when a more polemical, even aggrandizing tone enters the discussion that the possibility of a rational distinction between different objectives becomes hard to maintain. In this regard, Kurt Eissler is at least candid in his book on Leonardo. The first section of the book is frankly called "Polemics," and in a chapter called "The Historian vs. the Psychoanalyst" Eissler makes no bones about what he believes and, moreover, expects of those who disagree with him:

> There can, of course, be no doubt that the psychoanalyst has to know the results of historical and iconographic research; but what he does with that knowledge in order to reach psychological conclusions will more frequently than not strike the historian as far-fetched and inconclusive. [Meyer] Schapiro dismisses us with the admonition that the analyst should inform himself better about Leonardo's life and art and the culture of his time before applying his science to the psychological study of that life. Wohl and

Trosman, with their little understanding of the subtleness of the genius, believe the problem could have been solved if Freud had "allowed his manuscript to be scrutinized" by an expert in history. These writers bypass the essential question that is at issue between the historical sciences and psychoanalysis and that cannot be resolved as long as the historian and philologist do not acquire full insight into psychoanalysis and are restrained by the bias of our time from obtaining maximum knowledge of the structure of the human mind by consistent and long-lasting clinical work.[10]

No doubt somewhere there is a historian prepared to insist that any psychoanalyst who wants to write about history take a full graduate course and spend a few years doing "proper" historical research. But some scholars have to some degree combined the two disciplines—the historian Bruce Mazlish, for example, or the political scientist E. Victor Wolfenstein. Both men have psychoanalytic knowledge—of an order Dr. Eissler would doubtless find acceptable—as well as training in their professions.

Professor Mazlish has been an especially active proponent of what he and others (Robert Jay Lifton, Joel Kovel, John Demos) call "psychohistory." Each of these men has his own particular way of working with historical materials from a psychological (more precisely, psychoanalytic) point of view. They share a common interest in drawing upon several disciplines in the hope of seeing human experience more broadly, and escaping the rigidities and biases inherent in any particular psychoanalytic formulation. Robert Wallerstein has perhaps made the best case for such activity:

> Consider the impact on the assessment of an individual's psychological functioning if the limiting social postulate were changed from that of the "average expectable environment" to that of a "systematically fluctuating or a turbulent environment"; compare a campus in unrest set within a world in turmoil. That is, the simplifying assumptions made for its purposes by one behavioral science, if *looked at as variables* as they are in another behavioral science which makes them its central subject matter, would influence the explanations arrived at in important ways.[11]

Yet as one goes through Mazlish's *In Search of Nixon: A Psychohistorical Inquiry* or Wolfenstein's *The Revolutionary Personality: Lenin, Trotsky, Gandhi*, it seems clear that both scholars have as many dangers to avoid as opportunities to grasp. In both books we are warned that psychoanalytic "reductionism" is offensive and perhaps a thing of the past. Nevertheless, Nixon is called "oral" and "anal" at various points, as are Lenin, Trotsky, and Gandhi. Ambivalences are discussed, problems with mothers and fathers are described at length.

In the case of Mazlish's book an interesting dialectic of sorts takes place. First the President is described or typed. ("Orality is an important element in Nixon's character.") Then the reader is informed that such a description merely makes Richard Nixon a human being. If he has used a "genital metaphor and an anal one," then "others frequently use similar metaphors." After we have read two-thirds of his book, in which words or phrases like "passivity," "death anxiety," and "survivor guilt" are pervasive, Mazlish makes this statement: "What we have been discussing up to now may be thought of as the psychological banalities of Nixon's character." One wonders, at this point, why the author has bothered to write this book at all, especially since the rest of the book offers nothing else about the President's "character," only an extensive justification of the value of "psychohistory" as "science."

Understandably, Professor Mazlish has singled out Nixon, who has, after all, singled himself out. This "search" for Nixon ends with the discovery of "three traits," which he characterizes as "role identification," "ambivalence," and "denial." We have already been informed that any of us can possess these qualities. But Nixon apparently has more of them: "ambivalence, of course, is in all of us. Yet as a scholar I have never dealt with a public figure as ambivalent as Nixon." Exactly how does one quantify "ambivalence?" Has Mazlish studied other public figures? If so, which ones, and on what basis has he made his judgment? How are we to compare Nixon's "ambivalence" with, say, Wilson's? How does a psychiatrist distinguish among the degrees of ambivalence he finds in his various ambivalent patients? If the "degrees" of those three traits are at issue, one can find many patients who qualify as intensely ambivalent and who are also inclined to "deny" and resort to "role identification."

Nor do such patients become, on that account, hard to "know," as the President is claimed to be. "The three traits have made Nixon one of the most difficult political figures to analyze." Maybe the problem lies elsewhere; maybe the tools of psychoanalysis are inappropriate to the task at hand. In contrast, intelligent political journalists like Jules Witcover or Garry Wills, whose mind has been disciplined by the Jesuits, can "analyze" Nixon suggestively. Wills has evoked brilliantly those aspects of America's social reality that President Nixon has, one suspects, never overlooked or failed to understand. Wills understands the power of a certain kind of religious piety, even when it has become thoroughly secularized.

Richard Nixon's carerr—assisted, one should not forget, by Lee Harvey Oswald and Sirhan Sirhan—can be seen as the discerning response of an able and ambitious man to currents in American life he fully appreciates, and even manages to evoke with some credibility, in spite of the widespread distrust he also generates. When Wills analyzes our country's conflicting ideals and assumptions he gets as close to the "real" Nixon as any of us may find possible or desirable.

It is sad to find toward the end of Mazlish's book this remark: "Earlier we acknowledged that many people are wary of applying psychoanalysis to historical figures (and usually distrust therapy as well, a problem with which we cannot deal here)." It may be that many clinicians, who every day trust "therapy" enough to show up in an office and try hard to work with other human beings, have good reason to be wary: to repeat, so much that goes on in "treatment" is mysterious, intangible, elusive; one hesitates to apply to politics concepts already of very circumscribed or indeterminate value. Perhaps some of those wary clinicians would want to say what the psychoanalyst Leslie Farber did in response to the way human beings, from great men of history to ordinary workers and citizens, continue to be treated by members of his profession:

> Without examining these normative statements in detail, the reader can see why psychiatry is so often charged with being reductive. For while the creatures described above may bear some resemblance to animals or to steam engines or robots or electronic brains, they do not sound like people. They are in fact constructs of theory, more humanoid than humans; and whether they are based on the libido theory or on one of the new interpersonal theories of relationships, it is just those qualities most distinctively human which seem to have been omitted. It is a matter of some irony, if one turns from psychology to one of Dostoyevsky's novels, to find that no matter how wretched, how puerile, or how dilapidated his characters may be, they all possess more humanity than the ideal man who lives in the pages of psychiatry.[12]

True, psychiatric jargon can be defended: it is a kind of shorthand for busy doctors who are not interested in describing "life," as novelists like Dostoevski are, but in understanding and "curing" patients. Even assuming that such a way of thinking and speaking about people helps clinical understanding and doesn't itself affect "treatment"—an assumption I would certainly not want to make— one has to insist on the obvious, so far as men like Leonardo or Nixon go: they are not "patients" in treatment by "psychohistorians" and so nothing absolves us of the responsibility to measure up to the standards Dr. Farber suggests.

When the theoretical intent of the writing Farber describes becomes more ambitious, as it does in Wolfenstein's book, among others—when we are after the roots of genius or the specific "drives" or "psychohistorical contexts" that make for a gifted artist or writer or politician, we are likely to find the same sorry results. Generalizations are heaped on one another and they turn out to be mirages, deceptively intriguing, but ultimately susceptible to being dismissed on the most elementary logical grounds. Lenin, Trotsky, and Gandhi, we are told, "each had an unusually ambivalent relationship with his father." Even the word "unusually" does not deprive those men of the company of thousands and thousands of others. Because those men were "ambivalent" they couldn't take orders. But they must be singled out even further, the author knows:

> the inability to be a follower, of course, does not account for the ability to be a leader. For this something more is needed, namely a firm identification with parental authority, an underlying feeling of connection with the moral standards and behavior of one parent or another.

Does that formulation work, though? Are those leaders thereby distinguished from many men and women who have become "doctors, lawyers, Indian chiefs," factory workers and white-collar workers, maybe even psychiatrists and historians?

No discussion of "psychohistory" can even begin without mention of Erik Erikson, yet I come to him toward the end of this essay. Most of the "psychohistorians" I have mentioned refer to him constantly. His influence rivals Freud's; on those historians and political scientists I have discussed, I think it is fair to say his influence surpasses Freud's. Philosophers and theologians, also, have been especially indebted to him. "Religion," he writes in *Young Man Luther,* "elaborates on what feels profoundly true even though it is not demonstrable: it translates into significant words, images, and codes the exceeding darkness which surrounds man's existence, and the light which pervades it beyond all desert or comprehension.

One can look at such a sentence and be grateful for the subtlety of its content and expression. One can note the absence of heavy-handed "interpretations"; it is clear the writer does not intend to denigrate religion as an "illusion"; to "get" Luther, "explain" him, "expose" him, use him to prove a theory of his own— but rather to write a biography, an imaginative response to a series of facts about a particular person's life. Those facts are assembled to tell a story, to interest and maybe bestir the reader, to allow a writer with, say, psychological or philosophical interests (and how many writers are without such interests?) a medium for self-expression through another's life.

But there are obligations: to the letter and to the spirit of the subject's life. Though *Young Man Luther* has been widely praised, it has also been subject to serious criticism. Roland H. Bainton, Professor of Ecclesiastical History at Yale Divinity School, and an authority on Luther, has taken strong issue with a number of Erikson's assumptions. He has emphasized how vague, ambiguous, and sometimes severely distorted are those "sources" which even the best of Luther scholars ultimately have had to rely upon.

Bainton is not opposed to psychological speculation—with regard to Luther or anyone else. He mentions in what respects *Young Man Luther* was helpful to him, even suggests further issues Erikson might have profitably explored. But he insists that much of Erikson's thesis necessarily has to depend on his translation of remarks by Luther, and on the validity of various statements attributed to Luther, often at second-, third- and fourthhand. He takes issue with several of Erikson's translations. He also points out that sometimes there is contradictory information about Luther—so much so that several different yet plausible conclusions can be drawn, depending on which sources, letters, anecdotes are cited.[13]

Even so, in spite of such hazards Erikson's book provides opportunities: to connect the past with the present, to show with discretion how the application of a particular discipline, psychoanalysis, developed in the twentieth century, makes more intelligible to us events that had a different kind of coherence for others who lived long ago. It is not enough to call Erikson a gifted writer or an unusually sensitive psychoanalyst. He is more than these. He has dared to bring up subjects like "virtue"; not just "conflict-free" or "neutralized" energy or "ego-strengths," but various ethical strivings. He has insisted that those who would write about historical figures openly examine what their own prejudices might be, what their purposes are in studying a particular "life" or historical issue.

Erikson's prose is the product of careful struggle because he knows the damage that has been done, particularly in psychology and the social sciences, by the use of "becauses," "contexts," and "interrelationships." Erikson talks about "trust" and "initiative" and "industry," plain and risky words that bring us closer to life and imply judgments on human experience. By doing so, he is also choosing not to rely on an evasive technical vocabulary. "Conflicts" there are; but also resolutions to them—and beyond that, affirmations that have their own authority, momentum, and, yes, psychohistory: a thoughtful father here, a kind-spirited mother there, a friend who helped, a husband or wife who helped even more, a time that begged for something from someone.

In Wolfenstein's book we are told that Lenin lacked "trust" in comparison to Trotsky and Gandhi, and all three went through an "exceptionally stormy" adolescence, which, we are told, is "the period of the 'crisis of identity'." Here a phrase of Erikson's has been turned into a new label. His ability to pull together in a single formulation many observations or ideas can be a mixed blessing. What is meant to inspire in others one kind of response (does this way of putting things fit? is it helpful? or ought I look elsewhere, perhaps use my own words, or simply keep looking and listening?) gets quite another response (that is the answer, or what I want to prove, or what I had better well prove, since everyone else these days is doing so).

In December of 1871, the first book of George Eliot's *Middlemarch* was published; within a year the eight sections of that long and demanding novel had appeared. She had spent years preparing for the writing, and as an unashamed moralist, she wanted not only to tell a story but to instruct. She hoped in *Middlemarch* to show how certain individuals live—and thereby raise the old philosophical questions that some of us in psychiatry claim to have new ways of approaching: Who am I? What makes me behave as I do?

Middlemarch is "about" life in the English provinces from 1829 to 1832; it offers a detailed picture of a nation on the brink of political reform, social upheaval, economic change, and it also offers an astonishing breadth of sociological "data": dialects, customs, beliefs, prejudices. A novel of manners, a philosophical novel, a psychological novel, a Victorian novel, a novel which, as Henry James said, "sets a limit" to what "the old-fashioned English novel" can be—it is all of those, but is is also in class by itself.

George Eliot combed through the available medical literature to prepare for her study of Dr. Lydgate. She knew English provincial life from personal experience, but she read newspapers, books, articles to supplement her knowledge. She paid especially close attention to historical sources; like Tolstoy in *War and Peace* she was writing about a generation that immediately preceded her own, and she was aware that sometimes it is harder to be accurate about the recent past than about a more distant time. She knew theology and religious archaeology, and as a result Casaubon is unforgettable; he draws our sympathy as well as our scorn. She had a thorough grasp of the workings of the unconscious mind, so that Bulstrode's agonizing struggle with himself is presented with a keen eye for psychological nuance.

As she wrote she kept a notebook, published some time ago as *Quarry for Middlemarch*. All the facts in it, all the information she had gleaned, all her ideas and theories about human nature, all the historical veins she had tapped somehow came together in a story, in her characters. She condensed an era into a book. She transformed psychological characteristics into people—men and women who are not mechanisms or bundles of reflexes or drives or "needs." In *Middlemarch* history lives through the individuals whose lives, large and small, go to make up history.

I suppose we could call Eliot a psychological novelist, or a novelist interested in how social forces mold individual "behavior" or how particular men and women respond to the demands of a given era. Certainly she knew how to "integrate" her "perspectives." She meticulously fitted her knowledge into the novel, as Jerome Beatty in "History by Indirection: the Era of Reform in *Middlemarch*," *(Victorian Studies.* December, 1957) and Asa Briggs in *"Middlemarch* and the Doctors" (*Cambridge Journal,* pp. 749–762) have shown. It might be useful for some of us today to study how she went about her work, rather than to try to figure out her "personality." Maybe she was just a woman of broad sensibility who had taste and diligence and an extraordinary capacity to evoke the human complexity she saw about her.

In the same way, when one reads C. Vann Woodward's *Tom Watson* or Isaac Deutscher's three-volume biography of Leon Trotsky, one gets a notion of how that impoverished Georgia youth or that Russian student, so fiercely determined and so high-minded, slowly came to terms with themselves—and with the historical currents of their times. We are not given the "mind" of Tom Watson or Leon Trotsky; rather their lives, their concrete struggles, their disappointments, their blind spots, their inevitable pride. Eventually we come to know them well, as well as we can know anyone we have not met or spent time with.

True, not all scholars can glimpse as much as. C. Vann Woodward; few can give biography the power and drama of a novel, while providing the most vivid and searching kind of history. We certainly need more psychologically sophisticated historians—and more psychiatrists with a sense of history. But will that need be met by creating yet another "field" called "psychohistory"? One suspects that good historians like Woodward have no need of old or new psychological terminology or "perspectives," even as an analyst like Erikson calls upon history naturally and wisely because he is an intelligent and learned man—possessing a quality of mind which no college degree, and maybe no course of study, necessarily provides.

Meanwhile Bruce Mazlish may well have offered us an "objective" when he described the historian William L. Langer's suggestion that historians take a greater interest in psychology as an appeal for such an attempt on "a rather low level of theory." That would do—along with plain old thoughtfulness, tact, and the hope that a measure of grace, so mysterious in origin, so impossible to define, so evident and satisfying when present, will somehow come to inform what is written.

NOTES

1 Volume XI of *Complete Psychological Works of Sigmund Freud* (Macmillan, 1964).
2 *The Dynamics of Creation* (Atheneum, 1972).
3 Foreword to *Vincent Van Gogh: A Psychological Study* by Humberto Nagera (International Universities Press, 1968).
4 *Psychoanalysis and History,* edited by Bruce Mazlish (Grosset & Dunlap, 1971).
5 "Charismatic Leadership in Crisis" by George Devereux, in *Psychoanalysis and the Social Sciences,* edited by Warner Muensterberger and Sidney Axelrad (International Universities Press, 1955).
6 Ibid.
7 "Dictatorship and Paranoia" by Gustav Bychowski, ibid.
8 Ibid.
9 We are spared the absurd generalities of Gustav Bychowski's study a few years later on the same man (*Dictators and Disciples: A Psychoanalytic Interpretation of History,* International Universities Press, 1948).

   The repressions of his psycho-sexual development did not permit the proper integration and sublimation of his aggressive-sadistic drives, which, to begin with, were not utilized for the construction of normal erotic aggression. The intended identification with his father was not even psychically successful, and instead of the expected masculinity, the constantly competing passive, female attitude appeared.

10 One wants to read Eissler with respect and detachment but his persistent arrogance and rudeness make it hard to do so. We have reason to be grateful to Meyer Schapiro for the first-rate critical essays in which, without rancor, and with great sensitivity, he showed how Freud had erred. Eissler's book on Leonardo was largely prompted by Schapiro's observations, particularly his essay "Leonardo and Freud: An Art-Historical Study," first published in the *Journal of the History of Ideas,* Spring, 1956, and reprinted in *Renaissance Essays,* edited by P. Kristeller and P. Wiener (Harper & Row, 1968), and in *Ideas in Cultural Perspective,* edited by P. Wiener and A. Noland (Rutgers University Press, 1962).
11 *The Psychoanalytic Forum,* Vol. 4 (International Universities Press, 1972).
12 "Martin Buber and Psychiatry," *Psychiatry, A Journal for the Study of Interpersonal Processes,* XIX (1956), p. 110.
13 "Psychiatry and History: An Examination of Erikson's *Young Man Luther,*" *Religion in Life,* Winter, 1971.

8

Some Considerations on Psycho-History

Joseph M. Woods

In recent years an increasing number of historical works have been making use of psychoanalytic concepts in an effort to explain individual and group behavior in history. Despite the scepticism of many historians, it would seem that psycho-history, as it has come to be called, is winning a place for itself, or at the very least forcing those who write biographies or study political and social movements into the asking of some fresh questions. But there is another side to the development of psycho-history. In reviews by psychoanalysts of psycho-historical works and in debates among the practitioners of psycho-history itself there has come to the fore considerable argument about how this new discipline should be practiced. What does a historian need to know, and what training should he have to write psycho-history? Contrariwise, if only an analyst can write psychoanalytic history, what of his training in history? Or is the only fruitful path that of collaboration between analysts and historians? And how can this best be achieved? In short, before psycho-historical works can be critically examined, something must be known about the arguments over the nature of the discipline. It is to some of these arguments that the present essay will largely address itself. Its emphasis will be on psycho-biography.

Early in 1973, Robert Coles, a psychiatrist and the author of a recently published study of the work of Erik Erikson as well as several other works, published two essays on psycho-history in *The New York Review of Books.*[1] His arguments and viewpoints are a useful jumping-off place for discussion of the subject and some of its dilemmas.

Some of Coles' arguments have value, his criticism of jargon, for instance. Perhaps historians, unsure of their professional identities, of what history means, and what it means to be a historian, have embraced psychoanalytic jargon uncritically, as if the use of a private and developed professional language could endow them with a professional identity. The question of jargon is an especially

Reprinted from *The Historian,* vol. 36 (1974), pp. 722–35.

significant one because even among "classical" or "orthodox" psychoanalysts,[2] crucial terms such as depression, masochism, and narcissism, are not used in the same way.[3] But Coles' argument about psycho-history seems questionable at many points. He charges the psychologists and those historians who apply psychoanalytical concepts with envy of the creative energy displayed by great artists and historical leaders, with stinginess in praise, with negativism, with reducing the achievements of the great to weakness, problems, conflict.[4] No doubt he has a point, but should he not be equally alarmed about historians who idealize the figures they are writing about, who seem to endow historical personages with all the great qualities they themselves desire to possess, who minimize, leave unexamined, or put into footnotes the acts of selfishness, cruelty, self-deception, and self-destruction of their heroes? As Naomi Bliven has pointed out in a recent review of Antonia Fraser's *Oliver Cromwell,*[5] biographers of politicians are not as hard on their subjects as biographers of artists. Artists do not get credit for their unfulfilled intentions, but politicians do. They are praised for what they achieved and usually they are not blamed for what they promised but did not achieve. At least psychoanalysis provides a theory for noticing these facts, and perhaps understanding why a leader's reach exceeds his grasp.

One gets the impression from Coles that the insights of such thinkers as Pascal, Kierkegaard and Nietzsche, and of the great novelists, may instruct the historian about the human condition but that the developed body of psychoanalytic theory cannot do so for it is a set of concepts "of very circumscribed and indeterminate value,"[6] but one is not clear why Coles believes the insights of thinkers he admires should be more useful to the historian than a developed body of clinical evidence. Presumably it is because psychoanalytic concepts were devised to deal with sickness, and since the psycho-historian is hardly attempting to cure a patient, he cannot and should not apply them, and in applying them give us historical figures that are "more humanoid than human." But psychoanalytic concepts are not merely concepts devised for treating the sick. There are two branches in psychoanalytic literature: papers concerned with the technique and practice of psychoanalysis, and theoretical statements which purport to offer a general theory of mind and personality.[7] Coles does not give reasons for rejecting the claim of psychoanalytic theory to be a general psychology.[8] His argument also seems to ignore the fact that psychoanalytic theory has been built on the study of many patients who, whatever their sickness, have been successful in their careers even though they have not been made content or happy by their success.[9] But on the other hand many so-called great men in history have failed to take satisfaction in their successes—Luther, Rousseau, Lincoln, Woodrow Wilson to name a few— however much they longed for success. It would seem that psychoanalytic theory again enables the historian to notice and perhaps explain this fact.

Coles argues in criticizing Walter Langer's recently published *The Mind of Adolf Hitler*[10] that Hitler's weaknesses do not explain how he became Führer of all Europe. How many thousands of others who employed such mechanisms as "identification with the aggressor" got nowhere, and how many paranoid schiz-ophrenics have "messiah complexes"? Such a criticism is not, however, a valid criticism of psycho-history alone, but of any explanation of why any figure, in Erikson's phrase, "daydreams his way into history." Every historian comes up with some notion of the motives of the character he is dealing with, and one can always argue that ten or ten thousand other people in that time and place had (or might have had) the very same motives, and yet did not take the historical stage. No historian can really explain this mystery of why X, instead of these ten thousand other people, who may have had similar motives, becomes noteworthy. It seems to me one of those unproductive questions like why does Shakespeare have the Friar leave the tomb in *Romeo and Juliet*. We are reminded by Coles that whereas psycho-historians have, by and large, given us persons who are il-lustrations of theory, it is the great novelists like Dostoevski and George Eliot who give us people in all the fullness of life. But what historian of any school can rival the great novelists in characterization? It is hardly a just criticism of psycho-historians to say that they are inferior to major novelists. Furthermore, Coles, decrying the negativism of the psycho-historian, tells us that historical fig-ures have been given more by their parents and bring more from their child-hoods than burdens, complexes, conflicts, and inhibitions. To be sure. But the remark may well be beside the point. The point is rather that many great artists and famous historical figures do not acknowledge those debts to parents and others, and the biographer, often with the aid of psychoanalytic theory, attempts to explain why. Surely one of the major findings of psychoanalysis is that children internalize distorted images of early authority figures, having invested those fig-ures with their own hostile and sadistic impulses, and that in many cases these images are lasting and unmodified by experience. Thus V. S. Pritchett's recent biography of Balzac, which seems to me to understand Balzac in a psychoan-alytical way (although Pritchett does not acknowledge any influence and writes a prose unhindered by jargon), notes that Balzac was given to presenting him-self—usually to women—as someone deprived of a mother's love and as "ruined" by his mother, whereas it would be more accurate to say that he had ruined his mother, financially at least.[11]

Many psychoanalysts, however, would seem to believe that psychoanalytic the-ory can contribute to the understanding of historical personages.[12] To be sure these psychoanalysts are critical of those historians who have not seriously studied psychoanalytic theory and who seem to be, at this late date, laboring under the impression that psychoanalytic theory begins and ends with Freud and who are almost completely unaware of the revisions and elaborations in theory since the 1940s.[13] What has been criticized is that psycho-biographers have often not taken into account the shift in emphasis in psychoanalytic theory from (a) the instincts and their vicissitudes to (b) the development of the ego and the early object-relationships, especially the importance of the mother in the development of the child—that is to say, the importance of the pre-oedipal stages of life. These developments in theory would seem to be of special importance to the historian because they provide an explanation of how one relates—or fails to relate—to others. Assuming that "good enough mothering" takes place in the pre-oedipal mother-child relation, the child moves from a phase in which there is no awareness of self apart from the other to the phase where the other is regarded by the child as existing only to gratify his needs, to the phase where the other is regarded as a person in his own right with needs and feelings of his own. In the relationship with the mother, the child's ego, availing itself of its own inherent energies and with additional neutralized energy from the drives, begins to build up "internalized object relations"—that is, good and bad self-images and good and bad object-images. These images "result from continuous daily contact with the mothering person and reflect countless pleasureable and frustrating experiences in the infant's daily life."[14]

These images must become (a) differentiated and (b) stabilized. In normal development, the self-images are differentiated from the object-images, and the good and bad self-images are integrated as are the good and bad object-images. The differentiation between the self and object-images and the respective integration of the good and bad self and object-images constitute the basis for (1) individual identity and relationship with others, (2) the achievement of "psychological birth"—that is, psychological separation from the mother and the continuing process of becoming a separated individuated person, (3) the ability of the child to make necessary identifications with others, which are the basis for a developing identity and expansion of the functioning of the ego by acquiring skills and roles, (4) the appropriate development of the superego—that is, the development of a structure in which (a) personal goals, ideals and aspirations (called the ego-ideal) are toned down from the magical, grandiose aspirations of the child and (b) the internalized versions of the punitive parents have also been toned down by more realistic perceptions of parental demands and prohibitions and (c) the idealized and punitive aspects of the superego are harmonized.[15] Disturbances in the mother-child relationship of the pre-oedipal period are usually regarded as the cause of those character disorders which fall on the scale of pathology between psychosis and neurosis—the "borderline" states and certain narcissistic personality disturbances. These disorders have received much attention in psychoanalytic literature over the last decade.[16]

Because of the importance, then, of the mother-child relationship for the development of personality, psychoanalysts have been critical of much work done in psycho-biography on the ground that all too confidently the biographer focuses on the Oedipus complex of a given figure—as if all problems and conflicts were rooted in an unresolved oedipal conflict, and as if the pre-oedipal stages of development were not significant. As Gertrude and Rubin Blanck point out, if a father is resentful of a male child and of the attention the child receives from its mother, that may indicate that the father has not resolved his own Oedipus complex. But the father's behavior may also be "a manifestation of pre-oedipal object relations and of need-gratification wishes which render the individual unable to take the needs of either wife or son into account."[17] Which of these interpretations is true depends on the other evidence the clinician has available about the life of the patient. Since the biographer of an historical figure does not have direct access to his subject and has no way of uncovering repressed material, some analysts believe that he cannot be certain about the source of the character's "problems."[18] Psychoanalysts are agreed in criticizing the biographer who goes beyond the evidence and fabricates unconscious desires and fantasies.[19]

Since, then, the biographer often does not have, and cannot get enough information about his subject, some psychoanalysts believe that full analytic study of an historical figure is not possible and that the psycho-historian should restrict himself to "partial efforts, highlighting what general biographers have ignored and failed to understand, to undo denials and idealizations and to correct distortions aided by freedom from unconscious reactions to our subjects."[20] But must psycho-historians restrict themselves to critical corrections? The method used by Miles F. Shore in his essay on Henry VIII is suggestive.[21] Instead of speculating about what Henry's feeling for and early relationships with parents and siblings "must have been," Shore points out that Henry received treatment at the hands of tutors and servants that vacillated between extravagant adulation and brutal discipline, and that the hypocrisy and self-serving nature of this adulation by what were in effect "paid foster parents," had the result that his upbringing did not offer the possibilities for forming permanent important relationships. All of these conditions fostered the development of Henry's pathological narcissism. Shore then goes on to show how Henry's narcissism operated: how a series of defeats and disappointments offended Henry's grandiose self-image, and caused the series of actions which led to the break with Catherine and with Rome, and to later events in Henry's career as well.

Actually, is it necessary to postulate anything about a subject's childhood to do an analytic study? This is a central question because there is rarely enough reliable and available evidence about any given childhood and about a subject's feelings about the significant figures in childhood. But psychoanalytic theory enables the biographer to see, in examining the mature life of a character, behavior that he might not otherwise notice: alteration between active and passive states, how he relates to people, or whether his behavior indicates that he has not relinquished fantasies of omnipotence, whether he is burdened with an unconscious sense of guilt; and to show how these constructs enable us to understand the character more clearly. One does not, in short, have to know the earliest reasons why a character seems incapable of regarding other people except as "there" to meet his needs, in order to notice that he does relate to people in such an infantile way. Furthermore, psychoanalytic writing makes clear that the same effects (or "symptoms") do not always result from the same early "causes." Ralph Greenson has pointed out that compulsive gambling can be the result of (a) deprivation, (b) over-gratification, or (c) a combination of these in childhood.[22] Since this is true, the biographer is hardly—given the lack of evidence about a subject's childhood—entitled to assume causes.

The psychoanalytic work done over the last decade or so on the narcissistic personality may be useful to the historical biographer in understanding certain so-called "great men" in history.[23] What are the features of this type of character? A defective superego or conscience. Instead of having ideals, standards, values, goals, narcissistic personalities are possessed by fantasies of omnipotence, dreams of limitless greatness. They do not have ideals; rather, as Edith Jacobson says, the demandingness and exhibitionism of His Majesty the Baby are masquerading as ideals.[24] The narcissistic personality has not renounced infantile fantasies of omnipotence—more precisely, he has not renounced the wish for magical participation in the omnipotence of idealized early authority figures.[25] As Ralph Greenson points out, these personalities do not simply long for omnipotence, they feel they are omnipotent.[26] Unconsciously, their wishes are facts. They want to have their cake and eat it. They act upon their grandiose fantasies to be assured that they are superhuman. Their participation in the omnipotence of early figures may manifest itself in a belief in a special relationship with God, Fate, History, the mystical Nation, the General Will. They are subject to rapid oscillations of mood, feeling at times that they are God, at other times that they are nothing.[27] Usually narcissistic personalities deceive themselves into believing that they are serving noble causes, making nations great, rescuing and avenging the oppressed. Actually they are preoccupied with their own greatness.

Nevertheless, the grandiose self-concept which the narcissistic personality tries to live up to often does make for real achievement. As Max Weber said of charismatic leaders, because they attempt the impossible they attain the possible. Historians have often recognized the absence in so-called "great men" of any genuine values, standards, commitments, and of any coherent identity. They have recognized that one looks in vain for a consistent ideology, that great men often lack fidelity to the values of their group, their class, or their nation. Of Lloyd George, John Maynard Keynes wrote that he was "rooted in nothing"; General Beck said of Hitler, "this fellow has no Fatherland at all"; of Napoleon III, Marx wrote, "being nothing himself, he could be everything to everyone." Going along with the self-preoccupation of narcissistic personalities is the absence in them of any feeling that other persons are persons in their own right with needs and feelings of their own. Others are regarded instead as existing to meet their needs and demands, or as mirrors before whom they display themselves, or as containers into which the narcissistic personality deposits his own characteristics when they do not accord with his idealized self.[28] One is always right, good, and superior: others are wrong, bad, and inferior. These narcissistic types may be extremely dependent on other people but they really use them to live up to their own dreams of glory. Those on whom they depend are soon devalued and blamed if reality proves resistant (as reality usually does). Other helpers are often soon substituted—as if people were interchangeable parts; notice, for example, Henry VIII's succession of *alter rexes*. There is little human give-and-take in these relationships. Above all, this personality type usually does not experience conscious guilt feelings for greed, selfishness, hostility and aggression against others. Absence of conscious guilt feelings is one of the leading characteristics of their pathology.[29] They are given to projecting the guilt they should feel or the feelings and actions they should feel guilty about. Hitler, for instance, who had sponged off his mother and had earned no money until he was twenty-two, accused the Jews of being parasites on the German nation.[30] Yet the very defects of the narcissistic personality may be an advantage to a political leader.[31] The absence of any real values and principles and of any center seem to make it possible for him to play many roles and to tell other people what they want to hear in order to get their support. He pretends to be conservative to conservatives and radical to radicals. The defects in the structure of his superego make it possible for him to lie, exploit, manipulate, divide and conquer, crush opposition—not to speak of provoking wars and inaugurating "final solutions." Political leaders of this type seem to have an uncanny ability to use their "sickness" for purposes of gaining public support and attention. As Erikson writes of Hitler, "It is hard to say where personal symptom ends and shrewd propaganda begins."[32]

There is no need to dwell on the inadequacies of Walter Langer's *The Mind of Adolf Hitler*. It was written in 1943 as a secret report for the OSS but not published until 1972. It was composed before many of the developments in and revisions of psychoanalytic theory that I have been discussing had taken place. It emphasizes Hitler's pervasive Oedipus complex which was developed "to an extraordinary degree." The interpretation, and the evidence and reasoning behind it, have been criticized by clinicians and historians alike.[33] More recent analytic work on Hitler focuses on the pre-oedipal period and on a disturbed mother-child relationship.[34]

Of more interest to historians than speculating on childhood traumas is the theory recently proposed by a psycho-historian that Hitler unconsciously wanted (or needed) to fail. That theory holds that because of Hitler's unconscious guilt feelings about the possibility of his having Jewish blood, about his incestuous desires, and about his "massively masochistic sexual perversion," Hitler had to punish himself by "bringing about the kind of global war that he could not conceivably win."[35] But we do not really know what Hitler's unconscious guilt feelings were "about." They might just as well have been about his destructive wishes and deeds. But that is not the important point. The important point is rather that recent psychoanalytic theory has, on the basis of more and more clinical evidence, cast doubt on the earlier theory that self-destructive behavior is caused by unconscious guilt feelings seeking punishment. There may be some cases where self-defeat is produced by guilt needing punishment, but those cases involve neurotics with overly severe superegos.[36] An overly severe superego was hardly Hitler's problem. If it had been, as Erikson has pointed out, Hitler would have been "paralyzed"; he would not have been one of the great actors and destroyers

in history.[37] Rather Hitler's case might correspond to those borderline personalities whose self-destructive tendencies are the product of inner structural defects. Neither the ego nor the superego are well enough constructed to tame
and regulate aggressive impulses. As a result aggression is released both against
the world and against the self.[38] This is but one possible explanation for Hitler's
self-destructiveness.

There has been almost an embarrassment of riches in explaining self-defeating
behavior in recent psychoanalytic literature—none of them stressing guilt in
search of punishment. Some of these are: self-defeat may result from grandiosity,
from the need to be beyond limits. Gamblers going for broke—and Hitler so
characterized himself—do not necessarily need to lose. They may lose, but that
is not the intention of the gambling. Proving themselves omnipotent *is* the intention. That Hitler committed suicide when he didn't get away with it might
also be ascribed to shame because of failure to live up to his exalted self-image.[39]
Or a person may invite defeat in order to rescue self-esteem—paradoxical as
this may seem. Unconsciously he can say to himself: I control the circumstances;
I have arranged for failure; it did not come upon me from outside myself.[40] Or
a person may be self-defeating not just to punish himself but to punish someone
else—"victory through defeat"—whether the someone else be hated and envied
early figures or later figures.[41] I do not know which of the many current psychoanalytic explanations for self-destructiveness might work in Hitler's case. I
am simply saying that an explanation that stresses guilt seeking punishment is,
given the state of theory today, the least plausible.

Much has been written on methodology in psycho-history—how to proceed,
what evidence to credit, which psychoanalytic model to apply, what to do in the
absence of the evidence that an analyst has available in healing a patient, whether
the historian must have clinical experience as well as formal study in psychoanalytic theory, whether psycho-history must be a collaborative effort between historians and psychoanalysts. One can hardly imagine a line of inquiry more likely
to vex the founder of psychoanalysis. Freud had little love for discourses on
method. Those who were preoccupied with methodology were, he said, forever
polishing their glasses and never putting them on.

It may be true that psycho-history cannot be written except as a collaborative
effort. This surely depends on what is meant by psycho-history. Isn't any work
that makes use of psychoanalytic theory to understand a given individual or group
movement, a work of psycho-history? Could not Edmund Wilson, "Our American
Plutarch,"[42] be called a psycho-historian? Certainly he used psychoanalytic theory
not only to understand the creative process in literature but also to understand
historical figures such as Marx, Lenin, Lincoln, Woodrow Wilson. His use of psychoanalytic theory has always shown tact and judgment. It was never used explicitly, let alone self-consciously. Wilson did not invoke diagnostic labels or worry
about what level of pathology a given character displayed. Nor did he use psychoanalysis in such a way that his subject became an illustration of a theory. Nor

was he inclined to go beyond the evidence, imagining what childhoods "must have been." He criticizes, for example, Carl Sandburg's trumped-up version of Lincoln's childhood. Wilson himself is content to establish Lincoln's towering ambition, his heroic conception of himself by referring to one of his speeches in 1838: "Towering genius ... thirsts and burns for distinction; and, if possible, it will have it, whether at the expense of emancipating slaves or enslaving free men."[43] Wilson interprets: "it is evident that Lincoln has projected himself into the role against which he is warning [his audience]."[44] He was "describing this figure with a fire that seemed to derive as much from admiration as from apprehension."[45] Wilson shows that to justify his ambition and the aggression that it involved Lincoln grew increasingly to believe that God was on the side of the Union and against slavery and had willed the Civil War. And Wilson believes that this religious mysticism about the Union was not merely contrived by Lincoln "to express himself in phrases congenial to his public" but was a "vision" that had imposed itself. Yet while thirsting and burning for distinction at the expense of sending "thousands to their deaths" and referring one's will and actions to God is hardly a flattering picture of Lincoln, the reader at no point feels that Lincoln has been put down, reduced, or that Edmund Wilson is attacking a national idol or moralizing about his faults. Wilson's tone, his ability not to trivialize or patronize a figure seems to spring from his sense that "thirsting and burning for distinction" or sadistic and masochistic tendencies (which Wilson so clearly brings out in his treatment of Marx) are human qualities, not occasions for shocked surprise of outraged morality or disappointment that some of history's movers and shakers have "base" motives. He realizes that achievement has its price, and writes of Karl Marx:

> Certainly his character was domineering; certainly his personality was arrogant, and abnormally mistrustful and jealous; certainly he was capable of vindictiveness and of what seems to us gratuitous malignity. But if we are repelled by these traits in Marx, we must remember that a normally polite and friendly person could hardly have accomplished the task which it was the destiny of Marx to carry through—a task that required the fortitude to resist and to break off all those ties which—as they involve us in the general life of society—limit our views and cause our purposes to shift.[46]

One doubts if many psychoanalysts would agree with this favorable verdict on Marx, would agree that his isolation, aggression, and cruelty are to be excused, still less explained, by his "destiny," though they may have made possible his achievement. Wilson seems to admire those figures who need to be great, who thirst and burn for distinction at whatever cost; but he does not withhold or suppress whatever information is available to him that makes possible a harsher or different judgment. Psychoanalysis is not an orthodoxy; two psychoanalysts regarding the same historical figure will not necessarily come to the same interpretation of his behavior or to the same judgment of his goodness or badness.[47] Thus Erik Erikson has been criticized by a psychoanalyst for "idealizing" Gandhi, for not giving enough attention to his sadism and to the irresponsibility, given the poverty of India, involved in his contempt for science, birth control, industrialization, and mass education.[48] It would seem, then, that psychoanalysis is not going to make history itself different from what it has always been and what Pieter Geyl said it was: "argument without end."

NOTES

1 February 22, and March 8, 1973.

2 We refer here to psychoanalysts who have received their training at Institutes accredited by the American Psychoanalytic Association. For further detail see *A Glossary of Psychoanalytic Terms and Concepts*, ed. by Burnes E. Moore and Bernard D. Fine (2nd ed.; New York, 1968), 9–11.

3 Myer Mendelson, *Psychoanalytic Concepts of Depression* (Springfield, Ill., 1960), 137. Mendelson points out that there is "but limited consensus among psychoanalytic writers on depression. Disagreement is acute on numerous issues."

4 Coles, *New York Review of Books,* Feb. 22, 1973, 18, 19, 21.

5 *The New Yorker,* Jan. 14, 1974.

6 Coles, *New York Review of Books,* Mar. 8, 1973, 27.

7 Lionel Trilling, Introduction to *The Life and Work of Sigmund Freud* by Ernest Jones. Edited and abridged by Lionel Trilling and Steven Marcus (New York, 1963), vii.

8 See *Makers of Modern Social Science: Sigmund Freud,* ed. Paul Roazen (Englewood Cliffs, N.J., 1973), editor's introduction.

9 See Helen H. Tartakoff, "The Normal Personality in Our Culture and the Nobel Prize Complex," in R. M. Loewenstein et al., *Psychoanalysis: A General Psychology* (New York, 1966), 222–52; and Annie Reich, "Pathologic Forms of Self-Esteem Regulation," *Psychoanalytic Study of the Child,* 25 (1960), 215–32.

10 *The Mind of Adolf Hitler: The Secret Wartime Report* (New York, 1972).

11 V. S. Pritchett, *Balzac* (New York, 1973).

12 Panel. "The Methodology of Psychoanalytic Biography," reported by John E. Gedo, *Journal of the American Psychoanalytic Association,* 20 (1972), 638–49. Cited hereafter as Gedo. Also Bernard C. Meyer, "Some Reflections on the Contributions of Psychoanalysis to Biography," in *Psychoanalysis and Contemporary Science,* I, ed. R. R. Holt and E. Peterfreund (New York, 1972), 373–91. Cited hereafter as Meyer.

13 By psychoanalytic theory here, I mean that body of theory which, to speak only of the United States, is taught at psychoanalytic training institutes accredited by the American Psychoanalytic Association and to the literature which appears in such journals as *International Journal of Psychoanalysis, Journal of the American Psychoanalytic Association, Psychoanalytic Quarterly, American Imago,* and such annuals as *The Psychoanalytic Study of the Child.*

14 Rubin Blanck and Gertrude Blanck, *Marriage and Personal Development* (New York, 1968), 12.

15 This brief summary of the importance of the mother-child relationship for the development of personality is derived from Rubin Blanck and Gertrude Blanck, *Marriage and Personal Development,* especially Chapters 2, 5, 6, and 7 and from Otto F. Kernberg, "Early Ego Integration and Object Relations," *Annals of the New York Academy of Science,* 193 (August 25, 1972), 233–47. Some of the major contributors to ego psychology and object relations theory are John Bowlby, Erik Erikson, W. R. D. Fairbairn, Anna Freud, Heinz Hartmann, Edith Jacobson, Otto Kernberg, Melanie Klein, Margaret Mahler, René Spitz, D. W. Winnicott. A list of significant writings will be found in the bibliography of the Blancks' book and in the footnotes of the Kernberg article.

16 Otto F. Kernberg, "Borderline Personality Organization," *Journal of the American Psychoanalytic Association,* 15 (1967), 641–85; "Factors in the Psychoanalytic Treatment of Narcissistic Personalities," *Journal of the American Psychoanalytic Association,* 18 (1970), 51–85; and "A Psychoanalytic Classification of Character Pathology," *Journal of the American Psychoanalytic Association,* 18 (1970), 800–822.

17 Blanck and Blanck, *Marriage,* 78.

18 See Gedo, "The Methodology of Psychoanalytic Biography," 641–43. It would seem that analytic biography may be more successful with literary figures than with generals and politicians for the works of the former allow access to their fantasies.

19 Rudolf Binion's *Frau Lou: Nietzsche's Wayward Disciple* (Princeton, 1968) has been criticized by Bernard F. Meyer, for instance, as an example of "wild analysis" because Binion with neither evidence nor argument "unhesitatingly announces the cause of his subject's unhappy childhood: 'a craving for her father excited by excretion and attended by darkling visions of re-entering his bowel-womb to repossess his penis.' [p. 6] Now aside from wondering what this sentence might mean [Dr. Meyer continues] the reader may justly ask by what route the author arrived there, for there is nothing in the text up to this point—31 lines of the book so far—that has paved the way for any conclusion whatever, let alone this somewhat extravagant one. Psychoanalysis is not an arcanum for an exercise in revealed truth; neither is it in the nature of its methodology nor in that of any scientific discipline, for that matter, to initiate a study or an experiment with an unproved conclusion." Meyer, "Some Reflections . . . ," 374. Later in his essay, Meyer notes that Binion, in his preoccupation with Frau Lou's "charged up obsession with famous men, overlooks or minimizes the role of maternal influences both in his subject and in those who moved about her." Ibid., 378–79.

20 Gedo, "The Methodology of Psychoanalytic Biography," 641.

21 Miles F. Shore, "Henry VIII and the Crisis of Generativity," *Journal of Interdisciplinary History,* 2 (Spring, 1972), 359–90.

22 Ralph Greenson, "On Gambling," *American Imago,* 4 (April 1947), 70. Myer Mendelson has pointed out that there is disagreement among analysts about "the period in childhood which is most critical for the predisposition to depression." Mendelson, *Psychoanalytic Concepts of Depression,* 138.

23 Not all narcissistic personalities have the same degree of pathology. This category of mental illness falls between neurosis and psychosis, but some are closer to neurosis and some to psychosis (borderline personality disorders). Hitler, for instance, has been diagnosed as a "narcissistic personality with overt borderline characteristics." See Norbert Bromberg, "Hitler's Character and Its Development," *American Imago,* 28 (1971), 289–303. It should be noted that the narcissistic personality represents pathological narcissism. Normal narcissism is evident in "healthy self-esteem."

24 Edith Jacobson, *The Self and the Object World* (New York, 1964), 203–04.

25 Helen H. Tartakoff, "The Normal Personality in Our Culture and the Nobel Prize Complex," in Loewenstein, *Psychoanalysis,* 233, 242.

26 Ralph Greenson, "On Gambling," 68.

27 Annie Reich, "Pathologic Forms of Self-Esteem Regulation," 226.

28 Paulina F. Kernberg, "The Course of the Analysis of a Narcissistic Personality with Hysterical and Compulsive Features," *Journal of the American Psychoanalytic Association,* 19 (1971), 453.

29 Ibid.

30 Norbert Bromberg, "Hitler's Character and Its Development," 298.

31 Alexander and Juliet George suggest that high accomplishment in political life may be positively correlated not only with neurosis but with even more pathological states. *Psychology Today* (June 1973), 98.

32 *Childhood and Society* (New York, 1963, paperback edition), 341.

33 See Coles, *New York Review of Books,* March 8, 1973, 25–26; Hans Gatzke, "Hitler and Psychohistory," in *American Historical Review,* 78 (April 1973), 394–401. See also Erik H. Erikson, *Childhood and Society,* 329–30. Erikson is not criticizing Langer's book directly, and his essay gives no indication that he has seen the original report; he is criticizing, however, the view that Hitler's behavior can be adequately explained by the "Oedipus complex."

34 Norbert Bromberg, "Hitler's Character and Its Development."

35 R. G. L. Waite, "Adolf Hitler's Guilt Feelings: A Problem in History and Psychology," *Journal of Interdisciplinary History,* I (Winter, 1971), 229–49. This article gives many instances of Hitler's self-defeating behavior which historians might ordinarily pass over, but not all of them are equally plausible.

36 Otto F. Kernberg, "Prognostic Considerations Regarding Borderline Personality Organization," *Journal of the American Psychoanalytic Association,* 19 (1971), 610.

37 *Childhood and Society,* 329.

38 Otto F. Kernberg, "Early Ego Integration and Object Relations," 242, and "Prognostic Considerations Regarding Borderline Personality Organization," 608–11.

39 Charles Rycroft, *Neurosis and Anxiety* (London, 1971, Pelican paperback), 54.

40 L. Eidelberg, "Humiliation and Masochism," *Journal of the American Psychoanalytic Association,* 7 (1959), 274–84.

41 Otto F. Kernberg, "Prognostic Considerations Regarding Borderline Personality Organization," 610.

42 The phrase is Alfred Kazin's.

43 Edmund Wilson, *Patriotic Gore* (New York, 1969, paperback edition), 107.

44 Ibid., 108.

45 Ibid., 129.

46 Wilson, *To the Finland Station* (New York, 1972), 178–79.

47 For a discussion of different interpretations by two analysts of an important episode in Goethe's life and the impossibility of deciding which interpretation is valid, see Gedo, "Methodology of Psychoanalytic Biography," 640.

48 H. Robert Blank, review of Erikson's *Gandhi's Truth, Psychoanalytic Quarterly,* 41 (1972), 123–27.

9

Why Did Van Gogh Cut Off His Ear? The Problem of Alternative Explanations in Psychobiography

William McKinley Runyan

Late Sunday evening December 23, 1888, Vincent Van Gogh, then thirty-five years old, cut off the lower half of his left ear and took it to a brothel, where he asked for a prostitute named Rachel and handed the ear to her, requesting that she "keep this object carefully."

How is this extraordinary event to be accounted for? Over the years a variety of explanations have been proposed, and more than a dozen of them will be sketched below. Is one of these explanations uniquely true, are all of them true in some way, or perhaps, are none of them true? What criteria and procedures are there for critically evaluating and deciding among these alternative interpretations? This incident is examined in order to explore the problem of alternative explanations in the study of individual lives, a problem of central importance in psychobiography (Anderson, 1981a; Crosby, 1979), in personality psychology (Allport, 1961; Hogan, 1976; Murray, 1938), and in the clinical professions (Horowitz, 1979; Spence, 1976).

A VARIETY OF EXPLANATIONS

1. One explanation of Van Gogh's behavior is that he was frustrated by two recent events: the engagement of his brother Theo, to whom he was very attached, and the failure of an attempt to establish a working and living relationship with Paul Gauguin. The aggressive impulses aroused by these frustrations were first directed at Gauguin, but then were turned against himself (Lubin, 1972).

2. A second interpretation is that the self-mutilation resulted from a conflict over homosexual impulses aroused by the presence of Gauguin. According to this account, the ear was a phallic symbol (the Dutch slang word for penis, *lul*, resembled the Dutch word for ear, *lel*), and the act was a symbolic self-castration (Lubin, 1972; Westerman Holstijn, 1951).

3. A third explanation is in terms of Oedipal themes. Van Gogh was sharing a house with Gauguin, and Gauguin reported that on the day before the ear mutilation Van Gogh had threatened him with a razor but, under Gauguin's powerful gaze, had then run away. According to this interpretation, Gauguin represented Van Gogh's hated father and that, failing in his initial threat, Van Gogh "finally gratified his extraordinary resentment and hate for his father by deflecting the hatred onto his own person. In so doing Van Gogh committed, in phantasy, an act of violence on his father with whom he identified himself and at the same time he punished himself for committing the act" (Schnier, 1950, p. 153). Then "in depositing his symbolic organ at the brothel he also fulfilled his wish to have his mother" (pp. 153–54).

4. Another interpretation is that Van Gogh was influenced by bullfights he had seen in Arles. In such events the matador is given the ear of the bull as an award, displays his prize to the crowd, and then gives it to the lady of his choice. The proponent of this interpretation, J. Olivier (in Lubin, 1972) says: "I am absolutely convinced that Van Gogh was deeply impressed by this practice.... Van Gogh cut off the ear, his own ear, as if he were at the same time the vanquished bull and the victorious matador. A confusion in the mind of one person between the vanquished and the vanquisher" (p. 158). Then like the matador, Van Gogh presented the ear to a lady of his choice. (The following explanations, unless otherwise noted, are also from Lubin's (1972) comprehensive analysis.)

5. In the months preceding Van Gogh's self-mutilation, there were fifteen articles in the local paper about Jack the Ripper, who mutilated the bodies of prostitutes, sometimes cutting off their ears. "These crimes gave rise to emulators, and Vincent may have been one of them. As a masochist instead of a sadist, however, it is conceivable that he would reverse Jack's act by mutilating himself and bringing the ear to a prostitute" (Lubin, 1972, p. 159).

6. Van Gogh was emotionally and financially dependent on his brother Theo, and usually spent the Christmas holidays with him. This year, however, Vincent learned that Theo would spend the holiday with his new fiancée and her family. One interpretation suggests that Van Gogh's self-mutilation was an unconscious strategy for holding on to his brother's attention, and a way of getting Theo to come and care for him rather than spending the holidays with his fiancée.

7. Van Gogh had recently been painting a picture of a woman rocking a cradle, using Madame Roulins as his model. He felt great affection for the Roulins family and may have envied the love and attention their children received. In mutilating himself, Van Gogh may have been attempting to obtain care and love from these substitute parents. The immediate response of Madame Roulins is not known,

but Monsieur Roulins came to Van Gogh's aid on the night of the injury and helped to care for him afterward.

8. Van Gogh had a great sympathy for prostitutes and identified with their status as social outcasts. One suggestion is that his self-mutilation was a reflection of this identification. "In June, just a few months before butchering his ear, he had written that 'the whore is like meat in a butcher shop': when he treated his own body as 'meat in a butcher's shop,' he reversed their roles, identified himself with the whore, and showed his sympathy for her" (Lubin, 1972, p. 169).

9. Vincent felt that his mother saw him as too rough and as a bad boy. During the psychotic state surrounding this incident, primitive symbolic thought processes may have led Van Gogh to cut off his ear from a desire to be perceived more positively by his mother. "Because the unconscious mind tends to regard protuberances as masculine and aggressive, removing the protuberant part of the ear may have been to inform the prostitute, a substitute for his mother, that he was not an aggressive, hurtful male—the 'rough' boy whom his mother disliked—but helpless, penetrable, the victim of a hurt" (Lubin, 1972, p. 173).

10. It is likely that Van Gogh experienced frightening auditory hallucinations during his psychotic attack similar to those he experienced in other attacks. Afterward, while in the sanatorium, he wrote that other patients heard strange sounds and voices as he had and speculated in one case that this was probably due to a disease of nerves in the ear. Thus, in a psychotic state, Van Gogh could have felt that his own ear was diseased and cut it off to silence the disturbing sounds.

11. In the Garden of Gethsemane scene in the Bible, Simon Peter cut off the ear of Malchus, a servant of the high priest, who had come to seize Christ. This scene had been on Van Gogh's mind. He attempted to paint it in the summer of 1888, and also mentioned it in a letter to his sister in October. In his delirium, Van Gogh may have acted out the scene at Gethsemane, carrying out the roles of both victim and aggressor.

12. Another explanation is that Vincent identified with the crucified Jesus and that the Virgin Mary lamenting over the dead body of Christ represented Vincent's mother. "In giving the mother surrogate, Rachel, a dead segment of his body, Vincent symbolically repeated the scene on Calvary" (Lubin, 1972, p. 179).

13. Vincent Van Gogh lived in the shadow of a dead brother, also named Vincent, who died at birth exactly one year before Vincent the painter was born. It is suggested that Vincent had the feeling he was unloved by a mother who continued to grieve over an idealized lost son. Killing part of himself may have been an attempt to win his mother's love. Vincent's self-mutilation "represented a symbolic death, exhibiting Vincent in the image of his dead brother, the first Vincent—someone mother adored. As a gift, the severed ear was specifically the gift of a baby, a dead baby. Thus it was both a reliving of wishes to unite him with mother and a bitter mockery of his mother's attachment to her dead son" (Lubin, 1972, pp. 182–83.)

124   **William McKinley Runyan**

What to Make of These Alternative Explanations?

Here are thirteen different psychodynamic explanations for why Van Gogh cut off his ear and gave it to a prostitute, and additional interpretations have been proposed (Lubin, 1972; Nagera 1967; Schneider, 1950; Schnier, 1950; Untermeyer, 1955; Westerman Holstijn, 1951). There is a substantial list of explanations for Van Gogh's disturbances which also consider biological factors (Monroe, 1978; Tralbaut, 1969). How should we interpret these alternative explanations? Are all of them true, are some true and some false, or, perhaps, are none of them true? Do the various explanations conflict, so that if one is chosen then one or more of the others must be rejected, or do a number of them supplement each other? Is there, perhaps, some other explanation that would replace all of these possibilities? Do we end up with a feeling that we understand Van Gogh's behavior, that we know why he acted as he did?

Individuals may vary widely in their responses to this material. From one point of view, it is a richly woven tapestry connecting a single event to many themes, conflicts, symbols, and unconscious wishes and processes in Van Gogh's life. According to the principle of "overdetermination," which suggests that actions typically have multiple causes and meanings, this material can be seen as a rich set of complementary explanations for Van Gogh's behavior. Lubin (1972) for example, after discussing a number of possible explanations, suggests that "there may be truth in all of these suggestions. One's motivations include the superficial factors that are well known to oneself as well as deep, troubling factors that one would vehemently deny when confronted with them. Man carries his conflicts from one period of life to the next, and each stage of development puts its mark on the next" (p. 163). From the standpoint of overdetermination, it would be surprising to find a single explanation for any human action, and events can be expected to have more than one cause, more than one meaning. At other points, Lubin states that "various aspects of Vincent's life converged in this single episode" (p. 155) and that what we have is a set of "interrelated" explanations (p. 182).

A second way of making sense of these multiple explanations is to note that several of the different explanations are concerned with different aspects or features of the larger episode. For example, the choice of an ear may have been related to Van Gogh's observation of bullfights, the fact that it happened at Christmastime may have been associated with the presentation of the ear as a gift, and his choice of a prostitute as the recipient may have been related to recent publicized accounts of Jack the Ripper. A substantial number of interpretations, however, are concerned with similar aspects of the event. His choice of the ear has been related to his observation of bullfights, the newspaper accounts of Jack the Ripper, the ear as a phallic symbol, a belief that auditory hallucinations may have come from diseased nerves in the ear, and his concern with the Gethsemane scene.

A third approach is to work from the assumption that several of these explanations may be valid while the others are not, and that procedures for critically evaluating alternative explanations are needed in order to assess their relative credibility. The doctrine of overdetermination may be correct in that psychological events often have multiple causes and meanings, but to assume that all possible interpretations "are ultimately members of one happy family is to abandon critical thinking altogether" (Hirsch, 1967, p. 164). For therapeutic purposes, it may be useful to explore as many meanings as possible for a single event, but for scientific or explanatory purposes, it is necessary both to critically assess the plausibility of alternative explanations and then to examine the extent to which the remaining explanations supplement or conflict with one another.

A fourth possible response is to think that all of this symbolic interpretation is somewhat arbitrary, perhaps even hopelessly arbitrary. If interpretations can be generated merely by noting similarities between the event in question and earlier events and experiences, then connections "are embarrassingly easy to find" and "the number of possible (and plausible) explanations is infinite" (Spence, 1976, pp. 377, 379). It can be argued that the process of interpretation is so loose and flexible that it can be used to explain anything, and its opposite, not only once but in many different ways. A milder version of this criticism is that the process of psychodynamic interpretation is perfectly legitimate but that it has been used with insufficient constraint in this particular example.

THE CRITICAL EVALUATION OF EXPLANATORY CONJECTURES

This incident forcefully raises several basic questions about the logic of explanation in psychobiography. What procedures exist, or can be developed, for critically evaluating alternative explanations of life events? How can we know whether we do or do not have a "good" explanation of a particular event or set of events in a life history? The Van Gogh example is useful in that it pushes the explanatory endeavor further than usual by suggesting a wide range of possible interpretations, with supporting evidence for each. In doing so, it raises with unusual clarity questions about the generation of explanatory hypotheses, about the critical evaluation of such hypotheses, and about the choice among, or integration of, a variety of explanatory possibilities.

It seems helpful, following Popper (1962), to distinguish between the processes of conjecture and refutation and to make a distinction between the processes of generating and critically evaluating explanatory conjectures. The literature on Van Gogh provides an excellent example of the processes of explanatory conjecture, and can also be used to illustrate the process of critically evaluating such conjectures. Consider, for example, the hypothesis that Van Gogh may have been influenced by contemporary newspaper accounts of Jack the Ripper. This particular explanation depends on the assumption that Van Gogh read these stories in the local paper, that he noticed the ear-cutting detail mentioned in two of the fifteen stories, that it made a lasting impression on him, and that it influenced him the night he mutilated his own ear. This explanation depends on a chain of assumptions, none of which has direct empirical support, which leaves this particular conjecture relatively unsubstantiated.

In comparison, the probability that he was influenced in his actions by visions of a matador and bull may be somewhat higher (although still perhaps low on an absolute basis) in that his letters indicate that he had attended bullfights in Arles. There is evidence that he had at least witnessed this scene, and that it had made an impression on him, whereas we can only presume that he may have read about Jack the Ripper and his cutting of ears.

Consider also the theory that he identified with a prostitute by treating his own body like meat in a butcher shop. The phrase "the whore is like meat in a butcher's shop" occurred in a letter in June of 1888, six months before the ear-cutting incident. Without further supporting evidence that this image occurred to Van Gogh nearer in time to the ear-cutting incident, there is little reason to believe that it played a significant part in his self-mutilation.

Part of the evidence supporting an Oedipal interpretation of the incident also seems open to question. Gauguin did not report that Van Gogh threatened him with a razor until fifteen years after the incident; indeed, in Gauguin's account to a friend four days after the event, this was not mentioned. Gauguin left Arles for Paris immediately after Van Gogh's self-mutilation. It has been suggested by Rewald (1956) that Gauguin was concerned about the propriety of his conduct, and may have invented the threat story later as a justification for having abandoned Van Gogh in a moment of crisis.

In yet another explanation, Untermeyer (1955) suggested that Van Gogh "had cut off an ear and sent it to one of the prostitutes he and Gauguin had visited. It was a Christmas present, a return for being teased about his over-sized ears" (p. 235). There are several reasons for being suspicious of this particular explanation. As far as I have been able to determine, there is no evidence that Van Gogh was teased by the prostitute about the size of his ears. This highly relevant circumstance is not mentioned in such primary sources as Van Gogh's letters or Gauguin's memoirs or in far more extensive biographies of Van Gogh, such as Tralbaut's (1969) or Lubin's (1972), which contain detailed analyses of the ear-cutting episode. Furthermore, the same paragraph containing this assertion has at least two other factual errors in its description of the incident. Instead of supposing that Untermeyer's book of ninety-two biographical sketches has access to information unavailable to scholars such as Tralbaut, who has spent more than fifty years studying and writing about Van Gogh, it seems more reasonable to conclude that there is no reliable evidence supporting this explanatory conjecture and that the evidence was fabricated in order to produce a plausible account. Similar criticisms may be made of Meier-Graeffe's (1933) story that the prostitute had earlier asked Van Gogh for a five-franc piece, he had refused, and that she then said that "if he could not give her a five-franc piece he might at least honour her with one of his large lop-ears for a Christmas present" (p. 163).

An explanation not based on such unreliable evidence rests on Van Gogh's report several months later in the sanatorium that other patients heard words and voices, just as he had, probably because of diseased nerves of the ear. Such beliefs may have played a part in the ear-mutilation episode.

The evidence presented must, in addition to being reliable in itself, be shown to have explanatory relevance or explanatory force in relation to the events in question. This explanatory relevance may, according to various construals, be obtained through deductive use of a theory or law relating the available evidence to the event to be explained (Hempel, 1965), through identifying reasons that the agent had for acting as he or she did (Dray, 1957), or through constructing a coherent narrative linking the evidence to the event to be explained (Sherwood, 1969). Consider, for example, the explanation which suggests that Van Gogh identified with the crucified Jesus, and that in giving the mother surrogate, Rachel, a dead segment of his body, he symbolically repeated the scene on Calvary. In his presentation of the ear, Van Gogh hoped that his mother would adore him as Mary adored the crucified Jesus (Lubin, 1972, p. 180). This explanation is based on a set of symbolic equivalencies, with Vincent representing Jesus, the severed ear representing the dead body, and Rachel representing the Virgin Mary. The events of his ear-mutilation can be translated into these terms, but what is the explanatory force of such a translation? It is not sufficient to suggest such possible symbolic equivalences; it is also necessary to provide reasons for believing that such representations were causally relevant to the actual course of events, in other words, that Van Gogh, either consciously or unconsciously, made such symbolic connections and that they influenced his actions. At various times in his life, such as in his struggles to be a minister and in his compassion for the downtrodden, Van Gogh did indicate an identification with Jesus; but that the severed ear represented to him the dead body of Christ, that Rachel represented the Virgin Mary, or that images of the Calvary scene influenced his self-destructive actions that night remains to be demonstrated.

Perhaps the single most strongly supported explanatory factor in Vincent's breakdown was the perceived loss of his brother's care. Specifically, the ear-cutting incident and two later mental breakdowns coincided with learning of Theo's engagement, his marriage, and the birth of his first child. In each case, Vincent was threatened by the prospect of losing his main source of emotional and financial support, as it seemed that Theo might redirect his love and money toward his new family (Tralbaut, 1969).

A masochistic response under situations of rejection or loss of love was not alien to Van Gogh. In 1881, he had visited the parents of Kee Voss, a woman he loved but who was avoiding him. When he heard that Kee had left the house in order to avoid seeing him, Van Gogh "put his hand in the flame of the lamp and said, 'Let me see her for as long as I can keep my hand in the flame' " (Tralbaut, 1969, p. 79). They blew out the lamp and said that he could not see her. These other incidents make it seem more likely that Van Gogh's self-mutilation was influenced by a perceived loss of love from his brother.

It is no easy task to winnow through a range of explanatory hypotheses, and given limitations in the accessible evidence about historical events, it is sometimes impossible to directly test every explanatory conjecture. However, substantial progress can still be made in identifying faulty explanations and in gathering corroborative evidence in support of others. Explanations and interpretations can be evaluated in light of criteria such as (1) their logical soundness, (2) their comprehensiveness in accounting for a number of puzzling aspects of the events in question, (3) their survival of tests of attempted falsification, such as tests of derived predictions or retrodictions, (4) their consistency with the full range of available relevant evidence, (5) their support from above, or their consistency with more general knowledge about human functioning or about the person in question, and (6) their credibility relative to other explanatory hypotheses (Bromley, 1977, chap. 8; Cheshire, 1975; Crosby, 1979; Hempel, 1965, 1966; Sherwood, 1969).

For each explanatory problem we can imagine a tree of explanatory inquiries, with the trunk representing the initial question or puzzle, each limb representing an explanatory conjecture, and smaller branches off the limb representing tests of that particular hypothesis or conjecture. Any single explanatory hypothesis can be submitted to a variety of tests, with each test providing partial, although not definitive, corroboration or disconfirmation of the hypothesis.

The least developed inquiries would consist of a trunk with a single bare limb, representing a single explanatory conjecture that has received little or no critical examination. A comprehensive explanatory inquiry would resemble a well-developed tree, filled out with limbs and branches, representing a great variety of explanatory conjectures, with extensive testing of each explanatory hypothesis. This picture of an ideal tree, or of a fully rational explanatory inquiry, provides a framework for assessing the progress of particular explanatory inquiries and for visualizing what has been done in relation to what could be done.

THE SEARCH FOR SINGLE EXPLANATIONS

Psychobiographical studies of individual lives are often criticized for being open to a variety of explanations. For instance, it is claimed that Freud's case studies "suffer from the critical flaw of being open to many interpretations" (Liebert and Spiegler, 1978, p. 50). Popper (1962) states: "Every conceivable case could be interpreted in the light of Adler's theory, or equally of Freud's.... I could not think of any human behavior which could not be interpreted in terms of either theory. It was precisely this fact—that they always fitted, that they were always confirmed—which in the eyes of their admirers constituted the strongest argument in favour of these theories. It began to dawn on me that this apparent strength was in fact their weakness" (p. 35). Similarly, Gergen (1977) says: "The events of most people's lives are sufficiently variegated and multifarious that virtually any theoretical template can be validated. The case study simply allows the investigator freedom to locate the facts lending support to his or her pre-formulated convictions" (p. 142).

These criticisms are, I believe, overstated and apply most readily to poorly developed explanatory inquiries. It may be possible to interpret any life with any theory, but often only at the cost of distortion or selective presentation of the evidence. Any explanatory conjecture *can* be made, but not all of them stand up under critical examination. In legal proceedings, self-serving explanations of the course of events by a guilty defendant often crumble under rigorous cross-examination. Similarly, explanations of a life history using a particular theory sometimes fail to stand up under critical examination. For example, the disorders of George III had widely been seen as manic-depressive psychosis until Macalpine and Hunter (1969) persuasively reinterpreted them as symptoms of porphyria, a hereditary metabolic disturbance. Even if some evidence can be found in a life history that is consistent with a wide variety of theories, this does not mean that all of these theories provide an adequate interpretation of the events in question.

Critical testing of the claims and implications of various explanations can lead to the elimination of many of them as implausible or highly unlikely. Ideally, this process will lead to a single well-supported explanation. In some cases, though, even after a great number of unsatisfactory conjectures are eliminated, more than one explanation that is consistent with the available evidence may remain. We are sometimes faced with "many possible explanations, all of which may be equally valid theoretically and which the facts equally fit, and when this happens there is no way we can say which explanation is the most correct" (Pye, 1979, p. 53).

This problem may not be frequently encountered in everyday practice, where minimal resources are available for inquiry, where investigation ceases once a single plausible explanation is reached, or where inquiry stops once an interpretation consistent with a prevailing theoretical orthodoxy is produced. However, if an explanatory problem is extensively investigated, if it is approached from a variety of theoretical perspectives, or if it touches on conflicting social and political interests, it becomes more likely that a variety of alternative explanations will be generated.

CONCLUSION

It is sometimes suggested that the interpretation of single cases is little more than an arbitrary application of one's theoretical preferences. No doubt this happens at times, but *any* method can be poorly used. Effective use of the case study method requires not only the formulation of explanations consistent with some of the evidence but also that preferred explanations be critically examined in light of all available evidence, and that they be compared in plausibility with alternative explanations. After the implausible alternatives have been eliminated, more than one explanation consistent with the available evidence may remain, but this is far different from saying that the facts can be adequately explained in terms of any theoretical conjecture.

When faced with a puzzling historical or clinical phenomenon, investigators are sometimes too ready to accept the first psychodynamic interpretation that makes previously mysterious events appear comprehensible. The case of Van Gogh's ear illustrates the dangers of this approach, as further inquiry often yields a variety of other apparently plausible explanations. When this happens, it is not sufficient to suggest that all of the explanations may be simultaneously true; rather, the situation requires that the alternative explanatory conjectures be critically evaluated and compared in terms of their relative plausibility.

REFERENCES

Allport, G. W. *Pattern and growth in personality.* New York: Holt, Rinehart and Winston, 1961.

Anderson, J. W. The methodology of psychological biography. *Journal of Interdisciplinary History,* 1981, II, 455–75.

Bromley, D. B. *Personality description in ordinary language.* New York: Wiley, 1977.

Cheshire, N. M. *The nature of psychodynamic interpretation.* London: Wiley, 1975.

Crosby, F. Evaluating psychohistorical explanations. *Psychohistory Review,* 1979, 7(4), 6–16.

Dray, W. H. *Laws and explanation in history.* Oxford: Oxford University Press, 1957.

Gergen, K. J. Stability, change, and chance in understanding human development. In N. Datan & H. Reese (Eds.), *Life-span developmental psychology: Dialectical perspectives on experimental research.* New York: Academic Press, 1977.

Hempel, C. G. *Aspects of scientific explanation.* New York: Free Press, 1965.

———. *Philosophy of natural science.* Englewood Cliffs, N.J.: Prentice-Hall, 1966.

Hirsch, E. D., Jr. *Validity in interpretation.* New Haven: Yale University Press, 1967.

Hogan, R. *Personality theory: The personological tradition.* Englewood Cliffs, N.J.: Prentice-Hall, 1976.

Horowitz, M. J. *States of mind: Analysis of change in psychotherapy.* New York: Plenum Medical, 1979.

Liebert, R. M. & Spiegler, M. D. *Personality: Strategies and issues.* Homewood, Ill.: Dorsey Press, 1978.

Lubin, A. J. *Stranger on the earth: A psychological biography of Vincent Van Gogh.* New York: Holt, Rinehart & Winston, 1972.

Macalpine, I., & Hunter, R. *George III and the mad business.* New York: Pantheon, 1969.

Meier-Graeffe, J. *Vincent Van Gogh: A biographical study.* (J. Holroyd-Reece, Trans.). New York: Blue Ribbon Books, 1933.

Monroe, R. R. The episodic psychoses of Vincent Van Gogh. *Journal of Nervous and Mental Disease,* 1978, 166, 480–88.

Murray, H. A., et al. *Explorations in personality.* New York: Oxford University Press, 1938.

Nagera, H. *Vincent Van Gogh: A psychological study.* London: Allen & Unwin, 1967.

Popper, K. R. *Conjectures and refutations.* New York: Basic Books, 1972.

Pye, L. Letter to the editor. *Psychohistory Review,* 1979, 8 (3), 50–53.

Rewald, J. *Post-impressionism from Van Gogh to Gauguin.* New York: Museum of Modern Art, 1956.

Schneider, D. E. *The psychoanalyst and the artist.* New York: International Universities Press, 1950.

Schnier, J. The blazing sun: A psychoanalytic approach to Van Gogh. *American Imago,* 1950, 7, 143–62.

Sherwood, M. *The logic of explanation in psychoanalysis.* New York: Academic Press, 1969.

Spence, D. P. Clinical interpretation: Some comments on the nature of evidence. In T. Shapiro (Ed.), *Psychoanalysis and contemporary science* (Vol. V). New York: International Universities Press, 1976.

Westerman Holstijn, A. J. The psychological development of Vincent Van Gogh. *American Imago,* 1951, 8, 239–73.

10

Some Uses of Dynamic Psychology in Political Biography: Case Materials on Woodrow Wilson

Alexander L. George

More so than historical writing at large, biography is selective. By choosing a single individual as his concern, the biographer can focus on those aspects of the historical process which interacted most directly with his subject. The nature of this interaction and, particularly, the extent to which it is reciprocal, is one of the central problems of biography. To what extent was the behavior of the subject culturally and situationally determined? To what extent did it reflect the individuality of his personality? Though variously worded by different writers, this twofold task of the biographer is a familiar and perplexing one.

In a brief but acute statement of the problem, the Committee on Historiography emphasized that the writing of biography requires both a systematic field theory of personality and hypotheses as to social roles.[1] While agreeing with this twofold emphasis, we have chosen for several reasons to focus attention in the present article upon the need for a systematic approach to personality factors. First, it would appear that historians generally are already more favorably disposed to the cultural approach, and better prepared to employ it, than to a systematic handling of personality components in biography. Second, we wish to show by introducing concrete case materials that a systematic personality approach may be necessary and particularly rewarding in the biographical study of innovating leaders, those who attempt to reinterpret and expand the functions of existing roles or to create new roles. We are particularly interested, that is, in "role-determining" as against "role-determined" leadership. At the same time, we agree that the creation or reinterpretation of leadership roles can only be understood in the context of social-historical dynamics and the institutional setting. The "great leader," as Gerth and Mills observe, has often been a man who has successfully managed such institutional dynamics and created new roles of leadership.[2]

We shall draw upon our previously reported study of Woodrow Wilson[3] in order to demonstrate how the personality component in a biography may be handled in a systematic fashion. And we shall attempt to show that dynamic psychology provides a number of hypotheses which can supplement a cultural or role analysis of Wilson's interest in constitution-writing and which permit the biographer to view the relationship between his "Presbyterian conscience" and his political stubbornness in a new light.

SOME DEFICIENCIES OF PSYCHOLOGICAL BIOGRAPHIES

In the past three or four decades historians have occasionally turned to the new field of dynamic psychology for assistance in this task. At the same time, specialists in psychology, especially psychoanalysts, have themselves occasionally attempted to apply the insights and theories of their practice to historical figures.[4] The results of such efforts, from both sides, to merge history and psychology in the writing of political biography have not been encouraging. Even when their purpose was not to debunk a historical figure, most psychoanalytical biographies suffered from pronounced and basic deficiencies.

Three major deficiencies in this type of biography may be briefly mentioned. In the first place, in varying degrees such biographies exaggerate the purely psychological determinants of the political behavior of their subjects. In the cruder of these studies, the subject is represented as if in the grip of powerful unconscious and irrational drives which dictate his every thought and action. Even in more discriminating analyses, the revelation of human motive resulting from incisive insights into the subject's personality can easily oversimplify the complexity of motivation and political action.

Secondly, in viewing adult character and behavior as the legacy of certain early childhood experiences, psychological biographies often oversimplify the process of personality formation and the intricacy of personality structure and functioning. Such a psychological approach is by today's standards inadequate for it overlooks the relevance of important developments in "ego psychology" in the past few decades.[5] Contemporary students of personality emphasize that in the course of his development the individual develops a variety of defenses against underlying anxieties and hostilities. He may learn ways of curbing and controlling tendencies which handicap him in various situations; and he may even devise *constructive* strategies for harnessing personal needs and motivations and directing them into fruitful channels. In other words, the individual attempts to cope simultaneously with the demands of impulse, conscience and reality in developing a philosophy of life, a system of values, a set of attitudes and interests, and in choosing in various situations from among alternative courses of action.[6]

And, finally, to conclude this brief review of the major deficiencies encountered in psychological biographies, one is struck by the fact that the actions of the subject are often interpreted in ways which seem highly speculative and arbitrary. Few investigators in this field have come to grips with the admittedly difficult problem of making rigorous reconstructions of personality factors and plausible interpretations of their role in behavior from the types of historical materials usually available to the biographer. The result is that the use which the biographer makes of dynamic psychology often appears to consist in little more than borrowing certain terms and hypotheses, and superimposing them, more or less arbitrarily upon a smattering of the available historical materials concerning the subject.

PERSONALITY TYPES: THE PROBLEM OF DIAGNOSIS AND CLASSIFICATION

Typologies of personality or character are provided by most of the various schools of psychoanalysis and dynamic psychology. The depiction of a type is usually on the basis of one or more traits, or behavioral tendencies. Often, the characterization of types also includes some indication of the origins and underlying psychodynamics of that type of behavior, which enhances the usefulness of the typology to the biographer. We do not propose to review these typologies here or to attempt to assess their relative worth to the biographer.[7] Rather we wish to consider the status or nature of these personality types and some of the problems which arise in efforts to utilize them in biography.

Most of the types in question are to be understood as being general constructs, or *ideal types*. Though derived from empirical observation, they abstract and deliberately oversimplify reality.[8] Accordingly, their value to the biographer is necessarily limited, since his task is to describe and explain a particular individual in all his concreteness and complexity.

The biographer cannot be satisfied merely to label his subject as constituting an instance of, or bearing a certain resemblance to, a certain personality or character type. To do so oversimplifies the task of making fruitful use of the theories and findings of dynamic psychology and yields results of a limited and disappointing character. Many investigators whose initial attempt to use a personality approach in biography is of this character become disillusioned and abandon the task. They sense that to type their subject, as a "compulsive" for example, tends to caricature him rather than to explain very much of the richness, complexity and variety of his behavior throughout his career.

We are concerned here with a problem not always clearly recognized in the writing of psychological biographies. *Classification* is often confused with *diagnosis*. To tag the subject of the biography with a label or to pigeonhole him in one of a number of existing categories does not in itself provide what the biographer will need most: namely, a discriminating "theory," i.e., a set of assumptions or hypotheses, as to the structure and dynamics of his subject's personality system.

The "diagnosis *vs.* classification" problem also exists in clinical psychiatry where a distinction is sometimes made between the "sponge" and the "file-drawer" clinician.[9] The "sponge"-type clinician attempts to approach his patient with a relatively open mind, trying to derive a theory about that particular patient from an intensive analysis of his behavior and case history. In contrast, the "file-drawer"-type of clinician is more inclined to orient himself to the patient on the basis of general theories and past experience. The one attempts to construct a theory about the patient *de nouveau,* a theory that, as a result, may be highly particularistic; the other stresses gaining insight into the patient by making an astute classification of him on the basis of accumulated theory and experience.

The difference between these clinical approaches is mentioned here in order to point up alternative approaches available to the biographer. As will become clear, we are suggesting that though the biographer should indeed be familiar with available personality theories, he should nonetheless approach his subject as does the "sponge"-type clinician and undertake to develop as discriminating and refined a theory as possible of that particular personality.

In attempting to account for the subject's actions throughout his career, the biographer will have to make specific diagnoses of the operative state of his personality system in numerous situations. To this end, the biographer starts with as good a theory of the subject's personality as he can derive from secondary accounts and from a preliminary inspection of historical materials. Then he reviews chronologically, or developmentally, the history of his subject's behavior, attempting to assess the role that situational and personality factors played in specific instances.[10]

In utilizing a preliminary theory of the subject's personality to make specific diagnoses the biographer in a real sense also "tests" that theory. Detailed analysis of the subject's actions in a variety of individual situations provides new insights into the motivational dynamics of the subject's behavior; these insights, in turn, enable the biographer to progressively refine and improve the theory of the subject's personality with which he started. What the biographer hopes to achieve eventually is an account of the subject's personality that gives coherence and depth to the explanation of his behavior in a variety of situations and that illuminates the more subtle patterns that underlie whatever seeming "inconsistencies" of character and behavior he has displayed.

TWO USES OF PERSONALITY TYPES IN BIOGRAPHY

Despite the general nature of personality and character types, they may be of substantial use to the biographer in several ways. First, knowledge of these types assists the biographer in developing the kind of *preliminary* theory about the personality of his subject to which reference has already been made. Second, familiarity with the psychodynamics of behavior associated with a particular personality or character type provides the biographer with hypotheses for consideration in attempting to account for the actions of his subject, especially those that cannot be easily explained as adequate responses to the situation which confronted him. Let us consider these two general uses in somewhat greater detail.

A major shortcoming in many conventional biographies, including those of Wilson, is that they lack a systematic theory about the subject's personality and motivations. The biographer is usually satisfied to catalogue individual traits exhibited by the subject without exploring their possible interrelationship and their functional significance within the personality as a whole.[11] Various of Wilson's biographers,[12] for example, have called attention to his marked "conscientiousness," "stubbornness," "single-track mind," and various other traits. They have done so, however, without indicating awareness that, according to Freudian theory, these traits are commonly exhibited by "compulsive" persons.

The term "compulsive" today is commonly applied to persons whose lives are regulated by a strict super-ego, or conscience, which dominates their personalities. Perhaps not generally known, however, is the fact that this type of behavior has been carefully studied over a period of many years by many clinicians; as a result, there are a number of detailed analyses and theories of compulsiveness and the compulsive type that attempt to account for the genesis and underlying dynamics of this type of behavior. Later in this paper we shall attempt to show how this rich body of observation and theory can be used by the biographer. It suffices here to observe that biographers of Wilson, being generally unfamiliar with such materials, have not been in a position to assess the significance of individual traits displayed by Wilson in terms of their underlying dynamics.[13]

Occasionally biographers of Wilson have been able, on the basis of an intensive analysis of a particularly well-documented episode in Wilson's career, to infer or to suggest that his choice of action in a particular situation was apparently governed by personal motives other than the aims and values which he was publicly espousing.[14] But generally they have hesitated to make diagnoses of the operative state of Wilson's personality system in specific situations, to explore in any systematic fashion the complexity and deeper levels of his motivation, or to postulate in detail the role of his personality in his political behavior. Therefore, while these biographers have sensed Wilson's personal involvement in politics and called attention to his many contradictions, their portraits of Wilson's personality are inevitably somewhat flat, even though accurately depicting behavioral tendencies at a surface level.

A familiarity with personality and character types identified in the literature of dynamic psychology will assist the biographer to construct a *preliminary* theory, or model, as to the structure and functioning of his subject's personality. For this purpose there are available to the biographer a variety of typologies of personality and character. Some of these are predominantly sociopsychological rather than clinical in their conception and orientation. Not all typologies of personality are comparable, since they have been constructed from different theoretical standpoints, for different purposes and applications. An overlapping can be noted, however, particularly among some of the typologies provided by various schools of psychoanalysis. Thus, for example, the "aggressive" person in Karen Horney's system bears a substantial resemblance to the Freudian concept of the compulsive type. Similarly, Alfred Adler's central emphasis upon the drive to power and superiority as a means of compensation for real or imagined defects finds a place in many other personality theories as well.

Given the variety of alternative typologies available, the biographer must obviously consider a number of them before choosing the type or types that seem most appropriate to his subject and most useful for the specific questions about the subject's motivations and behavior he is trying to clarify.

Personality theorists, Freudian and non-Freudian, have emphasized that the type-constructs formulated by them are not pure types. Rather, they view the personality functioning of an individual as a mixture of several trends, or types, in a more or less dynamic relationship to each other. This observation applies with particular force to Wilson, in whom several diverse trends can be detected.[15] Nonetheless, the present account is limited to discussing the applicability of the compulsive type to Wilson, partly because of limitations of space and partly because we feel that the compulsive component of his personality is particularly important for illuminating the self-defeating aspects of his behavior.

In any case, having found much evidence of compulsiveness and of the compulsive syndrome in the historical accounts of his life and career, we felt justified in adopting as a tentative working theory that Wilson had a compulsive personality.

We then considered his development and behavior in detail from this standpoint, examining the voluminous documentation of his career that is available to the biographer. In doing so, we encountered increasing evidence of behavior on his part that could not easily be subsumed under the simple model of the compulsive type. This forced us to refine and elaborate the theory as to his compulsiveness, and to attempt to state the *conditions* and to characterize the *situations* in which he did and did not behave in a way (for example, stubbornly) that was in accord with the expectations explicit or implicit in the personality model with which we were working.[16]

Gradually, then, the general construct of the compulsive type (which, as already mentioned, is to be taken as an abstraction and deliberate oversimplification of reality) was modified and brought into consonance with the complexities encountered in the individual case at hand. The point was reached when the picture of Wilson's personality that was emerging became too complex to be retained within the bounds of the compulsive model with which we had started. What remained of that model or theory was the notion of an important compulsive component in his personality and functioning. This component, we shall attempt to show, remained of considerable value as an explanatory principle for some of Wilson's political behavior that has puzzled and distressed many of his contemporaries and biographers.

Another major use of typologies and theories of personality to the biographer is that of providing alternative hypotheses for consideration in attempting to account for the actions and behavioral patterns of his subject. Such general hypotheses are not ready-made explanations to be employed arbitrarily or to be superimposed upon the data. Rather, as a statement of the dynamics of behavior and motivation often or typically associated with a certain personality type, they may serve to orient the biographer's effort to explain the actions of his subject.[17] A familiarity with such hypotheses broadens and deepens the biographer's assessment of the aims and values that the subject pursues in a given situation or in a series of situations. Furthermore, it sensitizes him to historical evidence of the possible operation of unconscious or unstated motives he might otherwise overlook.

During the preparation of our study of Wilson we combed the technical literature for hypotheses about the dynamics of motivation and behavior associated with compulsiveness that might illuminate the nature of Wilson's personal involvement in political activities.[18] We hoped to find clues to certain inept and apparently irrational actions on his part and to discover, if possible, a consistent pattern or thread in the various inconsistencies of behavior and character he displayed.

If Wilson is not the simple clinical stereotype of a compulsive, neither can he be regarded as a full-blown neurotic. True, one cannot read, for example, Karen Horney's insightful and penetrating descriptions of neurotic drives and of the neurotic character structure without being struck by the applicability of much of what she says to Wilson. But these descriptions are applicable only to a certain point and, upon reflection, one is on balance equally or more impressed with the extent to which Wilson's behavior and career *diverge* from those of her patients. This divergence from the clinical picture concerns precisely the critical question whether the neurotically disposed individual is able to deal adequately with his conflicts and hence retains the ability to function effectively.

For Wilson was, after all, a highly successful person. He was able to overcome a severe disturbance in childhood development; thereafter, not only did he keep fairly well in check the compulsive and neurotic components of his personality but he succeeded in large measure in harnessing them constructively to the achievement of socially productive purposes.[19] To the clinical psychologist, therefore, Wilson is interesting as much because he was able to overcome childhood difficulties and to perform as successfully as he did in public life, as he is because of the pathological pattern of self-defeating behavior he tended to repeat on several occasions during his public career.[20]

COMPULSIVENESS AND THE COMPULSIVE TYPE

To indicate briefly what is meant by compulsiveness and the compulsive type of personality is not an easy task since these concepts are employed somewhat differently within the various theoretical schools which comprise dynamic psychology. The point to be made here is that the existence of different theoretical orientations and, particularly, of important lacunae in knowledge and theory within the field of dynamic psychology need not prevent the biographer from making fruitful use of systematic personality theory as a source of hypotheses that serve to orient and give direction to his own research.[21]

In any case, the usefulness of the technical literature to the biographer will be enhanced if the distinction is kept in mind between the question of the *origins* of compulsiveness and compulsive traits, about which there are various views, and the *dynamics* of such behavior, about which there is less disagreement. Similarly, the biographer will observe that specialists seem able to agree more readily on a characterization of the quality of compulsive behavior than on a list of specific traits common to all compulsive persons.

In Freudian theory various correlations are predicted between disturbances of different stages in libido development and the emergence of certain adult character traits. Disturbances in one of these stages of development leads, according to the theory, to the presence of orderliness, stinginess, and stubbornness in adult behavior.[22] These are general traits, or broad tendencies, that manifest themselves more specifically in a variety of ways. By combing the technical literature one can easily construct a richer, more elaborate list of traits which together comprise the syndrome or constellation.[23]

Thus, for example, the general trait "orderliness" may manifest itself in (a) "cleanliness" (corporeal, symbolic); (b) "conscientiousness" (single-track mind, concentration, drive, pedantism, reliability, punctuality, punctiliousness and thoroughness); (c) "regularity" (according to spatial and temporal aspects); (d) "plannedness"; (e) "norm conformity."[24]

Most personality and character types are usually described, at least in the first instance, in terms of certain manifest behavioral traits such as those that have been listed. If the description of a type does not link the traits in question with a theory of personality structure and motivational dynamics, the type-construct will obviously be of little value for motivational and situational analysis of an individual's behavior. At the same time, however, it is overly sanguine to expect that relationships between most manifest behavior traits and their inner, subjective functions for the personality will be of a simple one-to-one character. For, as clinical psychologists have particularly emphasized, the same item of manifest behavior may fulfill different functions for different personalities or, at different times, for the same individual. Particularly the political and social behavior of an individual, in which the biographer is most interested, is not likely to reflect single motives; it is more likely to be the outcome of a complex interplay of several motives and of efforts on the part of the person to adjust inner needs and strivings to one another as well as to external reality considerations.

A personality type construct is potentially more useful, therefore, if it is associated with a more or less distinctive type of motivational dynamics, whether or not this be invariably accompanied by a set of distinctive behavioral traits.

From this standpoint, leaving aside for the present the question of its validity, the Freudian concept of the compulsive type is a particularly rich one in that it includes, in addition to the syndrome of traits already noted, a rather explicit and detailed set of structural-dynamic hypotheses of this kind.

We shall not attempt to recapitulate the rather involved and technical set of structural-dynamic hypotheses associated with the compulsive type in Freudian theory. Of immediate interest here is the fact that orderliness and stubborness in persons of this type are said to derive in part from a desire for power or domination, which in turn is said to be related to a more basic need for self-esteem, or security.[25] Thus, according to the technical literature compulsives often show a marked interest in imposing orderly systems upon others, an activity from which they derive a sense of power. They also hold fast obstinately to their own way of doing things. They dislike to accommodate themselves to arrangements imposed from without, but expect immediate compliance from other people as soon as they have worked out a definite arrangement, plan or proposal of their own.

In the spheres of activity in which they seek power gratifications, compulsives are sensitive to interference. They may take advice badly (or only under special circumstances). Often they exhibit difficulties in deputing work to others, being convinced at bottom that they can do everything (in this sphere) better than others. This conviction is sometimes exaggerated to the point that they believe they are unique. Negativeness, secretiveness and vindictiveness are traits often displayed by compulsives. (Considerable evidence of most of these traits and tendencies, too, can be found in the historical materials on Wilson, many of them being noted by contemporaries and biographers.)[26]

While particularly that aspect of Freudian theory that regards interferences with libido development as the genesis of adult character traits has been criticized, the existence of certain constellations of adult traits, as in this instance, is less controversial and, in fact, appears to enjoy some empirical support.[27]

In revisions and elaborations of Freudian theory somewhat less emphasis is often placed upon specifying a distinctive content of compulsive behavior. Karen Horney, for example, regards compulsiveness as a characteristic quality of all neurotic needs. Thus, the craving for affection, power and prestige, and the ambition, submissiveness and withdrawal which different neurotics manifest all have a desperate, rigid, indiscriminate and insatiable quality, i.e., the quality of compulsiveness.[28]

Much of common to various of these formulations has been summarized in Harold D. Lasswell's account of the functional role of the compulsive dynamism in the personality system and of the general character of the circumstances in which it is adopted.[29] Thus, the compulsive dynamism is one of several possible defensive measures a child may adopt as a way out of an acute tension-producing situation that may arise during the course of socialization and learning. Tension is produced when a relatively elaborate set of requirements are imposed upon the child and reinforced by a system of rewards and punishments of a special intensity and applied in such manner so that deprivations and indulgences are balanced. One possible defensive measure against the ensuing tension is the adoption of a blind urge to act with intensity and rigidity, i.e., the dynamism of compulsiveness.

The reasons and conditions for the emergence of compulsiveness are, as has been suggested, somewhat difficult to formulate precisely. However, in making use of available knowledge of the compulsive personality for purposes of political biography, an answer to the causal question is not essential. Whatever creates a given personality dynamism, the dynamism itself—which is what interests the biographer the most—can be fairly readily identified in accounts of the subject's behavior.

In Wilson's case, even the circumstances under which the compulsive dynamism was adopted are richly suggested in materials collected by the official biographer.[30] Thus, accounts of early efforts at the boy's education, in which the father played a leading role, strongly suggest the sort of acute tension-producing situation that, we have already noted, is considered by specialists as predisposing to the adoption of the compulsive dynamism. This, however, evidently was not Wilson's initial method of coping with the tension-inducing situation; rather, for quite a while his method of defense took the form of a tendency to withdraw from the situation. For the time being the boy was unable, perhaps out of fear of failure, or unwilling, perhaps out of resentment, to cooperate with his father's efforts to advance his intellectual development. Wilson's early "slowness" (which specialists today might well consider a case of reading retardation based on emotional factors) was a matter of considerable concern to his family; it manifested itself most strikingly in his not learning his letters until he was nine and not learning to read readily until the age of eleven.[31]

At about this time the boy showed signs of beginning to cooperate actively with his father's efforts to tutor him and to make prodigious efforts to satisfy the perfectionist demands that the Presbyterian minister levied upon his son.[32] One can only speculate at the reasons for the change at this time; possibly it was connected with the birth of a younger brother when Wilson was ten. (Wilson had two older sisters but no younger brothers or sisters until this time; he himself recalled that he had clung to his mother and was laughed at as a "mama's boy" until he was a great big fellow.)

In any case, it is easy thereafter to find evidence of a compulsive bent to the young adolescent's personality. It requires no great familiarity with the technical literature on such matters to detect indications of compulsiveness in the youth's extreme conscientiousness, the manner in which he drove himself repeatedly to physical breakdowns, and the singleness of purpose he displayed in applying himself to the task of achieving knowledge and skill in the sphere of competence—politics and oratory—with which he quickly identified his ambitions.[33]

WILSON'S INTEREST IN CONSTITUTIONS

In the remainder of this paper we should like to develop the case, mainly by way of illustrative materials from the study of Wilson, for supplementing cultural and historical components in biography by an intensive and relatively systematic appraisal of personality.

A number of Wilson's biographers, including the official biographer,[34] have been struck by the interest in constitutions he displayed from early youth. Beginning in his fourteenth year he wrote or revised a half dozen constitutions, an activity that culminated in the Covenant of the League of Nations. It is our thesis that this activity on his part reflects the type of interest in order and power that compulsive persons often display. (See above, p.140.) In other words, he was motivated in part (though not exclusively) by a desire to impose orderly systems upon others, deriving therefrom a sense of power or domination.

The historian will quickly object, and rightly so, offering a more obvious counter-hypothesis, which is certainly plausible; namely that Wilson's interest in writing constitutions was culturally determined. After all, it was part of the belief system of the age that progress in human affairs was to be achieved by such instrumentalities as better constitutions, institutional reform, etc. The fact that Wilson wrote or revised many constitutions, therefore, does not necessarily attest to a personal interest in order and power.

Is it possible to demonstrate that Wilson's motivation in the matter did not stem exclusively from identification with a role that was socially approved? Or is such a question entirely out of the reach of the historian? In the following remarks we shall attempt to show that such questions are capable of being dealt with on the basis of the materials and method of the historian.

First, why Wilson and not someone else? Why, in other words, did the belief system in question impress itself particularly on Wilson? Is it not more than a coincidence that in every club he joined as a youth he seized the earliest opportunity, often making it the first order of business, to revise its constitution in order to transform the club into a miniature House of Commons? Granted that constitution-making was part of the existing cultural and political ethos and that admiration for the British system was already widespread among American students of government, why should the task of revising the constitution and political structure of these groups always fall to Wilson? Why were none of these constitutions revised along desirable lines by others, before Wilson joined these clubs? It would seem that among his contemporaries it was Wilson who found constitution-making a particularly attractive occupation. The readiness with which he accepted for himself a role that was, to be sure, culturally sanctioned makes the inference plausible that personal motives were strongly engaged by the possibility that constitution writing afforded of ordering the relations of his fellow-beings.[35]

Secondly, what evidence can be found of an unconscious motive or need to impose orderly systems upon others? If such a motive exists, we may expect appropriate pleasurable feelings to ensue from its gratification. However, we cannot reasonably expect that the pleasure experienced by the individual in such instances will be fully articulated under ordinary circumstances. Hence, in the type of historical materials on the subject's inner life usually available to the biographer we can expect only episodic and fragmentary evidence of the fact that an activity on his part has satisfied deeply felt personality needs. This is in fact what we find in this case. For example, after rewriting the constitution of the Johns Hopkins debating society and transforming it into a "House of Commons," Wilson reported to his fiancee the great pleasure he had derived from the project: "It is characteristic of my whole self that I take so much pleasure in these proceedings of this society. . . . I have a sense of power in dealing with men collectively that I do not feel always in dealing with them singly."[36]

That constitution-writing had a deep personal meaning for Wilson is further suggested by the fact that such activities were always instrumental to his desire to exercise strong leadership. It is rather obvious even from historical accounts that rewriting constitutions was for Wilson a means of restructuring those institutional environments in which *he* wanted to exercise strong leadership. He wished to restructure the political arena in these instances in order to enhance the possibility of influencing and controlling others by means of oratory. This was a skill in which he was already adept as an adolescent and to the perfection of which he assiduously labored for years. In the model House of Commons which Wilson created, and in which as the outstanding debater he usually became "Prime Minister," independent leadership was possible and, as Wilson had foreseen, the skillful, inspirational orator could make his will prevail.[37]

From an early age, then, Wilson's scholarly interest in the workings of American political institutions was an adjunct of his ambition to become a great statesman. He wished to exercise power with great initiative and freedom from crippling controls or interference. The relationship between Wilson's theories of leadership and his own ambitions and changing life situation, which we cannot recapitulate here, is revealing in this respect.[38] Suffice it to say that when Wilson's career development is studied from this standpoint considerable light is thrown on the intriguing question of the role of personal motivations in political inventiveness and creativity. Political psychologists have hypothesized that a compulsive interest in order and power is often to be found in strong political leaders who were great institution-builders and who made it their task to transform society. The case study of Wilson lends support to this general hypothesis.

To posit such personal, unconscious components in the political motivation of some leaders by no means excludes the simultaneous operation of cultural determinants. There is no doubt in Wilson's case that his personal interest in order and power was defined and channelized by the cultural and political matrix of the times. Moreover, concrete opportunities to rewrite constitutions and to exercise and perfect his talents as orator-leader were provided by existing situations in which he found himself or that he actively sought out.

Thus, the external situation in which the individual exists necessarily defines and delimits the field in which personality develops and in which personality needs and traits find expression. On the other hand, the interaction between the personality of a political leader and the milieu in which he operates may be, in an important sense, a reciprocal one. A leader's basic needs and values, his motives and dispositions, shape his perception of the situations that confront him and influence his definition and evaluation of the choices of action open to him.[39]

What is gained by attributing motivations of this character to a political leader? In this case, what difference does it make whether Wilson's interest in writing constitutions had the type of personal motivation in question? The postulate of a deep-seated, unconscious interest in imposing orderly systems upon others as a means of achieving a sense of power, we believe, accounts in part (but only in part) for Wilson's peculiar involvement in the League Covenant and in the making of the peace, the many strands of which we have attempted to document in our book. The biographer who is sensitive to the possible role of unconscious motivation is struck, for example, by the fact that it was Wilson's constant concern to reserve to himself final authorship of the Covenant, even though none of the ideas that entered into it were original with him, and that he appeared to derive peculiar pleasure from giving his own stamp to the phraseology of the document.[40]

Similarly, the postulate that Wilson derived from constitution-writing gratification of unconscious personal needs for power and domination may account in part (again only in part) for the tenacity with which he resisted efforts by various Senators to rewrite parts of the Covenant, which in some cases amounted merely to an alteration of its wording. Wilson appears to have subconsciously experienced all such efforts as attempts to "interfere" with or "dominate" him in a sphere of competence that he regarded as his own preserve.

Such an interpretation, taken alone, will seem highly speculative. The reader, we hope, will find it more plausible in the context of the theory of Wilson's personality that we have worked out and utilized in detail for purposes of analyzing Wilson's entire development and career. Briefly paraphrased here, the theory is that political leadership was a sphere of competence Wilson carved out for himself (from early adolescence on!) in order to derive therefrom compensation for the damaged self-esteem branded into his spirit as a child. Particularly when performing in his favored role as interpreter and instrument of the moral aspirations of the people, he considered himself as uniquely endowed and virtually infallible. His personality needs were such that in the sphere of competence, which he regarded as peculiarly his own, he had to function "independently" and without "interference" in order to gain the compensatory gratification he sought from the political arena. These we believe to have been the underlying dynamics of his somewhat autocratic style of leadership to which many contemporaries and biographers have called attention.[41]

THE RELATIONSHIP BETWEEN WILSON'S MORALITY AND HIS STUBBORNNESS

The extraordinary role of "conscience" and "stubbornness" in Wilson's political behavior has been noted by numerous of his contemporaries and biographers. It has often been said that Wilson's refusal to compromise on certain notable occasions, particularly as President of Princeton and as President of the United States, was a reflection of his "Presbyterian conscience." When great principles were at stake, as on these occasions, he could not bring himself to compromise. In such situations Wilson characteristically portrayed himself as confronted by a choice between dishonorable compromise of principles and an uncompromising struggle for moral political goals. Accordingly, for him, there could be no alternative but to fight for truth and morality against all opposition, whatever the consequences.

No matter that others (including careful historians such as Arthur S. Link)[42] find his characterization of the situation in these terms unconvincing; that in fact Wilson was not really confronted by such an unpleasant either-or choice. The fact remains that *Wilson* saw it thus. However much one may deplore the political consequences of his refusal to compromise, so the argument goes, surely the only valid conclusion that can be drawn is that Wilson was possessed by an unusually strong sense of morality and rectitude that exercised a determining influence upon his political behavior.

It has seemed plausible, therefore, to attribute great importance to the Presbyterian culture in which Wilson was reared and from which, to condense this familiar thesis, he derived his unusual conscience and sense of morality.

Such a thesis must cope with various questions that can be legitimately raised. For example: If Wilson's refusal to compromise in certain instances is simply a matter of his Presbyterian conscience, then what of the numerous instances in which that same conscience was no bar to highly expedient, if not opportunistic political behavior on his part?[43] Clearly, at the very least a more refined theory as to the nature of the Presbyterian conscience and of its influence on political behavior is needed.

This general question is merely posed here. Instead of pursuing it further on this occasion let us consider, rather, the usefulness of looking at the relationship between Wilson's morality and his political stubbornness in terms of what is known about the dynamics of the compulsive type. To examine the problem of Wilson in these terms is not to deny the importance of his Presbyterian upbringing or related cultural factors. Nor does it thereby ignore the possibility, which need not be explored here, that compulsive personalities are or were frequently to be found among members of the Presbyterian subculture. Indeed, the Presbyterian ethos no doubt provided reinforcement and rationalization for Wilson's stubbornness. We have elsewhere observed that such a creed produces men of conviction who find it possible to cling to their principles no matter what the opposition. The feeling that they are responsible, through their conscience, only to God, gives them a sense of freedom from temporal authority and the opinions of their fellow men.[44]

The problem of Wilson's convictions that he was "right" in refusing to compromise, and was acting in conformity with moral standards, however, is more complex than it appears at first glance, as we will try to show.

The analysis of "stubborn" behavior in compulsive personalities indicates that it is often a form of aggression. Thus aggressive tendencies, usually repressed, find expression in situations that actually comprise, or can be represented by the individual to himself as comprising, struggles on behalf of goals that receive strong endorsement by the conscience. The operative mechanism is referred to as "idealization" and has been described in the following terms: "The realization that an ideal requirement is going to be fulfilled brings to the ego an increase in self-esteem. This may delude it into ignoring the fact that through the idealized actions. There is an expression of instincts that ordinarily would have been repressed. . . .the ego relaxes its ordinary testing of reality and of impulses so that instinctual [in this case, aggressive] impulses may emerge relatively uncensored."[45] One is reminded in this connection of Wilson's repeated expressions of his "pleasure" and "delight" at an opportunity for a good fight, on behalf of a good cause, and his highly aggressive outbursts against opponents who blocked his high moral purposes. The instinctual nature of these eruptions is suggested by their extreme and intemperate quality; they were often personally unbecoming as well as politically inexpedient, and on occasion left Wilson shortly thereafter much chagrined at his loss of self-control.

Whatever the satisfactions of an uncompromising fight for what is "right," it may lead the compulsive person into essentially immoral behavior, behavior which strongly conflicts with role requirements and expectations. Given a culture in which political power is shared and in which the rules of the game enjoin compromise among those who participate in making political decisions for the community, to insist stubbornly that others submit to your own conception of what is truth and morality may in fact contravene political morality. The "right" thing for Wilson to do in the critical phases of his struggles at Princeton and with the Senate in the League matter, in terms of the prevailing political mores, was to have worked together with others who legitimately held power in order to advance as far as possible towards desirable political goals.

Wilson was well aware of this requirement. As a historian and astute student of American political institutions, he knew very well that the "right" thing for a statesman to do is to be practical and accomplish what he can. And he had expressed himself often on this very problem. In an address before the McCormick Theological Seminary, in the fall of 1909, for example, he had said: "I have often preached in my political utterances the doctrine of expediency, and I am an un-abashed disciple of that doctrine. What I mean to say is, you cannot carry the world forward as fast as a few select individuals think. The individuals who have the vigor to lead must content themselves with a slackened pace and go only so fast as they can be followed. They must not be impractical. They must not be impossible. They must not insist upon getting at once what they know they cannot get."[46]

However, at several critical junctures in his public career, when he found his righteous purposes blocked by opponents who would not bend to his will, Wilson did not do the "right" thing; he did not compromise or accommodate, even when friends and political associates enjoined him to do so. Rather, he stubbornly per-sisted in his course and helped bring about his own personal defeat and the defeat of worthwhile measures which he was championing.

It seems, then, that we are confronted here by a form of self-defeating behavior in which the role of "conscience" in political stubbornness is perhaps much more complex than is implied in the familiar thesis of Wilson's "Presbyterian con-science" and his stiff-necked "morality."

But why must stubborn refusal to compromise be pushed to the point of self-defeat and the frustration of desirable legislation if not for Wilson's stated reason that he would have found it immoral to compromise great principles? Once again the literature on compulsiveness provides an alternative set of hypotheses with which to assess the available historical data. It is our thesis, which we have tried to document elsewhere,[47] that Wilson's stubborn refusals to compromise in sit-uations where true morality and the requirements of his role demanded accom-modation created feelings of guilt within him. He was vaguely disturbed by what he subconsciously sensed to be his own personal involvement in the fights with his opponents. The greater the stubbornness (a form of aggression against his opponents), the greater the inner anxiety at violating the moral injunction to compromise, which was a very real requirement of his political conscience.

This predicament was worked out in the following manner: stubborn refusal to compromise was maintained to the point where Wilson could demonstrate his "moral superiority" over his opponents. This could be achieved by manip-ulating the situation so that his opponents were also involved in "immoral" be-havior, for example, by permitting their dislike of Wilson to warp their political good sense, by conspiring to defeat Wilson despite the merits of the issue at stake, by refusing to support desirable proposals just because he was championing them, etc. Thus, stubbornness was maintained so that, should it not succeed in forcing the capitulation of his opponents, it would provoke his defeat by selfish and immoral opponents. Thereby, he could at least assuage his anxiety and guilt for, whatever his "crime," it was outweighed by the demonstration in defeat of his "moral superiority" over his opponents.

These, we believe, were the underlying dynamics of the search for martyrdom which other writers[48] as well have seen in Wilson's ill-fated Western speaking tour on behalf of the League of Nations. Whether the available historical materials which we have cited in support of this thesis render it sufficiently plausible and convincing must be left to individual judgment. Instead of rephrasing the evidence and reasoning already presented on its behalf in our book, we shall confine our-selves here to noting that the mechanisms described above, as underlying the possible quest for martyrdom, are very well described in the literature on com-pulsive stubbornness.

> What is usually called stubbornness in the behavior of adult persons is an attempt to use other persons as instruments in the struggle with the super-ego. By provoking people to be unjust, they strive for a feeling of moral superiority which is needed to increase their self-esteem as a counter-balance against the pressure of the super-ego.[49]
>
> The stubborn behavior is maintained the more obstinately, the more an inner feeling exists that it is impossible to prove what needs to be proven, and that one is actually in the wrong.... The feeling, "Whatever I do is still less wicked than what has been done to me," is needed as a weapon against the super-ego and, if successful, may bring relief from feelings of guilt.[50]

In brief, therefore, the very "morality" in terms of which Wilson could initially legitimize the open expression of pent-up aggression and hostility ensnared him in profoundly immoral political behavior. His repeated protestations as the struggle with his opponents wore on that he had to do what was "right" and what conscience demanded were, in fact, a cloak for activity that was contrary to the requirements of his leadership role and some of the demands of his own conscience. The repeated protestations that he was acting merely as an instrument of the people's will and had no personal stakes in the battle were the external manifestation of desperate efforts to still inner doubts of the purity of his mo-tivation in refusing compromise and to controvert the knowledge that gnawed from within that he was obstructing his own cause.[51] We have here an instance not of stern morality but of a type of rationalization which has been labelled the "moralization" mechanism, i.e., a tendency to interpret things as if they were in accord with ethical standards when they are actually (and subconsciously known to be) in striking contrast to them.[52]

Thus did Wilson go down to tragic defeat. A subtle personal involvement in political struggle prevented him from anchoring his actions in the profound wis-dom of the maxim: "There comes a time in the life of every man when he must give up his principles and do what he thinks is right."[53]

THE SELF-DEFEATING PATTERN IN WILSON'S CAREER

The thesis of a self-defeating dynamism in Wilson's personality gains in plausibility from evidence that it was part of a pattern which tended to repeat itself under similar conditions during his career.[54] A number of Wilson's biographers have noted that Wilson's defeat in the fight for the League fits into a pattern of behavior he had displayed earlier in public life. Thus, after a painstaking analysis of the bitter and unsuccessful struggle Wilson waged with his opponents at Princeton, Professor Link was led to remark that "a political observer, had he studied carefully Wilson's career as president of Princeton University, might have forecast accurately the shape of things to come during the period when Wilson was president of the United States." Calling the former period a microcosm of the latter, Link ascribed to Wilson's uncompromising battles both in the graduate college controversy and in the League of Nations battle with the Senate "the character and proportions of a Greek tragedy."[55]

Similarly, writing many years before, Edmund Wilson, the distinguished man of letters, saw in the same events of Wilson's career evidence of a curious cyclical pattern that can be detected in the lives of other historical figures as well:

> It is possible to observe in certain lives, where conspicuously superior abilities are united with serious deficiencies, not the progress in a career or vocation that carries the talented man to a solid position or a definite goal, but a curve plotted over and over again and always dropping from some flight of achievement to a steep descent into failure.[56]

The type of enigmatic personality described here by a humanist is one which has been of long-standing interest to the clinician as well. Influenced by Freud's earlier description and analysis of neurotic careers, Franz Alexander in 1930 presented what has become a classical psychoanalytical account of this general character type.[57] In many cases, driven by unconscious motives, persons of this type alternate between committing a transgression and then seeking punishment. Thereby, their careers may exhibit "alternating phases of rise and abrupt collapse," a pattern indicating that "aggressive and self-destructive tendencies" run along together. "The neurotic character," Alexander continues, "has fired the literary imagination since time immemorial. They are nearly all strong individualities who struggle in vain to hold the anti-social tendencies of their nature in check. They are born heroes who are predestined to a tragic fate."

Let us examine more closely the repetitive pattern of behavior that observers working from different standpoints have detected in his career.[58] As President of Princeton, Governor of New Jersey, and President of the United States, Wilson gained impressive early successes only to encounter equally impressive political deadlocks or set-backs later on. He entered each of these offices at a time when reform was the order of the day, and with a substantial fund of goodwill to draw upon. In each case there was an initial period during which the type of strong leadership he exercised in response to his inner needs coincided sufficiently with the type of leadership the external situation required for impressive accomplishment. He drove the faculty and trustees at Princeton to accomplish an unprecedented series of reforms. The New Jersey legislature of 1911 was a triumph of productivity in his hands. Later, he exacted a brilliant performance from the Sixty-Third Congress of the United States.

We are forced to recognize, therefore, that Wilson's personal involvements contributed importantly to the measure of political accomplishment he attained. In each position, however, his compulsive ambition and imperious methods helped in time to generate the type of bitter opposition that blocked further successes and threatened him with serious defeats. Wilson was skillful in the tactics of leadership only so long as it was possible to get exactly what he wanted from the trustees or the legislature. He could be adept and inventive in finding ways of mobilizing potential support. He could be, as in the first year of the Governorship and in the "honeymoon" period of the Presidency, extremely cordial, if firm; gracious, if determined; and generally willing to go through the motions of consulting and granting deference to legislators whose support he needed. It is this phase of his party leadership that excited the admiration of contemporaries, historians, and political scientists alike. It is essential to note, however, that Wilson's skillfulness in these situations always rested somewhat insecurely upon the expectation that he would be able to push through his proposed legislation in essentially unadulterated form. (As Wilson often put it, he was willing to accept alterations of "detail," but not of the "principles" of his legislative proposals.)

Once opposition crystalized in sufficient force to threaten the defeat or marked alteration of his proposed legislation, however, Wilson was faced with a different type of situation. Skillful political behavior—the logic of the situation—now demanded genuine consultation to explore the basis of disagreement and to arrive at mutual concessions, bargains, and formulas that would ensure passage of necessary legislation. In this type of situation Wilson found it difficult to operate on the basis of expediential considerations and at times proved singularly gauche as a politician. Once faced with genuine and effective opposition to a legislative proposal *to which he had committed his leadership aspirations,* Wilson became rigidly stubborn and tried to force through his measure without compromising it.[59] The greater the opposition, the greater his determination not to yield. He must win on his own terms or not at all!

Personally involved in these struggles, Wilson was incapable of realistically assessing the situation and of contriving skillful strategies for dividing the opposition and winning over a sufficient number to his side. Both at Princeton and later in the battle with the Senate over ratification of the treaty, Wilson was incapable of dealing effectively in his own interest with the more moderate of his opponents. In the heat of the battle, he could tolerate no ambiguity and could recognize no legitimate intermediate position. He tended to lump together all of his opponents. In such crises, therefore, his leadership was strongly divisive rather than unifying. He alienated the potential support of moderate elements who strongly sympathized with his general aims but felt some modification of his proposals to be necessary. Instead of modest concessions to win a sufficient number of moderates over, he stubbornly insisted upon his own position and rudely rebuffed their overtures, thus driving them into the arms of his most bitter and extreme opponents.[60] It was his singular ineptness in the art of political accommodation, once the battle was joined, which was at bottom responsible for some of Wilson's major political defeats at Princeton and in the Presidency.

In these situations—when opposition crystalized and threatened to block Wilson's plan—the desire to succeed in achieving a worthwhile goal, in essence if not in exact form, became of less importance than to maintain equilibrium of the personality system. He seems to have experienced opposition to his will in such situations as an unbearable threat to his self-esteem. To compromise in these circumstances was to submit to domination in the very sphere of power and political leadership in which he sought to repair his damaged self-esteem. Opposition to his will, therefore, set into motion disruptive anxieties and brought to the surface long-smouldering aggressive feelings that, as a child, he had not dared to express. The ensuing struggle for his self-esteem led, on the political level, to the type of stubborn, self-defeating behavior and the search for moral superiority over his opponents that we have already described.

NOTES

1 *The Social Sciences in Historical Study: A Report of the Committee on Historiography,* Social Science Research Council, Bulletin 64, 1954, pp. 153–54. By "field theory of personality" the Committee had in mind one which takes into account the fact that " 'external factor,' not just childhood training, set norms and incentives and influence motivation and codes of conduct," (See also ibid., p. 61.).

2 Hans Gerth and C. Wright Mills, *Character and Social Structure* (New York, 1953), chapter xiv, "The Sociology of Leadership," See also fn. 35, pp. 87, 88.

3 A. L. George and J. L. George, *Woodrow Wilson and Colonel House: A Personality Study* (New York, 1956). (Hereafter referred to as *WW & CH.*)

4 For a recent review of such studies see John A. Garraty, "The Interrelations of Psychology and Biography," *Psychological Bulletin* 51, No. 6 (1954): 569–82. See also Gordon W. Allport, *The Use of Personal Documents in Psychological Science,* Social Science Research Council Bulletin 49, 1942.

5 For a brief review of this development see Calvin S. Hall and Gardner Lindzey, *Theories of Personality* (New York, 1957), pp. 64–65, 271–72.

6 For a useful statement of major trends in social psychology and personality theory see Chapter 2, "Converging Approaches," in M. Brewster Smith, Jerome S. Bruner and Robert W. White, *Opinions and Personality* (New York, 1956).
For a useful summary and synthesis of the ways in which unconscious needs find expression in political behavior see Robert E. Lane, *Political Life* (Glencoe, Illinois, 1959), chapter 9.

7 Useful accounts of some of these typologies, and others drawn partly from social-psychological standpoints, are available in Ruth L. Monroe, *Schools of Psychoanalytic Thought* (New York, 1955); Harold D. Lasswell, *Power and Personality* (New York, 1948); Robert E. Lane, "Political Character and Political Analysis," *Psychiatry* 16(1953):387–98. On trends in the study of political leadership, see Lester G. Seligman, "The Study of Political Leadership," *American Political Science Review* 44(December 1950):904–15.

8 On this general point, see Gardner Murphy, *Personality: A Biosocial Approach to Origins and Structure* (New York and London, 1974), pp. 749–52.

9 I am indebted to Dr. David Hamburg, Chairman, Psychiatry Department, Stanford University, for bringing this to my attention.

10 The need for developmental analysis of personality that starts with some preliminary theory, or set of hypotheses, has been frequently emphasized by those writing on the problems of biography. See for example the following statement by the historian Thomas C. Cochran: "Faced with the task of constructing an interpretive biography, the investigator trained in

psychological methods would formulate hypotheses as he started work on the early life of his subject-hypotheses as to what sort of person the man would prove to be when he later became involved in different types of situations. A systematic testing of these hypotheses against the evidence provided at different stages in the life history would not only provide clues to the understanding of motives but would also focus the biography sharply on the processes of personality development." (In *The Social Sciences in Historical Study: A Report of the Committee on Historiography,* Social Science Research Council, Bulletin 64, 1954, p. 67.)

11 Much dissatisfaction has been expressed in recent times with the conventional "trait" approach to the study of personality and leadership. See, for example, Cecil A. Gibb, "The Principles and Traits of Leadership," *Journal of Abnormal and Social Psychology* 42(1947):267–84: Alvin Gouldner, *Studies in Leadership* (New York, 1950).

12 Among the many useful personality sketches and interpretations of Wilson see particularly those recently provided by Arthur S. Link, *Wilson: The New Freedom* (Princeton, 1956), pp. 61ff., 93–144; John A. Garraty, "Woodrow Wilson: A Study in Personality," *The South Atlantic Quarterly* 56, No. 2 (April, 1957):176–85; John Morton Blum, *Woodrow Wilson and the Politics of Morality* (Boston, 1956).
The importance of personality is emphasized particularly in Garraty's account, which runs parallel to our own at many points.

13 Thus Blum refers only parenthetically to Wilson's "compulsiveness" and his "obsessive sense of unrest" (op. cit., pp. 5, 11, 75). Though he has explored the technical literature on compulsive behavior, Blum did not attempt a methodical exploitation of it in preparing his study of Wilson. (Personal communication to the author.)
The compulsive nature of Wilson's ambition and political style, his inability to pace his demands for reform more expediently, was earlier grasped by the official biographer (Ray Stannard Baker, *Woodrow Wilson: Life and Letters* (New York, 1927), II, pp. 153, 244–45; V. p. 119); by Link (see for example Wilson: *The Road to the White House* (Princeton, 1947), pp. viii–ix, 45, 90); by Edmund Wilson, "Woodrow Wilson at Princeton," *Shores of Light* (New York, 1952), pp. 312–13; and by Edward S. Corwin, in *Woodrow Wilson: Some Princeton Memories,* ed. William Starr Myers, pp. 34–35.

14 See, for example, Arthur L. Link's perceptive account of Wilson's highly revealing reaction when his opponents at Princeton unexpectedly offered to accept a compromise proposal to which he had earlier committed himself. (Op. cit., pp. 69–71, 75–76; see also *WW & CH,* 42–43.)

15 Thus, a fuller statement of the personality trends or types that can be detected in Wilson's personality would, in Freudian terms, probably have to include reference to the "oral character" and the "neurotic character" (see pp. 92–93), as well as to the compulsive type. Similarly, if Karen Horney's typology is employed Wilson would probably have to be described as an amalgam of her "compliant," "aggressive" and "detached" personality types. See K. Horney, *Our Inner Conflicts* (New York, 1945).
It should be noted that some of the "contradictions" in Wilson's character, often noted by contemporaries and biographers, can be understood in terms of the combination of trends, or types, of which his personality was composed.

16 See *WW & CH,* pp. 115–22.

17 I have omitted from this paper a discussion of the historian's method for explaining the "subjective" side of action (the "logic-of-the-situation" approach), and of the prospects for merging it with that of the clinician's. These prospects are not unfavorable, though the task is admittedly difficult. Both the historian and the clinician (as well as the political scientist!) are interested in intensive causal analysis of the single case and employ for this purpose a variant of the same type of interpretive procedure.

18 A useful, detailed summary of theories about the dynamics of behavior in compulsives is provided in Otto Fenichel, *The Psychoanalytic Theory of Neurosis* (New York, 1945), pp. 268–310, 487–88, 530–31.

19 On this point see also *WW & CH,* p. 320.

20 We must reserve for another occasion an effort to account for Wilson's development of a viable personality organization and the ability to function as successfully as he did.

21 The fact that there are various specialized terminologies within the field of dynamic psychology and that members of the various schools at times state their differences polemically tends to obscure the wide area of fundamental agreement among them and the fact that an important body of knowledge and insight into human behavior has been gradually developed around a common dynamic point of view. Moreover, dynamic psychology has based itself more recently upon a core of assumptions common to a number of approaches to the study of behavior: psychoanalysis, social anthropology, social psychology and learning theory. (See, for example, O. H. Mowrer and C. Kluckhohn, "Dynamic Theory of Personality," in J. McV. Hunt, ed., *Personality and the Behavior Disorders,* I (New York, 1944), pp. 69–135.)

22 These traits, comprising the so-called "anal" or "anal compulsive" character, are sometimes formulated in different terms as instances of sublimations or reaction formations. Freud's statement of the type appears in his "Character and Anal Erotism," *Collected Works,* II (London, 1950), pp. 45–50. For more recent formulations, see Fenichel, loc. cit., especially pp. 278–84.

An important restatement and interpretation of Freud's libido theory is provided by Erik H. Erikson in his *Childhood and Society* (New York, 1950). See also the attempt to clarify and elaborate operationally the Freudian character types in Henry A. Murray, *Explorations in Personality* (New York, 1938), pp. 361–85.

23 For this purpose, in addition to the sources cited in the preceding footnote, see for example, William Healy and Augusta F. Bronner, *The Structure and Meaning of Psychoanalysis as Related to Personality and Behavior* (New York, 1930); William C. Menninger, "Characterologic and Symptomatic Expressions Related to the Anal Phase of Psychosexual Development," *Psychoanalytic Quarterly* 12, 1943: 161–93.

24 In the initial phase of our research we collected a large amount of evidence of the presence of most of these orderly traits in Wilson. Contemporaries and biographers have been impressed by various orderly traits in Wilson. For example, Wilson was "a stickler for accuracy" (David Lawrence, *The True Story of Woodrow Wilson,* p. 342); he had an extraordinary ability to concentrate and compartmentalize (Baker, op. cit., II, p. 44) and himself often referred to his "single-track" mind (Alfred Maurice Low, *Woodrow Wilson—An Interpretation,* p. 282); he attempted to rigidly separate thinking and emotions and leaned over backwards to prevent private and personal considerations from interfering with public duties (Baker, op. cit., II, p. 2; III, pp. 160–61; Edith Bolling Wilson, *My Memoir,* p. 162; Joseph Tumulty, *Woodrow Wilson As I Know Him,* pp. 473–74); he was pedantic, dogmatic and fastidious as a teacher (C. W. Mosher, Jr., "Woodrow Wilson's Methods in the Classroom," *Current History* 32(June 1930):502–03; Baker, op. cit., II, p. 13); he was reliable and scrupulous in keeping his word, no matter what the inconvenience (E. B. Wilson, op. cit., p. 171; Tumulty, op. cit., p. 469); his punctuality was well-known and it was said that one could set one's watch from his comings and goings (Eleanor Wilson McAdoo, *The Woodrow Wilsons,* pp. 22, 60, 213; Lawrence, op. cit., p. 126); he was punctilious, thorough and methodical (Baker, op. cit., I, pp. 86–87, 182; E. W. McAdoo, op. cit., pp. 24, 188; E. B. Wilson, op. cit., pp. 90, 307, 347; A. S. Link, *Wilson: The Road to the White House,* p. 94); he was strikingly neat, orderly and regular in personal working habits (Baker, op. cit., II, p. 46; V. p. 138; E. W. McAdoo, op. cit., p. 20; E. B. Wilson, op. cit., p. 79).

25 The hypothesis that certain types of (compulsive or neurotic) personalities pursue power as a means of obtaining compensation for low self-esteem can be and has been divorced from the distinctive structural-dynamic framework and terminology of the Freudian school. Various versions of a similar hypothesis are provided by other schools of dynamic psychology. (See fn. 25).

26 In his personality profile of Wilson, Arthur S. Link, for example, identifies the following traits: a demand for unquestioning loyalty, egotism and a belief in the infallibility of his own

judgment, vanity and a belief in his own superior wisdom and virtue, inability to rely upon others, indulgence in narrow prejudices and vindictiveness, intolerance of advice and resentment of criticism, a tendency to equate political opposition with personal antagonism, susceptibility to flattery. (*Wilson: The New Freedom,* pp. 67–68.) In his *Wilson: The Road to the White House,* the same biographer referred to his subject as possessing an "imperious will and intense conviction," a "headstrong and determined man who was usually able to rationalize his actions in terms of the moral law and to identify his position with the divine will" (p. ix).

In compulsives, too, an overrevaluation and high development of the intellect is often found. At the same time, however, intellectualization is curiously combined with archaic features (superstitiousness and magical beliefs). It is noteworthy, therefore, that many writers (e.g., ibid, p. 94) have been struck by the curious streak of superstitiousness in Wilson, a man otherwise noted for his emphasis on the intellect and on being guided by reason.

27 See, for example, Robert R. Sears, *Survey of Objective Studies of Psychoanalytic Concepts,* Social Science Research Council Bulletin 51, 1943, pp. 67–70.

28 Karen Horney, *The Neurotic Personality of Our Time* (New York, 1937); *Our Inner Conflicts* (New York, 1945).

29 H. D. Lasswell, *Power and Personality* (New York, 1948), pp. 44–49.

30 Some of these materials are presented in volume I (pp. 36ff.) of Ray Stannard Baker, *Woodrow Wilson: Life and Letters* (New York, 1927). However, other relevant materials on Wilson's childhood, and, especially, on his relationship with his father were not included in the official biography and are to be found in the Baker Papers, Library of Congress. A fuller summary and interpretation of this material than is possible here is given in *WW & CH,* Chapter I.

31 The significance of this childhood developmental problem has been overlooked in the otherwise authoritative biography by Arthur S. Link. There is no reference to it in Link's account of Wilson's formative years. On the contrary, Link asserts that "Wilson's boyhood was notable, if for nothing else, because of his normal development." (*Wilson: The Road to the White House,* p. 2.) The fact of Wilson's "slowness" is also omitted in the biographies by Garraty and Blum, though it is mentioned (and glossed over) by Baker, op. cit., I. pp. 36–37. The stern, domineering and caustic manner of Wilson's father, a source of acute tension and discomfort for Wilson, is also muted in Baker's published account, though not in the materials which Baker collected for his biography. (See note 30 above.)

32 A belated identification with his father appears to have accompanied Wilson's adoption of the compulsive dynamism at this time. The identification with the father was extremely strong on the manifest level and was rigidly maintained throughout Wilson's lifetime. At the same time, however, feelings of inferiority vis-á-vis the father, who had been the chief instrument of Wilson's damaged self-esteem, persisted throughout Wilson's life. For this and other reasons, accordingly, we have felt it necessary to postulate that the father-son conflict persisted in Wilson at an unconscious level. (Readers familiar with the technical literature will be reminded of the Freudian theory of the Oedipal basis of the inferiority complex.)

We have also postulated that aspects of Wilson's behavior in the struggles with Dean West and Senator Lodge constituted a displacement, or "acting out," of the unconscious hostility that he had experienced towards his father as a child but had not dared to express. (For a fuller statement of the thesis concerning the father-son relationship, see *WW & CH,* Chapter I, also pp. 46, 114–15, 270–73.) On the conditions under which Wilson's latent aggressive impulses could find overt expression against political opponents, see the discussion of "idealization," p. 90.

33 Baker, op. cit., I.

34 Baker, op. cit., I, pp. 45, 75–76, 94, 123–24, 148, 198–200, 302–03.

35 In more general terms we are asserting the possibility that personality needs and motives of an unconscious character may govern an individual's selection of social and political roles and that these needs and motives may infuse themselves into the individual's performance

of those roles. The fact that a person's behavior can be interpreted in terms of role theory, therefore, does not relieve the investigator from considering the possibility that aspects of basic personality are also expressing themselves in such behavior. It is incorrect, therefore, to define the problem as some proponents of role theory tend to do in terms of "role vs. personality." Rather, the interplay of role and personality needs to be considered.

36 Baker, op. cit., I, p. 199; *WW & CH,* p. 22.

37 Ibid.

38 See *WW & CH,* pp. 144–48, 321–22.

39 *WW & CH,* p. xvii.

40 See *WW & CH,* pp. 208–10, 223, 226–28.

41 This theory is a special application of a general hypothesis concerning the pursuit of power as a means of compensation for low self-estimates, which Harold D. Lasswell has extracted from the findings and theories of various schools of dynamic psychology. (See his *Power and Personality,* p. 39ff.) The hypothesis is evidently of wide, though not universal application in the study of political leaders.

   We have discussed some of the problems of applying this general hypothesis to someone like Wilson, who pursued other values as well as power, in *WW & CH,* pp. 319–22, and in the paper, "Woodrow Wilson: Personality and Political Behavior," presented before a panel of the American Political Science Association, Washington, D.C., September, 1956.

   As already noted, the pervasiveness of power strivings as compensation for organic or imagined defects was given early emphasis by Alfred Adler. The fruitfulness of Adler's theories for subsequent social psychological approaches to personality is now widely recognized. See, for example, Gardner Murphy, op. cit., Chapter 24, "Compensation for Interiority."

42 Wilson: *The Road to the White House,* p. 76.

43 See particularly Arthur S. Link, *Wilson: The Road to the White House,* and *WW & CH,* chapters III and IV.

44 *WW & CH,* pp. 4–5.

45 Otto Fenichel, *Psychoanalytic Theory of Neurosis,* pp. 485–86.

46 Baker, op. cit., II, p. 307.

47 *WW & CH,* pp. 290–98.

48 See, for example, Richard Hofstadter, *The American Political Tradition,* 2nd ed. (New York, 1954), pp. 281–82; Thomas A. Bailey, *Woodrow Wilson and the Great Betrayal* (New York, 1945).

49 Fenichel, op. cit., p. 279.

50 Ibid., p. 497. See also Christine Olden, "The Psychology of Obstinancy," *Psychoanalytic Quarterly* 12(1943):240–55.

51 *WW & CH,* pp. 297–98.

52 See, for example, Fenichel, op. cit., p. 486.

53 It might be added that we have encountered no evidence that Wilson subsequently ever expressed or experienced any self-doubts as to the wisdom or correctness of his refusal to compromise in the struggle to ratify the peace treaty. On the contrary, his defeat and physical breakdown seem to have provided relief from the feelings of uneasiness experienced at the time.

54 It should be emphasized that whether, to what extent, and how often the self-defeating dynamism referred to here finds expression depends upon the character of the situations encountered by the subject during his lifetime. Similarly, we have postulated that this destructive tendency was held in check to some extent by the development in Wilson's personality system of a constructive strategy whereby he generally committed his need for domination and achievement only to political projects which were about ready for realization. (On this point, not discussed further in this paper, see *WW & CH,* pp. 118, 320–22.)

55 Arthur S. Link, *Wilson: The Road to the White House,* pp. 90–91. A similar observation is made by Blum, op. cit., p. 36.

56 Edmund Wilson, "Woodrow Wilson at Princeton," reprinted in his *Shores of Light* (New York, 1952), p. 322.

57 "The Neurotic Character," *International Journal of Psychoanalysis* 11(1930):292–311. In contrast to true neurotics who squander their energy in futile inactivity, Alexander noted, persons of this character type live active and eventful lives; they "act out" repressed unconscious motives that are unacceptable to their ego. The neurotic element in such persons appears, that is, not so much in the form of circumscribed symptoms but permeates the personality and influences their entire behavior.

58 The following paragraphs are a brief paraphrase of materials presented in *WW & CH*, pp. 116–21, 320–22, and in a paper at the meetings of the American Political Science Association, Washington, D.C., September, 1956.

59 The italicized phrase is an important qualification to the general proposition. In the case of legislative proposals which were not "his" or to which he had not committed his aspirations for high achievement, for example the military "preparedness" legislation of 1915–16, Wilson was more flexible when confronted by effective Congressional opposition. (*WW & CH*, pp. 116, 121.)

60 *WW & CH*, pp. 38, 45; chapter XIV, especially 286–89.

11

The Georges' Wilson Reexamined: An Essay on Psychobiography

Robert C. Tucker

ON PSYCHOBIOGRAPHY

Forty-five years have passed since Harold Lasswell wrote into the first paragraph of *Psychopathology and Politics* the ringing declaration that "political science without biography is a form of taxidermy." The kind of biographical study needed in the discipline, if taxidermy was not to be its fate, was not conventional biography but biography as "life history." Biography as "life history," or "natural history" as Lasswell also called it, would be "concerned with facts which are *developmentally* significant,"[1] i.e., what nowadays is generally described as "psychological biography."

The distinction between psychological biography (or psychobiography for short) and conventional biography is real though not absolute. Conventional biography has been characterized by one of its scholarly practitioners as "... the simulation, in words, of a man's life, from all that is known about that man."[2] That is to say, it is a form of portrait painting, where the subject is a person's life and the medium of expression is language. As such it has had not only a very long history but one that shows many significant changes in life-writing conventions. Thus English biography in the nineteenth century, unlike much biography in England and elsewhere in the twentieth, observed the convention that "the fundamental reason for writing a man's life was that he was admirable."[3] Whatever the prevailing conventions, however, conventional biography has rarely been devoid of some psychological characterization of its subject—typically as an informed mind's intuitive judgment of character expressed in terms of everyday discourse.

What is distinctive of psychobiography as a scholarly enterprise is that the biographer is attempting to make sense out of the subject's life-course, or key

Reprinted from the *American Political Science Review*, vol. 71 (1977), pp. 606–18.

phases of it, *in terms of a consciously thought-out psychological interpretation of that subject's personality*. This is not to say that he will be oblivious of the role of circumstance in the life course, or that his study will not contain descriptive passages or whole sections which might just as easily appear in a regular biography of the same individual.

It follows that all psychobiographies have in common a mooring in personality theory, either in one of its particular forms (Freudian, post-Freudian, or non-Freudian) or in some eclectic combination of interpretive-theoretical orientations. Beyond this, we can draw a distinction between two different ways in which the psychobiographer may make use of the theoretical position he has selected in the effort to "make sense" out of the subject's life-course psychologically. He may, on the one hand, treat the subject as an illustrative example of a general psychological formula or paradigm that he believes is applicable, e.g., the "compulsive personality" as conceptualized in Freudian thought or the "paranoid personality" as described in clinical textbooks. Or, having used one or another formula or paradigm as a *springboard* for interpretive analysis of the individual case at hand, he may work out an individualized psychological theory or set of hypotheses concerning the personality of his subject—referring, for example, to that person's life-goal or goals as rooted in a particular character structure, pattern of motivation, and modes of response to people and situations. It seems to me that psychobiography as a form of scholarship is developing, and fruitfully so, from the first to the second sort of approach. As Alexander George has expressed it, "to tag the subject of the biography with a label or to pigeonhole him in one of a number of existing categories does not in itself provide what the biographer will need most: namely, a discriminating 'theory,' i.e., a set of assumptions or hypotheses, as to the structure and dynamics of his subject's personality system."[4]

Since, in either of these two approaches, personality theory will give guidance to the psychobiographer's interpretation of his subject, the question arises whether it matters very much which personality theory or whose psychological perspective is chosen for this purpose, so long as the psychobiographer adheres to it as rigorously as possible and follows it as far as it will take him in his interpretive quest. In short, isn't any one of the major psychological perspectives acceptable in principle as a guideline, and what possible basis is there for preferring one over another?

One could argue that it is best to avoid a comparative analysis of different theoretical perspectives, given the overlap among them and given the inevitable difficulties of adjudication. Alternatively, one may take the view, as I do, that despite difficulties, the critical task in psychobiography is to compare alternatives and try to discover which of various possible theoretical perspectives is most fruitful for dealing with the case at hand. But then the question arises: by what criteria do we decide which theoretical perspective can do more, interpretively or explanatorily, than the alternative preferred and used by the psychobiographer whose work is under consideration?

Two criteria appear particularly applicable. First, which of the two leaves the psychobiographer with a smaller residue of refractory material, of actions, characteristics, etc., that do not easily submit to explanation in terms of the given perspective? Second, which of the two is more effective for interpreting the key points or key patterns in the subject's life, those phenomena which are most significant for the subject's influence upon people and events and hence most in need of explanation by the psychobiographer of a political leader? From the standpoint of a psychobiography that attempts to be, likewise, a psychohistory—that is, a contribution to history writing as well as to life-writing—the matter of key points or patterns is often very important; and this is where the comparison of alternative modes of psychological interpretation may be most needed and most useful for scholarship.

GETTING OFF THE GROUND

Lasswell proved excessively optimistic in his early belief that biography as "natural history," or psychobiography, was close at hand.[5] Progress has in fact been slow. We might compare the recent past and present in psychobiography in political science with the dawn of the age of the heavier-than-air flying machine. Such a contraption had been conceived by various minds, inspired by a belief in its possibility, and here and there an effort was being made to construct one that would fly. Finally, a success occurred: the Wright brothers, at Kitty Hawk, got their machine off the ground and it flew. Alexander and Juliette George have in a way been the Wright brothers of psychobiography in political science. Their *Woodrow Wilson and Colonel House* has been widely appraised as a psychobiographical effort that succeeded.[6]

It may be helpful to pinpoint the sense in which the Georges succeeded. There has not been anything approaching a consensus among political scientists that a political leader's personality is a factor of potentially great or even decisive importance in explaining his conduct in the leader-role that he acquires. Many believe that the pressures and role requirements of political office, along with the political logic of the situations encountered, suffice to explain the leader's conduct; and that an individual not disposed to be responsive to these pressures and situational demands is also not likely to rise to power at all, owing to the screening process involved in any society's mode of leader selection.

The Georges demonstrate impressively, in the single but significant case of Wilson, that his performance in a succession of leader-roles was deeply affected by the psychodynamics of his personality; and portentously so, since what was involved in his personality-determined conduct in the nation's presidency was ultimately nothing less than United States entry into the League of Nations. As one early reviewer appropriately remarked in the light of such considerations, "this book is a good antidote to the irrepressible tendency of political scientists, as well as laymen, to think of high politics as something carried on by disembodied spirits, whose larger actions may vary in degree of shrewdness and fore-sight but are seldom affected by submerged and hidden passions."[7]

I fully share the view just cited, and propose to reexamine the Georges' *Wilson* in the belief that it is a work of outstanding scholarly merit and a path-finding achievement which has done much to inaugurate the psychobiographical en-terprise as a vital part of political science. Moreover, I believe any genuine classic requires to be re-reviewed from time to time as scholarship develops sufficiently to permit fresh assessment. My treatment will focus on three themes: the book's underlying Lasswellian hypothesis about political man; the Georges' application of the hypothesis; and a comparison of the resulting psychological interpretation of Wilson's character and political conduct with an alternative possible inter-pretation based upon Karen Horney's conception of the neurotic personality.

LASSWELL'S ASSUMPTIONS ABOUT POLITICAL MAN

Woodrow Wilson and Colonel House was the product of fifteen years of study and research. From the outset, it was conceived as a psychobiography as defined above. In the early phase, the Georges worked with the hypothesis that Wilson was a "compulsive personality" as that type has been conceived in Freudian the-ory. At length, they found this approach inadequate and adopted a new theoretical point of departure in Lasswell's psychological characterization of political man.

Over many years, Lasswell's effort to give the study of politics a psychological foundation issued in a search for a psychologically defined "political type," a *"homo politicus."* In *Psychopathology and Politics,* political man was characterized as one who displaces "private affects" onto "public objects" and rationalizes this in terms of the public interest.[8] Eighteen years later, in *Power and Personality,* Lasswell moved to a more Adlerian position in his continuing effort to concep-tualize political man. In Alfred Adler's post-Freudian "Individual Psychology," a person with one or another form of congenital weakness or organ inferiority is seen as compensating for the resultant inferiority feelings by developing a life-goal of superiority and a corresponding "style of life." Adapting this idea to his purposes as a political scientist, Lasswell now hypothesized that, apart from dis-placing private affects onto public objects, political man seeks power "as a means of compensation against deprivation," and specifically that: *"Power is expected to overcome low estimates of the self,* by changing either the traits of the self or the environment in which it functions."[9] The Georges adopted this "compen-sation" hypothesis as the basis for psychological interpretation of Wilson. In their words, "power was for him a compensatory value, a means of restoring the self-esteem damaged in childhood."[10]

In a later methodological essay, Alexander George has spoken in broader terms about the Lasswellian formula, attributing to it a general usefulness to the political scientist concerned with psychobiography. While the hypothesis provides, he writes, a "relatively 'shallow' account of the origins of the need for power," still:

The problems of interest to the political scientist do not require the same level of explanation in matters of this kind that the psychoanalyst is interested in. Moreover, the political scientist lacks the data, observational opportunities and diagnostic skills for making fuller in-depth reconstructions. Under these circumstances, attempts to do so are likely to be difficult, frustrating and unduly speculative—as well as often being unnecessary.[11]

I am not convinced that the political scientist as psychobiographer is in any better position to dispense with fuller in-depth reconstructions than any other psychobiographer,[12] although it may be true in some instances. Moreover, Lasswell's conception of the politician as one who seeks power to overcome low estimates of the self, useful though it may be up to a point, presents a serious problem.

The conception has value insofar as it takes us beyond the old stereotype of the politician as one who seeks power simply for power's sake. It makes allowance for what is probably the frequent fact that people seek the power of political office for motives other than power *per se*. What needs to be called into question is the assumption that the power-drive of would-be political leaders derives from low estimates of the self. This seems *prima facie* doubtful. "Low estimates of the self" would take the form of conscious feelings of self-depreciation or self-belittlement. Very possibly, there have been exemplars in political history. But it would seem that in most cases, political power-seeking is a form of activity that appeals to expansive personalities, to people who possess very considerable (if not unusually strong) self-esteem and self-confidence, reflecting high rather than low estimates of self. Those in whom feelings of self-belittlement or self-depreciation are salient would tend to shun active involvement in the political arena, and not to be successful if they ventured into it.

Curiously, Lasswell himself, in one place, recognizes or half-recognizes this. He writes that "the accentuation of power is to be understood as a compensatory reaction against low estimates of the self *(especially when coexisting with high self-estimates)* ..."[13] But he does not explain, psychologically, the paradox of high self-estimates coexisting with low ones. He could have done so, however, had he referred to the work of Karen Horney on the neurotic personality. This form of personality, as she analyzes it, shows high *and* low estimates of the self coexisting.

In the revision of psychoanalysis made by Horney, human beings are endowed with a growth tendency or urge toward actualization of their capacities and potentialities as persons. When, however, psychologically adverse experience in early childhood results in a condition of "basic anxiety," defined as a "feeling of being isolated and helpless in a world conceived as potentially hostile," the child typically responds by, among other things, forming an "idealized image" of himself to make up for his inadequate sense of personal identity and insecurity about his personal significance.[14] The idealized image is a picture of himself as a perfect or superhuman being along one or another line as dictated by the tendency to move *against* others in a drive for "mastery," *toward* others in search for "love," or *away from* others in quest of "freedom."

Unless the psychic conditions generating the basic anxiety change for the better, the individual in time takes a fateful further step: he identifies the idealized image as the person he really is. In Horney's terms, the idealized image turns into an "idealized self." When and if this happens, the energies available for growth or self-realization are henceforth invested in the effort to prove in action, i.e., to demonstrate to himself and others, that he *is* in fact the idealized self. Since any failure along this line incurs painful anxiety, the effort to actualize the idealized self (Horney calls this the "search for glory") takes on a compulsive character, meaning that the person in question feels driven involuntarily to prove himself (i.e., the idealized self) in action. Failures are, however, unavoidable given the individual's human fallibility, on the one hand, and the godlike or absolute character of the idealized self on the other.

Awareness of such discrepancies causes the person—again compulsively—to turn in a fury of self-accusation, self-condemnation and self-hatred against his "empirical" self, which begins to seem to him an alien being. Hence the neurotic personality is above all the victim of an inner conflict, a person "at war with himself." Being thus at odds with himself, moreover, he is virtually certain to be at odds with others. For others, if only unwittingly, are likely to inflict painful blows upon the neurotic person's "pride system" by failing, in word or deed, to treat him in accordance with the claims of the idealized self. Whence his hypersensitivity to criticism (an implicit denial of the idealized self's lofty attributes or perfection) and the vindictive hostility aroused in him toward those enemies (as he perceives them) who have given him affront by criticism or other forms of failure to affirm the idealized image. To gain a vindictive triumph over them by hitting back at them is his way of attempting to restore the injured pride. Furthermore, one of his unconscious ways of dealing with the self-hatred aroused in him by his violations of his impossibly high standards is to "externalize" it, i.e., to project it outwards and experience it as his hatred of *other* persons— against whom it is realistically possible to fight and win a pride-restoring triumph. This increases the likelihood that the neurotic's inner conflict will impair, at least at certain times in life, his relationships with others.

Here, then, in the neurotic personality, we see the coexistence of both unnaturally high and unnaturally low estimates of the self. The high ones take the form of an idealized self-image possessing attributes of imagined genius, perfection, or greatness along one or another line; the low ones, in a despised empirical self experienced as an offensive stranger because of its inevitable inability to fulfill the superhuman demands and specifications of the idealized self. Through such inner mechanisms as repression, externalization, and rationalization, the neurotic does his best to preserve the pride system intact and act out successfully the role of greatness and glory in which he has cast himself in his self-idealization. But no matter how herculean his efforts along this line, he is virtually condemned to suffer a series of experiences which bring the despised self into the forefront of his self-consciousness or threaten to do so. On the one hand, he strives by every possible means to keep the "high" self-estimate salient in his experience of himself; on the other, the "low" one keeps threatening to intrude.

Although references in *Power and Personality* show that Lasswell was at the time of writing familiar with the views Horney had expressed in various writings then available, his parenthetical mention of coexisting high and low self-estimates did not betoken an attempt to make use of her theory of the neurotic personality for his purposes. His formula for "the political type" remained the one already cited: the power-seeker pursues power in order to "overcome low estimates of the self."

THE GEORGES' APPLICATION OF LASSWELL'S HYPOTHESIS

The first question I want to raise is: how consistently do the Georges follow Lasswell's compensation hypothesis in their psychological interpretation of Wilson, and how well does it serve them? They do postulate, as already indicated above, that Wilson's desire for power and for a career of political leadership was motivated by a desire to overcome the low self-estimates generated during his early childhood. Wilson's father humiliated the boy by regularly making him the target of a caustic wit. The son "never retorted and he never rebelled. Instead, he accepted his father's demands for perfection, tried to emulate him, and interpreted his stinging criticisms as humiliating evidence that, try as he might, he was inadequate."[15] The Georges note that the boy did not learn the written alphabet until he was nine and couldn't read readily until he was eleven. Wilson's recollections of his youth, the authors go on,

> furnish ample indication of his early fears that he was stupid, ugly, worthless and unlovable.... It is perhaps to this core feeling of inadequacy, of a fundamental worthlessness which must ever be disproved, that the unappeasable quality of his need for affection, power and achievement, and the compulsive quality of his striving for affection may be traced. For one of the ways in which human beings troubled with low estimates of themselves seek to obliterate their inner pain is through high achievement and the acquisition of power. The trouble is that no matter how dazzling, their accomplishments are likely to prove only momentarily satisfying because the deep-seated low estimates persist and in short order begin to clamor anew for assuagement.[16]

Thus for the Georges, Lasswell's compensatory hypothesis explains the urge for power and achievement which made Wilson dissatisfied with being a professor (in this connection, they quote him as saying: "I want to *do* something!") and drove him to win a succession of important leader-roles: the presidency of Princeton University (1902–10), the governorship of New Jersey (1910–12), and finally the presidency of the United States (1913–21). Lasswell's compensation hypothesis serves more as a generalized explanation of Wilson's lifelong quest for leader-roles than as a means of explaining specific actions taken along the way. From time to time, however, the authors invoke the hypothesis in concrete explanatory contexts. For example, they write in one place that the need to struggle against the self-depreciating tendencies from Wilson's early years "crippled his capacity to react objectively to matters at hand."[17] Again, in dealing with his troubled relations with Congress in 1913, they suggest that what dictated his leadership tactics was "his need for domination as a means of countering his low self-estimates."[18]

Wilson's impressive successes in winning leader-roles were counterbalanced and ultimately overshadowed by a number of failures in his performance as a leader, most notably the long and losing battle with Dean West at Princeton over the location of the projected new Graduate College and the battle with Senator Lodge and others over ratification of the Versailles Treaty by the United States Senate. Even in his short career as governor, his successful passage of reforms in the New Jersey legislature of 1911 was followed by what Arthur Link calls "the debacle of the session of 1912," which was (writes Link) "the result of his own failures and personal limitations." Apart from his absences from the state at the time, the failure of leadership reflected Wilson's "temperamental inability to cooperate with men who were not willing to follow his lead completely; he had not lost his habit, long since demonstrated at Princeton, of making his political opponents also his personal enemies, whom he despised and loathed."[19]

The explanation of this pattern of recurrent leadership failure is an obvious major challenge for any psychobiography of Wilson. The Georges recognize this fact. They begin their concluding "Research Note" in *Woodrow Wilson and Colonel House* by citing Edmund Wilson's description of the career of Wilson:

> As President of the United States, he repeated after the War his whole tragedy as president of Princeton—with Lodge in the role of West, the League of Nations in the place of the quad system, and the Senate in the place of the Princeton trustees. It is possible to observe in certain lives, where conspicuously superior abilities are united with serious deficiencies, not the progress in career or vocation that carries the talented man to a solid position or a definite goal, but a curve plotted over and over again and always dropping from some flight of achievement to a steep descent into failure.[20]

Alexander George calls this the "self-defeating pattern" and "self-defeating dynamism" in Wilson's career.[21] One of the authors' chief concerns in their study of Wilson is to explain this pattern.

Their way of doing so involves a certain shift of explanatory perspective. Lasswell's compensatory hypothesis has been invoked to explain Wilson's quest for power, his need to dominate people in order to assuage inadequacy feelings. The self-defeating pattern manifested itself, however, *after* Wilson had attained various leader-roles and was exercising the authority that they conferred upon him. Specifically, when as leader he was confronted with determined opposition to a project which he had proposed and was trying to put through—the Graduate College location issue at Princeton and the League issue are the two principal instances—he would grow rigid and uncompromisingly insistent upon having his way *in toto* and upon utterly defeating and humbling those who led the opposition against him—even though this meant the loss of the project itself in a form that intrinsically ought to have been acceptable to him.

The Georges recognize that Wilson's conduct in these recurring situations of challenge to his authority as leader calls for a more concrete, a more *ad hoc* explanation than the generalized urge for power and achievement which they see as stemming from low estimates of self. In constructing this explanation, they shift their emphasis from a need for domination to a need for "freedom *from* domination" or a "fear *of* being dominated."[22] This in turn is speculatively derived from the vicissitudes of Wilson's childhood relationship to his father. The argument runs as follows: children generally experience a certain amount of resentment of their parents, and this tendency would have been intensified in Wilson's case by his father's harsh ridicule of him. But the anxiety aroused by these hostile feelings caused Wilson to repress them from consciousness and assume an attitude of "surpassing devotion" to his father, so that "there is not a shred of evidence that he ever once openly rebelled against his father's authority. Instead, he submitted and became an extravagently devoted son," so much so that "even in successful maturity, he retained a feeling of incompetence in his father's presence."[23]

The final step in the argument is that the Dean Wests of Wilson's career as a leader—those who opposed and threatened to defeat his cherished projects—were father-figures against whom he was determined to express the rebellious and hostile feelings that he had suppressed in relation to his real father, on the implicit motto of "never again." The authors' statement of the argument runs as follows:

> He bristled at the slightest challenge to his authority. Such a characteristic might well have represented a rebellion against the domination of his father, whose authority he had never dared openly to challenge. Throughout his life his relationships with others seemed shaped by an inner command never again to bend his will to another man's. He seems to have experienced men who were determined to make their viewpoints prevail against his own—men like Dean West at Princeton or, later, Senator Lodge—as an unbearable threat. They seem to have stirred in him ancient memories of his capitulation to his father and he resisted with ferocity. *He* must dominate, out of fear of being dominated.[24]

The fact that the authors have introduced a new line of reasoning (outside of or going beyond the Lasswellian compensatory formula) to explain Wilson's self-defeating pattern is not objectionable, although it would seem desirable, if possible, to account for the latter in terms of the same *system of explanation* that applies to Wilson's other characteristic patterns of behavior. The new line of reasoning does, however, present some problems. As acknowledged in the first of the statements cited above, it is speculative. There is no direct evidence for "the violence he had once felt but never ventured to express in response to his father's overwhelming domination," and the only indirect evidence—his notable slowness to learn the alphabet and to read—is presumably interpretable in more than one way. As the Georges emphasize, Wilson's lifelong demeanor toward his father was admiring and deferential; in short, anything but hostile, violent, rebellious. They interpret this as signifying repressed violent feelings against the elder Wilson.[25] This is no more subject to disproof than it is to proof. Certain questions might, however, be raised. If Wilson so successfully (through reaction-formation) managed to suppress his underlying rebelliousness against his dominating father, might he not have shown a like tendency in relations with father-like dominating figures encountered later in life, the very Wests and Lodges against whom he fought so uncompromisingly? Or, if we allow that he was driven to act out against other would-be dominators the rebellious violence that he had repressed in himself with reference to his own father, why do we not see a pattern of rebellious violence against numerous potential father-figures encountered earlier in life, e.g., school teachers, or superiors in academic life with whom he had dealings prior to his presidency at Princeton? Why did the suppressed aggressive violence come out in him only in these few instances in middle and later life?

None of what has been said here invalidates the Georges' interpretive approach to Wilson. At most it suggests that the problem of working out a fully satisfactory psychological interpretation of him remains unsolved, and that an alternative to the Georges' approach may be worth trying out. It seems to me that the most promising basis for such an alternative is the conception of the neurotic personality presented by Karen Horney in her final and most important work of synthesis, *Neurosis and Human Growth*. That Woodrow Wilson was a neurotic personality and that much of his behavior which is of special interest to students of politics invites interpretation on this hypothesis will be the burden of the argument in what follows, and the evidence will be drawn from the Georges' study itself.

AN ALTERNATIVE INTERPRETATION

In his review of the Georges' book cited above, Bernard Brodie writes: "Wilson was intensely neurotic—though the authors refrain from using this or like terms throughout the book—and to get into the dynamics of his actions inevitably requires recourse to concepts and· insights that have developed out of the discoveries of Sigmund Freud."[26] Brodie was correct, I believe, in saying that Wilson was "intensely neurotic," although the Georges avoidance of the term apparently reflects doubt about this on their part. The Horneyan conception of the neurotic personality, at any rate, was not, in their view, fully applicable to Wilson. As Alexander George says elsewhere,

> If Wilson is not the simple clinical stereotype of a compulsive, neither can he be regarded as a full-blown neurotic. True, one cannot read, for example, Karen Horney's insightful and penetrating descriptions of neurotic drives and of the neurotic character structure without being struck by the applicability of much of what she says to Wilson. But these

descriptions are applicable only to a certain point and, upon reflection, one is on balance equally or more impressed with the extent to which Wilson's behavior and career *diverge* from those of her patients. This divergence from the clinical picture concerns precisely the critical question whether the neurotically disposed individual is able to deal adequately with his conflicts and hence retains the ability to function effectively. For Wilson was, after all, a highly successful person. He was able to overcome a severe disturbance in childhood development; thereafter, not only did he keep fairly well in check the compulsive and neurotic components of his personality but he succeeded in large measure in harnessing them constructively to the achievement of socially productive purposes. To the clinical psychologist, therefore, Wilson is interesting as much because he was able to overcome childhood difficulties and to perform as successfully as he did in public life, as he is because of the pathological pattern of self-defeating behavior he tended to repeat on several occasions during his public career.[27]

I have quoted this statement at length not only because it sets forth a distinctly skeptical, not to say negative, view of the applicability of Horneyan theory to Wilson, but also because it raises an important general question.

This is "the critical question whether the neurotically disposed individual is able to deal adequately with his conflicts and hence retains the ability to function effectively." Professor George implies that Horney would answer in the negative— a position that I believe is mistaken. Horney at least allows for the *possibility* of effective functioning on the social plane. In her view, as I read it, neurosis is often a mighty motive force for achievement, including achievement of what for many would be "socially productive purposes" in the political realm. Notwithstanding the egocentricity of the neurotic individual's "search for glory," he may in some instances be spurred on to impressive political success, even triumph, by the driving inner need to prove the idealized self in action and gain public recognition of it.[28] Especially in those societies whose cultural norms or mores place a high value on power, fame, etc., individuals of exceptional ability who are motivated by neurotic ambition may be highly successful in the achievement of their goals and may thereby, through very much of their careers, find in this external success at least the mirage of a solution for their inner conflicts. Of course, the person who is inwardly conflicted ("at war with himself") because of neurosis will pay a high psychological price for this form of solution. Moreover, by virtue of the psychodynamics of neurosis, summarized earlier, the neurotic's inner conflicts will place a heavy strain on his relations with others. They may, in fact, impair his effectiveness in an organizational role. But the neurotically generated social animosities or conflict may at times be, or appear, socially "functional" depending upon the nature and situation of the organization itself, e.g., if in some sense it is a fighting organization with an ideology of militance in terms of which an enmity born of neurosis can credibly be rationalized.

Whatever position we take on this general issue, when we turn to Wilson the case against the thesis that he was a neurotic personality is weak. For here we clearly see both sides of the coin. On the one hand, enormous ambition combined with extraordinary political talents drove him to dizzy heights of success in a career of leadership that ran in a single decade from the presidency of a university to the presidency of the United States. None of this success is incompatible with the possibility that Wilson and his ambition were neurotic in character. On the other hand, his stunningly successful career was bedeviled by repeated searing personal conflicts in which Wilson's response to those who incurred his enmity by opposing his projects comprised a "pattern of self-defeating behavior" which Professor George himself calls "pathological." Such a duality of accomplishment and failure, of greatness come to grief, would suggest the possibility of neurosis even if we knew nothing more about the individual in question. To argue the proposition in positive terms, however, we must turn to the evidence.

Horney discusses the neurotic personality in general terms and at the same time, as indicated earlier, suggests a threefold typology of neurotic personalities. She distinguishes (1) those who seek "expansive" solutions in one or another form of mastery; (2) those who seek "self-effacing" solutions in love; and (3) those whose solution is "resignation" through aloofness from others or freedom. She also suggests that these various "solutions" are at best dominant trends in a neurotic life-course and that many cases (if not all) are mixed ones. Those who seek expansive solutions are, moreover, divided into "narcissistic," "perfectionistic," and "arrogant-vindictive" subtypes characterized respectively by the need for admiration, extreme perfectionism, and the need for a vindictive triumph over those perceived as enemies. A neurotic who makes a career of political leadership will almost self-evidently belong to the expansive category, although it has been hypothesized that the appeal of mastery through political accomplishment could be accompanied in some instances by self-effacing tendencies expressing the appeal of love.[29] That this hypothesis applies to Wilson may be suggested by such a statement as the following in a letter to his first wife: "I have an uncomfortable feeling of carrying a volcano about with me. My salvation is in being loved. . . . There surely never lived a man with whom love was a more critical matter than it is with me!"[30] Yet Wilson's dominant solution was certainly the expansive one, with elements of all three subtypes or subtendencies present. As we shall see, the last of these, i.e., the need for a vindictive triumph over enemies, is especially relevant to the self-defeating pattern.

On the basis of Horney's generalized description of the neurotic process and the detailed biographical material provided by the Georges in their book, Wilson was a classic case of the neurotic personality. It is quite clear from their account of the boy's early life, of "the crushing feelings of inadequacy which had been branded into his spirit as a child,"[31] that he experienced the basic anxiety that in Horney's view fosters neurosis. Second, we see in the young Wilson ample evidence of the self-idealization which Horney explains as the anxiety-ridden youngster's method of finding a sense of personal worth and significance in such circumstances. As a boy at the dinner table, he was heard to say, "papa, when I get to be a man, I'm going to have a lofty position." "He spent his childhood and youth," the Georges write, "industriously preparing to be a great man."[32] Also, he soon began to visualize the political realm as the scene of his destined greatness. At sixteen, while conversing with his cousin Jessie, he referred to a portrait on the wall and said: "That is Gladstone, the greatest statesman that ever lived. I intend to be a statesman, too."[33]

Young Wilson created an image of himself as a future great statesman, and eventually identified himself with it; the idealized image became, in Horney's terms, an "idealized self," which he felt driven to prove in practice. Since the idealized self was a statesman-self, the goal of his compulsive striving to demonstrate it in practice *can* be described as "power," but it would be more accurately designated a quest for great political accomplishment or "search for glory." In the Georges' words, "what attracted him, apparently, was the prospect of exercising leadership *per se*. He was ..., throughout his career, a leader in search of a cause. One feels, almost, that the various causes for which he fought so passionately in later years were in themselves almost incidental to him. A man cannot exercise power in a vacuum, after all."[34] An indication of the importance of seeing the search for glory as the driving force of Wilson's life is that he especially sought public acknowledgment and applause, which need not have been the case if power *per se* were his object. From boyhood, his ambition was to become a great orator, and as a political man he was, all his life, above all a magnificent *performer*. This was true of him as a teacher as well: "Wilson's performance at Princeton, from the very start, was superlative. His class lectures were celebrated.... Sometimes, at the end of a particularly brilliant performance— and they were *performances*—the students would impulsively burst into applause."[35]

What is salient in this personality is a lofty self-estimate, not a low one, although the latter may have lurked below the surface in the form of repressed or semirepressed self-condemnatory tendencies arising from the empirical Wilson's inability always and wholly to *be* the idealized self in actual practice. In short, we have here that very combination of high and low self-estimates which was discussed earlier. Public plaudits, and in particular those of the political communities over which he successively presided as leader, would have represented to Wilson a proof of success in fulfilling his ambition to be a new Gladstone. Political success, as attested by public approval, was confirmation of the idealized self, and all the more necessary because the suppressed self-doubts and self-condemnatory tendencies inevitably made him insecure in his lofty self-estimate and hence in need of constant support in the form of praise and admiration.

Speaking of neurotic pride, Horney writes:

> With all his strenuous efforts toward perfection and with all his belief in perfection attained, the neurotic does not gain what he most desperately needs: self-confidence and self-respect.... The great positions to which he may rise, the fame he may acquire, will render him arrogant but will not bring him inner security. He still feels at bottom unwanted, is easily hurt, and needs incessant confirmation of his value.[36]

Wilson emerges in the Georges' account as just such a person. They speak of "that undercurrent of restless dissatisfaction which was the man's fundamental mood."[37] Elsewhere, they write that "Wilson's thirst for accomplishment was unquenchable. A project successfully completed might for a moment still his inner doubts—but only for a moment."[38] Horney's line of reasoning, based on the concept of the idealized image of self and the never-ending and yet never fully successful quest to actualize and gain confirmation of it, explains all this better than the Lasswellian formula does.

The same is true of Wilson's way of responding to approval and admiration from those around him or from strangers, and his way of responding to disapproval or disagreement. Because of the inevitable insecurity of the pride structure, the neurotic personality is, as Horney explains, in constant need of reassurance from others that he *is* the paragon that he believes himself to be; and he is hypersensitive to criticism because it threatens to mobilize and bring him face to face with his suppressed *self*-critical, *self*-condemnatory tendencies. Consequently, he tends to react with vindictive hostility to the source of the criticism or opposition, upon whom his self-condemnation is projected. Wilson's enormous need for reassurance and admiration, and his resulting manner of responding to flattery, of which Colonel House took such active advantage—all this is abundantly documented in the biographical facts cited by the Georges. So is his hostility against his detractors or those who in any way threatened to outdo him in a leader-role, as Dean West did at Princeton. "All of Wilson's close friends—the men, the women, the professors, the politicians, the socialites— shared one characteristic: they were or at least had to seem to him to be *uncritical* admirers of the man and of everything he did."[39] Further, the authors note as "truly remarkable" the "vast number of letters Wilson wrote to friends fervently expressing his gratitude for their faith and affection. So far from reducing his energy for this type of letter-writing, the pressure of public business, particularly when he was under attack, seemed to intensify his need to turn for solace to those who restored him with their uncritical approval."[40] Naturally, he was most in need of this uncritical approval when "under attack," because public attack would intensify the insecurity of his idealized self.

The Georges' way of explaining Wilson's compulsive need for uncritical admiration and agreement with his views differs from the Horneyan explanation suggested in the foregoing paragraph. As they see it:

> Intellectual disagreement or the feeling that a friend disapproved of some project he had in hand aroused intolerable anxieties, the echoes of indelible boyhood impressions. For the boy Wilson had learned that if he did not earn his father's approval by instantly accepting his every opinion and behaving accordingly, he stood in danger of forfeiting his father's love. To the man Wilson, identity of opinion and love were inseparably linked. . . . To him, if a friend disagreed with him about a matter of importance, it signified that the friend no longer cared for him. He reacted in the way he once had feared his father would react in similar circumstances—he broke the relationship.[41]

To me this explanation is not cogent: it simply transposes to the adult Wilson a way of relating to persons that corresponds to his father's way of relating to *him* when he was a child. But it is not self-evident that Wilson would have taken over this trait from his father; he might have rebelled against it. Whereas in terms of Horneyan theory, we do get a dynamic explanation of the behavior in question. Approval of him and his projects, especially by those whose opinions mattered most to him, was a vital need because it ministered to his craving for reassurance that he *was* his "true self," i.e., the idealized one. It was for this reason that he required "the soothing balm of flattery," as the Georges put it in describing Colonel House's way of approaching Wilson.[42] Significantly, the Georges themselves seem at times to see the behavior in these terms:

> He needed his friends to confirm his faith—so easily shaken by outer attack because so savagely preyed upon from within—in *his great destiny,* in *his human worth.* He needed their tributes to his *selfless idealism,* particularly when the detractors rudely stripped away his carefully wrought rationalizations and, with cruelly used insight, broadcast the power-seeking, self-centered, arrogant aspects of his behavior.[43]

THE SELF-DEFEATING PATTERN: TWO VIEWS

We come, finally to Wilson's repeated rigidity and vindictiveness in response to challenges to his authority as expressed in such cherished projects as his Graduate College conception at Princeton and the League of Nations Covenant. I have summarized the Georges' interpretation of this behavior as Wilson's effort to gain "freedom from domination" by figures whom he may have experienced as reincarnations of his domineering father, and I have questioned that view, believing that an alternative interpretation in Horneyan terms is more persuasive.

The Georges draw a useful distinction between "Wilson the power-seeker" and "Wilson the power-holder." As power-seeker, he was "free to devote every ounce of his intelligence and energy to waging a realistic campaign to attain his goal." Indeed, "he proved himself a practical politician without peer, a prodigy in the art of elevating himself to power."[44] Certainly, Wilson demonstrated notable flexibility in the process of power seeking, and a capacity to adapt his policy positions to the requirements for success. This was shown, for example, in his shift from a conservative political stance before winning the governorship to the reformism which powerfully assisted him along the path to the presidency. His flexibility was repeated in his quick shift to an antibossism posture in state politics after encouraging the Democratic party bosses of New Jersey who groomed him for the governorship to believe that he would remain loyal to them. His troubles always emerged *after* he had won a position of power. Of Wilson the power-holder the Georges write that "having attained an opportunity for exercise of power, first as President of Princeton and finally as President of the United States, he was no longer able to suppress his inner impulses toward aggressive leadership."[45] Further: "Having legitimized his drive to exercise power by laborious self-preparation and by adopting worthy goals, Wilson felt free to indulge his wish to force others into immediate and complete compliance with his demands."[46]

But Wilson the power-holder did not become immediately and indiscriminately aggressive in his leadership tactics. As the Georges take care to point out:

> In each of the major executive posts he occupied during his life there was an initial period during which the type of leadership he exercised in response to his inner needs coincided with the type of leadership the external situation required for impressive accomplishment. He drove the faculty and trustees at Princeton to accomplish an unprecedented series of reforms. The New Jersey legislature of 1911 was a triumph of productivity in his hands. Later, he was to exact a brilliant performance from the Sixty-Third Congress of the United States.

They go on:

> Wilson's difficulties arose when he encountered opposition, often evoked partly in reaction to his own driving demands, and when the chance for further success hinged upon his ability to alter his tactics. . . . Indeed, he was usually least capable of flexible responses in the situations which most required them. For angry opposition only intensified his anxieties and the more surely dictated a stubborn determination to subjugate his foes.[47]

This passage suggests that the opposition to which Wilson responded in this manner was wittingly or unwittingly provoked ("often evoked partly in response to his own driving demands") by the man himself. The Georges reinforce this inference when they say a little further on: "His *provocative behavior* attracted the personal hostilities of his opponents. They, then, attacked him and his programs in a vindictive spirit."[48]

Now if, in the initial periods, Wilson as leader was capable of prodigious accomplishment (and the flexibility it requires), the distinction between Wilson the power-seeker and Wilson the power-holder, for all its usefulness as a starting point, does not take us to the core of the problem. What has to be explained is not a generalized aggressiveness in Wilson's enactment of his leader-roles, but specifically his opposition-provoking behavior *in office* and the vindictiveness which this opposition typically aroused in him—with politically self-defeating consequences. Approaching this problem in terms of the hypothesis that Wilson was a neurotic personality in Horney's terms, a solution suggests itself along the following lines. His motivation, as has been argued, was never a desire for power *per se;* it was the search for glory, and more concretely the drive to prove the idealized Wilson in action through leadership success. The prime test of such success was winning a leadership role that would bring him fame, honor, acclaim and acknowledgment of his talents, along with the opportunity to reap more such rewards by demonstrating in the office won his greatness as a leader.

Accordingly, no sooner had he obtained a particular leadership role than he would take advantage of it to espouse and strive to put through new ideas, new departures in policy, new programs which, if successful, would bring greater glory and possibly, also, open the way to a still higher leadership role with its still greater opportunities for further leadership success. Since in his initial periods in office he found not only real needs for change but also real opportunities to persuade the given establishment and community of the desirability of the proposed reforms, the initial scale of Wilson's accomplishment was impressive. But he would be driven by his compulsive need for glory, reinforced now by the initial leadership success, to press for further dramatic and acclaim-producing leadership projects despite the inevitable growth of resistance to further change; or else, as in the governorship, he would lose interest after exploiting the potentialities of the post for his purposes and thus allow the success in the legislative session of 1911 to give way to the failure of that in 1912.

To cite an especially important instance of Wilson's motivation as leader, we may refer to his espousal of the League of Nations. Colonel House appealed to Wilson's desire for glory in this connection: "All through the war, in seeking to stimulate Wilson's interest in international affairs, House shrewdly assured him that he could achieve immortality by pioneering a world organization which would insure peace."[49] And further: "He had always wanted—*needed*—to do immortal work. Devising a peace settlement which would prevent future wars was a task which appealed to everything within him which strove for self-vindication through accomplishment. For what greater good could a man do than engineer the end to human strife?"[50] But the moral motivation was inextricably intertwined with the egocentricity of Wilson's search for glory. Once he had taken up the project, Wilson was highly possessive about it. As House confided to his diary:

> I wish again to call attention to the selfishness which seems to lurk in the minds of those in authority. The President is anxious to state his peace terms before Lloyd George and Clemenceau have an opportunity to forestall him. It is not team work. . . . It is the thing I have complained of so often in this diary, that is, that it is not so much general accomplishment that those in authority seem to desire as accomplishment which may redound to their personal advantage.[51]

Whoever rose to challenge Wilson in such a situation, by opposing the plan or Wilson's particular version of the plan, aroused him to a vindictive fury as compulsive as the need for glory which underlay his espousal of the plan. For such a challenge was implicitly a challenge to the validity of Wilson's exalted self-appraisal, his idealized statesman-self and its attributes of wisdom, nobility, farsightedness. Having difficulty in imagining that the plan (and hence he, himself, as its sponsor) was deficient in any way, Wilson could only interpret the opposition as motivated by the ugly ulterior designs of an evil opponent. Such a rationalization was his only means of defending the idealized self in that situation.

Consequently, Wilson became not only utterly intransigent toward the challenge, he also became enraged against the challenger. Very likely this rage was compounded by the projection upon the opponent of Wilson's own repressed self-hate. His only recourse now was to do everything possible to expose the opponent as malign and to defeat him humiliatingly. Gaining such a pride-restoring vindictive triumph eventually became more important to Wilson than putting through the project itself, no matter how much effort he had invested in it. As Horney notes in discussing such motivation in the neurotic personality, "compulsively he has to drag his rival down or defeat him."[52] I submit that the psychodynamics of Wilson's self-defeating pattern find explanation in these terms.

To conclude with a speculative postscript to this argument, let us recall the Georges' distinction between Wilson the power-seeker and Wilson the power-holder and their reference to his "provocative behavior" while in power. We might hypothesize that underlying the provocative behavior was not only the search for glory through great leadership that led him to drive too hard, but also *an unconscious need to provoke opposition in order that, by overcoming it, he could experience the winning of the leader-role again,* for example by appealing to his mass constituency over the heads of his establishmentarian opposition. As the Georges say in their final paragraph, "Wilson sought vindication."[53] This meant, we might add, not alone the sought-for vindictive triumph over the evil challenger, but the rewinning of legitimate power in the very process of gaining that political victory.

This reasoning would suggest that Wilson had an unconscious fantasy of being challenged and of overcoming the challenge gloriously, thereby gaining vindication both of himself and some immediate threatened project expressive of his greatness as a leader. His provocative behavior may be seen from this viewpoint as a way of creating, while in the leader-role, situations that made it necessary for him, as it were, to win it all over again. His tendency, then, was *not* to defeat himself, but to produce challenges to himself that would enable him to win the leadership, and the plaudits, again in the face of the very resistance that he himself had provoked. So, *after* winning a leader-role, Wilson was driven, while enacting that role, to go on reenacting the experience of winning it, to go on being a "power-seeker."[54]

This re-examination of the Georges' psychological interpretation of Woodrow Wilson has been accompanied by the outlining of an alternative approach based on the hypothesis that Wilson was a neurotic personality. Earlier, some criteria were suggested for measuring the relative explanatory values of differing psychological approaches in psychobiography. Perhaps the most fitting words with which to bring the essay to a close would be those of the Georges: "Let the reader consider whether these patterns of behavior become more consistently comprehensible in terms of the explanations herein offered than in terms of other explanations. That will be the best test of their usefulness."[55]

NOTES

1 Harold D. Lasswell, *Psychopathology and Politics,* new ed. (New York: Viking Press, 1960), p. 9. Here and throughout italics are in the original unless otherwise indicated in footnotes.

2 Paul Murray Kendall, *The Art of Biography* (New York: Norton, 1965), p. 15.

3 A. O. J. Cockshut, *Truth to Life: The Art of Biography in the Nineteenth Century* (New York: Harcourt, Brace Jovanovich, 1974), p. 16.

4 Alexander L. George, "Some Uses of Dynamic Psychology in Political Biography: Case Materials on Woodrow Wilson," in *A Source Book for the Study of Personality and Politics,* ed. Fred I. Greenstein and Michael Lerner (Chicago: Markham, 1971), p. 80.

5 In his "Afterthoughts—Thirty Years Later," appended to the 1960 new edition of *Psychopathology and Politics,* he himself noted that ". . . the study of politicians (and of politics in general) by methods largely inspired by psychoanalysis has made but modest progress to date" (p. 290). Since 1960, however, the psychobiographical study of political leaders has shown notable signs of progress, in Erik H. Erikson, *Gandhi's Truth: On the Origins of Militant Non-Violence* (New York: Norton, 1969), and a number of other studies.

6 For example, according to Betty Glad, "Contributions of Psychobiography," *Handbook of Political Psychology,* ed. Jeanne N. Knutson (San Francisco: Jossey-Bass, 1973), p. 298, "the systematic use of psychobiography for the exploration of the interface between personality, attitudes, and political behavior did not really begin until 1956, with the publication of the Georges' book—*Woodrow Wilson and Colonel House*—and Smith, Bruner, and White's *Opinions and Personality.*" Fred Greenstein devotes most of a chapter of his *Personality and Politics.* 2nd ed. (New York: Norton, 1975) to an analysis of the Georges' study as a model of procedure in psychobiography.

7 Bernard Brodie, "A Psychoanalytic Interpretation of Woodrow Wilson," in *Psychoanalysis and History,* ed. Bruce Mazlish (Englewood Cliffs: Prentice-Hall, 1963), p. 123. This review appeared originally in *World Politics,* 9 (1957), 413–22.

8 Lasswell, *Psychopathology and Politics,* pp. 74–75.

9 Harold D. Lasswell, *Power and Personality* (New York: Norton, 1948), p. 39.

10 *Woodrow Wilson and Colonel House,* p. 320.

11 Alexander L. George, "Power as a Compensatory Value for Political Leaders," *The Journal of Social Issues,* Vol. XXIV, no 3 (July, 1968), 30.

12 Greenstein has reasoned along similar lines in *Personality and Politics,* pp. 68–69, 92–93.

13 Lasswell, *Power and Personality,* p. 53. Italics added.

14 Karen Horney, *Neurosis and Human Growth: The Struggle Toward Self-Realization* (New York: Norton, 1950), pp. 18, 22. The following exposition of the concept of the neurotic personality is a summary of Horney's analysis in this book.

15 *Woodrow Wilson and Colonel House,* p. 6.

16 Ibid., p. 8.

17 *Woodrow Wilson and Colonel House,* p. 114.

18 Ibid., p. 151.

19 Arthur S. Link, *Woodrow Wilson: The Road to the White House* (Princeton: University Press, 1947), pp. 206–07.

20 *Woodrow Wilson and Colonel House,* p. 317.

21 George, "Some Uses of Dynamic Psychology," p. 92.

22 *Woodrow Wilson and Colonel House,* pp. 43, 12. Italics added.

23 *Woodrow Wilson and Colonel House,* p. 9.

24 Ibid., pp. 11–12.

25 Noting the importance placed by the Georges on the pattern of reading retardation in boyhood, Greenstein finds that the Georges' interpretation of Wilson's idealization of his father involved "reaction-formation" (*Personality and Politics,* p. 84). This is fully plausible although the Georges do not use the term itself. In Freudian theory, reaction-formation represents an individual's attempt to defend against a certain repudiated tendency in himself by going to the opposite extreme.

26 Brodie, "A Psychoanalytic Interpretation of Woodrow Wilson," p. 115.

27 George, "Some Uses of Dynamic Psychology," p. 83. From one of the references to this article (p. 97) it appears that the quoted comment on Horney was based on a reading of

two of her earlier works: *The Neurotic Personality of Our Time* (New York: Norton, 1937) and *Our Inner Conflicts* (New York: Norton, 1945). The latter work presaged in many ways the fuller and more systematic account of the dynamics of the neurotic personality presented in *Neurosis and Human Growth*.

28 A notable historical example which I have attempted to document in detail, in terms basically of Horneyan theory, is Stalin. See Robert C. Tucker, *Stalin As Revolutionary 1879–1929: A Study in History and Personality* (New York: Norton, 1973), chaps. 3–4 and 12–14.

29 This hypothesis has been suggested by Mr. Harry Hirsch of the Princeton Politics Department in a seminar discussion. For Horney's classification of neurotic personality types and analysis of the main types and subtypes, see *Neurosis and Human Growth,* chaps. 8, 10 and 11.

30 *Woodrow Wilson and Colonel House,* p. 21. One's interpretation of this statement would turn on what one took to be the precise meaning that Wilson placed on "love." It could have carried, for example, the connotation of admiration or adulation, which in turn would be consonant with the "expansive" solution.

31 Ibid., p. 114.

32 Ibid., pp. 8, 9.

33 Ibid., p. 3.

34 Ibid., p. 29.

35 *Woodrow Wilson and Colonel House,* p. 28. During his Princeton period Wilson made this statement, which I believe was unwittingly self-revelatory: ". . . I am covetous for Princeton of all the glory that there is, and the chief glory of a university is always intellectual glory. The chief glory of a university is the leadership of the nation in the things that attach to the highest ambitions that nations can set themselves, those ideals which lift nations into the atmosphere of things that are permanent and do not fade from generation to generation" (Link, *Wilson: The Road to the White House,* p. 44).

36 Horney, *Neurosis and Human Growth,* p. 86.

37 *Woodrow Wilson and Colonel House,* p. 24.

38 Ibid., p. 119.

39 Ibid., p. 31.

40 Ibid., p. 122.

41 *Woodrow Wilson and Colonel House,* pp. 31–32.

42 Ibid., p. 126.

43 Ibid., p. 122. Italics added.

44 Ibid., pp. 58, 116.

45 Ibid., p. 116.

46 Ibid., pp. 117–118.

47 *Woodrow Wilson and Colonel House,* pp. 118–19. On these points the Georges are in full agreement with Link. See Link, *Woodrow Wilson: The Road to the White House,* p. 45.

48 *Woodrow Wilson and Colonel House,* p. 121. Italics added. See also the authors' statement in the Introduction (p. xx) that: "As President of the United States, his provocative behavior all but invited the catastrophic defeat he suffered when the Senate refused to ratify the Versailles Peace Treaty with the League of Nations in it."

49 *Woodrow Wilson and Colonel House,* p. 189.

50 Ibid., p. 197.

51 Quoted in *Woodrow Wilson and Colonel House,* p. 189. By "those in authority" House, of course, meant the president.

52 Horney, *Neurosis and Human Growth,* p. 198.

53 *Woodrow Wilson and Colonel House,* p. 315.

54 I am indebted to Dr. Joseph Slap for elucidating in a personal communication the way in which unconscious fantasies can underlie certain repetitive forms of conduct or lead an individual to recreate situations which activate such forms of conduct.

55 *Woodrow Wilson and Colonel House,* p. 12.

12

Woodrow Wilson's Political Personality: A Reappraisal

Edwin A. Weinstein
James William Anderson
Arthur S. Link

Historians, biographers, and political scientists, as well as psychiatrists and psychologists, have long been intrigued by Woodrow Wilson's personality and its relationship to the events of his academic, political, and diplomatic careers. Although interpretations have varied, there is universal agreement that Wilson's personality was of major importance in both his successes and failures.

Along with the conventional descriptions of Woodrow Wilson's character by his major biographers, Ray Stannard Baker and Arthur S. Link, there have been two book-length psychoanalytic studies. The first, *Thomas Woodrow Wilson*, by Sigmund Freud and William C. Bullitt, was written during the 1930s but not published until 1967.[1] This study, a biased application of a simplistic and distorted version of psychoanalytic theory, is not regarded either by historians or psychoanalysts as a scholarly contribution. In one review,[2] Link demonstrated that the evidence on which the psychological interpretations are based is wildly inaccurate and at times even fabricated. In another review,[3] the psychoanalyst, Erik H. Erikson, pointed out that the crude psychological propositions used in the book were certainly not the handiwork of Freud; he added, however, that Freud's involvement with the book, no matter how minimal,[4] remains an embarrassment to psychoanalysts.

The second study, *Woodrow Wilson and Colonel House: A Personality Study*, by Alexander L. and Juliette L. George, was published in 1956 and reprinted with a new preface in 1964.[5] In contrast to the Freud-Bullitt book, the Georges' study has received wide acclaim, and political scientists interested in psychology have

Reprinted with permission from *Political Science Quarterly*, 93(Winter 1978–79):585–98.

held it up as a model of a psychodynamically oriented political biography. For example, Bernard Brodie calls the book "the first interpretation of the character of [Wilson] which impressed one as having depth, coherence, and consistency."[6] Fred I. Greenstein and Michael Lerner write that it is "one of the most rigorous and convincing of the psychobiographies of political figures."[7] Elmer E. Cornwell, Jr., in a recent review of books on the presidency, characterized *Woodrow Wilson and Colonel House* as "perhaps the best portrait ... drawn." "Their analysis of the impact on the future President of a strict Calvinistic creed and demanding Presbyterian-minister father," Cornwell adds, "remains the most successful 'psychohistorical' treatment of any President."[8]

It is our view, however, that the Georges' book (along with an explanatory article that Alexander George published in 1960), although not deserving of immediate dismissal, as is the Freud-Bullitt work, presents an essentially incorrect interpretation of the personality of Woodrow Wilson and its effect on his career.

The style of the book is graceful and concise, and the Georges have an unusual ability to translate psychological concepts into readily grasped, non-technical language. They are basically sympathetic to Wilson and have great admiration for his achievements. In addition, as Robert C. Tucker has noted in a recent essay on the book,[9] the Georges deserve credit for advancing, through their case study of Wilson, the understanding that a political leader's personality may play a large or even decisive role in determining his conduct in public affairs. The Georges also made a contribution to the development of the methodology of psychobiography. The two authors, in their Research Note and in the 1964 Preface, and Alexander George in the essay of 1960, described the methods they had used while writing the book and their reasons for adopting these methods; they were the first psychobiographers to attempt to conceptualize the process of applying psychology to biography. Finally, some of the book's shortcomings reflect the time in which it was written. Psychological theory has advanced since the mid-1950s, and a great deal of new evidence about Wilson's life has been discovered since the book's original publication in 1956. The Georges, of course, had to work with the psychological theories and the historical sources which were available at the time.[10]

Nonetheless, the Georges' book, in our opinion, suffers from three major deficiencies, which, taken together, result in an inaccurate portrayal of Wilson's personality. The principal failing of the book is that the research on which it rests is inadequate. Second, the Georges fail to recognize the limitations of their psychological model and misrepresent evidence to fit their theory. Third, they ignore Wilson's neurological disorders as conditions affecting his behavior.

The remainder of this essay will examine in detail two of the topics most crucial to the Georges' interpretation of Wilson's personality—Wilson's childhood and the Princeton graduate college controversy; present data, which though available to them, was not investigated; and comment on their use of psychological theory.

I

The Georges claim that Wilson suffered from a troubled relationship with his father, the Rev. Dr. Joseph Ruggles Wilson, a distinguished southern Presbyterian minister. Although Woodrow Wilson overcame his childhood difficulties to some extent, they state, pathological patterns continued to plague him periodically throughout his political career. The main evidence offered for this view is Wilson's early learning experience. The facts are well-known: Wilson did not learn the alphabet until he was nine and did not read with even minimal facility until he was eleven. He entered school at the age of ten and performed poorly. The explanation offered by the Georges reads:

> Perhaps the Doctor's scorn of fumbling first errors was so painful (or perhaps the mere expectation of such a reaction was so distressing) that the boy renounced the effort altogether. Perhaps, too, failing—refusing—to learn was one way in which the boy dared to express his [unconscious] resentment against his father.[11]

It is improbable that Wilson's slowness in learning to read was due to emotional factors and highly likely that it was a manifestation of developmental dyslexia. Undiagnosed in Wilson's childhood, the condition was well-known to neurologists at the time that the Georges wrote their book. However, a number of psychiatrists and psychologists still believed that the condition was an emotional rather than a neurological problem, and the Georges simply chose an explanation that was currently popular. The condition is a frequent one, occurring in about 10 percent of the school population, significantly more frequently in boys. Research over the past seventy years indicates that developmental dyslexia is caused by a delay in the establishment of the dominance of one cerebral hemisphere—usually the left—for language. One theory is that, with the maturational lag, there is representation of language in both hemispheres and performance suffers in the competition for control of the same function.

The specific evidence that Wilson had developmental dyslexia can be summed up in three groups. First, by his own admission he was a slow reader into adult life. At the Johns Hopkins, the amount of assigned reading was his bane. "Steady reading," he wrote his fiancée, "always demands of me more expenditure of resolution and dogged energy than any other sort of work."[12] Second, difficulties in calculation are commonly associated with developmental dyslexia, and Wilson was extremely poor in arithmetic. Third, when, as a result of a stroke in 1896, he could not write with his right hand, he was able, within a few days and without practice, to write with his left hand in perfectly formed script. This ability strongly suggests that he had mixed cerebral dominance for language.

The reading disability affected Wilson's development and his relationship with his parents, but hardly in the way that the Georges state. It probably made him more dependent on his family. Also, he may have feared that his reading problems indicated that he was stupid or lazy. The condition probably made Dr. Wilson more pedagogic and insistent on drilling his "lazy" son. To judge from Wilson's pleasant memories of having his family read to him, they seem to have been tolerant of his problem. During the Civil War, Dr. Wilson was away from home some of the time serving as a chaplain in the Confederate Army. Much of the reading was done by other family members and, if the Georges' hypothesis were true, Wilson must have been expressing his "unconscious hostility" toward his mother, sisters, and other relatives. We do not have a good record of Wilson's childhood such as might be gained from contemporary letters, diaries, or autobiographies; like any other child, he may have felt insecurities. However, it is certain that they did not come about in the manner postulated by the Georges.

According to the Georges, Wilson's relationship with his father was nothing less than devastating. They say that Wilson's father "ridiculed his intellectual capacities and made him feel mediocre." They add that Wilson had to endure "barbed criticism," "sarcastically made demands" and "aspersions on his moral and intellectual worth," and that Wilson interpreted these criticisms "as humiliating evidence, that, try as he might, he was inadequate." As a result of this treatment, they conclude, Wilson feared that he was "stupid, ugly, worthless and unlovable."[13] The Georges' entire interpretation of Wilson's personality revolves around their portrayal of his relationship with his father. They argue that, because of this relationship, Wilson forever harbored a deep sense of worthlessness and also carried a burden of rage which he later turned against adversaries, such as Dean Andrew F. West and Senator Henry Cabot Lodge of Massachusetts.

The sole evidence for this view of Wilson's relationship with his father, aside from the Georges' interpretation of Wilson's reading disability, consists of comments made to Baker in the mid-1920s. Wilson's daughter, Margaret, talking of Dr. Wilson said: "His idea was that if a lad was of fine tempered steel, the more he was beaten, the better he was."[14] The metaphor, a favorite of both Wilson and his father, may be interpreted in various ways and at several levels of concreteness. Probably Dr. Wilson was boasting about Woodrow. But any interpretation should take into account Margaret Wilson's feelings about her grandfather. Margaret did not know Dr. Wilson well until she was fourteen years old, when, because of his deteriorating health, he came to live with his son in Princeton. Affected by severe cerebral arteriosclerosis, Dr. Wilson had become testy and puerile, and his grandchildren were afraid of him.[15] Margaret Wilson's statement can hardly be regarded as indicative of Wilson's relationship with his father while the boy was growing up.

The other recollection is a more substantial one. Wilson's cousin, Helen Woodrow Bones, told Baker:

> Uncle Joseph was a cruel tease, with a caustic wit and a sharp tongue, and I remember hearing my own family tell indignantly of how Cousin Woodrow suffered under his teasing. He was proud of WW, especially after his son began to show how unusual he was, but only a man as sweet as Cousin Woodrow could have forgotten the severity of the criticism to the value of which he so often paid tribute, in after life.[16]

This recollection, more than fifty years after the alleged events, may or may not have been accurate. However, Helen Bones (who was the first Mrs. Wilson's private secretary from March 1913 until Mrs. Wilson's death in August 1914, served as mistress of the White House until Wilson married again in December 1915, and continued to live off and on with the president and his second wife) was fiercely and passionately devoted to Wilson. She deeply resented any criticism of the man she idolized.[17] She would probably have exaggerated and magnified the importance of such stories about Dr. Wilson's treatment of his son. She most likely heard the stories from her parents, and there is evidence of bad blood between them and Dr. and Mrs. Wilson.

The Georges cite an additional recollection to give an idea of the nature of this teasing. One morning, according to another cousin, Jessie Bones Brower (Helen Bones's sister), Wilson's father apologized when his son arrived late for breakfast and explained that he had been so greatly excited at the discovery of another hair in his mustache that it had taken him longer to wash and dress. "I remember very distinctly the painful flush that came over the boy's face," the cousin recalled.[18] If this is typical of Dr. Wilson's teasing, it does not sound harsh or excessive and certainly does not suggest the type of father-son relationship that would handicap Wilson for the rest of his life. Wilson's father was a great wit and punster and used his family as an audience, but there is no indication that he was malicious.

Let us grant that these recollections offer some support for the Georges' interpretation. However, they must be weighed against contrary evidence, which is much more substantial. There are many reports from people who knew Wilson and his father well—sources available to the Georges—about the extraordinarily warm relationship that existed between Wilson and his father during Wilson's childhood.[19] They spent a great deal of time together, and Dr. Wilson read to him and talked to him at length. Early in the week, Wilson's father would visit parishioners while they were at work, and he would take his son along to share the experiences. As evidence of Wilson's submissive attitude toward his father, the Georges cite his helping his father, as a young man, with the dull task of writing the minutes of the General Assembly of the southern Presbyterian Church. If one is to judge by the bitter controversy that led to Dr. Wilson's resignation from the Columbia Theological Seminary,[20] the minutes were anything but dull. In pursuit of their theme of Wilson's "unconscious hostility" toward and fear of his father, the Georges go so far as to interpret Wilson's tender care of his father, over the last years of his life, and his singing of the old man's favorite hymns to him, as evidence of Wilson's guilt and submission!

The Georges emphasize that Wilson was extremely dependent on his father until the latter's death. In support of their view, they cite the observation of a Princeton colleague, Winthrop More Daniels, that Wilson was always the pupil of his father. They fail to cite evidence to the contrary, such as that of Bliss Perry, who commented on the comradely relationship between the two men.[21] It is true that Wilson was financially dependent on his father into his late twenties. However, after the death of Wilson's mother in 1888, he, Woodrow Wilson, became the effective head of the family and the one to whom his brother, sisters, and *father* came for advice and support. Yet the Georges maintain that Wilson's early dependence never changed. As further evidence, they cite the famous "my incomparable father" letter written when Wilson was thirty-two and in the first year of his professorship at Wesleyan. The letter reads:

> My precious father,
> My thoughts are full of you and dear "Dode" [Wilson's younger brother, Joseph] all the time. Tennessee seems *so* far away for a chap as hungry as I am for a sight of the two men whom I love. As the Christmas recess approaches I realize, as I have so often before, the *pain* there is in a season of holiday and rejoicing away from you. As you know, one of the chief things about which I feel most warranted in rejoicing is that I am your son. I realize the benefit of being your son more and more as my talents and experience grow: I recognize the strength growing in me as of the nature of your strength: I become more and more conscious of the hereditary wealth I possess, the capital of principle, of literary force and skill, of capacity for first-hand thought; and I feel daily more and more bent toward creating in my own children that combined respect and tender devotion for their father that you gave your children for you. Oh, how happy I should be, if I could make them think of me as I think of you! You have given me a love that grows, that is stronger in me now that I am a man than it was when I was a boy, and which will be stronger in me when I am an old man than it is now— a love, in brief, that is rooted and grounded in *reason,* and not in filial instinct merely— a love resting upon abiding foundations of *service,* recognizing you as in a certain very real sense the author of all I have to be grateful for! I bless God for my noble, strong, and saintly mother and for my incomparable father. Ask "Dode" if he does not subscribe? and tell him that I love my brother passionately.
> ...Ellie joins me in unbounded love to you both.
>
> Your devoted son,
> Woodrow[22]

Although still an important figure in the southern Presbyterian Church, Dr. Wilson had encountered disappointments in his work and was frequently discouraged and depressed. His career had not advanced, while Woodrow's had, and he had become increasingly identified with and somewhat envious of his son. Wilson, busy in his new position at Wesleyan and involved with writing *The State* (1889), had not written to his father for some time. Could not Wilson, feeling his neglect of his father, now a lonely widower, have written the letter to raise the old man's spirits and self-esteem? And could he not in fact have been expressing his feelings toward his father?

The Georges claim that Dr. Wilson became proud of his son only after the latter began to show how unusual he was. There could be some argument about when Woodrow Wilson began to display extraordinary talent. Probably it was during his senior year at Princeton, when he was managing editor of *The Princetonian* and had an article accepted by a national review. Yet the many letters that Joseph R. Wilson wrote to his son before 1878–79 reveal affection, admiration, pride in his son, and helpful criticism, but never denigration.[23] Wilson dedicated *Congressional Government* to his father. He wrote:

> To his father, the patient guide of his youth, the gracious companion of his manhood, his best instructor and most lenient critic, this book is affectionately dedicated by the author.

Dr. Wilson had a tremendous influence on his son, and probably no boy grows up without some resentment toward his father. However, on the basis of the evidence there is no reason to believe that the dedication of *Congressional Government*[24] was not a valid representation of Wilson's feelings toward his father.

It is almost incredible that a psychobiography tracing the development of Wilson's personality should make so little mention of his mother, Janet, or Jessie, Woodrow Wilson, about whom a great deal was known when the Georges wrote their book. They spend less than half a page on the subject, quoting from the memories of her that Wilson expressed at the time of her death: "As the first shock and the acute pain of the great, the irreparable blow passes off, my heart is filling up with tenderest memories of my sweet mother, memories that seem to hallow my whole life—which seem to explain to me how it came about that I was given the sweetest, most satisfying of wives for my daily companion. My mother, with her sweet womanliness, her purity, her intelligence, prepared me for my wife. I remember how I clung to her (a laughed-at 'mamma's boy') till I was a great big fellow: but love of the best womanhood came to me and entered my heart through her apron-strings."[25]

A discerning reading of all the evidence about Jessie available to the Georges and of the Wilson family correspondence, which was not available to them, would have shown that this description of Wilson's relationship with his mother was far from complete. Jessie Wilson was indeed a saintly, intelligent woman, devoted to her family, and Wilson was a very loving son. But she was extremely overprotective, and the mutual dependence that she fostered was responsible for the relatively late age at which Wilson achieved emotional and heterosexual maturity. Shy, reserved, and deferential to the outgoing Dr. Wilson, she was intensely ambitious for her husband and son. She was also extraordinarily sensitive to what she felt were slights of others; and, when Wilson or his father encountered setbacks, she invariably attributed them to the spite and malice of their opponents. While Wilson's father pointed out his son's faults and tried to temper his impatience and aggressiveness, she was completely uncritical. Much more than Dr. Wilson, she gave Woodrow the feeling that he was not only intellectually, but morally, superior to his colleagues—a trait that contributed to one of Wilson's greatest failings, his overconfidence. Her influence had a great deal to do with Wilson's shyness and uneasiness with people who were not close to him, and his particular dependence on women. Mrs. Wilson was often ill—probably on a psychosomatic basis—and extremely anxious and worrisome about Woodrow's health. Wilson's attitudes toward illness, derived from both parents, had most important consequences for his career. There is also good evidence that Mrs. Wilson suffered from chronic depression; her son later said many times that he had inherited his tendency toward melancholy from his mother's side.

II

No study of Wilson's behavior during the great crises of his career can be complete without taking into account the effects of the cerebral vascular disease from which he suffered, intermittently, from the age of thirty-nine until his death in 1924. In 1896, Wilson had a stroke which caused a marked weakness of his right hand, and he had recurrences in 1900, 1904, 1906, and 1907. The stroke of 1906 caused not only weakness of his right arm but almost complete blindness of his left eye, a syndrome indicative of an embolus from the left internal carotid artery. Wilson's attempts to adapt to the consequences of the stroke caused changes in his behavior and helped set into motion events relevant to his defeats in the quadrangle plan and graduate college controversies at Princeton. The course of carotid artery disease is very variable, with frequent remissions, and, in the light of today's knowledge, it is not surprising that Wilson was in good health while governor of New Jersey and when he became president of the United States. The disease, however, is ultimately a progressive one and, by the end of World War I, Wilson was showing signs of generalized cerebral involvement. In Paris, he had an attack of influenza, probably a virus encephalopathy, which, super-imposed on pre-existing brain damage, produced changes in behavior which may have influenced the outcome of the peace negotiations. In October 1919 he had a massive stroke that completely paralyzed the left side of his body and produced mental attitudes and personality changes which were important factors in his failure to obtain ratification of the Treaty of Versailles.[26]

The Georges are not neurologists or psychiatrists, and some of the information on which the above reconstruction is based was not available to them. Yet even lay observers, such as Herbert Hoover, had commented on the changes of Wilson's mental functioning after the Paris illness. Any behavioral scientist should have wondered about the effects of the massive stroke of 1919. Similarly, the Georges ignored Wilson's stroke of 1906 as a factor in his behavior and explained his problems during the quadrangle (or "quad") plan and graduate college controversies as stemming from an emotionally disturbed childhood.

The controversy over the location and character of the graduate college was the most dramatic event of Woodrow Wilson's term as president of Princeton University. A wealthy alumnus, William C. Procter, in 1909 offered to donate $500,000 to help build a graduate college to house graduate students, but he included an important stipulation—that the building be located on the golf course, nearly a mile from the center of the campus. It was the site which the dean of the small existing graduate school, Andrew Fleming West, a close friend of Procter, had selected. West favored an off-campus site so that graduate students might study undisturbed by undergraduates. Wilson consistently argued that they should live close together, in order, as he put it, that the graduate students might energize the intellectual life of the undergraduates.[27] It was the same idea that had led Wilson to institute the preceptorial system and to propose his quadrangle plan. Originally, both West and Wilson had advocated a central location, but West had changed his view. West believed that Wilson had delayed action on the graduate college in favor of his preceptorial and quad plans—which indeed he had—and charged that Wilson had gone back on his promise of support, given in 1906, at the time when West turned down an offer of the presidency of the Massachusetts Institute of Technology. Wilson believed, with ample reason, that West was an intellectual dilettante, who wished to maintain dominion over an elitist world of his own. Some months before the Procter offer, Wilson had reorganized the faculty committee on the graduate school and broken West's absolute control of the policies of the graduate school.

The Georges see the conflict as based on Wilson's perception of West as a father figure. In their view, the situation caused Wilson to give vent to the unconscious hostility which he had felt, but had never been able to release, toward his own father. They regard the issue of the location of the college as merely an excuse for Wilson to release this unconscious hostility by doing battle with West. At some level, they say, West evoked in Wilson the image of his father. Therefore Wilson resisted West "with all the violence he had once felt, but never ventured to express, in response to his father's overwhelming domination." But, they add, Wilson could not confess, even to himself, that he experienced West as "an unbearable threat," and, consequently, he "disguised all his volcanic feelings against West in terms of a great moral crusade in which he championed the 'right.' "[28]

We have already examined the Georges' previous evidence for Wilson's "unconscious hostility" toward his father. Before considering further their interpretation of the graduate college controversy, additional background is necessary. The situation was already a tense one because of the bitter struggle that had occurred over the quadrangle plan. This was a proposal by Wilson to abolish the exclusive undergraduate eating clubs and construct quadrangles, or residential colleges, assignment to which would be made by lot. Opposition, often violent, soon developed and was led by the eastern alumni. The trustees, who had approved the plan "in principle," when Wilson presented it in June 1907, withdrew their support in October. Wilson continued to press for it, and the battle became so acrimonious that a wealthy trustee and generous contributor to the university, M. Taylor Pyne, threatened to withdraw his support if Wilson ever mentioned the quad plan again.[29] Dean West led the minority faction of the faculty who were in opposition, which, to Wilson's great sorrow, included his best friend, John Grier Hibben.

Wilson's illness was an important factor in the defeat of his quad plan and also laid the groundwork for his defeat in the graduate college controversy. In 1906 he was at the height of his popularity and power at Princeton: the curriculum had been reformed, the faculty upgraded, and the preceptorial system successfully launched. Except for an episode of weakness in his right arm lasting several months in 1904, he had been in excellent health during his presidency. The stroke of 1906 was the first one to be recognized as such, and Wilson received a gloomy prognosis. He and his wife were aware that the condition was similar to that which had robbed his father of his mental faculties. Characteristically, Wilson's reaction was to immerse himself in his work. Originally, he had thought that the quad plan would take twenty years; now he thought it immediately attainable. In the interests of his health, he cut down on his social life. He took regular naps, reduced his personal contacts, and, in contrast to his previous habits, now decided to meet members of the Princeton community only on official business. Prior to the formal announcement to the trustees of the plan in June 1907, he had mentioned the idea to only three intimate friends on the faculty and not at all to the alumni. This lack of preparation contrasted markedly with the way he had organized support for the preceptorial system and must be judged an important cause of his failure. Wilson's increased overconfidence was one of a number of behavioral changes that occurred after the stroke in 1906; he became less empathic, more stubborn, and more prone to overgeneralize and personalize his problems.

The question of the site of the graduate college was far more than a pretext for Wilson to destroy West. At stake were Wilson's control of the university and the character of its educational program. It is debatable whether close association between graduates and undergraduates would have yielded the advantage that Wilson envisaged. However, his emphasis on such an association in the preceptorial and quadrangle plans indicates that the issue was important in itself. The Georges' treatment of the graduate college controversy makes it seem that Wilson stood practically alone in pressing his arguments. Actually, many others shared his point of view. Approximately half of the trustees supported Wilson, and the various votes related to the controversy were all close. Although the evidence is not conclusive, it appears that a large majority of the faculty, particularly the professors who were doing most of the graduate instruction, preferred that the college be built in the midst of the campus. In fact, members of the faculty (and of the board of trustees) were constantly pressing Wilson to stand firm and even to remove West or reduce his influence over the graduate program and college.[30]

Wilson's personality and his pattern of behavior under stress had a great deal to do with the events of the controversies over the quad plan and graduate college. But Wilson's aversion to Dean West did not come about because of unconscious feelings toward his father. Wilson detested West because West was the condensed symbol of so many of the social, educational, economic, and political problems that Wilson faced at Princeton. Moreover, Wilson did not "disguise" his feelings toward West. He expressed them quite openly.[31]

It is impossible in a single article to provide detailed analysis of and commentary on an entire book. It must suffice to say that we believe that the Georges' view of the relationship between Wilson and Edward M. House was highly distorted by overreliance on the House diary, which often presents a one-sided and unreliable account of events; that we find their explanation for Wilson's attempts to remain out of World War I almost arcane; and that recent research has considerably revised their explanation for the so-called break between Wilson and House at the Paris Peace Conference.[32]

III

By today's standard, the Georges' use of psychological theory is inadequate. Their formulations have been largely superseded by the views of ego psychology and by considerations of the development of the self and of social roles and interactions. While the Georges cannot be criticized for not anticipating these approaches, it should be pointed out that the works of Harry Stack Sullivan, Karen Horney, and Erich Fromm were available to them. Also, the common-sense view that most children identify with their parents and grow to resemble them does not seem to have played a part in their thinking. By the 1950s, the idea of fixed childhood hostilities, locked deep in the unconscious, impervious to change, and ready to burst forth in pristine fury, was being challenged. For the Georges to suggest that Wilson simply and directly transferred his hatred of his father to West and Senator Lodge during the fight over the Versailles Treaty is highly mechanistic, reductionistic, and deterministic. The formulation leaves no room for consideration of character development or identity formation.

The authors could have given a more realistic view of Wilson's relationship with his parents had they taken up family values and cultural norms. For example, Wilson's reluctance to express any negative feelings toward members of his family was shared by them and was a facet of their subculture. It is difficult to accept any theory of personality that does not take into consideration a subject's relationship with his mother, particularly Wilson's mother, who instilled so much anxiety in him. Then, the Georges give the impression that all that one has to know about Wilson is that his self-esteem was disastrously low. Yet self-esteem is rarely unitary. One may feel confident in some areas, insecure in others. Wilson was bothered by feelings that he was ugly; he seems to have identified himself in this respect with his rather physically unattractive mother. Yet he rarely had doubts about his intellectual and leadership qualities after reaching maturity.

Even without detailed knowledge of Wilson's childhood, one would assume, from his compulsive personality traits and his need to control his environment, that he had anxieties and insecurities. Yet to translate such insecurities into an insatiable drive for political power is to provide far too simple an explanation for a complex, multidetermined process. Further, the Georges state:

His [Wilson's] stern Calvinistic conscience forbade an unabashed pursuit of power for personal gratification. He could express his desire for power only insofar as he convincingly rationalized it in terms of altruistic service and fused it with laudable social objectives.[33]

It is true that Wilson often validated pragmatically arrived at decisions in moral terms, but when in the world of human affairs is concern for the public good divorced from personal gratification?

Woodrow Wilson and Colonel House has important implications for writers of psychobiography. They should be aware that personality theories derive, not only from scientific investigations, but also from ideology, the social milieu, and the personal problems of their authors. Theories are dated, as the Georges themselves point out; theories not only change with the years, but proponents of the same theory differ in their interpretations of it. In an interdisciplinary endeavor, more than superficial knowledge of areas outside of one's primary field is necessary. The historian or political scientist should be familiar, not only with psychoanalytic theory, but also with the many aspects of behavioral science, which, in recent years, have so profoundly influenced psychoanalysis. Above all, the psychobiographer should immerse himself in the primary biographical sources, not least of all for the reason that the criteria for clinical evidence may be quite different from those for historical work.[34] The great acclaim accorded the Georges' book may have helped give the impression that psychobiography can be written by furnishing "deep" interpretations of the work of others. No psychobiography is better than the research on which it rests.

NOTES

1 Sigmund Freud and William C. Bullitt, *Thomas Woodrow Wilson* (Boston: Houghton Mifflin, 1967).

2 Arthur S. Link, "The Case for Woodrow Wilson," *Harper's,* April 1967. pp. 85–93.

3 Erik H. Erikson, in *The New York Review of Books,* February 9, 1967, pp. 3–6; reprinted in *The International Journal of Psychoanalysis* 48(1967):462–68.

4 The degree of Freud's involvement will not be known until the Bullitt Papers at Yale are opened and we can see what Freud actually wrote. It is well known that Freud disliked Americans in general and Wilson in particular, who he thought was the embodiment of the Puritan moralist and was responsible for the breakup of the Austro-Hungarian Empire.

5 Alexander L. George and Juliette L. George, *Woodrow Wilson and Colonel House: A Personality Study* (New York: Dover Publications, Inc., 1964). Although the book includes an analysis of Wilson's relationship with Colonel House, the central concern is to provide a portrait of Wilson's personality and political behavior (see p. xxi), and it is this portrait, not the analysis of the relationship between Wilson and House, that is the focus of the present essay.

6 Bernard Brodie, "A Psychoanalytic Interpretation of Woodrow Wilson," in Bruce Mazlish, ed., *Psychoanalysis and History* (New York: Grossett & Dunlap, 1971), pp. 115–23.

7 Fred I. Greenstein and Michael Lerner, eds. *A Source Book for the Study of Personality and Politics* (Chicago: Markham, 1971), p. 77.

8 *The Wilson Quarterly* 1 (Winter 1977):68.

9 Robert C. Tucker, "The Georges' Wilson Reexamined: An Essay on Psychobiography," *American Political Science Review* 71(June 1977):606–18.

10 However, Alexander George, in an article published ten years ago ("Power as a Compensatory Value for Political Leaders," *Journal of Social Issues* (July 1968):29–49), still confidently advanced the theory that Wilson's damaged self-esteem, caused by his tyrannical and demanding father, was an important factor in propelling him into politics. The first, second, and perhaps the third, volumes of *The Papers of Woodrow Wilson,* which shed much new light on the relationship between Wilson and his father, were available when George's article was written. He presumably did not read these volumes; in any event, he did not cite them.

11 George and George, *Woodrow Wilson and Colonel House,* p. 7.

12 Wilson to Ellen Louise Axson, March 29, 1884, Arthur S. Link et al., *The Papers of Woodrow Wilson,* 28 vols. to date (Princeton, N.J.: Princeton University Press, 1966–) 3: 496; hereinafter cited as *PWW.*

13 George and George, *Woodrow Wilson and Colonel House,* pp. 114, 272, 6, 8.

14 Ibid., p. 8.

15 Margaret Axson Elliot, *My Aunt Louisa and Woodrow Wilson* (Chapel Hill, N.C.: University of North Carolina Press, 1944), p. 122.

16 George and George, *Woodrow Wilson and Colonel House,* p. 8.

17 Expressions of her feelings occur again and again in Helen W. Bones to Jessie Bones Brower, February 12 and 23, April 1 and 12, May 3, and June 1, 7, and 18, 1913. Woodrow Wilson Collection, Princeton University Library.

18 George and George, *Woodrow Wilson and Colonel House,* p. 8.

19 See for example, Ray Stannard Baker, *Woodrow Wilson, Life and Letters: Youth, 1856–1890* (Garden City, N.Y.: Doubleday, Page and Co., 1927); Josephus Daniels, *The Life of Woodrow Wilson* (Philadelphia: The John C. Winston Co., 1924); William Bayard Hale, *Woodrow Wilson; The Story of His Life* (Garden City, N.Y.: Doubleday, Page and Co., 1912); William Allen White, *Woodrow Wilson* (Boston and New York: Houghton Mifflin, 1924).

20 About this episode, see John M. Mulder, *Woodrow Wilson: The Years of Preparation* (Princeton, N.J.: Princeton University Press, 1978), pp. 15–17.

21 Bliss Perry, *And Gladly Teach* (Boston: Houghton Mifflin, 1935), p. 153.

22 Wilson to Joseph Ruggles Wilson, December 16, 1888, *PWW,* 6:30–31.

23 None of these letters was written during Wilson's early childhood; they date from the year 1875, when Wilson was eighteen years old, and they include seventy-six letters written before September 1885, when Wilson began his first teaching job at Bryn Mawr College. They are printed in *PWW,* vols. 1–5.

24 *Congressional Government: A Study in American Politics* (Boston: Houghton Mifflin, 1885), p. iii.

Thirty years later, long after his father's death, we hear Wilson saying about his father: "I remember my father as essentially humble and devout before God, spirited and confident before men. A natural leader, with a singular gift of clear, eloquent, convincing speech. Generous, playful, full of high spirits, and yet given to most laborious industry, alike in the use of books and in the administration of church affairs. A man who believed much more in the efficacy of Christian simple and pure living than in dogmatic advice or spiritual conversation—a robust Christian.

"The description I naturally associate with his name would be something like this: "Generous, high-spirited, thoughtful, studious, a master of men and of thought, who sought the life of dogma in conduct and preferred a pure life to a pious profession" (c. May 25, 1914).

And again: "As I look back on my boyhood, it seems to me that all the sense I got, I got by association with my father. He was good fun: he was a good comrade; and the experience he had had put a lot of sense in him that I had not been endowed with by birth, at any rate; and by constant association with him, I saw the world and the tasks of the world through his eyes, and because I believed in him I aspired to do and be the thing that he believed in" (May 29, 1914).

25 WW to Ellen A. Wilson, April 18, 1888, *PWW,* 5:719.

26 See Edwin A. Weinstein, "Woodrow Wilson's Neurological Illness," *Journal of American History* 57(September 1970):324–51. On a basis of new evidence, it is not likely, as was stated in this article, that Wilson had a stroke in Paris.

27 As Wilson put it in an address before the Princeton Club of New York on April 7, 1910: "As I look back upon my own studies as a graduate student, I realize that ... the intellectual limitations of the men with whom I was associated in the great graduate school I attended, was that their thought was so centered upon special lines of study that they had become impatient of everything that drew them away from them. I have heard these men again and again deplore the necessity they would some day be under of going through the drudgery of teaching stupid undergraduates,—a state of mind and a point of view which utterly unfitted them for the very profession they were approaching. That was due, in my mind, to the dissociation of graduate study in the life of the university from the undergraduate body.
"Not only that, but I believe that our universities lack the impulse of advanced study, so far as their undergraduates are concerned, largely because their undergraduates are not sufficiently brought into contact with the graduates. You know, gentlemen, that the process of education is a process of contagion. If you want to educate a man, put him in close association with the kind of intellectual fire you wish him to be touched by" (*PWW*, 20–345).

28 George and George, *Woodrow Wilson and Colonel House,* pp. 40, 43.

29 Melancthon W. Jacobus to Wilson, November 5, 1907, *PWW,* 17:468–69.

30 Arthur S. Link wishes to state that much new evidence discovered since the publication of his *Wilson: The Road to the White House* in 1947 has convinced him that his treatment of Wilson and West and the graduate college controversy is inadequate and unbalanced.

31 The entire graduate college controversy is amply documented in *PWW*, vols. 18–20.

32 The most authoritative study of House at the Paris Peace Conference, Inga Floro, *Colonel House in Paris: A Study of American Policy at the Paris Peace Conference 1919* (Aarhus, Denmark: Universitetsforlaget, 1973), proves conclusively that the cause of the so called break between the two men was House's failure to follow Wilson's explicit instructions while the latter was in the United States.

33 George and George, *Woodrow Wilson and Colonel House,* p. 117.

34 The best example in the past few years of a psychiatrist's use of primary historical sources is John E. Mack, *A Prince of Our Disorder: The Life of T. E. Lawrence* (Boston: Little, Brown, 1976).

13

Woodrow Wilson and Colonel House: A Reply to Weinstein, Anderson, and Link

Juliette L. George
Alexander L. George

Arthur S. Link of Princeton University has been studying and writing about Woodrow Wilson for some forty years, and he is the editor of *The Papers of Woodrow Wilson*. The thirty-six volumes thus far published in this series are a tribute to his prodigious scholarship. By common consent, Professor Link is the preeminent Wilson scholar of our time. If Link finds serious fault with an interpretation of Wilson, it behooves those who advanced it to reexamine their work in the light of his criticisms. As authors of *Woodrow Wilson and Colonel House: A Personality Study,* we felt placed under such an obligation upon the publication in *Political Science Quarterly* three years ago of an article by Link in collaboration with Edwin A. Weinstein (a psychiatrist and neurologist who has been studying and writing about Wilson for almost fifteen years), and James William Anderson (a clinical psychologist). In their article, Weinstein, Anderson, and Link characterized *Woodrow Wilson and Colonel House* as "an essentially incorrect interpretation of the personality of Woodrow Wilson and its effect on his career."[1]

Over the past few years, therefore, we have reviewed our work and have incorporated into our research a great deal of manuscript material that has become available since the publication of *Woodrow Wilson and Colonel House* in 1956. This review in the light of all the evidence, old and new, has served to confirm our belief in the validity of the interpretation of Wilson we offered in *Woodrow Wilson and Colonel House*. Indeed, the data now available permit a much fuller delineation of the relationship between Wilson and his father—of the extraordinary bond that existed between them, the very intensity of which, in our view, is related to the intensity of Wilson's early self-doubt, his suffering and need for approval (all of which now also may be more fully documented). We continue

Reprinted with permission from *Political Science Quarterly,* 96(Winter 1981–82):641–65.

191

to view Wilson as a great tragic figure whose "tragic flaw"—a ruinously self-defeating refusal to compromise with his opponents on certain issues that had become emotionally charged for him—evolved out of low self-estimates that we believe he developed as a child in response to his father's demands.

We consider it unfortunate, moreover, that Weinstein, Anderson, and Link present as though it were an indisputable fact Dr. Weinstein's *hypothesis* that beginning in 1896, Woodrow Wilson suffered a series of brain-damaging strokes that significantly and adversely affected his political functioning even so early as during his Princeton presidency. That Weinstein's retrospective interpretation of Wilson's medical problems is open to question among qualified medical specialists is obvious from the statement by Michael F. Marmor, M.D., of the Stanford University School of Medicine (see appendix). Of even greater concern, however, is the fact that Professor Link has permitted himself to state unequivocally in *The Papers of Woodrow Wilson* that Wilson suffered such strokes. In numerous notes and other editorial apparatus to several volumes of *The Papers,* Link asserts that Wilson had small strokes in 1896 and 1907 and "a major stroke" in 1906.[2] We believe he has thereby compromised the objectivity of that otherwise superb series and therefore compromised its value to historians, both present and future.

Weinstein, Anderson, and Link state in their critique that *Woodrow Wilson and Colonel House*

> suffers from three major deficiencies, which, taken together, result in an inaccurate portrayal of Wilson's personality. The principal failing of the book is that the research on which it rests is inadequate. Second, the Georges fail to recognize the limitations of their psychological model and misrepresent evidence to fit their theory. Third, they ignore Wilson's neurological disorders as conditions affecting his behavior.[3]

We shall address these criticisms in turn.

SOURCE MATERIALS FOR *WOODROW WILSON AND COLONEL HOUSE*

Weinstein, Anderson, and Link disparage our research—*Woodrow Wilson and Colonel House* furnishes " 'deep' interpretations of the work of others."[4] In our book, we characterized our work as "largely a synthesis and reinterpretation of well-known facts of Wilson's career."[5] We did not claim to be historians, nor was it our aim to uncover new data: rather, we hoped to cast a fresh eye on that which was already known. Indeed, we extracted a great deal of useful information from the published literature. To the extent that we could gain access to them at the time we were doing our research, however, we also studied the major primary sources.

The three principal relevant manuscript collections were: the Wilson papers at the Library of Congress, the papers of Ray Stannard Baker at the Library of Congress, and the papers of Colonel House at the Sterling Memorial Library at Yale University. Mrs. Wilson, who was notoriously chary of granting scholars access to the Wilson papers, rejected our periodically renewed requests until our study was almost complete. Then we were allowed to read a series of documents which, Katharine E. Brand (Mrs. Wilson's representative in the Manuscript Division of the Library of Congress) assured us, was all the collection contained for the years of Wilson's childhood and youth. We found little of significance in what we were allowed to see that Baker had not already published.

Miss Brand herself had charge of Baker's papers and she granted us access to them. We studied the Baker papers, over a period of years, to the great enrichment of our comprehension of Woodrow Wilson. For Baker, with Mrs. Wilson's help, had collected the reminiscences of scores of Wilson's family, friends, and associates. His papers remain an indispensable source for Wilson researchers.

Access to Colonel House's papers was controlled by Charles Seymour, president-emeritus of Yale University. Shortly after Seymour announced that Colonel House's diary would be open to scholars, we applied for, and were granted, permission to read it. It is a source of abiding satisfaction to us that, although we do not consider ourselves historians, we found and published for the first time numerous passages in House's diary (which Seymour had omitted from *The Intimate Papers of Colonel House*) revealing of certain significant aspects of the Colonel's attitude toward Wilson.

Inga Floto, whose book *Colonel House in Paris: A Study of American Policy at the Paris Peace Conference 1919* Weinstein, Anderson, and Link refer to as "the most authoritative study of House at the Paris Peace Conference," characterizes *Woodrow Wilson and Colonel House* as "epoch making," a " 'coup' from an historian's point of view."[6] We find it awkward to cite her generous praise but consider the disparagement of our research by Weinstein, Anderson, and Link justification for doing so. *Woodrow Wilson and Colonel House,* Floto writes, is "the first attempt at a consistent utilization of House's voluminous diary in its full, chronological scope," and she credits us with having made available material of "decisive importance."[7]

Weinstein, Anderson, and Link make no reference whatever to our use of primary source materials, let alone to the fact that we unearthed new data. We consider this an unfair omission and their criticism of our research unjustified.

WOODROW WILSON'S PERSONALITY

We turn now to the second of our "principal failings": ". . .the Georges fail to recognize the limitations of their psychological model and misrepresent evidence to fit their theory."[8] It seems to us that we were not only aware but scrupulous to convey to readers an awareness that what we were presenting for their consideration is an interpretation of Wilson based on certain hypotheses, which we articulated and invited them to examine on the basis of data, which we also presented. We explicitly stated in our book that the validity of our interpretations is necessarily a matter of opinion:

> No incontrovertible proof can be offered. Nor can any one incident be relied upon to sustain this or any other theory of Wilson's motivation. It is only when the man's career

is viewed as a whole that a repetition of certain basically similar behavior is discernible. Let the reader consider whether these patterns of behavior become more consistently comprehensible in terms of the explanations herein offered than in terms of other explanations. That will be the best test of their usefulness.[9]

Weinstein, Anderson, and Link evince no such restraint in the presentation of their hypotheses. Consider, for example, the way they conclude their statement concerning Wilson's inability to read until he was eleven, which they attribute to developmental dyslexia, physiologically determined, and which we, on the other hand, suggest in *Woodrow Wilson and Colonel House* may have derived from feelings of inadequacy and been an unconscious expression of resentment of his father's perfectionist demands.[10] Say Weinstein, Anderson, and Link: "We do not have a good record of Wilson's childhood such as might be gained from contemporary letters, diaries, or autobiographies; like any other child, he may have felt insecurities. However, it is certain that they did not come about in the manner postulated by the Georges."[11] Whence, in the absence of adequate data, these authors' certainty? Is peremptory assertion a substitute for reasoned argument? So apparently Weinstein, Anderson, and Link think; for so many of their interpretations and medical diagnoses are couched in categorical language— language that we consider inappropriate to the speculative nature of their enterprise.

The Dyslexia Hypothesis

Let us get down to specific cases: we do not think our hypothesis about Wilson's delayed acquisition of reading skills can be thus handily dispatched. Nor do we consider it irrelevant that Link's present certainty about the cause of Wilson's reading problem follows decades of his failing to recognize that a problem requiring explanation even existed. In *Wilson: The Road to the White House,* published in 1947, he did not even refer to Wilson's early learning difficulties and wrote that "Wilson's boyhood was notable, if for nothing else, because of his normal development."[12] (This notwithstanding that years before, Baker, whose work Link cites, had specifically drawn attention to Wilson's early slow development.)[13]

Twenty years later, in 1967—long after we, in *Woodrow Wilson and Colonel House,* had again drawn attention to the data of Wilson's early learning problems and he himself had mentioned in passing that Wilson "was a late starter"—Link was still arguing that "all evidence indicates that Wilson had a normal boyhood, at least as normal as was possible for boys growing up in the South during the Civil War and Reconstruction."[14]

By 1968, Link was at least referring, however doubtfully, to the "family tradition" which "may or may not be correct" according to which Wilson "did not learn to read until he was nine." (Actually the data indicate he had learned only his letters when he was nine. He could not read until he was eleven.) To be sure, Link was now willing to acknowledge that the boy "seems to have suffered from insecurity on account of his inability to achieve as rapidly as he thought he should," but he was quick to pronounce it "normal insecurity." "His personal advantages and precocity aside," Link wrote, "Wilson seems to have been a remarkably normal person during the first forty years of his life. His childhood was serene. . . ."[15]

The article in *Political Science Quarterly* by Weinstein, Anderson, and Link provides gratifying indication that Link has at last taken notice of what he joins his colleagues in correctly describing as the "well-known" facts of Wilson's boyhood learning difficulties. However, the diagnosis he joins them in offering—developmental dyslexia—seems to us to collapse under scrutiny.

Weinstein, Anderson, and Link speak of developmental dyslexia as if it were a now thoroughly understood disability of established etiology.

> Undiagnosed in Wilson's childhood, the condition was well-known to neurologists at the time that the Georges wrote their book. However, a number of psychiatrists and psychologists still believed that the condition was an emotional rather than a neurological problem, and the Georges simply chose an explanation that was currently popular. The condition is a frequent one, occurring in about 10 percent of the school population, significantly more frequently in boys. Research over the past seventy years indicates that developmental dyslexia is caused by a delay in the establishment of the dominance of one cerebral hemisphere—usually the left—for language.[16]

A far less confident tone about the nature of reading disabilities and various types of dyslexia is taken by several of the experts who participated in the conference on dyslexia conducted in 1977 by the National Institute of Mental Health. For example, Michael Rutter, a British psychiatrist, contends that the term "dyslexia" has not yet been even satisfactorily defined and that "the presumption of a neurological basis is just that—namely a presumption." He considers it "meaningless" at this time to attempt any estimate of the prevalence of dyslexia.[17] While there is great interest in the hypothesis that a delay in the acquisition of left-hemisphere dominance may be associated with some cases of reading difficulty, Rutter believes that "the evidence on this point remains inconclusive." John Hughes of the Department of Neurology, University of Illinois School of Medicine, writes: "Satz (1976) has summarized the data relating cerebral dominance and dyslexia and has claimed that information is still lacking on this crucial issue." As for the etiology of reading disorders, a number of eminent psychiatrists *continue* to believe that emotional factors are the basis for some of them.[18]

Our purpose in citing the continuing perplexities of specialists in dyslexia research is to counter the impression that readers might well gain from Weinstein, Anderson, and Link that medical research has solved the mystery of reading disabilities and that psychological explanations have been eliminated for all varieties. According to Rutter the very concept of developmental dyslexia "constitutes a hypothesis—the hypothesis that within the large overall group of disabled readers there is a subgroup with a distinct constitutionally determined condition."[19] Very well. Weinstein, Anderson, and Link claim that "Tommy" Wilson was such an intrinsically impaired child. What is their evidence?

"Specific evidence" of developmental dyslexia, Weinstein, Anderson, and Link claim, is that Wilson "was a slow reader into adult life. At the Johns Hopkins, the amount of assigned reading was his bane. 'Steady reading,' he wrote his fiancée, 'always demands of me more expenditure of resolution and dogged energy than any other sort of work.' "[20]

The sentence from Wilson's letter to his fiancée, Ellen Axson, that Weinstein, Anderson, and Link quote in support of their thesis is incorrectly cited as having been written on 29 March 1884. This is an error of some consequence, since its correct date, 29 *November* 1884, places it within the period that Wilson was making a heroic effort to toil through the reading required for obtaining a Ph.D. It was an effort he detested, which only weeks before he had decided to abandon on the grounds, he had written Ellen Axson, that "a forced march through fourteen thousand pages of dry reading" would jeopardize his health. "I am quite sure that I shall profit much more substantially from a line of reading of my own choosing, in the lines of my own original work. . . ."[21]

Nonetheless, in those days, as in these, a degree made a man more marketable. Wilson, avid to equip himself for a job that would give him the wherewithal to marry, reluctantly embarked on the hateful "forced march" shortly after he had renounced it. The drudgery was all but unbearable. His letters to Ellen Axson during these weeks and until mid-February, 1885, chronicle his growing distress. He is tempted "to throw down these heavy volumes and run out into the glories of the open air." He berates himself for not accepting the necessity of complying with the requirements. Try as he will to submit, "I often grow savagely out of humour with my present state of pupilage. . . ."[22]

Reading for the Ph.D. was not the full measure of his problem. "I am handicapped for my degree," he wrote to a friend, "because of the extra work with which I was indiscreet enough to saddle myself." He had committed himself to collaborate on a history of political economy with one of his professors. "I am to wade—am wading, indeed—through innumerable American text writers," he continued, "for the purpose of writing . . . about one-third of the projected treatise." As for the degree, "it's this year or never."[23] The burden proved too great and, finally, on 19 February 1885, he wrote to his fiancée: "I have given up—this time conclusively—the struggle for the degree. . . . Cramming kills me; reading in development of a subject improves and invigorates me."[24]

Is the sentence that Weinstein, Anderson, and Link pluck from one of the letters Wilson wrote in the midst of the struggle described above credible evidence of developmental dyslexia? That construction of it strikes us as tortured. It seems to us much more likely that Wilson's statement indicates his distress at the *kind* of reading that was being demanded of him and the crushing amount of it.

If the record suggested that Wilson was generally a reluctant reader, slow because the very act of reading was difficult for him, the case for Weinstein, Anderson, and Link's hypothesis of developmental dyslexia would gain some ground. The record fails them, however. One has but to look through the diary he kept during the summer after his freshman year at Princeton to see that he was in fact an omnivorous reader, provided only that he had a taste for the matter at

hand: Macaulay, Shakespeare, Gibbon, Plutarch, Pepys, Dickens, novels, magazines, encyclopedia articles—all passed under his frequently enthusiastic but, by
preference, unhurried scrutiny.[25] The argument may be summed up in a simple
statistic: it takes no less than thirty pages of quite fine print in the index to the
first twelve volumes of *The Papers of Woodrow Wilson* to cover the subject category, "Woodrow Wilson—Reading."[26]

Weinstein, Anderson, and Link claim two other "groups" of "specific evidence
that Wilson had developmental dyslexia": he was "extremely poor in arithmetic,"
an ineptitude commonly associated with developmental dyslexia; and he quickly
"and without practice" mastered writing with his left hand when in 1896 (as the
result of a stroke, they say, an assertion about which more later) he was unable
to write with his right hand. This ability "strongly suggests that he had mixed
cerebral dominance for language."[27]

We question that the dyslexia hypothesis finds support from these "groups"
of evidence. Being "extremely poor in arithmetic" can have a score of explanations other than developmental dyslexia; moreover, whatever his difficulties
with arithmetic, Wilson's capabilities ranged from keeping meticulous personal
financial records to overseeing the formulation of national economic policy and
the negotiation of intricate international economic questions. As for his left-
handed writing, given Wilson's considerable artistic talents and his intense per-
severance, it is not surprising that he succeeded in acquiring that skill. It was
not the easy accomplishment that Weinstein, Anderson, and Link suggest, however. We know from Stockton Axson's account that Wilson set about the task
with "customary determination."[28] We know from Wilson himself that he practiced
"laboriously," notwithstanding which writing with his left hand remained "clumsy
and uncertain," "awkward," "tedious," "a painfully slow process"—"it takes me
half an hour to [write] one of these pages."[29] In short, Wilson does not seem to
have been naturally ambidextrous. Even with practice, writing with his left hand
seems to have remained an uncomfortable occasional necessity rather than an
easy alternative to the use of his clearly preferred right hand.

The dyslexia hypothesis suffers further when one considers two aspects of
dyslexia about which the experts generally agree: that it is strongly associated
with disordered handwriting and with persistently atrocious spelling.[30] Wilson's
handwriting—as surely Weinstein, Anderson, and Link would agree—is a very
model of beautiful penmanship. Even his check registers look like copperplate.
And he was an excellent speller. His errors were few and far between.

For the purpose of pursuing our critics' train of thought, however, let us grant
for a moment that "Tommy" Wilson suffered from some inborn defect, that it
was indeed developmental dyslexia that impeded his learning to read. What
would the psychological consequences of such a disability have been, both upon
the boy and his parents? The literature on dyslexia is clear that every poor reader,
no matter what the cause of his problem, is predisposed to feeling inadequate,
"bad," or "stupid."[31]

Weinstein, Anderson, and Link give passing recognition to the fact that "the reading disability affected Wilson's development and his relationship with his parents," but they immediately add "but hardly in the way that the Georges state." How, then, *was* the boy affected? "It probably made him more dependent on his family," they say. They acknowledge that "he may have feared that his reading problems indicated that he was stupid or lazy" and that "the condition probably made Dr. Wilson more pedagogic and insistent on drilling his 'lazy' son." Having edged up to the dread explanation, Weinstein, Anderson, and Link hurry away and remove Dr. Wilson with them: during the Civil War he was sometimes away from home; other family members read to Wilson and he enjoyed that; and the data are lacking, but whatever insecurities Wilson might have felt "it is certain that they did not come about in the manner postulated by the Georges."[32]

This account by Weinstein, Anderson, and Link leaves some nagging loose ends that not only deserve but demand consideration. What would the effect be on a boy to fear that he was stupid or lazy—and, by the way, there is no "may have" about it: years later when he was president, Wilson often reminisced about his boyhood with his physician and friend, Cary Grayson, and Grayson recalls that "he often spoke of himself as being a lazy boy."[33] What attitudes toward himself would his father's "insistent drilling" have engendered—his father, a master of the English language, a brilliant expositor of Calvinist doctrine, which says nothing about developmental dyslexia but a great deal about wickedness and sin and dereliction of duty? Would this devoted father, a man of his times, not have had an especially poignant stake in the intellectual progress of this, his third child but first son, and been frustrated and disappointed at the boy's poor performance? And would "Tommy's" self-concept not almost inevitably have suffered? Would he not have felt humiliated, unworthy, inadequate? In short, would this family situation not have fostered the ripening in a boy's heart of those low estimates of himself that these authors deny existed? It seems to us they overlook the ample evidence that this was the case and refuse to draw the conclusion obvious even from their prettified account of the family interaction.

Woodrow Wilson and His Father

For the sake of evaluating Weinstein, Anderson, and Link's thesis on its own ground, we have thus far omitted the ingredient of Dr. Wilson's propensity for sarcasm and severe criticism and how these are likely to have impinged upon his son's development. "The Georges claim that Wilson suffered from a troubled relationship with his father," write Weinstein, Anderson, and Link, and they reject the idea.[34] Having attempted to subtract Wilson's reading problem as indication of father-son stress, they try to belittle the significance of the testimony of young family members that Joseph R. Wilson, a man of many virtues to be sure, was also a sarcastic tease.

The evidence cannot be so handily dispatched, however. And now there is a good deal more of it than was available at the time we were writing *Woodrow*

Wilson and Colonel House. There is, for example, an unpublished manuscript by Dr. Stockton Axson, the much younger brother of the first Mrs. Wilson, who lived with the Woodrow Wilsons for a number of years. Axson was not only Woodrow Wilson's devoted friend for over forty years; he was also a great favorite of Wilson's father. The two were fast friends to the day Joseph Ruggles Wilson died, and Stockton Axson thought the old minister a great man. Yet he wrote at length of the forbidding side of Dr. Joseph Wilson and of how, when displeased, his humor "bubbled *hot*" in "scalding sarcasms" which could be "really withering." He had in him, Axson tells us, "a certain savage humor which caused him to say sometimes cruel things even to those who loved him and whom he loved." Notwithstanding his qualities of greatness, he was a "ruthless sort of a man," Axson wrote, "a man with a distinct streak of perversity in him." In his sarcasm, he reminded Axson of Jonathan Swift.[35]

The sarcasm, the mordant wit, the cruel teasing, the relentless drilling to which he subjected his son obviously constituted only one facet of Dr. Joseph Wilson's personality. We do not for a moment deny—nor did we in *Woodrow Wilson and Colonel House*—that there is rich and persuasive evidence of the comradeship between Wilson and his father, of abiding love, and of the transmission from father to son of moral values and of a range of skills and perceptions that fostered the greatness of Woodrow Wilson.[36] Recognizing and giving full weight to this evidence, however, does not necessitate refusing to recognize, as we think our critics refuse to do, that *all* facets of Joseph Wilson entered into his interaction with his son and that the syndrome we tried to trace in *Woodrow Wilson and Colonel House* also had important consequences. Weinstein, Anderson, and Link write as though they consider it beyond the realm of possibility that the demanding father may have generated in his sensitive son feelings of inadequacy and also of unconscious resentment. Is it likely that the boy never inwardly rebelled at the stern religious teachings graven into his soul? Did Woodrow Wilson enjoy some divine dispensation from experiencing conflicting emotions about a beloved parent? Is it really unthinkable to Weinstein, Anderson, and Link that Wilson may have had to deal with ambivalence?

There is the briefest intimation—half a sentence—that such questions crossed our critics' minds. "Dr. Wilson had a tremendous influence on his son," they write, "and probably no boy grows up without *some* resentment toward his father."[37] Weinstein, Anderson, and Link write as though any unconscious resentment Wilson felt toward his father was of minor dimensions and without significant repercussions for the understanding of his political behavior. They write as though his early learning difficulties neither resulted from nor led to psychological problems that importantly affected his development. They leave unmentioned and show no sign of having considered the implications of many self-revealing statements Wilson made in private conversations or of dozens of self-characterizations to be found in his letters, in his diaries, and sometimes even in his public utterances which bespeak great inner turmoil.

Wilson's Enduring Anxieties

We shall cite just one such statement to convey the flavor of the evidence. In 1884, at age twenty-eight—long before any of the "strokes" that Weinstein, Anderson, and Link claim altered his personality—Wilson wrote to his fiancée:

> It isn't pleasant or convenient to have strong passions: and it is particularly hard in my case to have to deal with unamiable feelings; because the only whip with which I can subdue them is the whip of hard study and that lacerates *me* as often as it conquers my crooked dispositions. I hope that none of my friends—and much more none of my enemies!—will ever find out *how much it costs me to give up my own way*. I have the uncomfortable feeling that I am carrying a volcano about with me.[38]

In other letters to Ellen Axson Wilson he refers to himself as "a man of a sensitive, restless, overwrought disposition." He speaks of his "sombre, morbid nature," his "fears," "anxieties," "morose moods," of "my poor, mixed, inexplicable nature." "Deep perturbations are natural to me, deep disturbances of spirit." He writes of "my natural self-distrust," of having "never been sanguine," of often falling when irritated into "the stern, indignant, defiant humour, the scarcely suppressed belligerent temper for which there are abundant materials in my disposition." "I have to guard my emotions from painful overflow," he confides.[39]

Such feelings, so persistently and intensely expressed, require explanation. Weinstein, Anderson, and Link offer none. We believe that these emotions were related to his ceaseless effort to maintain his self-esteem; that for Wilson carving out a sphere of competence in public life and striving for high achievement were a means of overcoming feelings of unimportance, of moral inferiority, of weakness, of mediocrity, of intellectual inadequacy; that in certain crucial situations in his public career, Wilson's self-defeating stubbornness and unwillingness to defer (or at least make expedient gestures of deference) to men whose cooperation was essential to the accomplishment of his goals were irrational manifestations of underlying low self-estimates against which he had constantly to struggle. It remains our conviction that the hypotheses advanced in *Woodrow Wilson and Colonel House,* applied to the vast body of data concerning Woodrow Wilson, have consistent explanatory power.[40]

WOODROW WILSON'S MEDICAL PROBLEMS

The third "principal failing" of *Woodrow Wilson and Colonel House,* according to Weinstein, Anderson, and Link, is that we "ignore Wilson's neurological disorders as conditions affecting his behavior." Undaunted by the virtual absence of medical records for this period of Wilson's life, they assert unequivocally that he suffered strokes in 1896, 1900, 1904, 1906, and 1907. They say that "by the end of World War I, Wilson was showing signs of generalized cerebral involvement." They state further that an episode of illness (which Weinstein had earlier diagnosed as a stroke) in April 1919 while he was negotiating the Versailles Peace

Treaty in Paris was not only influenza but "probably a virus encephalopathy, which, superimposed on pre-existing brain damage, produced changes in behavior which may have influenced the outcome of the peace negotiations." The massive stroke of October 1919 which, as is well known, paralyzed Wilson's left side also, according to Weinstein, Anderson, and Link, resulted in personality changes "which were important factors in his failure to obtain ratification of the Treaty of Versailles."[41]

It is certainly the case that we did not think that brain damage became a factor to consider in Wilson's political behavior until the autumn of 1919. While doing our research for *Woodrow Wilson and Colonel House,* we were alert to the possibility that personality changes affecting his handling of the League controversy in the Senate may have followed the catastrophic stroke of October 2. There was indeed evidence that he was given to outbursts of tears and of temper. His pathetic hope that the Democratic convention might renominate him and that he could win a third term in 1920 suggested impairment of his judgment of the political realities. A moving memorandum by Katharine E. Brand detailing Woodrow Wilson's last years made it clear that in many ways he was but a shadow of his former self. Nonetheless it was our conclusion then and it is our conclusion now that his behavior on the League issue remained intact. Whatever the nature of the brain damage he sustained in the fall of 1919, it altered neither his grasp of his problem with the Senate nor his strategy to deal with it. He had struck his unyielding position long before October 1919—a position that anguished practically everyone who cared personally about him or supported U.S. entry into the League of Nations. Wilson's conduct in this respect after the stroke was entirely consistent with his behavior before it. Both before and after, ample warnings were conveyed to him of the all but inevitable consequences of his refusal at every turn to compromise. Both before and after the stroke, he rejected these warnings, using the same arguments against compromise and cogently communicating them from his sickbed. The stroke seemed not to modify his behavior one whit in this respect.

Of course, it is possible to argue that he *would* have changed his position had he not been stricken. One can only speculate. Our own guess, given his history, is that he would not have yielded, that his stubbornness was in the deepest sense an expression of the integrity of his functioning on the public issue of supreme value to him. To the day he died, he expressed the conviction that history would vindicate him. To those who knew and loved him best, his refusal to compromise was a source of sorrow rather than of surprise. A sense of some terrible inner logic to his self-defeating behavior in terms of stable, persistent characteristics that they had long since recognized pervades their narratives.

His implacable enemy, Senator Henry Cabot Lodge, too, sensed that Wilson was held to his course by some invincible inner compulsion. The leading opponent of Senate ratification of the Treaty as submitted by Wilson, Lodge based his strategy upon a shrewd assessment of Wilson's personality. He calculated that Wilson would never agree to accept even minor reservations, that rather than compromise with the Senate and particularly with him (Lodge), Wilson would allow the treaty—League of Nations and all—to be defeated.[42]

The drama unfolded quite as Lodge had foreseen. His tactical finesse in maneuvering Wilson from one excruciating refusal to compromise to another testifies to his deadly insight into the tragic flaw in Wilson's character. He was not confounded by any perplexing "changes" in Wilson. His success at predicting Wilson's reactions suggests their constancy through all the vicissitudes of Wilson's health.

There was a time when Link recognized the relationship between Wilson's character and the recurrent defeats he suffered. In his book, *Wilson: The Road to the White House,* Link wrote:

> The Princeton period was the microcosm of a later macrocosm, and a political observer, had he studied carefully Wilson's career as president of Princeton University, might have forecast accurately the shape of things to come during the period when Wilson was president of the United States. What striking similarities there are between the Princeton and the national periods![43]

Link's comment pertained to the quad and graduate school controversies that fractured the Princeton community in 1907 and continued to reverberate bitterly for years after Wilson's resignation from the Princeton presidency in 1910. The quad controversy revolved about Wilson's plan to build quadrangles in which upper and lower classmen, some graduate students, and unmarried preceptors would live and eat together thereby, Wilson argued, stimulating intellectual exchange outside of the classroom. Opponents, among whom were wealthy alumni on whose contributions any construction would depend, viewed the plan as a threat to the eating clubs to which many were sentimentally attached and as having high-handedly been presented to the Board of Trustees before discussion with faculty and alumni. Moreover, they regarded Wilson's quad plan as a brazen attempt to divert attention and resources from the long-planned development of the graduate college under the leadership of its dean, Andrew Fleming West. In 1906, at Wilson's own behest, West had declined an invitation to become president of the Massachusetts Institute of Technology in favor of remaining at Princeton in order to put the graduate college into operation. A bitter dispute erupted between Wilson and his supporters and West and his supporters which crystallized around the ostensible issue of where the proposed graduate college should be located. Various concessions to Wilson's views were offered including substantial reform of the eating clubs, stripping Dean West of much of his authority, and compromising on the site issue. Wilson refused them all.

Writing in *Wilson: The Road to the White House* about what he then considered Wilson's unreasonable behavior, Link said: "The vagaries of his mind during this period are unfathomable." At that time he found the most striking fact about the whole Princeton controversy "the absence of any clear-cut issue" and that Wilson had shifted from one issue to another so that "it was almost impossible to tell where he really stood."[44] He attributed Wilson's difficulties at Princeton and later in his career explicitly to his *character* rather than to the logic of the situations he confronted:

> Wilson was a headstrong and determined man who was usually able to rationalize his actions in terms of the moral law and to identify his position with the divine will.... The time came at Princeton, Trenton, and Washington when Wilson did not command the support of the groups to whom he was responsible. Naturally, he was not able to change his character even had he wanted to change it, with the result that controversy and disastrous defeat occurred in varying degrees in all three cases.[45]

Link now holds a different view of the Princeton imbroglio, as he indicates in a footnote to the article by Weinstein, Anderson, and Link: "Arthur S. Link wishes to state that much new evidence discovered since the publication of his *Wilson: The Road to the White House* in 1947 has convinced him that his treatment of Wilson and West and the graduate college controversy is inadequate and un-balanced."[46]

The account of the Princeton controversy given by Weinstein, Anderson, and Link suggests that Wilson's actions in fact derived from a reasonable assessment of the situation rather than from characterological idiosyncrasies. If this is indeed Link's current interpretation, it collides with the simultaneous claim that "changes" in Wilson's behavior due to brain damage from the alleged strokes of 1896, 1900, 1904, 1906, and 1907 impaired his performance and played a critical role in his defeat. To us it seems that to the extent that they consider Wilson's refusal to compromise in the quad and graduate college battles a reasonable defense of his principles, they reduce the grounds for arguing the significance of the alleged personality and behavioral changes in consequence of the alleged strokes.

Wilson's Behavior in Paris

If in their article Professor Link repudiates the interpretive structure of *Wilson: The Road to the White House,* Dr. Weinstein also discloses a significant change of view involving one of his key diagnoses: that of Wilson's brief illness in Paris in April 1919. In his widely read and widely quoted article, "Woodrow Wilson's Neurological Illness," published in 1970, Weinstein stated that the most likely cause of Wilson's illness during the Peace Conference was a "cerebral vascular occlusion (blood clot in the brain)"—in short, a stroke. He construed certain aspects of Wilson's behavior during and after his illness as evidence of the kind of behavioral change that would confirm brain damage caused by a stroke. Weinstein described the "cerebral vascular occlusion" as "a lesion in the right cerebral hemisphere extending to include deeper structures in the limbic-retic-ular system. With the history of lesions of the left side of the brain, indicated by the attacks of right-sided paresthesia and left monocular blindness from 1896 to 1908, he now had evidence of bilateral damage, a condition affecting emotional and social behavior more severely than a unilateral lesion."[47]

This medical description was so precise and authoritative in tone that few lay-men would dare to take issue with it. The problem is that the major evidence on which it relied—the allegedly strange changes in Wilson's behavior—is tittle-tattle which has gained momentum and grown in absurdity in its passage from one source to another. The historical record, as we shall shortly attempt to show, provides a background against which Wilson's "strange behavior," viewed in context, seems reasonable and rational.

The speculative nature of Weinstein's diagnoses is revealed by the fact that in the article by Weinstein, Anderson, and Link the minutely described stroke of his earlier article is withdrawn. A footnote states that new evidence indicates that it is not likely to have occurred after all.[48] Now readers are informed that Wilson had an attack of influenza in Paris in April 1919 (as most historians have thought all along). A crucial aspect of the brain-damage thesis is salvaged, however, for Weinstein, Anderson, and Link also say that it was not merely influenza but "probably a virus encephalopathy." In short, as a result of one disease or another, according to Weinstein, Woodrow Wilson sustained brain damage in April 1919 that significantly affected his judgment in the conduct of the negotiations. In both articles "strange" changes of behavior are cited as evidence of altered brain function.[49]

Let us examine some of this allegedly irrational behavior: one manifestation cited by Weinstein in his earlier article (which presumably constitutes part of the documentation of the "changes in behavior" alleged by Weinstein, Anderson, and Link) was Wilson's instruction to his personal staff in Paris that they use official limousines only for official business. Irwin "Ike" Hoover, White House head usher who served as chief of Wilson's household staff in Paris, is the source of this tale, which he recorded in his book, *42 Years in the White House*. This gentlemen, as his letters to his wife indicate, had grown accustomed to taking joyrides practically every day—sometimes two and three times a day. ("It is fine to order up a big limousine, say 'to the hotel' and off it goes," he wrote to his wife. "Come out, say 'home' and you are on the way back." Of the scores of letters he wrote home, there is scarcely a handful—except when he was at sea en route to or from the conference—in which he did not articulate his use or non-use of the limousines for the particular day covered. "Ike" missed his fam-ily—and also his Dodge automobile to which he referred affectionately in several letters.)[50] Other staff members fell into the same habit of rushing for the cars the moment the president and Mrs. Wilson went out.

One day during his illness in April 1919 the president sent for one member of his staff after the other and found that they were all out in the cars. This an-gered him and he ordered the staff to curtail use of the cars for personal plea-sure.[51] We see nothing "strange" or "irrational" in Wilson's crackdown—unless it be that he did not sooner lose his temper at Hoover's profligate abuse of priv-ilege.

On the basis of "Ike" Hoover's account, Weinstein also accepted as "markedly irrational behavior" after his April 1919 illness that Wilson was concerned that the French servants in the house the French government had placed at his disposal were spies. The fact is that many Americans at the conference were worried about spies. Joseph Grew, secretary of the American commission, issued directives warning of the need for the secure handling of confidential papers, for burning trash, for being alert to the possibility that telephones were being tapped, and that French employees might be spying for their government. During the very week of Wilson's illness, Dr. Grayson wrote in his diary that one of the servants who claimed not to speak English had been found to know English fluently and that the French government was engaged in spying on the president. Mrs. Wilson's secretary, Edith Benham, noted in her diary on 29 March 1919 that conversations at meals had to be restrained because "Colonel House says there are spies here in the house who report everything to the Foreign Office." Colonel House noted in his diary at the beginning of the conference that the private wire between his study and Wilson's "is constantly 'covered' to see that it is not tapped."[52]

It seems to us grotesque that Wilson's concern for security at the conference should be interpreted by Weinstein and others as evidence of brain damage. Was Joseph Grew also brain damaged? And Dr. Grayson, Colonel House, and Miss Benham too?

The Question of Strokes

And what about the earlier episodes of illness in 1896, 1900, 1904, 1906, and 1907 which Weinstein, Anderson, and Link state were strokes, the one in 1906 being "the first one to be recognized as such"?[53] By all accounts, Wilson's illness in 1906 was the most serious of his prepresidential years. One spring morning in that year, he awakened unable to see out of his left eye. He immediately consulted two eminent Philadelphia specialists (an ophthalmologist and an internist). The medical records, unfortunately, are missing. Surviving letters and later reminiscences, however, indicate that Wilson was told that a burst blood vessel had caused a hemorrhage in the eye, that he had arteriosclerosis and high blood pressure, and that he needed prolonged rest. Wilson obediently delegated his duties to Princeton colleagues, spent a quiet summer in England and, with medical approval, resumed his work in the fall.

Nowhere could we find evidence that this illness had been diagnosed as a stroke or "recognized as such." We wrote to Weinstein and asked when Wilson's illness in 1906 was recognized as a stroke and by whom. In his reply, Weinstein cited sources that simply contain no mention of a stroke.[54] He further wrote in this letter that Wilson's ophthalmologist and internist knew that he had arteriosclerosis and high blood pressure and that strokes are very common in these conditions; and that they may not have told Wilson in so many words that he had had a stroke but used a euphemism instead. Such speculation on Weinstein's part consisting of what he thinks must have been in other people's minds strikes us as utterly inadequate justification for the unqualified claim by Weinstein, Anderson, and Link that the 1906 illness was a stroke "recognized as such," much less for Link's assertion in *The Papers of Woodrow Wilson* that it was "a major stroke."

Of course the question to which all the foregoing discussion leads is: how would competent, independent medical authority evaluate Woodrow Wilson's illnesses throughout his career and Weinstein's diagnoses of them? For a response to this question, we turned to Michael F. Marmor, M.D., associate professor of Ophthalmology at the Stanford University School of Medicine. We placed at Marmor's disposal all the data in our possession relating to Wilson's health[55] and made available to him the relevant volumes of *The Papers of Woodrow Wilson* as well as the source materials cited by Weinstein in his various articles.

Marmor embodied the results of his review in a letter to us dated 18 May 1981 (see appendix for the text). The letter speaks for itself and we need only note here Marmor's main conclusions: that in the absence of documented findings or medical records, Weinstein's analysis is necessarily speculative; that his own reading of the evidence leads him to question both the medical interpretations of Weinstein and the propriety of presenting such views as historical fact.

As a matter of fact, questions about the validity of Weinstein's diagnoses have been raised previously and were brought to the attention of both Link and Weinstein a decade ago. In 1971, Robert T. Monroe, M.D., an internist long associated with the Harvard University School of Medicine, wrote four pages of comments on Weinstein's article, "Woodrow Wilson's Neurological Illness," which had been published the preceding year. He detailed the medical grounds for doubting Weinstein's interpretations and expressed his overall evaluation as follows: "Professor Weinstein seeks to prove that Wilson 'had a long history of cerebral vascular disease,' and that it 'was associated with alterations in behavior and personality.' In my view he has failed on both counts." Weinstein dismissed Monroe's comments as uninformed, and the following year, volume sixteen of *The Papers of Woodrow Wilson* appeared with the statement in the preface that Wilson's illness in 1906 was "a major stroke."[56]

IMPLICATIONS FOR *THE PAPERS OF WOODROW WILSON*

In conclusion, we should like to say a few words about *The Papers of Woodrow Wilson,* of which Professor Link is editor. The publication of Wilson's papers is one of the major projects in historiography in our time. These volumes are meant to preserve for posterity a true and unbiased record concerning Woodrow Wilson. Scholars today consult *The Papers of Woodrow Wilson* on the assumption—an assumption upon which they ought to be able to rely—that the facts stated in the informational notes to various documents are true and accurate. Scholars will continue to consult *The Papers of Woodrow Wilson* on this assumption for many generations to come. As we noted at the beginning of this article, the editorial matter of several volumes of *The Papers* contains (in prefaces and in numerous notes as well as in listings in various indices) unqualified allusions to Wilson's so-called strokes between the years 1896 and 1907. (The volumes covering the period of the Paris Peace Conference into which Wilson's illness of April 1919 falls have not yet been published.) We believe that these allusions have prejudiced the objectivity of *The Papers of Woodrow Wilson* and have already misled a number of writers.[57] We also believe that those in charge of the project have a reverence for the truth and a fidelity to their scholarly duties. We suggest that a reconsideration and emendation of the editorial matter that elevates Dr. Weinstein's controversial medical hypotheses to the status of historical fact is in order.*

POSTSCRIPT

A book by Edwin A. Weinstein, *Woodrow Wilson: A Medical and Psychological Biography,* has appeared since this article was completed. We can only note here that Weinstein persists in presenting, as if it were indisputable fact, his theory that Wilson suffered a series of disabling strokes dating back to 1896. The book contains numerous statements implying the existence of medical data and opinion which, so far as we know, simply are not available in the historical record.[58] An even more serious concern is that Weinstein has omitted data of critical diagnostic significance, thus precluding an objective evaluation of his hypotheses by his medical peers. His account of Wilson's episode of visual loss in 1906 is an important case in point.

In describing the 1906 episode, Weinstein writes that Mrs. Wilson "searched for evidence that would bear out the Doctor's opinion that her husband's stroke had been brought on by strain and overwork." He also writes that the Princeton trustees "agreed that the stroke had been caused by overwork." However, we know of no evidence (and Weinstein offers none) that Wilson's doctors, Mrs. Wilson, or the Princeton trustees stated, implied, or even believed that Wilson had suffered a stroke.

Weinstein titles his chapter about the 1906 episode, "A Major Stroke and Its Consequences," and he begins with a general description of carotid occlusive disease. In this disorder, blood clots or arteriosclerotic plaques in the neck may

*We wish to express our cordial thanks to the staff of the Manuscript Division, Library of Congress, for facilitating our research there and especially to Dr. David Wigdor, specialist, twentieth-century political history. At the Yale University Library, Arthur Walworth took precious time from his own work on Woodrow Wilson and the Paris Peace Conference to direct our attention to documents of particular interest from his own files and in the papers of Colonel House. Professor Link and Dr. David W. Hirst accorded us many courtesies, for which we thank them, at the Firestone Library, Princeton University. At all stages of our work on this project we have benefited from the expert knowledge and wisdom of Margaret M. Stuart, M.D. We are indebted to Joseph M. Goldsen, A.E. Hanson, Elise F. Kendrick, and Lee R. Lombard for helpful comments on the first version of this article, which was presented at the annual meeting of the International Society of Political Psychology in Mannheim, Germany, in June 1981.

fragment and form emboli that lodge in smaller arteries such as those within the eye. He then writes that Wilson's ophthalmologist (Dr. George E. de Schweinitz) "told him that he had sustained a blood clot in the eye," the obvious implication being that "clot" refers to an embolus from the carotid. We believe this is a misleading description because important evidence has been omitted. What de Schweinitz actually told Wilson is not known. It can only be inferred from letters written by Wilson and Mrs. Wilson at the time, and from the later recollections of such knowledgeable people as John Grier Hibben (who had accompanied Wilson to Dr. de Schweinitz's office), Stockton Axson, Drs. Cary Grayson and E.P. Davis, and Eleanor Wilson McAdoo. *All* of these sources say that Wilson's loss of vision was caused by a hemorrhage or burst blood vessel within his eye. Yet Weinstein omits any mention of hemorrhage in his book, even though the distinction between hemorrhage and embolic clot is critical, because bleeding within the eye is *not* characteristic of carotid occlusive disease and indeed militates against that diagnosis. Weinstein's only cited source for the word "clot" is a letter from Ellen Axson Wilson to a cousin in which she says: "Two weeks ago yesterday Woodrow waked up perfectly blind in one eye!—it turned out from the bursting of a blood vessel in it. . . . The clot in the eye is being absorbed with extraordinary rapidity." The word "clot" in the context of Mrs. Wilson's letter seems clearly to refer to a coagulum from the burst blood vessel rather than to an embolus.

We (Michael F. Marmor, Juliette L. George, and Alexander L. George) hope to comment more fully on Weinstein's book elsewhere.

APPENDIX

May 18, 1981

Dr. and Mrs. Alexander George
Department of Political Science
Stanford University
Stanford, California 94305

Dear Dr. and Mrs. George:

I have reviewed at length the medical and historical source material which bears upon the possibility that Woodrow Wilson had neurologic disease. I am preparing a comprehensive analysis of this material for publication and this letter represents a summary of my impressions and conclusions.* You have my permission to quote from this letter, with the proviso that statements should not be taken out of context or used without sufficient material to provide a balanced picture of my views.

*See Michael F. Marmor, "Wilson, Strokes, and Zebras," *New England Journal of Medicine*, 307 (August 26, 1982) 528–35. See also Marmor, "The Eyes of Woodrow Wilson," *Ophthalmology*, 92 (March 1985) 454–65—eds.

Let me say at the outset that the medical analysis of historical figures is by nature a speculative process. In the absence of documented findings or medical records, one must rely upon guesswork and judgment to analyze lay descriptions of disease. Physicians are trained to consider all of the rare and unlikely disease which might afflict their patients, lest one be missed. However, in looking back over history, the approach should probably be the opposite: given the symptoms, search for the most common and likely causes. Under these constraints, historical diagnoses will rarely have the certainty of scientific fact, and should in general be considered hypothesis.

In a series of articles, psychiatrist Edwin Weinstein has argued that Wilson suffered from serious cerebrovascular disease over a period of nearly thirty years, and that discrete strokes accounted for behavioral changes at several critical junctures in Wilson's professional life. This view has been accepted by the eminent historian Arthur Link, who has referred to these "strokes" without qualification in the current edition of *The Papers of Woodrow Wilson*. My own reading of the evidence leads me to question both the medical interpretations of Dr. Weinstein, and the propriety of presenting such views as historical fact.

Weinstein's thesis is that Wilson suffered for many years from cerebrovascular disease, primarily carotid artery insufficiency, and had discrete strokes which influenced his professional behavior. Weinstein contends cerebrovascular disease first became manifest as disability of the right arm, resulting from one or more small strokes in 1896. The strongest and most direct evidence for stroke is considered to be Wilson's episode of left visual loss in 1906, which Weinstein describes as diagnostic of left carotid occlusive disease. Finally the illness which Wilson suffered during the 1919 Peace Conference is viewed as viral encephalopathy superimposed on preexisting brain damage. Each of these points merits careful analysis.

Wilson had difficulty with his right hand and arm for more than twenty years, and referred on numerous occasions to "writer's cramp" which was apparently diagnosed as a "neuritis." The precise symptoms are not spelled out, but the hand and arm were often painful, especially while writing. These symptoms began long before the alleged stroke of 1896, and references to this complaint can be found in the Wilson papers as far back as 1884. There are no references to suggest a sudden onset of symptoms (as from a stroke) in either 1884 or 1896, and the symptoms are too chronic to call them a result of transient ischemic attacks. Furthermore, Wilson also had occasional discomfort and pain in his *left* arm.

"Writer's cramp" is poorly understood as a clinical entity. Some cases may have an organic basis from pathology such as arthritic joint damage or inflammation of the nerves, but many are thought to represent an occupational neurosis. Characteristically, the patient has difficulty writing more than a few words, but lacks any major disability for other activities. This fits the descriptions of Wilson's disorder, and there is evidence that even during his severe periods of disability he was able to write brief ledger entries with his right hand which rules out any serious paralysis or limitation of movement. To accept this condition as writer's cramp (even without a precise definition of that term) seems perfectly reasonable in view of the nature and duration of the symptoms, whereas to fit these symptoms into a stroke syndrome places them in the category of unusual manifestations.

The 1906 episode is interpreted by Weinstein as direct evidence for cerebrovascular disease, since right-sided weakness and left-sided blindness are often associated with insufficiency or occlusion of the left carotid artery. However, the ocular findings in Wilson's case argue *against* a diagnosis of carotid occlusion. Wilson awoke one morning aware of poor vision in his left eye, which numerous sources indicate was found to result from bursting of a blood vessel and hemorrhage inside the eye. The fact of the matter is that retinal hemorrhage is *not* a sign of carotid occlusive disease. Carotid disease most characteristically leads to occlusion of the retinal arteries which causes a loss of vision but produces a very different picture (without hemorrhage) inside the eye. Arterial occlusion would not have been described in the language used by Wilson and his family members.

Wilson's doctors noted signs of arteriosclerosis and mild hypertension, and there seems little doubt that he had systemic vascular disease. The most likely cause for Wilson's eye disease would be a retinal vein occlusion, which is often associated with hypertensive vascular disease, and which produces diffuse hemorrhages in the retina. Other possibilities include hemorrhagic macular degeneration. The point to emphasize is that these ocular hemorrhages occur frequently as isolated events; they give evidence of generalized vascular pathology but they do not constitute strokes or carry any direct implication of cerebral ischemia or symptomatology.

There are other reasons to doubt a stroke in 1906. The stroke would have affected the left cerebral hemisphere which has major control over language and speech, yet Wilson clearly suffered no impairment in these areas. Weinstein implies that a stroke caused personality changes that affected Wilson's subsequent activities, but the literature on strokes is quite clear in emphasizing that personality changes are not a characteristic of the stroke syndrome in the absence of cognitive changes or dementia. Weinstein carefully qualifies his argument to state that Wilson's behavioral changes in 1906 were an adaptation to his illness and could result from stress as well as brain damage. Considering that Wilson had indeed suffered an ocular hemorrhage, and that he was working with intensity as president of Princeton University, why should it be necessary to invoke strokes or cerebral pathology to account for his actions?

Similar problems arise in analyzing the illness that began on April 3, 1919, during the Peace Conference. Weinstein initially concluded that Wilson had suffered a stroke to explain his behavior during the conference, but the tenuousness of the stroke hypothesis is shown by Weinstein's shift to a diagnosis of viral encephalopathy when new evidence made it clear that Wilson had had respiratory disease. I fail to see the need for postulating any diagnoses beyond severe influenza to account for Wilson's behavior. Wilson was ill with respiratory symptoms and high fever, and there are surely few of us who cannot attest to the debilitating effect of severe flu. Wilson was confined to bed for five days but was incapacitated only on the first day, after which he resumed conferring and decision making from his bedroom. The term "viral encephalopathy" may apply to a broad range of symptoms, from minimal headache and irritability, to severe somnolence, convulsions, and death. Wilson clearly did not have the latter, and some would argue that the former are in fact a routine component of the flu syndrome. Wilson's activities for the remainder of April 1919 seem quite consistent with a history of severe but uncomplicated influenza, and I should think the burden of proof would be to show otherwise.

Wilson probably had systemic vascular disease for a good part of his life, and there is no question that he ultimately suffered a severe stroke in the fall of 1919. Neither of these observations, however, can be construed as evidence for multiple strokes or for significant neurologic dysfunction during the earlier years of his career. Chronic vascular disease may cause subtle changes in mentation, ultimately resulting in dementia. Could Wilson have had very mild degrees of change accumulating over the years? Certainly this is possible, but how does one distinguish this type of subtle degeneration from other aspects of maturation and aging which are evident in everyone? This man actively ran one of the major universities in the United States, campaigned articulately for the presidency, and was clearly a lucid and powerful thinker in political affairs up to the moment of his serious stroke in 1919.

The interpretations which I have chosen to emphasize focus upon common and ordinary conditions, rather than the unusual or the extreme. I think the odds favor such an interpretation, but these views are admittedly hypothetical and open to review or criticism by others. I hope that my arguments will, at the least, raise reasonable doubts about the stroke theory and return it to a position of hypothesis rather than fact in historical source material.

With warm regards,

(Signed) Michael F. Marmor, M.D.*
Associate Professor
Division of Ophthalmology
Chief, Ophthalmology Section
Veterans Administration Medical Center
Palo Alto, California

---

*Doctor Marmor is currently Head, Division of Ophthalmology, Stanford University School of Medicine—eds.

NOTES

1 See Edwin A. Weinstein, James William Anderson, and Arthur S. Link, "Woodrow Wilson's Political Personality: A Reappraisal," *Political Science Quarterly* 93(Winter 1978–79):586; and Alexander L. George and Juliette L. George, *Woodrow Wilson and Colonel House: A Personality Study* (New York: John Day Company, 1956: Dover Publications, 1964). We are exiled in good company. Some years ago Arthur Link wrote of Ray Stannard Baker that his eight-volume *Woodrow Wilson: Life and Letters* (Garden City, New York: Doubleday, Page and Co., 1927–1939) suffered from Baker's having "to a large degree imposed his own personality profile upon Wilson." Moreover, claims Link (without justification, in our opinion), Baker portrayed Wilson "as being mainly feminine in personality, if not virtually a sexual neuter." This of the man in whose early volumes Woodrow Wilson fairly springs to life. Baker's prodigious research resulted in the collection of that rich raw data upon which Link's own work—and that of every other Wilson scholar—heavily rests. See Arthur S. Link, ed., *Woodrow Wilson: A Profile* (New York: Hill and Wang, 1968), pp. vii–viii.

2 We shall here cite two of the two dozen instances we have thus far found in Arthur S. Link et al., ed. *The Papers of Woodrow Wilson,* 36 vols. to date (Princeton, N.J.: Princeton University Press, 1966–). Of Wilson's illness in May 1906, it is stated in the introduction to vol. 16: "Years of excessive work take their toll in late May 1906, when Wilson suffers a major stroke that seems for a moment to threaten his life. . . ." (p. vii). In December 1907, Moses Taylor Pyne, a Princeton trustee, wrote to Wilson saying he was sorry to learn "that you were suffering from an attack of Neuritis" (ibid., vol. 17, p. 549). Link's editorial footnote to the word "Neuritis" reads: "In fact, Wilson had unquestionably suffered a slight stroke" (ibid., p. 550).

3 Weinstein, Anderson, and Link, "A Reappraisal," p. 587.

4 Ibid., p. 598.

5 George and George, *Woodrow Wilson and Colonel House,* p. 323.

6 Inga Floto, *Colonel House in Paris: A Study of American Policy at the Paris Peace Conference 1919* (Aarhus, Denmark: Universitetsforlaget, 1973; Princeton, N.J.: Princeton University Press, 1980); Weinstein, Anderson, and Link, "A Reappraisal," p. 597.

7 Floto, *Colonel House in Paris,* pp. 13, 20, 21. We cite Floto solely on the question of our research and do not mean to suggest that she endorses our interpretation of the House-Wilson relationship. To be sure, she credits us with "elucidating the 'mechanism' " of the friendship in an unassailable" fashion, but she is critical of our analysis of the "break." Her book is an important contribution to a continuing discussion among historians. We think, however, that the assertion by Weinstein, Anderson, and Link that Floto "proves conclusively that the cause of the so-called break between the two men was House's failure to follow Wilson's explicit instructions while the latter was in the United States" ("A Reappraisal," p. 597) is an oversimplification.

8 Weinstein, Anderson, and Link, "A Reappraisal," p. 587.

9 George and George, *Woodrow Wilson and Colonel House,* p. 12. See also ibid., p. 114.

10 See ibid., p. 7.

11 Weinstein, Anderson, and Link, "A Reappraisal," pp. 588–89.

12 Arthur S. Link, *Wilson: The Road to the White House* (Princeton, N.J.: Princeton University Press, 1947), p. 2.

13 Baker, *Life and Letters,* vol. 1, pp. 36–37.

14 George and George, *Woodrow Wilson and Colonel House,* p. 7; and Arthur S. Link, "The Case for Woodrow Wilson," *Harper's Magazine* 234(April 1967):91. In anticipation of the argument that Wilson did poorly because his schooling was disrupted in consequence of the disrupted times, let us point out that "Tommy" was a conspicuously poor student compared to his peers. According to Baker, " 'Tommy' Wilson's school work was decidedly below average" and his teacher compained to Dr. Joseph Wilson that "Tommy" was at the foot of his class not for want of ability but because he would not study (Baker, *Life and Letters,*

vol. 1, p. 42; also the Papers of Ray Stannard Baker, Series 1B, Box 3, "Memo for the Augusta Period," Library of Congress, Washington, D.C., p. 10). Link had referred to Wilson as a "late starter" in *Woodrow Wilson: A Brief Biography,* Cleveland, Ohio: World Publishing Co., 1963), p. 18.

15 Link, *A Profile,* pp. xiv–xv.
16 Weinstein, Anderson, and Link, "A Reappraisal," p. 588.
17 Michael Rutter, "Prevalence and Types of Dyslexia," in *Dyslexia: An Appraisal of Current Knowledge,* eds. A. L. Benton and D. Pearl (New York: Oxford University Press, 1978), pp. 5, 24. The chapters in this book were written for the National Institute of Mental Health conference.
18 Ibid., p. 9; John R. Hughes, "Electroencephalographic and Neurophysiological Studies in Dyslexia," p. 234 and O. Spreen, "The Dyslexias: A Discussion of Neurobehavioral Research," pp. 178–79, both in *Dyslexia,* Benton and Pearl; also see Leon Eisenberg, "Psychiatric Aspects of Language Disability," in *Reading, Perception and Language: Papers from the World Congress on Dyslexia,* ed., D. D. Duane and M. B. Rawson (Baltimore, Md.: York Press, 1975), p. 225.
19 Rutter, "Prevalence and Types of Dyslexia," p. 24.
20 Weinstein, Anderson, and Link, "A Reappraisal," p. 588.
21 Wilson to Ellen Axson, 8 November 1884, *Papers of Woodrow Wilson,* vol. 3, p. 415.
22 Wilson to Ellen Axson, 20 January 1885, ibid., p. 623; 13 February 1885, ibid. vol. 4, pp. 244–45.
23 Wilson to Heath Dabney, 14 February 1885, ibid., vol. 4, pp. 248–49.
24 Wilson to Ellen Axson, 19 February 1885, ibid., p. 269.
25 See ibid., vol. 1, pp. 83–128, and 132ff. for a still earlier diary and "Commonplace Book" in which Wilson recorded his enjoyment of reading. See also Wilson to his sister, Annie Howe, on 19 April 1876 in which he reports "employing most of the last week in reading" and finding "a great deal of enjoyment" in it (ibid., p. 128).
26 See ibid., vol. 13, pp. 267–97.
27 Weinstein, Anderson, and Link, "A Reappraisal," p. 588.
28 "Material on Woodrow Wilson Prepared by Dr. Stockton Axson with Occasional Assistance of Admiral Cary T. Grayson," a memoir owned personally by Professor Link. See chapter entitled "Health and Recreations," p. 15. We wish to thank Professor Link for granting us access to this manuscript.
29 Wilson to Dr. Azel W. Hazen, 29 March 1897, *Papers of Woodrow Wilson,* vol. 10, p. 201. Wilson to Ellen Axson Wilson, 17, 21, and 23 June 1896, and 3 July, 18 August 1896, ibid., vol. 9, pp. 519, 523, 527, 532, 573. Also see Wilson to Ellen Axson Wilson, 29 June 1908, ibid., vol. 18, p. 345.
30 Macdonald Critchley, *The Dyslexic Child* (Springfield, Ill.: Charles C. Thomas, Publisher, 1970), pp. 36–40. See also Rutter "Prevalence and Types of Dyslexia," p. 18.
31 Eisenberg, "Psychiatric Aspects of Language Disability," p. 220. See also D. Duane, "Summary of the World Congress on Dyslexia," in *Reading, Perception and Language,* Duane and Rawson, p. 5; and Critchley, *The Dyslexic Child,* p. 97.
32 Weinstein, Anderson, and Link, "A Reappraisal," pp. 588–89.
33 "Memorandum of Interviews with Dr. Cary T. Grayson on February 18, 19, 1926 at Washington," Papers of Ray Stannard Baker, Box 109.
34 Weinstein, Anderson, and Link, "A Reappraisal," p. 587. Space limitations preclude further discussion of Wilson's childhood and relationship with his father. For relevant data, see George and George, *Woodrow Wilson and Colonel House,* pp. 6–13, 31–32, 271–72; see also George and George, "*Woodrow Wilson and Colonel House:* A Reply to Weinstein, Anderson and Link" (Paper delivered at the 1981 meeting of the International Society of Political Psychology, Mannheim, Germany, June 1981), pp. 10–78. We hope to publish elsewhere a fuller account, made possible by the data now available, about Wilson's father as his re-

lentlessly driving (as well as wonderfully incisive) critic; and of Wilson's longing to do—as he put it—"immortal work," work of such noble service to humanity that to further it he felt morally justified to indulge his aggressions against those who stood in his way in that sphere of authority in which he sought compensatory gratifications.

One interesting vein of data—a good deal of which Professor Link, unfortunately, has omitted from *The Papers of Woodrow Wilson*—is contained in letters to Wilson from his parents about their difficulties in raising Wilson's much younger brother Joseph R. Wilson, Jr. ("Josie"), ten years Wilson's junior. Dr. and Mrs. Wilson complain to the now studious and increasingly successful "Woodrow" that "Josie" is "lazy"—even as Wilson himself, as a boy, had been made to feel. They disparage "Josie's" nascent competences, express concern about his lack of will to study, seek Wilson's advice about what to "do" about the hapless boy (as, when Wilson was a lad, his father had conferred with the family's distinguished elders about what to "do" about his poor performance in school). They poke fun at "Josie," squelch his wish to play, disparage his popularity with his fellows, express surprise and amusement at his accomplishments. In short, years after publication of our book, further documentation has emerged of a parental style that includes the seriously ego-damaging characteristics which we—on the basis of practically no evidence, according to Weinstein, Anderson, and Link— were able to describe in *Woodrow Wilson and Colonel House.*

35 "Material on Woodrow Wilson Prepared by Dr. Stockton Axson," chapter entitled "Woodrow Wilson and His Father," pp. 5, 8, 15–16; chapter entitled "Dr. Joseph R. Wilson," pp. 1, 2, 9, 12–13; chapter entitled "The Personality of Woodrow Wilson," Part II, p. 24; and untitled chapter, pp. 4–5.

36 George and George, *Woodrow Wilson and Colonel House,* pp. 3, 12–13.

37 Weinstein, Anderson, and Link, "A Reappraisal," p. 592 (emphasis added).

38 Wilson to Ellen Axson, 7 December 1884, *Papers of Woodrow Wilson,* vol. 3, p. 522 (emphasis added).

39 See in ibid. Wilson to Ellen Axson (Wilson), 17 February 1885 (vol. 4, p. 263), 13 March 1892 (vol. 7, p. 483), 20 July 1908 (vol. 18, p. 372), 9 August 1902 (vol. 14, p. 68), 23 February 1900 (vol. 11, p. 436), 28 January 1895 (vol. 9, p. 137), 20 March 1885 (vol. 4, p. 389), and 29 August 1902 (vol. 14, p. 118).

40 See also Alexander L. George, "Power as a Compensatory Value for Political Leaders," *Journal of Social Issues* 24(July 1968):29–49.

41 Weinstein, Anderson, and Link, "A Reappraisal," pp. 587, 594. It is useful throughout this discussion to bear in mind Dr. Weinstein's criteria for accepting impaired brain function as an etiological or causal agent in political behavior. He stated them in his article, "Woodrow Wilson's Neurological Illness," *Journal of American History* 57(1970), as follows: "First, the appearance of clinical evidence of brain damage should coincide with behavioral change. Second, the behavioral change should involve some impairment in performance. Third, it should be possible to classify actions in the political field into behavioral syndromes known to be associated with certain types of brain damage" (p. 325).

42 See Henry Cabot Lodge, *The Senate and the League of Nations* (New York: Charles Scribner's Sons, 1925). Wilson, Lodge wrote, "was simply an element to be calmly and coolly considered in a great problem of international politics" (p. 226). It was "of vital moment to me" to make "a correct analysis of Mr. Wilson's probable attitude" (p. 219; see also pp. 212–13). Lodge's insight was based upon years of hostile but astute observations stretching back to the beginning of Wilson's administration—a period during which, if we understand Weinstein, Anderson, and Link correctly, they believe Wilson to have been relatively free of manifestations of the brain damage from which they say he suffered.

43 Link, *The Road to the White House,* p. 90.

44 Ibid., pp. 76, 78.

45 Ibid., pp. viii–ix.

46 Weinstein, Anderson, and Link, "A Reappraisal," p. 596, n. 30.

47 Weinstein, "Woodrow Wilson's Neurological Illness," pp. 341–42.

48 Weinstein, Anderson, and Link, "A Reappraisal," p. 594, n. 26. We wished to include as part of the data we were assembling for independent medical review the "new evidence" that led Dr. Weinstein to abandon his "stroke" diagnosis. For over a year and a half, however, we were unable to gain access to it. Both Professor Link and Dr. Weinstein stated in reply to our several requests that they were bound by a promise of confidentiality not to reveal it. We were especially interested to know how the new evidence related to Dr. Weinstein's current diagnosis of "virus encephalopathy," upon which the hypothesis that Wilson sustained brain damage in Paris must now rest. We therefore wrote Dr. Weinstein and asked whether the new evidence proved or suggested the diagnosis of virus encephalopathy. In a letter dated 12 September 1979, he replied that the confidential data did not go beyond confirming the diagnosis of influenza.

On 22 October 1980, Professor Link wrote to us that he had been released from the pledge of confidentiality and he granted us access to the diary of Dr. Cary T. Grayson, Wilson's physician throughout his presidency. We thank him for this courtesy.

49 Weinstein, Anderson, and Link make repeated references to physiologically induced behavior and personality changes in Wilson without delineating the characteristic behavior patterns, the underlying personality, upon which the alleged changes impinged. Changes, after all, are comprehensible only in terms of that which preexists. Did the postulated brain damage accentuate certain aspects of a well-established behavior system or did it, in these authors' view, cause quite alien behavior to become manifest?

50 Papers of Irwin Hoover, Box 2, Library of Congress.

51 Diary of Cary T. Grayson, 5 April 1919; Gilbert Close to Arthur Walworth, 7 May 1951. Papers of Arthur Walworth, Yale University Library, New Haven, Conn.

52 Memoranda nos. 29, 32, 47 from Secretary of the American Commission to Negotiage Peace to members of the commission and their staffs, Papers of Tasker H. Bliss, Container 286, Library of Congress; Diary of Cary T. Grayson, 8 April 1919; Diary of Edith Benham Helm, 29 March 1919, Library of Congress; Diary of Edward M. House, 7 January 1919, Yale University Library.

53 Weinstein, Anderson, and Link, "A Reappraisal," p. 596.

54 Alexander L. George and Juliette L. George to Edwin A. Weinstein, M.D., 19 July 1979 and his reply 12 September 1979. Dr. Weinstein cited Baker, Mrs. Wilson, Stockton Axson, and Moses Taylor Pyne. In a subsequent letter (3 October 1979), Dr. Weinstein said he had no other sources.

55 This included the diary of Dr. Cary T. Grayson as well as our correspondence with both Professor Link and Dr. Weinstein concerning the data upon which they relied for the preparation of their article and, most particularly, for Dr. Weinstein's diagnoses of Wilson's illnesses in 1906 and in Paris in April 1919. Professor Link informed us (letter dated 1 March 1979) that he had no medical records concerning Wilson that have not already been published in the *Papers of Woodrow Wilson* or are not available in the Wilson papers at the Library of Congress.

56 See the Papers of Arthur Walworth, Yale University Library, for Dr. Monroe's comments and Dr. Weinstein's reaction to them.

57 See, for example, John Mulder, *Woodrow Wilson: The Years of Preparation* (Princeton, N.J.: Princeton University Press, 1978), pp. 143, 145, and 147 for unequivocal references to Wilson's "stroke" of 1896 and its supposed effect on his thinking; see also his account of Wilson's illness in 1906 in which the stroke hypothesis also appears (pp. 185–86). There are numerous other references to the effects of Wilson's alleged strokes on his thinking and behavior. For a further discussion of this issue, see Juliette L. George, Michael F. Marmor, and Alexander L. George, "Issues in Wilson Scholarship: References to Early 'Strokes' in the *Papers of*

Woodrow Wilson," Journal of American History 70(March 1984):845–53; Arthur S. Link et al., "Communication," ibid., 945–55; George, Marmor, George rejoinder, ibid. 955–56. See also George, Marmor, George, "Communication," ibid., 71(June 1984):198–212—eds.

58 Edwin A. Weinstein, *Woodrow Wilson: A Medical and Psychological Biography* (Princeton, N.J.: Princeton University Press, 1981), pp. 165–67. See also Ellen Axson Wilson to Mary Hoyt, 12 June [1906], *Papers of Woodrow Wilson,* vol. 16, p. 423; Wilson to Nicholas Murray Butler, I June 1906, ibid., p. 413; "Memorandum of Interviews with Grayson," Papers of Ray Stannard Baker, Box 109, p. 3; ibid., Box 5, Notebook XXII, pp. 56–57; Cary T. Grayson, *Woodrow Wilson: An Intimate Memoir* (New York: Holt, Rinehart and Winston, 1960 and 1977), p. 81; Stockton Axson, "Material on Woodrow Wilson," chapter entitled "Health and Recreations," p. 23, and chapter entitled "The Physical Man," p. 10. In the Papers of Ray Stannard Baker, see conversation with John Grier Hibben, 18 June 1925, Box 111; conversation with E. P. Davis, M.D., 12 November 1925, Box 106; E. P. Davis, "Memoranda Concerning Woodrow Wilson"; and Gilbert Close to Ray Stannard Baker, 26 September 1925, Box 103. See also Eleanor Wilson McAdoo, *The Priceless Gift* (New York: McGraw-Hill Book Company, 1962), p. 241. It is interesting to note that Weinstein himself, in his article "Woodrow Wilson's Neurological Illness," stated: "De Schweinitz found that the blindness had been caused by the bursting of a blood vessel in the eye" (p. 334). De Schweinitz's finding of a burst blood vessel is also reported in a footnote in *The Papers of Woodrow Wilson,* vol. 16, p. 412, n.1.

Part II
Bibliography

Suggestions for additional readings in psychobiography are grouped below under two headings. The first contains general works on the relationship between psychoanalysis and biography. These readings amplify some of the arguments put forth by Mack, Coles, and Runyan in the selections reprinted above. The second heading consists of comparative readings and contrasting interpretations of notable historical figures; they are arranged roughly chronologically.

Psychohistorians rarely discuss in theoretical terms the relationship between psychology and biography. Erik Erikson is perhaps the most notable exception. As a clinician, he is not surprisingly strongly influenced in his view of the past by the scientific and clinical ideas attributed to psychoanalysis. In *Childhood and Society* (New York, 2d ed., 1963), he wrote: "psychologies and psychologists are subject to historical laws and . . . historians and historical records are subject to those of psychology" (p. 403). For a succinct statement, see Erikson's *Insight and Responsibility* (New York, 1964), pp. 201–08. A growing connection between clinical work and psychobiography was reported by John Gedo in "The Methodology of Psychoanalytic Biography," *Journal of the American Psychoanalytic Association,* vol. 20 (1972), pp. 638–49. However, the literary biographer Leon Edel maintains that biographers should not be influenced by the therapeutic intent: see his "The Biographer and Psycho-Analysis," *International Journal of Psychoanalysis,* vol. 42 (1961), pp. 458–66. Similarly, W. F. Mandle warns the biographer against the therapeutic overtones of psychoanalytic theory. A biographer is not in any way a therapist, he wrote; his task rather is "to understand and explain the past" ("Psychology and History," *The New Zealand Journal of History,* vol. 2, no. 1 [April, 1968], pp. 1–17). The most thorough recent discussion of theory and method in psychobiography is William McKinley Runyan's *Life Histories and Psychobiography* (New York, 1982), from which chapter three, "Why Did Van Gogh Cut Off His Ear?" has been reprinted above. Two other important works which review psychobiographies and their methods should be mentioned here. They are: John Mack, "Psychoanalysis and Historical Biography," *Journal of the American Psychoanalytic Association,* vol. 19 (1971), pp. 143–79; and Miles Shore, "Biography in the 1980's: A Psychoanalytic Perspective," *Journal of Interdisciplinary History,* vol. 12, no. 1 (Summer 1981), pp. 89–113.

II

Psychobiographers have ranged widely over the past and with varying degrees of success in attempting to explain past lives. Their difficulties have been exacerbated by a scarcity of historical evidence. Only a few psychohistorians have been bold enough to tackle ancient history, where more than the usual evidentiary problems exist. The case for a psycho-historical interpretation of this early period has been made by Thomas W. Africa, "Psychohistory, Ancient History, and Freud," *Arethusa,* vol. 12, no. 1 (Spring 1979), pp. 5–33. Africa's attempt at a psychobiography of the Roman era may be found in "The Mask of an Assassin: A Psychohistorical Study of M. Junius Brutus," *Journal of Interdisciplinary History,* vol. 8, no. 4 (Spring 1978), pp. 599–626.

Erik Erikson's *Young Man Luther* (New York, 1958)—generally considered to be the model for contemporary psychobiography—is not without its deficiencies in historical evidence. For critical reviews of this important work see, for example, the *Journal for the Scientific Study of Religion,* vol. 2, no. 2 (April 1963), pp. 238–52. Other comments may be found in Roland H. Bainton, "Luther: A Psychiatric Portrait," *The Yale Review,* vol. 48 (1959), pp. 405–10; Lewis W. Spitz, "Psychohistory and History: The Case of Young Man Luther," *Soundings,* vol. 56 (1974), pp. 182–209; and a special issue of *The Psychohistory Review* on Erikson, vol. 5, no. 3 (December 1976). Especially useful is R. A. Johnson (ed.), *Psychohistory and Religion: The Case of Young Man Luther* (Philadelphia, 1977). For a general critical treatment of Erikson, see Joel Kovel, "Erik Erikson's Psychohistory," *Social Policy,* vol. 5 (1974), pp. 60–64.

The tendency of some psychobiographers to emphasize theory over fact is best exemplified by J. C. Flugel's early study (first published in 1920) of a contemporary of Luther's, King Henry VIII of England. Flugel makes much of Henry's unconscious "desires," "feelings," "complexes," "mind," and "tendencies"—as they are variously described in his "On the Character and Married Life of Henry VIII," in Bruce Mazlish (ed.), *Psychoanalysis and History* (Englewood Cliffs, 1963). A more recent psychological portrait of Henry is less reductive. Miles Shore combines Eriksonian stage-modeling with Heniz Kohut's psychology of narcissism in "Henry VIII and the Crisis of Generativity," *Journal of Interdisciplinary History,* vol. 2 (1972), pp. 359–90.

To overcome the scarcity of relevant personal detail so important to psychobiography, Elizabeth Marvick utilizes an early medical record kept during the childhood of her subject Louis XIII, king of France from 1610 to 1642. See her two articles "The Character of Louis XIII: The Role of his Physician," *Journal of Interdisciplinary History,* vol. 4, no. 3 (Winter 1974), pp. 347–74; and "Childhood History and Decisions of State: The Case of Louis XIII," in L. de Mause (ed.), *The New Psychohistory* (New York, 1975). Another seventeenth-century figure has captured the attention of Roger Howell, who cautiously reviews the evidence for a psychobiographical study of that elusive Puritan, Oliver Cromwell, in "Cromwell's Personality: The Problems and Promises of a Psychohistorical Approach," *Biography,* vol. 1, no. 1 (Winter 1978), pp. 41–60.

Ernst Lewy uses evidence—which he considers "as reliable as material supplied by patients"—in combination with Freudian Oedipal theory to discuss an eighteenth-century Prussian monarch: see "The Transformation of Frederick the Great: A Psychoanalytic Study," in *The Psychoanalytic Study of Society,* vol. 4 (1967), pp. 252–311. Less explicit about his theoretical structure, Harold T. Parker explains Napoleon Bonaparte's ambition and rise to power as a need for approval from his mother and later (by extension) approval from France. Parker's argument is in "The Formation of Napoleon's Personality: An Exploratory Essay," *French Historical Studies,* vol. 7 (1971), pp. 6–26.

A particularly useful article because it is unusually self-conscious about its methodology is the collaborative work by Frederick Wyatt and William B. Willcox, "Sir Henry Clinton: A Psychological Exploration in History," *William and Mary Quarterly,* vol. 16 (1959), pp. 3–26. Wyatt (a clinical psychologist) and Willcox (a historian) observe that Clinton, who was a commander of the British forces during the American Revolution, had a career marked by curious episodes of maladaptive behavior. They argue that it can be explained by "an unconscious conflict over authority." Clinton's colonial opponent, Benjamin Franklin, was well known for an opposite trait: Franklin was a diplomat and negotiator of great skill. In a satisfyingly modest approach, Richard L. Bushman avoids speculation about Franklin's infancy and childhood and explains the life from firmly established adult behavior patterns: see "On the Uses of Psychology: Conflict and Conciliation in Benjamin Franklin," *History and Theory,* vol. 5 (1966), pp. 225–40.

Another military figure in American history who, like Clinton, was not known for his conciliatory nature was General George Custer. Custer's last stand has gone down in history as a courageous battle against insurmountable odds, but to Charles K. Hofling, it was another "rash and self-destructive" act characteristic of Custer's life. Hofling, following the theories of self psychology advocated by Heinz Kohut, believes that Custer had a narcissistic personality disorder: see Hofling's *Custer and the Little Big Horn* (Detroit, 1981).

Kohutian interpretations seem to have made significant headway in recent psychobiographical studies. Charles Strozier's *Lincoln's Quest for Union* (New York, 1982) places Lincoln's leadership within a broad framework of a Kohutian "cohesive group self" (the United States in the 1850s). Lincoln's rage and fears of a dominant Southern slave power was emblematic of the North as a whole, and contributed to a war spirit. Other aspects of Lincoln's personality—such as his self-deprecating humor—Strozier sees as part of a Kohutian self-therapy to ward off depression. See also Strozier's article, "Heinz Kohut and the Historical Imagination," *Psychohistory Review,* vol. 7, no. 2 (Fall 1978), pp. 36–39. A more contemporary subject explained in Kohutian terms is the former Australian prime minister, Gough Whitlam. James Walter's *The Leader: A Political Biography of Gough Whitlam* (University of Queensland, 1980) portrays Whitlam as a "narcissistic personality type": see especially chapter six.

One of the few psychohistorical studies with a woman as its subject is Donald R. Allen's analysis of Florence Nightingale. Relying on Helene Deutsch's notion of feminine masochism, Allen believes that a strong masochistic strain in Nightingale "helped her to choose and pursue a career in nursing" at a time when this was not a respectable occupation for upper-class women. The discussion may be found in detail in Allen's article, "Florence Nightingale: Toward a Psychohistorical Interpretation," *Journal of Interdisciplinary History,* vol. 4, no. 1(Summer 1975), pp. 23–45. Other recent psychobiographies have diverged from Deutsch's orthodox Freudian view of women: see John Cody, *After Great Pain: The Inner Life of Emily Dickinson* (Cambridge, Mass., 1971); Jean Strouse, *Alice James: A Biography* (Boston, 1980); and Alice Wexler, *Emma Goldman: An Intimate Life* (New York, 1984).

As one might expect, historical subjects living closer to our own time promise a greater harvest of useful evidence. But this has led neither to a consensus of methodological approach nor to an agreement in interpretation. Even within the psychodynamic tradition, there is great variation. Good examples are three differing treatments of Otto von Bismarck, the nineteenth-century German statesman. Otto Pflanze gives a rather eclectic psychodynamic portrayal, Reichian in parts, in his "Toward a Psychoanalytic Interpretation of Bismarck," *American Historical Review,* vol. 77 (1974), pp. 419–44. Charlotte Sempel's "Bismarck's Childhood: A Psychohistorical Study," *History of Childhood Quarterly,* vol. 2 (1974), pp. 107–24 draws upon Anna Freud, Erikson, and selected articles in the *Psychoanalytic Study of the Child* for its theoretical framework. (See also Sempel's "1866: Bismarck's Gamble," *Psychohistory Review,* vol. 7, no. 2 [Fall, 1978], pp. 25–29.) Judith M. Hughes, "Toward the Psychological Drama of High Politics: The Case of Bismarck," *Central European History,* vol. 10 (1978), pp. 271–85, relies on object relations theory. Hughes has expanded her article into a longer study, *Emotion and High Politics* (Berkeley, 1983)— a somewhat insoluble mixture of diplomatic policy and personality in late-nineteenth-century Germany and Britain.

It is upon another German, Adolf Hitler, that the most extensive psychohistorical scrutiny of all has fallen. While Hitler was still in power psychological studies were begun, notably Walter Langer's classified wartime study for the OSS, *The Mind of Adolf Hitler* (New York, 1972); and Erik Erikson's "Hitler's Imagery and German Youth," *Psychiatry,* vol. 5 (1942), pp. 475–93. Langer's book applies an orthodox Freudian scheme to public and intelligence material available during the war. Correctly noting the importance of Hitler's fantasies, Langer's analysis nevertheless suffers from theoretical rigidity. Erikson's essay, later published in revised form in his *Childhood and Society* (New York, 1950), portrays the mixture of unconscious urges and shrewd propaganda that filled Hitler's *Mein Kampf* and suggests the historically determined unconscious reasons for the Germans' response to their Führer's dreams and appeals.

More recent psychohistorical studies of Hitler include Robert Waite, *The Psychopathic God* (New York, 1977) and Rudolph Binion, *Hitler and the Germans* (New York, 1976). Waite's book relies heavily upon Langer's study, which was declassified and published in 1972. Waite sees Hitler as a "'borderline personality," suffering from a sadomasochistic guilt complex, a severe Oedipus complex, castration anxiety, and an undescended testicle. Waite provides a great deal of clinical material to support his interpretation of the evidence and there is much that rings true in his depiction of the private Hitler. Some of his conclusions, however, are based more upon theoretical assumptions than upon direct evidence from Hitler's childhood and adolescent years. Binion's work is a unique attempt to isolate the determinative causes for Hitler's rise and fall. By immersing himself in the relevant documents, Binion claims to detect empathically a link between Hitler's trauma over his mother's death at the hands of a Jewish doctor and the trauma suffered by the German people in 1918, twin traumas that led, respectively, to Auschwitz and Stalingrad. Binion's method is probably too intensely subjective for most historians: see, for example, Fred Weinstein's critique in *Psychohistory Review,* vol. 6, no. 1 (Summer 1977), pp. 50–61.

Works on Hitler constitute only the most prominent outcropping of the mountain of psychohistorical work on Nazi Germany. Psychohistorians have also undertaken the study of other subjects connected with Nazism. Historian and psychoanalyst Peter Loewenberg has produced representative studies such as "The Unsuccessful Adolescence of Heinrich Himmler," *American Historical Review,* vol. 76 (1971), pp. 612–41; "The Psychohistorical

Origins of the Nazi Youth Cohort," *American Historical Review,* vol. 76 (1971), pp. 1457–1502; and a comprehensive review essay, "Psychohistorical Perspectives on Modern German History," *Journal of Modern History,* vol. 47 (1975), pp. 229–79.

Political and social disorders of the twentieth century, represented by Hitler's rise to power, have given psychohistorians much to think about. Revolutionary studies especially would seem to be a promising field. The relationship between personal psychological traits and revolution is treated by George D. Jackson's "Lenin and the Problems of Psychohistory," *Canadian Slavonic Papers,* vol. 19, no. 2 (June 1977), pp. 207–22. Jackson puts aside the simplistic Freudian theories of E. Victor Wolfenstein's *The Revolutionary Personality* (Princeton, 1971) and suggests instead a more clinical approach based on the work of Carl Rogers and Abraham Maslow. This, Jackson claims, would avoid the misleading monolithic interpretations of personality based on childhood traumas and substitute a study of personalities at a given point of time in a life. A different psychobiographical approach to revolutions is suggested by Bruce Mazlish's *The Revolutionary Ascetic* (New York, 1976). Mazlish believes that the "Robespierres win out over Dantons" in revolutions because the puritanical revolutionary with a "displaced libido" who denies bonds of friendship and feeling can devote everything to the revolution. Among Mazlish's examples are Oliver Cromwell, Robespierre, Lenin, and Mao Tse-tung. Mazlish's thesis has been questioned. Peter Loewenberg suggests in the *American Historical Review,* vol. 82, no. 2 (April 1977), pp. 336–37 that Mazlish relied too heavily on the Oedipal dynamics of Freudian libido theory: Loewenberg recommends object relations theory. Chalmers Johnson is more critical, and wonders how Mao can be considered an ascetic with "his pot belly, his chain smoking, and his three wives." See "Pregnant with 'Meaning!' Mao and the Revolutionary Ascetic," *Journal of Interdisciplinary History,* vol. 7, no. 3 (Winter 1977), pp. 499–508.

An ascetic mode of leadership would also seem to characterize Woodrow Wilson's presidency. Wilson is second only to Hitler as a psychobiographical subject. In addition to the three articles reprinted above, readers may want to peruse the biography that initiated the present debate on the psychological travails of Wilson, Alexander and Juliette George's *Woodrow Wilson and Colonel House: A Personality Study* (New York, 1956). We recommend the Dover edition (1964): here the Georges add a helpful preface and a concluding research note. Alexander George elaborates on his theoretical model in "Power As a Compensatory Value for Political Leaders," *Journal of Social Issues,* vol. 24, no. 3 (1968), pp. 29–49. A recent issue of *Political Psychology,* vol. 4, no. 2 (June 1983), pp. 289–331, debates the various interpretations of Wilson. Dorothy Ross provides a timely survey of the issues in her "Review Essay/Woodrow Wilson and the Case for Psychohistory," *Journal of American History,* vol. 69, no. 3 (December 1982), pp. 659–68. Much of the controversy swirls around Edwin Weinstein's evaluation of Wilson's health during critical moments of his presidency. Weinstein's views are given in the article reprinted above, but readers desiring additional information should read Weinstein's recent book, *Woodrow Wilson: A Medical and Psychological Biography* (Princeton, 1981), cited in note 13 of our introduction.

The life of T. E. Lawrence, scholar, author, and as "Lawrence of Arabia," a guerrilla leader against the Turks in World War I, has become an intriguing psychobiographical subject. Digging deeply into Lawrence's background and utilizing a sophisticated eclectic—though essentially psychodynamic—model, John Mack places a debased self-esteem at the center of Lawrence's curious fall from fame into obscurity after the war. Mack's first advanced his thesis in "T. E. Lawrence: A Study of Heroism and Conflict," *American Journal of Psy-*

chiatry, vol. 125 (1969), pp. 1083–92: Mack later expanded his ideas into a full-scale biography of Lawrence, *A Prince of Our Disorder* (Boston, 1976).

The perils of writing a psychobiography of a contemporary figure are well illustrated in the case of Richard Nixon. Many attempts have been methodologically unsophisticated and politically biased. A representative work is David Abrahamsen's *Nixon vs Nixon: An Emotional Tragedy* (New York, 1976). An analyst, Abrahamsen claims to be basing his study upon "years of training and experience" and to rest his conclusions upon "a vast body of scientific knowledge," yet he seems unable to distinguish between historical fact and bald speculation. Bruce Mazlish obtains somewhat better results in his "Toward a Psychohistorical Inquiry: The 'Real' Richard Nixon," *Journal of Interdisciplinary History*, vol. 1 (1970), pp. 49–105. In Mazlish's longer psychobiography, *In Search of Nixon* (New York, 1972), especially worth noting is chapter six, "The Psychohistorical Approach." Stanley Allen Renshon's review article, "Psychological Analysis and Presidential Personality: The Case of Richard Nixon," *History of Childhood Quarterly*, vol. 2 (1975), pp. 415–50 provides a thoughtful comparison of four psychological approaches to Nixon.

PART III

THE PSYCHOLOGY OF
THE GROUP IN HISTORY

14

Group Psychology and Problems of Contemporary History

Bruce Mazlish

Events of recent history have begged for explanation in terms of group psychology and group behaviour. The omnipresent reality of totalitarianism, especially, calls for its interpretation in the very terms—growing "irrationality," and hence psychology—that shape the phenomenon itself. Somehow, we must make what seems almost totally irrational submit to rational explanation. The term "cult of personality" itself emphasizes the psychological dimension. So, too, our increased interest in, and awareness of, racial situations provokes an inquiry into the inter-personal relations that underlie an otherwise irrational, and often uneconomical, system. Colonial relations, messianic cults, all ask similar questions.

Yet, since the publication of William McDougall's *Introduction to Social Psychology* in 1908, perhaps the earliest text in the field, little seems to have been done here that satisfies the historian's quest for greater understanding. As for psychoanalytically-oriented work, the theories of Freudian individual psychology, even for those convinced of their validity, seem not to have been satisfactorily connected to the problems of group psychology. Thus the stern and demanding challenge of group psychology and its relation to history still confronts us, unsmilingly. The cheerful note in this situation is that a fresh look at the problem, however unsuccessful, can hardly be compared too unfavourably to its predecessors.

I propose, therefore, to note some of the new theories of group psychology and group behaviour as applied to contemporary history; then to glance at their possible application to national character; at their application in work on group psychoses and neuroses, as well as inter-group rivalry and persecutions (all closely related phenomena); and, lastly, to discuss briefly a case study in inter-

This article first appeared in the *Journal of Contemporary History*, 3,2 (April 1968), pp. 163–77.

group relations, O. Mannoni's study of the colonial relationship in Madagascar.

The new theories of group psychology, or at least the non-Freudian ones, appear to me to have little applicability to history. What is known as the theory of cognitive dissonance does not help to explain historical phenomena.[1] Similarly, the work done at the Massachusetts Institute of Technology by Richard Held and his colleagues on the connection between motor activity and the perception of reality, on the distortion of even the simplest perceptions when action is inhibited, is fascinating, but it is difficult to see how it can be usefully applied by the historian. The same applies to the recent work by other psychologists, showing that one's judgment is affected by what others around one think: if six "primed" subjects claim a black object is white, the innocent seventh subject will in all probability also pronounce it white. Suggestions about the lack of motor activities in totalitarian countries leading to distortion, or about the influence of propagandized peers on a person, while undoubtedly true, simply do not advance us far in history.

It may be that the failure is mine. However, in what follows I shall only be able to remark on a few instances of what is, generally speaking, non-Freudian group psychology as applied to historical material.

David McClelland's *The Achieving Society* (1961) is by now a well-known book. Its thesis is simple: the ethos of "achieving" is crucial to a flourishing society, and its presence in personality can be measured empirically, even for past societies. The method of application is elaborate: scales and tables, based on present-day questionnaires and polling techniques, are used to investigate Greek pottery as well as the German school system, and to see how high on the "achieving scale" they measure. Obviously, the book attracts as an effort to shed light on the psychological factor in developing underdeveloped countries today, and as an empirical corrective and extension to Max Weber's theory of the Protestant ethos. Alas, most critics have not been persuaded by either the tables (which too often seem to have shaky conclusions drawn from them) or the sweeping nature of the theory.

McClelland's book does point to the increasing interest in the factor of group psychology as part of the economic development process. It has gradually become clear even to the econometricians that human beings are what make economies tick, and that economic development does not take place on paper, in terms of nicely manipulated figures. Thus, in addition to generalized theories of growth in which the psychological factor is merely presumed, such as Rostow's theories of economic stages, there are important efforts, such as Everett Hagen's *Theory of Social Change* (1962), in which the psychological is explicitly made central to the theory. As Hagen, a professional economist, says elsewhere, "The theory of the economics of economic development will mainly elaborate details, rather than making major advances, until advances in sociology and personality theory give it new insights."[2]

Along with economic development, political development has become a subject of current interest. Here, too, the psychological has received much emphasis, centring to a large extent on the idea of identity. Perhaps it is only natural that the 'search for identity' by new nations attracts more attention than the analysis of the identity of established nations. Thus, Lucian Pye deals with the "identity crisis," both on the individual and the public level, in Burma, in his book *Politics, Personality, and Nation Building;* and Harold Isaacs has done a whole series of studies based on this concept, covering the untouchables, Americans in Israel, the Filipinos, American Negroes, and so forth. Isaacs' other overriding interest in these studies is to observe how individuals and groups perceive others, and how they are, in turn, perceived (see, for example, *Scratches on our Minds: American Images of China and India*); and he relates this aspect of the psychology of perception (used at a low level of theory) to his examination of the search for identity; part of a group's self-identity, for example, is based on how it is perceived by other groups.

Leaving development aside for the moment, psychological and semi-psychological studies have been made also on how existing political systems function in terms of their leadership element (and, of course, such studies can quickly be extended to the developing nations).[3] An instance is Lewis J. Edinger's *Kurt Schumacher: A Study in Personality and Political Behavior* (1965). The basic theory behind this book is clearly Harold Lasswell's classic notion (e.g., in *Psychopathology and Politics,* 1930) that the political actor, to use Edinger's phrases, "strives to satisfy personal needs through the assumption and performance of certain roles"(p. 5). One then asks what expectations the "actor" brings to his roles, and what are the expectations of the "counter-players." Alas, the "satisfaction of conscious or unconscious personal goals may not correspond to rationally posited or group-oriented goals and norms" (p. 4). Worse, the "actor" in the leading role may even reject new information when it clashes with cherished beliefs, needs, etc. (our old friend perception again). Other conclusions are that what works in one situation may not work in another: what was manifestly functional for Schumacher in securing leadership of the SPD was dysfunctional in the larger context of post-war German politics (p. 306); and a concluding hypothesis: "that behaviour which may have been self-defeating in terms of Schumacher's manifest aspirations may have served latent personality needs" (p. 282).

Obviously, work such as Edinger's is not very Freudian. It is more concerned with actors, roles, communication networks, and group-oriented goals. It will be interesting to see, therefore, what comes out of the conference on "Leadership," planned by Dankwart Rustow, Columbia University. (The papers are to appear as an issue of *Daedalus.*) Its stated purpose is to "look at rulers, at founders of states, or at founders of social or intellectual movements from a variety of perspectives, including the interplay between private personality and public role, the relationship between leaders, followers, rivals, and antagonists, the tactics of leadership, and a leader's successes, failures, and place in history." A central problem is conceived to be that of "the social and psychological congruence between leaders and followers," and in pursuing the psychological theme, we are informed, correctly of course, that "David Truman, summing up the trend of studies in social psychology, has stressed that 'the conception of leadership as a functional relationship rules out the possibility that all leaders have in common certain "traits" that set them off from followers.' " Robert C. Tucker will deliver a paper on The Theory of Charismatic Leadership; Stanley Hoffman on General de Gaulle; Dankwart Rustow on Ataturk as State Founder, and so forth, all emphasizing social, or group, psychology, Freudian or otherwise.

What of the more Freudian, or Neo-Freudian, efforts? We can take the work of Erik Erikson as the most outstanding contribution. His *Young Man Luther* (1959) was a brilliant, pioneering example of the new work in the emerging field of psycho-historical process. Now Erikson has turned to contemporary history, in the figure of Mahatma Gandhi. As yet only bits and pieces of this study have emerged, but the full-scale work is promised soon. It will provide an examination of the methodological problems involved in such work, much deeper even than that of the Luther volume, and will analyse Gandhi explicitly in the political and religious group settings in which he functioned. For those interested in contemporary history, the book may well have an even wider interest, for Erikson uses Gandhi, and his theory of non-violence, as a way of analysing the phenomena of war and violence in our time. Erikson is taking his theories of basic trust and of mutuality in the individual and seeking to extend them to the public arena. Deeply affected, I believe, by Konrad Lorenz's *On Aggression* (1966), he is trying to provide a "ritualization" for aggressive impulses, a training in "mutuality" that will keep man from going for the jugular, so to speak, and thus to supply the deficiency created by our lack of instinctive restraints. Gandhi shows the way.

Further discussion will have to await the appearance of Erikson's book. If, as I suspect, it takes up where Freud left off (one thinks, for example, of his "Thoughts for the Times on War and Death," 1915), we may well have an important theoretical contribution, not only to the study of Gandhi's leadership and to the problem of Indian identity, which it is sure to be, but to what is perhaps the most important phenomenon of contemporary history: war. If so, one hopes that it will stimulate further empirical studies.[4]

National character has always been an intriguing subject simply because everyone can play. The dour Scotsman, the energetic American, the volatile Italian, each can be nicely ticketed. Serious scholars, such as David Potter *(People of Plenty)*, Margaret Mead *(And Keep Your Powder Dry)*, Geoffrey Gorer and John Rickman *(The People of Great Russia)*, and even Erik Erikson (see his essays on American, German, and Russian character in *Childhood and Society*), have also tried their hand at the subject.

In my judgment it is an impossible subject. The only thing to do with so-called national character is to dissolve it into its parts. Certainly, in trying to understand contemporary domestic or international history, the concept of a unitary national character is a poor—indeed, non-existent—analytic tool.[5] To begin with, the subject of nationalism itself is still one of the least well-defined and manageable topics. The very definition of a "nation" and the basis on which it rests is up in the air. (At one extremity, we have African "nations" only a few years old, trying to compress into one generation changes that took centuries in Europe; and at the other extremity we have centuries-old European nations trying to transcend their present existence and achieve a supranational "European" identity.) Why not first study "tribal" character? Or regional character? And then examine how these are synthesized into something larger, called "national character" (e.g., what "characteristics" are held in common, in America, by a New Englander; a Mississippian—white or Negro; a Texan; and a Minnesotan?).

"National character," in other words, may mask the hard questions of dynamic process and functional relationship. For example, take character: on the individual level, a classic psychoanalytic definition is Fenichel's "The habitual mode of bringing into harmony the tasks presented by internal demands and by the external world" (*The Psychoanalytic Theory of Neurosis,* 1945, p. 467). The first part of this definition refers to defences, and is a useful notion in so far as most individuals develop characteristic patterns of defence (denial, projection, repression, etc.). Internal demands might seem constant but, as Erikson has insisted, they at least manifest themselves differently at different stages of the individual's life cycle. And the external world—that is in fact the realm of history (in this case, personal history). The point of all this is that, today, the emphasis in psychoanalysis is on "character" as a dynamic process, where even the defences shift during different periods of life and in relation to changing external demands.

How can these notions be extended to group psychology? The Eriksonian position, for example, and it is conceptually admirable, is that the individual's character is developed mainly in terms of the group character, that is, of the values and patterns of behaviour of the group as these are manifested in bringing up children: hence *Childhood and Society* (1951). Thus, by studying a "great man," a Luther or Gandhi, we may come to understand as well the society within which he is nurtured and to which he in turn contributes his creativity. There is much to be said for this approach; but it is no longer effectively in terms of "national character."

What about functional relationship? Let us assume an American "national character." If, for example, we are trying to understand American military policy today, can we use the generalized national character as a base from which to begin analysis? Or must we ask whether a distinct sub-group—say, a Southern "character"—plays a disproportionate role in formulating and carrying out military policy? Moreover, must we ask more narrowly how the Southern sub-group character and the Eastern sub-group character interact with one another, so that an outcome unintended by either emerges from the confrontation of character?

And, given the structure of American executive power, ought we to ask about the "character" of the President, and how it interrelates to something called the national character? In short, national character is an overgeneralized notion, when what counts most is the character of the men who actually wield power. (How representative of Japanese national character were the militarists who wielded power in the second world war? Were the surprise attacks preceding almost all Japanese military involvements in modern times a characteristic Japanese "defence," or a particular policy and offensive tactic of the generals?)

What national character points at is important. We do want to inquire about characteristic defences of a people, but we need to see these as dynamic, changing according to who the leaders are, to the demands of external reality, and to the period of history and the particular generation concerned. In short, concepts such as "national character," "spirit of the age," and so forth, start at the wrong end. They are stereotyped and posit as explanatory concepts what may only emerge, momentarily, as a result of particular empirical relations in a functioning system, subject to rapid change again. Consequently, we need to inquire into what is behind "national character," not into "national character" itself.

Under the heading, "Group Psychoses and Neuroses, and Intergroup Rivalry and Persecution," we find such unalluring topics as anti-Semitism and the authoritarian personality. As parts of the totalitarian phenomena of our time, these topics press for explanation in the same "irrational" terms as appear to produce them. "Sane," "rational" interest politics of the nineteenth century have given way to "cultural" or "status" politics, and the latter tend to rest on unconscious, rather than conscious, foundations: hence the appeal to social psychology, especially psychoanalysis.[6]

Anti-Semitism, of course, existed long before totalitarianism, but it is only with the advent of modern psychology that we have tried to probe its nature deeply. Such works as Ernst Simmel's "Anti-Semitism and Mass Psychopathology," along with essays by various scholars in the book he edited, *Anti-Semitism, a Social Disease* (1946); Ackerman and Jahoda, *Anti-Semitism and Emotional Disorder: A Psychoanalytic Interpretation* (1950); and numerous other studies have done much to illuminate the subject. Such studies form part of a general inquiry into racial or religious prejudice (anti-Negroism, anti-Catholicism, and so forth), and we can regard them as prototypic.

The first thing to note is that anti-Semitism is not to be classified as an individual mental disease. In fact it is a character defence, used to prevent mental illness. Unfortunate as this may be, it is true. Emotional conflicts typically displayed by anti-Semites—unsatisfactory relations with the opposite sex, unsatisfactory resolution of feelings towards the father and mother, strong tendency to regress to primitive and childlike destructive impulses, general immaturity, and general confusion as to development of self (lack of "identity")—all these are dealt with by various defence mechanisms (especially projection and introjection) in an effort to substitute prejudice for more threatening neurotic, or psychotic, symptoms. The same conflicts, however, may lead to other "ideological" solutions.

In any case, it is the social setting that turns, or does not turn, a personal solution into, say, the "final solution" of history. Norman Cohn sees this very well, in his *Warrant for Genocide* (1967): "Though the individuals who make up a group of Jew-killers are well within the bounds of reality, and most of them are not even fanatics, and even the fanatics are far from mad—yet it is perfectly true that the group as a whole behaves like a paranoiac in the grip of his delusion." Such a group "psychosis" arises, however, only where there is a hard core of fanatics, supported by public indifference, and allowed to run amuck, or even encouraged, by the government. In this sense, then, Simmel is absolutely right in calling anti-Semitism a "social disease."

Let us now turn to *The Authoritarian Personality* (1950), as typical of a certain range of studies. While it, too, deals with anti-Semitism, it seeks to describe a larger entity: the authoritarian, or fascist, personality. Like McClelland's *Achieving Society,* it tries to set up an objective scale, derived from questionnaires, by which to measure the presence of the phenomenon. To this, however, it adds the "confirming evidence" of depth interviews. Methodologically, it has raised many important questions, and these have been gone into exhaustively by other scholars. So, too, has the point that should concern us most here, both about this particular study and the anti-Semitic studies touched on above: admit, for argument's sake, that some people have a "tendency" to an "authoritarian" or "anti-Semitic" personality, how do we go from this to political or social action, which is what we are interested in? What is the actual link between such personality factors and the public arena (note that this is the same question asked about Lasswell's formulation thirty years earlier of the relation between private motivations and public acts, where the individual "displaced" the former onto the latter)?[7] The answers to these questions have not been forthcoming and this points to the real difficulties. Psychological explanation is not the same as historical explanation.

While the studies on anti-Semitism and authoritarian personalities are most interesting and valuable, they do not shed much light on the phenomena of contemporary history. To begin with, such personality traits have existed for a long time: it is like trying to explain culture by climate, when the climate has stayed the same for centuries. If we add to this the sort of criticisms implicit in the brief discussion above, we find ourselves not far advanced. In short, the problem of group psychology and contemporary history cannot be resolved until we look more closely at this particular problem in the light of the general problem of historical explanation.

One of the crucial points in the specifically psychoanalytic approach in relation to history concerns causation and determinism; and it is a point that disturbs unsympathetic critics of psychoanalysis. Freud insisted that strict determination prevailed in respect of psychic acts; there are no "accidents." For example, "free association," the basis of dream analysis and of therapy, is "free" only in the sense that it is not hampered by the censorship of "logical," "rational" thought and mores. It is not, however, undetermined. In fact, free association, as almost all the other processes in psychoanalysis, is *over-determined*. Indeed, it is the latter phenomenon—the fact that the same word or symbol refers to many elements in the unconscious thought process, on the one hand, and that the single unconscious drive or pattern of behaviour will manifest itself in innumerable different conscious manifestations, on the other hand—that warrants the historian in his use of the evidence. Because the psychological phenomena are over-determined, the evidence can be abundant and self-confirming.

Nevertheless, determined and over-determined as it is, psychoanalytic evidence is not generally *causal* in nature; and this is the first fallacy. Psycho-historical inquiry does not offer us causal explanations, but only explanations in terms of correspondence and co-existing processes. This fact is clearer, for example, in Erikson than in Freud. In discussing the case of a little boy, Erikson declares:

> We cannot escape the conviction that the meaning of an item which may be "located" in one of the three processes [the somatic, the ego, and the societal] is co-determined by its meaning in the other two. An item in one process gains relevance by giving significance to and receiving significance from items in the others. Gradually, I hope, we may find better words for such relativity in human existence. Of the catastrophe described in our first specimen, then, we know no "cause." Instead we find a convergence in all three processes of specific intolerances which made the catastrophe retrospectively intelligible, retrospectively probable. The plausibility thus gained does not permit us to go back and undo causes. It only permits us to understand a continuum, on which the catastrophe marked a decisive event, which now throws its shadow back over the very items which seem to have caused it (*Childhood and Society,* 1963, pp. 37–8).

Put another way, "Being unable to arrive at any simple sequence and causal chain with a clear location and a circumscribed beginning, only triple bookkeeping (or, if you wish, a systematic going around in circles) can gradually clarify the relevances and the relativities of all the known data" (p. 46). In sum, psycho-historical inquiry helps us to understand the "meaning" of an event, but does not—in fact, cannot—offer us a simple causal explanation of it.

It follows directly that history cannot be *reduced* to psychoanalytic explanation. This reductionism is the second great fallacy in the field. As we have seen in discussing *The Authoritarian Personality,* psychoanalysis adds to other explanations in history; it is no substitute for them.

The third fallacy is the pathological one. Analysis of a "leader" (or, indeed, of a whole people, "national character"), may simply reduce the subject to its neurotic or psychotic elements, and it becomes a matter of wonder how he functions at all; the sources of his creativity, of his positive appeal to his followers, seem never to be exposed. Without labouring this point, it must be said that mere description, for example of an Oedipal complex, while valuable, is not enough;

we need to see it in its adaptive aspect, and to study it as part of what Erikson called his "triple bookkeeping," where our prime concern is with "relativity" and "meaning."

One of the most interesting efforts in analysing a group situation, especially because it does not approach the subject via a great man and his relations to his followers, is to be found in O. Mannoni's fascinating work, *The Psychology of Colonization* (1950), a pioneering, imaginative, and marvellously intuitive book. Put simply, Mannoni's analysis of the relationship in Madagascar, around 1948 (and the uprising that then occurred), between the natives and the colonial rulers is that the former have a need for dependency relations, starting from their cult of the dead, but inculcated in them by all their family arrangements, while the latter act in terms of a "superiority complex" (in reality, a fear of inferiority). To the colonialist, the native's dependency looks like inferiority, and, in certain cases, lack of gratitude (the natives, for example, take support for granted). To the native, the colonialist's effort to shake himself free of the dependency relationship (by giving him "freedom") is perceived as betrayal. And so on, in a complex series of misunderstandings (and "understandings"?).

Without exploring the book's thesis any further, it will be useful to look briefly at the methodology, for it points to some of the problems in relating group psychology to contemporary history. The first thing to notice is Mannoni's admitted personal involvement in the situation. As he tells us, he was himself being analysed, and the events of 1948 were a sort of "conversion crisis" for him; his experience raises the question of what, for shorthand purposes, we can call the "counter-transference" problem. To what extent does the historian distort his materials because of his own psychological reactions? Obviously, the problem of distortion exists in all historical work, but when it draws on the deepest elements of unconscious processes, it is more difficult to deal with. New techniques, new training, and new methodology will have to be evolved to deal with this situation.

Next, Mannoni's analysis of the natives is based on his own ethnological observation. He brought to this book various theories from Alfred Adler and Melanie Klein, but, as he admits, the natives would never tell him their dreams nor submit to psychoanalysis. How trustworthy, then, is such an analysis? How adequate the Adlerian theories used? Mannoni does offer some explanations of otherwise inexplicable native behaviour that seem suggestive; but we have no way of checking on them. What does become obvious is that he talks of the natives as if they were a homogeneous group, when in fact they are composed of more than a score of separate tribes, each, apparently, with somewhat different customs and motivations. Certainly the Hova are different: they came to Madagascar as conquerors and rulers, just as did the Europeans, and think of themselves as rather superior to the "natives." Yet today they are in the culturally marginal situation of being between the colonial rulers (French) and the "natives." In short, we are up against some of the social-context problems raised earlier in relation to national character.

As for the colonialists, what materials does Mannoni use in analysing them? His appeal is to European literature, and he offers us, for example, fascinating analyses of Defoe's *Robinson Crusoe* and Shakespeare's *The Tempest,* as well as of Descartes's character.[8] Mannoni's intention is to demonstrate the European fear of dependency and abandonment, successfully kept at bay, however, by a deliberate confrontation of isolation and by a resolution of Oedipal feelings into characteristics of independence and superiority. Once again, persuasive as this work is, we must ask how suitable it is as explanation? Were the twentieth-century Europeans who became colonialists "typical" sixteenth or eighteenth-century characters? Or with rather special drives and needs? Why not analyse *them,* directly? In short, again we need particular empirical work in terms of a significant sociological context: the correct identification and then analysis of the actual colonial elite.

Whatever the weaknesses in Mannoni's book (and I have touched on them merely to illustrate some general problems), it has one overpowering virtue: he places his colonialists and natives in a direct psychological confrontation. This is perhaps the crux of his special addition to psycho-historical inquiry. Character is not something isolated and static, but is something developed and expressed in relation to other persons and groups.

To take as illustration the case of Hitler, the nazis, and the German people: it is not enough to analyse them in terms of the role of guilt in their personal and collective behaviour (incidentally, a fascinating topic). One must also analyse the role of guilt in those with whom they are interacted, say, the English and French at Munich. The "guilt" of Versailles, after all, was experienced, though differently, by both sides, and both sides were trying to "do" and "undo," as they "acted out" their deepest psychological impulses.[9] It is this confrontation aspect of psycho-historical inquiry that Mannoni's work brings so strongly to the fore, and which is methodologically its most important contribution.

Out of such a confrontation and interaction comes, as it does for individuals, a sense of identity (or else a failure of such a sense), and this brings us back full circle to the problems of national character and the economic and political development of underdeveloped countries. Perhaps now we can see that it is identity—a sense of inner sameness and continuity, perceived as such by oneself and confirmed by the perception of others—that we must study, rather than national character. Such sameness as found in identity is, of course, paradoxically, a dynamic characteristic (requiring moreover constant reaffirmation), of a person or group.[10]

We would no doubt all agree that many of the major problems of contemporary history can be summarized under such headings as totalitarianism, war, modernization, development, and revolution.[11] Existing studies using the theories and techniques of some form of group psychology oblige the historian to deal with such an approach as he seeks to understand the historical phenomena surrounding him. It is to be hoped, however, that the historian will seek comprehension in contemporary history not only by the utilization of existing studies (which, admittedly, are lamentably few in number and deficient in methodology and data), but by entering the field himself. Once it is seen that group psychology (especially of the psychoanalytic kind) is neither a substitute for history, nor a cosmetic to be applied externally to Clio, but an intrinsic and meaningful part of historical explanation, it will be difficult for any really honest historian to evade a confrontation on this level with himself and, consequently, with his fellow men and their destinies.

NOTES

1 See Leon Festinger, *A Theory of Cognitive Dissonance* (1957). Professor F. C. Iklé offers a summary: "Studies show that in certain circumstances people tend to reduce discrepancies between their behavior and what they know by distorting what they know. A person who has chosen among alternatives that seemed equally attractive to him tends to suppress or modify information that suggests his choice was wrong. He will inflate the data that makes the chosen alternative look preferable and belittle the advantages of the rejected alternative that he belatedly discovers," F. C. Iklé, "Can Social Predictions Be Evaluated," *Daedalus,* Summer 1967, p. 734.

2 Professor Hagen made this statement when delivering a yet unpublished paper to the Group for Applied Psychoanalysis in Boston, 1967.

3 Perhaps the best known of such studies is Nathan Leites's *A Study of Bolshevism* (1953). Here, a "code" of Bolshevik behavior, a way of psychological response, was worked out. But the book is much more an example of content analysis than of psychoanalysis. The dynamic element is simply missing. If, however, one does take the book seriously in its own terms—content analysis—then one is forced to ask why no comparable work on the "code" of American behavior has been forthcoming? And this immediately leads to the point that the "code" of Bolshevik and the "code" of American behavior would have to be studied as a highly dynamic psychological interplay in international affairs rather than as a rigid, self-contained set of rules for one party only.

4 Brief mention should be made of two of Erikson's disciples. The first is Robert Lifton, best known for his study, *Thought Reform and the Psychology of Totalism* (1961), which seeks to examine, by means of modified Freudian theory, the general subject of totalitarian thought control (incidentally, from a non-Freudian, Pavlovian point of view, there is the interesting, and even earlier, work, *Battle for the Mind,* by William Sargent, which seems to reach similar conclusions). Lifton is now engaged on a study of Hiroshima and the impact of the atom bomb, which joins in a significant way with Erikson's interest in war and its psychology. In his "Death and Death Symbolism," already published, Lifton seeks to use new data—immediate historical materials—to inspire new concepts of psychology and historical behavior, concepts which relate to twentieth-century themes of violence, inhumanity, guilt, and anxiety, and which contrast with the sexual vocabulary of Freud originating in the Victorian era of the late nineteenth century. In short, new times and experiences are seen as calling forth new psychological concepts by which to explain them.

The second disciple is Susanne Rudolph, who has produced two articles on Gandhi. The first one, in *World Politics* (October 1963), on "The New Courage: An Essay on Gandhi's Psychology," implicitly raises the problem of using western theories and perceptions in relation to non-western groups and cultures; it also explores from a psychological viewpoint the topic of "marginality." The other paper, "Self-Control and Political Potency" (*The American Scholar,* Winter 1965–6), is on the general phenomenon of asceticism, with particular reference to Gandhi, as a means of political power; here, too, the problem of differing cultural values enters meaningfully. In this last paper we also have an effort to extend Freud's notion of the leader as free of libidinal ties.

5 Of course, this is not to say that intuitions about national character, such as are found in most of the studies I have named, are not both interesting and valuable. The admirable article on the subject by Alex Inkeles and Daniel J. Levison, "National Character: The Study of Modal Personality and Sociocultural Systems" (*Handbook of Social Psychology,* ed. G. Lindsey, vol. 2, 1954), is more sanguine about the possibilities of the subject, though the authors admit that even a successful *a priori* definition of "national character" does not mean that the entity necessarily exists empirically.

6 On the shift away from "interest" politics, see, for example, Hannah Arendt, *The Origins of Totalitarianism* (1961), or *The New American Right,* ed. Daniel Bell (1955).

7 One of the best criticisms along these lines is Edward Shill's article in the collection on the *Authoritarian Personality,* ed. by Christie and Jahoda. See also Lucian Pye, "Personal Identity and Political Ideology' (1962), reprinted in *Psychoanalysis and History,* ed. B. Mazlish (1963).

8 For further analysis of Shakespeare's *The Tempest* and the psychology of race relations, see Philip Mason, *Prospero's Magic* (1962).

9 Obviously, such an analysis must take into account not only the "confrontation" aspect of the situation—what the behavior of one party triggers off psychologically in the behaviour of the other—but the reality aspect, the political, military, economic, and social circumstances surrounding the two parties.

10 The difficulties of achieving such an identity for underdeveloped countries are also well expressed by Lucian Pye: "Erikson's concept of identity thus suggests that the problem of consensus in transitional societies runs deeper than mere agreement over political forms and over the appropriate ends and means of political action; it involves the creation of an inner coherence of values, theories and actions for the entire polity. The implication is that in underdeveloped countries there is a vicious circle at the subjective level, which is more crucial to the problem of national development than the more manifest vicious circle of poverty, ill-health and illiteracy. Those who hope that national identity can come from modernization cannot escape the pressing psychological fact that modernity, in the mind of these people, has always been the monopoly of those who were their former masters. If they hated their colonial rulers, then they cannot expect to find their identities by following the same path. If they did not hate their former rulers, there might still be the problem of preferring dependency to autonomy, which would confuse the quest for identity. National identity cannot be built upon doing less well what one's former master excelled at" ("Personal Identity and Political Ideology," in *Psychoanalysis and History,* p. 172).

11 Chalmers Johnson, however, cautions us about the use of psychology in relation to revolutions: "The aspect of psychological studies of revolution that we do not find useful is the misinformed generalization of micro-data without reference to a macro-model—namely, the derivation of revolution from psychological studies of individual revolutionaries and the resultant value judgment that because some revolutionaries are lunatics, revolution is a form of social lunacy." Johnson then concludes: "Psychological data on revolutionaries must be related to the social system; otherwise they are only of propaganda value, useful in denigrating movements of which we may disapprove" (*Revolution and the Social System,* 1964, pp. 25–6). It should be clear from what I said earlier that I agree with Johnson about the need for relating psychological data to the social system. I am distressed, however, at his implied notion that all psychological studies of revolutionaries are "denigrating"; this is to embrace the pathological fallacy.

15

The Sociological Endeavor
and Psychoanalytic Thought

Gerald M. Platt

Attempts at integrating psychoanalytic and sociological thought have focused upon aggregate behavior, that is, on "national character" studies, on studies of collective action in political and religious movements, or on revolutionary activity, and so on. However, analyses of such group action employing psychosocial frameworks have not fared well in sociology: either they did not meet the scientific standards of the sociological discipline or they did not seem to lead anywhere. Today there is mostly apathy, ambivalence, or outright hostility toward psychoanalytically oriented frameworks in sociology.

However, not all the forms of integration between the two disciplines are held in equal disesteem, and even within the several forms there are more and less well-regarded works. This essay will suggest four forms of integration between psychoanalysis and sociology and will use these as categories in terms of which we may amplify the discussion. A word of caution is in order: psychosocial thought is not neatly organized around a topic such as American Studies. Sociologists want to develop universals applicable to the here and now and to distant times and places. Thus, it will be difficult to confine this discourse to American society, although special attention will be given to this substantive focus.

PSYCHOBIOGRAPHY OF ELITES: THE ONTOGENETIC MODEL

Suggesting that sociologists have not pursued ontogenetic studies of prominent figures should not imply that they are uninterested in this approach or that they eschew it simply on sectarian grounds. There are certainly sufficient numbers of psychobiographical "leadership" studies so that a sociologist could construct

First published in the *American Quarterly,* 28 (1976), pp. 343–59. Copyright © 1976, American Studies Association.

a course entitled, "The Sociology of American Elites." American presidents, for example, have especially attracted psychobiographers and it would be possible in a sociology course of this nature to review the lives, personalities, and political styles of Jefferson, Lincoln, Theodore Roosevelt, Wilson, Kennedy, and Nixon.[1] Why then do not sociologists more thoroughly delve into this intellectual endeavor?

The answer to this question resides in a number of issues all connected with the theoretical framework employed by psychobiographers. For example, no matter how often psychobiographers write that the objective of "psychobiographical investigation is to try to relate the particular identity need of a given leader to the 'typical identity needs' of his historical times,"[2] sociologists will not accept such an assertion. Robert Bellah points out that it is problematic to infer the personality of the mass from the analysis of an elite figure, no matter how sensitive and detailed the analysis.[3] Thus, sociologists recoil from generalizations like "these qualities and experiences [regarding Theodore Roosevelt] were shared by many of his contemporaries."[4]

At one level this is no more than a criticism based upon statistical representativeness; sociologists would never infer from a single case to a total population. But this criticism has a deeper and more important meaning. Sociologists know that such generalizations violate the very ontogenetic theory the psychobiographer employs. In the ontogenetic model the adult personality is a result of the organization of drives and defenses as these became fixed through infant handling by caretaker persons during the early phases of child rearing. But that theory stresses the idiosyncratic development of personality and sociologists have suggested two systematic features of the caretaking process which contribute to personal idiosyncrasy: variation in meaning and thus in the effect of the same caretaking event; and variation in caretaking events as a result of spatial and temporal differences, such as those produced by birth order and familial differentiation within a society.

These two sources of variation in concerted effect upon personality can be illustrated by referring again to the Theodore Roosevelt biography; in this instance we are reviewing the different meaning of caretaking events in relation to birth order in personality formation. It has been argued that Theodore Roosevelt's aggressive political style was a result of anger engendered in him through maternal oral deprivation in combination with emulation of paternal phallic character (i.e., "hardness"). Interestingly, however, the passive retreatism, personal and occupational failure, and alcoholism of Teddy's younger brother Elliott are explained in terms of the same constellation of parental caretaking events. Thus, if two children raised in a single family and assumedly experiencing similar caretaking events can develop such divergent personalities, the theory cannot claim for a population congruent personalities even if they are touched by similar child rearing experiences, unless the theory can specify the conditions under which similar treatment or environmental impingements will produce personality convergence and/or divergence. But psychoanalytic literature admits to the lack of understanding of why one psychic economy rather than another emerges out of similar circumstances.[5]

In sum, psychobiographers have not convinced sociologists that it is possible to assert psychological congruence between a leader and mass simply by studying the leader, no matter how effectively the leader is related to the mass. The willingness of a population to be moved and the capacity to move a population can be explained entirely in sociological terms.

Tenuous inferences regarding the relation of the leader's personality to that of the mass is not the only issue which has turned sociologists away from psychoanalytically oriented work. Additionally, sociologists wish to understand how contemporary and historical actors realistically deal with the circumstances they face. But the ontogenetic model employed in describing such uniquely capable adult personalities must resort to anomalous child rearing practices and consequences to explain such development. The result of this is that such persons described in these terms, no matter how cogent their actions and how exceptional their accomplishments, end up being "neurotics."[6]

This creates a dilemma for psychobiographers which they have never resolved. How are such regressed persons so acutely perceptive, so able to evaluate the problems they face, so capable of acting upon realistic grounds, so cognitively controlled when their egos are hemmed in by drives and defenses? The capacity to perceive and to deal with the world objectively at any time, but especially when the ego is confronted with realistic difficulties and perplexities, as so many of the central figures in psychobiographies are, necessitates some concept of ego processes independent of sexual energies, that is, an ego relatively autonomous from drives and from excessive moralizing.[7]

But the typical psychobiography describes its protagonist in exactly the opposite manner, that is, as an individual relating to contemporary problems and persons in terms of fixed energies and displaced symbols of a personal past. The dilemma is exacerbated by the incaution psychobiographers manifest in locating the point of fixation in the ontogenetic process. Characters described in oral and anal terms would be hard pressed to operate in everyday life, let alone solve significant social and intellectual problems. The oedipally fixed individual would be obsessive and rigid, lacking the fluidity for creative solutions associated with psychobiographical heroes. By contrast, it is to Erikson's credit that he fixed his identity crisis in terms of social features for performance; at a minimum this associates personal conflict with a social reality.[8]

Thus, the ontogenetic model itself is at the root of many of the difficulties that sociologists associate with psychobiographical endeavors. But the model in fact has been used in two ways. The first and most prevalent way is the literal clinical view, i.e., in which child rearing determines adult personality. The second way has been to treat the parent-child relationship as a metaphoric prism through which to view other human relationships in society. Thus, a psychobiographer may seek in adult relationships features which resemble the parent-child relationship—identifying oedipal struggles over authority, dependence, autonomy, intellectual and cultural commitments, etc., as Mazlish has done in his excellent study of James and John Mill.[9]

The literal use of psychoanalytic theory has been rightfully labeled "reductionist" because every present situation is treated as a return of a repressed personal past.[10] However, the second, metaphoric, form of the theory's use has led to important theoretical and empirical accomplishments in overcoming the criticisms of spurious inference, or of deriving creativity from mental illness. The metaphoric use of the ontogenetic model should dominate psychohistory in the coming decade.

SHARED SOCIALIZATION, SHARED PERSONALITY

Sociology conceives of society as differentiated into segments associated by distinguishable bases of solidarity, attitudes, and behaviors. The bases of solidarity are variables—like age, sex, class, ethnicity—and institutions—like family, education, religion, the political and economic orders. Socialization is a term employed in connection with child rearing but more generally refers to any social context in which individuals experience cognitive, emotive, and moral learning and undergo personal transformation. Social differentiation and socialization are independent conceptions and thus it has been possible to examine their coincident effects, such as age-socialization, sex-socialization, class-socialization and so on.

Sociological works explicitly addressed to age-socialization have only recently begun to appear.[11] Sex-socialization has had a long history in psychoanalytic work, now negatively evaluated by contemporary scholars. A reinvigorated interest in sex-socialization has been stimulated by the women's movement.[12] Socialization studies in institutions, especially occupational socialization, have received a great deal of attention in sociology since the 1950s.[13] However, class and ethnic childhood socialization has been a sociological preoccupation for almost half a century.[14]

Freud's analysis of the relationship between adult character and the treatment of infantile sexuality and aggression began to pervade class and ethnic socialization studies in the 1940s. One group of sociologists investigated breast feeding, weaning, toilet training, sexual play, and so on among families distinguished by class and ethnic background. The "mediating variables" for such activities were parental permissiveness, control, punishment, expressivity, and authority. The investigators were also interested in the effects of child rearing practices on adult personality formation.

Another group of sociologists, anthropologists, and psychoanalysts with neo-Freudian orientations studied similar relationships among preliterate peoples and in foreign nations. These two groups of social scientists shared an important dimension in their approach to the topic. Both wanted to find consistent treatment of infantile impulses in relation to consistent adult behavioral expressions. Psychoanalytic theory would thus be integrated with sociology by demonstrating that social patterns of behavior were derivative of fixed personality dispositions developed from child rearing practices.

While the two groups shared a single objective, they were distinguishable by their methodologies. The former group was composed of research sociologists and social psychologists investigating statistically sampled populations, usually within our society, and employing the techniques of personal interviews, personality inventories, and projective tests. The latter group was composed of sociologists, anthropologists and psychoanalysts doing ethnographic field observation, collecting dreams, myths, and folklore, though also using projective instruments.

The distinction between the two groups is not clear cut, but it is worth making because it permits us to discuss the findings of each group separately. The generalizations reported by the experimental group in 1946 indicated that the American lower classes were more permissive in socialization practices than the middle classes, and that, holding class constant, black Americans tended to be more permissive than whites. Further, middle class parents produced more psychologically troubled children and adults.[15]

Almost immediately following the publication of these findings a series of contradictory child rearing studies appeared. These publications suggested that the earlier psychoanalytically informed socialization studies were incorrect and that there was no difference in infant treatment by class. Later studies reported that the middle classes were more permissive and tolerant of their children than were the lower classes.[16] Finally, Urie Bronfenbrenner compiled all of these studies, restructured the data so that they were comparable, and reanalyzed the findings. Bronfenbrenner hypothesized that the middle classes were more susceptible to influences from popular culture and thus changed their child rearing patterns more quickly than the lower classes. Martha Wolfenstein had already demonstrated that popular advice to parents since 1914 had been in the direction of greater permissiveness in child rearing.[17]

In light of the durability of class and ethnic culture, and the instability of child rearing practices, the assumed causative association between the two was rendered problematic. And William Sewell, an experimental sociologist, was particularly incensed by the indictment of the middle classes as productive of "neurotic" individuals. Sewell and his students set out, in a series of carefully designed studies, to test whether any association between infant caretaking and adult personality existed. His work was devastating for psychoanalytic theory. In a summary article published in 1961 he reported that childhood treatment and adult personality characteristics were statistically unrelated. More specifically, Sewell was saying that most relationships such as longer and shorter breastfeeding periods, or harsh or permissive toilet training, led to no measurable differences in adult 'personality. A very small number of associations were statistically significant but the majority of these relationships contradicted expectational associations that derived from psychoanalytic theory. Sewell and his students pursued this research well over ten years and calculated hundreds of associations between specific child handling practices and adult personality characteristics. Every experiment, whether directed at the study of orality, anality, or whatever, led to the same conclusion: there was no evidence for the assumed psychoanalytic relationship between child rearing and adult personality.[18]

Finally, in a summary article on class and ethnic influences on socialization published in 1970, Robert Hess reported, "No recent studies of any scope deal with the questions of social class differences in patterns of child rearing. The familiar variables—toilet training, feeding, concern about sex play, and the like— no longer dominate the research stage."[19] In part the decline of these studies can be explained in terms of their scientific, i.e., statistical failure. But as noted in the discussion of psychobiography the underlying problem is in psychoanalytic theory itself.

Concepts of breast feeding, toilet training, sex play, permissiveness, authority, family, social class, ethnicity are all important to study in themselves, but they are too global to serve as bases for understanding adult actions in particular situations. Too much intervenes between childhood and adult years. In sum, then, the research sociologists attempted to relate social differentiation, socialization, and psychoanalytic theory while still employing the ontogenetic family model, hoping to find congruent personality dispositions and thus consistent social action on this basis. But even if class and ethnic caretaking events had held constant over time (and they did not), this framework would still be confronted with other sources of variation in personality formation, as explained above.[20]

PSYCHOANALYTIC THEORY IN CULTURE AND PERSONALITY STUDIES

The logic governing the integration of psychoanalytic theory with anthropological studies has been noted, i.e., infantile discipline shapes adult dispositions to action and thus determines consistent group patterns of behavior. This field tends to be characterized by an intelligent caution regarding the limitations of psychoanalytic integration with anthropology.[21] There is, however, considerable variation in the quality of the work and the degree and kind of psychoanalytic conceptualizations employed.

The integration of psychoanalysis and anthropology started early in this century and the production has been intimidating.[22] For example, in 1959, John Honigmann, in a summary paper entitled "Psychocultural Studies," recorded 407 publications in the years 1955 to 1958; the vast bulk of these integrated psychoanalytic theory with cultural anthropology. In 1961 and 1963 considerable production was again reported in this area, and summary articles entitled "Culture and Personality" showed that the field was still dominated by psychoanalytic psychology. However, by 1965, the biennial summary entitled "Psychology and Anthropology" indicated that anthropologists were drawing from a much broader spectrum of psychological orientations. By 1971, only a small proportion of the items cited in the relevant article of the *Biennial Review of Anthropology* employed psychoanalytic theory.[23]

This change in the field of culture and personality raises two questions; first, the more theoretical: why the decline of interest in psychoanalytic theory in culture and personality studies? second, the more practical: how is it possible to review this enormous production? We will address the latter question first; the focus of this article permits circumscription of the culture and personality works to those which analyze American society. The more difficult theoretical question will be addressed later.

Culture and personality studies of America can be divided into three broad substantive categories: psychocultural studies of, respectively, American WASP society, of American blacks, and of American Indian societies.[24] One of the best known psychocultural American national character studies is Geoffrey Gorer's *The American People: A Study of National Character.*[25] Gorer begins his analysis with America's relationship to Britain and to Europe, characterized as a form of father rejection (read "destruction"). And once America accomplished this break with its paternal past, the rest of the Oedipal drama ensued: American men became dominated by their own morality, castrates in their homes, slaves to their ambitious strivings, and alienated adjuncts of their machines and offices. Americans seek after individualism but fear isolation. Their heterosexual relationships are dependent and filled with ambivalence. American character, in the presence of material abundance, is held together by a thin psychological thread. All of this followed because America became a child-centered, mother-dominated society; indeed, American superego was "maternalized."

Gorer disclaimed any moralizing intention on several occasions,[26] but after a quarter-century it is not difficult to see his bias. Gorer at one point unfolds the American wife-husband relationship by analogy with the "Blondie" cartoon, and this says more about the usefulness of the analysis than do all the scholarly pages in the volume together. In brief, Gorer's work is a thinly disguised British intellectual's characterization of white middle class Protestant American society as neurotically and crudely materialist.

Only a few years after Gorer's portrayal of American character, Erik Erikson's chapter on "American Identity" appeared in *Childhood and Society*. Erikson's characterization was similar to Gorer's, especially in its emphasis on "mom" in the development of American personality. But unlike Gorer's depiction of a "smotherer," Erikson's mother is in the business of producing compulsive male adults capable of working in an industrial society. For Erikson, mother represents society's morality; one envisions a 1950s suburban matron as drill sergeant, preparing her children for the rigors of competitive social warfare.[27] Although these works by Gorer and Erikson were not of primary interest to Sewell, he did note in passing the slipshod quality of their analyses and inferences.[28]

References to Gorer's and Erikson's depictions of American national character are now largely absent from the sociological literature.[29] However, the framework on which they were based did survive to some degree, especially in the study of American student life. In 1960 Kenneth Keniston explained alienated youth in terms of dominating mothers and passive fathers. In the years 1968–1973, though, Keniston reversed himself, characterizing student activists as heightened in their consciousness, that is, as being concerned for others and as being desirous of creating an open, flexible community—because they had been socialized, after all, in democratic families.[30] While Lewis Feuer could still see student activism in very traditional ontogenetic terms (i.e., angry sons symbolically killing symbolic fathers),[31] Stanley Rothman and his colleagues described Jewish student radicals as attacking a hated WASP establishment which had undermined their fathers and had wished to emasculate them.[32] Needless to say, it would be difficult to reconcile Keniston's image of mobilized, determined, and independent youth with Gorer's and Erikson's notion of their socialization.

With regard to the earlier period in American national life, John Demos has suggested that Puritans socialized their children by stressing "law and order" in the anal phase of development (Demos, following Erikson, actually refers to this stage in terms of "autonomy"). However, Demos is quick to note that Puritan parental efforts which structure this stage of life are continuous throughout the socialization process, so that the emphasis on obedience to a rigid moral code is "maintained with little significant change for quite a number of years."[33]

An excellent companion work to Demos is Kai T. Erikson's *Wayward Puritans: A Study in the Sociology of Deviance.*[34] Though Kai Erikson's work is only minimally psychoanalytic, he demonstrates that deviance is a form of behavior which helped define the boundaries of Puritan morality and thus helped keep the community intact. The narrowness of appropriate forms of Puritan behavior underscores the salience of Demos' analysis.

Sociologists do not typically employ psychoanalytic concepts in their own historical studies.[35] Psychosocial studies of slavery, however, being consistent with a concern for present-day black identity, have particularly interested sociologists. Stanley Elkins' *Slavery* is most notable in this regard.[36] Elkins' Sullivanian analysis, grounded in the thought of George Herbert Mead, the eminent American sociological theorist, helped his work achieve its impact. It should be noted, for example, that Erving Goffman's conception of "total institution," an important corrective to the concentration camp analogy employed by Elkins (it suggests less stress on internationalization and more stress on variant forms of slave role-playing) nevertheless seems to be based on the fundamental logic laid out by Elkins.[37]

The study of the development of oppressive social conditions analogous to slavery in the post-Civil War period has yielded a number of psychosocial works regarding the consequences for black identity. Works by John Dollard, Abram Kardiner and Lionel Ovesey, Robert Coles, Kenneth B. Clark, Joel Kovel and

Thomas J. Cottle are able to integrate psychological with sociological levels of analysis without reducing one to the other.[38] Because these analyses give credence to social variables, they are popular among sociologists.[39]

Black identity studies, of course, have a built-in corrective against reductionism; the pervasive racial discrimination which must affect black identity can hardly be denied. However, the workers who studied American Indian societies, which are relatively segregated from white culture, were less constrained by these social realities. The result is that psychosocial studies of American Indians exhibit a great deal of variation in the degree to which they exclusively employ the child rearing model to explain social organization. The massive amount of ethnographic works precludes an exhaustive review; we can at best illustrate only some of the extremes in approach.

Geza Roheim, one of the most orthodox psychoanalytically oriented workers in this group, wrote of preliterate societies in general that: "Culture or subli-mation in a group are evolved through the same processes as in the individual"; "Cultural areas are conditioned by typical infantile situations in each area"; "Hu-man culture as a whole is the consequence of our prolonged infancy"; "Typically human forms of adjustment are derived from the infantile situation."[40] Compare these comments to Cora DuBois' remarks regarding orality among the Alor:

> To avoid the possibility of simplistic interpretations, it must be stressed again that no single tension like hunger and the habits associated with its gratification will explain either the totality of the culture or the dominant and stressed personality traits of its bearers. It will be only by examining the whole variety of such individual life experiences and searching for the formalized and unformalized cultural correlates that any progress will be made, not only in defining more sharply the interaction of personality and culture, but also in elucidating the stability of attitudes and value systems.[41]

There are, then, some common themes among the works of the culture and personality group, but obviously there are also important differences. The work of this group is not unidimensional in orientation nor in quality. The general principle for judging quality, besides that of professional standards of scholarly excellence, is the degree to which culture and personality studies avoid a re-ductionist psychoanalytic explanation of societal or group patterns of behavior.

This standard is shared by many critics of the culture and personality school. The most extensive criticism of the approach was offered by Harold Orlansky in 1949. Following an exceedingly detailed review of the literature in the field, Orlansky suggested that

> we are led to reject the thesis that specific ... disciplines have specific, invariant psy-chological impact upon the child. Instead, it appears that the effect of a particular dis-cipline can be determined only from knowledge of the parental attitude associated with it, the value which the culture places upon discipline, the organic constitution of the infant, and the entire socio-cultural situation in which the individual is located. In short, it is contended that personality is not the resultant of instinctual infantile libidinal drives

mechanically channelled by parental disciplines, but rather that it is a dynamic product of the interaction of a unique organism undergoing maturation and a unique physical and social environment.[42]

Orlansky's stance was not new to the field, but it was an unpopular position at the time of its publication. Still his argument for the autonomy of the effects of cultural and social variables sufficed to promote a negative attitude toward psychoanalytic theory in ethnographic work. But there was an additional pressure on anthropological and sociological ethnographers to break the psychoanalytic alliance. This was, and is, the pressure on these social scientists to offer descriptions of societies which are both richly empirical and readily recognizable as "correct" from the perspective of societal members, i.e., the subjects of their investigations. A less elaborate image of a society, subjectively inconsistent with the knowledge and experience of its members, is referred to in sociology as a "gloss." Ethnographic descriptions which articulate only with professional categories of description are referred to as a "professional gloss." Regrettably, much of what passed for "scientific" psychoanalytically oriented national character and culture and personality studies came to be viewed in terms of "professional gloss." These studies could be considered valid descriptions only by psychoanalytic "true believers."

A NEW SYNTHESIS

At the same time, however, a few sociologists began to reexamine the theoretical bases for the integration of psychoanalysis and sociology. Talcott Parsons contributed significantly to the revisions which followed. In a series of papers on the topic, most of which are reprinted in his *Social Structure and Personality,* Parsons asserted that causal relationships had to proceed from society to personality.[43] Parsons went much further in other important ways, suggesting, for example, that there was no level of the personality unaffected by society and culture, including the instinctual. Parsons, however, did not break with the familial ontogenetic model.

It was, rather, the implicit suggestion of a group of psychoanalytically oriented social psychologists, who were performing laboratory studies on interactive patterns in small groups, that caused a break with the ontogenetic familial model. Their writings indicated that symbolic enactments of Freudian sociological descriptions could be generated in group therapy sessions. The analysis suggested, however, that symbol systems could be independent of instinctual sublimation and it thus rendered problematic the need for a family socialization model to explain shared morality in a group.[44]

Influenced by these sources, I began with Fred Weinstein to rethink psychosocial approaches to social organization, to collective action, and to historical studies. The culmination of this was our publication of *The Wish to Be Free* and *Psychoanalytic Sociology.*[45] There are important theoretical discontinuities between our two works, but their general points of agreement include: establishing the primacy of cultural and social factors in collective action; a stress upon reality orientations in mass movements; the explanation of psychic forces in collective action in terms of responses to particular conditions of strain and as binding and unifying mechanisms; the capacity to explain class, age, family background, etc.,—that is, to explain heterogeneity of membership in collective movements— as a situationally produced and hence contingent feature, bypassing any need for an ontogenetic socialization model; a theoretical framework that allows for the organization of empirical work in a manner consistent with sociological and historical demands for validity and in conformity with members' descriptions of their own experience. We have our doubts that a closed theoretical system is possible in social science; at this point, however, we have not come to any firm conclusions on the matter.[46]

The field of psychohistory and psychosocial studies is evolving. The production is now almost too massive to catalogue. I have approached the topic of the relationship of psychoanalysis to sociology from the perspective of modes or styles of integration, as a technique for categorizing different efforts. Some modes of integration properly have disappeared from the literature, while others have changed and improved.

NOTES

1 Carl Binger, "Conflicts in the Life of Thomas Jefferson," *American Journal of Psychiatry,* 125 (1969), 1,098–1,107; Fawn Brodie, "Jefferson Biographers and the Psychology of Canonization," *Journal of Interdisciplinary History,* 2 (1971), 155–72; and *Thomas Jefferson: An Intimate History* (New York: Norton, 1973); Ramon I. Harris, "Thomas Jefferson: Female Identification," *American Imago,* 25 (1968), 371–88; Pierce L. Clark, *Lincoln: A Psycho-Biography* (New York: Scribner, 1933), and "Unconscious Motives Underlying the Personalities of Great Statesmen and Their Relation to Epoch-Making Events: A Psychoanalytic Study of Abraham Lincoln," *Psychoanalytic Review,* 8 (1921), 1–21; Bronson A. Feldman, "Lincoln: The Psychology of a Cult," *Journal of the National Psychological Association for Psychoanalysis,* I (1952), 7–24; Edward J. Kempf, *Abraham Lincoln's Philosophy of Common Sense: An Analytical Biography of a Great Mind* (New York: Academy of Sciences, 1965); George W. Wilson, "A Prophetic Dream Reported by Abraham Lincoln," *American Imago,* 1 (1940), 92–98; Glenn Davis, "The Early Years of Theodore Roosevelt: A Study of Character Formation," *History of Childhood Quarterly,* 2 (1975), 461–92; Glenn Davis, "The Maturation of Theodore Roosevelt: The Rise of an Affective Leader," *History of Childhood Quarterly,* 3 (1975), 43–74; Morton Prince, "A Scientific Vivisection of Mr. (T.) Roosevelt," *Current Literature,* 52 (1912), 518–22; Bernard Brodie, "A Psychoanalytic Interpretation of Woodrow Wilson," in *Psychoanalysis and History,* Bruce Mazlish, ed., rev. ed., (New York: Grosset and Dunlap, 1971), 115–23; Sigmund Freud and William G. Bullitt, *Thomas Woodrow Wilson: A Psychological Study* (Boston: Houghton Mifflin, 1967); Alexander L. and Juliette L. George, *Woodrow Wilson and Colonel House: A Personality Study* (New York: Day, 1956); William Bayard Hale, *The Story of Style: A Psychoanalytic Study of Woodrow Wilson* (New York: Viking, 1920); Philip Rieff, "Fourteen Points on Wilson," *Encounter,* (1967), 85; David Shannon, "Woodrow Wilson's Youth and Personality: An Essay Review," *Pacific Northwest Quarterly,* 58 (1967), 205–07; Nancy G. Clinch, *The Kennedy Neurosis* (New York: Grosset and Dunlap, 1973);

Joseph Katz, "President Kennedy's Assassination," *Psychoanalytic Review,* 51 (1964–65, #4), 121–24; James Barber, "President Nixon and Richard Nixon: Character Traps," *Psychology Today,* 8 (Oct. 1974), 112–21; Eli Chesen, *President Nixon's Psychiatric Profile* (New York: Wyden, 1973); Bruce Mazlish, *In Search of Nixon: A Psychohistorical Inquiry* (New York: Basic Books, 1972); Stanley Allen Renshon, "Psychological Analysis and Presidential Personality: The Case of Richard Nixon," *History of Childhood Quarterly,* 2 (1975), 115–50. Also see Erwin Hargrove, *Presidential Leadership: Personality and Political Leadership* (New York: Macmillan, 1966); James Barber, *The Presidential Character: Predicting Performance in the White House* (Englewood Cliffs, N.J.: Prentice-Hall, Inc.. 1972).

2 Richard Evans, *Dialogue with Erik Erikson* (New York: Norton, 1967), 66.

3 Robert Bellah, *Beyond Belief: Essays on Religion in a Post-Traditional World* (New York: Harper, 1970), 13.

4 Glenn Davis, "The Early Years of Theodore Roosevelt."

5 George R. Krupp, "The Bereavement Reaction," in Warner Muensterberger and Sidney Axelrad, eds., *The Psychoanalytic Study of Society* (1962), Vol. 2, 42–74; the relevant passages are on pp. 43–44. David Shapiro, *Neurotic Styles* (New York: Basic Books, 1965), 5. Robert Wallerstein, "Psychoanalytic Reflections on the Problem of Reality," *Journal of American Psychoanalytic Association,* 21 (1973), 5–33. Also see F. Weinstein and G. M. Platt, *Psychoanalytic Sociology: An Essay on the Interpretation of Historical Data and the Phenomena of Collective Behavior* (Baltimore: Johns Hopkins University Press, 1973), 45.

6 On the problem of reality and realistic action in psychoanalytic discourse, see Weinstein and Platt, op. cit. On the need for reality orientation in historical studies, see Gerald Izenberg, "Psychohistory and Intellectual History," *History and Theory,* (1975), 139–55. See also Fred Weinstein's review of Arthur Mitzman's *Iron Cage, American Historical Review,* (June 1971), 1,399–1,401. Weinstein suggests that Weber, as portrayed by Mitzman, would have been hard pressed to make his intellectual contributions given this psychological characterization.

7 General statement on the place of ego in psychoanalytic theory can be found in Robert White, "Ego and Reality in Psychoanalytic Theory," *Psychological Issues* (monograph 11, 1963); also see George S. Klein, "The Ego in Psychoanalysis: A Concept in Search of an Identity," *Psychoanalytic Review,* 56 (1969–70), 511–25. The concept "ego"—indeed, the entire "ego psychology" is theoretically problematic. That is, concepts—introduced by Freud and elaborated by Heinz Hartmann, Ernst Kris, Rudolph Lowenstein, and Anna Freud—pertaining to the "structural theory" and psychoanalytic metapsychology lend themselves too easily to reification and distortion. The leading critics of "ego psychology" and the structural theory are George Klein, Roy Schafer, and Robert R. Holt. For a summary view, see Robert R. Holt, "The Past and Future of Ego Psychology," *Psychoanalytic Quarterly,* 44 (1975), 550–76, and the companion article by Emanuel Peterfreund, "The Need for a New General Theoretical Frame of Reference for Psychoanalysis," ibid., 534–49. While I approve of the criticism, I will continue to use the customary language, pending some agreement on replacements for the structural terms. Changing the language here would only lead to confusion. Any reader interested in the way terms might change is referred to, e.g. Roy Schafer, "Action: Its Place in Psychoanalytic Interpretation and Theory," *Annual of Psychoanalysis,* 1 (1973), 159–96. More traditional psychoanalysts have always eschewed the main implications of the ego psychology. Thus, Edward Glover referred to Heinz Hartmann—generally considered to be the leading ego psychoanalytic theoretician in the post-Freudian era—as a neo-Freudian and said that Hartmann's concept of "secondary autonomy" is "a comforting narcissistic myth." See Glover, "Metapsychology or Metaphysics?" *Psychoanalytic Quarterly,* 35 (1966), 173–90. Beyond these criticisms it is still necessary to address ourselves to the main problem, the ability of people to define and cope with their problems in everyday life.

8 For a sociological exploration of this problem, see G. Platt and F. Weinstein, "Alienation and the Problem of Social Action," in Edward A. Tiryakian, ed., *The Phenomenon of Sociology*

(New York: Appleton-Century-Crofts, 1971), 284–310. For Erik H. Erikson's most detailed statement on identity, see his "Identity and the Life Cycle: Selected Papers" (with a Historical Introduction by David Rapaport), in *Psychological Issues* (New York: International Universities Press, 1959), 1–171. Also see in this connection Kathleen Dalton, "Theodore Roosevelt, 1858–1901; A Social Psychological Interpretation," (Diss. Johns Hopkins University).

9 Bruce Mazlish, *James and John Stuart Mill: Father and Son in the Nineteenth Century* (New York: Basic Books, 1975).

10 William Gilmore, "The Problem and Danger of 'Originitis' in Psycho-History: The Early Years of Orestes Brownson," paper presented at the annual convention of the Organization of American Historians, April 13, 1973, Chicago, Ill. See also Peter Blos, "The Epigenesis of Adult Neurosis," *Psychoanalytic Studies of the Child,* 27 (1972), 105–35; and Erik Erikson, *Young Man Luther* (New York: Norton, 1958), 18.

11 See Matilda White Riley, Marilyn Johnson, and Anne Foner, *Aging and Society: A Sociology of Age Stratification* (New York: Russell Sage Foundation, 1972), Vol. III. Also see Anne Foner, "Age in Society," *American Behavioral Scientist,* 19 (1975), 144–65; Ann P. Parelius "Lifelong Education and Age Stratification," ibid., 206–23; Joan M. Waring, "Social Replenishment and Social Change," ibid., 237–56; Bernice L. Neugarten, Joan W. Moore, and John C. Lowe, "Age Norms, Age Constraints, and Adult Socialization," *American Journal of Sociology,* 70 (1965), 710–17. In the field of psychology see Kenneth Keniston, "Youth: A 'New' Stage of Life," *American Scholar* (Autumn 1970), 631–54; this same topic is discussed from a sociological perspective by T. Parsons and G. M. Platt, "General Education and Studentry Socialization: The Undergraduate College," Ch. 4, *The American University* (Cambridge: Harvard University Press, 1973).

12 Eleanor E. Maccoby, ed., *The Development of Sex Differences* (Stanford: Stanford University Press, 1966); Paul H. Mussen, "Early Sex-Role Development," in David A. Goslin, ed., *Handbook of Socialization Theory and Research* (Chicago: Rand McNally, 1969), 707–29; Walter Mischel, "Sex-Typing and Socialization," in Paul H. Mussen, ed., *Carmichael's Manual of Child Psychology,* 3rd. ed. (New York: Wiley, 1970), vol. 2, Ch. 20, 3–72; Alice Rossi, "Feminist History in Perspective: Sociological Contributions to Biographic Analysis," in Dorothy Gies McMuigan, ed., *A Sampler of Women's Studies* (Ann Arbor: University of Michigan, Center for Continuing Education of Women, 1973), 85–108; Nancy Chodorow, "Family Structure and Feminine Personality," in Michael Zimbalist Rosaldo and Louise Lamphere, eds., *Women, Culture and Society* (Stanford: Stanford University Press, 1974), 43–66; Carroll Smith-Rosenberg, "Puberty to Menopause: The Cycle of Femininity in Nineteenth-Century America," in Mary Hartman and Lois W. Banner, ed., *Clio's Consciousness Raised: New Perspectives on the History of Women* (New York: Harper Torchbooks, 1974), 23–37. A recent review essay on psychology offers several sources related to sex-socialization: Mary Brown Parlee, "Psychology," *Signs: A Journal of Women in Culture and Society,* 1 (1975), No. 1, 119–38.

13 For general and recent statements on "adult socialization," see Orville Brim and Stanton Wheeler, *Socialization After Childhood: Two Essays* (New York: Wiley, 1966); John A. Clausen, ed., *Socialization and Society* (Boston: Little, Brown, 1968); Howard S. Becker, "The Self and Adult Socialization," in *Sociological Work: Method and Substance* (Chicago: Aldine, 1970), 289–303; Howard S. Becker and Anselm L. Strauss, "Careers, Personality and Adult Socialization," *American Journal of Sociology,* 57 (1952), 470–77; Robert R. Faulkner, "Coming of Age in Organizations: A Comparative Study of Career Contingencies and Adult Socialization," *Sociology of Work and Occupations,* 1, No. 2 (May 1974), 131–73.

14 Bronfenbrenner reports class-socialization studies performed in 1928 and 1932, the former out of Berkeley, the latter a national study. See Urie Bronfenbrenner, "Socialization and Social Class Through Time and Space," in Eleanor E. Maccoby, Theodore M. Newcomb, and Eugene L. Hartley, ed., *Readings in Social Psychology,* 3d ed. (New York: Henry Holt, 1958), 400–25.

15 Arnold W. Green, "The Middle Class Male Child and Neurosis," *American Sociological Review,* 11 (1946), 31–41; Allison Davis and Robert J. Havighurst, "Social Class and Color Differences in Child-Rearing," ibid., 698–710; Martha C. Ericson, "Child-rearing and Social Status," *American Journal of Sociology,* 52 (1946), 190–92.

16 Eleanor E. Maccoby and Patricia K. Gibbs, "Methods of Child Rearing in Two Social Classes," in W. E. Martin and C. B. Stendler, eds., *Readings in Child Development* (New York: Harcourt, Brace, 1954); Robert R. Sears, Eleanor E. Maccoby, and Harry Levin, *Patterns of Child Rearing* (Evanston, Ill.: Pow, Patterson and Co., 1957); Daniel R. Miller and Guy E. Swanson, *The Changing American Parent: A Study on the Detroit Area* (New York: Wiley, 1958), and *Inner Conflict and Defense* (New York: Schocken, 1966). See also in this connection, Robert J. Havighurst and Allison Davis, "A Comparison of the Chicago and Harvard Studies of Social Class Differences in Child Rearing," *American Sociological Review,* 20 (1955), 438–42.

17 Urie Bronfenbrenner, "Socialization and Social Class Through Time and Space"; Martha Wolfenstein, "Trends in Infant Care," *American Journal of Orthopsychiatry,* 23 (1953), 120–30.

18 William H. Sewell, "Social Class and Childhood Personality," *Sociometry,* 24 (1961), 340–56; most of the relevant bibliography of Sewell and his co-workers is cited in this article.

19 "Social Class and Ethnic Influences upon Socialization," in Carmichael's *Manual of Child Psychology,* 457–557.

20 This methodological difficulty plagues even impressive psychohistorical works such as Peter Lowenberg's study of "The Psychohistorical Origins of the Nazi Youth Cohort," *American Historical Review,* 76 (1971), 1,457–1,502. In light of these considerations a position such as de M·use's—that all social meaning derives from child care—flies in the face of established social sc.entific knowledge. Indeed, it would be impossible to explain social order if we took such a statement as deMause's seriously. See Lloyd deMause, *The History of Childhood* (New York: Psychohistory Press, 1974).

21 Kluckhohn points to a summary of the criticism raised regarding the integration of psychoanalysis into anthropology in his "The Influence of Psychiatry on Anthropology in America During the Past One Hundred Years," in J. K. Hall, G. Zilboorg, and H. A. Bunker, eds., *One Hundred Years of American Psychiatry* (New York: American Psychiatric Association. Columbia University Press, 1944), 580–617, esp. 614–15. The best of these efforts avoided analytic reductionism and integrated social, economic, and political institutions and cultural patterning with the psychodynamic variables. In this connection, see from the anthropological side, Cora DuBois, *The People of Alor* (Minneapolis: University of Minnesota Press, 1941), and from the psychoanalytic side, Abram Kardiner, *The Psychological Frontiers of Society* (New York: Columbia University Press, 1945).

22 Edward Sapir was initiator of the culture and personality field; he published a series of papers starting in 1929. See Edward Sapir, *The Unconscious: A Symposium* (New York: Knopf, 1929), 114–42; "Cultural Anthropology and Psychiatry," *Journal of Abnormal and Social Psychology,* 27 (1932), 234–35; "The Emergence of the Concept of Personality in the Study of Cultures," *Journal of Social Psychology,* 5 (1934), 408–15; "The Constribution of Psychiatry to Understanding Behavior in Society," *American Journal of Sociology,* 29 (1937), 862–71; "Anthropology and the Psychiatrist," *Psychiatry,* 1 (1938), 7–13.

23 John J. Honigmann, "Psychocultural Studies," *Biennial Review of Anthropology,* 1 (1959), 67–106; Anthony F. C. Wallace and Raymond D. Fogelson, "Culture and Personality," *Biennial Review of Anthropology,* 2 (1961), 42–78; Robert A. LeVine, "Culture and Personality," *Biennial Review of Anthropology,* 3 (1963) 107–45. J. L. Fischer, "Psychology and Anthropology," *Biennial Review of Anthropology,* 4 (1965), 211–61, Harry C. Triandis, Roy S. Malpass, and Andrew R. Davidson, "Cross-Cultural Psychology," *Biennial Review of Anthropology,* 7 (1971), 1–84.

24 The outstanding anthologies of the culture-personality orientation were Clyde Kluckhohn,

Henry A. Murray, and David M. Schneidner, eds., *Personality in Nature, Society and Culture* (New York: Knopf, 1956: first published in 1948), and Douglas G. Haring, ed., *Personal Character and Cultural Milieu* (Syracuse: Syracuse University Press, 1956). Additional materials can be found in the *Biennial Reviews of Anthropology* (formerly the *Annual Review of Anthropology*). See also, A. Irving Hallowell, "Culture, Personality, and Society," in *Anthropology Today,* 597–620; Margaret Mead, "National Character," and Alex Inkeles, "National Character and Modern Political Systems," in F. Hsu, ed., *Psychoanalytic Anthropology* (Homewood: Dorsey, 1961), 172–208. And there have been some recent anthologies on psychoanalysis and society and culture; see Hendrik M. Ruitenbeek, ed., *Psychoanalysis and Social Science* (New York: Dutton, 1962), and *Varieties of Modern Social Theory* (New York: Dutton, 1963); Warner Muensterberger, ed., *Man and His Culture: Psychoanalytic Anthropology after "Totem and Taboo"* (London: Rapp and Whiting, 1969).

25 (New York: Norton, 1948).

26 Gorer, *The American People,* 144.

27 (New York: Norton, 1950).

28 William H. Sewell, "Infant Training and the Personality of the Child," *American Journal of Sociology,* 58 (1952), 150–59.

29 Margaret Mead, *And Keep Your Powder Dry: An Anthropologist Looks at Amerca* (New York: Morrow, 1942) is an earlier and much less psychoanalytically influenced American national character study which has worn better than these two. Other sociologically influential national character studies employ psychoanalytic concepts, but they are not so literal in terms of the clinical ontogenetic socialization model. See, for example, David Riesman, *The Lonely Crowd* (New Haven: Yale University Press. 1950); Winston White, *Beyond Conformity* (New York: Free Press, 1961); Snell and Gail Putney, *Normal Neurosis: The Adjusted American* (New York: Harper and Row, 1964); Alexander Mitscherlich, *Society Without Father: A Contribution to Social Psychology,* trans. Eric Moxbacker (New York: Harcourt, 1963); Hendrick M. Ruitenbeek, *The Individual and the Crowd: A Study of Identity in America* (New York: Nelson, 1964). Summaries of relevant bibliography can be found in Michael McGiffert, *American Quarterly,* 15 (1963), summer supplement #2, part 2), 330–49; Thomas L. Hartshorne, "Recent Interpretations of the American Character," *American Studies International* (supplement to the December 1975 *AQ*), 10–17.

30 Kenneth Keniston, *The Uncommitted* (New York: Harcourt, 1960), *Young Radicals* (New York: Harcourt, 1968), *Youth and Dissent* (New York: Harcourt, 1971), and *Radicals and Militants* (Lexington, Mass.: Heath, 1973).

31 Lewis Feuer, *The Conflict of Generations* (New York: Basic Books, 1969).

32 Stanley Rothman, Anne H. Bedlington, Phillip Isenberg, and Robert Schnitzer, "Ethnic Variations in Student Radicalism: Some New Perspectives," unpublished paper, 1976. For a thesis similar to Rothman, et al., see John Murray Cuddihy, *Ordeal of Civilty: Freud, Marx and Levi-Strauss, and the Jewish Struggle with Modernity* (New York: Basic Books, 1974).

33 John Demos, *A Little Community: Family Life in Plymouth Colony* (New York: Oxford University Press, 1970), 139.

34 (New York: Wiley, 1966).

35 See in this connection, Werner J. Cahnman and Alvin Boskoff, eds., *Sociology and History: Theory and Research* (New York: Free Press, 1964). Philip Rieff constitutes an exception to this rule. See his "History, Psychoanalysis, and the Social Sciences," *Ethics,* 63 (1953), 107–20, reprinted in Edward N. Saveth, ed., *American History and the Social Sciences* (New York: Free Press, 1964), 110–26.

36 Stanley M. Elkins, *Slavery: A Problem in American Institutional and Intellectual Life* (Chicago: University of Chicago Press, 1959). For example, David Brion Davis, *The Slave Power Conspiracy and the Paranoid Style* (Baton Route: Louisiana State University Press, 1969), and Earl E. Thorpe, *Eros and Freedom in Southern Life and Thought* (Durham, N.C.: Seeman

Printery, 1967), are hardly known among sociologists. However, other historical and social scientific works on the South and slavery are used by sociologists, especially the writings of Tannenbaum, Stampp, and Genovese. Recently Robert W. Fogel and Stanley L. Engerman made a flap in sociology, but this was primarily because of their complex statistical analysis: see their *Time on the Cross: The Economics of American Negro Slavery* (Boston: Little, Brown, 1974). For a concise historical overview of the debate regarding the origins of slavery, see Joseph Boskin, *Into Slavery: Racial Decisions in the Virginia Colony* (Philadelphia: Lippincott, 1976)

37 Ann J. Lane, *The Debate Over Slavery: Stanley Elkins and His Critics* (Urbana: University of Illinois Press, 1971).

38 John Dollard, *Caste and Class in a Southern Town* (New York: Doubleday, 1937); Abram Kardiner and Lionel Ovesey, *The Mark of Oppression: Explorations in the Personality of the American Negro* (New York: World Publishing, 1951); Robert Coles, *Children of Crisis: A Study of Courage and Fear* (Boston: Little, Brown, 1964) Vol. 1; Kenneth B. Clark, *Dark Ghetto: Dilemmas of Social Power* (New York: Harper Torchbooks, 1965); Joel Kovel, *White Racism: A Psychohistory* (New York, Pantheon, 1970); Thomas J. Cottle, *Black Children, White Dreams* (Boston: Houghton Mifflin, 1974). We should also mention in this connection Allison Davis and John Dollard, *Children of Bondage: The Personality Development of Negro Children in the Urban South* (Washington, D.C.: American Council on Education, 1940); William H. Grier and Price M. Cobbs, *Black Rage* (New York: Basic Books, 1968); Frantz Fanon, *The Wretched of the Earth* (New York: Grove Press, 1968), and *Black Skin, White Masks* (New York: Grove Press, 1967).

39 Although not directly concerned with black identity but rather with ethnic prejudice, the classic *Authoritarian Personality* needs to be noted for its ground-breaking work in the integration of personality and culture and society. See T. W. Adorno, Else Frenkel-Brunswik, Daniel J. Levinson, and R. Nevitt Sanford, *The Authoritarian Personality* (New York: Harper, 1950). Also see in this connection, Richard Christie and Marie Jahoda, *Studies in the Scope and Method of "The Authoritarian Personality": Continuities in Social Research* (Glencoe, Ill.: Free Press, 1954), and Milton Rokeach, *The Open and Closed Mind* (New York: Basic Books, 1960).

40 Geza Roheim, "The Psychoanalytic Interpretation of Culture," originally published *International Journal of Psychoanalysis,* 22 (1941) and reprinted in Warner Muensterberger, ed., *Man and his Culture,* 31–51; quotes from p. 50.

41 Cora DuBois, "Attitudes Toward Food and Hunger in Alor," originally published in Leslie Spier, A. Irving Hallowell, and Stanley S. Newman, eds., *Language, Culture and Personality: Essays in Memory of Edward Sapir* (1941), 272–81, and reprinted in Douglas G. Haring, ed., *Personal Character and Cultural Milieu* (Syracuse, N.Y.: Syracuse University Press, 1948), 240–53, quote from p. 253. See also Esther Goldfrank, "Socialization, Personality, and the Structure of Pueblo Society (with particular reference to Hopi and Zuni)," originally published in *American Anthropologist,* 47 (1945), 516–39, and reprinted in Douglas G. Haring, ed., *Personal Character and Cultural Milieu,* 303–27, quote from p. 322.

42 "Infant Care and Personality," *Psychological Bulletin,* 46 (1949), 1–48; A. R. Lindesmith and A. L. Strauss, "A Critique of Culture-Personality Writings," *American Sociological Review,* 15 (1950), 587–600. For a pointed refutation of Orlansky's work from a traditional psychoanalytic point of view, see Sidney Axelrad, "Infant Care and Personality Reconsidered: A Rejoinder to Orlansky," *The Psychoanalytic Study of Society,* Vol. II (New York: International Universities Press, 1962), 75–132.

43 (New York: Free Press, 1964). Some exceedingly interesting papers on the relation of personality to culture and society are included in Anne Parsons, ed., *Belief, Magic and Anomie: Essays in Psychosocial Anthropology* (New York: Free Press, 1969).

44 Philip E. Slater, *Microcosm: Structural, Psychological and Religious Evolution in Groups*

(New York: Wiley, 1966); Theodore Mills, "Authority and Group Emotion," in W. Bennis and E. Schein, ed., *Interpersonal Dynamics* (Homewood, Ill.: Dorsey, 1964), 94–108; Theodore Mills, *Transformation: An Analysis of a Learning Group* (Englewood Cliffs, N.J.: Prentice-Hall, 1964); W. G. Bennis, "Defenses Against 'Depressive Anxiety' in Groups: The Case of the Absent Leader," *Merrill-Palmer Quarterly* 7 (1961), 3–30; W. G. Bennis and H. A. Shepart, "A Theory of Group Development," *Human Relations,* 9 (1957), 415–37.

45 *The Wish to Be Free: Society, Psyche and Value Change* (Berkeley: University of California Press, 1969); *Psychoanalytic Society* (1960); see also, "The Coming Crisis in Psychohistory," *Journal of Modern History,* 47 (June 1975).

46 For related psychosocial investigations, see Edwin G. Burrows and Michael Wallace, "The American Revolution: The Ideology and Psychology of National Liberation," *Perspectives in American History,* 6 (1972); Jack P. Greene, "Autonomy and Stability: New England and the British Colonial Experience in Early Modern America," *Journal of Social History,* 7 (1974), 171–94; Edward Shorter, "Illegitimacy, Sexual Revolution, and Social Change in Modern Europe," *Journal of Interdisciplinary History,* 2 (1971), 237–72; Bruce Mazlish, *James and John Stuart Mill;* E. A. Wrigley, "The Process of Modernization and the Industrial Revolution in England," *Journal of Interdisciplinary History,* 3 (1972), 225–59; Peter Shaw, *The Character of John Adams* (Chapel Hill: University of North Carolina Press, 1976).

16

Accusers, Victims, Bystanders: The Innerlife Dimension

John Demos

The organizing structures of inner life have little to do with logic, proportion, balance, and the like; seemingly disparate elements are frequently joined on the basis of symbolic or experiential association. And there is one thematic cluster in the witchcraft materials that vividly exemplifies this point. The main ingredients, described at length in the preceding pages, can be summarized as follows. (1) Infants seemed to make an especially likely, and vulnerable, target for witchcraft; among all the fatalities explained in this way there was clearly disproportionate representation for the very young. (2) Many witches were believed to have an inordinate, and envious, interest in infants and small children. (Some were, in fact, childless.) (3) A number of witches were accused of interfering in the process of infant "nursing." (They would cause soreness or ulcers in the breast; they would make the milk dry up.) (4) Another notorious target of witchcraft was livestock, including (and especially?) milk cows. (5) Witches themselves were thought to "give suck" to their imps and familiars. (6) Courts, local officials, and private citizens would search the bodies of suspected witches for the preternatural "teats" that marked them as the Devil's own.

There is a central preoccupation here with maternal function, especially in regard to infants and small children, which invites further study. Of course, infants of this time and place were very much at risk, relative to other age-groups in the population.[1] Moreover, the forms of their morbidity and mortality may have seemed especially perplexing. (Infant illness was often sudden and dramatic; and communication—in particular, verbal communication—between patient and caretaker was limited or nil.) In short, there was good reason to be anxious about the care of the very young, and it hardly seems surprising that witchcraft belief should have picked up this anxiety. But something else was involved as well. The figure of the witch suckling her imps conveyed a scornful reflection on maternity itself: what has been termed above the witch-as-nurse displayed, in the unconscious, a reverse face—the nurse-as-witch. Here one senses the viewpoint of an aggrieved and angry child, caught up in an archaic form of "sibling rivalry": "I hate my mother who has so unfairly shifted her love from (all-deserving) me to her other (wicked and undeserving) children." Hence the aforementioned cluster of witch-related beliefs seems to have expressed, more or less simultaneously, a parent's fear that infant children may sicken and die, and a child's wish that infant siblings would suffer precisely that fate.

Here once again is the issue of attack-aggression-rage, which looms so large throughout the witchcraft material. Its importance in the psychology of victims; accusers, bystanders (and even the accused themselves) can scarcely be overemphasized: this was what witchcraft most chiefly concerned. Yet infantile sibling rivalry will not alone suffice as explanation; it needs some larger framework of understanding. The succeeding paragraphs propose such a framework—and, by a very roundabout route, return eventually to the subject of aggression.

Recall, for a start, the figure of the witch-as-intruder: this, too, embraced a very large theme. It was as if the witch and her victim were battling back and forth across a vital territory where *boundaries* had assumed the greatest possible significance. On the manifest level the victim and his supporters would labor strenuously to keep the witch at a distance, while she, for her part, was forever "thrusting in." Countermagical strategies were designed to establish clear and impermeable boundaries (for example, the placement of bay leaves or horseshoes, usually near the threshold of the victim's house). At the level of fantasy, as well, the same theme was powerfully evident. Time and again a spectral witch attacked her victim at home and in bed (coming "through the window" or "in at the keyhole"); there was no way to prevent a "shape" from gaining whatever access she desired. Her favorite targets included the victim's children, his livestock, his personal effects; in short, no part of his household was beyond reach. His private conversation, indeed his very thoughts, might be known to her—also embarrassing events in his past, and important prospects in his future. Of course, the most dramatic of all forms of victimization was outright "possession" by the Devil, a process in which the center of personality was invaded from outside. Here was a total failure of boundary-maintenance.

But concern for boundaries was inseparable from the matter of *control*. The intrusions of the witch were meant to demonstrate, and to enlarge, her power over important aspects of the victim's experience. This issue was articulated with special clarity in the course of fits and the various "spectral" encounters. Could the witch force others to do her bidding (that is, to sign the Devil's book)? Could she manipulate their feelings? (Said one shape, "I will make you afraid before I have done with you.")[2] Could she dictate the details of their behavior? (Said one victim, *"They* say I must not speak it [God's name]. . . . They say I must not go in. . . . They say I shall not eat it . . ." etc. And an afflicted girl, under the watchful care of Cotton Mather, asked her tormentors simply, "Is my life in your hands?")[3] Affliction itself was a direct manifestation of the power of the witch. She attacked in places, and by methods, of her own choosing—and the results corresponded in detail to her plan. Her touch, her look, her words could be instantly efficacious. Occasionally she reduced her victims to small images—to "puppets," in both the literal and the figurative meanings of that term. On the other hand, the witch herself could sometimes be manipulated; a careful application of countermagic might simply reverse the roles of puppet and puppeteer.

Considered from an explicitly psychological standpoint, these elements denote a distinctive mode of "object relations." Subject and object, self and non-self, are poorly distinguished—or, at best, are separated only by brittle, easily movable borders. Connections across (or through) such borders are fluid, dense, more or less continuous. Control is indeed a lively issue here—along with its obverse, autonomy. Important sectors of experience are compressed into the two categories of pleasure and pain; and motives are reduced to love and hate (expressed as succor and attack). To all this is added a heavy reliance on the "defense mechanism" of projection.

But to put matters thus is to raise further questions of cause, of source, of origins. Where, in short, did such patterns come from? The prominence throughout the witchcraft material of projective process offers an important clue. Projection (along with introjection) belongs with the most "archaic" of the defenses; its roots lie buried in the earliest phase of life. Freud himself identified the key link: "The original pleasure ego wants to introject into itself everything that is good and to eject from itself everything that is bad. . . . Expressed in the language of the oldest—the oral—instinctual impulses, the judgement is: 'I should like to eat this,' or 'I should like to spit this out.' "[4] Amidst the turmoil of infant sensation, projection and introjection provide a modicum of order. At best they serve the long-term goal of "structure building" (sorting and connecting constituent parts within the early self); at the least, they help to sharpen the boundaries between self and non-self (since their operation depends on boundaries of some sort).[5]

They remain, forever afterwards, associated with a cluster of "unconscious ego activities."[6] And they carry an implicit reference to the most primitive perceptual experiences of the very young child, who regards his "primary object" (caretaker) as a virtual appendage bound to perform his entire bidding. When this expectation runs afoul of reality, rage is the certain result. Expressed subjectively, the initial impression "She will not do as I want" quickly becomes "She does not love me," which is further elaborated into "She hates me and seeks to hurt me." In later life sudden reversals—such as illness or other misfortune—may recall the feelings of helplessness and frustration of infancy. And these, in turn, may reactivate the characteristically infantile modes of perception. Then—and again later—the sense of being well seems to depend on the care, the loving compliance, of others. Conversely, being unwell has the subjective meaning of being unloved and unprotected, or even of being hated.

These processes can be directly related to the development of the "self-system." They belong to that very early and formative period which Freud designated by the term "primary narcissism" but left for later psychoanalytic theorists—most especially Heinz Kohut—to explore in detail.[7] The building of the "nuclear self" is indeed a central theme here. From the diffuse and disorganized experiences of the newborn infant a core of personality gradually evolves. This core has increasing qualities of cohesiveness (in its internal composition), of boundedness (vis-à-vis the external world), and of continuity (over time). Objects (internal representations of other people) are distinguished with growing clarity, but from an inherently "narcissistic" viewpoint. The budding self conceives a "grandiose fantasy," encompassing power, knowledge, beauty, perfection—and looks for confirmation in all this from the available objects. At the same time the self invests the objects with a perfection of their own—in which it may then share by way of an enduring attachment. (This is, in brief, a matter of "idealization," of primitive hero-worship.) Encounters with reality, and a growing appreciation of intrinsic limitations, bring about the gradual modification of these early narcissistic structures. Infantile grandiosity is rescaled and reworked into "healthy ambition," and infantile idealization yields a stable system of (internalized) values. Meanwhile the nuclear self becomes an effective center for the myriad experiences of later life and the locus of a continuing "esteem" (especially *self*-esteem).[8]

This is but a schematic outline based on *optimal* development, and of course the particulars of individual experience are never so tidy or so happily successful. Indeed, the chief concern here is the negative side—the failures, the deficits, the distortions in the self-system. For witchcraft expressed such things, was rooted in them, to a quite unmistakable degree. The implicit concern with boundary-maintenance was itself a diagnostic sign. Victims were thought to be attached to witches, invaded by witches, overcome by witches—notions that suggest a certain fragility in the nuclear self. The presence of so much angry affect points in a similar direction. However, anger is an insufficiently strong description of the attitudes expressed toward—or, more frequently, projected into—the figure of the witch. There was something raw, uncompromising, altogether "primitive" about these attitudes—a quality readily associated with the clinical category "narcissistic rage."[9] Behind narcissistic rage there usually lies an experience of "narcissistic injury" or insult. And this, in turn, calls attention to the numerous situations of conflict with which accusations of witchcraft were typically bound up. Slighting remarks, threats, petty aspersions on character or behavior often evoked a strong response. There was a prickly side to the early New Englanders which shows through in many sectors of their experience, not least in their concern with witches.[10] Consider, too, the matter of display, the claims of "special-ness" implicit in attack by witchcraft. Such claims were most vividly dramatized in full-blown "fits," but, in a lesser measure, they may be imputed to all self-described victims: "The forces of evil have chosen *me* as their target. And you—the standers-by—must attend to me in my hour of affliction."

This discussion has alluded more than once to infantile "ties" with a "primary object." But such terminology may seem excessively abstract, even obfuscating. *Who ordinarily was—and is—the actual, flesh-and-blood "primary object"?* And what is the lasting significance of the "ties" involved here? To raise these ques-tions is to return to a most important problem. Recall the conclusion of Chapter 3 that accused witches were predominantly adult women; recall, too, the difficulty of understanding *why*. Social conditions—the (partially) inferior status of New England women vis-à-vis men—seemed to "fit" with the witch/woman equation, but hardly to explain it.[11] The transcultural aspect of this phenomenon—the common tendency in otherwise disparate societies to define witches as *female*—suggested that interpretive effort might need to reach beyond the particular cir-cumstances of a single time and place. The involvement of both sexes—women no less than men—in prosecuting witches implied another set of parameters. But sociological inquiry yielded no clear line of interpretation, no answers, sat-isfying these general specifications.

Now, as the problem of gender appears once again, there is a more promising outlook. For the theory of early object relations does furnish some answers (which is to say that the problem itself belongs more to the psychology than to the sociology of witchcraft). The key point is what Dorothy Dinnerstein has called the "female monopoly of early child care," the fact that "for virtually every human the central infant-parent relationship, in which we form our earliest, intense and wordless, feelings toward existence, is a relationship with a woman."[12] Beneath the manifold forms of this relationship (across different cultures, and for different individuals within the same culture), there are certain fundamental regularities.

Infants are, in the first place, entirely dependent on their mothers: for food, for warmth, for nurturance, for entertainment, for virtually all the "good" they know. A mother's power to supply these needs, or not to supply them (depending on her own wishes and resources), lies at the center of infantile experience. She seems, from the infant's own standpoint, "omnipotent and responsible for every blessing and curse of existence."[13] For the blessings she is gratefully loved—but for the curses she is angrily blamed. And every child, no matter how well cared for, knows some discomfort, some disappointment, some moments of loss and separation. These are, moreover, experienced with an immediacy and intensity unmatched in any subsequent phase of life.

But there is more to the infant-mother relationship than helplessness and de-pendence on the one side and (seemingly) limitless powers on the other. For the mother is critically implicated in the infant's evolving experience of its own center, its own will, its own subjectivity. She is the "non-self" from which self is progressively distinguished; she plays "it" to the infantile "I." She is "the over-whelming, external will"—again the words are Dinnerstein's—"in the face of which the child first learns the necessity for submission." She disposes a vital power "to foster or forbid, to humble or respect, our first steps toward auton-omous activity."[14]

As an overall result, "female sentience . . . carries permanently for most of us the atmosphere of that unbounded, shadowy presence toward which all our needs were originally directed." And, also as a result, we attribute to "female intentionality" a menacing aspect of

> the rampant and limitless, the alien and unknowable. It is an intentionality that needs to be . . . corralled and subjugated if we . . . are to feel at all safe in its presence. It needs to be corralled . . . not only because its boundaries are unclear, but also because its wrath is all-potent and the riches it can offer or refuse us [are] bottomless.[15]

These images—to repeat—arise and flourish in all "mother-raised children," that is, in women as well as men. Their lasting power derives from their very early provenance. Their association with "pre-verbal" development is, in fact, of the greatest importance; for since they are "formed entirely without words," they continue thereafter to have a "subterranean life of their own, unmodified by that limited part of human sensibility which we call intelligence."[16] Their force and their distinctiveness are highlighted when they are set alongside the comparable imagery of men. "Male sentience" and "male intentionality" have—within the same context of innerlife experience—a much clearer shape, a far more even coloration. Men appear to stand for reason, for logic, for balance, for whatever is most "cleanly human." This, in turn, reflects developmental circumstance. Men (fathers) are not ordinarily much of a factor in infantile experience. And when (later on) men do begin significantly to impinge on the child's life, they enter an "object world" which is in all ways more developed. The child has some ca-pacity to appreciate their separate "subjectivity"—they are more "you" than "it"—and to take their measure as creatures of human, although still quite outsized, dimensions. Fathers, in short, seem far less "magically formidable" than mothers, from the standpoint of the child.[17]

The "magically formidable" qualities of mothers—enlarged to embrace women in general—are, of course, of the greatest importance here. Indeed, the term would serve nicely to describe witches, as perceived by their victims and accusers. Other elements in the figure of the witch have an equally clear reference to infantile experience: the (seeming) malevolence, the intrusiveness, the capacity to inflict all-consuming hurt and harm. To be sure, impressions received *after* infancy must also be credited: most especially, castration anxiety (in its two dif-ferent, gender-related forms), and the (awesome, mysterious) role of women as bearers of new life.* But these serve, by and large, to elaborate on themes rooted in the earliest object-world.

There is little doubt, finally, that New England was populated by "mother-raised children."** Childbirth itself was entirely in the hands of women (midwives, and female kin and friends of the mother); it seems, indeed, that men and all younger children were effectively excluded from such occasions.[19] Breast-feeding—which continued, in the average case, for about one year—would establish a special bond between the mother and her newborn.[20] And this bond seems to have been maintained also in other areas of infant care (judging from scattered notations in personal and local records).[21] By contrast, fathers do not appear in any significant relationship to children until the latter are at least two or three years old. Of course, this division of responsibility for infant nurture is characteristic of virtually every known culture, past and present. It fosters, in turn, a virtually universal "antagonism to women," a misogynous substrate of transcultural dimensions. Its visible outgrowths were—and are—extremely varied, even within a single social setting. But among all such outgrowths none has been more compelling than the figure of the witch. Here was something that the New Englanders shared with countless other specimens of humankind. *

There is one additional way to consider this material, involving a shift of reference from the self system and early object relations to what Erik Erikson has called "psychosocial adaptation."[22] Erikson's well-known schedule of developmental stages posits an unfolding of specific "ego qualities" (each encompassing positive and negative "potentialities"). And among such qualities the one associated with the second stage invites particular attention. The issue in this period (roughly the second and third years of life) is defined as "autonomy vs. shame

---

*The link between castration anxiety and more generalized fears of women has been summarized as follows by Karen Horney: "It [castration anxiety] is an anxiety of psychogenic origin that goes back to feelings of guilt and old childhood fears. Its anatomical-psychological nucleus lies in the fact that during intercourse the male has to entrust his genitals to the female body, that he presents her with his semen and interprets this as a surrender of vital strength to the woman, similar to his experiencing the subsiding of erection after intercourse as evidence of having been weakened by the woman." Woman's biological role in bearing children elicits both fear and jealousy. On the one hand, there is the [preconscious] idea that a person who gives life is also capable of taking it away. (Thus, as Simone de Beauvoir has written, "From the day of his birth man begins to die: this is the truth incarnated in the Mother.") On the other hand, childbearing seems awesome, wonderful, enviable. There is a considerable scientific literature on these issues, and on their relation to misogynous feeling at large.[18] Their presence among the psychological forces that generated witchcraft belief can scarcely be doubted. However, they reflect a specifically *male* viewpoint, and could apply, at most, to the men within the victim-group. And since the *animus* toward witches so clearly embraced persons of both sexes, other factors (e.g. the residues of "early object relations") have greater explanatory power in the present context.

**The implicit reference of the term "raised" continues, for these purposes, to be very *early* childhood.

and doubt." If all goes well, boundaries are defined, and "limits" are set, around a "vital perimeter of personal space." Within this space the child seeks "a gradual and well-guided experience of the autonomy of free choice." And the legacy to later life—again, given a favorable result—is "a sense of self-control without loss of self-esteem," accompanied by "a lasting sense of good will and pride." But often, of course, the result is not so favorable, and the "negative potentialities" come into play. Thus an inordinate propensity to shame is usually grounded in the experience of this developmental stage. But it is "doubt" which seems especially pertinent here. Erikson writes,

> Doubt is the brother of shame. Where shame is dependent on the consciousness of being upright and exposed, doubt ... has much to do with a consciousness of having a front and a back ... and especially a "behind." For the reverse area of the body ... cannot be seen by the child, and yet it can be dominated by the will of others. The "behind" is the small being's dark continent, an area of the body which can be magically dominated and effectively invaded by those who would attack one's power of autonomy.... This basic sense of doubt ... finds its adult expression in paranoiac fears concerning hidden persecutors and secret persecutions threatening from behind.*[23]

This *potpourri* of interpretive deduction yields some common implications about development—about source-points of the stresses and conflicts that found outward expression in witchcraft belief. To recapitulate: (1) "Projection" was everywhere central to witchcraft accusations. And projection, with its "oral" foundation, rates as one of the earliest of all the psychological "defenses." (2) Witchcraft belief displayed important elements of "magical thinking," especially with respect to implicit stereotypes of women. And these have their roots in the "preverbal" substrate of infantile experience. (3) The symptoms and fantasies associated with witchcraft suggest a certain vulnerability in the "self system." Here, too, the genetic line leads far back toward infancy. (4) The same evidence, considered from the standpoint of "ego qualities," underscores the issue of "autonomy" (and its negative correlate "doubt"). And this issue is said to belong especially to the "second stage" of psychosocial adaptation, encompassing roughly the second and third years of life. (5) The extreme symptoms of one particular victim-group, the "af-

---

*The passage, as quoted, implies a biological reference for the psychosocial "potentialities" of the second stage. In short, Erikson links specifically "anal" concerns to the child's struggle for autonomy and his corresponding vulnerability to shame and doubt. However, the strength of this link presumably varies, depending on the personal (and cultural) reinforcement in any given case. In settings where much is made of "toilet training," the anal reference is likely to be central and obvious. But in a different context—i.e., where such matters are downplayed— it may have only minimal importance. For an anthropological example of a culture in which the developmental attainment of autonomy is not much joined to anal preoccupation, see Jean L. Briggs, "The Issues of Autonomy and Aggression in the Three-year-old: The Utku Eskimo Case," in *Seminars in Psychiatry*, IV (1972), 317–29. In this respect, Puritan child-rearing was more like the "Eskimo case" than, e.g., the usual pattern of our own time.

flicted girls," denote unresolved conflicts in relation to "maternal objects." And the cast of those conflicts seems largely "pre-oedipal."

Of course, no such interpretations can be made to yield a precise set of chronological markings, for individual development necessarily sets something of its own pace. Yet the convergent emphasis on *very early* experience seems impressive. Terms like "preverbal" and "pre-oedipal" imply an upper bound of about age three. On the other hand, these tasks and concerns do not belong to the condition of neonates. They require some glimmerings of psychic structure, or at least some movement in that direction; hence age one seems plausible as an approximate lower bound.

Do these numbers find explicit confirmation in the witchcraft materials themselves? There is one documentary fragment which deserves at least a mention: an allegation, from the Salem trials, that one of the accused witches "appeared [i.e. in her spectral shape] as little as a child of two years old."[24] In general, however, the records are devoid of developmental reference—hence the need to revert once again to procedures of inference. What is known generally about the experience of early childhood in seventeenth-century New England? And can this experience be plausibly connected with the themes explored above in relation to witchcraft?

There are, in fact, grounds for thinking that age two was an especially important—and difficult—time in the life of a Puritan child. It was about then that he was most likely to face the arrival of a younger sibling, since in most New England families pregnancies were spaced at intervals of twenty to thirty months.[25] This would mean, in turn, the loss of his mother's special attention: no longer was he the littlest, and most vulnerable, member of the family. But beyond such intimations from demography lie important and explicit prescriptions of Puritan child-rearing. The central task for parents, as defined by the leading exemplars of New England culture, was "training the will" of their young. Indeed, their phrase "training the will" was regularly equated with "breaking the will." Every child was thought to come into the world with inherent tendencies to "stubbornness and stoutness of mind": these must be "beaten down" at all costs.[26] One aspect of such tendencies was the wilful expression of *anger*—and anger was, by Puritan reckoning, the most dangerous and damnable of human affects.[27] Children must therefore be trained to compliance, to submission, to "peace." To effect such training, drastic means were sometimes needed. Puritan parents were not inclined to spare the rod; but more important than physical coercion was the regular resort to shaming.[28] (Here lies another line of connection to the vital "second stage" in Erikson's formulation, defined as it is around the polarity of "autonomy vs. shame and doubt.")

Published statements about child-rearing from the period emphasize that this regime must start early, in order to be fully effective. And while they are not additionally specific, they do direct attention to the second and third years of life. For these are the years when much of development seems to center on the expression of personal "will." The child stands, and walks, and moves more or less freely about; he achieves great progress in the coordination of hand and eye; he begins consciously to control important bodily processes (e.g. the eliminative ones). Much of cognition remains preverbal; yet he gains at least the rudiments of speech (e.g. those which permit him to give or withhold his assent— "yes" and, above all, "no"). Most two-year-old children are eager to test their new-found capacities in relation to other people. And such testing inevitably yields a quotient of frustration and anger, even where it contributes most directly to the growth of "autonomy."

Now imagine how all this might seem against a backdrop of Puritan values. Wilfulness, self-assertion, competitive struggle, surges of infantile grandiosity, sudden outbursts of anger: thus the markings of "original sin," displayed in unvarnished form. To allow such traits room for growth was to open a way for the Devil, whose own character was defined in virtually the same terms. There could be little doubt where parental and social obligation lay. . . .

Developmental theory and clinical data from our own time; seventeenth-century notions of child-rearing; Puritan values in a larger sense; and the particulars of witchcraft proceedings: such are the ingredients of our interpretive model. The model does not constitute "proof" in the traditional manner of historical research, for the connections between one element and the next lie, in part, beyond a scholar's sight-range. Yet there is a sense of fit about the whole, which carries its own persuasiveness.

Some cautions and disclaimers are needed, by way of conclusion. It would be unwise to assign an exclusive "causal" significance to specifically traumatic events forced on New England children in the first few years of life. Any such "reductionist" argument misleads—on at least two counts. For one, it underestimates the importance of manifest cultural tradition. Witchcraft, in all its rich detail, was a subject of *explicit communication,* between persons, communities, and whole generations. Expressed differently: witchcraft was a matter of conscious belief no less than inward (and unconscious) propensity. In addition, the earliest developmental impressions must not be overemphasized at the expense of all succeeding ones. The present investigation has been pressed to the level of roots and sources, but there is no doubting the importance of subsequent reinforcement. Indeed, such reinforcement can be virtually assumed: if New England children encountered in earliest life a strenuous resistance to their deepest autonomous strivings, they must surely have had similar experiences in later childhood. The value-system which supported all this made no intrinsic distinctions as to age. Older children and "youths" would hear from all sides the Puritan message of "peace," of "harmony," of submission—with its corollary warnings against anger and the open assertion of self. Presumably the same message was received, without words, in countless personal transactions.

These psychological inferences must not, finally, be construed as a diagnosis of outright pathology. The great majority of the New Englanders who believed in witchcraft were in no meaningful sense "sick" or otherwise "disturbed." Most of them, like most of us, fell within some normal range of mental and emotional adaptation. On the other hand, most of them—again, like most of us—knew certain areas of inner conflict and vulnerability. And—perhaps to a greater degree for them than is true for us—such areas obtained similar shape and substance among otherwise different individuals; for theirs was a more unified, less heterogeneous culture.

To be sure, some few among them showed in their attitudes toward witchcraft a vulnerability that ran very deep and proved ultimately disabling. For these few— and the "afflicted girls" come first to mind—the language of sickness does indeed apply. Their troubles bear direct comparison to clinical experience today; their fits and related behavior were the outward signs of a disturbance at the center of personality. Though little is known of their individual histories prior to their involvement in witchcraft proceedings, one many reasonably infer psychic "lesions" of a large, and long-standing, kind.

And yet pathology is always a matter of *relative,* not absolute, distinctions. Hence even the most extreme instances of affliction would remain in some sense comprehensible to the whole community of New Englanders. A girl "in her fits," an older person attributing specific misfortune to the malefic power of his neighbor, the legion of ordinary folk who maintained a general belief in the reality and power of witchcraft: all were joined by strong bonds of inner preoccupation. The difference and distance between them embraced quantity, not quality; as individuals they represented a variety of points along a single psychological spectrum. Every attack by witchcraft summoned deeply responsive echoes in a host of "bystanders," for the victim was acting out—although (sometimes) to an "extremity"—pressure-points and vulnerabilities that were widely shared.

Two points deserve a final restatement. Strong, purposeful, effective as they undeniably were, many of the New Englanders seem to have felt persistently vulnerable in their core sense of self. Tremors of uncertainty plagued their struggle to grow and endure as free-standing individuals; they could not feel confident of maintaining the existential boundaries of their lives. And, in ways examined above at great length, such feelings were evoked with particular intensity by the figure of the witch.

By a separate but parallel route she evoked other feelings as well. The intrusive, demanding traits so widely attributed to her are best viewed as projections. Her victims were presumably uncomfortable about similar tendencies in themselves, about their own wishes to intrude, to encroach, to dominate, to attack—their whole assertive side. As frequently happens in such situations, they dealt with their conflict by externalizing it. Not they, but rather their neighbor—the "witch"—possessed the traits they so deeply despised.

NOTES

1 Maris A. Vinovskis, "Mortality Rates and Trends in Massachusetts before 1830," *Journal of Economic History,* XXXII (1972), 195–201; David E. Stannard, *The Puritan Way of Death,* 54–55; Demos, *A Little Commonwealth,* 131–32; Kenneth A. Lockridge, "The Population of Dedham, Massachusetts, 1636–1736," in *Economic History Review,* 2nd ser., XIX (1966), 329; James K. Somerville, "A Demographic Profile of the Salem Family, 1660–1700," unpublished paper presented at the conference on social history, Stony Brook, New York. (1969).

2 Deposition by Mary Hale, in the trial of Katherine Harrison; Willys Papers, W017, Brown University Library.

3 Cotton Mather, "Memorable Providences, Relating to Witchcrafts and Possessions," in Charles Lincoln Burr, ed., *Narratives of the Witchcraft Cases* (repr. New York, 1968), 112, 116, III; Cotton Mather, "A Brand Plucked Out of the Burning," in ibid., 269.

4 Sigmund Freud, "Negation," in Strachey, ed., *The Standard Edition of the Complete Psychological Works of Sigmund Freud,* XIX, 237.

5 Anna Freud, *The Ego and the Mechanisms of Defense,* 51–52.

6 The term—and the main elements of the argument presented in this paragraph—are taken from the work of Abraham Kardiner. See his *The Individual and His Society* (New York, 1939), 305–10.

7 Sigmund Freud, "On Narcissism," in Strachey, ed., *The Standard Edition of the Complete Psychological Works of Sigmund Freud,* XIV, 69–102, and "An Outline of Psychoanalysis," in ibid., XXIII, 150ff. Kohut's work is most fully presented in his two books, *The Analysis of the Self* (New York, 1971) and *The Restoration of the Self* (New York, 1977). See also Otto Kernberg, *Borderline Conditions and Pathological Narcissism* (New York, 1975).

8 For an excellent summary of recent work by Kohut and his colleagues, see Ernest S. Wolf, "Recent Advances in the Psychology of the Self: An Outline of Basic Concepts," in *Comprehensive Psychiatry,* XVII (1976), 37–46.

9 Heinz Kohut, "Thoughts on Narcissism and Narcissistic Rage," in *The Psychoanalytic Study of the Child,* XXVII (1972), 360–400; see also Kohut, *The Restoration of the Self,* 116ff.

10 Demos, *A Little Commonwealth,* 49–51; Richard L. Bushman, *From Puritan to Yankee: Character and the Social Order in Connecticut, 1690–1765* (Cambridge, 1967), ch. 1.

11 See pp. 63–64.

12 Dorothy Dinnerstein, *The Mermaid and the Minotaur: Sexual Arrangements and Human Malaise* (New York, 1976), 33. Dinnerstein's extraordinary book—easily the best of all studies on the psychological underpinnings of misogyny—provides the basis for this discussion of the woman/witch equation.

13 Ibid., 108.

14 Ibid., 28–29, 165.

15 Ibid., 164.

16 Ibid., 84.

17 Ibid., 175–76.

18 Karen Horney, *Feminine Psychology,* Harold Kelman, ed. (New York, 1967); see especially "The Distrust Between the Sexes," 107–18. Wolfgang Lederer, *The Fear of Women* (New York, 1968). H. R. Hays, *The Dangerous Sex* (New York, 1964). Joseph Rheingold, *The Fear of Being a Woman* (New York, 1964). Bruno Bettelheim, *Symbolic Wounds* (New York, 1954). Marjorie C. Barnett, " 'I Can't' versus 'He Won't,' " in *Journal of the American Psychoanalytic Association,* XVI (1968), 588–600. Edith Jacobson, "Development of the Wish for a Child in Boys," in *The Psychoanalytic Study of the Child,* V (1950), 139–52. Daniel S. Jaffe, "The Masculine Envy of Woman's Procreative Function," in *Journal of the American Psychoanalytic Association,* XVI (1968), 121–48. Kato van Leeuwen, "Pregnancy Envy in the Male," in *International Journal of Psychoanalysis,* XLVII (1966), 319–24. Robert C. Bak, "The Phallic Woman," in *The Psychoanalytic Study of the Child,* XXIII (1968), 15–36.

19 This, at any rate, is the strong impression gained from personal and legal records dealing with episodes of childbirth, and from manuals of midwifery. See the brief account of colonial practice in Richard W. Wertz and Dorothy C. Wertz, *Lying In: A History of Childbirth in America* (New York, 1977).

20 Demos, *A Little Commonwealth,* 133.

21 Whenever infants are mentioned in records from the period, their mothers are invariably found with them.

22 See Erik H. Erikson, *Childhood and Society,* 2nd ed. (New York, 1963), ch. 7, "Eight Ages of Man."

23 Ibid., 253–54.

24 Testimony by Hannah Post, printed in Massachusetts Historical Society, *Collections,* III, 224.

25 Demos, *A Little Commonwealth,* 68.

26 Robert Ashton, ed., *The Works of John Robinson,* 2 vols. (Boston, 1851), I, 245–47.

27 Ibid., I, 226.

28 See, for example, the opinions of Cotton Mather on discipline of the young in his little treatise "Some Special Points Relating to the Education of My Children," reprinted in Perry Miller and Thomas A. Johnson, ed., *The Puritans,* 2 vols. (New York, 1963), II, 724–27. See also the words which Mather attributed (elsewhere) to his clerical colleague, Nathaniel Ward: "Of young persons he would himself give this advice: 'Whatever you do, be sure to maintain shame in them,' for if that once be gone, there is no hope that they'll ever come to good"; *Magnalia Christi Americana* (Hartford, 1853), I, 522.

17

Non-Psychoanalytic Approaches to National Socialism

Harvey Asher

This paper attempts to answer the questions of why and how the Germans were led so far by Hitler and the Nazis, without recourse to psychological theories that focus primarily on abnormal behavior. Instead, attention will be directed to those findings of social psychologists that support the notion that many Germans followed a regime whose ideas they did not necessarily share and whose actions they may have abhorred.

It can of course be argued that the policies Hitler pursued exposed the wishes (sometimes unconsciously held) of the populace, and that the link between leaders and led was the German historical tradition, a shared set of beliefs, attitudes, and values created by exposure to common experiences, institutions, crises, and behaviors. With varying degrees of sophistication, historians subscribing to revelationist positions try to isolate those thinkers in the German past whose ideas they believe resemble or seem potentially compatible with Hitler's *Weltanschauung*.[1] Or they may point to idiosyncratic German ways of apprehending reality that were sufficiently congruent with the Nazi outlook so as to be politically exploitable.[2] Specific historical events responsible for the distorted mind set of the Germans may be cited, such as the bitter reaction to the wars of the French Revolution, which led to an exaggerated rejection of rationalism and cosmopolitanism.

The notion that the German past prepared the way for Hitler is not restricted to a discussion of intellectual precursors. It also takes the form of trying to establish continuity between the political heritage of an earlier era, e.g., Bismarckian authoritarianism, and a modern version of the same paradigm, e.g., Nazi authoritarianism. At its extreme, the revelationist school asserts that the German past irrevocably prepared the way for Hitler, that the Germans got what they

Reprinted from *Psychohistory Review,* 7:3 (Winter, 1978), pp. 13–21.

deserved.[3] More sensibly, it is noted that an anachronistic authoritarian state—by preventing the mature development of liberalism, democratic socialism, left-wing Catholicism, and responsible conservatism—provided the prototype for Nazism or made it impossible to offer effective resistance to a Fascist onslaught.[4]

The importance of historical continuity is also stressed in efforts directed toward establishing a German national character, as displayed in an authoritarian personality, family, or similar characterological syndrome.[5] Such studies are of three basic types: (1) in-depth personality assessments seeking to explore the latent or underlying character structure of individual Germans; (2) analyses of German collective, institutional, and political phenomena; and (3) social anthropological accounts of childrearing patterns among Germans, and their manifestation in the adult personality.[6] Authoritarian personality traits on the individual level are supposedly created and reinforced by familial patterns of paternal dominance and maternal submission, producing a national character high in submission and obedience to authority which Hitler manipulated for his own "warped" ends. The psychological consequences of these authoritarian developments on German history include repressed hostility (individual and collective), and the inhibition of soft, so-called feminine feelings such as tenderness and love.

In turn, the Germans' repressed hostility was projected onto others and "acted out" under the Nazis. The implication is that Germans supported the Third Reich because the Nazis embodied their collective frustration and more importantly, because they offered the psychiatric casualties of unhealthy childrearing patterns the opportunity to release those pent-up frustrations. More astute writers of the character distortion school specify particular historical conditions which activated resentments that had hitherto remained latent. Particular groups in German society are singled out as being especially susceptible to infection.[7] In any case, the Nazis and their supporters remain linked by mutual pathology. Tragically for mankind and the Germans "a successful leader (Hitler) gives expression to the subliminal needs of the culture and is able to project an image that fuses with and meets these cultural attitudes (abnormalities)."[8]

And yet, even if we could establish the existence of pathology on the individual or small-group level,[9] some serious difficulties remain. One is that most Germans failed to join the Party.[10] Of equal concern, the Germans never gave Hitler an electoral majority.[11] Nor can it be demonstrated conclusively that most Nazis came from authoritarian homes;[12] or, since so many who did come from authoritarian homes did not become Nazis, it is not possible to single out this factor as the main etiological agent.[13]

While it is virtually impossible to prove that most Germans were Nazi supporters by virtue of shared psychological pathology and common authoritarian upbringing, might it not be that in Hitler's Germany a large number of deviants (ten to fifteen percent of the population) gained control over a majority of "normal" people? Selzer makes just such an argument, but his explanation of the

Nazi success is both weak and confusing. Having rejected authoritarian cultural and social characteristics in the German population as the primary link between the Nazis and the masses, Selzer then suggests that "the Nazi ethos appealed to certain aspects of their personality, even though they did not conform to the Nazi type."[14] Elsewhere he remarks on how "the chance emergence of a highly effective leadership resulted in the politicization to a most unusual degree of the psychologically aberrant population of Germany."[15] *Chance* turns out to be the connection between Hitler and the German masses, who, it turns out, do share at least some of the personality traits of their pathological leaders after all.

The use of national character to account for German submission to Hitler and the Nazis is fraught with problems: (1) authoritarianism is not peculiar to Germans; (2) it is not clear if all Germans succumbed to it; and (3) it is not possible to specify how much of the authoritarian trait the individual must possess to become a Nazi supporter or sympathizer. National character arguments essentially account for Hitler's hold over the Germans by postulating reciprocal pathologies, overt for the former, covert for the latter; the Nazis represent a distorted and disguised mirror-image of their authoritarian German brethren. The Freudian perspective is evident here—all men are basically evil, though some are more so than others. They possess uncontrollable impulses and death instincts which constantly threaten to crash through the shaky barriers that uphold civilization.[16] The Nazis are the example *par excellence* of this universal tendency; the authoritarian structure of the Reich produced circumstances under which if one scratched a German, one found a potential Nazi.

Freudian notions also appear in those theories which focus on mass movements and the politics of mass mobilization to explain German acceptance of Hitler. These writers argue that the breakdown of class structure and the disappearance of autonomous groups with limited goals produced anomie and rootlessness, reactions to the massive dislocations spawned by industrialization. The victims of uncontrolled technology respond by becoming irrational and malleable; they are then seduced by manipulative leaders who capture the dispossessed and alienated with histrionic strategies.[17] Predictably, the virulence of the German reaction to these disruptive forces is attributed to national history. In truth then, we wind up with a subtler version of the national character thesis, with somewhat greater emphasis on a charismatic leadership harnessing the energies of *mindless* and hate-ridden masses—a twentieth century Teutonic version of collective insanity.

Theories centering on irrational mass-man in many ways represent a throwback to Gustav Le Bon's earlier work on crowd behavior.[18] The Frenchman described the impulsivity of crowds which he ascribed to a weakening in intellectual aptitude and the suspension of critical judgment. The individual in the crowd becomes an automaton, displaying extreme credulity, fleeting sentiments, irritability, intolerance, and absence of reason; in short, behaviors "which are almost always observed in beings belonging to inferior forms of evolution—in women, savages, and children." (p. 16) Le Bon endorses the primacy of the unconscious personality in guiding crowd behavior: "The heterogeneous is swamped by the homogenous and the unconscious qualities obtain the upper hand." (p. 8) The loosening of rational bonds make the group particularly susceptible to suggestion and contagion, mindless automatons dominated by strong-willed leaders who exercise "a veritible magnetic fascination on those around them" (p. 120) by "calling up in the souls of their fellows that formidable force known as faith, which renders a man the absolute slave of his dream." (p. 114)

Of special interest here is Le Bon's belief that "an entire nation may become a crowd under the action of certain influences," (p. 3) a view which sounds rather similar to the national character position described earlier. That crowds display different forms of irrational behavior is, in Le Bon's opinion, due to racial differences. (p. 159) The similarity of this line of thought to modern versions highlighting the German national character and its collective "madness" is transparent.

Although his terminology is different, Freud expressed many of the same views on crowd behavior as Le Bon.[19] "In a group the individual is brought under conditions which allow him to throw off the repressions of his unconscious instinctual impulses." (p. 74) Freud explains how inhibitions and individual instincts are removed in the group. He contends that the suggestibility of group members results from their having "put one and the same object (the Leader) in place of their ego ideal (personal aspirations) and have consequently identified themselves with one another in their ego (leading to espirit de corps, group identity)." (p. 116) Group actions recapitulate the dynamics of the ancient primal horde, that archaic heritage which in times immemorial made the individual compliant toward his parents. (p. 123) "The leader of the group is still the dreaded primal father" (p. 123) to whom the individual surrenders his ego ideal. (p. 129)

Several difficulties prevent Le Bon and Freud's versions of contagion theory from being employed as a sufficient explanation of the relationship between Hitler, the Nazis, and the Germans. For one thing they assert that in a crowd, all individuals experience the same emotions and engage in the same kind of response to a single, compelling source of suggestion.[20] Always seeing the group as a total unit blinds these authors "to any diversity or differing degree of individual conviction backing up the apparent behavior of the group."[21] It is assumed that all individuals in the group share common motives and attitudes, all possess the same unconscious impulses, and all display regressive behavior. More colloquially, the picture drawn is of people going crazy together, no longer able to function with the least bit of rationality.

While this theory is somewhat efficacious for explaining short-term mob actions such as Kristallnacht, in the case of Nazi Germany we are concerned with explaining a long-term relationship between leaders and led which showed few signs of severance even after it became clear that the leader was pursuing a disastrous course. While it may be shown that Hitler exhibited self-destructive tendencies,[22] it would be virtually impossible to demonstrate that the Germans continued to support him because he was leading them in pursuit of Thanatos, a conclusion strongly suggested by the Freudian model.

Some modern day psychohistorical studies of Hitler also aim at increasing our understanding of the relationship between the Nazis and the German masses, although such is not always their primary intent. Those that do have such intent share a common interest in demonstrating the close affinity between Hitler's personal pathology (variously diagnosed), his political decisions, his Weltanschauung, and style of leadership. Most germane to our purpose is the contention, shared by several psychohistorians, that what likely saved Hitler from psychotic disintegration was his ability to get the German people to buy into his projections, albeit for reasons transcending his own pathology.[23] In other words Hitler avoided going crazy by getting the Germans to equate his bizarre perceptions with reality, which they did because of some unresolved, unconscious conflicts in their own past that in some mysterious way overlapped with Hitler's personal hangups.[24] Rudolph Binion attempts to demystify the situation by specifying the content of the traumas experienced by Hitler and the Germans and by showing how they intertwined. He cites three traumas: (1) Klara Hitler's over the death of her children; (2) Adolf Hitler's over the death of his mother; and (3) the German people's over their unwillingness to accept defeat in World War I. While a complete discussion of the Binion theses is beyond the scope of this article,[25] we can at least question his assertion that *all* Germans were traumatized and that following Hitler was the *only* way the trauma could be resolved.

This brief survey of several traditional and psychoanalytic studies of Hitler's hold over the Germans revealed a number of methodological difficulties and questionable assumptions. I now want to look at the contributions of social learning theory to the subject. Social learning theorists are highly critical of fundamental Freudian constructs, e.g., the unconscious. They are concerned with overt behavior—how responses are learned, maintained, increased or extinguished. They advocate a strong empirical grounding to confirm their hypotheses. Very broadly speaking, this orientation can be labeled behavioristic;[26] the individual is seen as responding to factors in the external world rather than projecting his own internal states (drives) onto the environment.

One dimension of learning theory relevant to our discussion is the concept of modeling. According to Bandura and Walters, there are at least three possible effects of exposure to a model: (1) to imitate precisely responses *not previously* in the observer's repertoire (new behaviors); (2) to inhibit or increase the frequency and/or intensity of a *previously* acquired response more or less similar to those exhibited by the model; and (3) to serve as a cue, whereby the model's responses elicit *similar* observer responses that are neither entirely novel nor inhibited as a result of prior learning.[27] Cumbersome language aside, what this social learning model suggests is that the behavior of some Germans toward Hitler's regime was acquired not as the result of character deficiency or historical conditioning to authority, but through imitating the behavior of the new Nazi authority figures, behavior which was encouraged and rewarded by the Führer and his entourage. New behaviors were learned, for example, to act out aggression or to disavow reason. Previously learned behaviors increased in frequency or intensity—prejudice against Jews justified beating them up and eventually exterminating them. Much of Hitler and his cohorts' hold over the masses flowed from the dynamics of the interaction itself—that is, Nazis served as new models for citizens to emulate. How the Nazis acquired power is largely an historical question. That *the achievement of power* gave them greater potency as model is beyond question. Quite possibly the tradition of obedience among Germans augmented the process of imitating strong political authority figures. It is a truism that winners are more imitated than are losers: an important aspect of Hitler's control was that behaviors he endorsed were rewarded by the regime, for example by increased status, or a better job. It is likely that specific individuals and constituencies who did not necessarily approve of Nazi attitudes or behaviors adopted them not out of fervent conviction or mindless conformity, but by the process of imitation. The standards of acceptable behavior were redefined by a new group of models who gained maximum exposure through their monopolistic control of the mass media. Skillful use of propaganda and the provision of opportune setting, e.g., Nuremburg rallies, in which to act out the new rituals and responses increased the likelihood of imitation.

The concept of imitation helps to remind us that loss of critical faculties need not be the only or primary reason a person surrenders his individuality; he can do so while remaining critically aware and knowledgeable. While a Heydrich, Himmler, or Goebbels may have jumped on the Nazi band-wagon because it provided a vehicle for coping with his own particular pathology,[28] it does not follow that all or most Germans were similarly motivated unless one assumes, as do many Freudians, that one can generalize from the abnormal to the so-called normal. Imitation of potent models rather than psychopathy or a flawed personality thesis helps augment our understanding of the average German's response to the Nazis.

Individuals may imitate a group for several reasons. Their emulation may result from:

a. Reward power, based on a member's perception that others have the ability to mediate rewards for him.
b. Coercive power, based on the member's perception that others have the ability to mediate punishment for him.
c. Legitimate power, based on the perception by members that others have a legitimate right to prescribe behavior for them.
d. Referent power, based on the member's identification with others.
e. Expert power, based on the perception that the other has some special knowledge or expertise.[29]

Most of the theories discussed in the early part of this article focus exclusively on legitimate and referent power. Earlier totalitarian theories exphasized coercive power.[30] Traditional biographers have referred to expert power, e.g., Hitler's ability to dazzle army leaders by rattling off military statistics.[31] The importance of reward powers for understanding part of the relationship between Hitler and the Germans has been noted. We will also be looking at categories of legitimate and referent powers, but in a somewhat different manner than traditional or psychoanalytic historians.

Cognitive dissonance is another social psychological tool useful for explaining why some Germans followed the Nazis. The supposition here is that cognitive systems tend toward a state of harmony, balance, consistency, or consonance. Cognitive dissonance arises when people at any one time *know* things that have opposing behavioral implications. If one stimulus implies "do this" and another indicates "do the opposite" then the individual is in a state of cognitive dissonance.[32] To cope with discrepancies between opposing cognitions, or cognitions and behaviors held simultaneously, the dissonant person has recourse to several strategies. He can exaggerate the value of what was chosen. In the Germans' case, the citizen could glorify the value of submitting to the Führer over the value of independent action, or he could devalue the rejected alternative, for example by assessing the Weimar Republic as completely bankrupt.

Still another way of reducing dissonance is to find others who agree with us or who are in the same situation as we are. This technique, called bolstering, enables the person to say: "There is nothing wrong with me; see how many are just like me."[33] In contradistinction to the Freudian defense mechanism of projection, the individual who "bolsters" need not *unconsciously* cast out the unwanted "evil" by attributing it to others. Rather he consciously accommodates others to his position: "Yes, I may be treating Jews terribly, but so is everyone else, which makes me no worse than them."

Obviously the three responses can be used in various combinations.[34] The point is that when a person is induced to do or say something which is contrary to his private opinion, there will be a tendency for him to change his opinion so as to align it with what he has done or said. It seems plausible to suggest that the Nazi experiment increased the proclivity to cognitive dissonance among Germans because Hitler and the Nazi value system *were not compatible* with their personal beliefs. While certainly not a complete explanation of the willingness of many to perform actions they *consciously* loathed, the theory of cognitive dissonance offers a helpful qualification to those theories which assume the primacy of unconscious processes or postulate national character deficiencies. It highlights the willingness of human beings to pursue consistency in thought, though sometimes at the expense of a realistic world view.

In line with cognitive dissonance theory, there is some evidence that "individuals who go through a severe initiation to gain admission to a club or organization ... tend to think more highly of that organization than those who do not go through severe initiation to gain admittance."[35] If motivation is held con-

stant, severity of initiation may be the decisive factor in determining one's assessment of the group experience, not what the group actually *does*. While most
relevant for explaining the loyalty of the Nazi elite, this tendency suggests that
some who joined the Party retained their membership and positive appraisal not
because of what the party did for them, nor out of ideological conviction, but
because of what they gave up to join.

Here a word is also in order about how inaccurate views may be sustained
in light of contrary evidence. The problem is how to prevent new knowledge
from effecting a change of opinion or action.[36] One way is by contextual twisting.
This involves the reinterpretation of contradictory information in the context of
what is already known. Undoubtedly, some Germans knew Jews whose characteristics did not fit Hitler's stereotype. A maneuver to justify ignoring this piece
of information would have been to proclaim that Jew an exception to the rule,
thereby allowing the stereotype to be maintained. Or the disturbing fact may be
placed in the context of data compatible with the prevalent attitude. Instead of
acknowledging that some Jews possessed "intelligence" and "business acumen"
these key characteristics were perceived and classified as "shrewdness" and "ex-
ploitativeness"—enabling the stereotype to remain unassailed. New information
as such is not even processed, let alone evaluated. One might also reject an unpleasant fact on the grounds that it conflicts with other, presumably more complete data. Although the Jews in a given German community might not have
exhibited a particularly invidious trait, their brethren elsewhere were assumed
to display the hated characteristic conspicuously.[37]

Another tactic for retaining a static world view is to discredit those sources
which would challenge it. In the German context, this involved denying that ex-
termination was being implemented, because the source of information, whether
the foreign press or an acquaintance, was unreliable.

A last resort is simply to discard the relevance of new information. People
may have "learned" that the Jewish stereotype was false or that a "final solution"
was being enacted. Given the fact that the new information did not interfere
with their daily activities, their comments may have been, "So what?" Such conduct is a way of leaving a field of potential conflict by withdrawing from it both
physically and psychologically.

The procedures just described are far from passive; it requires effort to de-
sensitize oneself to facts, to avoid perceiving them or to keep them out of focus.

> To protect himself from coming in conflict with the social order, the individual adopts
> measures the consequences of which are *not* to observe, *not* to understand, *not* to
> feel.[38]

It is not the purpose of this article to discuss the psychic costs levied by these
distortive processes. What I have attempted is to counter the facile notion of
passive, uniform German masses unconsciously seduced by fiendish deviants who

found responsive chords in a defective population infected by "historical pathology."[39] Rather, I have made an effort to illustrate some of the conscious ways in which many Germans avoided unpleasant situations.

I remain all too aware that in the German case we are at times dealing with the behavior of evil people. I am also cognizant that Nazi goals and conduct were elsewhere emulated, that there were other fascist experiments, and that virulent anti-Semitism was not confined to Germany—some Poles, Ukrainians, and Frenchmen enthusiastically joined the SS.[40] It is also likely that people partly meet those who manipulate them, and that propaganda and coercion enhance the process. Yet it remains equally true that much of German collective behavior toward National Socialism operated on a conscious level, is rationally analyzable, and that psychosocial approaches are efficacious in dealing with these behaviors. While the historian employing psychosocial theory must be chary of making the facts fit the generalization, knowledge of group behavior augments his ability to grapple with the dynamics of the historical process. Psychosocial concepts offer a corrective to contagion theories—the argument that collective behavior follows from the more or less automatic transmission and unconscious, uncritical reception of moods and emotions from person to person. Likewise, it eliminates nebulous concepts such as multiple trauma and collective neurosis, while avoiding the overuse of paradox which frequently permeates psychoanalytic explanations of connections between leaders and led.

The effects of group pressure must be assigned weight in accounting for the willingness of some Germans to submit to Hitler and the Nazis. The experiments of Solomon Asch are suggestive here.[41] A group of individuals were asked to judge the size of various lines. Outside of the experimental setting subjects made mistakes one percent of the time. Then the situation was changed so that all but one member of the group were told to make wrong judgments. In thirty-three percent of the cases, the duped subject yielded to the majority. One fifth of the subjects were entirely independent; forty-two percent of the group were not appreciably affected by the experimental conditions. (p. 458) The reasons the deceived victims gave for yielding ranged from not wanting to offend, to fear of interfering with the experiment, to an imperative need not to be different, to actually coming to see reality the way the majority reported it. (pp. 468–73)

Asch did not believe that the contradiction between sense perception and group pressure was due to the past experience of the subject. Even those who remained independent throughout, exuding confidence, were still disturbed and assailed by doubts and the temptation to join with the others. (p. 466) In a later experiment, Asch increased the magnitude of line discrepancy to see if it would help the critical subjects to assert their independence and to repudiate the majority more decisively. The results were that "increasing the objective discrepancies did not abolish the majority effect or appreciably decrease it." (p. 475) However, when conditions were altered by reducing the opposition to *one* person, the change was sufficient almost to abolish the experimental effect. Asch concludes that the results described earlier were a function of the presence of a majority. (p. 476)

One further modification of the initial experiment bears mentioning. When Asch introduced a partner in the group who was supportive of the critical subject two changes occurred: (1) the majority effect was markedly weakened; and (2) the degree to which any single subject yielded diminished strikingly.

The Asch experiments underscore the importance of receiving confirmation from others for attitudes we hold, decisions we make, or actions we perform. Without such support it is very difficult for the individual to retain his independence against the group even if his values are different. Asch's work offers another corrective to undue focus on Hitler's charisma or the "religious" nature of the Nazi movement. Germans often followed the Nazis not out of any great sense of idealism or spiritual fervor, but because they did not want to offend a larger or more powerful group, especially when they perceived themselves as standing alone. While the Nuremberg rallies attracted men who obeyed because they were true believers,[42] the compliance of others was governed by the more mundane considerations of the Asch experiments.

To deny the prevailing view in society, however that view comes to predominate, requires of the individual a serious severence of social bonds, that familiar milieu which he knows and moves in and through which he acquires a sense of worth. An individual's decision to buck the system cannot always be made in reference to a specific issue of disagreement, such as the Nuremberg Laws. The price for assertion of self is costly. And as was the case with many Germans, although they *knew* better, they *chose* not to protest.

The work of Solomon Asch also suggests that much of the behavior (symptomology) exhibited by individuals and groups is a function of factors in the situation itself. If one manipulates external variables in a group interaction (such as proximity, location, and social support), it is possible to elicit behavior that individuals would not ordinarily exhibit. Unlike the psychoanalytic historian who moves from the world of the individual to the external environment and consequently must deduce states of internal mentation,[43] the social psychologist manipulates the external environment and observes behavioral change. Traditional descriptive history which analyzes specific external variables and assesses their impact, such as Hindenburg's decision to appoint Hitler Chancellor, would seem to be the natural ally of the social psychological approaches described in this article. Historians provide the raw data (events, decisions, statistics); the social psychologist can show how major historical episodes became operational at the group level. That is how one moves from the event to changes in human behavior.

In 1935, Muzafer Sherif began a number of experiments to study social factors in perception as a means of getting at the problem of norm formation.[44] In a completely darkened room, a single point of light appears to move when in fact it does not. This phenomenon is called the autokinetic effect. Judgment of the distance of apparent light movement differs markedly from individual to individual and in different spatial arrangements of the room. This unstructured situation arouses considerable anxiety in the individual. (pp. 202–03)

One group of subjects was first asked to estimate the light movement individually and then brought into a group setting to make "new" estimates. A second batch began its estimates within a group setting and proceeded to render individual judgment. Sherif found that in the absence of an objective range or scale of stimuli and an externally given reference, both groups (individual and collective) built up their own ranges on an internal reference point, that is they established a range within which all subsequent judgments were rendered. Although in both cases the ranges and norms of individuals tended to converge, convergence was greater when subjects first worked in a group setting. (p. 206) Moreover, when a group member was subsequently experimented on alone, "he perceived the situation in terms of the range and norm that he brought with him from the group." (p. 206)

In the Asch experiments (a more structured situation), the conditions produced error in the majority direction in only one third of the cases despite the obvious discrepencies. In the more ambiguous design of Sherif, *every* subject converged toward an introduced standard unless it was extraordinarily discrepant, e.g., twelve times the person's largest previous judgment. (p. 121)

While caution is indicated in extrapolating the results of these experiments to historical phenomena, they remain suggestive for our subject. They indicate that norms form when individuals interact in problem situations that involve uncertainties and choice among alternative modes of action. Norm formation develops in out-of-the-ordinary situations, where the usual rules and routine of daily living are not applicable. This would seem to be a fit description of the situation in Germany after World War I, suggesting that the *key* variable for understanding the Nazi phenomenon is not to be found in a long established national tradition but in those external events which made previous ways of responding to the environment difficult, inappropriate, or useless. It was the perceived ambiguity of the post World War I situation induced by concrete historical events, that led to a breakdown in the traditional authoritarian structure. Rather than augmenting receptivity to Nazism, the so-called authoritarian tradition may have acted to prevent submission to the Nazi model.

It is important to remember that the Freudian construct of bipolar traits allows that the defenses employed by the authoritarian character give rise to results that may be socially constructive as well as destructive. It is true, as many psychohistorians contend, that the defense mechanisms of the authoritarian personality can lead to submission, repressed aggression and sadism—qualities compatible with a "Nazi personality type." It is also true, but less emphasized, that "the culturally productive variations of the same defenses (can) result in control and discipline, precision and accuracy, dedicated performance and order,"[45] traits which under the appropriate circumstances may be antithetical to Nazism.

The question which psychoanalytic accounts of Nazism fail to answer, in my judgment, is why and how the "pathological" pole of a given trait came to predominate. Even if the dynamics of the process can be traced for a given individual or small group, is it not asking too much to assume that all Germans infected by authoritarianism came down with the same disease? Sherif's experiments suggest that any general conclusion about an alleged German collective pathology will have to be of a most general sort; at best we can say that the perceptions of the populace and of Hitler and the Nazis were not completely discrepant. This does not mean they were similar or that Hitler articulated what most Germans felt, if only unconsciously. Rather we must concentrate first and foremost on the specifics of the external environment which contributed to the Nazi success, such as the deficiencies of Weimar and the bitterness over Versailles. Then attention should move to those observable policies of the Nazis which increased their sources of support, e.g., reduction of class antagonism, foreign policy successes, reduction of unemployment, and terror. The final step is to turn to social psychological theories for an understanding of the different ways and motivations that led most Germans to enthusiastically support or reluctantly go along with the regime.

It also needs to be noted that the dynamics involved in the Nazis' *coming* to power and their *staying* in power are not synonymous. Common sense would indicate that many who are not enthusiastic about a cause will jump on the wagon if it seems to be moving forward, or if there is only one wagon available. The various psychosocial concepts discussed in this article have dealt with both sets of contingencies: how some Germans came to support the Nazis in their bid for power and why they didn't jump off the wagon when it began to go out of control.

On the latter contingency, the willingness of most Germans to stay with Hitler to the bitter end, the brilliant experiments of Stanley Milgram are instructive.[46] His studies were conducted on American subjects, and dealt with obedience that was willingly assumed in the absence of any sort of threat, "obedience that is maintained through the simple assertion by authority that it has the right to exercise control over the person." (p. xii)

The paradigmatic experiment, from which Milgram ran numerous variants, involved soliciting subjects to test the effects of punishment on learning. The "learner" was an accomplice of the experimenter. The "teacher" was a naive subject who was instructed to teach the learner word pairings, e.g., "green"/"ball." The learner-accomplice was seated in a chair, his arms strapped to prevent excessive movement, and an electrode attached to his wrist.

In the experiment, the "teacher" sat behind a generator with thirty switches, ranging from fifteen volts to four hundred fifty volts. There were also verbal designations which ranged from Slight Shock to Danger—Severe Shock. The "teacher" was told to increase the level of shock each time the learner responded incorrectly. At seventy-five volts the learner grunted; at one hundred twenty volts he complained verbally; at one hundred fifty he demanded to be released; at two hundred eighty-five volts "his response can only be described as an agonized scream." (p. 4) The distressing result of the experiment was that "a substantial proportion (of teachers) continued to the last shock on the generator." (p. 5) "It is the extreme willingness of adults to go to almost any lengths on the command of authority that constitutes the chief finding of the study." (loc. cit.)

The primary explanation that Milgram offers for obedience to authority is that a person comes to view himself as the instrument for carrying out another person's wishes and therefore no longer regards himself as responsible for his actions. (p. 8) The individual's moral sense reverts to a consideration of how well he is living up to the expectations authority has of him.

This psychological shift, as Milgram's experiments demonstrate, is not peculiar to Germans. Nor am I contending that it is a complete explanation for German obedience. What I am proposing is that many Germans obeyed Hitler not because they sympathized with his ideas, nor because he performed mass hypnotism, nor because he offered a substitute religion. They were not wicked or evil, or irreversibly conditioned by the German past, or in the thrall of a collective trauma. Rather they obeyed him for the banal reason that for most individuals, as Milgram's findings imply, it is very difficult *not* to obey authority.[47]

In conclusion I would like to state that I do not believe that any single psychological approach to history can by itself definitively answer the questions of why and how the Germans were led so far by the Nazis. I close by offering a three-stage division of labor for historians working on these questions.

a. *Traditional historians.* This group can help to isolate those factors in the German past that made Hitler's accession to power a possibility, e.g., the Bismarckian legacy, the failures of Weimar politicians, historical accidents, Hitler's own skills. They can describe and analyze the import of significant events and personages on the Nazi climb to and retention of power.

b. *Psychoanalytic historians.* These scholars contribute most to increasing our empathic understanding of the private world of Hitler and other Nazi personages. They may discern nonobvious patterns and interconnections between Hitler's childhood, adolescence, and subsequent actions. They enable us to share in the intensity of Hitler's feelings and beliefs and aid us in perceiving how Hitler's internal, subjective world became externalized and politically significant.

c. *Historians using non-Freudian concepts.* These individuals are most effective in showing the dynamics involved in Hitler's and the Nazi's domination over the German masses. They seek to describe the relationship between Hitler and the masses by the same "laws" that govern other known forms of social and group behavior. They are most interested in the rational and conscious aspects of collective behavior and avoid postulating metaphysical collective

Limited neither by birth nor by death, the duration of *What is* replaces and transcends the unending survival which characterized the Olympian gods."[21] In other words, *Being*, birthless as well as deathless, replaced for the philosophers the mere deathlessness of the Olympian gods; Being became the true divinity of philosophy because, in the famous words of Heraclitus, it was "made by none of the gods or men, but always was and is and shall be: an ever-living fire, fixed measures kindling and fixed measures going out."[22] The gods' immortality could not be trusted; what had come into being could also cease to be—were not the pre-Olympian gods dead and gone?—and it was this flaw in the gods' everlastingness (much more, I think, than their frequent immoral conduct) that made them so vulnerable to Plato's ferocious attacks. The Homeric religion was never a creed that could be replaced by another creed; "the Olympian gods were laid low by philosophy."[23] That the new and everlasting divinity, which Heraclitus in the fragment just quoted still calls *kosmos* (not the world or the universe but their order and harmony), is finally, starting with Parmenides, given the name "Being" seems due, as Charles Kahn suggests, to the *durative* connotations this word had from the beginning. It is indeed true, and by no means a matter of course, that "the durative aspect, being inseparable from the stem, colors every use of the verb, including every philosophical use."[24]

If Being replaced the Olympian gods, then philosophy replaced religion. Philosophizing became the only possible "way" of piety, and this new god's newest characteristic was that he was One. That this One was indeed a god and thus decisively different from what we understand by "being" becomes obvious when we see that Aristotle called his "First Philosophy" a "Theology," by which he did not mean a theory about the gods but what much later—in the eighteenth century—was called *ontologia* or "Ontology."

The great advantage of the new discipline was that man, to win his share of immortality, no longer needed to count on the uncertain ways of posterity. He could actualize it while he was alive without requiring any help from his fellow-men or from the poets, who in earlier days, by bestowing fame, could make his name last forever. The way to the new immortality was to take up one's abode with things that are forever, and the new faculty making this possible was called *nous* or mind. The term was borrowed from Homer, where *noos* encompasses all mental activities besides designating the specific mentality of one person. It is *nous* that corresponds to Being, and when Parmenides says "*to gar auto noein estin te kai einai*"[25]("to be and to think [*noein*, the activity of *nous*] are the same"), he is already saying implicitly what Plato and Aristotle then said explicitly: that there is something in man that corresponds exactly to the divine because it enables him to live, as it were, in its neighborhood. It is this divinity that causes Thinking and Being to be the same. By using his *nous* and by withdrawing mentally from all perishable things, man assimilates himself to the divine. And the assimilation is meant pretty literally. For just as Being is the god, *nous,* according to Aristotle (quoting from either Ermotimos or Anaxagoras), is "the god in us," and "every mortal life possesses the part of some god."[26] *Nous,* "as all wise men agree," said Plato, "is the king of heaven and earth";[27] hence it is above the whole universe, just as Being is higher in rank than anything else. The philosopher, therefore, who has decided to risk the voyage beyond "the gates of Day and Night" (Parmenides), beyond the world of mortals, "shall be called the friend of god, and if ever it is given to man to put on immortality, it shall be given to him."[28] In short, to engage in what Aristotle called the *theōrētikē energeia* that is identical with the activity of the god (*hē tou theou energeia*) means to "immortalize" (*athanatizein*), engage in an activity that in itself makes us immortal "as far as that is possible, and [to] do our utmost to live in accordance with what is highest in us."[29]

For us, it is of some importance to note that the immortal and divine part within man does not exist unless it is actualized and focused on the divine outside; in other words, the *object* of our thoughts bestows immortality on thinking itself. The object is invariably the everlasting, what was and is and will be, and therefore cannot be otherwise than it is, and cannot *not* be. This everlasting object is primarily the "revolutions of the universe," which we can follow mentally, thus proving that we are "not an earthly but a heavenly growth," creatures who have their "kindred" not on earth but in heaven.[30] Behind this conviction, we can easily detect the aboriginal wonder, in itself philosophical. It is wonder that sends the scientist on his course of "dispelling ignorance" and that made Einstein say: "The eternal mystery of the world [i.e., the universe] is its comprehensibility." Hence all subsequent "development" of theories to match the universe's comprehensibility "is in a certain sense a continuous flight from 'wonder.' "[31] The God of the scientists, one is tempted to suggest, created man in his own image and put him into the world with only one Commandment: Now try to figure out by yourself how all this was done and how it works.

At any rate, to the Greeks, philosophy was "the achievement of immortality,"[32] and as such it proceeded in two stages. There was first the activity of *nous*, which consisted in contemplation of the everlasting and was in itself *aneu logou*, speechless; then followed the attempt to translate the vision into words. This was called *alētheuein* by Aristotle and does not just mean to tell things as they really are without concealing anything, but also applies only to propositions about things that always and necessarily are and cannot be otherwise. Man qua man, as distinct from other animal species, is a composite of *nous* and *logos*: "his essence is set in order according to *nous* and *logos*"—*ho anthrōpos kai kata logon kai kata noun tetaktai autou hē ousia*.[33] Of these two, it is only *nous* that enables him to partake of the everlasting and the divine, while *logos*, designed "to say what is," *legein ta eonta* (Herodotus), is the specifically, uniquely human ability that is also applied to mere "mortal thought," opinions or *dogmata*, to what happens in the realm of human affairs and to what merely "seems" but *is* not.

Logos as distinguished from *nous* is not divine, and the translation of the philosopher's vision into speech—*alētheuein*, in the philosophers' strict sense—created considerable difficulties; the criterion of philosophical speech is *homoiōsis* (in opposition to *doxa* or opinion), "to make a likeness" or assimilate in words as faithfully as possible the vision provided by *nous*, which itself is without discourse, seeing "directly, without any process of discursive reasoning."[34] The criterion for the faculty of vision is not "truth" as suggested by the verb *alētheuein*, derived from the Homeric *alēthes* (truthful), where it is used only for the *verba dicendi*, in the sense of: tell me without hiding (*lanthanai*) within yourself, that is, do not deceive me—as though the common function of speech, here implied in the *alpha privativum*, were precisely deception. Truth remains the criterion of speech, though now, when it has to assimilate itself to and take its cue, as it were, from the vision of *nous*, it changes character. The criterion for vision is only the quality of everlastingness in the seen object; the mind can partake in that directly, but "if a man is engrossed in appetites and ambitions and spends all his pains on these . . . he cannot fall short of becoming mortal altogether, since he has nourished the growth of his mortality." But "if he has set his heart" on contemplating the everlasting objects, he cannot "fail to possess immortality in the fullest measure that human nature admits."[35]

It is generally admitted that philosophy, which since Aristotle has been the field of inquiry into things that came after the physical and transcended them (*tōn meta ta physika*, "about what comes after the physical"), is Greek in origin. And being Greek in origin it set itself the original Greek goal, immortality, which seemed even linguistically the most natural aim for men who understood themselves as *mortals, thnētoi* or *brotoi*, for whom, according to Aristotle, death was "the greatest of all evils," and who had as their kindred, their blood relations, as we would say, "drawing breath from one mother," the immortal gods. Philosophy did nothing to change this natural goal; it only proposed another way to attain it. Summarily speaking, the goal disappeared with the decline and fall of the Greek people and disappeared from philosophy altogether with the arrival of Christianity, bearing its "good news," telling men they were not mortals, that, contrary to their former pagan beliefs, the world was doomed to end, but they would be bodily resurrected after death. The last trace of the Greek quest for the everlasting may be seen in the *nunc stans*, the "standing now" of the medieval mystics' contemplation. The formula is striking, and we shall see later that it indeed corresponds to an experience highly characteristic of the thinking ego.

However, while the mighty incentive to philosophize disappeared, the topics of metaphysics remained the same and continued to prejudge throughout the centuries which things are worthy of being thought about and which are not. What for Plato was a matter of course—that "pure knowledge is concerned with the things that are always the same without change or mixture, or with what is most akin to them"³⁶—remained in manifold variations the chief assumption of philosophy up to the last stages of the modern age. Excluded by definition were all matters concerning human affairs, because they were contingent; they could always be different from what they actually were. So even when Hegel, under the influence of the French Revolution—in which, according to him, eternal principles such as freedom and justice had been actualized—took history itself as his field of inquiry, he could do it only on the assumption that not only the revolutions of the skies and sheer thought-things such as numbers and the like followed the iron laws of necessity, but that the course of human affairs on earth also followed such laws, the laws of the incarnation of the Absolute Mind. From then on, the goal of philosophizing was not immortality but necessity: "Philosophical contemplation has no other intention than to eliminate the accidental."³⁷

The originally divine metaphysical topics, the everlasting and the necessary, survived the need to "immortalize" through the mind's effort to "stay" and remain in the presence of the divine, an effort rendered otiose when, with the rise of Christianity, faith replaced thought as the bringer of immortality. And in a different way the evaluation of spectatorship as the essentially philosophical and best way of life also persisted.

In pre-Christian times that notion was still alive in the philosophical schools of late antiquity, when life in the world was no longer considered a blessing and involvement in human affairs no longer seen as a distraction from a more divine activity but, rather, as dangerous and joyless in itself. To keep yourself out of political involvement meant to occupy a position outside the turmoil and misery of human affairs and their inevitable shifts. The Roman spectators were no longer situated on the ascending rows of a theater where they could look down godlike on the game of the world; their place was now the secure shore or haven where they could watch, without being endangered, the wild and unpredictable upheavals of the storm-swept sea. These are the words of Lucretius praising the advantages of mere spectatorship: "What joy it is, when out at sea the stormwinds are lashing the waters, to gaze from the shore at the heavy stress some other man is enduring! Not that anyone's afflictions are in themselves a source of delight; but to realize from what troubles you yourself are free is joy indeed."[38] Here, of course, the philosophic relevance of spectatorship is entirely lost—a loss that befell so many Greek notions when they fell into Roman hands. What is lost is not only the spectator's privilege of judging, as we found it in Kant, and the fundamental contrast between thinking and doing, but also the even more fundamental insight that whatever appears is there to be seen, that the very concept of appearance demands a spectator, and that therefore to see and to behold are activities of the highest rank.

It was left to Voltaire to draw conclusions from Lucretius' proposition. According to him, the desire to see is nothing but cheap curiosity: it attracts people to the spectacle of a ship about to be shipwrecked; it drives people to climb trees or look at the massacres of battle or attend public executions. And this passion, according to Voltaire, man shares with monkeys and young dogs. In other words, if Lucretius is right and man's passion for seeing spectacles is due solely to his sense of safety, then the sheer lust for seeing can be ascribed only to an immature irrational drive that endangers our very existence. The philosopher, for whom Lucretius speaks, will not need to see the shipwreck to be warned against entrusting his safety to the wildness of the sea.

Unfortunately, it is in this rather shallow form that the beneficial and "noble" distance between the spectator and his object has been handed down in our tradition—if we leave out of consideration the high rank of contemplation in medieval philosophy with its altogether different connotations. And it is curious how frequently Lucretius is the implicit or explicit source. Thus Herder writes about the French Revolution: "We can look upon the French Revolution from the safe port as though we looked upon a shipwreck on the open, alien sea, unless bad fortune should throw us in against our will." And Goethe, asked after the battle of Jena how he had fared, answered with the same image: "I cannot complain. I was like a man who looks from a solid rock down upon the furious sea and who, though unable to assist the shipwrecked, cannot be reached by the breakers, and according to some ancient author this is supposed to be a rather comfortable feeling."[39]

As we come to the modern age, the nearer we get to our own time, the less is left—not in the textbooks but in actual experience—of the pre-philosophic assumptions that were actually the midwives of the "awesome" science (McKeon) called metaphysics.

15 Plato's answer and its echoes

In Greek philosophy, there exists, however, one answer to our question What makes us think? that has nothing to do with these pre-philosophic assumptions which became so very important for the history of metaphysics and which probably long ago lost their relevance. It is the saying of Plato I have already cited, namely, that the origin of philosophy is Wonder, an answer that in my opinion has lost nothing of its plausibility. For this wonder is in no way connected with the quest for immortality; even in Aristotle's famous interpretation of wonder as *aporein* (being puzzled on account of ignorance, which can be dispelled by knowledge), there is no mention of *athanatizein*, the immortalizing activity we know from the *Nicomachean Ethics*[40] and which indeed is entirely Platonic. Plato's remark about wonder occurs rather abruptly (and, so far as I can see, is nowhere repeated in his work) during a discussion of the relativity of sense perceptions. Speaking about something that is "out of order," the passage itself is somewhat out of order, as happens frequently in Plato, where the most telling sentences can easily be isolated and sound out of context, especially when, after getting involved in the logical and other perplexities typical of his century and of which one could rightly say they are dated, he suddenly breaks off discussing them. Here Theaetetus has said that he was "wondering"—in the ordinary sense of being "puzzled"—whereupon Socrates compliments him: "This is the true mark of the philosopher," and never comes back to the issue under consideration. The short passage reads: "For this is chiefly the passion (*pathos*) of the philosopher, to wonder (*thaumazein*). There is no other beginning and principle (*archē*) of philosophy than this one. And I think he [namely Hesiod] was not a bad genealogist who made Iris [the Rainbow, a messenger of the gods] the daughter of Thaumas [the Wonderer]."⁴¹ At first glance, this seems merely to say that philosophy as understood by the Ionian school is a child of astronomy; it springs from marveling at the miracles of the sky. As the rainbow connecting the sky with the earth brings its message to men, so thinking or philosophy, responding in wonder to the daughter of the Wonderer, connects the earth with the sky.

Upon closer inspection, these few words hint at much more. The word "Iris," rainbow, also occurs in the *Cratylus*,⁴² where Plato derives it "from the verb *to tell* (*eirein*), because she was a messenger," whereas the word for "wonder" (*thaumazein*), which he here divests of the ordinary sense in which Theaetetus had used it by giving its genealogy, occurs regularly in Homer and is itself derived from one of the many Greek verbs for seeing in the sense of "beholding": *theasthai*— the same root we met earlier in Pythagoras' *theatai*, spectators. In Homer, this wonder-struck beholding is usually reserved for men to whom a god appears; it is also used as an adjective for men in the sense of O admirable one!—namely worthy of the admiring wonder we usually reserve for the gods, a godlike man. Moreover, the gods who appeared to men had this peculiarity: they appeared in familiar human disguise and were recognized as divinities only by those whom they approached. The responding wonder, therefore, is not something men can summon up by themselves; the wonder is a *pathos*, something to be suffered, not acted; in Homer, it is the god who acts, whose appearance men have to endure, from whom they must not run away.

In other words, what sets men wondering is something familiar and yet normally invisible, and something men are forced to *admire*. The wonder that is the starting-point of thinking is neither puzzlement nor surprise nor perplexity; it is an *admiring* wonder. What we marvel at is confirmed and affirmed by admiration which breaks out into speech, the gift of Iris, the rainbow, the messenger from above. Speech then takes the form of praise, a glorification not of a particularly amazing appearance or of the sum total of things in the world, but of the harmonious order behind them which itself is not visible and of which nevertheless the world of appearances gives us a glimpse. "For the appearances are a glimpse of the non-revealed" (*"opsis gar tōn adēlōn ta phainomena"*), in the words of Anaxagoras.[43] Philosophy begins with an awareness of this invisible harmonious order of the *kosmos*, which is manifest in the midst of the familiar visibilities as though these had become transparent. The philosopher marvels at the "non-visible harmony," which, according to Heraclitus, is "better than the visible" (*"harmoniē aphanēs phanerēs kreittōn"*).[44] Another early word for the invisible in the midst of the appearances is *physis*, nature, which according to the Greeks was the totality of all things that were not man-made and not created by a divine maker but that had come into being by themselves; and of this *physis* Heraclitus said that "it likes to hide itself,"[45] namely behind the appearances.

I have introduced Heraclitus by way of explication, because Plato himself does not specify what his admiring wonder is directed at. Nor does he say how this original marveling transforms itself into the dialogue of thinking. In Heraclitus, the significance of *logos* is at least suggested in the following context: Apollo, he says, "the lord of the Delphian oracle" and, we may add, the god of the poets, "does not speak out nor does he conceal but indicates" (*"oute legei oute kryptei alla sēmainei"*),[46] that is, hints at something ambiguously, to be understood only by those who have an understanding of mere hints (the god *winkt,* as Heidegger translates). Even more tantalizingly suggestive is another fragment: "Bad witnesses are eyes and ears for men if they have barbarian souls,"[47] that is, if they do not possess *logos*—for the Greeks not just speech but the gift of reasoned argument that distinguished them from the barbarians. In short, wonder has led to thinking in words; the experience of wonder at the invisible manifest in the appearances has been appropriated by speech, which at the same time is strong enough to dispel the errors and illusions that our organs for the visible, eyes and ears, are subject to unless thinking comes to their help.

From this, it should be obvious that the wonder that befalls the philosopher can never concern anything particular but is always aroused by the whole, which, in contrast to the sum total of entities, is never manifest. Heraclitus' harmony comes about through the sounding together of opposites—an effect that can never be the property of any particular sound. This harmony in a way is separate (*kechōrismenon*) from the sounds that produce it, just as the *sophon,* which one "may not and may call by the name of Zeus,"[48] is "set apart from all other things."[49] In terms of the Pythagorean parable, it is the beauty of the game of the world, the meaning and meaningfulness of all the particulars acting together. As such this is manifest only to a beholder in whose mind the particular instances and sequences are invisibly united.

Since Parmenides, the key word for this invisible imperceptible whole implicitly manifest in all that appears has been *Being*—seemingly the most empty and general, the least meaningful word in our vocabulary. What happens to a man who suddenly turns about to become aware of Being's all-pervasive presence in the world of appearances was described with great precision thousands of years after its first discovery in Greek philosophy. The passage is relatively modern and therefore more insistent on personal, subjective emotions than any Greek text would be, and for that very reason perhaps more persuasive to psychologically trained ears. Coleridge writes:

Hast thou ever raised thy mind to the consideration of existence, in and by itself, as the mere act of existing? Hast thou ever said to thyself thoughtfully, It is! Heedless in that moment, whether it were a man before thee, or a flower, or a grain of sand, — without reference, in short, to this or that particular mode or form of existence? If thou hast indeed attained to this, thou wilt have felt the presence of a mystery, which must have fixed thy spirit in awe and wonder. The very words, — There is nothing! or, — There was a time, when there was nothing! are self-contradictory. There is that within us which repels the proposition with as full and instantaneous a light, as if it bore evidence against the fact in the right of its own eternity.

Not to be, then, is impossible: to be, incomprehensible. If thou hast mastered this intuition of absolute existence, thou wilt have learnt likewise, that it was this, and no other, which in the earlier ages seized the nobler minds, the elect among men, with a sort of sacred horror. This it was that first caused them to feel within themselves a something ineffably greater than their own individual nature.[50]

The Platonic wonder, the initial shock that sends the philosopher on his way, was revived in our own time when Heidegger, in 1929, concluded a lecture entitled "What is Metaphysics?" with the words, already cited, "Why is there anything at all and not, rather, nothing?" and called this "the basic question of metaphysics."[51]

The question, expressing the philosopher's shock in modern terms, had been asked before him. It occurs in Leibniz' *"Principes de la nature et de la grâce"*: *"Pourquoi il y a plutôt quelque chose que rien?"* For since *"le rien est plus simple et plus facile que quelque chose,"*[52] this something must have a sufficient cause for its existence, and this cause in turn must have been caused by something else. Following this train of thought, one finally arrives at the *causa sui*, at something which is its own cause, so that Leibniz' answer arrives at the ultimate cause, called "God," an answer we already find in Aristotle's "unmoved mover"—the god of the philosophers. It was Kant, of course, who dealt the death blow to that god, and in his words on the subject we can clearly recognize what Plato only hinted at: the uncaused and "unconditioned necessity" our cause-and-effect thinking "so indispensably require[s] as the last bearer of all things, is for human reason the veritable abyss. . . . We cannot put aside, and yet also cannot endure the thought, that a being, which we represent to ourselves as supreme amongst all possible beings, should, as it were, say to itself: 'I am from eternity to eternity, and outside me there is nothing save what is there through my will, *but whence then am I?*' All support here fails us; and the *greatest* perfection, no less than the *least* perfection, is unsubstantial and baseless for the merely speculative reason, which makes not the least effort to retain either the one or the other, and feels indeed no loss in allowing them to vanish entirely."[53] What strikes us here as specifically modern is that in the restatement of Parmenides' early insight that nothingness is inconceivable, unthinkable, the emphasis has shifted, as it were, from nothing-ness to Being: Kant nowhere says that the abyss of nothing because of being inconceivable *is not,* and though he might have said that the antinomies of reason, rousing him from dog-matic slumber, had made him think, he nowhere says that the experience of this abyss—the other side of Plato's wonder—had done so.

Schelling quoted Kant's words emphatically and it was prob-ably from this passage, rather than from the more casual remark in Leibniz, that he derived his own repeated insistence on this "ultimate question" of all thinking—Why is something at all, why is there not nothing?[54] He calls it the "most despairing question."[55] This reference to sheer despair, as arising out of thinking itself, occurs in Schelling's late writings, and it is so very significant because the same thought had haunted him earlier, in his youth when he still believed that no more was needed to banish nothingness than "absolute affirmation," which he called "the essence of our soul." By virtue of it "we recognize that non-being is forever impossible," neither knowable nor understandable. And for the young Schelling, this ultimate question—Why is there not nothing, why is there anything at all?—posed by the intellect seized with vertigo at the rim of the abyss—is forever suppressed by the insight that "*Being* is necessary, [made so] that is, by the absolute affirma-tion of Being in cognition."[56]

All this would suggest a simple return to the position of Parmenides if Schelling had not felt that only the "absolute *positing* of the idea of God" could guarantee this affirmation, which according to him is "the absolute negation of nothingness": it is "as certain that reason forever negates nothingness, and that nothingness is nothing, as it is certain that reason affirms the All and that God is eternal." Hence, the only "completely valid answer to the question, *Why is there not nothing, why is there anything at all?* is not the something but the All *or God*."[57] Reason, unaided by the idea of God, according to "its mere nature," may "posit a Being that is forever," but then, confronting this thought which it is in reason's nature to posit, reason remains as it were "thunderstruck (*quasi attonita*), paralyzed, unable to move."[58] No Iris-like messenger, bringing the gift of speech, and with it the gift of reasoned argument and reasonable response, accompanies the philosophical shock; and the affirmation of Being, clearly corresponding to the element of admiration in Plato's wonder, needs faith in a Creator-God to save human reason from its speechless dizzy glance into the abyss of nothingness.

What happens to thought's "ultimate question," once this faith is resolutely rejected and human reason is left completely alone with its own capacities, we can trace in Sartre's *Nausea*, by far the most important of his philosophical works. There the hero of the novel, looking at the root of a chestnut tree, has been suddenly overcome by "what 'to exist' meant . . .; existence usually hides itself. It is there, around us, in us, it is *us*, you can't say two words without mentioning it, but you can never touch it." But now "existence had suddenly unveiled itself. It had lost the harmless look of an abstract category: it was the very paste of things. . . . Or rather the root, the park gates, the bench, the sparse grass, all that had vanished: the diversity of things, their individuality, were only an appearance, a veneer." The reaction of Sartre's hero is not admiration, and not even wonder, but nausea at the opaqueness of sheer existence, at the naked thereness of the factually given, which indeed no thought has ever succeeded in reaching, let alone illuminating and making transparent: "You couldn't even wonder where all that sprang from, or how it was that a world came into existence, rather than nothingness." Now that all marveling had been eliminated, it was the scandal of Being that nothingness was "unthinkable." There had been nothing *before* it. Nothing . . . That was what worried me: of course

there was no *reason* for this flowing larval stuff to exist. *But it
was impossible* for it not to exist. It was unthinkable: to imagine nothingness you had to be there already, in the middle
of the world, alive, with your eyes wide open. . . . I felt with
boredom that I had no way of understanding. No way. Yet it
was there, waiting, looking at one." It is this completely meaningless thereness that makes the hero shout: " 'Filth! what
rotten filth!' . . . but it held fast and there was so much, tons
and tons of existence, endless."[59]

In this progressive shift from Being to nothingness, caused
not by the loss of wonder or perplexity but by the loss of admiration and willingness to affirm in thought, it would be
very tempting to see the end of philosophy, at least of that
philosophy whose beginning Plato had fixed. No doubt, the
turning from admiration to negation is easy enough to understand, not because it is occasioned by any tangible events or
thoughts but because, as Kant had already observed, speculative reason in itself "feels no loss" and no gain in turning to
either side of the matter. Hence, the notion that to think means
to say "yes" and confirm the factuality of sheer existence is also
found in many variations throughout the history of philosophy
in the modern age. We find it notably in Spinoza's "acquies-
cence" in the process in which everything that is swings and
in which the "big fish" forever eat the small fish. It appears in
Kant's pre-critical writings when he tells the metaphysician
that he should first ask: "Is it possible that nothing at all
exists?" which then should lead him to the conclusion that "if
no existence is given at all, there would also be nothing to
think about," a thought that in turn leads to a "concept of
absolutely necessary being "[60]—a conclusion Kant would hardly
have recognized in the critical period. More interesting is
a remark he makes a little earlier about living in "the best
possible world": he repeats the old consoling thought, "that
the whole is the best, and that everything is good for the
sake of the whole," but seems himself not quite convinced of
this ancient *topos* of metaphysics, for he suddenly injects: *"Ich
rufe allem Geschöpfe zu . . .* : *Heil uns, wir sind!"*—"I call out
to every creature . . . : Hail to us that we are!"[61]

This affirmation, or, rather, the need to reconcile thought

with reality, is one of the leitmotifs of the work of Hegel. It informs Nietzsche's *amor fati* and his notion of "eternal recurrence"—the "highest form of affirmation that can be reached"[62] precisely because it is at the same time the "heaviest weight."

How, if a . . . demon were to . . . say to you "This life as you now live it . . . you will have to live . . . innumerable times more; and there will be nothing new in it, but every pain and every joy and every thought and sigh . . . must return to you—all in the same succession and sequence. . . . The eternal hour glass of existence is upended over and over and you with it, a dust grain of dust." Would you not throw yourself down . . . and curse the demon who spoke thus? Or did you once experience a tremendous moment when you would have answered him, "You are a god and never have I heard anything more godly." . . . How well disposed would you have to become to yourself and to life to *crave nothing more fervently* than this ultimate eternal confirmation and seal.[63]

The point of these passages is that Nietzsche's notion of eternal recurrence is not an "idea" in the Kantian sense of regulating our speculations, nor, of course, is it anything like a "theory," a relapse, so to speak, into the ancient time-concept with its cyclical motion. It is indeed a mere thought or, rather, a thought-experiment, and its poignancy resides in the intimate connection that binds the thought of Being and the thought of nothingness together. Here the need for confirmation arises not out of a Greek admiration for the invisible harmony and beauty that bind together the infinite diversity of particular beings, but out of the simple fact that nobody can think Being without at the same time thinking nothingness, or think Meaning without thinking futility, vanity, meaninglessness.

The way out of this perplexity seems to be indicated by the old argument that without an aboriginal confirmation of Being, there would be nothing to think about and nobody to do the thinking; in other words, the very activity of thinking no matter what kind of thought already presupposes existence. But such merely logical solutions are always treacherous; nobody who clings fast to the notion that "there is no truth" will ever be convinced if it is pointed out to him that the proposition is self-defeating. An existential, meta-logical solution of the perplexity can be found in Heidegger, who, as we saw, evinced something like the old Platonic wonder in reiterating the question Why is there anything at all rather than nothing? According to Heidegger, *to think* and *to thank* are essentially the same; the very words derive from the same etymological root. This, obviously, is closer to Plato's wondering admiration than any of the answers discussed. Its difficulty lies not in the etymological derivation and the lack of an argumentative demonstration. It is still the old difficulty inherent in Plato, of which Plato himself seems to have been well aware and which is discussed in the *Parmenides*.

Admiring wonder conceived as the starting-point of philosophy leaves no place for the factual existence of disharmony, of ugliness, and finally of evil. No Platonic dialogue deals with the question of evil, and only in the *Parmenides* does he show concern about the consequences that the undeniable existence of hideous things and ugly deeds is bound to have for his doctrine of ideas. If everything that appears partakes in an Idea visible only to the eye of the mind and derives from this Form whatever reality it may possess in the Cave of human affairs—the world of ordinary sense perception—then everything that appears at all, by no means only admirable things, owes its very appearingness to such a suprasensory entity to explain its presence in this world. So, asks Parmenides, what about utterly "trivial and undignified objects" such as "hair and mud and dirt," which have never aroused admiration in anybody? Plato, speaking through Socrates, does not use the later common justification of evil and ugliness as necessary parts of the whole that appear evil and ugly only to the limited perspective of men. Instead, Socrates replies that it would be simply absurd to ascribe ideas to such stuff—". . . in these cases, the things are just the things we see" —and suggests that it is better to retreat at this point "for fear of falling into a bottomless pit of nonsense." (Parmenides, however, an old man in the dialogue, points out: "That . . . is because you are still young, Socrates, and philosophy has not yet taken hold of you so firmly as I believe it will someday. You will not despise any of these things then, but at present your youth makes you still pay attention to what the world will think."[64] But the difficulty is not resolved and Plato never again raises the question.) We are not interested here in the doctrine of ideas, or only to the extent that one might be able to demonstrate that the notion of ideas occurred to Plato because of beautiful things and would never have occurred to him had he been surrounded by nothing but "trivial and undignified objects."

There is, of course, a decisive difference between Plato's and Parmenides' quest for divine matters and the seemingly more humble attempts of Solon and Socrates at defining the "unseen measures" that bind and determine human affairs, and the relevance of the difference for the history of philosophy, as distinguished from the history of thought, is very great. What matters in our context is that in both instances thought is concerned with invisible things that are pointed to, nevertheless, by appearances (the starry sky above us or the deeds and destinies of men), invisibles that are present in the visible world in much the same way as the Homeric gods, who were visible only to those whom they approached.

16   *The Roman answer*

In my attempt to isolate and examine one of the basic sources of non-cognitive thinking I have emphasized the elements of admiration, confirmation, and affirmation, which we encounter so powerfully in Greek philosophical and prephilosophic thought and can trace throughout the centuries, not as a matter of influence but of often-repeated first-hand experience. I am not at all sure that what I have been describing runs counter to present-day experiences of thinking but I am quite sure that it runs counter to present-day opinion on the subject.

Common opinion on philosophy was formed by the Romans, who became the heirs of Greece, and it bears the stamp, not of the original Roman experience, which was exclusively political (and which we find in its purest form in Virgil), but of the last century of the Roman republic, when the *res publica*, the public thing, was already in the process of being lost, till finally, after Augustus' attempt at restoration, it became the private property of the imperial household. Philosophy, like the arts and letters, like poetry and historiography, had always been a Greek import; in Rome culture had been looked upon with some suspicion as long as the public thing was still intact, but it was also tolerated and even admired as a noble pastime for the educated and a means of beautification of the Eternal City. Only in the centuries of decline and fall, first of the republic and then of the empire, did these occupations become "serious," and did philosophy, for its part, Greek borrowings notwithstanding, develop into a "science," Cicero's *animi medicina*—the opposite of what it had been in Greece.[65] Its usefulness was to teach men how to cure their despairing minds by escaping from the world through thinking. Its famous watchword—which sounds almost as though it had been formulated in contradiction of the Platonic admiring wonder—became *nil admirari:* do not be surprised at anything, admire nothing.[66]

But it was not just the popular image of the figure of the philosopher, the wise man whom nothing can touch, that we owe to the Roman transmittal; Hegel's well-known saying about the relation of philosophy and reality ("the owl of Minerva begins its flight when dusk is falling")[67] bears the mark of the Roman rather than the Greek experience. For Hegel, Minerva's owl exemplified Plato and Aristotle rising, as it were, out of the disasters of the Peloponnesian war. Not philosophy, but the *political* philosophy of Plato and Aristotle grew out of the decline of the polis, "a shape of life grown old." And with respect to this political philosophy there is considerable evidence for the truth of Pascal's splendidly impertinent remark in the *Pensées:*

We can only think of Plato and Aristotle in grand academic robes. They were honest men, and like others laughing with their friends, and when they wanted to divert themselves, they wrote the *Laws* or the *Politics*, to amuse themselves. That part of their life was the least philosophic and the least serious. . . . If they wrote on politics, it was as if laying down rules for a lunatic asylum; if they presented the appearance of speaking of a great matter, it was because they knew that the madmen, to whom they spoke, thought they were kings and emperors. They entered into their principles in order to make their madness as little harmful as possible.[68]

In any event, the profound Roman influence on even so metaphysical a philosopher as Hegel is quite manifest in his first published book,[69] where he discusses the relation between philosophy and reality: "The need for philosophy arises when the unifying power has disappeared from the life of men, when the opposites have lost the living tension of their relatedness and their mutual interdependence and have become autonomous. Out of disunity, out of being torn apart, arises thought," namely, the need for reconciliation (*"Entzweiung ist der Quell* des Bedürfnisses der Philosophie"). What is Roman in the Hegelian notion of philosophy is that thinking does not arise out of reason's need but has an existential root in unhappiness—whose typically Roman character Hegel with his great sense of history recognized very clearly in his treatment of the "Roman World" in the late lecture course published as the *Philosophy of History.* "Stoicism, Epicureanism, and Scepticism ... although ... opposed to each other, had the same general purport, viz., rendering the soul absolutely indifferent to everything which the real world had to offer."[70] What he apparently did not recognize is the extent to which he himself had generalized the Roman experience: "The History of the World is not the theatre of happiness. Periods of happiness are blank pages in it, for they are periods of harmony."[71] Thinking then arises out of the disintegration of reality and the resulting *dis*-unity of man and world, from which springs the need for another world, more harmonious and more meaningful.

And this sounds very plausible. How often indeed must the first thought-impulse have coincided with an impulse to escape a world that has become unbearable. It is improbable that this escape-impulse is less old than the admiring wonder. Yet we look in vain for its expression in conceptual language before the long centuries of decline that began when Lucretius and Cicero transformed Greek philosophy into something essentially Roman—which meant, among other things, something essentially practical.[72] And following these precursors with their mere foreboding of disaster—"everything is gradually decaying and nearing its end, worn out by old age," in the words of Lucretius[73]—it took over a hundred years before those thought-trains were developed into a sort of consistent philosophical system. That occurred with Epictetus, the Greek slave and the most acute mind, possibly, among the late Stoics. According to him, what must be learned to make life bearable is not really thinking, but "the correct use of imagination," the only thing we have entirely within our power. He still uses a deceptively familiar Greek vocabulary, but what he calls "the reasoning faculty" (*dynamis logikē*) has as little to do with Greek *logos* and *nous* as what he appeals to as "will" has to do with Aristotelian *proairesis*. He calls the faculty of thinking in itself "sterile" (*akarpa*);[74] for him the subject matter of philosophy is each man's own life, and what philosophy teaches man is an "art of living,"[75] how to deal with life, in the same fashion that carpentry teaches an apprentice how to deal with wood. What counts is not "theory" in the abstract but its use and application (*chrēsis tōn theōrēmatōn*); to think and to understand are a mere preparation for action; to "admire the mere power of exposition"—the *logos*, the reasoned argument and train of thought itself—is likely to turn man "into a grammarian instead of a philosopher."[76]

In other words, thinking has become a *technē*, a particular kind of craftsmanship, perhaps to be deemed the highest—certainly the most urgently needed, because its end product is the conduct of your own life. What was meant was not a way of life in the sense of a *bios theōrētikos* or *politikos*, a life devoted to some particular activity, but what Epictetus called "action"— an action in which you acted in unison with no one, which was supposed to change nothing but your self, and which could become manifest only in the *apatheia* and *ataraxia* of the "wise man," that is, in his refusal to react to whatever good or evil might befall him. "I must die, but must I also die sighing? I can't help being chained, but can't I help weeping? . . . You threaten to handcuff me. Man, what are you saying? You can't handcuff me; you manacle my hands. You are threatening to behead me; when did I say that my head could not be cut off?"[77]

Obviously, these are not just exercises in thinking but exercises in the power of the will. "Ask not that events should happen as you will, but let your will be that events should happen as they do, and you shall have peace" is the quintessence of this "wisdom"; for "it is impossible that what happens should be other than it is."⁷⁸

This will be of considerable interest to us when we come to deal with the phenomenon of the will, an altogether different mental capacity, whose chief characteristic, compared with the ability to think, is that it neither speaks in the voice of reflection nor does it use arguments but only imperatives, even when it is commanding nothing more than thought or, rather, imagination. For in order to obtain the radical withdrawal from reality that Epictetus demands, the emphasis on thinking's ability to have present what is absent shifts from reflection to imagination, and this not in the sense of a utopian imagining of another, better, world; rather, the aim is to strengthen the original absent-mindedness of thought to such an extent that reality disappears altogether. If thinking is normally the faculty of making present what is absent, the Epictetian faculty of "dealing with impressions aright" consists in conjuring away and making absent what actually is present. All that existentially concerns you while living in the world of appearances is the "impressions" by which you are affected. Whether what affects you exists or is mere illusion depends on your decision whether or not you will recognize it as real.

Wherever philosophy is understood as the "science" that deals with the mind sheerly as consciousness—where therefore the question of reality can be left in suspense, bracketed out altogether—we encounter in fact the old Stoic position. Only missing is the original motive for making thought a mere instrument which does its business at the bidding of the will as master. In our context, the point is that this bracketing of reality is possible, and not because of the force of will power but because of the very nature of thinking. If one may count Epictetus among the philosophers, it is because he discovered that consciousness makes it possible for mental activities to recoil upon themselves.

If while perceiving an object outside myself I decide to

concentrate on my perception, on the act of seeing instead of the seen object, it is as if I lost the original object, because it loses its impact upon me. I have, so to speak, changed the subject—instead of the tree I now deal merely with the perceived tree, that is, with what Epictetus calls an "impression." This has the great advantage that I am no longer absorbed by the perceived object, something outside myself; the seen tree is inside me, invisible to the outside world as though it had never been a sense-object. The point here is that the "seen tree" is not a thought-thing but an "impression." It is not something absent that needed memory to store it up for the de-sensing process that prepares the mind's objects for thinking and is always preceded by experience in the world of appearances. The seen tree is "inside" me in its full sensory presence, the tree itself deprived only of its realness, an image and not an after-thought about trees. The trick discovered by Stoic philosophy is to use the mind in such a way that reality cannot touch its owner even when he has not withdrawn from it; instead of withdrawing mentally from everything that is present and close at hand, he has drawn every appearance inside himself, and his "consciousness" becomes a full substitute for the outside world presented as impression or image.

It is at this moment that consciousness indeed undergoes a decisive change: it is no longer the silent self-awareness that accompanies all my acts and thoughts and guarantees my identity, the simple I-am-I (nor is it a question here of the strange difference that inserts itself into the core of this identity, which we shall come to later, an insertion peculiar to mental activities because of their recoil upon themselves). Since I am no longer absorbed by an object given to my senses (even though this object, unchanged in its "essential" structure, remains present as an object of consciousness—what Husserl called the "intentional object"), I myself, as sheer consciousness, emerge as an entirely new entity. This new entity can exist in the world in complete independence and sovereignty and yet seemingly remain in possession of this world, namely, of its sheer "essence," stripped of its "existential" character, of its realness that could touch and threaten me in my own.

I have become I-for-myself in an emphatic way, finding in myself everything that was originally given as "alien" reality. It is not so much the mind as this monstrously enlarged consciousness that offers an ever-present, seemingly safe refuge from reality.

This bracketing of reality—getting rid of it by treating it as though it were nothing but a mere "impression"—has remained one of the great temptations of the "professional thinkers," till Hegel, one of the greatest of them, went even further and built his philosophy of the World Spirit on the experiences of the thinking ego: reinterpreting this ego on the model of consciousness, he carried the whole world into consciousness as though it were essentially nothing but a mental phenomenon.

The efficiency, for the philosopher, of turning away from the world into the self is beyond doubt. Existentially speaking, Parmenides was wrong when he said that only Being manifests itself in, and is the same as, thinking. Non-being is also thinkable if the will commands the mind. Its force of withdrawal is then perverted into an annihilating power, and nothingness becomes a full substitute for reality, because nothingness brings relief. The relief, of course, is unreal; it is merely psychological, a soothing of anxiety and fear. I still doubt that there ever was anybody who remained master of his "impressions" when roasted in the Phalarian Bull.

Epictetus, like Seneca, lived under the rule of Nero, that is, under rather desperate conditions, though he himself, unlike Seneca, was scarcely persecuted. But over a hundred years earlier, during the last century of the republic, Cicero, well versed in Greek philosophy, had discovered the thought-trains by which one could take one's way out of the world. He found that such thoughts, by no means as extreme or as carefully elaborated as in Epictetus, were likely to offer comfort and help in the world as it then was (and, of course, always is, more or less). Men who could teach this way of thinking were highly esteemed in Roman literary circles; Lucretius calls Epicurus—who more than two hundred years after his death finally got a pupil worthy of him—"a god" because "he was the first to invent a way of life which is now called wisdom and through his art rescued life from such storms and so much darkness."⁷⁹ For our purposes, however, Lucretius is not such a good example; he does not insist on thinking but on knowing. Knowledge acquired by reason will dispel ignorance and thus destroy the greatest evil—fear, whose source is superstition. A more appropriate example is Cicero's famous "Dream of Scipio."

To understand how extraordinary this concluding chapter of Cicero's *Republic* actually is and how strange its thoughts must have sounded to Roman ears, we must briefly recall the general background against which it was written. Philosophy had found a kind of foster home in Rome during the last century before Christ, and in that thoroughly political society it had first of all to prove that it was good for something. In the *Tusculan Disputations*, we find Cicero's first answer: it was a question of making Rome more beautiful and more civilized. Philosophy was a proper occupation for educated men when they had retired from public life and had no more important things to worry about. There was nothing essential about philosophizing. Nor did it have to do with the divine; to the Romans, founding and conserving political communities were the activities most closely resembling those of the gods. Nor had it any connection with immortality. Immortality was human as well as divine, but was not the property of individual men, "for whom death is not only necessary but frequently desirable." By contrast, it was definitely the potential property of human communities: "If a commonwealth (*civitas*) is destroyed and extinguished, it is as though—to compare small things with great—this whole world were to perish and collapse."⁸⁰ For communities, death is neither necessary nor ever desirable; it comes only as a punishment, "for a community ought to be so constituted that it be eternal."⁸¹ All this is from the treatise that finishes with Scipio's Dream—hence, Cicero, though old now and disappointed, had clearly not changed his mind. As a matter of fact, nothing even in his *Republic* itself prepares us for the Dream of Scipio at the end—except the lamentations of Book 5: "Only in words and because of our vices, and for no other reasons, do we still retain and keep the public thing [the *res publica*, the subject matter of the treatise]; the thing itself we have lost long since."⁸²

And then comes the dream.[83] Scipio Africanus, the victor of Carthage, relates a dream he had shortly before he destroyed the city. The dream showed him a hereafter where he met an ancestor who told him he would destroy Carthage and warned him that after the destruction of the city he would have to restore the public thing in Rome by assuming the supreme authority of Dictator, if only he could escape being assassinated—which, it turned out, he could not. (Cicero meant to say that Scipio might have been able to save the republic.) And in order to do the job properly, to summon up the necessary courage, he is told that he should hold (*sic habeto*) the following to be true: Men who have preserved the *patria* are certain to find their place in heaven and be blessed with eternal time. "For the highest god who governs the world likes nothing better than the assemblies and the intercourse of men which are called commonwealths; their governors and conservators return to heaven after having left this world. Their job on earth is to stand guard over the earth." This, of course, does not imply a Christian promise of resurrection in a hereafter; and although the citation of divine wishes is still in the vein of Roman traditions, there sounds an ominous note: it is as though, failing the promise of such a reward, men might no longer want to do what the public thing demands of them.

For—and this is essential—the rewards of this world, Scipio's ancestor informs him, are in no way sufficient to compensate you for your labors. They are insubstantial and unreal if you think about them from the right perspective: high up in heaven, Scipio is invited to look down on the earth, and the earth appears so small that "he was pained to see our empire as a mere dot." Whereupon he is told: if the earth appears small to you from here, then always look up to the sky so that you may be able to despise human matters.

For what kind of fame is it that you may be able to attain in the conversation of men or what kind of glory among them? Don't you see how narrow the space is in which glory and fame reside? And those who speak about us today, how long will they talk? And even if there were reason to place our trust in tradition and the memory of future generations, one day there will be natural catastrophes—

floods or fire—so that we cannot obtain a long-lasting fame, let alone an eternal one. If you raise your eyes you will see how futile all this is; fame was never eternal, and the oblivion of eternity extinguishes it.

I have given the gist of this passage at some length to make clear how much these proposed thought-trains stand in open contradiction to what Cicero, in common with other educated Romans, had always believed in *and* had expressed even in the same book. In our context, I wanted to offer an example (and an eminent one, perhaps the first recorded in intellectual history) of how certain trains of thought actually aim at thinking oneself out of the world, and by means of *relativization*. In relation to the universe, the earth is but a dot; what does it matter what happens on her? In relation to the immensity of time, centuries are but moments, and oblivion will finally cover everything and everybody; what does it matter what men do? In relation to death, the same for all, everything specific and distinguishing loses its weight; if there is no here-after—and life after death for Cicero is not an article of faith but a moral hypothesis—whatever you do or suffer does not matter. Here thinking means following a sequence of reasoning that will lift you to a viewpoint outside the world of appearances as well as outside your own life. Philosophy is called upon to compensate for the frustrations of politics and, more generally, of life itself.

This is the mere beginning of a tradition that culminated philosophically in Epictetus and reached a climax of intensity about five hundred years later, at the end of the Roman Empire. Boethius' *On the Consolation of Philosophy,* one of the most popular books throughout the Middle Ages and hardly read by anyone today, was written in a condition of extremity of which Cicero had no premonition. Boethius, a noble Roman, had fallen from the height of fortune, found himself in jail, and was awaiting his execution. Because of that setting, the book has been likened to the *Phaedo*—a rather strange analogy: Socrates in the midst of his friends after a trial in which he had been permitted to speak at length in his own defense, awaiting an easy, painless death, and Boethius jailed without a hearing, absolutely alone after the death sentence has been pronounced in a mock trial at which he was not even present, much less given the opportunity to defend himself, and now waiting for execution by slow and abominable tortures. Although he is a Christian, it is Philosophy and neither God nor Christ that comes to console him; and although, while still in high office he had spent his "secret leisure" in studying and translating Plato and Aristotle, he consoles himself with typically Ciceronian and also Stoic thought-trains. Except that what was mere relativization in Scipio's dream is now turned into violent annihilation. The "immense spaces of eternity" to which in duress you must direct your mind annihilate reality as it exists for mortals; the ever-changing nature of Fortune annihilates all pleasures, for even if you enjoy what Fortune has given you (riches, honor, fame), you are in constant fear of losing it. Fear annihilates all happiness. Everything you unthinkingly believe to exist does not exist once you begin to think about it—that is what Philosophy, the goddess of consolation, tells him. And here the question of evil, which is hardly touched upon by Cicero, comes up. The thought-train concerning evil, still rather primitive in Boethius, already contains all the elements we find later in a much more sophisticated and complex form throughout the Middle Ages. It runs thus: God is the final cause of everything that is; God as the "highest good" cannot be the cause of evil; everything that is must have a cause; since there are only apparent causes of evil but no ultimate cause, evil does not exist. The wicked ones, he is told by Philosophy, not only are not powerful, they *are not.* What you unthinkingly consider evil has its place in the order of the universe, and insofar as it is, it is necessarily good. Its bad aspects are an illusion of the senses which you can get rid of by thinking. It is old Stoic advice: What you negate by thought—and thought is in your power—cannot affect you. Thinking makes it unreal. Immediately, of course, we are reminded of Epictetus' glorification of what today would be called will power; and undeniably there is an element of willing in this kind of thinking. To think along these lines means to act upon yourself—the only action left when all acting in the world has become futile.

What is so very striking about this thinking of late antiquity is that it is centered exclusively on the self. To that, John Adams, living in a world in his day not completely out of joint, had an answer: "A death bed, it is said, shows the emptiness of titles. That may be. [However] . . . shall laws and government, which regulate sublunary things, be neglected because they appear baubles at the hour of death?"[84]

I have dealt with two sources from which thinking as we know it historically has sprung, the one Greek, the other Roman, and they are different to the point of being opposites. On the one hand, admiring wonder at the spectacle into which man is born and for whose appreciation he is so well equipped in mind and body; on the other, the awful extremity of having been thrown into a world whose hostility is overwhelming, where fear is predominant and from which man tries his utmost to escape. There are numerous indications that this latter experience was by no means alien to the Greeks. Sophocles' "Not to be born surpasses every *logos;* second-best by far is to go as swiftly as possible whence we came"[85] seems to have been the poet's variation on a proverbial saying. The remarkable fact is that, so far as I know, this mood is nowhere mentioned as a source of Greek thought; perhaps even more remarkable, it has nowhere produced any great philosophy—unless one wants to count Schopenhauer among the great thinkers. But although the Greek and Roman mentalities were worlds apart and though the chief fault of textbook history of philosophy is smoothing out such sharp distinctions—till it sounds as if everybody somehow said vaguely the same thing—it is also true that the two mentalities do have things in common.

In both cases, thinking leaves the world of appearances. Only because thinking implies withdrawal can it be used as an instrument of escape. Moreover, as has already been emphasized, thinking implies an unawareness of the body and of the self and puts in their place the experience of sheer activity, more gratifying, according to Aristotle, than the satisfaction of all the other desires, since for every other pleasure we depend on something or somebody else.[86] Thinking is the only activity that needs nothing but itself for its exercise. "A generous man needs money to perform generous acts . . . and a man of self-control needs the opportunity of temptation."[87] Every other activity of high or low rank has something to over- come outside itself. This is true even of the performing arts, such as flute-playing, whose end and purpose is in the exercise itself—to say nothing of productive works, which are under- taken for their result and not for themselves and where happi- ness, the satisfaction of a job well done, comes after the ac- tivity itself has come to an end. The frugality of philosophers has always been proverbial, and Aristotle mentions this: "a man engaged in theoretical activity has no needs . . . and many things are only a hindrance to it. Only insofar as he is a human being . . . will he need such things for the business of being human [*anthrōpeuesthai*]"—having a body, living together with other men, and so on. In the same vein, Democ- ritus recommends abstinence for thinking: it teaches how the *logos* derives its pleasures from itself (*auton ex heautou*).[88]

The unawareness of the body in the thinking experience combined with the sheer pleasure of the activity explains better than anything else not only the soothing, consoling effects certain thought-trains had on the men of late antiquity but also their curiously extreme theories of the power of mind over body—theories clearly refuted by common experi- ence. Gibbon writes in his comments on Boethius: "Such topics of consolation, so obvious, so vague, or so abstruse, are in- effectual to subdue the feelings of human nature," and the final victory of Christianity, which offered these "topics" of philoso- phy as literal facts and sure promises, proves how right Gibbon was.[89] He added: "Yet the sense of misfortune may be diverted by the labour of thought," and he hinted at least at what actually is the case, namely, that fear for the body disappears as long as the "labour of thought" lasts, not because the con- tents of thought can overcome fear but because the thinking activity makes you unaware of having a body and can even overcome the sensations of minor discomforts. The inordinate strength of this experience may elucidate the otherwise rather strange historical fact that the ancient body-mind dichotomy with its strong hostility to the body could be adopted virtually intact by the Christian creed, which was based after all on the dogma of the incarnation (the Word become Flesh) and on belief in bodily resurrection, that is, on doctrines that should have spelled the end of the body-mind dichotomy and its unsolvable riddles.

Before turning to Socrates, I want to mention briefly the curious context in which the word "philosophize," the verb, not the noun, makes its first appearance. Herodotus tells us of Solon, who, having framed the laws for Athens, set out upon ten years of travel, partly for political reasons but also for sight-seeing—*theōrein*. He arrived at Sardis, where Croesus was at the height of his power. And Croesus, after having shown Solon all his riches, addressed him thus: "Stranger, great word has come to us about you, your wisdom and your wandering about, namely, that you have gone visiting many lands of the earth *philosophizing* with respect to the spectacles you saw. Therefore it occurred to me to ask you if you saw one whom you considered the happiest of all."[90] (The rest of the story is familiar: Croesus, expecting to be named the happiest man on earth, is told that no man, no matter how lucky he is, can be called happy before his death.) Croesus addresses Solon not because he has seen so many lands but because he is famous for philosophizing, reflecting upon what he sees; and Solon's answer, though based on experience, is clearly beyond experience. For the question, Who is the happiest of all?, he had substituted the question, What is happiness for mortals? And his answer to this question was a *philosophoumenon*, a reflection on human affairs (*anthrōpeiōn pragmatōn*) and on the length of human life, in which not one day is "like the other," so that "man is wholly chance." Under such conditions it is wise "to wait and mark the end,"[91] for man's life is a story and only the end of the story, when everything is completed, can tell you what it was all about. Human life, because it is marked by a beginning and an end, becomes whole, an entity in itself that can be subjected to judgment, only when it has ended in death; death not merely ends life, it also bestows upon it a silent completeness, snatched from the hazardous flux to which all things human are subject. This is the gist of what later became a proverbial *topos* throughout Greek and Latin antiquity—*nemo ante mortem beatus dici potest.*⁹²

Solon himself was well aware of the difficult nature of such deceptively simple propositions. In a fragment that ties in very well with the story told by Herodotus, he is recorded as saying: "Most hard it is to perceive the hidden (*aphanes*) measure of judgment, which nevertheless [even though it does not appear] holds the limits of all things."⁹³ Here Solon sounds like a predecessor of Socrates, who also, as they said later, wanted to bring philosophy down from the sky to the earth and hence began to examine the invisible measures by which we judge human affairs. When asked who is the happiest among men, Solon responded by raising the question, And what if you please is happiness, how are you to measure it?— in the same way that Socrates was to raise the questions, What are courage, piety, friendship, *sōphrosynē*, knowledge, justice, and so on?

But Solon gives a kind of answer, and this answer, rightly understood in its implications, even contains what people today would call a whole philosophy in the sense of *Weltanschauung*: the uncertainty of the future makes human life miserable, "danger is inherent in all works and deeds, nobody knows how a thing begun will turn out, one who does well fails to foresee what ill fortune may befall him, while a god gives good luck in everything to the evildoer."⁹⁴ Hence, the "No man can be called happy while he is still alive" actually means: "No man is happy; all mortals on whom the Sun gazes are wretches."⁹⁵ This is more than a reflection; it is already a kind of doctrine and as such un-Socratic. For Socrates, confronted with such questions, concludes virtually every strictly Socratic dialogue by saying: "I have failed utterly to discover what it is."⁹⁶ And this aporetic character of Socratic thinking means: admiring wonder at just or courageous deeds seen by the eyes of the body gives birth to such questions as What is courage? What is justice? The existence of courage or justice has been indicated to my senses by what I have seen, though they themselves are not present in sense perception, and hence not given as self-evident reality. The basic Socratic question—What do we *mean* when we use this class of words, later called "concepts"?—arises out of that experience. But the original wonder is not only not resolved in such questions, since they remain without answer, but even reinforced. What begins as wonder ends in perplexity and thence leads back to wonder: How marvelous that men can perform courageous or just deeds even though they do not know, can give no account of, what courage and justice are.

17   *The answer of Socrates*

To the question What makes us think? I have been giving (except in Solon's case) historically representative answers offered by professional philosophers. These answers are dubious for precisely that reason. The question, when asked by the professional, does not arise out of his own experiences while engaged in thinking. It is asked from outside—whether that outside is constituted by his professional interests as a thinker or by the common sense in himself that makes him question an activity that is out of order in ordinary living. And the answers we then receive are always too general and vague to have much sense for everyday living, in which thinking, after all, constantly occurs and constantly interrupts the ordinary processes of life—just as ordinary living constantly interrupts thinking. If we strip these answers of their doctrinal content, which of course varies enormously, all we get are confessions of a need: the need to concretize the implications of the Platonic wonder, the need (in Kant) of the reasoning faculty to transcend the limitations of the knowable, the need to become reconciled with what actually is and the course of the world—appearing in Hegel as "the need for philosophy," which can transform occurrences outside yourself into your own thoughts—or the need to search for the meaning of whatever is or occurs, as I have been saying here, no less generally, no less vaguely.

It is this helplessness of the thinking ego to give an account of itself that has made the philosophers, the professional thinkers, such a difficult tribe to deal with. For the trouble is that the thinking ego, as we have seen—in distinction from the self that, of course, exists in every thinker, too—has no urge to appear in the world of appearances. It is a slippery fellow, not only invisible to others but also, for the self, impalpable, impossible to grasp. This is partly because it is sheer activity, and partly because—as Hegel once said—"[as] an abstract ego it is liberated from the particularity of all other properties, dispositions, etc., and is active only with respect to the general, which is the same for all individuals."⁹⁷ In any case, seen from the world of appearances, from the marketplace, the thinking ego always lives in hiding, *lathē biōsas.* And our question, What makes us think?, is actually inquiring about ways and means to bring it out of hiding, to tease it, as it were, into manifestation.

The best, in fact the only, way I can think of to get hold of the question is to look for a model, an example of a thinker who was not a professional, who in his person unified two apparently contradictory passions, for thinking and acting—not in the sense of being eager to apply his thoughts or to establish theoretical standards for action but in the much more relevant sense of being equally at home in both spheres and able to move from one sphere to the other with the greatest apparent ease, very much as we ourselves constantly move back and forth between experiences in the world of appearances and the need for reflecting on them. Best suited for this role would be a man who counted himself neither among the many nor among the few (a distinction at least as old as Pythagoras), who had no aspiration to be a ruler of men, no claim even to be particularly well fitted by his superior wisdom to act in an advisory capacity to those in power, but not a man who submitted meekly to being ruled either; in brief, a thinker who always remained a man among men, who did not shun the marketplace, who was a citizen among citizens, doing nothing, claiming nothing except what in his opinion every citizen should be and have a right to. Such a man ought to be difficult to find: if he were able to represent for us the actual thinking activity, he would not have left a body of doctrine behind; he would not have cared to write down his thoughts even if, after he was through with thinking, there had been any residue tangible enough to set out in black and white. You will have guessed that I am thinking of Socrates. We would not know much about him, at least not enough to impress us greatly, if he had not made such an enormous impression on Plato, and we might not know anything about him, perhaps not even from Plato, if he had not decided to lay down his life, not for any specific belief or doctrine—he had none—but simply for the right to go about examining the opinions of other people, thinking about them and asking his interlocutors to do the same.

I hope the reader will not believe that I chose Socrates at random. But I must give a warning: there is a great deal of controversy about the historical Socrates, and though this is one of the more fascinating topics of learned contention, I shall ignore it[98] and only mention in passing what is likely to be the chief bone of contention—namely, my belief that there exists a sharp dividing line between what is authentically Socratic and the philosophy taught by Plato. The stumbling block here is the fact that Plato used Socrates as *the* philosopher, not only in the early and clearly "Socratic" dialogues but also later, when he often made him the spokesman for theories and doctrines that were entirely un-Socratic. In many instances, Plato himself clearly marked the differences, for example, in the *Symposium,* in Diotima's famous speech, which tells us expressly that Socrates does not know anything about the "greater mysteries" and may not be able to understand them. In other instances, however, the line is blurred, usually because Plato could still reckon on a reading public that would be aware of certain enormous inconsistencies—as when he lets Socrates say in the *Theaetetus*[99] that "great philosophers . . . from their youth up have never known the way to the marketplace," an anti-Socratic statement if ever there was one. And yet, to make matters worse, this by no means signifies that the same dialogue does not give fully authentic information about the real Socrates.[100]

No one, I think, will seriously dispute that my choice is historically justifiable. Less easily justifiable, perhaps, is the transformation of a historical figure into a model, for there is no doubt that some transformation is necessary if the figure in question is to perform the function we assign to it. Etienne Gilson, in his great book about Dante, wrote that in *The Divine Comedy* "a character . . . conserves . . . as much of its historical reality as the representative function that Dante assigns to it requires."[101] It seems easy enough to grant this kind of freedom to poets and to call it license—but worse when non-poets try their hand at it. Yet, justified or not, that is precisely what we do when we construct "ideal types"—not out of whole cloth, as in the allegories and personified abstractions so dear to the hearts of bad poets and some scholars, but out of the crowd of living beings past or present who seem to possess a representative significance. And Gilson hints at least at the true justification of this method (or technique) when he discusses the representative part assigned by Dante to Aquinas: the real Thomas, Gilson points out, would not have done what Dante made him do—eulogize Siger of Brabant—but the only reason that the real Thomas would have declined to pronounce such a eulogy would have been a certain human weakness, a defect of character, "the part of his make-up," as Gilson says, "which he had to leave at the gate of the *Paradiso* before he could enter."[102] There are a number of traits in the Xenophonian Socrates, whose historical credibility need not be doubted, that Socrates might have had to leave at the gate of Paradise.

The first thing that strikes us in Plato's Socratic dialogues is that they are all aporetic. The argument either leads nowhere or goes around in circles. In order to know what justice is, you must know what knowledge is, and in order to know that, you must have a previous, unexamined notion of knowledge.[103] Hence, "a man cannot try to discover either what he knows or what he does not know. If he knows, there is no need of inquiry; if he does not know . . . he does not even know what he is to look for."[104] Or, in the *Euthyphro:* in order to be pious you must know what piety is. The things that please the gods are pious; but are they pious because they please the gods or do they please the gods because they are pious?

None of the *logoi*, the arguments, ever stays put; they move around. And because Socrates, asking questions to which he does *not* know the answers, sets them in motion, once the statements have come full circle, it is usually Socrates who cheerfully proposes to start all over again and inquire what justice or piety or knowledge or happiness are.[105] For the topics of these early dialogues deal with very simple, everyday concepts, such as arise whenever people open their mouths and begin to talk. The introduction usually runs as follows: to be sure, there are happy people, just deeds, courageous men, beautiful things to see and admire, everybody knows about them; the trouble starts with our nouns, presumably derived from the adjectives we apply to particular cases as they *appear* to us (we *see* a happy man, *perceive* the courageous deed or the just decision). In short, the trouble arrives with such words as *happiness, courage, justice,* and so on, what we now call concepts—Solon's "non-appearing measure" (*aphanes metron*) "most difficult for the mind to comprehend, but nevertheless holding the limits of all things"[106]—and what Plato somewhat later called ideas perceivable only by the eyes of the mind. These words are part and parcel of our everyday speech, and still we can give no account of them; when we try to define them, they get slippery; when we talk about their meaning, nothing stays put any more, everything begins to move. So instead of repeating what we learned from Aristotle, that Socrates was the man who discovered the "concept," we shall ask what Socrates did when he discovered it. For surely these words were part of the Greek language before he tried to force the Athenians and himself to give an account of what they and he meant—in the firm belief, of course, that no speech would be possible without them.

Today that is no longer so certain. Our knowledge of the so-called primitive languages has taught us that the grouping together of many particulars under a name common to all of them is by no means a matter of course; these languages, whose vocabulary is often so remarkably rich, lack such abstract nouns even in relation to clearly visible objects. To simplify matters, let us take a noun which to us no longer sounds abstract at all. We can use the word "house" for a great number of objects—for the mud hut of a tribe, for the palace of a king, the country home of a city dweller, the cottage in the village, the apartment house in town—but we can hardly use it for the movable tents of some nomads. The house in and by itself, *auto kath'auto,* that which makes us use the word for all these particular and very different buildings, is never seen, either by the eyes of the body or by those of the mind; every imagined house, be it ever so abstract, having the bare minimum to make it recognizable, is already a particular house. This other, invisible, house, of which we must have a notion in order to recognize particular buildings as houses, has been explained in different ways and called by different names in the history of philosophy; with this we are not concerned here, although we might find it less hard to define than such words as "happiness" or "justice." The point here is that it implies something considerably less tangible than the structure perceived by our eyes. It implies "housing somebody" and being "dwelt in" as no tent, put up today and taken down tomorrow, could house or serve as a dwelling place. The word "house" is the "unseen measure," "holds the limits of all things" pertaining to dwelling; it is a word that could not exist unless one presupposed thinking about being housed, dwelling, having a home. As a word, "house" is shorthand for all these things, the kind of shorthand without which thinking and its characteristic swiftness would not be possible at all. *The word "house" is something like a frozen thought that thinking must unfreeze* whenever it wants to find out the original meaning. In medieval philosophy, this kind of thinking was called "meditation," and the word should be heard as different from, even opposed to, contemplation. At all events, this kind of pondering reflection does not produce definitions and in that sense is entirely without results, though somebody who had pondered the meaning of "house" might make his own look better.

Socrates, at any rate, is commonly said to have believed in the teachability of virtue, and he seems indeed to have held that talking and thinking about piety, justice, courage, and the rest were likely to make men more pious, more just, more courageous, despite the fact that neither definitions nor "values" were given them to direct their future conduct. What

Socrates actually believed in such matters can best be illustrated by the similes he applied to himself. He called himself
a gadfly and a midwife; in Plato's account somebody else
called him an "electric ray," a fish that paralyzes and numbs
by contact, and Socrates recognized the likeness as apt, provided that his hearers understood that "the electric ray paralyzes others only through being paralyzed itself. . . . It isn't
that, knowing the answers myself, I perplex other people. The
truth is rather that I infect them also with the perplexity I feel
myself."[107] Which, of course, sums up neatly the only way thinking can be taught—even though Socrates, as he repeatedly
said, did not teach anything, for the simple reason that he had
nothing to teach; he was "sterile" like the midwives in Greece,
who were beyond the age of childbearing. (Since he had nothing to teach, no truth to hand out, he was accused of never
revealing his own view [*gnōmē*]—as we learn from Xenophon,
who defended him against the charge.)[108] It seems that he,
unlike the professional philosophers, felt the urge to check
with his fellow-men to learn whether his perplexities were
shared by them—and this is quite different from the inclination
to find solutions for riddles and then demonstrate them to
others.

Let us look briefly at the three similes. First, Socrates is
a gadfly: he knows how to sting the citizens who, without him,
will "sleep on undisturbed for the rest of their lives" unless
somebody comes along to arouse them. And what does he
arouse them to? To thinking and examination, an activity without which life, in his view, was not only not worth much but
was not fully alive. (On this subject, in the *Apology* as in other
cases, Socrates is saying very nearly the opposite of what Plato
made him say in the "improved apology" of the *Phaedo*. In
the *Apology*, Socrates tells his fellow-citizens why he should
live and also why, though life is "very dear" to him, he is not
afraid of death; in the *Phaedo*, he explains to his friends how
burdensome life is and why he is glad to die.)

Second, Socrates is a midwife: in the *Theaetetus*, he says
that it is because he is sterile himself that he knows how to
deliver others of their thoughts; moreover, thanks to his

sterility, he has the expert knowledge of the midwife and can decide whether the child is a real child or a mere wind-egg of which the bearer must be cleansed. But in the dialogues, hardly anybody among Socrates' interlocutors has brought forth a thought that is not a wind-egg and that Socrates considered worth keeping alive. Rather, he did what Plato in the *Sophist*, certainly thinking of Socrates, said of the sophists: he purged people of their "opinions," that is, of those unexamined pre-judgments that would prevent them from thinking —helping them, as Plato said, to get rid of the bad in them, their opinions, yet without making them good, giving them truth.[109]

Third, Socrates, knowing that we do not know, and nevertheless unwilling to let it go at that, remains steadfast in his own perplexities and, like the electric ray, paralyzed himself, paralyzes anyone he comes into contact with. The electric ray, at first glance, seems to be the opposite of the gadfly; it paralyzes where the gadfly rouses. Yet what cannot fail to look like paralysis from the outside—from the standpoint of ordinary human affairs—is *felt* as the highest state of being active and alive. There exist, despite the scarcity of documentary evidence about the thinking experience, a number of utterances of thinkers throughout the centuries to bear this out.

Hence, Socrates, gadfly, midwife, electric ray, is not a philosopher (he teaches nothing and has nothing to teach) and he is not a sophist, for he does not claim to make men wise. He only points out to them that they are not wise, that nobody is—a "pursuit" keeping him so busy that he has no time for either public or private affairs.[110] And while he defends himself vigorously against the charge of corrupting the young, he nowhere pretends that he is improving them. Nevertheless, he claims that the appearance in Athens of thinking and examining represented in himself was the greatest good that ever befell the City.[111] Thus he was concerned with what thinking is good for, although, in this, as in all other respects, he did not give a clear-cut answer. We may be sure that a dialogue dealing with the question What is thinking good for? would have ended in the same perplexities as all the others.

If there had been a Socratic tradition in Western thought,

if, in Whitehead's words, the history of philosophy were a collection of footnotes not to Plato but to Socrates (which, of course, would have been impossible), we certainly would find in it no answer to our question, but at least a number of variations of it. Socrates himself, well aware that he was dealing with invisibles in his enterprise, used a metaphor to explain the thinking activity—the metaphor of the wind: "The winds themselves are invisible, yet what they do is manifest to us and we somehow feel their approach."[112] We find the same metaphor in Sophocles, who (in the *Antigone*)[113] counts "windswift thought" among the dubious, "awe-inspiring" (*deina*) things with which men are blessed or cursed. In our own time, Heidegger occasionally speaks of the "storm of thought," and he uses the metaphor explicitly at the only point in his work where he speaks directly of Socrates: "Throughout his life and up to his very death Socrates did nothing other than place himself in this draft, this current [of thinking], and maintain himself in it. This is why he is the purest of the West. This is why he wrote nothing. For anyone who begins, out of thinking, to write must inevitably be like those people who run for shelter from a wind too strong for them . . . all thinkers after Socrates, their greatness notwithstanding, were such refugees. Thinking became literature." In a later explanatory note he adds that to be the "purest" thinker does not mean to be the greatest.[114]

In the context in which Xenophon, always anxious to defend the master with his own vulgar arguments against vulgar accusations, mentions this metaphor, it does not make much sense. Still, even he indicates that the invisible wind of thought was manifest in the concepts, virtues, and "values" with which Socrates dealt in his examinations. The trouble is that this same wind, whenever it is roused, has the peculiarity of doing away with its own previous manifestations: this is why the same man can be understood and understand himself as gadfly as well as electric ray. It is in this invisible element's nature to undo, unfreeze, as it were, what language, the medium of thinking, has frozen into thought—words (concepts, sentences, definitions, doctrines) whose "weakness" and inflexibility Plato denounces so splendidly in the *Seventh Letter*. The conse-

quence is that thinking inevitably has a destructive, under-
mining effect on all established criteria, values, measurements
of good and evil, in short, on those customs and rules of conduct we treat of in morals and ethics. These frozen thoughts,
Socrates seems to say, come so handily that you can use them
in your sleep; but if the wind of thinking, which I shall now
stir in you, has shaken you from your sleep and made you
fully awake and alive, then you will see that you have nothing
in your grasp but perplexities, and the best we can do with
them is share them with each other.

Hence, the paralysis induced by thinking is twofold: it is
inherent in the *stop* and think, the interruption of all other
activities—psychologically, one may indeed define a "problem"
as a "situation which for some reason appreciably holds up
an organism in its effort to reach a goal"[115]—and it also may
have a dazing after-effect, when you come out of it, feeling
unsure of what seemed to you beyond doubt while you were
unthinkingly engaged in whatever you were doing. If what
you were doing consisted in applying general rules of conduct
to particular cases as they arise in ordinary life, you will find
yourself paralyzed because no such rules can withstand the
wind of thought. To take again the example of the frozen
thought inherent in the word "house," once you have thought
about its implied meaning—dwelling, having a home, being
housed—you are no longer as likely to accept for your own
home whatever the fashion of the time may prescribe; but this
by no means guarantees that you will be able to come up with
an acceptable solution to what has become "problematic."

This leads to the last and, perhaps, even greatest danger
of this dangerous and profitless enterprise. In the circle around
Socrates, there were men like Alcibiades and Critias—God
knows, by no means the worst among his so-called pupils—
who had turned out to be a real threat to the polis, and this
not because they had been paralyzed by the electric ray but,
on the contrary, because they had been aroused by the gadfly.
What they had been aroused to was license and cynicism.
Not content with being taught how to think without being
taught a doctrine, they changed the non-results of the Socratic
thinking examination into negative results: If we cannot define

what piety is, let us be impious—which is pretty much the opposite of what Socrates had hoped to achieve by talking about piety.

The quest for meaning, which relentlessly dissolves and examines anew all accepted doctrines and rules, can at any moment turn against itself, produce a reversal of the old values, and declare these contraries to be "new values." To a certain extent, this is what Nietzsche did when he reversed Platonism, forgetting that a reversed Plato is still Plato, or what Marx did when he turned Hegel upside down, producing a strictly Hegelian system of history in the process. Such negative results of thinking will then be used with the same unthinking routine as before; the moment they are applied to the realm of human affairs, it is as though they had never gone through the thinking process. What we commonly call "nihilism"—and are tempted to date historically, decry politically, and ascribe to thinkers who allegedly dared to think "dangerous thoughts"—is actually a danger inherent in the thinking activity itself. There are no dangerous thoughts; thinking itself is dangerous, but nihilism is not its product. Nihilism is but the other side of conventionalism; its creed consists of negations of the current so-called positive values, to which it remains bound. All critical examinations must go through a stage of at least hypothetically negating accepted opinions and "values" by searching out their implications and tacit assumptions, and in this sense nihilism may be seen as an ever-present danger of thinking.

But that danger does not arise out of the Socratic conviction that an unexamined life is not worth living, but, on the contrary, out of the desire to find results that would make further thinking unnecessary. Thinking is equally dangerous to all creeds and, by itself, does not bring forth any new creed. Its most dangerous aspect from the viewpoint of common sense is that what was meaningful while you were thinking dissolves the moment you want to apply it to everyday living. When common opinion gets hold of the "concepts," that is, the manifestations of thinking in everyday speech, and begins to handle them as though they were the results of cognition, the end can only be a clear demonstration that no man is wise. Practically, thinking means that each time you are confronted with some difficulty in life you have to make up your mind anew.

However, non-thinking, which seems so recommendable a state for political and moral affairs, also has its perils. By shielding people from the dangers of examination, it teaches them to hold fast to whatever the prescribed rules of conduct may be at a given time in a given society. What people then get used to is less the content of the rules, a close examination of which would always lead them into perplexity, than the *possession* of rules under which to subsume particulars. If somebody appears who, for whatever purposes, wishes to abolish the old "values" or virtues, he will find that easy enough, provided he offers a new code, and he will need relatively little force and no persuasion—i.e., proof that the new values are better than the old—to impose it. The more firmly men hold to the old code, the more eager will they be to assimilate themselves to the new one, which in practice means that the readiest to obey will be those who were the most respectable pillars of society, the least likely to indulge in thoughts, dangerous or otherwise, while those who to all appearances were the most unreliable elements of the old order will be the least tractable.

If ethical and moral matters really are what the etymology of the words indicates, it should be no more difficult to change the mores and habits of a people than it would be to change their table manners. The ease with which such a reversal can take place under certain conditions suggests indeed that everybody was fast asleep when it occurred. I am alluding, of course, to what happened in Nazi Germany and, to some extent, also in Stalinist Russia, when suddenly the basic commandments of Western morality were reversed: in one case, "Thou shalt not kill"; in the other, "Thou shalt not bear false witness against thy neighbor." And the sequel—the reversal of the reversal, the fact that it was so surprisingly easy "to re-educate" the Germans after the collapse of the Third

Reich, so easy indeed that it was as though re-education was automatic—should not console us either. It was actually the same phenomenon.

To come back to Socrates. The Athenians told him that thinking was subversive, that the wind of thought was a hurricane sweeping away all the established signs by which men orient themselves, bringing disorder into the cities and confusing the citizens. And though Socrates denies that thinking corrupts, he does not pretend that it improves anybody either. It rouses you from sleep, and this seems to him a great good for the City. Yet he does not say that he began his examining in order to become such a great benefactor. As far as he himself is concerned, there is nothing more to be said than that life deprived of thought would be meaningless, even though thought will never make men wise or give them the answers to thought's own questions. The meaning of what Socrates was doing lay in the activity itself. Or to put it differently: To think and to be fully alive are the same, and this implies that thinking must always begin afresh; it is an activity that accompanies living and is concerned with such concepts as justice, happiness, virtue, offered us by language itself as expressing the meaning of whatever happens in life and occurs to us while we are alive.

What I called the "quest" for meaning appears in Socrates' language as love, that is, love in its Greek significance of Erōs, not the Christian agapē. Love as Eros is primarily a need; it desires what it has not. Men love wisdom and therefore begin to philosophize because they are not wise, and they love beauty, and do beauty, as it were—philokaloumen, as Pericles called it in the Funeral Oration[116]—because they are not beautiful. Love is the only matter in which Socrates pretends to be an expert, and this skill guides him, too, in choosing his companions and friends: "While I may be worthless in all other matters, this talent I have been given: I can easily recognize a lover and a beloved."[117] By desiring what it has not, love establishes a relationship with what is not present. In order to bring this relationship into the open, make it appear, men want to speak about it—just as the lover wants to speak about the beloved. Because thought's quest is a kind of desirous love, the objects of thought can only be lovable things—beauty, wisdom, justice, and so on. Ugliness and evil are almost by definition excluded from the thinking concern. They may turn up as deficiencies, ugliness consisting in lack of beauty, evil, *kakia,* in lack of the good. As such, they have no roots of their own, no essence that thought could get hold of. If thinking dissolves positive concepts into their original meaning, then the same process must dissolve these "negative" concepts into their original meaninglessness, that is, into nothing for the thinking ego. That is why Socrates believed no one could do evil voluntarily—because of, as we would say, its ontological status: it consists in an absence, in something that is not. And that is also why Democritus, who thought of *logos,* speech, as following action in the same way that the shadow accompanies all real things, thus distinguishing them from mere semblances, counseled against speaking of evil deeds: ignoring evil, depriving it of any manifestation in speech, will turn it into a mere semblance, something that has no shadow.[118] We found the same exclusion of evil when we were following Plato's admiring, affirming wonder as it unfolds into thinking; it is found in almost all Occidental philosophers. It looks as though Socrates had nothing more to say about the connection between evil and lack of thought than that people who are not in love with beauty, justice, and wisdom are incapable of thought, just as, conversely, those who are in love with examining and thus "do philosophy" would be incapable of doing evil.

18   *The two-in-one*

Where does this leave us in regard to one of our chief problems—the possible interconnectedness of non-thought and evil? We are left with the conclusion that only people inspired by the Socratic *erōs,* the love of wisdom, beauty, and justice, are capable of thought and can be trusted. In other words, we are left with Plato's "noble natures," with the few of whom it may be true that none "does evil voluntarily." Yet the implied and dangerous conclusion, "Everybody wants to do good," is not true even in their case. (The sad truth of the matter is that most evil is done by people who never made up their minds to be or do either evil or good.) Socrates, who, unlike Plato, thought about all subjects and talked with everybody, cannot have believed that only the few are capable of thought and that only certain objects of thought, visible to the eyes of the well-trained mind but ineffable in discourse, bestow dignity and relevance on the thinking activity. If there is any-thing in thinking that can prevent men from doing evil, it must be some property inherent in the activity itself, regardless of its objects.

Socrates, that lover of perplexities, made very few positive statements. Among them are two propositions, closely inter-connected, that deal with this subject. Both occur in the *Gorgias*, the dialogue about rhetoric, the art of addressing and convincing the many. The *Gorgias* does not belong among the early Socratic dialogues; it was written shortly before Plato became the head of the Academy. Moreover, its very subject matter is an art or form of discourse that would seemingly lose all sense if it were aporetic. And yet, this dialogue is still aporetic, except that Plato concludes it with one of his myths of a hereafter of rewards and punishments which apparently— that is, ironically—resolve all difficulties. The seriousness of these myths of his is purely political; it consists in their being addressed to the multitude. Yet the myths, certainly non-Socratic, of the *Gorgias* are of importance because they con-tain, albeit in a non-philosophical form, Plato's admission that men do commit evil acts voluntarily, and the additional im-plied admission that he, no more than Socrates, knew what to do philosophically with that disturbing fact. We may not know whether Socrates believed that ignorance causes evil and that virtue can be taught; but we do know that Plato thought it wiser to rely on threats.

The two positive Socratic propositions read as follows.

The first: "It is better to be wronged than to do wrong," to which Callicles, the interlocutor in the dialogue, replies as all Greece would have replied, "To suffer wrong is not the part of a man at all, but that of a slave for whom it is better to be dead than alive, as it is for anyone who is unable to come either to his own assistance when he is wronged or to that of anyone he cares about."[119] The second: "It would be better for me that my lyre or a chorus I directed should be out of tune and loud with discord, and that multitudes of men should disagree with me rather than that I, *being one*, should be out of harmony with myself and contradict me."[120] Which causes Callicles to tell Socrates that he is "going mad with eloquence," and that it would be better for him and everybody else if he would leave philosophy alone.[121]

And there he has a point. It was indeed philosophy, or, rather, the experience of thinking, that led Socrates to make these statements—although, of course, he did not start his enterprise in order to arrive at them, any more than other thinkers embarked upon theirs in order to be "happy."[122] (It would be a serious mistake, I believe, to understand these statements as the results of some cogitation about morality; they are insights, to be sure, but insights of experience, and as far as the thinking process itself is concerned they are at best incidental by-products.)

We have difficulty realizing how paradoxical the first statement must have sounded when it was made; after thousands of years of use and misuse, it reads like cheap moralizing. And the best demonstration of how difficult it is for modern readers to understand the thrust of the second is the fact that its key words, *"Being one"* (preceding "it would be worse for me to be at odds with myself than in disagreement with multitudes of men"), are frequently left out in translation. As to the first, it is a subjective statement; it means: it is better *for me* to suffer wrong than to do wrong. And in the dialogue where it occurs, it is simply countered by the opposite equally subjective statement, which, of course, sounds much more plausible. What becomes apparent is that Callicles and Socrates are talking about a different I: What is good for one is bad for the other.

If, on the other hand, we look at the proposition from the point of view of the world, as distinguished from those of the two speakers, we would have to say: What counts is that a wrong has been done; and for this, it is irrelevant who is better off, the wrong-doer or the wrong-sufferer. As citizens, we must prevent wrong-doing because the world in which we all live, wrong-doer, wrong-sufferer, and spectator, is at stake; the City has been wronged. Our law codes, with their distinction between crimes where indictment is mandatory and transgressions that pertain only to the private affairs of individuals who may or may not want to sue, take this into account. We could almost define a crime as that transgression of the law that demands punishment regardless of the one who has been wronged; the wronged one may feel like forgiving and forgetting, and there may be no danger for others if it can be assumed that the wrong-doer is altogether unlikely to do wrong again. Still, the law of the land permits no option because it is the community as a whole that has been violated.

In other words, Socrates is not talking here in the person of the citizen, who is supposed to be more concerned with the world than with his self; he talks as the man chiefly devoted to thinking. It is as though he said to Callicles: If you were like me, in love with wisdom and in need of thinking about everything and examining everything, you would know that if the world were as you depict it, divided into the strong and the weak, where "the strong do what they can and the weak suffer what they must" (Thucydides), so that no alternative exists but to either do or suffer wrong, then it is better to suffer than to do. But the presupposition is of course: *if you are in love with wisdom and philosophizing; if* you know what it means to examine.

To my knowledge there is only one other passage in Greek literature that, in almost the same words, says what Socrates said. "More unfortunate [*kakodaimonesteros*] than the wronged one is the wrong-doer,"[123] reads one of the fragments of Democritus, Parmenides' great adversary, who probably for this reason is never mentioned by Plato. The coincidence seems noteworthy because Democritus, as distinguished from Socrates, was not particularly interested in human affairs but he seems to have been quite interested in the experience of thinking. It looks as though what we are tempted to understand as a purely moral proposition actually arose out of the thinking experience as such.

And this brings us to the second statement, which in fact is the prerequisite for the first one. It, too, is highly paradoxical. Socrates talks of being one and *therefore* not being able to risk getting out of harmony with himself. But nothing that is identical with itself, truly and absolutely *One*, as A is A, can be either in or out of harmony with itself; you always need at least two tones to produce a harmonious sound. Certainly when I appear and am seen by others, I am one; otherwise I would be unrecognizable. And so long as I am together with others, barely conscious of myself, I am as I appear to others. We call *consciousness* (literally, as we have seen, "to know with myself") the curious fact that in a sense I also am for myself, though I hardly appear to me, which indicates that the Socratic "being one" is not so unproblematic as it seems; I am not only for others but for myself, and in this latter case, I clearly am not just one. A difference is inserted into my Oneness.

We know of this difference in other respects. Everything that exists among a plurality of things is not simply what it is, in its identity, but it is also different from others; this being different belongs to its very nature. When we try to get hold of it in thought, wanting to define it, we must take this otherness (*altereitas*) or difference into account. When we say what a thing is, we must say what it is *not* or we would speak in tautologies: every determination is negation, as Spinoza has it. Touching on this matter, the problem of identity and difference, there is a curious passage in Plato's *Sophist* that Heidegger has pointed to. The Stranger in the dialogue states that of two things—for instance, rest and motion—"each one is different [from the other], but itself *for itself* the same" (*hekaston heautō tauton*).[124] In interpreting the sentence, Heidegger puts the emphasis on the dative, *heautō*, for Plato does not say, as we would expect, *hekaston auto tauton*, "each one itself [taken out of context] is the same," in the sense of the tautological A is A, where difference arises out of the plurality of things. According to Heidegger, this dative means that "each thing itself is returned to itself, each itself is the same for itself [because it is] with itself. . . . Sameness implies the relation of 'with,' that is, a mediation, a connection, a synthesis: the unification into a unity."[125]

The passage Heidegger is examining occurs in the *Sophist's* final section about the *koinōnia*, the "community," the fitting and blending together, of the Ideas, and especially about the possible community of Difference and Identity, which seem to be contraries. "What is different is always so called with reference to other things" (*pros alla*),[126] but their opposites, things "that are what they are in themselves" (*kath' hauta*), partake in the "Idea" of difference insofar as they "refer back to themselves"—they are the same with or for themselves, so that each *eidos* is different from the rest, "not by virtue of its own nature, but because it partakes of the character of Difference,"[127] that is, not because it has a relation to something else from which it is different (*pros ti*), but because it exists among a plurality of Ideas, and "every entity qua entity harbors the possibility of being looked upon as different from something."[128] In our terms, wherever there is a plurality—of living beings, of things, of Ideas—there is difference, and this difference does not arise from the outside but is inherent in every entity in the form of duality, from which comes unity as unification.

This construction—Plato's implication as well as Heidegger's interpretation—seems to me erroneous. To take a mere thing out of its context with other things and to look on it only in its "relation" to itself (*kath' hauto*), that is, in its identity, reveals no difference, no otherness; along with its relation to something it is *not*, it loses its reality and acquires a curious kind of eeriness. In that way, it often appears in works of art, especially in Kafka's early prose pieces or in some paintings of van Gogh where a single object, a chair, a pair of shoes, is represented. But these art works are thought-things, and what gives them their meaning—as though they were not just themselves but *for* themselves—is precisely the transformation they have undergone when thinking took possession of them. In other words, what is being transferred here is the experience of the thinking ego to things themselves. For nothing can be itself and at the same time for itself but the two-in-one that Socrates discovered as the essence of thought and Plato translated into conceptual language as the soundless dialogue *eme emautō*—between me and myself.[129] But, again, it is not the thinking activity that constitutes the unity, unifies the two-in-one; on the contrary, the two-in-one become One again when the outside world intrudes upon the thinker and cuts short the thinking process. Then, when he is called by his name back into the world of appearances, where he is always One, it is as though the two into which the thinking process had split him clapped together again. Thinking, existentially speaking, is a solitary but not a lonely business; solitude is that human situation in which I keep myself company. Loneliness comes about when I am alone without being able to split up into the two-in-one, without being able to keep myself company, when, as Jaspers used to say, "I am in default of myself" (*ich bleibe mir aus*), or, to put it differently, when I am one and without company.

Nothing perhaps indicates more strongly that man exists *essentially* in the plural than that his solitude actualizes his merely being conscious of himself, which we probably share with the higher animals, into a duality during the thinking activity. It is this *duality* of myself with myself that makes thinking a true activity, in which I am both the one who asks and the one who answers. Thinking can become dialectical and critical because it goes through this questioning and answering process, through the dialogue of *dialegesthai*, which actually is a "traveling through words," a *poreuesthai dia tōn logōn*,[130] whereby we constantly raise the basic Socratic question: *What do you mean when you say* . . . ? except that this *legein*, saying, is soundless and therefore so swift that its dialogical structure is somewhat difficult to detect.

The criterion of the mental dialogue is no longer truth, which would compel answers to the questions I raise with myself, either in the mode of Intuition, which compels with the force of sense evidence, or as necessary conclusions of reckoning with consequences in mathematical or logical reasoning, which rely on the structure of our brain and compel with its natural power. The only criterion of Socratic thinking is agreement, to be consistent with oneself, *homologein autos heautō*:[131] its opposite, to be in contradiction with oneself, *enantia legein autos heautō*,[132] actually means becoming one's own adversary. Hence Aristotle, in his earliest formulation of the famous axiom of contradiction, says explicitly that this is axiomatic: "we must necessarily believe it because . . . it is addressed not to the outward word [*exō logos,* that is, to the spoken word addressed to someone else, an interlocutor who may be either friend or adversary] but to the discourse *within the soul,* and though we can always raise objections to the outward word, to the *inward discourse* we cannot always object," because here the partner is oneself, and I cannot possibly want to become my own adversary.[133] (In this instance, we can watch how such an insight, won from the factual experience of the thinking ego, gets lost when it is generalized into a philosophical doctrine—"A cannot be both B and A under the same conditions and at the same time"—for we find the transformation being achieved by Aristotle himself when he discusses the same matter in his *Metaphysics*.[134])

A close reading of the *Organon,* the "Instrument," as the collection of Aristotle's early logical treatises has been called since the sixth century, clearly shows that what we now call "logic" was by no means originally meant as an "instrument of thought," of the inward discourse carried on "within the soul," but was designed as the science of correct talking and arguing when we are trying to convince others or give an account of what we state, always starting, as Socrates did, with premises most likely to be agreed on by most men or by most of those generally believed to be the wisest. In the early treatises, the axiom of non-contradiction, decisive only for the inward dialogue of thinking, has not yet been established as the most basic rule for discourse in general. Only after this special case had become the guiding example for all thought could Kant, who in his *Anthropology* had defined thinking as "talking with oneself . . . hence also inwardly listening,"[135] count the injunction "Always think consistently, in agreement with your-

self" (*"Jederzeit mit sich selbst einstimmig denken"*) among
the maxims that must be regarded as "unchangeable commandments for the class of thinkers."[136]

In brief, the specifically human actualization of consciousness in the thinking dialogue between me and myself
suggests that difference and otherness, which are such outstanding characteristics of the world of appearances as it is
given to man for his habitat among a plurality of things, are
the very conditions for the existence of man's mental ego as
well, for this ego actually exists only in duality. And this ego—
the I-am-I—experiences difference in identity precisely when
it is not related to the things that appear but only related to
itself. (This original duality, incidentally, explains the futility
of the fashionable search for identity. Our modern identity
crisis could be resolved only by never being alone and never
trying to think.) Without that original split, Socrates' statement about harmony in a being that to all appearances is
One would be meaningless.

Consciousness is not the same as thinking; acts of consciousness have in common with sense experience the fact that they
are "intentional" and therefore *cognitive* acts, whereas the
thinking ego does not think something but *about* something,
and this act is dialectical: it proceeds in the form of a silent
dialogue. Without consciousness in the sense of self-awareness,
thinking would not be possible. What thinking actualizes in its
unending process is difference, given as a mere raw fact
(*factum brutum*) in consciousness; only in this humanized form
does consciousness then become the outstanding characteristic
of somebody who is a man and neither a god nor an animal. As
the metaphor bridges the gap between the world of appearances and the mental activities going on within it, so the
Socratic two-in-one heals the solitariness of thought; its inherent duality points to the infinite plurality which is the law
of the earth.

To Socrates, the duality of the two-in-one meant no more
than that if you want to think, you must see to it that the two
who carry on the dialogue be in good shape, that the partners

be *friends*. The partner who comes to life when you are alert and alone is the only one from whom you can never get away—except by ceasing to think. It is better to suffer wrong than to do wrong, because you can remain the friend of the sufferer; who would want to be the friend of and have to live together with a murderer? Not even another murderer. In the end, it is to this rather simple consideration of the importance of agreement between you and yourself that Kant's Categorical Imperative appeals. Underlying the imperative, "Act only on that maxim through which you can at the same time *will* that it should become a universal law,"[137] is the command "Do not contradict yourself." A murderer or a thief cannot will that "Thou shalt kill" and "Thou shalt steal" be general laws, since he naturally fears for his own life and property. If you make yourself an exception, you have contradicted yourself.

In one of the contested dialogues, the *Hippias Major*, which even if not by Plato may still give authentic testimony about Socrates, Socrates describes the situation simply and accurately. It is the end of the dialogue, the moment of going home. He tells Hippias, who has shown himself to be an especially thickheaded partner, how "blissfully fortunate" he is in comparison with poor Socrates, who at home is awaited by a very obnoxious fellow who always cross-examines him. "He is a close relative and lives in the same house." When he now will hear Socrates give utterance to Hippias' opinions, he will ask "whether he is not ashamed of talking about a beautiful way of life, when questioning makes it evident that he does not even know the meaning of the word 'beauty.' "[138] When Hippias goes home, he remains one, for, though he lives alone, he does not seek to keep himself company. He certainly does not lose consciousness; he is simply not in the habit of actualizing it. When Socrates goes home, he is not alone, he is *by* himself. Clearly, with this fellow who awaits him, Socrates has to come to some kind of agreement, because they live under the same roof. Better to be at odds with the whole world than be at odds with the only one you are forced to live together with when you have left company behind.

What Socrates discovered was that we can have intercourse with ourselves, as well as with others, and that the two kinds of intercourse are somehow interrelated. Aristotle, speaking about friendship, remarked: "The friend is another self"[139]—meaning: you can carry on the dialogue of thought with him just as well as with yourself. This is still in the Socratic tradition, except that Socrates would have said: The self, too, is a kind of friend. The guiding experience in these matters is, of course, friendship and not selfhood; I first talk with others before I talk with myself, examining whatever the joint talk may have been about, and then discover that I can conduct a dialogue not only with others but with myself as well. The common point, however, is that the dialogue of thought can be carried out only among friends, and its basic criterion, its supreme law, as it were, says: Do not contradict yourself.

It is characteristic of "base people" to be "at variance with themselves" (*diapherontai heautois*) and of wicked men to avoid their own company; their soul is in rebellion against itself (*stasiazei*).[140] What kind of dialogue can you conduct with yourself when your soul is not in harmony but at war with itself? Precisely the dialogue we overhear when Shakespeare's Richard III is alone:

> What do I fear? Myself? There's none else by:
> Richard loves Richard: that is, I am I.
> Is there a murderer here? No. Yes, I am:
> Then fly: what! from myself? Great reason why:
> Lest I revenge. What! myself upon myself?
> Alack! I love myself. Wherefore? For any good
> That I myself have done unto myself?
> O! no: alas! I rather hate myself
> For hateful deeds committed by myself.
> I am a villain. Yet I lie, I am not.
> Fool, of thyself speak well: fool, do not flatter.

Yet all this looks very different when midnight is past and Richard has escaped his own company to join that of his peers. Then:

> Conscience is but a word that cowards use,
> Devis'd at first to keep the strong in awe. . . .

Even Socrates, so much in love with the marketplace, has to go home, where he will be alone, in solitude, in order to meet the other fellow.

I have drawn attention to the passage in *Hippias Major* in its stark simplicity because it provides a metaphor that can help simplify—at the risk of over-simplification—matters that are difficult and therefore always in danger of over-complication. Later times have given the fellow who awaits Socrates in his home the name of "conscience." Before its tribunal, to adopt Kantian language, we have to appear and give account of ourselves. And I chose the passage in *Richard III*, because Shakespeare, though he uses the word "conscience," does not use it here in the accustomed way. It took language a long time to separate the word "consciousness" from "conscience," and in some languages, for instance, in French, such a separation never was made. Conscience, as we understand it in moral or legal matters, is supposedly always present within us, just like consciousness. And this conscience is also supposed to tell us what to do and what to repent; before it became the *lumen naturale* or Kant's practical reason, it was the voice of God.

Unlike this ever-present conscience, the fellow Socrates is talking about has been left at home; he fears him, as the murderers in *Richard III* fear conscience—as something that is absent. Here conscience appears as an after-thought, roused either by a crime, as in Richard's own case, or by unexamined opinions, as in the case of Socrates. Or it may be just the anticipated fear of such after-thoughts, as with Richard's hired murderers. This conscience, unlike the voice of God within us or the *lumen naturale*, gives no positive prescriptions (even the Socratic *daimōn*, his divine voice, only tells him what *not* to do); in Shakespeare's words "it fills a man full of obstacles." What causes a man to fear it is the anticipation of the presence of a witness who awaits him only *if* and when he goes home. Shakespeare's murderer says: "Every man that means to live well endeavors . . . to live without it," and success in that comes easy because all he has to do is never start the soundless solitary dialogue we call "thinking," never

go home and examine things. This is not a matter of wickedness or goodness, as it is not a matter of intelligence or stupid-
ity. A person who does not know that silent intercourse (in
which we examine what we say and what we do) will not mind
contradicting himself, and this means he will never be either
able or willing to account for what he says or does; nor will he
mind committing any crime, since he can count on its being
forgotten the next moment. Bad people—Aristotle to the contrary notwithstanding—are *not* "full of regrets."

Thinking in its non-cognitive, non-specialized sense as a
natural need of human life, the actualization of the difference
given in consciousness, is not a prerogative of the few but an
ever-present faculty in everybody; by the same token, inability
to think is not a failing of the many who lack brain power but
an ever-present possibility for everybody—scientists, scholars,
and other specialists in mental enterprises not excluded. Everybody may come to shun that intercourse with oneself whose
feasibility and importance Socrates first discovered. Thinking
accompanies life and is itself the de-materialized quintessence
of being alive; and since life is a process, its quintessence can
only lie in the actual thinking process and not in any solid
results or specific thoughts. A life without thinking is quite
possible; it then fails to develop its own essence—it is not
merely meaningless; it is not fully alive. Unthinking men are
like sleepwalkers.

For the thinking ego and its experience, conscience that
"fills a man full of obstacles" is a side effect. No matter what
thought-trains the thinking ego thinks through, the self that
we all are must take care not to do anything that would make
it impossible for the two-in-one to be friends and live in
harmony. This is what Spinoza meant by the term "acquies-
cence in one's self" (*acquiescentia in seipso*): "It can spring
out of reason [reasoning], and this contentment is the greatest
joy possible."[141] Its criterion for action will not be the usual
rules, recognized by multitudes and agreed upon by society,
but whether I shall be able to live with myself in peace
when the time has come to think about my deeds and words.
Conscience is the anticipation of the fellow who awaits you if
and when you come home.

For the thinker himself this moral side effect is a marginal affair. And thinking as such does society little good, much less than the thirst for knowledge, which uses thinking as an instrument for other purposes. It does not create values; it will not find out, once and for all, what "the good" is; it does not confirm but, rather, dissolves accepted rules of conduct. And it has no political relevance unless special emergencies arise. That while I am alive I must be able to live with myself is a consideration that does not come up politically except in "boundary situations."

This term was coined by Jaspers for the general, unchanging human condition—"that I cannot live without struggling and suffering; that I cannot avoid guilt; that I must die"—to indicate an experience of "something immanent which already points to transcendence" and which, if we respond to it, will result in our *"becoming the Existenz we potentially are."*[142] In Jaspers, the term gets its suggestive plausibility less from specific experiences than from the simple fact that life itself, limited by birth and death, is a boundary affair in that my worldly existence always forces me to take account of a past when I was not yet and a future when I shall be no more. Here the point is that whenever I transcend the limits of my own life span and begin to reflect on this past, judging it, and this future, forming projects of the will, thinking ceases to be a politically marginal activity. And such reflections will inevitably arise in political emergencies.

When everybody is swept away unthinkingly by what everybody else does and believes in, those who think are drawn out of hiding because their refusal to join in is conspicuous and thereby becomes a kind of action. In such emergencies, it turns out that the purging component of thinking (Socrates' midwifery, which brings out the implications of unexamined opinions and thereby destroys them— values, doctrines, theories, and even convictions) is political by implication. For this destruction has a liberating effect on another faculty, the faculty of judgment, which one may call with some reason the most political of man's mental abilities. It is the faculty that judges *particulars* without subsuming them under general rules which can be taught and learned until they grow into habits that can be replaced by other habits and rules.

The faculty of judging particulars (as brought to light by Kant), the ability to say "this is wrong," "this is beautiful," and so on, is not the same as the faculty of thinking. Thinking deals with invisibles, with representations of things that are absent; judging always concerns particulars and things close at hand. But the two are interrelated, as are consciousness and conscience. If thinking—the two-in-one of the soundless dialogue—actualizes the difference within our identity as given in consciousness and thereby results in conscience as its by-product, then judging, the by-product of the liberating effect of thinking, realizes thinking, makes it manifest in the world of appearances, where I am never alone and always too busy to be able to think. The manifestation of the wind of thought is not knowledge; it is the ability to tell right from wrong, beautiful from ugly. And this, at the rare moments when the stakes are on the table, may indeed prevent catastrophes, at least for the self.

Where Are We When We Think?

IV

19 "Tantôt je pense et tantôt je suis"
(Valéry): the nowhere

As I approach the end of these considerations, I hope that
no reader expects a conclusive summary. For me to make
such an attempt would stand in flagrant contradiction to
what has been described here. If thinking is an activity that
is its own end and if the only adequate metaphor for it,
drawn from our ordinary sense experience, is the sensation of
being alive, then it follows that all questions concerning the
aim or purpose of thinking are as unanswerable as questions
about the aim or purpose of life. I am putting the question—
Where are we when we think?—at the end of our examination
not because the answer could supply any conclusion but only
because the question itself and the considerations it raises can
make sense only in the context of this whole approach. Since
what is to follow rests so heavily on my previous reflections,
I shall briefly summarize them in what must appear (but
are not meant) to be dogmatic propositions:

First, thinking is always out of order, interrupts all
ordinary activities and is interrupted by them. The best illustration of this may still be—as the old story goes—Socrates'
habit of suddenly "turning his mind to himself," breaking off
all company, and taking up his position wherever he happened
to be, "deaf to all entreaties" to continue with whatever he
had been doing before.[1] Once, we are told by Xenophon, he
remained in complete immobility for twenty-four hours in a
military camp, deep in thought, as we would say.

Second, the manifestations of the thinking ego's authentic
experiences are manifold: among them are the metaphysical
fallacies, such as the two-world theory, and, more interestingly,
the non-theoretical descriptions of thinking as a kind of dying
or, conversely, the notion that while thinking we are members of another, noumenal, world—present to us by intima-

197

tion even in the darkness of the actual here-and-now—or Aristotle's definition of the *bios theōrētikos* as a *bios xenikos,* the life of a stranger. The same experiences are reflected in the Cartesian doubt of the reality of the world, in Valéry's "At times I think, and at times I am" (as though to be real and to think were opposites), in Merleau-Ponty's "We are truly alone only on the condition that we do not know we are; it is this very ignorance which is our [the philosopher's] solitude."[2] And it is true that the thinking ego, whatever it may achieve, will never be able to reach reality qua reality or convince itself that anything actually exists and that life, human life, is more than a dream. (This suspicion that life is but a dream is, of course, among the most characteristic traits of Asian philosophy; examples from Indian philosophy are numerous. I shall give a Chinese example which is very telling because of its briefness. It reports a story told about the Taoist (i.e., anti-Confucian) philosopher Chuang Tzu. He "once dreamt he was a butterfly flitting and fluttering around, happy with himself and doing as he pleased. He didn't know he was Chuang Chou. Suddenly he woke up and there he was, solid and unmistakable Chuang Chou. But he didn't know if he was Chuang Chou who had dreamt he was a butterfly, or a butterfly dreaming it was Chuang Chou. Between Chuang Chou and a butterfly there must be *some* distinction!")[3]

The intensity of the thinking experience, on the other hand, manifests itself in the ease with which the opposition of thought and reality can be reversed, so that only thought seems to be real whereas all that merely is seems to be so transitory that it is as though it were not: "What is being *thought,* is; and what *is, is* only insofar as it is thought" (*Was* gedacht *ist, ist; und was* ist, ist *nur, insofern es* Gedanke *ist*).[4] The decisive point here, however, is that all such doubts disappear as soon as the thinker's solitude is broken in upon and the call of the world and our fellow-men changes the inner duality of the two-in-one into a One again. Hence the notion that everything that is might be a mere dream is either the nightmare that rises out of the thinking experience or the consoling thought to be summoned up, not when I have withdrawn from the world, but when the world has withdrawn from me and become unreal.

Third, these oddities of the thinking activity arise from the fact of withdrawal, inherent in all mental activities; thinking always deals with absences and removes itself from what is present and close at hand. This, of course, does not prove the existence of a world other than the one we are part of in ordinary life, but it means that reality and existence, which we can only conceive in terms of time and space, can be temporarily suspended, lose their weight and, together with this weight, their meaning for the thinking ego. What now, during the thinking activity, become meaningful are distillations, products of de-sensing, and such distillations are not mere abstract concepts; they were once called "essences."

Essences cannot be localized. Human thought that gets hold of them leaves the world of the particular and goes out in search of something generally *meaningful*, though not necessarily universally valid. Thinking always "generalizes," squeezes out of many particulars—which, thanks to the de-sensing process, it can pack together for swift manipulation—whatever meaning may inhere. Generalization is inherent in every thought, even though that thought is insisting on the universal primacy of the particular. In other words, the "essential" is what is applicable everywhere, and this "everywhere" that bestows on thought its specific weight is spatially speaking a "nowhere." The thinking ego, moving among universals, among invisible essences, is, strictly speaking, nowhere; it is homeless in an emphatic sense—which may explain the early rise of a cosmopolitan spirit among the philosophers.

The only great thinker I know of who was explicitly aware of this condition of homelessness as being natural to the thinking activity was Aristotle—perhaps because he knew so well and spelled out so clearly the difference between acting and thinking (the decisive distinction between the political and the philosophical way of life) and, drawing the obvious inference, refused to "share the fate" of Socrates and to let the Athenians "sin twice against philosophy." When a charge of impiety was brought against him, he left Athens and "withdrew to Chalcis, a stronghold of Macedonian influence."[5] He had counted homelessness among the great advantages of the philosopher's way of life in the *Protreptikos,* one of his early works, which was still well known in antiquity but has come down to us only in fragments. There he praises the *bios theōrētikos* because it needed "neither implements nor special places for [its] trade; wherever on earth somebody devotes himself to thinking, he will attain the truth everywhere as though it were present." Philosophers love this "nowhere" as though it were a country (*philochōrein*) and they desire to let all other activities go for the sake of *scholazein* (doing nothing, as we would say) because of the sweetness inherent in thinking or philosophizing itself.[6] The reason for this blessed independence is that philosophy (the cognition *kata logon*) is not concerned with particulars, with things given to the senses, but with universals (*kath' holou*), things that cannot be localized.[7] It would be a great mistake to look for such universals in practical-political matters, which always concern particulars; in this field, "general" statements, equally applicable everywhere, immediately degenerate into empty generalities. Action deals with particulars, and only particular statements can be valid in the field of ethics or politics.[8]

In other words, it may well be that we were posing a wrong, inappropriate question when we asked for the location of the thinking ego. Looked at from the perspective of the everyday world of appearances, the everywhere of the thinking ego— summoning into its presence whatever it pleases from any distance in time or space, which thought traverses with a velocity greater than light's—is a *nowhere.* And since this nowhere is by no means identical with the twofold nowhere from which we suddenly appear at birth and into which almost as suddenly we disappear in death, it might be conceived only as the Void. And the absolute void can be a limiting boundary concept; though not inconceivable, it is unthinkable. Obviously, if there is absolutely nothing, there can be nothing to think about. That we are in possession of these limiting boundary concepts enclosing our thought within unsurmountable walls—and the notion of an absolute beginning or an absolute end is among them—does not tell us more than that we are indeed *finite* beings. To assume that these limitations could serve to map out a place where the thinking ego could be localized would be just another variation of the two-world theory. Man's finitude, irrevocably given by virtue of his own short time span set in an infinity of time stretching into both past and future, constitutes the infrastructure, as it were, of all mental activities: it manifests itself as the only reality of which thinking qua thinking is aware, when the thinking ego has withdrawn from the world of appearances and lost the sense of realness inherent in the *sensus communis* by which we orient ourselves in this world.

In other words, Valéry's remark—when we think, we *are* not—would be right if our sense of realness were entirely determined by our spatial existence. The everywhere of thought is indeed a region of nowhere. But we are not only in space, we are also in time, remembering, collecting and recollecting what no longer is present out of "the belly of memory" (Augustine), anticipating and planning in the mode of willing what is not yet. Perhaps our question—Where are we when we think?—was wrong because by asking for the *topos* of this activity, we were exclusively spatially oriented—as though we had forgotten Kant's famous insight that "time is nothing but the form of inner sense, that is, of the intuition of ourselves and of our inner state." For Kant, that meant that time had nothing to do with appearances as such—"neither with shape nor position" as given to our senses—but only with appearances as affecting our "inner state," in which time determines "the relation of representation."⁹ And these representations—by which we make present what is phenomenally absent—are, of course, thought-things, that is, experiences or notions that have gone through the de-materializing operation by which the mind prepares its own objects and by "generalizing" deprives them of their spatial properties as well.

Time determines the way these representations are related to each other by forcing them into the order of a sequence, and these sequences are what we usually call thought-trains. All thinking is discursive and, insofar as it follows a train of thought, it could by analogy be presented as "a line progressing to infinity," corresponding to the way we usually represent to ourselves the sequential nature of time. But in order to create such a line of thought we must transform the *juxtaposition* in which experiences are given to us into a *succession* of soundless words—the only medium in which we can think—which means we not only de-sense but de-spatialize the original experience.

20 *The gap between past and future:
the* nunc stans

In the hope of finding out where the thinking ego is located in time and whether its relentless activity can be temporally determined, I shall turn to one of Kafka's parables, which, in my opinion, deals precisely with this matter. The parable is part of a collection of aphorisms entitled "HE."[10]

He has two antagonists; the first presses him from behind, from his origin. The second blocks the road in front of him. He gives battle to both. Actually, the first supports him in his fight with the second, for he wants to push him forward, and in the same way the second supports him in his fight with the first, since he drives him back. But it is only theoretically so. For it is not only the two antagonists who are there, but he himself as well, and who really knows his intentions? His dream, though, is that some time in an unguarded moment—and this, it must be admitted, would require a night darker than any night has ever been yet—he will jump out of the fighting line and be promoted, on account of his experience in fighting, to the position of umpire over his antagonists in their fight with each other.

For me, this parable describes the time sensation of the thinking ego. It analyzes poetically our "inner state" in regard to time, of which we are aware when we have withdrawn from the appearances and find our mental activities recoiling characteristically upon themselves—*cogito me cogitare, volo me velle*, and so on. The inner time sensation arises when we are not entirely absorbed by the absent non-visibles we are thinking about but begin to direct our attention onto the activity itself. In this situation past and future are equally present precisely because they are equally absent from our sense; thus the no-longer of the past is transformed by virtue of the spatial metaphor into something lying *behind* us and the not-yet of the future into something that *approaches* us from ahead (the German *Zukunft,* like the French *avenir,* means, literally What comes toward). In Kafka, this scene is a battleground where the forces of past and future clash with each other. Between them we find the man Kafka calls "He," who, if he wants to stand his ground at all, must give battle to both forces. The forces are "his" antagonists; they are not just opposites and would hardly fight with each other without "him" standing between them and making a stand against them; and even if such an antagonism were somehow inherent in the two and they could fight each other without "him," they would have long ago neutralized and destroyed each other, since as forces they clearly are equally powerful.

In other words, the time continuum, everlasting change, is broken up into the tenses past, present, future, whereby past and future are antagonistic to each other as the no-longer and the not-yet only because of the presence of man, who himself has an "origin," his birth, and an end, his death, and therefore stands at any given moment between them; this in-between is called the present. It is the insertion of man with his limited life span that transforms the continuously flowing stream of sheer change—which we can conceive of cyclically as well as in the form of rectilinear motion without ever being able to conceive of an absolute beginning or an absolute end—into time as we know it.

This parable in which two of time's tenses, the past and the future, are understood as antagonistic forces that crash into the present Now, sounds very strange to our ears, whichever time concept we may happen to hold. The extreme parsimony of Kafka's language, in which for the sake of the fable's realism every actual reality that could have engendered the thought-world is eliminated, may cause it to sound stranger than the thought itself requires. I shall therefore use a curiously related story of Nietzsche's in the heavily allegorical style of *Thus Spake Zarathustra*. It is much easier to understand because it concerns, as its title says, merely a "Vision" or a "Riddle."[11] The allegory begins with Zarathustra's arrival at a gateway. The gateway, like every gateway, has an entrance and an exit, that is, can be seen as the meeting-place of two roads.

Two paths meet here; no one has yet followed either to its end. This long lane stretches back for an eternity. And the other long lane out there, that is another eternity. They contradict each other, these roads; they offend each other face to face—and it is here, at this gateway, that they come together. The name of the gateway is inscribed above: "Now" [*"Augenblick"*]. . . . Behold this Now! From this gateway Now, a long eternal lane leads *backward;* behind us lies an eternity [and another lane leads forward into an eternal future].

Heidegger, who interprets the passage in his *Nietzsche*,[12] observes that this view is not the view of the beholder but only that of the man who stands in the gateway; for the onlooker, time passes in the way we are used to think of it, in a succession of nows where one thing always succeeds another. There is no meeting-place; there are not two lanes or roads, there is only one. "The clash is produced only for the one who *himself is* the now. . . . Whoever stands in the Now is turning in both directions: for him Past and Future run against *each other.*" And, summing up in the context of Nietzsche's doctrine of Eternal Recurrence, Heidegger says: "This is the authentic content of the doctrine of Eternal Recurrence, that Eternity *is* in the Now, that the Moment is not the futile Now which it is only for the onlooker, but the clash of Past and Future." (You have the same thought in Blake— "Hold infinity in the palm of your hand / And eternity in an hour.")

Returning to Kafka, we should remember that all these instances are dealing not with doctrines or theories but with thoughts related to the experiences of the thinking ego. Seen from the viewpoint of a continuously flowing everlasting stream, the insertion of man, fighting in both directions, produces a rupture which, by being defended in both directions, is extended to a gap, the present seen as the fighter's battleground. This battleground for Kafka is the metaphor for man's home on earth. Seen from the viewpoint of man, at each single moment inserted and caught in the middle between *his* past and *his* future, both aimed at the one who is creating his present, the battleground is an in-between, an extended Now on which he spends his life. The present, in ordinary life the most futile and slippery of the tenses—when I say "now" and point to it, it is already gone—is no more than the clash of a past, which is no more, with a future, which is approaching and not yet there. Man lives in this in-between, and what he calls the present is a life-long fight against the dead weight of the past, driving him forward with hope, and the fear of a future (whose only certainty is death), driving him backward toward "the quiet of the past" with nostalgia for and remembrance of the only reality he can be sure of.

It should not unduly alarm us that this time construct is totally different from the time sequence of ordinary life, where the three tenses smoothly follow each other and time itself can be understood in analogy to numerical sequences, fixed by the calendar, according to which the present is today, the past begins with yesterday, and the future begins tomorrow. Here, too, the present is surrounded by past and future inasmuch as it remains the fixed point from which we take our bearings, looking back or looking forward. That we can shape the everlasting stream of sheer change into a time continuum we owe not to time itself but to the continuity of our business and our activities in the world, in which *we continue* what we started yesterday and hope to finish tomorrow. In other words, the time continuum depends on the continuity of our everyday life, and the business of everyday life, in contrast to the activity of the thinking ego—always independent of the spatial circumstances surrounding it—is always spatially determined and conditioned. It is due to this thoroughgoing spatiality of our ordinary life that we can speak plausibly of time in spatial categories, that the past can appear to us as something lying "behind" us and the future as lying "ahead."

Kafka's time parable does not apply to man in his everyday occupations but only to the thinking ego, to the extent that it has withdrawn from the business of everyday life. The gap between past and future opens only in reflection, whose subject matter is what is absent—either what has already disappeared or what has not yet appeared. Reflection draws these absent "regions" into the mind's presence; from that perspective the activity of thinking can be understood as a fight against time itself. It is only because "he" thinks, and therefore is no longer carried along by the continuity of everyday life in a world of appearances, that past and future manifest themselves as pure entities, so that "he" can become aware of a no-longer that pushes him forward and a not-yet that drives him back.

Kafka's tale is, of course, couched in metaphorical language, and its images, drawn from everyday life, are meant as analogies, without which, as has already been indicated, mental phenomena cannot be described at all. And that always presents difficulties of interpretation. The specific difficulty here is that the reader must be aware that the thinking ego is not the self as it appears and moves in the world, remembering its own biographical past, as though "he" were *à la recherche du temps perdu* or planning his future. It is because the thinking ego is ageless and nowhere that past and future can become manifest to it as such, emptied, as it were, of their concrete content and liberated from all spatial categories. What the thinking ego senses as "his" dual antagonists are time itself, and the constant change it implies, the relentless motion that transforms all Being into Becoming, instead of letting it *be*, and thus incessantly destroys its being *present*. As such, time is the thinking ego's greatest enemy because—by virtue of the mind's incarnation in a body whose internal motions can never be immobilized—time inexorably and regularly interrupts the immobile quiet in which the mind is active without doing anything.

This final meaning of the parable comes to the fore in the

concluding sentence, when "he," situated in the time gap, which is an immovable present, a *nunc stans*, dreams of the unguarded moment when time will have exhausted its force; then quiet will settle down on the world, not an eternal quiet but just lasting long enough to give "him" the chance of jumping out of the fighting line to be promoted to the position of umpire, the spectator and judge outside the game of life, to whom the meaning of this time span between birth and death can be referred because "he" is not involved in it.

What are this dream and this region but the old dream Western metaphysics has dreamt from Parmenides to Hegel, of a timeless region, an eternal presence in complete quiet, lying beyond human clocks and calendars altogether, the region, precisely, of thought? And what is the "position of umpire," the desire for which prompts the dream, but the seat of Pythagoras' spectators, who are "the best" because they do not participate in the struggle for fame and gain, are disinterested, uncommitted, undisturbed, intent only on the spectacle itself? It is they who can find out its meaning and judge the performance.

Without doing too much violence to Kafka's magnificent story, one may perhaps go a step further. The trouble with Kafka's metaphor is that by jumping out of the fighting line "he" jumps out of this world altogether and judges from outside though not necessarily from above. Moreover, if it is the insertion of man that breaks up the indifferent flow of everlasting change by giving it an aim, namely, himself, the being who fights it, and if through that insertion the indifferent time stream is articulated into what is behind him, the past, what is ahead of him, the future, and himself, the fighting present, then it follows that man's presence causes the stream of time to deflect from whatever its original direction or (assuming a cyclical movement) ultimate non-direction may have been. The deflection seems inevitable because it is not just a passive object that is inserted into the stream, to be tossed about by its waves that go sweeping over his head, but a fighter who defends his own presence and thus defines what otherwise might be indifferent to him as *"his"* antagonists: the past, which he can fight with the help of the future; the future, which he fights supported by the past.

Without "him," there would be no difference between past and future, but only everlasting change. Or else these forces would clash head on and annihilate each other. But thanks to the insertion of a fighting presence, they meet at an angle, and the correct image would then have to be what the physicists call a parallelogram of forces. The advantage of this image is that the region of thought would no longer have to be situated beyond and above the world and human time; the fighter would no longer have to jump out of the fighting line in order to find the quiet and the stillness necessary for thinking. "He" would recognize that "his" fighting has not been in vain, since the battleground itself supplies the region where "he" can rest when "he" is exhausted. In other words, the location of the thinking ego in time would be the in-between of past and future, the present, this mysterious and slippery now, a mere gap in time, toward which nevertheless the more solid tenses of past and future are directed insofar as they denote that which *is* no more and that which *is* not yet. That they *are* at all, they obviously owe to man, who has inserted himself between them and established his presence there. Let me briefly follow the implications of the corrected image.

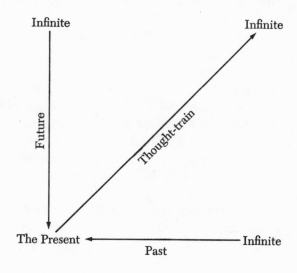

Ideally, the action of the two forces that form our parallelo-gram should result in a third force, the resultant diagonal whose origin would be the point at which the forces meet and upon which they act. The diagonal would remain on the same plane and not jump out of the dimension of the forces of time, but it would in one important respect differ from the forces whose result it is. The two antagonistic forces of past and future are both indefinite as to their origin; seen from the view-point of the present in the middle, the one comes from an infinite past and the other from an infinite future. But though they have no known beginning, they have a terminal ending, the point at which they meet and clash, which is the present. The diagonal force, on the contrary, has a definite origin, its starting-point being the clash of the two other forces, but it would be infinite with respect to its ending since it has resulted from the concerted action of two forces whose origin is infinity. This diagonal force, whose origin is known, whose direction is determined by past and future, but which exerts its force toward an undetermined end as though it could reach out into infinity, seems to me a perfect metaphor for the activity of thought.

If Kafka's "he" were able to walk along this diagonal, in perfect equidistance from the pressing forces of past and future, he would not, as the parable demands, have jumped out of the fighting line to be above and beyond the melee. For this diagonal, though pointing to some infinity, is limited, enclosed, as it were, by the forces of past and future, and thus protected against the void; it remains bound to and is rooted in the present—an entirely human present though it is fully actualized only in the thinking process and lasts no longer than this process lasts. It is the quiet of the Now in the time-pressed, time-tossed existence of man; it is somehow, to change the metaphor, the quiet in the center of a storm which, though totally unlike the storm, still belongs to it. In this gap between past and future, we find our place in time when we think, that is, when we are sufficiently removed from past and future to be relied on to find out their meaning, to assume the position of "umpire," of arbiter and judge over the manifold, never-ending affairs of human existence in the world, never arriving at a final solution to their riddles but ready with ever-new answers to the question of what it may be all about.

To avoid misunderstanding: the images I am using here to indicate, metaphorically and tentatively, the location of thought can be valid only within the realm of mental phenomena. Applied to historical or biographical time, these metaphors cannot possibly make sense; gaps in time do not occur there. Only insofar as he thinks, and that is insofar as he is *not,* according to Valéry, does man—a "He," as Kafka so rightly calls him, and not a "somebody"—in the full actuality of his concrete being, live in this gap between past and future, in this present which is timeless.

The gap, though we hear about it first as a *nunc stans,* the "standing now" in medieval philosophy, where it served, in the form of *nunc aeternitatis,* as model and metaphor for divine eternity,[13] is not a historical datum; it seems to be coeval with the existence of man on earth. Using a different metaphor, we call it the region of the spirit, but it is perhaps rather the path paved by thinking, the small inconspicuous track of non-time beaten by the activity of thought within the time-space given to natal and mortal men. Following that course, the thought-trains, remembrance and anticipation, save whatever they touch from the ruin of historical and biographical time. This small non-time space in the very heart of time, unlike the world and the culture into which we are born, cannot be inherited and handed down by tradition, although every great book of thought points to it somewhat cryptically— as we found Heraclitus saying of the notoriously cryptic and unreliable Delphic oracle: *"oute legei, oute kryptei alla sēmainei"* ("it does not say and it does not hide, it intimates").

Each new generation, every new human being, as he becomes conscious of being inserted between an infinite past and an infinite future, must discover and ploddingly pave anew the path of thought. And it is after all possible, and seems to me likely, that the strange survival of great works, their relative permanence throughout thousands of years, is due to their having been born in the small, inconspicuous track of non-time which their authors' thought had beaten between an infinite past and an infinite future by accepting past and future as directed, aimed, as it were, at themselves— as *their* predecessors and successors, *their* past and *their* future —thus establishing a present for themselves, a kind of timeless time in which men are able to create timeless works with which to transcend their own finiteness.

This timelessness, to be sure, is not eternity; it springs, as it were, from the clash of past and future, whereas eternity is the boundary concept that is unthinkable because it indicates the collapse of all temporal dimensions. The temporal dimension of the *nunc stans* experienced in the activity of thinking gathers the absent tenses, the not-yet and the no-more, together into its own presence. This is Kant's "land of pure intellect" (*Land des reinen Verstandes*), "an island, enclosed by nature itself within unalterable limits," and "surrounded by a wide and stormy ocean," the sea of everyday life.[14] And though I do not think that this is "the land of truth," it certainly is the only domain where the whole of one's life and its meaning—which remains ungraspable for mortal men (*nemo ante mortem beatus esse dici potest*), whose existence, in distinction from all other things which begin to *be* in the emphatic sense when they are completed, terminates when it *is* no more—where this ungraspable whole can manifest itself as the sheer continuity of the I-am, an enduring presence in the midst of the world's ever-changing transitoriness. It is because of this experience of the thinking ego that the primacy of the present, the most transitory of the tenses in the world of appearances, became an almost dogmatic tenet of philosophical speculation.

Let me now at the end of these long reflections draw attention, not to my "method," not to my "criteria" or, worse, my "values"—all of which in such an enterprise are mercifully hidden from its author though they may be or, rather, *seem* to be quite manifest to reader and listener—but to what in my opinion is the basic assumption of this investigation. I have spoken about the metaphysical "fallacies," which, as we found, do contain important hints of what this curious out-of-order activity called thinking may be all about. In other words,

I have clearly joined the ranks of those who for some time now have been attempting to dismantle metaphysics, and philosophy with all its categories, as we have known them from their beginning in Greece until today. Such dismantling is possible only on the assumption that the thread of tradition is broken and that we shall not be able to renew it. Historically speaking, what actually has broken down is the Roman trinity that for thousands of years united religion, authority, and tradition. The loss of this trinity does not destroy the past, and the dismantling process itself is not destructive; it only draws conclusions from a loss which is a fact and as such no longer a part of the "history of ideas" but of our political history, the history of our world.

What has been lost is the continuity of the past as it seemed to be handed down from generation to generation, developing in the process its own consistency. The dismantling process has its own technique, and I did not go into that here except peripherally. What you then are left with is still the past, but a *fragmented* past, which has lost its certainty of evaluation. About this, for brevity's sake, I shall quote a few lines which say it better and more densely than I could:

> Full fathom five thy father lies,
>   Of his bones are coral made,
> Those are pearls that were his eyes.
>   Nothing of him that doth fade
> But doth suffer a sea-change
>   Into something rich and strange.
> *The Tempest,* Act I, Scene 2

It is with such fragments from the past, after their sea-change, that I have dealt here. That they could be used at all we owe to the timeless track that thinking beats into the world of space and time. If some of my listeners or readers should be tempted to try their luck at the technique of dismantling, let them be careful not to destroy the "rich and strange," the "coral" and the "pearls," which can probably be saved only as fragments.

> 'O plunge your hands in water,
>   Plunge them in up to the wrist;
> Stare, stare in the basin
>   And wonder what you've missed.

'The glacier knocks in the cupboard,
The desert sighs in the bed,
And the crack in the tea-cup opens
A lane to the land of the dead. . . .'
                          W. H. Auden[15]

Or to put the same in prose: "Some books are undeservedly forgotten, none are undeservedly remembered."[16]

21   Postscriptum

In the second volume of this work I shall deal with willing and judging, the two other mental activities. Looked at from the perspective of these time speculations, they concern matters that are absent either because they are not yet or because they are no more; but in contradistinction to the thinking activity, which deals with the invisibles in all experience and always tends to generalize, they always deal with particulars and in this respect are much closer to the world of appearances. If we wish to placate our common sense, so decisively offended by the need of reason to pursue its purposeless quest for meaning, it is tempting to justify this need solely on the grounds that thinking is an indispensable preparation for deciding what shall be and for evaluating what is no more. Since the past, being past, becomes subject to our judgment, judgment, in turn, would be a mere preparation for willing. This is undeniably the perspective, and, within limits, the legitimate perspective of man insofar as he is an acting being.

But this last attempt to defend the thinking activity against the reproach of being impractical and useless does not work. The decision the will arrives at can never be derived from the mechanics of desire or the deliberations of the intellect that may precede it. The will is either an organ of free spontaneity that interrupts all causal chains of motivation that would bind it or it is nothing but an illusion. In respect to desire, on one hand, and to reason, on the other, the will acts like "a kind of *coup d'état*," as Bergson once said, and this implies, of course, that "free acts are exceptional": "although we are free whenever we are willing to get back into ourselves, *it seldom happens that we are willing"* (italics added).[17] In other words, it is impossible to deal with the willing activity without touching on the problem of freedom.

I propose to take the internal evidence—in Bergson's terms, the "immediate datum of consciousness"—seriously and since I agree with many writers on this subject that this datum and all problems connected with it were unknown to Greek antiquity, I must accept that this faculty was "discovered," that we can date this discovery historically, and that we shall thereby find that it coincides with the discovery of human "inwardness" as a special region of our life. In brief, I shall analyze the faculty of the will in terms of its history.

I shall follow the experiences men have had with this paradoxical and self-contradictory faculty (every volition, since it speaks to itself in imperatives, produces its own counter-volition), starting from the Apostle Paul's early discovery of the will's impotence—"I do not do what I want, but I do the very thing I hate"[18]—and going on to examine the testimony left us by the Middle Ages, beginning with Augustine's insight that what are "at war" are not the spirit and the flesh but the mind, as will, with itself, man's "inmost self" with itself. I shall then proceed to the modern age, which, with the rise of the notion of progress, exchanged the old philosophical primacy of the present over the other tenses against the primacy of the future, a force that in Hegel's words "the Now cannot resist," so that thinking is understood "as essentially the negation of something being directly present" (*"in der Tat ist das Denken wesentlich die Negation eines unmittelbar Vorhandenen"*).[19] Or in the words of Schelling: "In the final and highest instance there is no other Being than Will"[20]—an attitude that found its final climactic and self-defeating end in Nietzsche's "Will to Power."

At the same time I shall follow a parallel development in the history of the Will according to which volition is the inner capacity by which men decide about "whom" they are going to be, in what shape they wish to show themselves in the world of appearances. In other words, it is the will, whose subject matter is projects, not objects, which in a sense creates the *person* that can be blamed or praised and anyhow held responsible not merely for its actions but for its whole "Being," its *character*. The Marxian and existentialist notions, which play such a great role in twentieth-century thought and pretend that man is his own producer and maker, rest on these experiences, even though it is clear that nobody has "made" himself or "produced" his existence; this, I think, is the last of the metaphysical fallacies, corresponding to the modern age's emphasis on willing as a substitute for thinking.

I shall conclude the second volume with an analysis of the faculty of judgment, and here the chief difficulty will be the curious scarcity of sources providing authoritative testimony. Not till Kant's *Critique of Judgment* did this faculty become a major topic of a major thinker.

I shall show that my own main assumption in singling out judgment as a distinct capacity of our minds has been that judgments are not arrived at by either deduction or induction; in short, they have nothing in common with logical operations—as when we say: All men are mortal, Socrates is a man, hence, Socrates is mortal. We shall be in search of the "silent sense," which—when it was dealt with at all—has always, even in Kant, been thought of as "taste" and therefore as belonging to the realm of aesthetics. In practical and moral matters it was called "conscience," and conscience did not judge; it told you, as the divine voice of either God or reason, what to do, what not to do, and what to repent of. Whatever the voice of conscience may be, it cannot be said to be "silent," and its validity depends entirely upon an authority that is above and beyond all merely human laws and rules.

In Kant judgment emerges as "a peculiar talent which can be practised only and cannot be taught." Judgment deals with particulars, and when the thinking ego moving among generalities emerges from its withdrawal and returns to the world of particular appearances, it turns out that the mind needs a new "gift" to deal with them. "An obtuse or narrow-minded person," Kant believed, ". . . may indeed be trained through study, even to the extent of becoming learned. But as such people are commonly still lacking in judgment, it is not unusual to meet learned men who in the application of their scientific knowledge betray that original want, which can never be made good."²¹ In Kant, it is reason with its "regulative ideas" that comes to the help of judgment, but if the faculty is separate from other faculties of the mind, then we shall have to ascribe to it its own *modus operandi,* its own way of proceeding.

And this is of some relevance to a whole set of problems by which modern thought is haunted, especially to the problem of theory and practice and to all attempts to arrive at a halfway plausible theory of ethics. Since Hegel and Marx, these questions have been treated in the perspective of History and on the assumption that there is such a thing as Progress of the human race. Finally we shall be left with the only alternative there is in these matters—we either can say with Hegel: *Die Weltgeschichte ist das Weltgericht,* leaving the ultimate judgment to Success, or we can maintain with Kant the autonomy of the minds of men and their possible independence of things as they are or as they have come into being.

Here we shall have to concern ourselves, not for the first time, with the concept of history, but we may be able to reflect on the oldest meaning of this word, which, like so many other terms in our political and philosophical language, is Greek in origin and derived from *historein,* to inquire in order to tell how it was—*legein ta eonta* in Herodotus. But the origin of this verb is again Homer (*Iliad* XVIII) where the noun *histor* ("historian," as it were) occurs, and that Homeric historian is the *judge.* If judgment is our faculty for dealing with the past, the historian is the inquiring man who by relating it sits in judgment over it. If that is so, we may reclaim our human dignity, win it back, as it were, from the pseudo-divinity named History of the modern age, without denying history's importance but denying its right to being the ultimate judge. Old Cato, with whom I started these reflections—"never am I less alone than when I am by myself, never am I more active than when I do nothing"—has left us a curious phrase which aptly sums up the political principle implied in the enterprise of reclamation. He said: *"Victrix causa deis placuit, sed victa Catoni"* ("The victorious cause pleased the gods, but the defeated one pleases Cato").

Editor's Postface

Hannah Arendt died suddenly on December 4, 1975. It was a Thursday evening; she was entertaining friends. The Saturday before, she had finished "Willing," the second section of *The Life of the Mind*. Like *The Human Condition*, its forerunner, the work was conceived in three parts. Where *The Human Condition*, subtitled *The Vita Activa*, had been divided into Labor, Work, and Action, *The Life of the Mind*, as planned, was divided into Thinking, Willing, and Judging, the three basic activities, as she saw it, of mental life. The distinction made by the Middle Ages between the active life of man in the world and the solitary *vita contemplativa* was of course present to her thought, although her own thinker, willer, and judger was not a contemplative, set apart by a monkish vocation, but everyman insofar as he exercised his specifically human capacity to withdraw from time to time into the invisible region of the mind.

Whether or not the life of the mind is superior to the so-called active life (as antiquity and the Middle Ages had considered) was an issue she never pronounced on in so many words. Yet it would not be too much to say that the last years of her life were consecrated to this work, which she treated as a task laid on her as a vigorously thinking being—the highest she had been called to. In the midst of her multifarious teaching and lecture commitments, her service on various round tables and panels and consultative boards (she was a constant recruit to the *vita activa* of the citizen and public figure, though seldom a volunteer), she remained immersed in *The Life of the Mind*, as though its completion would acquit her not so much of an obligation, which sounds too onerous, as of a

217

compact she had entered into. All roads, however secondary, on which chance or intention put her in her daily and professional existence, led back to that.

When an invitation came, in June 1972, to give the Gifford Lectures at the University of Aberdeen, she chose to use the occasion for a kind of try-out of the volumes already in preparation. The Gifford Lectures also served as a stimulus. Endowed in 1885 by Adam Gifford, a leading Scottish justice and law lord, "for the purpose of establishing in each of the four cities of Edinburgh, Glasgow, Aberdeen, and St. Andrews . . . a Chair . . . of Natural Theology, in the widest sense of that term," they had been given by Josiah Royce, William James, Bergson, J. G. Frazer, Whitehead, Eddington, John Dewey, Werner Jaeger, Karl Barth, Etienne Gilson, Gabriel Marcel, among others—an honor roll to which she was quite proud to accede. If she was normally superstitious, she must have seen them too as a *porta-fortuna: The Varieties of Religious Experience*, Whitehead's *Process and Reality*, Dewey's *The Quest for Certainty*, Marcel's *The Mystery of Being*, Gilson's *The Spirit of Medieval Philosophy* had first seen the light as Gifford Lectures. . . . Having accepted, she drove herself harder perhaps than she ought to have to get hers ready in the time available; she delivered the first series, on Thinking, in the spring of 1973. In the spring of 1974, she returned for the second series, on Willing, and was interrupted by a heart attack after she had given her first lecture. She was intending to go back, in the spring of 1976, to finish the series; meanwhile she had given most of Thinking and Willing to her classes at the New School for Social Research in New York. Judging, she had not started, though she had used material on Judgment in courses she gave at the University of Chicago and at the New School on Kant's political philosophy. After her death, a sheet of paper was found in her typewriter, blank except for the heading "Judging" and two epigraphs. Some time between the Saturday of finishing "Willing" and the Thursday of her death, she must have sat down to confront the final section.

Her plan was for a work in two volumes. Thinking, the

longest, was to occupy the first, and the second was to contain Willing and Judging. As she told friends, she counted on Judgment to be much shorter than the other two. She also used to say that she expected it to be the easiest to handle. The hardest had been the Will. The reason she gave for counting on Judgment to be short was the lack of source material: only Kant had written on the faculty, which before him had been unnoticed by philosophers except in the field of aesthetics, where it had been named Taste. As for ease, she no doubt felt that her lectures on Kant's political philosophy, with their careful analysis of *The Critique of Judgment*, had pretty well prepared the ground to be covered. Still, one can guess that Judging might have surprised her and ended by taking up a whole volume to itself. In any case, to give the reader some notion of what would have been in the concluding section, an appendix has been joined to the second volume containing extracts from her classroom lectures. Aside from a seminar paper, not included here, on the Imagination, which touches briefly on its role in the judging process, this is all we now have of her thoughts on the subject (though something further may turn up in her correspondence, when that is edited). Mournful that there is not more; anyone familiar with her mind will feel sure that the contents of the appendix do not exhaust the ideas that must already have been stirring in her head as she inserted the fresh page in her typewriter.

About the editing. As far as I know, all of Hannah Arendt's books and articles were edited before reaching print. Those written in English, naturally. It was done by publishers' editors, magazine editors (William Shawn on *The New Yorker,* Robert Silvers on *The New York Review of Books,* Philip Rahv, in the old days, on *Partisan Review*), and also by friends. Sometimes several hands, unknown to each other, went to work on her manuscripts, with her consent and usually, though not always, with her collaboration; those she had learned to trust, she tended to leave rather free with the blue pencil. She referred to all this wryly as her "Englishing." She had taught herself to write English as an exile, when she was over thirty-five, and never felt as comfortable in it even as a spoken tongue as she had once felt in French. She chafed against our language and its awesome, mysterious constraints. Though she had a natural gift, which would have made itself felt in Sioux or Sanskrit, for eloquent, forceful, sometimes pungent expression, her sentences were long, in the German way, and had to be unwound or broken up into two or three. Also, like anybody writing or speaking a foreign language, she had trouble with prepositions. And with what Fowler called "cast-iron idiom." And with finding the natural place for adverbs; for that in English there are no rules—only an unwritten law, which appears tyrannous and menacing to a foreigner because it can also, unpredictably, be broken. Besides, she was impatient. Her sentences could be unwieldy not only because her native language was German, with its affection for strings of modifiers and subordinate clauses encumbering the road to the awaited verb, but also because she tried to get too much in at once. The mixture of hurry and generosity was very characteristic.

Anyway, she was edited. I worked on several of her texts with her, sometimes after another editor, amateur or professional, had preceded me. We went over "On Violence" together one summer in the Café Flore, and then I took it home for further attention. We worked on "On Civil Disobedience" in a *pensione* in Switzerland for several days, and we put some finishing touches on her last published article, "Home to Roost," in an apartment she had been lent in Marbach (Schiller's birthplace), handy to the *Deutsche Literaturarchiv*, where she was sorting Jaspers' papers. I worked with her on the Thinking section of *The Life of the Mind* in Aberdeen; in the photostat of the original manuscript, I can make out my penciled changes. The next spring, when she was in a ward in the Aberdeen hospital, for some days under an oxygen tent, I went over bits of Willing by myself, at her request.

When she was alive, the editing was fun, because it was a collaboration and an exchange. On the whole she accepted correction with good grace, with relief when it came to prepositions, for instance, with interest when some point of usage came up that was new to her. Sometimes we argued and continued the argument by correspondence; this happened over her translation of Kant's *Verstand* as "intellect"; I thought it should be "understanding" as in the standard translations. But I never convinced her and I yielded. Now I think we were both right, because we were aiming at different things: she clung to the original sense of the word, and I was after audience comprehension. In the present text it is "intellect." Most of the disagreements we had were settled by compromise or by cutting. But in the process her natural impatience, sooner or later, would reassert itself. She did not like fussing over details. "*You* fix it," she would say, finally, starting to cover a yawn. If she was impatient, she was also indulgent; for her, I figured as a "perfectionist," and she was inclined to humor the tendency, provided no proselytization was in view.

In any case, we never had a substantive difference. If at times I questioned the thought in one of her manuscripts, it was only to point out what seemed to be a contradiction with another thought she had been putting forward several pages back. It would usually turn out that I had failed to perceive some underlying distinction or, conversely, that she had failed to perceive the reader's need for the *distinguo*. Strange as it may seem, our minds were in some respects very close—a fact she often remarked on when the same notion would occur to each of us independently, while an ocean—the Atlantic—lay between us. Or she read some text I had written and found there a thought she had been silently pondering. This convergence of cast of mind, she decided, must have something to do with the theology in my Catholic background, which had given me, she believed, an aptitude for philosophy. Actually I had made far from brilliant marks in the two college courses in philosophy I had taken, bumbling and lethargically taught, it must be added. Otherwise, though, our studies had not been so far apart. In Germany, she had done her doctoral thesis on the Concept of Love in St. Augustine; in America, I had read him in an undergraduate course in Medieval Latin and been exhilarated by *The City of God*—my favorite. Possibly my medieval and Renaissance studies in French, Latin, and English, plus years of classical Latin and later home reading of Plato, had joined with a Catholic girlhood to make up the deficiency in formal philosopical training. There is also

Editor's Postface

the fact, which she did not consider, that in the course of years I had learned a great deal from her.

I mention these things now to cite my qualifications for editing *The Life of the Mind.* It was not a job I had applied for, and when, in January, 1974, she made me her literary executor, I doubt very much that she foresaw what was coming, i.e., that she would not live to finish those volumes and that it would be I, without benefit of her assistance, who would see them through the press. If finally she did foresee it, at least as a distinct possibility, after the heart attack a few months later in Aberdeen, she must have known how I would set about the work, with all my peculiarities and stringencies, and have accepted the inevitable in a philosophical spirit. Knowing me, she may even have foreseen the temptations that the new freedom from interference would dangle before me, freedom to do it "my" way, but if she read me as well as that, she would also have foreseen the resistance the mere glimmer of such temptations would muster in my still-Catholic conscience. . . . If she divined, in short, that there would be days when I would become a battlefield on which allegiance to the prose of my forefathers fought my sense of a duty to her, the picture of all that furious contention—the contest of the scruples and the temptations—so foreign to her own nature, would probably have amused her. I must assume that she trusted my judgment, had faith that in the end no damage would be done, that the manuscript would emerge unscarred from the fighting; lacking that basic confidence in *her* confidence, I would have soon had to throw in the sponge.

But whatever she foresaw, or failed to foresee, she is not here now to consult or appeal to. I have been forced to guess her reaction to every act of editorial interference. In most cases, previous experience has made that easy: if she knew me, I also knew her. But here and there problems have come up which in the past I would surely not have attempted to solve on my own, by guesswork. Whenever I was unsure, I would pepper a manuscript with question marks meaning "What do you want to say here?" "Can you clarify?" "Right word?" Today those points of interrogation ("What do you suppose

she means by that?" "Does she intend this repetition or not?")
are leveled at me. Yet not in my own person exactly; rather,
I put myself in her place, turn into a sort of mind-reader or
medium. With eyes closed, I am talking to a quite lively ghost.
She has haunted me, given pause to my pencil, caused erasures
and re-erasures. In practice, the new-found freedom has meant
that I feel less free with her typescript than I would have felt
if she were alive. Now and then I have caught myself leaning
over backwards for fear of some imagined objection and have
had to right myself with the reminder that in normal circumstances the page-long sentence staring at me would never have
been allowed to pass.

Or on the contrary it has happened that I have firmly
crossed out a phrase or sentence whose meaning was opaque
to me and substituted language that seemed to make better
sense; then, on a second reading, I have had misgivings,
gone back to consult the original text, seen that I had missed a
nuance, and restored the passage as written or else made a
fresh effort at paraphrase. Anybody who has done translating
will recognize the process—the repeated endeavors to read
through language into the mind of an author who is absent.
Here the fact that several years ago—and mainly, I suppose,
because of my friendship with her—I started taking German
lessons has turned out to be a benign stroke of fate. I know
enough of her native language now to make out the original
structure like a distant mountainous outline behind her English
phrasing; this has rendered many troublesome passages "trans-
latable": I simply put them into German, where they become
clear, and then do them back into English.

In any event, so far as I know, no change has been made
that in any way affects the thought. A few cuts, mostly small,
have been made, usually to eliminate repetitions, when I concluded that these were accidental rather than deliberate. In a
very few places, not more than two or three, I have added
something, for the sake of clarity, e.g., the words "Scotus was
a Franciscan" to a passage that otherwise would be obscure
to a reader lacking that information. But with these minor
exceptions, what has been done is just the habitual "Englishing" that all her texts underwent.

This does not apply to the material from her lectures printed in the appendix. These extracts are given verbatim, except for obvious typing mistakes, which have been corrected. It appeared to me that since the Kant lectures had never been intended for publication but to be delivered viva voce to a class of students, any editorial meddling would be inappropriate. It was not my business to tamper with history. Along with her other papers, the lectures from which the extracts have been taken are in the Library of Congress, where they can be consulted with permission from her executors.

I ought to mention one other group of changes. The manuscripts of both "Thinking" and "Willing" were still in lecture form, unchanged in that respect from the way they had been delivered in Aberdeen and New York, though in other respects much revised and added to (the last chapter of "Willing" was wholly new). Had she had time, obviously she would have altered that, turning listeners into readers, as she normally did when what had been given as a lecture came out in a book or magazine. In the present text, this has been done, except in the case of the general introduction, with its pleasant allusion to the Gifford Lectures. If something of the flavor of the spoken word nevertheless remains, that is all to the good.

A final remark about the Englishing should be interjected. Evidently personal taste plays a part in an editor's decisions. My own notion of acceptable written English is, like everybody's, idiosyncratic. I do not object, for instance, to ending a sentence with a preposition—in fact, I rather favor it—but I am squeamish when I see certain nouns, such as "shower" (in the sense of shower-bath) or "trigger," being used as verbs. So I could not let Hannah Arendt, whom I so greatly admired, say "trigger" when "cause" or "set in motion" would do. And "when the chips are down": I cannot say why the phrase grates on me, and particularly coming from her, who, I doubt, ever handled a poker chip. But I can see her (cigarette perched in holder) contemplating the roulette table or chemin de fer, so it is now "when the stakes are on the table"—more fitting, more in character. Would she have minded these small examples of interference with her freedom of expression? Did she set much store on "triggered"? I hope she would have indulged me in my prejudices. And though personal taste has occasionally marched in as arbiter (where once I would have sought to persuade), much care has been taken throughout to respect her characteristic tone. My own idiom has not been permitted to intrude; there is not a "Mary McCarthy word" in the text. In the one instance when, finding nothing better, I used such a word, it stuck out like a sore thumb from the galley proof and had to be hastily amputated. So that the text that the reader has been reading is hers; it *is* her, I hope, in the sense that the excisions and polishing reveal her, just as cutting away the superfluous marble from a quarried block lays bare the intrinsic form. Michelangelo said that about sculpture (as opposed to painting), and here at any rate there has been no hint of laying on or embellishment.

It has been a heavy job, which has kept going an imaginary dialogue with her, verging sometimes, as in life, on debate. Though in life it never came to that, now I reproach her, and vice versa. The work has gone on till late at night; then, in my dreams, pages of the manuscript are found all of a sudden to be missing or, on the contrary, turn up without warning, throwing everything, including the footnotes, out of kilter. But it has also been, if not fun, as in former days, rewarding. I have learned, for example, that I can understand the *Critique of Pure Reason*, which I had previously thought impenetrable by me. Searching for a truant reference, I have read some entire Platonic dialogues (the *Thaeatetus,* the *Sophist*) that I had never dipped into before. I have learned the difference between an electric ray and a sting ray. I have reread bits of Virgil's Bucolics and Georgics, which I had not looked at since college. Many of my old college textbooks have come down from their shelves, and not only mine but my husband's (he studied philosophy at Bowdoin) and my dear secretary's husband's (he had Rilke, some of the Aristotle we lacked, and more Virgil).

It has been a co-operative enterprise. My secretary, typing the manuscript, has gently interposed on behalf of commas and a sterner way with grammatical lapses: she is a Scruple, doing battle on the side of Temptation. Hannah Arendt's teaching assistant at the New School—Jerome Kohn—has hunted down

dozens of references and, quite often, answering the appeal
of those anxious question marks, been able to clarify, or else
we have pooled our bewilderment and arrived at reasonable
certainties. He has even (see the bad dream above) discovered
a page that, unnoticed by us, was missing from the photo-
statted manuscript. Other friends, including my German
teacher, have helped. Throughout this travail, there have been
times of positive elation, a mixture of our school days revisited
(those textbooks, late-night discussions of philosophic points),
and the tonic effect of our dead friend's ideas, alive and generative of controversy as well as of surprised agreement.
Though I have missed her in the course of these months—in
fact more than a year now—of work, wished her back to clarify,
object, reassure; compliment and be complimented, I do not
think I shall truly miss her, feel the pain in the amputated
limb, till it is over. I am aware that she is dead but I am simultaneously aware of her as a distinct presence in this room, listening to my words as I write, possibly assenting with her mus-
ing nod, possibly stifling a yawn.

A few explanations of practical matters. Since the manuscript, though finished in terms of content, was not in final
shape, not every quotation and allusion in the text was accompanied by a footnote. Thanks to Jerome Kohn and to Roberta
Leighton and her helpers at Harcourt Brace Jovanovich, many
of these have been run down. But as I write, a few are still
missing and if they cannot be found in time, the search will
have to continue and the results be included in a future edition.
Also, even where we do have references, a few of the footnotes
are incomplete, chiefly because the page or volume number as
given appears to be wrong and we have not yet been able
to locate the right passage. This too, I hope, will eventually
be rectified. We have been aided by having books from
Hannah Arendt's library that were used by her for reference.
But we do not have all the books she referred to.

It is clear that she often quoted from memory. Where her
memory did not correspond with a cited text, this has been
corrected. Except in the case of translations: here we have
sometimes corrected, sometimes not. Again it has been a

question of trying to read her mind. When she varied from a standard translation of a Greek or Latin or German or French original, did she do so on purpose or from a faulty recollection? Often one cannot be sure. As comparison shows, she did use standard translations: Norman Kemp Smith's of Kant, Walter Kaufmann's of Nietzsche, McKeon's Aristotle, the various translations of Plato in the Edith Hamilton–Huntington Cairns edition. But she knew all those languages well—a fact which prompted her to veer from the standard version when it suited her, that is, when she found Kemp Smith, for example, or Kaufmann imprecise, too far from the original, or for some other, purely literary reason. From an editorial point of view, this has created a rather chaotic situation. Do we credit Kemp Smith and Kaufmann in the footnotes when she has leaned heavily, but not entirely, on their versions? Not to do seems unfair, but in some eventualities the opposite could seem unfair too: Kaufmann, for instance, might not care to be credited with words and expressions that are not his. Kemp Smith is dead, like many of the Plato translators, but that does not mean that feeling for their feelings should die too.

Leaving the puzzles of credit aside for the moment, we have attacked the overall problem of translations in what may be a piecemeal, *ad hoc* way but which does meet the realities of the circumstance, for which no general and consistently applied rule seems to work. Where possible, each passage has been checked against the standard translation, often underlined or otherwise marked by her in the book she owned; when the variation is wide, we have gone back to the original language, and if Kemp Smith seems closer to Kant's German, we have used Kemp Smith. But when there is a shade of meaning overlooked in the standard translation that the Arendt translation brings out, we have used hers; also when the meaning is debatable. With practice, it soon becomes fairly easy to discern when a variant rendering corresponds to an intention on her part as opposed to inadvertence—a slip of memory or mistake in copying; differences in punctuation, for instance, we have treated as inadvertent.

Unfortunately, this common-sense solution does not meet

all contingencies. Unless the text cited was in her library, in English, we have no idea of what translation, if any, she used for reference. In the absence of further clues, I have assumed that she made her own translation and have felt free to alter it slightly, in the interests of English idiom or grammar, just as I would with her own text. (Once in a while, I have retranslated from the original myself. But I have lacked the effrontery to try that much with Heidegger, though I have dared with Master Eckhart.) In the case of classical authors, there is such a wealth of translations to choose among that one could hardly hope to find the one she might have been drawing on—a needle in a haystack. Once, by luck, I happened on a translation of Virgil which—it was apparent in a flash—she had used. My pencil moved (Eureka!) to indicate editor, date, and so on, in a footnote; then I looked again—no. Here, as so often, she had used a translation but had not stuck to it. And it is impossible to show in a footnote in which spots she diverged and which not.

Eventually we arrived at a policy, which has been to cite a translation only when it has been followed to the letter. Where no translator is named, it means that the version used is entirely or largely the author's or that we could not find the translation she drew on, if one exists. Yet even that policy requires qualification. The reader should know that some standard translations (McKeon, Kemp Smith, Kaufmann, the Hamilton-Cairns miscellany), even where not specifically mentioned, have served *grosso modo* as the author's guides.

The Bible has been a special problem. It seemed hard to tell at first whether she was using the King James version, the Revised Standard version, the Douai version, a German version which she then translated into English, or a mixture of all these. I even amused myself with the fond hypothesis that she had gone back to St. Jerome's Vulgate and done her own rendering from the Latin. My inclination was to use the King James version; aside from personal preference, there was the argument that the "thou shalt"s in the author's voice that appear repeatedly in the "Willing" volume should be matched by Biblical "thou" and "thee"s of the older version—otherwise it would sound peculiar. But Roberta Leighton has demonstrated to me that careful comparison shows that the manuscript is closest to the Revised Standard version; hence, that has been used, with a few exceptions, where the beauty of the King James language proved irresistible to us, as it evidently had to our author. At any rate, sticking on the whole to the Revised Standard has done away with one difficulty: the fact that the old version translates "love" (*agape*) as "charity." Since for modern ears, the word has a mainly tax-deductible connotation, or refers to "taking a charitable view" of something, it would have had to be changed to "love," in surrounding brackets, each time it occurred, which would have made awkward reading.

Such preoccupations with consistency and mirror-fidelity of reference will seem curious to the general reader. They are an occupational infirmity of editors and academics. Or they are the game-rules that scholarly writing agrees to and by their very strictness they add to the zest of the pursuit—a zest that cannot be shared by non-players. Hunting-the-slipper in the guise of an elusive footnote must be taken with dead seriousness, like any absorbing sport or game. Yet if it matters only to a few, mainly those engaged in it, where is the sense? What difference does it make whether God is "He" on one page and "he" on the next? Maybe the author just changed her attitude, which is her right. Why seek to divine her underlying preference and lock her, a free spirit, into a uniform "He" or "he"? Well, it is "He." And the will is "Will" when it is a concept and "will" when it is acting in a human subject.

I apologize to the general reader for mentioning these details of footnotes, capitalization, brackets, and so on, as devoid of interest to an outsider as a sportsman's pondered choice of trout-fly when a worm will catch the fish. That the fish is the point tends to be lost sight of by specialists, as Hannah Arendt would be the first to agree. She cared for the general reader, who for her remained a student in adult form. That was why she especially loved Socrates. Still, being a teacher and scholar, she knew about the game-rules and by and large accepted them, though more in the spirit of tolerance one brings to children's pastimes than with the zeal of a true participant. Anyhow, in the course of these months with the manuscript, my well-sharpened pencils have turned into stubs. And now I have talked enough shop-talk. It is time to leave the manuscript to itself.

Notes

Introduction

1. *Critique of Pure Reason*, B871. For this and later citations, see Norman Kemp Smith's translation, *Immanuel Kant's Critique of Pure Reason*, New York, 1963, which the author frequently relied on.
2. *Eichmann in Jerusalem*, New York, 1963.
3. Notes on metaphysics, *Kant's handschriftlicher Nachlass*, vol. V, in *Kant's gesammelte Schriften*, Akademie Ausgabe, Berlin, Leipzig, 1928, vol. XVIII, 5636.
4. Hugh of St. Victor.
5. André Bridoux, *Descartes: Oeuvres et Lettres*, Pléiade ed., Paris, 1937, Introduction, p. viii. Cf. Galileo: *"les mathématiques sont la langue dans laquelle est écrit l'univers,"* p. xiii.
6. Nicholas Lobkowicz, *Theory and Practice: History of a Concept from Aristotle to Marx*, Notre Dame, 1967, p. 419.
7. *De Republica*, I, 17.
8. *The Phenomenology of Mind*, trans. J. B. Baillie (1910), New York, 1964, "Sense-Certainty," p. 159.
9. See the note to "Vom Wesen der Wahrheit," a lecture first given in 1930. Now in *Wegmarken*, Frankfurt, 1967, p. 97.
10. See "Glauben und Wissen" (1802), *Werke*, Frankfurt, 1970, vol. 2, p. 432.
11. 11th ed.
12. *Werke*, Darmstadt, 1963, vol. I, pp. 982, 621, 630, 968, 952, 959, 974.
13. Introduction to his *The Basic Works of Aristotle*, New York, 1941, p. xviii. In citations from Aristotle, McKeon's translation has occasionally been used.
14. *Critique of Pure Reason*, B878. The striking phrase occurs in the last section of the *Critique of Pure Reason*, where Kant

claims to have established metaphysics as a science the idea of which "is as old as speculative human reason; and what rational human being does not speculate, either in scholastic or in popular fashion?" (B871). This "science" . . . "has now fallen into general disrepute" because "more was expected from metaphysics than could reasonably be demanded" (B877). Cf. also sections 59 and 60 of *Prolegomena to Any Future Metaphysics*.

15. *The Gay Science*, bk. III, no. 125, "The madman."
16. "How the 'True World' finally became a fable," 6.
17. "Nietzsches Wort 'Gott ist tot,'" in *Holzwege*, Frankfurt, 1963, p. 193.
18. B125 and B9.
19. René Char, *Feuillets d'Hypnos*, Paris, 1946, no. 62.
20. *Symposium*, 212a.
21. *Kant's handschriftlicher Nachlass*, vol. VI, Akademie Ausgabe, vol. XVIII, 6900.
22. *Werke*, vol. I, p. 989.
23. "Prolegomena," *Werke*, vol. III, p. 245.
24. *Critique of Pure Reason*, Bxxx.
25. *Kant's handschriftlicher Nachlass*, vol. V, Akademie Ausgabe, vol. XVIII, 4849.
26. Trans. John Macquarrie and Edward Robinson, London, 1962, p. 1. Cf. pp. 151 and 324.
27. "Einleitung zu 'Was ist Metaphysik?'" in *Wegmarken*, p. 206.
28. Hegel, *The Phenomenology of Mind*, Baillie trans., Introduction, p. 131.
29. *Ibid.*, p. 144.

Chapter I

1. The three ways of life are enumerated in *Nicomachean Ethics*, I, 5 and the *Eudemian Ethics*, 1215a35 ff. For the opposition of the beautiful to the necessary and the useful, see *Politics*, 1333a30 ff. It is interesting to compare the three Aristotelian ways of life with Plato's enumeration in the *Philebus*—the way of pleasure, the way of thinking (*phronēsis*), and a way of both mixed (22); to the way of pleasure Plato objects that pleasure in itself is unlimited in time as well as intensity: "it does not contain within itself and derive from itself either beginning or middle or end" (31a). And although

he "agrees with all sages (*sophoi*) . . . that *nous*, the faculty of thought and of truth, is for us king of heaven and earth" (28c), he also thinks that for mere mortals a life that "knows neither joy nor grief," though the most divine (33a-b), would be unbearable and that therefore "a mixture of the unlimited with what sets limits is the source of all beauty" (26b).

2. Thomas Langan, *Merleau-Ponty's Critique of Reason*, New Haven, London, 1966, p. 93.
3. Frag. 1.
4. *Republic*, VII, 514a–521b. *The Collected Dialogues of Plato*, eds. Edith Hamilton and Huntington Cairns, "Republic," trans. Paul Shorey, New York, 1961, has sometimes been drawn on, as has Francis MacDonald Cornford's *The Republic of Plato*, New York, London, 1941.
5. Kant, *Opus Postumum*, ed. Erich Adickes, Berlin, 1920, p. 44. Probable date of this remark is 1788.
6. *Critique of Pure Reason*, B565.
7. Maurice Merleau-Ponty, *The Visible and the Invisible*, Evanston, 1968, p. 17.
8. Maurice Merleau-Ponty, *Signs*, Evanston, 1964, Introduction, p. 20.
9. Hermann Diels and Walther Kranz, *Die Fragmente der Vorsokratiker*, Berlin, 1959, vol. II, B26.
10. *The Visible and the Invisible*, pp. 40–41.
11. *Das Tier als soziales Wesen*, Zürich, 1953, p. 252.
12. *Animal Forms and Patterns*, trans. Hella Czech, New York, 1967, p. 19.
13. *Ibid.*, p. 34.
14. *Das Tier als soziales Wesen*, p. 232.
15. *Ibid.*
16. *Ibid.*, p. 127.
17. *Animal Forms and Patterns*, pp. 112, 113.
18. *Das Tier als soziales Wesen*, p. 64.
19. *Biologie und Geist*, Zürich, 1956, p. 24.
20. *Of Human Understanding*, bk. III, chap. 1, no. 5.
21. Merleau-Ponty, *Signs*, Introduction, p. 17.
22. *The Visible and the Invisible*, p. 259.
23. *Signs*, p. 21.
24. *The Visible and the Invisible*, p. 259.
25. *De Anima*, 403a5–10.
26. *Ibid.*, 413b24 ff.

27. *De generatione animalium*, II, 3, 736b5–29, quoted from Lobkowicz, *op. cit.*, p. 24.
28. *De Interpretatione*, 16a3–13.
29. Mary McCarthy, "Hanging by a Thread," *The Writing on the Wall*, New York, 1970.
30. *Enarrationes in Psalmos, Patrologiae Latina*, J.-P. Migne, Paris, 1854–66, vol. 37, CXXXIV, 16.
31. Frag. 149.
32. Schelling, *Of Human Freedom* (1809), 414. Trans. James Gutmann, Chicago, 1936, p. 96.
33. Frag. 34.
34. *Critique of Pure Reason*, B354–B355.
35. *Ibid.*, A107. Cf. also B413: "In inner intuition there is nothing permanent," and B420: Nothing "permanent" is "given . . . in . . . intuition" "insofar as I think myself."
36. *The Visible and the Invisible*, pp. 18–19.
37. *Critique of Pure Reason*, A381.
38. *Critique of Pure Reason*, B565–B566. Kant writes here "transcendental" but means "transcendent." This is not the only passage in which he himself falls prey to the confusion that constitutes one of the pitfalls for the reader of his works. His clearest and simplest explanation of the use of the two words can be found in the *Prolegomena*, where he answers a critic, in the note on page 252 (*Werke*, vol. III), which reads as follows: "My place is the fruitful *bathos* of experience, and the word transcendental . . . does not signify something that transcends all experience, but what (*a priori*) precedes it in order to make it possible. If these concepts transcend experience I call their use transcendent." The object that determines appearances, as distinguished from experience, clearly transcends them as experiences.
39. *Critique of Pure Reason*, B566.
40. *Ibid.*, B197.
41. *Ibid.*, B724.
42. *Ibid.*, B429.
43. *The Philosopher and Theology*, New York, 1962, p. 7. In the same vein, Heidegger in the classroom used to tell the biography of Aristotle. "Aristotle," he said, "was born, worked [spent his life thinking], and died."
44. In his *Commentary* to I Corinthians 15.
45. *Critique of Pure Reason*, A381.
46. *Ibid.*, B157–B158.

235

47. *Ibid.*, B420.
48. The last and presumably best English translation, by John Manolesco, appeared under the title *Dreams of a Spirit Seer, and Other Writings*, New York, 1969. I have translated the passage myself from the German in *Werke*, vol. I, pp. 946–951.
49. "Allgemeine Naturgeschichte und Theorie des Himmels," *Werke*, vol. I, p. 384. English translation: *Universal Natural History and Theory of the Heavens*, trans. W. Hastie, Ann Arbor, 1969.
50. *The Bounds of Sense: An Essay on Kant's Critique of Pure Reason*, London, 1966, p. 249.
51. *The Visible and the Invisible*, pp. 28 ff.
52. *The Human Condition*, pp. 252 ff.
53. *Le Discours de la Méthode*, 3ème partie, in *Descartes: Oeuvres et Lettres*, pp. 111, 112; see, for first quotation, *The Philosophical Works of Descartes*, trans. Elizabeth S. Haldane and G. R. T. Ross, Cambridge, 1972, vol. I, p. 99.
54. Plato, *Philebus*, 67b, 52b.
55. *Ibid.*, 33b, 28c.
56. *Le Discours de la Méthode*, 4ème partie, in *Descartes: Oeuvres et Lettres*, p. 114; *The Philosophical Works*, vol. I, p. 101.
57. *The Visible and the Invisible*, pp. 36–37.
58. "Anthropologie," no. 24, *Werke*, vol. VI, p. 465.
59. Heidegger rightly points out: "Descartes himself stresses that the sentence [*cogito ergo sum*] is not a syllogism. The I-am is not a consequence of the I-think but, on the contrary, the *fundamentum*, the ground for it." Heidegger mentions the form the syllogism would have to take; it would read as follows: *Id quod cogitat est; cogito; ergo sum. Die Frage nach dem Ding*, Tübingen, 1962, p. 81.
60. *Tractatus*, 5.62; 6.431; 6.4311. Cf. *Notebooks 1914–1916*, New York, 1969, p. 75e.
61. Thomas Aquinas, *Summa Theologica*, pt. 1, qu. 1, 3 ad 2.
62. It seems that Gottsched was the first to speak of the common sense (*sensus communis*) as a "sixth sense." In *Versuch einer Kritischen Dichtkunst für die Deutschen*, 1730. Cf. Cicero, *De Oratore*, III, 50.
63. Quoted from Thomas Landon Thorson, *Biopolitics*, New York, 1970, p. 91.
64. *Summa Theologica*, pt. I, qu. 78, 4 ad 1.
65. *Op. cit., loc, cit.*

66. *Ibid.*
67. *Notebooks 1914–1916*, pp. 48, 48e.
68. *Politics*, 1324a16.
69. *The Visible and the Invisible*, p. 40.
70. *Philebus*, 25–26.
71. *Ibid.*, 31a.
72. Thomas S. Kuhn, *The Structure of Scientific Revolutions*, Chicago, 1962, p. 163.
73. *Critique of Pure Reason*, B367.
74. *De Interpretatione*, 17a1–4.
75. 980a22 ff.
76. *Monadology*, no. 33.
77. *Physics*, 188b30. Thomas Aquinas echoes the Aristotelian phrase: *"quasi ab ipsa veritate coacti"* (as though forced by truth itself), in his commentary on *De Anima*, I, 2, 43.
78. The *Dictionnaire de l'Académie* wrote in the same vein: *"La force de la vérité, pour dire le pouvoir que la vérité a sur l'esprit des hommes."*
79. W. H. Auden, "Talking to Myself," *Collected Poems*, New York, 1976, p. 653.
80. *Philosophie der Weltgeschichte*, Lasson ed., Leipzig, 1920, pt. I, pp. 61–62.
81. Notes on metaphysics, Akademie Ausgabe, vol. XVIII, 4849.
82. *Critique of Pure Reason*, A19, B33.
83. The only Kant interpretation I know of which could be quoted in support of my own understanding of Kant's distinction between reason and intellect is Eric Weil's consummate analysis of the *Critique of Pure Reason*, *"Penser et Connaître, La Foi et la Chose-en-soi,"* in *Problèmes Kantiens*, 2nd ed., Paris, 1970. According to Weil, it is inevitable *"d'affirmer que Kant, qui dénie à la raison pure la possibilité de* connaître *et de développer une* science, *lui reconnaît, en revanche, celle d'acquérir un savior qui, au lieu de connaître,* pense" (p. 23). It must be admitted, however, that Weil's conclusions remain closer to Kant's own understanding of himself. Weil is chiefly interested in the interconnection of Pure and Practical reason and hence states that *"le fondement dernier de la philosophie kantienne doit être cherché dans sa théorie de l'homme, dans l'anthropologie philosophique, non dans une 'théorie de la connaissance' . . ."* (p. 33), whereas my chief reservations about Kant's philosophy concern precisely his moral philos-

ophy, that is, the *Critique of Practical Reason*, although I agree of course that those who read the *Critique of Pure Reason* as a kind of epistemology seem to ignore completely the concluding chapters of the book (p. 34).

The four essays of Weil's book, by far the most important items in the Kant literature of recent years, are all based on the simple but crucial insight that *"L'opposition* connaître . . . *et* penser . . . *est fondamentale pour la compréhension de la pensée kantienne"* (p. 112, n. 2).

84. *Critique of Pure Reason*, A314.
85. *Ibid.*, B868.
86. *Ibid.*, Bxxx.
87. *Ibid.*
88. *Ibid.*, B697.
89. *Ibid.*, B699.
90. *Ibid.*, B702.
91. *Ibid.*, B698.
92. *Ibid.*, B714.
93. *Ibid.*, B826.
94. *Ibid.*, B708.

Chapter II

1. *De Veritate*, qu. XXII, art. 12.
2. *Critique of Pure Reason*, B171–B174.
3. *Critique of Judgment*, trans. J. H. Bernard, New York, 1951, Introduction, IV.
4. *Science of Logic*, Preface to the Second Edition.
5. *Philosophy of Right*, Preface.
6. Frag. 108.
7. Thucydides, II, 43.
8. *Critique of Pure Reason*, B400.
9. *Ibid.*, B275.
10. See Ernst Stadter, *Psychologie und Metaphysik der menschlichen Freiheit*, München, Paderborn, Wien, 1971, p. 195.
11. See the magnificent description of such a dream of "complete loneliness" in Kant's *Observations on the Feeling of the Beautiful and Sublime*, trans. John T. Goldthwait, Berkeley, Los Angeles, 1960, pp. 48–49.
12. *Critique of Pure Reason*, B157. Cf. chap. I of the present volume, pp. 43–45.
13. *Ibid.*, B158 n.

14. "Anthropologie," no. 28, *Werke*, vol. VI, p. 466.
15. *The Trinity*, bk. XI, chap. 3. English translation: *Fathers of the Church* series, Washington, D.C., 1963, vol. 45.
16. *Ibid.*
17. *Ibid.*, chap. 8.
18. *Ibid.*, chap. 10.
19. *An Introduction to Metaphysics*, trans. Ralph Manheim, New Haven, 1959, p. 12.
20. "Discours aux Chirurgiens," in *Variété*, Paris, 1957, vol. I, p. 916.
21. *Phaedo*, 64.
22. Diogenes Laertius, VII, 2.
23. *Sämmtliche Werke*, Leipzig, n.d., "Ueber den Tod," vol. II, p. 1240.
24. *Phaedo*, 64–67.
25. Cf. Valéry, *op. cit., loc. cit.*
26. See N. A. Greenberg's analysis, "Socrates' Choice in the *Crito*," in *Harvard Studies in Classical Philology*, vol. 70, no. 1, 1965.
27. Heraclitus, frags. 104, 29.
28. *Republic*, 494a and 496d.
29. *Ibid.*, 496a ff. Cornford, *The Republic of Plato*, pp. 203–204.
30. *Philebus*, 62b.
31. *Laws*, 935: In disputes, "all are wont to indulge in ridicule of their opponent." It is impossible "to abuse without seeking to ridicule." Hence, "every writer of comedy or iambic or lyric song shall be strictly forbidden to ridicule any of the citizens . . . and if he disobeys he shall be banished from the country." For the passages in the *Republic*, however, in which the fear of ridicule plays hardly any role, see 394 ff. and 606 ff.
32. *Theaetetus*, 174a–d.
33. "Träume eines Geistersehers," *Werke*, vol. I, p. 951.
34. *Phaedo*, 64.
35. *Ibid.*, 66.
36. *Ibid.*, 65.
37. *Protreptikos*, B43, ed. Ingemar Düring, Frankfurt, 1969.
38. *Ibid.*, B110.
39. *Republic*, 500c.
40. Letter of March 1638, *Descartes: Oeuvres et Lettres*, p. 780.
41. Editor's note: we have been unable to find this reference.
42. Akademie Ausgabe, vol. XVIII, 5019 and 5036.

43. Plato, in the *Phaedo*, 84a, mentions Penelope's web but in the opposite sense. The "soul of the philosopher," set free from the bondage of pleasure and pain, will not act Penelope-like, undoing her own weaving. Once rid (through the *logismos*), of pleasure and pain that "nail" the soul to the body, the soul (Plato's thinking ego) changes its nature and no longer reasons (*logizesthai*) but looks upon (*theāsthai*) "the true and the divine" and abides there forever.

44. "Ueber das Wesen der Philosophischen Kritik," *Hegel Studienausgabe*, Frankfurt, 1968, vol. I, p. 103.

45. *Philosophie der Weltgeschichte*, Lasson ed, Leipzig, 1917, pt. II, pp. 4–5.

46. *Reason in History*, trans. Robert S. Hartman, Indianapolis, New York, 1953, p. 89.

47. *Reason in History*, p. 69. Author's translation.

48. Preface to *The Phenomenology of Mind*.

49. *Politics*, 1269a35, 1334a15; see bk. VII, chap. 15.

50. Paul Weiss, "A Philosophical Definition of Leisure," in *Leisure in America: Blessing or Curse*, ed. J. C. Charlesworth, Philadelphia, 1964, p. 21.

51. VIII, 8. I follow the translation given in Kirk and Raven, frag. 278.

52. *Timaeus*, 34b.

53. "Der Streit der Fakultäten," pt. II, 6 and 7, *Werke*, vol. VI, pp. 357–362.

54. "Ueber den Gemeinspruch," *Werke*, vol. VI, pp. 166–167.

55. Hegel, *Philosophie der Weltgeschichte*, Introduction.

56. *Sophist*, 254.

57. *Republic*, 517b, and *Phaedrus*, 247c.

58. *Sophist*, 254a–b.

59. See chap. I of the present volume, pp. 33–34. In the beginning of *De Interpretatione*, Aristotle refers to his *De Anima*, as having dealt with some of the same points, but nothing in *De Anima* seems to correspond to the points raised in *De Interpretatione*. If my reading of the text is correct, Aristotle might have thought of the passage used by me in chap. I, that is, *De Anima*, 403a5–10.

60. *De Interpretatione*, 16a4–17a9.

61. "Reflexionen zur Anthropologie," no. 897, Akademie Ausgabe, vol. XV, p. 392.

62. *Monologion*.

63. In what follows here, I have relied closely on the first chapter,

on "Language and Script," of Marcel Granet's great book *La Pensée Chinoise*, Paris, 1934. I used the new German edition, which has been brought up to date by Manfred Porkert: *Das chinesische Denken—Inhalt, Form, Charakter*, München, 1971.

64. Kant, *Critique of Pure Reason*, B180.
65. B180–181.
66. *Tractatus*, 4.016 (*"Um das Wesen des Satzes zu verstehen, denken wir an die Hieroglyphenschrift, welche die Tatsachen, die sie beschreibt, abbildet. Und aus ihr wurde die Buchstabenschrift, ohne das Wesentliche der Abbildung zu verlieren"*).
67. *A Defence of Poetry.*
68. *Poetics*, 1459a5.
69. *Ibid.*, 1457b17 ff.
70. *Critique of Judgment*, no. 59.
71. *Ibid.*
72. *Ibid.*
73. *Prolegomena to Every Future Metaphysics*, no. 58, trans. Carl J. Friedrich, Modern Library, New York, n.d. Kant himself had been aware of this peculiarity of philosophical language in the pre-critical time: "Our higher rational concepts . . . usually take on a physical garment in order to achieve clarity." "Träume eines Geistersehers," p. 948.
74. No. 59. It would be interesting to examine Kant's notion of "analogy" from the early writing to the *Opus Postumum*, for it is striking how early it occurred to him that metaphorical thinking—that is, thinking in analogies—could save speculative thought from its peculiar unrealness. Already in the *Allgemeine Naturgeschichte und Theorie des Himmels*, published in 1755, he writes with respect to the "probability" of God's existence: "I am not so devoted to the consequences of my theory that I should not be ready to acknowledge . . . its being undemonstrable. Nevertheless, I expect . . . that such a chart of the infinite, comprehending as it does a subject which seems . . . to be forever concealed from human understanding, *will not on that account be at once regarded as a chimera, especially when recourse is had to analogy.*" (Italics added. English translation, by W. Hastie, quoted from *Kant's Cosmogony*, Glasgow, 1900, pp. 146–147.
75. See Francis MacDonald Cornford, *Plato's Theory of Knowledge*, New York, 1957, p. 275.

76. The essay, "The Chinese Written Character as a Medium for Poetry," edited by Ezra Pound, in *Instigations,* Freeport, N.Y., 1967, contains a curious plea for the Chinese script: "Its etymology is constantly visible." A phonetic word "does not bear its metaphor on its face. We forget that personality once meant, not the soul, but the soul's mask [through which the soul sounded, as it were—*per-sonare*]. This is the sort of thing one can not possibly forget in using the Chinese symbol. . . . With us, the poet is the one for whom the accumulated treasures of the race-words are real and active" (p. 25).

77. IX, 1–8.

78. Marshall Cohen's unfortunately unpublished manuscript "The Concept of Metaphor," which I was kindly permitted to consult, contains many examples, together with an excellent review of the literature on the subject.

79. *The Odyssey of Homer,* bk. XIX, ll. 203–209, trans. Richmond Lattimore, New York, 1967, p. 287.

80. "Das Homerische Gleichnis und der Anfang der Philosophie," in *Die Antike,* vol. XII, 1936.

81. Diels and Kranz, frag. B67.

82. *Aus der Erfahrung des Denkens,* Bern, 1947.

83. Bruno Snell, "From Myth to Logic: The Role of the Comparison," in *The Discovery of the Mind,* Harper Torchbooks, New York, Evanston, 1960, p. 201.

84. Hans Jonas, *The Phenomenon of Life,* New York, 1966, p. 135. His study of "The Nobility of Sight" is of unique help in the clarification of the history of Western thought.

85. Diels and Kranz, frag. 101a.

86. Aristotle seems to have thought along these lines in one of his scientific treatises: "Of these faculties, for the mere necessities of life and in itself, sight is the more important, but for the mind [*nous*] and indirectly [*kata symbebēkos*] hearing is the more important. . . . [It] makes the largest contribution to wisdom. For discourse, which is the cause of learning, is so because it is audible; but it is audible not in itself but indirectly, because speech is composed of words, and each word is a rational symbol. Consequently, of those who have been deprived of one sense or the other from birth, the blind are more intelligent than the deaf and the dumb." The point of the matter is that he seems never to have remembered this observation when he wrote philosophy. Aristotle, *On Sense and Sensible Objects,* 437a4–17.

87. *Op. cit.*, p. 152.
88. See Hans Jonas, chap. 3, on Philo of Alexandria, especially pp. 94–97, of *Von der Mythologie zur mystischen Philosophie,* Göttingen, 1954, which is the second part of *Gnosis und spätantiker Geist,* Göttingen, 1934.
89. *The Phenomenon of Life,* pp. 136–147. Cf. *Von der Mythologie,* pp. 138–152.
90. Bonn, 1960, pp. 200 f.
91. *Theaetetus,* 155d.
92. 982b11–22.
93. 983a14–20.
94. See, for instance, *Nicomachean Ethics,* VI, 8, where the *nous* is the mental perception (*aisthēsis*) of the "unchangeable primary or limiting terms" for which "there exists no *logos*" (1142a25–27). Cf. 1143b5.
95. *Seventh Letter,* 341b–343a, paraphrase.
96. On July 2, 1885.
97. No. 160.
98. *Nietzsche,* Pfullingen, 1961, vol. II, p. 484.
99. *Philosophical Investigations,* trans. G. E. M. Anscombe, New York, 1953, nos. 119, 19, 109.
100. *Phaedrus,* 274e–277c.
101. *Physics,* 209b15.
102. 286a, b.
103. 275d–277a.
104. *Philebus,* 38e–39b.
105. *Ibid.,* 39b–c.
106. 342.
107. *Ibid.,* 344b.
108. *Ibid.,* 343b.
109. *Ibid.,* 341e.
110. *Critique of Pure Reason,* B33. For: *"Nicht dadurch, dass ich bloss denke, erkenne ich irgend ein Objekt, sondern nur dadurch, dass ich eine gegebene Anschauung . . . bestimme, kann ich irgend einen Gegenstand erkennen"* ("I do not know an object merely in that I think, but only insofar as I determine a given intuition, can I know an object") (B406).
111. I am quoting from an early lecture-course of Heidegger's on Plato's *Sophist* (1924–25) according to a literal transcript, pp. 8, and 155, 160. See also Cornford's commentary on the *Sophist* in *Plato's Theory of Knowledge,* p. 189 and n. 1,

where *noein* is said to stand for the act of "intuition (*noēsis*) which *sees* directly, without . . . discursive reasoning."

112. 38 c–e.
113. P. 50 of chap. I of the present volume.
114. Aristotle, *Metaphysics*, 1003 a 21.
115. *Ibid.*, 984 b 10.
116. Thomas Aquinas, *De Veritate*, qu. I, art. 1.
117. *Critique of Pure Reason*, B82, B83.
118. *Sein und Zeit*, Tübingen, 1949, no. 44 (a), p. 217.
119. See Aristotle, *Posterior Analytics*, 100b5–17.
120. *An Introduction to Metaphysics* (1903), trans. T. E. Hulme, Indianapolis, New York, 1955, p. 45.
121. *Ibid.*
122. *Critique of Pure Reason*, B84 and B189–B191.
123. *An Introduction to Metaphysics*, p. 45.
124. *Protreptikos*, Düring ed., B87.
125. 1072b27.
126. 1072a21.
127. This mistranslation mars W. D. Ross's *Aristotle*, Meridian Books, New York, 1959, but is mercifully absent from his translation of the *Metaphysics* in Richard McKeon's *The Basic Works of Aristotle*.
128. *Philosophy of History*, Introduction, p. 9.
129. *Hegel's Philosophy of Right*, trans. T. M. Knox, London, Oxford, New York, 1967, addition to para. 2, p. 225.
130. *Wegmarken*, p. 19.
131. *Nicomachean Ethics*, 1175a12.
132. *Tractatus*, 401. It seems to me obvious that Wittgenstein's early language theory is solidly rooted in the old metaphysical axiom of truth as *adequatio rei et intellectus;* the trouble with this definition has always been that such an equation is possible only as intuition, namely, as an internal image that copies the sensorially given visible object. "The logical picture of a fact," which according to Wittgenstein is a "thought" (I am following Bertrand Russell's Introduction to the *Tractatus* in the bilingual edition, London, 1961, p. xii), is a contradiction in terms unless one takes "picture" as a metaphorical expression. There certainly exists a "relation which holds between language and the world," but whatever this relation may be, it is certainly not a "pictorial" one. If it were a pictorial relation, every proposition, unless it renders and repeats an accidental error in sensory perception (something looks like

a tree but turns out to be a man on closer inspection), would be true; however, I can make a great many propositions about a "fact" that say something quite meaningful without being necessarily true: "the sun turns about the earth" or "in September 1939 Poland invaded Germany"—the one being an error, the other being a lie. There are, on the other hand, propositions that are inherently unacceptable, as for instance "the triangle laughs," cited in the text, which is neither a true nor a false statement, but a meaningless one. The only internal linguistic criterion for propositions is sense or nonsense.

In view of these rather obvious difficulties and in view of the fact that Wittgenstein himself later rejected his "picture theory of propositions," it is rather interesting to find out how it occurred to him in the first place. There are, I think, two versions of this. He had been "reading a magazine in which there was a schematic picture depicting the possible sequence of events in an automobile accident. The picture there served as a proposition; that is, as a description of a possible state of affairs. It had this function owing to a correspondence between the parts of the picture and things in reality. It now occurred to Wittgenstein that one might reverse the analogy and say that a *proposition* serves as a *picture*, by virtue of a similar correspondence between *its* parts and the world. The way in which the parts of the proposition are combined—the *structure* of the proposition—depicts a possible combination of elements in reality." (See G. H. von Wright's "Biographical Sketch" in Norman Malcolm's *Ludwig Wittgenstein: A Memoir*, London, 1958, pp. 7–8.) What seems decisive here is that he did not take off from reality but from a *schematic reconstruction* of some event which itself had already been subjected to a process of thought, that is, he started from an illustration of a thought. In the *Philosophical Investigations* (663), there is an observation that reads like a refutation of this theory: "If I say 'I meant *him*,' very likely a picture comes to my mind . . . but the picture is only like an illustration to a story. From it alone it would mostly be impossible to conclude anything at all; only when one knows the story does one know the significance of the picture."

The second version of the origin of the "picture theory of propositions" is to be found in the *Tractatus* itself (4.0311) and sounds even more plausible. Wittgenstein, who replaced his earlier theory with the theory of language-games, seems to have been influenced by another game, frequently played in his time in society, the game of *tableaux vivants:* the rules demanded that somebody had to guess what proposition was expressed by the *tableau vivant* enacted by a number of persons. "One name stands for one thing, another for another thing, and they are combined with one another. In this way the whole group—like a tableau vivant—presents a state of affairs"; it actually is supposed to spell out a certain proposition.

I mention these things to indicate Wittgenstein's style of thinking. They may help explain "the puzzling thing about his later philosophy . . . that it is so piecemeal" and "has no master plan." (See the excellent presentation of David Pears, *Ludwig Wittgenstein*, New York, 1970, pp. 4 f.) The *Tractatus* also starts from a haphazard observation, from which, however, its author was able to develop a consistent theory that saved him from further haphazard observations and enabled him to write a continuous work. In spite of its frequent abruptness, the *Tractatus* is entirely consistent. The *Philosophical Investigations* shows how this ceaselessly active mind actually functioned, if it was not, almost accidentally, guided by a single assumption, for instance, by the thesis that "there must . . . be something in common between the structure of the sentence and the structure of the fact." (Russell, *op. cit.*, p. x, rightly calls this "the most fundamental thesis of Mr Wittgenstein's theory.") The most conspicuous property of the *Philosophical Investigations* is its breathlessness: it is as though somebody had actualized the *stop-and-think* inherent in thought to the point where it halted the whole thinking process and interrupted every thought-train by recoiling on itself. The English translation somehow mitigates this by rendering the ever-repeated *"Denk dir"* by a variety of words, such as "suppose," "imagine."

133. *Philosophical Investigations,* nos. 466–471.

Chapter III

1. *Timaeus,* 90c (see n. 35 below).
2. See the very instructive *Theory and Practice,* by Nicholas Lobkowicz, p. 7n.

3. *Symposium*, 204a.
4. Pindar, *Nemea*, 6; *The Odes of Pindar*, trans. Richmond Lattimore, Chicago, 1947, p. 111.
5. I, 131.
6. *Sophist*, 219b.
7. *Republic*, 518c.
8. *The Discourses*, bk. II, Introduction.
9. Bruno Snell, "Pindar's Hymn to Zeus," *op. cit.*, pp. 77–79.
10. *Nemea*, 4, *Isthmia*, 4, both Lattimore trans.
11. *Isthmia*, 4, Lattimore trans.
12. Thucydides, II, 41.
13. *Protreptikos*, Düring ed., B19 and B110. Cf. *Eudemian Ethics*, 1216a11.
14. *Protreptikos*, Düring ed., B109.
15. *De Finibus Bonorum et Malorum*, II, 13.
16. Heraclitus, B29.
17. *Symposium*, 208c.
18. *Ibid.*, 208d.
19. Anaximander seems to have been the first to equate the divine with the *apeiron*, the Non-Limited, whose nature it was to be forever—ageless, immortal, and imperishable.
20. Frag. 8.
21. Charles H. Kahn, in his fascinating study "The Greek Verb 'to be' and the Concept of Being," examines "the pre-philosophical use of this verb which . . . serves to express the concept of Being in Greek" (p. 245). In *Foundations of Language*, vol. 2, 1966, p. 255.
22. B30.
23. Snell, *op. cit.*, p. 40.
24. Kahn, *op. cit.*, p. 260.
25. Frag. 3.
26. *Protreptikos*, Düring ed., B110.
27. *Philebus*, 28c.
28. *Symposium*, 212a.
29. *Nicomachean Ethics*, 1178b3, 1178b22, 1177b33 (the last from Martin Ostwald trans., Indianapolis, New York, 1962).
30. *Timaeus*, 90d, a.
31. Quoted from Jeremy Bernstein's "The Secrets of the Old One—II," *The New Yorker*, March 17, 1973.
32. Francis MacDonald Cornford, *Plato and Parmenides*, New York, 1957, Introduction, p. 27.
33. *Protreptikos*, Düring ed., B65.

34. Cornford, *Plato's Theory of Knowledge*, p. 189.
35. *Timaeus*, 90c.
36. *Philebus*, 59b, c.
37. "Philosophie der Weltgeschichte," *Hegel Studienausgabe*, vol. I, p. 291.
38. *De Rerum Natura*, bk. II, first lines; *On the Nature of the Universe*, trans. Ronald Latham, Penguin, Harmondsworth, 1951, p. 60.
39. I owe the quotations from Herder and Goethe to the interesting study of navigation, shipwreck, and spectator as "existential metaphors" in Hans Blumenberg, "Beobachtungen an Metaphern," in *Archiv für Begriffsgeschichte*, vol. XV, Heft 2, 1971, pp. 171 ff. For Voltaire, see his article "Curiosité" in his *Dictionnaire Philosophique*. For Herder, see also *Briefe zur Beförderung der Humanität*, 1792, 17th Letter; for Goethe, *Goethes Gespräche*, Artemis ed., Zürich, 1949, vol. 22, no. 725, p. 454.
40. 1177b27–33.
41. *Theaetetus*, 155d.
42. *Cratylus*, 408b.
43. B21a.
44. B54.
45. B123.
46. B93.
47. B107.
48. B32.
49. B108.
50. *The Friend*, III, 192, as quoted by Herbert Read in *Coleridge as Critic*, London, 1949, p. 30.
51. Now together with two later explications, an Introduction and an Epilogue, in *Wegmarken*, pp. 19 and 210.
52. 1714, no. 7.
53. *Critique of Pure Reason*, B641.
54. *Werke*, 6. Ergänzungsband, ed. M. Schröter, München, 1954, p. 242.
55. *Ibid.*, p. 7.
56. See the posthumously published *System der gesammten Philosophie* of 1804, in *Sämtliche Werke*, Abt. I, Stuttgart and Augsburg, 1860, vol. VI, p. 155.
57. *Sämtliche Werke*, Abt. I, vol. VII, p. 174.
58. *Ibid.*, Abt. II, vol. III, p. 163. Cf. also Karl Jaspers, *Schelling*, München, 1955, pp. 124–130.

59. Paris, 1958, pp. 161–171.
60. See the *Preisschrift* "Uber die Deutlichkeit der Grundsätze der natürlichen Theologie und der Moral" (1764), 4th Consideration, no. 1, *Werke,* vol. I, pp. 768–769.
61. "Uber den Optimismus," *Werke,* vol. I, p. 594.
62. *Ecce Homo,* "Thus Spoke Zarathustra," 1.
63. *The Gay Science,* bk. IV, no. 341.
64. 130d, e.
65. *Tusculanae Disputationes,* III, iii, 6.
66. *Ibid.,* III, xiv, 30. Cf. Horace, *Epistolae,* I, vi, 1. Plutarch (in his *De recta Ratione,* 13) mentions the Stoic maxim and ascribes it—in Greek translation, *mē thaumazein*—to Pythagoras. Democritus is supposed to have praised *athaumastia* and *athambia* as Stoic wisdom, but seems to have had no more in mind than the "wise man's" imperturbability and fearlessness.
67. *Hegel's Philosophy of Right,* p. 13.
68. *L'Oeuvre de Pascal,* Pléiade ed., Bruges, 1950, 294, p. 901.
69. *Differenz des Fichte'schen und Schelling'schen Systems der Philosophie* (1801), Meiner ed., 1962, pp. 12 ff.
70. Trans. J. Sibree, New York, 1956, p. 318.
71. *Ibid.,* p. 26.
72. This transformation is especially telling when the borrowing from Greek philosophy is most obvious, as when Cicero says man is destined *ad mundum contemplandum* and then immediately adds: *et imitandum* (*De Natura Deorum,* II, xiv, 37), which he understands in a strictly moral-political sense, and not scientifically as, centuries later, Francis Bacon would have understood it: "Nature to be commanded must be obeyed; and that which in contemplation is as the cause, in operation is as the rule . . ." (*Novum Organon,* Oxford ed., 1889, p. 192).
73. *De Rerum Natura,* bk. II, 1174; *On the Nature of the Universe,* Latham trans., p. 95.
74. *Discourses,* bk. I, chap. 17.
75. *Ibid.,* bk. I, chap. 15.
76. *The Manual,* 49; *The Stoic and Epicurean Philosophers,* ed. Whitney J. Oates, New York, 1940, p. 482.
77. *Discourses,* bk. I, chap. 1.
78. *The Manual,* 8, Oates ed., p. 470; *Fragments,* 8, Oates ed., p. 460.

79. *Op. cit.*, V, 7 ff. Author's translation.
80. *De Republica*, I, 7.
81. *Ibid.*, III, 23.
82. *Ibid.*, V, 1.
83. Modeled, of course, on the myth of Er that concludes Plato's *Republic*. For the important differences, see the analysis of Richard Harder, the late eminent German philologist, "Uber Ciceros Somnium Scipionis," in *Kleine Schriften*, München, 1960, pp. 354–395.
84. "Discourses on Davila," *The Works of John Adams*, ed. Charles Francis Adams, Boston, 1850–1856, vol. VI, p. 242.
85. *Oedipus at Colonnus*.
86. *Politics*, 1267a12.
87. *Nicomachean Ethics*, 1178a29–30.
88. Frag. 146.
89. *The Decline and Fall of the Roman Empire*, Modern Library, New York, n.d., vol. II, p. 471.
90. I, 30; my translation of *hōs philosopheōn gēn pollēn theōriēs heineken epelēlythas*.
91. I, 32.
92. The thought content of that saying was fully explicated only in Heidegger's death-analyses in *Being and Time*, which take their methodological cue from the fact that human life—as distinguished from "things," which start their worldly existence when they are complete and finished—is complete only when it *is* no more. Hence, only by anticipating its own death can it "appear" as a whole and be subjected to analysis.
93. E. Diehl, ed., *Anthologia Lyrica Graeca*, Leipzig, 1936, frag. 16.
94. *Ibid.*, frag. 13, ll. 63–70.
95. *Ibid.*, frag. 14.
96. *Charmides*, 175b.
97. Hegel's *Encyclopädie der philosophischen Wissenschaften*, Lasson ed., Leipzig, 1923, 23: *"Das Denken . . . sich als abstraktes Ich als von aller Partikularität sonstiger Eigenschaften, Zustände, usf. befreites verhält und nur das Allgemeine tut, in welchem es mit allen Individuen identisch ist."*
98. It is surprising, in examining the literature, often very learned, to see how very little all this erudition has been able to contribute to an understanding of the man. The only exception I have been able to unearth is a kind of inspired profile

by the classicist and philosopher Gregory Vlastos, "The Paradox of Socrates." See the Introduction to his carefully selected *The Philosophy of Socrates: A Collection of Critical Essays,* Anchor Books, New York, 1971.

99. 173d.

100. On the Socratic problem, see the short, reasonable account given by Laszlo Versényi as an Appendix to his *Socratic Humanism,* New Haven, London, 1963.

101. *Dante and Philosophy,* trans. David Moore, Harper Torchbooks, New York, Evanston, London, 1963, p. 267.

102. *Ibid.,* p. 273.

103. Thus in *Theaetetus* and *Charmides.*

104. *Meno,* 80e.

105. The frequent notion that Socrates tries to lead his interlocutor with his questions to certain results of which he is convinced in advance—like a clever professor with his students—seems to me entirely mistaken even if it is as ingeniously qualified as in Vlastos' essay mentioned above, in which he suggests (p. 13) that Socrates wanted the other "to find . . . out for himself," as in the *Meno,* which however is not aporetic. The most one could say is that Socrates wanted his partners in the dialogues to be as perplexed as he was. He was sincere when he said that he taught nothing. Thus he told Critias in the *Charmides:* "Critias, you act as though I professed to know the answers to the questions I ask you and could give them to you if I wished. It is not so. I inquire with you . . . because I don't myself have knowledge" (165b; cf. 166c–d).

106. Diehl, frag. 16.

107. *Meno,* 80c. Cf. the above-mentioned passage, n. 105.

108. *Memorabilia,* IV, vi, 15 and IV, iv, 9.

109. *Sophist,* 226–231.

110. *Apology,* 23b.

111. *Ibid.,* 30a.

112. Xenophon, *Memorabilia,* IV, iii, 14.

113. *Antigone,* 353.

114. The German text, from *Was Heisst Denken?,* Tübingen, 1954, p. 52, reads as follows: "*Sokrates hat zeit seines Lebens, bis in seinen Tod hinein, nichts anderes getan, als sich in den Zugwind dieses Zuges zu stellen und darin sich zu halten. Darum ist er der reinste Denker des Abendlandes. Deshalb hat er nichts geschrieben. Denn wer aus dem Denken zu schreiben*

beginnt, muss unweigerlich den Menschen gleichen, die vor allzu starkem Zugwind in den Windschatten flüchten. Es bleibt das Geheimnis einer noch verborgenen Geschichte, dass alle Denker des Abendlandes nach Sokrates, unbeschadet ihrer Grösse, solche Flüchtlinge sein mussten. Das Denken ging in die Literatur ein."

115. G. Humphrey, *Thinking: An Introduction to Its Experimental Psychology*, London and New York, 1951, p. 312.

116. Thucydides, II, 40.

117. *Lysis*, 204b–c.

118. Frags. 145, 190.

119. *Gorgias*, 474b, 483a, b.

120. *Ibid.*, 482c.

121. *Ibid.*, 482c, 484c, d.

122. Aristotle frequently insisted that thinking "produces" happiness, but if so, not in the way that medicine produces health but in the way that health makes a man healthy. *Nicomachean Ethics*, 1144a.

123. Diels and Kranz, B45.

124. 254d.

125. *Identity and Difference*, trans. Joan Stambaugh, New York, Evanston, London, 1969, pp. 24–25.

126. 255d.

127. *Sophist*, 255e; Cornford, *Plato's Theory of Knowledge*, p. 282.

128. Heidegger, *Sophist* lecture transcript, p. 382.

129. *Theaetetus*, 189e; *Sophist*, 263e.

130. *Sophist*, 253b.

131. *Protagoras*, 339c.

132. *Ibid.*, 339b, 340b.

133. *Posterior Analytics*, 76b22–25.

134. 1005b23–1008a2.

135. No. 36, *Werke*, vol. VI, p. 500.

136. No. 56, *ibid.*, p. 549.

137. "Grundlegung zur Metaphysik der Sitten," *Werke*, vol. 4, pp. 51–55.

138. 304d.

139. *Nicomachean Ethics*, 1166a30.

140. *Ibid.*, 1166b5–25.

141. *Ethics*, IV, 52; III, 25.

142. *Philosophy* (1932), trans. E. B. Ashton, Chicago, London, 1970, vol. 2, pp. 178–179.

Chapter IV

1. *Symposium,* 174–175.
2. Merleau-Ponty, *Signs,* "The Philosopher and His Shadow," p. 174.
3. Quoted from Sebastian de Grazia, "About Chuang Tzu," *Dalhousie Review,* Summer 1974.
4. Hegel, *Encyclopädie der philosophischen Wissenschaften,* 465n.
5. Ross, *Aristotle,* p. 14.
6. *Protreptikos,* Düring ed., B56.
7. *Physics,* VI, viii, 189a5.
8. *Nicomachean Ethics,* 1141b24–1142a30. Cf. 1147a1–10.
9. *Critique of Pure Reason,* B49, B50.
10. *Gesammelte Schriften,* New York, 1946, vol. V, p. 287. English translation by Willa and Edwin Muir, *The Great Wall of China,* New York, 1946, p. 276–277.
11. Pt. III, "On the Vision and the Riddle," sect. 2.
12. Vol. I, pp. 311 f.
13. Duns Scotus, *Opus Oxoniense* I, dist. 40, q. 1, n. 3. Quoted from Walter Hoeres, *Der Wille als reine Vollkommenheit nach Duns Scotus,* München, 1962, p. 111, n. 72.
14. *Critique of Pure Reason,* B294 f.
15. "As I Walked Out One Evening," *Collected Poems,* p. 115.
16. W. H. Auden, *The Dyer's Hand and Other Essays,* Vintage Books, New York, 1968.
17. *Time and Free Will* (1910), trans. F. L. Pogson, Harper Torchbooks, New York, Evanston, 1960, pp. 158, 167, 240.
18. Romans 7:15.
19. *Encyclopädie,* 12.
20. *Of Human Freedom,* Gutmann trans., p. 8.
21. *Critique of Pure Reason,* B172–B173.

Index

256

Index

258

Index